The Encyclopedia of
Careers and Vocational Guidance

EIGHTH EDITION

The Encyclopedia of Careers and Vocational Guidance

WILLIAM E. HOPKE

Editor-in-Chief

VOLUME 1

Industry Profiles

J.G. FERGUSON PUBLISHING COMPANY

Chicago, Illinois

Library of Congress Cataloging-in-Publication Data

The Encyclopedia of careers and vocational guidance/ William E. Hopke, editor-in-chief. 8th ed.
    p. cm.
    Contents: v.1 Industry profiles — v.2. Professional careers — v.3. General and special careers —v.4. Technicians' careers.
Includes indexes.
    ISBN 0-89434-117-0 (set). —ISBN 0-89434-113-8 (v.1). —ISBN 0-89434-114-6 (v.2). —ISBN 0-89434-115-4 (V.3).
— ISBN 0-89434-116-2 (v.4)
    1. Vocational guidance—Handbooks, manuals, etc. 2. Occupations—Handbooks, manuals, etc. I. Hopke, William E.
HF5381.E52 1990
331.7'02—dc20
        90-3743
        CIP

ISBN 0-89434-117-0 (set)
      0-89434-113-8 (volume 1)
      0-89434-114-6 (volume 2)
      0-89434-115-4 (volume 3)
      0-89434-116-2 (volume 4)

Printed in the United States of America
N-8

Editorial Staff

Editorial Director: C.J. Summerfield

Assistant Editor: Amy I. Brown

Contributing Editors: Susan Ashby, John Morse, Nancy Parsegian, Mark Toch, James Unland

Writers: Pamela Dell, Lillian Flowers, Jim Garner, Phyllis Miller, Jeanne Rattenbury, Fran Sherman

Photo Editor: Carol Parden

Indexer: Carol Nielson

Designer: Shawn M. Biner, Biner Design

Copyeditors and Proofreaders: Wordsmiths

Production Manager: Tom Myles

Contents

Volume 1: Industry Profiles

Acknowledgements

The editorial staff of J.G. Ferguson would like to express its appreciation to the following companies, associations, organizations and individuals for their assistance in providing statistics, data, and descriptions for their fields. Their help has been enormously valuable to *The Encyclopedia of Careers and Vocational Guidance* and they have enhanced the contents of these volumes to the benefit of all readers seeking career information.

Aerospace Education Association
American Association for Advertising Agents
American Association for Leisure and Recreation
American Association of Professional Consultants
American Association of Political Consultants
American Bar Association
American Campaign Academy
American Consultants League
American Institute of Baking
American Institute of Mining, Metallurgical, and Petroleum Engineers
American Library Association
American Mathematical Society
American Mining Congress
American Newspaper Publishers Association
American Nuclear Society
American Physical Therapy Association
American Pulpwood Association
American Society for Engineering Education
American Society of Extracorporeal Technology
American Society for Metals
Army Recruiting Department
Association of Independent Video and Filmmakers
Association of National Advertisers
Association for Women in Mathematics
Chicago Board of Trade
College Sports Information Directors of America
Cook County Republic Committee
Dan Rostenkowski
Darren Carroll
Federal Express
Federal Reserve System
Folk Legacy
Future Aviation Professionals of America
Green Linnet Music
Hasbro

Howard Shenson
Institute of Mathematical Statistics
International Trade Commission
J. Walter Thompson
Military Entrance Processing Station, Cincinnati
National Aeronautics and Space Administration
National Association of Bank Women
National Association of Letter Carriers of the United States
National Association of Sports Officials
National Council of Teachers of Mathematics
National Federation of Interscholastic Coaches and Officials Association
National Oceanic and Atmospheric Administration
National Public Radio
National Recreation and Park Association
National Research Council
National Science Foundation
Norwegian Cruise Lines
Office of Public Affairs, The White House
Office of the Doorkeeper, U.S. House of Representatives
Playskool
Political Consultants Network
Polygram
Precision Metalforming Association
Rounder Records
Silo, Inc.
Society of Mining Engineers
Tonka
United States Coast Guard
United States Department of the Interior
United States Department of Health and Human Services
United States Department of State
United States Secret Service
United Parcel Service
WMAQ Broadcasting
WTTW Broadcasting
World Trade Center of New Orleans

Introduction

The Encyclopedia of Career and Vocational Guidance is approaching its twenty-fifth year in print. This eighth edition of the Encyclopedia has expanded into a four volume set from the two volumes first published in 1967. As the number of career choices has grown, *The Encyclopedia of Career and Vocational Guidance* has had to grow to accommodate all the information. There were about two dozen technicians' careers listed in the first edition; we now have an entire volume dedicated to the 128 technicians' careers covered. There are twenty-two industries covered for the first time. There are also 153 jobs in the careers volumes that have not had a separate article before. Overall, five hundred articles on careers in Volumes 2, 3, and 4 outline almost 1000 occupations. The original editors expressed a desire with that first edition to "bring together the greatest possible amount of accurate information about occupations." It is a goal we still set for the Encyclopedia.

The four volumes in the eighth edition cover two aspects of career information. Volume 1 covers the industries themselves—their structures, their career paths. The next three volumes cover the specific information on each particular job, including educational and training requirements.

The first volume is dedicated to an evaluation of seventy-six major industries. This volume differs in several ways from the earlier versions of Volume 1. We have structured each of the chapters so they cover quite specific elements of that particular industry. The opening section of each chapter covers general information and historical background for the industry. The historical information allows the reader to understand how that industry has developed and why it became important. Historical notes on each job are included in the job descriptions of Volumes 2, 3, and 4, but the Volume 1 histories paint a broad picture of industrial development. A variety of historical references were used to compile the histories, including museum studies of Egypt in 1500 B.C. and newspaper articles from the turn of the century.

Also included in the "General information" section are statistics on current employment and production. The section ends with the current status of the industry. From there the chapter moves into the second section, "The structure of the industry."

To understand how a particular job or career fits into the industry, the reader must have some understanding of the industry in which the job is located. This overview of the industry's structure is not specific to one corporation or business. It is a presentation of the generic setup of how that industry works. The section details the industries from beginning of their process through the completion of their end product. The information was obtained through interviews with leaders in the industry, through articles and publications on the industries, and through agencies involved in hiring and placing individuals in their specific field.

"Careers" follows the description of structure. This outlines the career titles and paths in brief that the industry involves. The career description may encapsulate a career to be found in its own article in one of the other volumes, or it may incorporate more than one job title. In the chapter on Politics and Public Service, the description of a campaign staff notes the different jobs available for that aspect of political life. For further details on jobs such as fundraiser or public relations specialist, the reader can go to those specific articles in Volume 2. At the end of each chapter is a list of the related articles the reader may want to consult for further information.

"Education" is the fourth section. This outlines the different levels of education and training for the different categories of careers covered in the industry. In Book Publishing, editors are often college graduates; printing press operators are more likely to have apprentice training. This gives the reader some idea of what education and training requirements are before narrowing in on one specific job title.

In the last section of the chapter, industry outlook is forecast. With information from the *Occupational Outlook Handbook*, the *U.S. Industrial Outlook*, statistics from the various associations and agencies, and other evaluative data, the best estimation of future performance and success is given. Following that information is a listing of organizations that can provide career information on training, education, internships, scholarships, and job placement. Related articles, as mentioned above, are also listed here to direct the reader to articles that provide further information on specific elements of the chapter's presentation.

Volumes 2, 3, and 4, cover the individual job descriptions. Volume 2 is dedicated to those jobs that may be catalogued under the heading "Professional, Administrative, and Managerial Occupations." Volume 3 describes the jobs listed in the following fields: Clerical; Sales; Service; Agriculture, forestry, and conservation; Processing; Machine trades; Bench work; Structural work; and Miscellaneous careers. Volume 4 details the technicians careers for these categories: Engineering and science; Agriculture, forestry, and conservation; Broadcast, media, and arts; Medical and health; and two non-specific categories. The first non-specific category is under the heading "Emerging technician occupations." Because new areas of examination and investigation are developing all the time, the specific field of study may not yet be classified or it may be a field that is completely new. Semiconductors and microelectronics are two of the new fields covered in this section. There is also a miscellaneous technicians category for established technicians careers that do not fall into one of the other five headings.

For each of the fourteen categories covered in Volumes 2, 3, and 4, there is a symbol that appears at the beginning of each section and at the top of every page. This symbol gives the reader a quick reference to the category in which the job is listed. A guide to the symbols follows the Table of Contents in each volume.

In each volume there is a complete index of job titles, covering all four volumes. This allows the reader to look up a specific job title and see references listed for all the volumes. With a broad job title such as editor, the reader would be directed to Book Publishing, Magazine Publishing, Newspaper Publishing, and Writers and editors.

At the end of Volume 4, there is one other index. The Dictionary of Occupational Titles (DOT) catalogues jobs by number. We have included in this edition an index that lists the job titles covered and their specific DOT code for cross-reference with government publications. At the end of each article in Volumes 2, 3, and 4 there are also codes for the relevant Standard Industrial Classification numbers (SIC), the Standard Occupational Classification numbers (SOC) used by the Department of Labor, and the Guide for Occupational Exploration numbers (GOE) used by the U.S. Employment Service.

Also at the end of the last volume are two appendices. The first lists organizations and associations that assist in training and job placement for the disabled and other special groups. These organizations can be contacted for further information relating to their services. The second appendix covers information on internships, apprenticeships, and special training programs available to students. Both are presented for supplemental information on the resources available for readers who wish to find out more on the specifics of programs offered and available to them.

We have endeavored to present as complete a picture as possible on the information needed to make a preliminary investigation of a career path. The only way to resolutely know if that career choice is a good one is to pursue it. The industry outlook, the job outlook, and the competition for employment are only here as a guideline. To the determined and dedicated applicant, a job is attainable despite the fiercest competition. This book is intended as a stepping stone to the decisions the reader needs to make to accomplish those career goals.

The editors

KEY TO OCCUPATIONAL CATEGORIES

 Industry Profiles. This represents the articles that outline descriptions of industries in Volume 1.

 Professional, Administrative, and Managerial Occupations. Covering careers that involve extensive academic training or practical training, these occupations include many of the jobs that require undergraduate or graduate school education. Volume 2

 Clerical Occupations. Clerical occupations are those involved with handling the records, communications, and general office duties required in every business. Volume 3

 Sales Occupations. This section includes sales careers for goods, services, and property, and careers for sales-related business. Volume 3

 Service Occupations. Careers in service comprise occupations that assist people in various aspects of life, from protection by law enforcement to physical care. Volume 3

 Agriculture, Forestry, and Conservation Occupations. Encompassing the occupations that work with various elements of nature, this category includes skilled and technicians' work related to farm production, mining, animal care, and wildlife services. Volume 3 and 4

 Processing Occupations. These are occupations that involve the mixing, treating, and recomposition of materials, chemicals, and products, normally through the use of machinery or tools. Volume 3

 Machine Trades Occupations. Careers in machine trades are those that work with machine assembly, maintenance, and repair. They work with metals, plastics, wood, paper, and stone in construction and repair. Volume 3

 Bench Work Occupations. With an emphasis on hand tools and dexterity skills, bench workers make and repair products that require manual deftness, such as jewelry or optical equipment. Volume 3

Structural Work Occupations. This category details the occupations involved in construction and repair of all large structures from bridges to homes. Volume 3

 Emerging Technician Occupations. Falling mainly into the fields of science and technology, these technicians occupations are either not yet catalogued into one of the sections following or will not be catalogued into an existing field. Volume 4

 Engineering and Science Technician Occupations. These technicians work with scientists and engineers as part of a team trained in the technical aspects of the work performed. Volume 4

 Broadcast, Media, and Arts Technicians Occupations. The technicians who operate, maintain, and repair the equipment involved in broadcasting and the arts are trained to run electronic, electrical, and mechanical equipment. Volume 4

 Medical and Health Technician Occupations. Responsible for the technical equipment used in medical fields, these technicians run the sophisticated machinery used by medical specialists. Volume 4

 Miscellaneous Occupations. In this section are the occupations that require skilled or semi-skilled levels of training. This includes a diverse range of job categories, including graphics arts, transportation and technicians in information services as well as other fields. Volume 3 and 4

Accounting

General information

Even before the introduction of currency, farmers kept track of their livestock and other valuable possessions in order to maintain some sense of where they stood financially. Having sixteen sheep, for example, meant the ability to trade up to sixteen sheep for something else of equal value. The farmer needed to know how many sheep to keep for continued offspring, and how many he could trade. This need established accounting in its most basic form.

Financial records have been found in the ruins of old Greek and Roman towns, showing that accountants and bookkeepers were at work balancing the financial records of businesses. Once currency was established, keeping track of money made the skills of an accountant important to business.

In 1494, Luca Pacioli, an Italian mathematician, wrote a treatise on accounting and bookkeeping that established the foundation for modern bookkeeping methods. The double entry method of bookkeeping was designed for business so that debits and credits were entered in separate columns in a financial ledger. This allowed businesses to keep better track of the movement of their funds.

Through the fifteenth century, instruction books were printed in Italy on bookkeeping. Since printing presses made reproductions of work relatively inexpensive, the disbursal of information on the new bookkeeping methods was swift. Presses in major cities in Italy were able to write and print their own manuals on bookkeeping and accounting.

As businesses became more complex with property investment and taxation and tax write-offs, the requirements for flexible, comprehensive bookkeeping methods was a necessity. In the late eighteenth century, the Industrial Revolution established large businesses that were involved in a vast array of production and manufacturing services. Management needed accurate financial records to determine the cost and effectiveness of the company's business.

The accounting profession in the United States dates back to the 1880s, when English and Scottish investors began buying stock in American companies. To keep an eye on their investments, they sent over British accountants. Many of these accountants stayed on to establish their own accounting businesses.

Federal legislation, such as the income tax in 1913 and the excess profits tax in 1917, helped bring about an accounting boom that has made the profession one of the largest in business today.

In order to establish some type of regularization and identification of qualified public accountants, the certified public accountant examination was developed in 1917. It is not required for practice in more than half of the United States, but the rest of the states do require certification through the American Institute of Certified Public Accountants, which sponsors the nationally recognized four-part CPA examination.

Other examinations followed the CPA examination in development. Certified Internal Auditors (CIA), the Certified Information Systems Auditor (CISA), and the Certificate in Management Accounting (CMA) are just a few of the possible licenses that can now be applied for. These credentials help establish an accountant's expertise, and thereby help potential clients identify which accountant they want to hire.

With the increasing number of large corporations during the last several decades, the job of the accountant has become more and more complex. It involves more than simply balancing daily financial journals and account ledgers for a business. Accountants must be able to draw pertinent financial data from a variety of sources. In addition, accountants must be able to analyze the figures and determine if all the

A partner of an accounting firm discusses new tax laws with her client. As a partial owner of the firm, she is responsible for generating new clients.

money transactions have been completed in an accurate fashion. Often accountants must work with figures representing large quantities of money. They must be able to do their job professionally, even if under tight time constraints.

The structure of the accounting industry

Accountants and auditors prepare, analyze, and verify financial reports for businesses and industrial and government organizations. The accounting department figures profits for the company, establishes how much in taxes the company has to pay, and keeps track of the cost of running the company. How the company does financially is the business of the accountants.

Accountants develop bookkeeping methods that allow the company to keep track of current assets and liabilities. They also establish methods that enable the company to keep track of the change in the assets and liabilities over a period of years. Accountants or auditors may be required to establish a system that breaks down spending into areas of expenditure or periods of expenditure. The bookkeeping system will depend on the role of the business and the needs of management.

Another major area of responsibility for most accountants is in the area of budgeting. Accountants use past and current financial records to forecast what a company can afford to spend in any one area. This plays a vital role when company executives decide how financial resources should be allocated.

Because each company has such specific needs, most companies, especially larger firms,

prefer that an accountant works for them exclusively. There are also large companies with different accounting divisions for each of the areas of financing and accounting. A full-time accountant may be referred to as a management accountant, private accountant, or industrial accountant.

Smaller businesses may hire a permanent accountant as part of the staff, or they may hire one who will work with them on a free-lance basis. Some small companies may hire a specific accountant to work with them on a particular project, especially if that accountant is known for having an expertise in that type of project.

The auditing department also works on the books for the company. Internal auditors keep track of company expenses to make sure that financial information is reported correctly. They are responsible for evaluating the financial information for possible fraud or waste. They may be responsible for developing more efficient methods of operation or new safeguards to assure the company is saving as much money as possible on operations. They should be knowledgeable on tax and business laws to make sure that the company is not violating any laws or rules in its manner of bookkeeping or operation.

In setting up and maintaining an accounting system for a business or individual, the needs of the account are assessed before designing the accounting methods. The accounting system to be set up will depend on the business needs. Particularly with large businesses, more than one accounting system may be needed to keep accurate track of the company's transactions.

A balance sheet system provides assets and liabilities, as well as other financial data. This gives stockholders and company officials some sense of the well-being of the business on a regular basis.

An income statement provides an account of the costs of operations and the intake of cash, so the overall cost of doing business can be appraised regularly, without calculating in other company investments.

Accounting systems can also be set up that provide earnings paid to stockholders and earnings that are reinvested in the company. A flow of funds can be organized that helps determine where and when company funds are paid out. If there are periods where a large amount of cash leaves the company, then arrangements may be requested to reschedule payments to remove high and low points in the cash flow.

For a larger company, a staff of accountants will divide the responsibilities of the business.

For firms requiring a temporarily large number of accountants, the services of an accounting firm are available.

During the last part of the 1980s, several small accounting firms merged to make larger corporations. The trend for accounting firms in the last part of the decade was to move into larger, more condensed groups to cover a broader range of territory, physically and professionally.

Large accounting firms have become one of the fastest growing areas of employment for accountants and auditors. These corporations hire staff accountants who work on the books of several outside companies. The businesses take on a number of clients for whom they will do the accounting and auditing. The accounting firm is able to increase the number of clients handled because one accountant may be able to handle more than one firm, and a group of accountants can handle a large client account.

The single largest employer for accountants and auditors is the United States government. Government accountants are responsible for maintaining the enormous quantity of financial records of government agencies. They also have the same responsibilities as the private accountants but, for some agencies, the budgets are immensely larger than private corporations. For the government accountants with the defense department, the annual expenditures are around $300 billion. More than 14,000 accountants and auditors work in the defense department, and the United States government employs almost 26,000 accountants and auditors for its budgeting needs.

In addition to the accountants and auditors who provide financial and bookkeeping services, some accountants work as teachers or administrators at business and professional schools. Some work part time as accountants or financial consultants.

As in many industries, computers are increasingly being used in accounting. Computer programs are available, for example, to summarize financial transactions or put financial data into special formats. This trend toward automation will continue in the future.

Careers

Accounting and auditing provide a number of career opportunities. Some accountants specialize in preparing tax- related material, while others provide more general services. A sampling of career options follows below.

Management accountants: Management accountants are company employees. They cover

A tax examiner at an IRS service center reviews tax returns to ensure that they are completed accurately. She also codes them for computer processing.

the financial aspects of the business, and may work in all or one of several possible areas: budget, property management and evaluation, systems accounting, or tax preparation. They are responsible for maintaining records, balancing financial books, and presenting financial information to company officers.

Treasurers: In charge of the business finances, a treasurer is responsible for the receiving, keeping, and disbursing of funds as the company requests it. He or she maintains the records of payments in and out of the company, and, with the investment officers, will develop a portfolio to successfully invest the company's money.

Public accountants: Public accountants are responsible for assisting businesses and individuals on an independent basis. They can aid in bookkeeping, preparing financial statements, and filing taxes with the government. They may work on their own or join with other accountants and run an accounting consultation business. There are several accounting agencies that have offices across the nation. The largest agencies bring in more than a billion dollars in business.

Public accountants have much the same function for the private citizen as the management accountant has for the business world. They develop and maintain financial record-keeping systems for individuals and businesses for tax purposes and they prepare tax returns and evaluate the financial records for compliance with the laws on income taxes and investments. They may work on auditing financial records of small businesses or self-employed businessmen. Public accountants are also available for consultation on investments, money management, or tax payment. They are authorities for the small businessman and the individual taxpayer on the best methods of maintain-

Accounting

A woman operates a computer that uses an optical devise to scan the written information on the 1040EZ tax returns.

ing a good, solid, legal financial system for income and investment.

Government accountants: A large number of the accountants hired by the government have the same job responsibilities as management accountants do in the private sector. For example, they organize and maintain the financial records of the organizations in the government. The Peace Corps office, the Foreign-Service office, and all the other departments have staff accountants.

The government also requires accountants who work at auditing and overseeing the financial status of private organizations. The two largest are the banks and the savings and loan industries. Because the deposits of citizens in these institutions are insured by the federal government, the government retains the power to oversee the activities of the institutions, and move in if they feel the institution is being poorly run (see Volume 1: Banking and Financial Services).

Chief bank examiners: These are the federal or state employees who make sure that the banking practices used by financial institutions are sound ones. They conduct examinations of the banking institutions to verify good business practices and compliance with banking laws.

Auditors: Auditors normally follow the tasks of the accountants. They check over the books and records to make sure that everything is accounted for correctly. They may be employed internally by a business or be brought in as consultants for a business or individual.

Internal Revenue Service workers: Since the Internal Revenue Service is the government department in charge of collecting taxes, the IRS must employ auditors and agents. The job of the auditors and agents are to ensure that the public and the professional world are paying the taxes they owe. Revenue agents verify tax filings and decide who may require investigation. An agent or an auditor will either request an interview in the government office or at the home or business of the subject being audited. The agent will then verify against the records kept by the taxpayer that the taxes were declared fairly and accurately. If taxes were not paid accurately, then the IRS will determine the taxes and fines to be paid.

Cost accountants: Cost accountants determine unit costs of products or services by analyzing records and depreciation reports. They classify and record all operating costs for use by management in controlling expenditures.

Tax accountants: Tax accountants prepare federal, state, or local tax returns for individuals or businesses. They must be fully knowledgeable on all tax laws and regulations.

Education

For almost all firms and for the federal government, the minimum educational requirements are four years of college with a major in accounting or a related field. Masters degrees in accounting or business administration are rapidly becoming a standard for the better jobs. These graduate programs have an emphasis on accounting and auditing courses.

Although graduate degrees are not yet a requirement for finding an accounting position, it is under consideration in several states that a master's degree be required merely to take the certification examination. This legislation is likely to pass at some point in the near future.

Courses that are required for most degree programs may include business finance, business administration, economics, English, mathematics, and other business related courses.

Internships with accounting firms are available for undergraduate and graduate programs. Summer work is also helpful, particularly when the student wishes to pursue a license in accounting or auditing.

In some states the certified public accountant license (CPA) is required before one can practice as a public accountant. In other states it is not required. The certified internal auditor examination (CIA) is an accepted measure of qualification for auditing. These licenses are normally preceded by at least two years of college study in accounting and auditing, and in some states two years of experience are also required.

Licensing is administered through an examination. Examination requirements vary from state to state, but most require four years of college.

The CPA examination is a four-part test given by the American Institute of Certified Public Accountants. The Certified Internal Auditor exam is a four-part test given by the Institute of Internal Auditors. Several other examinations are also sponsored in different specialties in accounting and auditing. Information on these examinations can be received through the accounting program in college, or through the board of accountancy in the state where the accountant is to practice.

In addition to educational requirements, aspiring accountants should have an aptitude for mathematics, be able to interpret facts and figures, and make good business decisions based on their analysis. They also must be patient and be able to concentrate on numerical information for long periods of time. Accountants must also be extremely trustworthy.

Industry outlook

Since the field of accounting and auditing is so large, the openings for people seeking employment are fairly frequent. According to the U.S. Department of Labor, the growth of the industry overall is expected to be much faster than the average during the 1990s. The field is one where the need for the staff will remain, regardless of the fluctuation of the economy. Businesses will continue to maintain records and pay taxes, so the accounting department will remain a requirement for businesses.

Other areas of growth expected for the industry include in the area of personal financial planning. More and more often people seek the assistance of an accountant or auditor when making investment decisions. Mergers and foreign investments are becoming frequent enough to encourage accountants to specialize in such transactions. Familiarity with trade laws, foreign taxes and such are an asset to an accountant specializing in international business affairs.

Turnover in the industry is slow, but since the growth is fast, the movement up the corporate ladder is fairly rapid. Opportunities for employment in the top accounting firms remains highly competitive. With the merging of several of the largest accounting firms, the competition for upper-level positions has increased

A data transcriber at an IRS service center operates a computerized machine that processes the taxpayers' checks on the day that the government has received them.

as the number of people qualified for promotion has surpassed the number of positions available. However, the increase in size of the accounting corporations has made the companies more likely to receive international business and has increased the international market for accounting firms. Expansion into international accounting and overseas posts has opened up the job area for international business specialists (see Volume 1: Foreign Trade).

According to *the New York Times*, although eight firms employ about 12 percent of the certified accountants, there are 48,000 other professional firms that hire corporate accountants. More than 250,000 certified accountants hold permanent jobs in the accounting industry. The diversity of positions available has allowed for flexibility in cost of the services and types of services offered by the firms. The competition in services between the larger firms and the smaller firms continues to create new business.

For people seeking employment in the accounting and auditing field, advanced degrees are becoming increasingly important to people who specialize or who wish to work in a more prestigious company. Overall, the industry outlook is good for students with a bachelor's degree or master's degree in accounting or a related field.

◇ SOURCES OF ADDITIONAL INFORMATION

American Institute of Certified Public Accountants
1221 Avenue of the Americas
New York, NY 10036

American Accounting Association
5717 Bessie Drive
Sarasota, FL 33583

National Society of Public Accountants
1010 North Fairfax Street
Alexandria, VA 22314

Institute of Internal Auditors
249 Maitland Avenue
Altamonte Springs, FL 32701

Foundation for Accounting Education
Pan-Am Building
200 Park Avenue
New York, NY 10166

◇ **RELATED ARTICLES**

Volume 1: Banking and Financial Services; Business Administration; Civil Service; Foreign Trade; Politics and Public Service
Volume 2: Accountants and auditors; Actuaries; City managers; Cost Estimators; Credit analysts, banking; Economists; Financial institution officers and managers
Volume 3: Billing clerks; Bookkeeping and accounting clerks; Financial institution clerks and related workers; Financial institution tellers; Securities and financial services sales representatives; Tax preparers
Volume 4: Data-processing technicians

Advertising

General information

Outdoor advertising is probably the oldest type of advertising; wall announcements were used by the ancient Romans. In Europe, merchants of all kinds used pictorial signboards for centuries. By the early 1900s, the outdoor poster developed into its familiar outdoor billboard form.

Without advertising, the rate of commercial progress would have been much slower. By the mid-1900s, many business people began to realize that advertising was necessary as a means of enhancing the image of a product. When some large companies decided that advertising was not necessary and that they could get along without it, sales began to drop. They quickly came back to advertising. Its importance was underscored by the breakfast cereal magnate C. W. Post: "I care not who manages production or sales, as long as I write the advertising."

Business owners continue to consider the cost of advertising to be a good investment. This is shown by the increasingly large sums of money spent on advertising every year. Effective advertising makes the job of the salesperson much easier. Less time is spent selling the product because the potential customer already often has positive feelings about the product.

The most effective advertising campaign was used on a product that is still sold today. In 1891, a druggist in Atlanta, Georgia, named Asa G. Candler, bought a carbonated beverage that was being sold at soda fountains under the name of Coca-Cola. He advertised the idea of refreshment, using crude oilcloth signs and woodcut posters. Sales grew from 47 gallons in the first year to 500,000 gallons by 1900, when $147,000 was invested in advertising. As sales rose so did advertising budgets. Coca-Cola became one of the best-known and most widely advertised products in the world. It spent over $370 million in advertising in 1988 and remains the top selling soda in the world.

In the early 1900s, merchants were the principal advertisers and they had to prepare their own advertising. Most of it was prepared for newspapers, which sometimes had employees help the advertiser write the ad. The person who did this was the agent who represented the newspaper and sold advertising space in it. For this service the newspaper paid the agent a commission. Some agents represented groups of papers, while others attempted to represent all of the papers. As time went on, however, it became clear that the agent who secured the account of an advertiser actually represented the advertiser more than the newspaper. Advertising agencies expanded and the number of their services increased.

Radio broadcasting began in the United States in 1922 when KDKA Radio in Pittsburgh went on the air to broadcast presidential election returns. The public quickly embraced radio and advertisers followed suit. Now, of course, advertisers use television as a major focus of many promotional campaigns, but radio continues to be an effective medium for advertising.

The structure of the advertising industry

Compared with $27.5 billion spent on advertising in 1975, the $100 billion tab spent on advertising each year in the late 1980s shows the increased acceptance and support of the advertising industry. Ad spending rose at an annual rate of about 8 percent in the 1980s.

Today, most of the advertising that runs nationally and much of that which appears locally is prepared by advertising agencies. A modern advertising agency is composed of writers, artists, buyers of space and time, researchers, and other specialists. Account executives represent the agency to clients.

An account executive at an advertising agency presents a finished copy of an advertisement to her client. If the client approves, the advertisement will be placed in several periodicals.

Modern marketing has been focused on the consumers' needs, wishes, and preferences. Under older ways of selling, a product would be made and a market sought for it after it was produced. The percentage of failures in this kind of selling was high. The modern way, called the new marketing concept, or the market-driven strategy, starts with the consumer or user and works backward. The product or service, the packaging of the product, and the advertising technique are all chosen in accordance with information secured from potential consumers before the product is actually manufactured. This can help clarify marketing goals and lead to greater effectiveness in the sales program.

As the importance of such marketing information increases, advertisers constantly measure the changing habits and attitudes of the market through surveys and other techniques. They do this continuously, and thereby plan their products and advertising campaigns based on the information gathered from potential consumers.

The advertiser has many ways to tell a product's story. Having first decided who the best potential customers are and where they are located, the advertiser tries to find an advertising medium or combination of media that will reach them. Each medium offers its own special values for particular purposes.

Local merchants, for example, may buy space in the newspapers that serve their area. They can present their merchandise every day, if they wish, and judge the results by the sales produced. Because the newspaper is a local medium, advertisers can plan their advertising to take advantage of local conditions, such as offering rainwear in wet weather and air conditioners for hot spells. Even large national advertisers such as automobile manufacturers can use national advertisements to promote general interest in their product and then direct those interested to local dealers.

Some advertisers, particularly those selling goods to special groups, such as sports enthusiasts, are willing to pay extra for placement in the sports section of a newspaper. Similarly, cosmetics advertisers may request fashion pages.

According to the *U.S. Industrial Outlook*, newspapers remain the top recipients of advertising dollars, receiving almost $30 billion in the late 1980s. National advertising, however, accounted for only 12 percent of newspaper ad billings. Television advertising revenues in 1988 were almost $24 billion (compared with $11.4 billion in 1980 and $3.6 billion in 1970).

During the 1980s, the cable television industry spent billions of dollars to build new systems and improve equipment. Cable TV and teletext advertising now promise to challenge the print media and network TV for advertising revenues.

TV allows advertisers to show their products in actual use. Commercials can suggest in dramatic ways the power of a car, the cleansing power of a detergent, or the amount of storage space in a refrigerator. With a television ad, an advertiser can design a message that appeals to the eye and the ear at the same time.

Commercials may vary in length, but the 30-second spot is used more than 80 percent of the time. Television commercials are usually produced on videotape (see Volume 1: Motion Pictures).

Advertisers usually rotate among various television shows, looking for reach and frequency. A. C. Nielsen and Arbitron ratings measure audiences. Use of home meters and diaries are widespread. By the 1990s, according to the Television Bureau of Advertising, there were some 168 million TV sets in U.S. homes, and the average time spent per household viewing TV reached more than seven hours a day.

The average household has more than five radios, with over a half billion radios in the U.S. alone. More than 85 percent of all automobiles are radio-equipped. Often, Americans rely on radio for news, information, weather, sports, and entertainment programming. Radio is the only medium that is entirely mobile.

Radio commercials are designed to deliver commercial messages on behalf of local and national advertisers. Radio commercials use straight voice copy, dramatic dialogues, music, and sound effects as primary production elements. Such production techniques are used individually or in combination. Radio commercial production is relatively inexpensive. A radio commercial reaches large audiences, yet each listener may conjure up an individual picture in his or her own mind. Therefore radio is said to be a more personal medium than television.

Radio is one of the primary advertising media for retail and local advertisers, who usually purchase commercials in 30 and 60 second units from local radio stations. National advertisers purchase radio commercials either through radio networks or on a "spot" basis (they purchase selected stations in specific markets to achieve specialized advertising objectives). The industry posted significant revenue increases during the last half of the 1980s. Radio ad expenditures in 1985 were estimated at $6.3 billion, and by 1988 they had reached $7.2 billion.

Magazines are a powerful force in the advertising industry. Occasionally, a magazine will achieve mass circulation, reaching millions of readers and appealing to people of various groups and backgrounds. Mass magazines may not always sustain their market position, however, and many successful periodicals are designed for special interest groups (see Volume 1: Magazine Publishing). There is a trade publication for almost every hobby, leisure-time activity, industry, and occupation. Each of these provides a ready-made audience for products or services that appeal to specific readers.

Magazine advertising offers certain special values not found in the other media. Magazines are kept longer than daily newspapers, for example, and may be picked up and read several times. Furthermore, many magazines are passed on from one reader to another, and the actual number of readers may be considerably higher than the circulation figures indicate. Magazines attract approximately 5 percent of the money spent in the U.S. on advertising, amounting to $5.6 billion in 1988.

Many advertisers find it profitable to use direct mail advertising, such as sales letters, leaflets, and folders that may be self-mailers. Direct mail is often supplied by manufacturers to their local dealers, who use it to call attention to special offers. Some mailings feature attention-grabbing devices, such as unusual folds and pop-ups. Nearly all direct mail seeks to get some kind of buying action, often with return cards or coupons. One type encloses coupons worth money if the product is bought; these have been widely used by food and soap manufacturers. Direct mail is often used in conjunction with other types of advertising.

The direct mail advertiser builds the mailing list carefully and tries to maintain its quality. Address lists can be bought from firms whose business it is to provide names of those with various interests and income levels. Highly specialized lists, such as those of art col-

The art director of an advertising agency must ensure that the quality of the art produced in the department is up to the usual high standards.

lectors or world travelers, can be provided when needed. As a rule, however, the more specialized the list, the higher the price.

Some of the oldest and most successful users of direct mail advertising are the mail order companies. They also use many other kinds of media to offer their goods. Their advertisements run in magazines and newspapers, as well as on radio and sometimes television. They seek immediate responses, and the ad that pulls best is often used again and again. The largest mail order houses rely on their catalogs, of which millions may be distributed annually. U.S. expenditures for direct-mail advertising were estimated at $19.1 billion in 1988.

Outdoor advertising signs, billboards, posters, and such are the most familiar and the oldest type of advertising. Most impressive and expensive of all forms of outdoor advertising is the electric sign. These can be any size from a few feet wide to a block long. Neon is a typical advertising method, and its popularity in the 1950s has given rise to a revived interest in the signs themselves. The neon light has become a modern art piece, with collectors spending thousands of dollars for an "Eat at Joe's" type sign. The outdoor medium has long been used by national advertisers who sell products used on the highways, such as automobiles and gasoline. It is also favored by local advertisers such as motels, supermarkets, and restaurants, who seek in this way to attract the passer-by. Those who design outdoor posters allow for what they call the five-second flash, since that is the estimated exposure of the message to the average motorist. This means that the message must be very short, and that the story should be instantly understood.

Transit advertising is displayed in such public places as subway cars, buses, and commuter trains. Posters known as 3–sheets are of-

A designer offers several renditions of the same advertisement. Though the changes may be subtle, they can make a big difference in the overall appearance and tone of the advertisement.

ten provided on station platforms. The message can be longer than on outdoor posters, because the passengers have more time to look at the advertisements.

Advertising agencies have a variety of accounts. A typical list might include a breakfast cereal manufacturer, a detergent company, a cosmetics firm, an automobile manufacturer, a hotel chain, a bank, an airline, and a beverage company. The size of the agency's business is indicated by the amount of advertising for which it bills its clients. Many agencies are small, billing less than $10 million a year. Most of the agency's income is in the form of the 15 percent commission from the media for ad placement, but some accounts are handled on a fee basis or by a combination of both methods. Agencies also charge commissions on work done by outside suppliers to prepare print advertisements or to produce TV and radio commercials. Some of the smaller agencies specialize in accounts in a single field. They may handle only financial accounts, while others take only hotels, book publishers, or industrial clients. Some agencies are known for their expertise in selling package goods. Others excel in retail and department store promotion. Almost every agency develops some distinctive quality that it uses in selling its services.

Many of the larger agencies maintain offices in key cities around the country from which to serve their clients. A number have expanded and offer service worldwide.

International advertising, small before the 1960s, began to increase significantly in the 1970s. The top ten U.S. agencies in worldwide gross income ($3.5 billion in 1984) earned 40 percent of their income from foreign accounts. Advertisers now require new services, such as special kinds of research and marketing counsel, and fees are negotiated for such services.

Once advertisers relied on intuition to tell them where to advertise and what to say. But today, with budgets that often run into millions of dollars, the advertiser and the agency try to get every fact that will help to make sound and profitable decisions. Such fact-finding must begin long before the plans are made and the first advertisement written. Indeed, many large advertisers now insist on a program of research that is planned just as thoroughly as the advertising program and that indicates at every step just how well the advertising is being received. Since modern advertising is concerned with everything that happens to the product along the chain of distribution, it follows that research must record everything that happens along that chain. Such research takes many forms.

Product research looks for improved features and design improvements that will make the product appeal to more people (see Volume 1: Marketing). Package research studies how the product looks on the shelf. Designers seek new color combinations, more convenient shapes, better patterns, and new materials (see Volume 1: Packaging).

In planning an advertising campaign, the agency planners rely on their media experts, who in turn study media research to decide which types of advertising will provide the greatest return for the least investment. Some of these facts are provided by the media themselves; others are secured by the agency. Then it is the duty of the media specialist to arrive at a recommendation as to which combination of media will do the best job.

As the plan goes forward and advertisements are written, copy research tests the eye appeal and persuasive interest of various ways of telling the product's story. Consumers are asked for their opinions on layouts using photographs, drawings, or cartoons. They are also queried as to their feelings on written copy, in which the copy treatment may involve a direct appeal or other approach. Results of such tests are then relayed to the creative people, who use the results in making the product seem more desirable. Each advertisement is usually built around a central theme, which is probably a promise of some kind, such as a claim of superior quality, longer wear proved in the laboratory, new uses for an old product, and the like. This selling appeal is often expressed in the form of a slogan, used over and over; some become part of the vernacular.

The effectiveness of the advertising campaign depends on how well the appeal is directed to the consumer. It must get attention, arouse interest, create desire, secure belief, and impel action. Such effectiveness is measured after the campaign has appeared by the various rating services. By questioning carefully chosen cross-sections of the public, research organizations rate the amount of reading, listening, and viewing the advertisements have managed to get. Usually the research organizations try to measure how many people were attracted to the message and how much of the message they remembered. This kind of research has shown that the most successful advertising sells its products or services for their consumer benefits. Beauty, comfort, convenience, and long life—these are the promises that sell all kinds of products, from furniture to motor cars.

When the research findings are complete, they are turned over to the creative people to be expressed in advertising. The copywriter begins to put down on paper thoughts about how the campaign should look and what it should say. The copywriter shows these initial attempts to the art director and they discuss them. Then the art director produces the first sketches of the layouts. Layouts and copy are shown to the creative director and then reviewed by the agency's plans board, composed of senior executives. At this point the rough layouts are put into more finished form, called "comprehensives." These are shown to the client, often with a preliminary presentation of the research facts that led to the choice of the content and appearance of this campaign. When the campaign has been approved, it goes to the production department. If it is a print campaign, advertisements must be set in type and prepared for the printer. The art director orders the finished art. The art and type proofs or film or other media ready for reproduction are sent directly to publications for printing.

In creating television commercials, the process is different. The TV writer has to think in sequences of words and pictures. The script is turned over to an art director, who sketches the scripted action on a storyboard, step by step. If approved, the storyboard is ready for the producer, who takes charge of all details, such as set design, props, casting characters, and the whole presentation for television. Commercials are usually put on video-tape.

Radio commercials differ from those prepared for TV in that they appeal to the ear only. The commercial writer is primarily responsible for the creative work and uses sound effects and music from a recorded library or by live musicians. In dramatic commercials, the words may be read by actors, who have their speeches timed with a stopwatch. Or the commercial message may be read straight by an announcer, in which case the commercial may be written for the announcer's speaking style.

Orders for insertion of advertisements are placed by the media department, which usually

Illustrators in advertising firms are hired to draw a range of sketches from cartoons to portraits.

delivers a schedule of insertion or air dates to the newspaper or broadcasting station. This department also deals with the people who sell space in magazines and newspapers and time on radio and television networks.

Careers

Many corporations and most large retail stores have an advertising department, whose advertising manager usually works in cooperation with the sales manager and often reports to a vice-president in charge of advertising and sales. There may be a number of writers and artists on the staff, as well as merchandising specialists whose job it is to work with dealers in the field. A sampling of career opportunities follows below.

Advertising managers: An advertising manager supplies information to the company's advertising agency and receives field reports from salespeople and analyzes them for ways to improve advertising effectiveness. He or she will work devising promotions for use by the company, which sometimes include incentive plans for the sales force. The advertising manager also often supervises the preparation of the company's annual reports, catalogs, and sales literature. Together with the agency's account executive, the ad manager works on planning the budget for the next year's campaign (see Volume 2: Marketing, advertising, and public relations managers).

Account managers: The account manager is responsible for establishing and maintaining an accurate budget for the advertising needs for the company. There are various ways that the account manager arrives at a figure for the advertising budget. One common method is to plan on spending a certain proportion of the

Always read the label.

This advertisement went through many stages before it appeared in this form. Many people were involved in the creation of the advertisement, from the inception of the idea to its final design. As a paid advertisement, the client had to give the final approval.

dollar amount generated through the sale of the item the previous year. Another is to figure the average for the industry and use that. A third method sets a sales goal and then estimates what volume of advertising will be needed to reach it. A successful account manager often requires a college background in accounting and management (see Volume 2: Advertising workers).

Merchandising managers: The merchandising manager plans sales and special events that will draw attention and attract shoppers to the store. This person is responsible for maintaining merchandise that is available for consumer purchase.

Media advertising managers: The function of a media advertising manager is to sell advertising space. Media advertising managers keep a running check on competitive media, and, using sales facts and figures on audiences, circulation, and readership, put together the best possible sales presentations. These are often directed at the specific type of advertiser the advertising manager is trying to attract (see Volume 2: Media specialists).

Copywriters: Copywriters are first and foremost, idea generators. Most advertising ideas come out of the copy department. It is the copywriters who create the basic framework of the advertisements, with headlines, text, and slogans. The copywriter should know how to use information sources and should have a nose for news, because much of the best advertising is news. In fact, many of the best copywriters have been news reporters before

entering advertising (see Volume 2: Writers and editors).

Copy chiefs: For every advertisement presented, as many as a dozen ads never get beyond the copy chief, the executive who decides which approach most appropriately expresses the selling theme.

Art directors: Art directors are in charge of creating and designing ads. They visualize how the advertisement will look. The art director sketches the design for the ad on a layout pad, with due regard for human interest, eye appeal, and the balance of shapes and elements. Usually the layout is done over and over until the art director is satisfied with it. Finished art and photography (the actual end-product of the art director's sketch) is usually done by artists and photographers who are self-employed. The art director will choose the artist or photographer who has a particular ability to do the sort of illustration desired, explaining just what is wanted and sometimes, in the case of a photograph, going to the studio while it is being taken (see Volume 1: Design).

Media buyers: Media buyers gather a vast amount of information about the relative size and type of audiences that can be reached through selected media, and the cost of advertising in each of these or any combination of them. The media director in an agency is told what kind of people the advertiser wants to reach; the director then makes a media plan that will reach the designated audience with greatest frequency and least cost. Statistical and cost computation and projections are aided by applications of computer programs written expressly for advertisers and agencies.

Research staff: Research workers gather and analyze the large amounts of factual data required in the planning and production of advertisements. The research worker uses mail questionnaires, personal interviews, and psychological tests. Research deals with broad social and economic trends, as well as human motives and patterns of human behavior. Research workers may make surveys of the buying habits of special groups, or may seek opinions of sample advertisements to find the best selling theme. (see Volume 1: Marketing).

Production staff: Production workers are concerned with all the technical processes of turning the final copy and artwork into printed advertisements, and in the case of television and radio, preparing the commercials for broadcast. Print production workers deal with outside printers, publishers, mailing houses, and typesetters (see Volume 1: Broadcasting; Design; and Volume 4: Graphics art technicians).

Account executives: Account executives are responsible for all the activities on the accounts that they supervise. The account executive handles relations between the agency and its clients and, in consultation with the client's advertising manager, studies the sales and advertising problems, develops a plan to meet them, and then seeks the client's approval of the plan.

Advertising managers: Advertising managers are the executives in charge of the advertising and promotion activities of corporations. Since most companies employ advertising agencies, there is usually a division of responsibility between the two organizations. Ideally, advertising managers and their assistants work closely with the agency people in planning and carrying out the advertising program. In some companies, the advertising manager is also responsible for company publications directed to employees, such as brochures, displays, and promotional activities.

Business managers: Business managers oversee the overall functioning of an agency. They are as important in advertising as in other lines of endeavor, and perhaps more so because the advertising business is a service in which all details must be attended to quickly and surely.

Education

Because advertising is a vocation that requires great breadth of interests and abilities, it is difficult for any one person to become expert in all aspects of the business. This explains the tend-

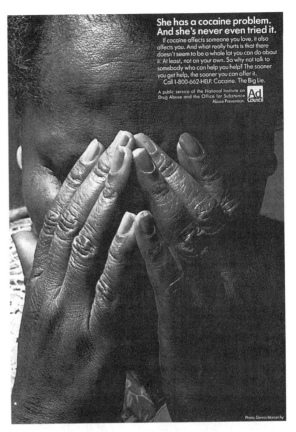

This is an example of a free advertisement, created at no charge by an advertising firm for the benefit of society. Part of a campaign to halt the use of cocaine, this advertisement ran as a public service of the National Institute on Drug Abuse and the Office of Substance Abuse Prevention.

ency of advertising people to specialize in one of the advertising skills. Such specialization may be required by the nature of the business, but if undertaken too soon it is often a distinct loss to the individual. To become a really well-rounded advertising person, the beginner is well advised to avoid specialization and, as much as possible, seek to get an overall view of the whole organization in which he or she is employed.

Many of the larger agencies and advertisers have training programs that help beginners acquire a range of skills. The copywriter who can also make a rough layout, set up a media schedule, and discuss production of an ad knowledgeably with artists and printers has advantages over one who cannot do those things. Although such a person may go on later to become a specialist, he or she will be a more valuable member of the staff because of such experience.

Some of the personal qualifications that help a person to advance in the business are imagination, curiosity, enthusiasm, and the ability to analyze problems. The ability to write and speak well is important, and selling experience is an asset. Educational qualifications include a good general college education, with courses in advertising and marketing. Some of the specialized skills required in advertising work are described below.

To prepare for art director and art production work, young people should get the best possible art training, with an emphasis on the practical aspects of communicating ideas visually. This kind of training is available in art schools or through more general colleges and universities. Since photography is so important in today's advertising, the art director should if possible, become adept in its use.

Many production people prepare for their jobs through on-the-job training, during which they specialize in some particular aspect of the production process. They should have knowledge of the various printing methods, and be familiar with characteristics of paper and inks. And since they work at the end of the production process, they must know how to get the job done even though the time allowed may seem to be impossibly short.

Those wishing to enter the administrative phase of advertising should get a comprehensive business education. Some of the best training for such jobs is given by the graduate business schools of universities. Such courses cover business history, organization, financing, development, expansion, and personnel policies. Qualities needed are foresight, calmness under stress, willingness to take a heavy load of responsibility, and the ability to make good decisions in complex situations. Management is a demanding activity. But for those who can make the grade, it pays well.

Copywriters and others involved in the creative process should be exposed to a wide range of ideas and methods of presentation. While a college degree is important, it is also important for writers and illustrators to develop original and exciting ideas.

Industry outlook

The advertising business grows in proportion to the growth of the national economy. Growth will be accelerated through the development of new products and services and the resulting increase in competition among producers of both industrial and consumer goods. In retail marketing the self-service emphasis requires advertising to keep the public informed about what is being offered.

In addition to the number of new workers needed each year, the advertising business has to replace several thousand persons who transfer to other types of work, retire, or leave the field for other reasons. The areas of greatest activity are New York and Chicago, but openings also occur in other large industrial centers throughout the country.

Agencies are to be found in cities coast to coast. Most are general agencies—that is, they take accounts of many kinds. Some, however, prefer to specialize. Usually the specialized agencies operate in the larger cities. In addition, there are many agencies run by one person. In these the owner, with perhaps one or two assistants, manages several accounts, writes all the copy (or has it written by freelance writers), orders the layouts and artwork from art studios, sends out media orders, and checks insertions. An owner often works long hours for a modest return, but has the satisfaction of running the enterprise, and some build the business to a point where a staff can be enlarged. Many account executives and copywriters in the larger agencies have had such experience and find it extremely valuable in providing both an overall view of the business and a sampling of the numerous skills required to operate an agency.

For both men and women, pay scales are usually highest in the larger organizations. Part of the satisfaction of advertising work is in the sense of creative accomplishment, such as seeing and hearing one's own ideas as they flash before millions of people. But there is much less glamour than is commonly supposed and much more of the day-to-day routine requires painstaking attention to detail.

◇ **SOURCES OF ADDITIONAL INFORMATION**

American Association of Advertising Agencies
666 Third Avenue
13th Floor
New York, NY 10017

American Advertising Federation
1400 K Street, NW
Suite 1000
Washington, DC 20005

Business/Professional Advertising Association
100 Metroplex Drive
Edison, NJ 08817

International Advertising Association
342 Madison, 20th Floor, Suite 2000
New York, NY 10017

Sales and Marketing Executives International
Statler Office Tower, Suite 458
Cleveland, OH 44115

American Marketing Association
250 South Wacker Drive, Suite 200
Chicago, IL 60606

For the most current information, contact:

Advertising Age
Crain Communications
740 North Rush Street
Chicago, IL 60611

◇ **RELATED ARTICLES**

Volume 1: Marketing; Design; Public Relations; Retailing
Volume 2: Advertising workers; Commercial artists; Cartoonists and animators; Demographers; Designers; Graphics programmers; Management trainees; Marketing, advertising, and public relations managers; Marketing research personnel; Media specialists; Photographers and camera operators; Public relations specialists; Writers and editors
Volume 3: Compositors and typesetters; Public opinion researchers; Radio, television, and print advertising sales workers
Volume 4: Graphic arts technicians; Layout technicians

Agriculture

General information

Agriculture and farming have changed the structure of society more significantly than any other industry. Before the development of farming, hunting and gathering were the methods for finding food. Prehistoric people moved from place to place, following the migration of animals, seeking food where he could find it. If he was unsuccessful for more than a very short period of time, he starved.

About 10,000 years ago, humans first developed the rudiments of farming. As prehistoric people figured out that seeds grew into plants, and certain seeds became certain plants, the idea of planting for future food took hold. The first evidence of farming from archeological records show that man first planted about 9000 B.C. According to archeological findings, it took another 1000 years for farming to become a primary source of food.

Farming was initially far more difficult than hunting; methods for developing fertile farmland and domesticating animals were learned by trial and error. However, as the skills were developed, it became easier for some groups to farm. This allowed them to develop permanent shelters and live in one region for several years.

This ability to remain in one place led to the development of villages, and then cities. It was only through the use of farming that people could remain in one location throughout the year, and develop the land for communal living and farming.

As the skills of farmers increased, it allowed for better production of food. Both animal husbandry and planting skills developed. As the quantity of food increased, this allowed some of the village members to work on something other than food production. Carpentry, pottery, weaving and such became the work of some of the village members, and farming was the work of the other part of the population.

Farming skills increased as new methods were developed. Leaving part of the farming land fallow, or unplanted, for a season allowed the ground to restore some nutrients needed for farming. Planting certain types of plants, like legumes, replaced minerals in the soil. This allowed for farmland to be used for much longer without depleting the soil entirely of its value.

The development of machines and tools assisted the farmer in food production. Prehistoric man developed the sickle for harvesting. The Egyptians developed irrigation and, at the same time as the Mesopotamians, a plow pulled by oxen. In the Middle Ages, horses were used for pulling plows. This shortened the time needed for plowing since horses worked faster than oxen. Jethro Tull developed the first modern farming machine around 1700, when he designed and built the first mechanical seed planter.

The agricultural revolution, from 1700 to the mid-1800s saw a boom in the ability of farmers to produce crops. Crop rotation allowed farm land to be used continually, and animal breeding improved dramatically. Because of the increase in production, towns became much larger as more people were able to move away from the farming communities and rely on work and markets in the cities.

As machinery improved, so did the size of the farm. When engines were used for tractors, the land that could be worked increased the size of farms. With pumps for irrigation, harvesters, and all of the other mechanical elements that now do the work that used to be done by hand, the production level has increased to the point where the United States produces more food than can be used in the country. Food is sent overseas, and farmers are paid to leave some land unplanted so the price of food does not drop too low.

Agriculture is one of the most progressive and dynamic industries in the United States.

Science and technology are playing a bigger role in agriculture, and as a result, the United States is unsurpassed in its production and quality of food. Scientists applying the principles of biochemistry, chemistry, physics, mathematics, genetics, microbiology, and other disciplines to the production and processing of farm products have unlocked many of nature's secrets and this knowledge has been used to the farmer's advantage.

As the proportion of human labor used in the production of farm goods has dropped approximately one-half, the proportion of capital represented by feed, machinery, fertilizer, and so on has increased tenfold. The farmer now relies heavily on these technological advancements to sustain and increase production.

Although farms have increased in size considerably since the end of World War II, the number of farms in the United States has declined. This is due in part to the fact that technology has allowed a family to operate a much larger farm than it did during the time of horse-drawn equipment, and in part to the growth of large-scale farms run by corporations.

Many functions that formerly were performed on the farm have now moved off the farm into large cities. For example, farmers use to keep large supplies of fresh meat on hand when the weather was cool enough to prevent the meat from spoiling. In the late fall of the year, a calf or sheep or pig would be slaughtered and the carcass would be hung outside to serve as the family meat supply through the winter. Today, this farm activity of the past may be performed in the city where large animal slaughterhouses and meat packing and processing industries have come into existence.

Another change is in the method of tilling the land. In the past, horses and mules pulled the plows that prepared the soil for farming. Today, agricultural engineers design tractors manufactured in large factories in the city. Tractors have allowed farmers to sow and harvest more efficiently, increasing the production of crops per acre. This shift in tilling methods has made many acres of land available for the production of crops for human consumption rather than to feed the animals that formerly pulled the plows. It also made farmers highly dependent on outside sources for their equipment and brought a new emphasis on the need for more sophisticated cash management.

These are only two examples of functions once performed on the farm that have shifted to industries in the city. There are many others, all of which have expanded the scope and increased the number of agricultural occupations and, therefore, the number of career opportunities available to young people.

Two farmers discuss the maintenance of a drainage system on a farm in southern Illinois.

The structure of the agriculture industry

American agriculture is a vast and diversified industry. The farmer who cultivates the land, raises livestock, and grows plants; the industries that process, distribute, or transport farm products and farm supplies; the organizations that supply services to the farmer and the consumer; the forester who cultivates forest land and timber; the conservationist who preserves and protects natural resources; and the schools and communications organizations that supply education and information about these occupations—all are working together in what is today known as the agriculture industry. Every day, in a variety of ways, it touches the lives of all persons, rural and urban, young and old.

At one time farming and agriculture meant the same thing, but this is no longer true. Today, agriculture includes not only farming and farm management but also many businesses and industries that produce goods and services the farmer uses to raise livestock and grow crops. Agriculture also includes industries that buy and process the products of the farm, as well as some industries that sell raw and processed farm products to the consumer. This

A farmer operates a new combine that harvests and separates corn. The forward thrust of the cabin allows the farmer to see more clearly and sit more comfortably.

whole complex of activities is often called agribusiness (see Volume 4: Agribusiness technicians).

The base for all agricultural work is the farm. The average farm will have a farm manager, who will probably have attended college for an agricultural degree. The manager will have farm laborers who will work either on a temporary basis during the planting or the harvest season, or permanent laborers who are in charge of regular production tasks.

Single crop farms are commonplace, with the cash crop (the crop that is grown for sales) being the only thing produced on the farm. Wheat farms and corn farms are obvious on any back road drive through the midwest and the plains states. Specialized livestock production is mainly centered on cattle and chicken farming in the United States. Sheep, goat, turkey, and fish farming are other livestock that are found on single livestock farms.

Diversified farms will produce several different crops or animals, or a mixture of both, for sale. The old-style family farm was frequently a diversified farm, with crops and a barn full of animals. It is less common now, partly because of the ease of specialized production, but mainly because the profit margin is often higher with single crop production. The land is normally well suited to only a few types of plants or animals and diversifying becomes difficult. But the diversified farm is less dependent on the success of production of a single item. Drought, disease, and other natural disasters may take less of a toll on the farm profits if many items are produced.

Agriculture (including forestry) produces about two-thirds of the raw materials in the United States. Over seven billion bushels of corn are produced each year in the United States. The United States also annually produces approximately 2 billion bushels of wheat, 140 million tons of hay, and more than 180 million boxes of oranges.

The off-the-farm industries provide farmers with seed, fertilizer, and machinery. The output industries then process and market the farm products. Storage, shipping, processing, packaging and canning are just some of the industries that assist the farmer in the sale of goods. The produce must reach the customer in the best condition for sale. It is also important, for example, that all the apples produced in September not arrive at the store on the same day. Storage for future sales, scheduling of deliveries, canning for off season sales, all these things are part of the agribusiness world.

To insure sales of their produce, farmers can arrange to have the crops sold before they are produced. Contract farming is an arrangement with a buyer, such as a food processor or marketer, to ship the produce to the buyer upon harvesting. The farmer must agree to a price at the time of the contract. This arrangement can be to the benefit of either the farmer or the buyer. If there are a lot of successful crops of the type the farmer sells, the farmer may get a higher price for the crops in a contract than if he had waited for the harvest and bid with many other farmers waiting to sell their goods.

If the crop production is low one year, then the buyer may have gotten a cheaper price on a product if the buyer arranged the contract early in the season, before the farmer knew that there would be less of the items produced than normal. In an open sale the farmer would be able to raise the price, because there would be more people trying to buy from him.

Aside from the goods and services, the off-the-farm portion of the agricultural industry also provides a large number of diversified careers. Of the approximately twenty-one million people working in various areas of agriculture, only about two million are located on farms, whereas about nineteen million work at agricultural jobs off the farm.

The Agricultural Experiment Station is the research center that normally works with the state universities that have agricultural schools. The agricultural schools are known as the land-grant universities. In 1862, Congress gave each state 30,000 acres of land for each senator and representative in Congress. The state was to sell the land and, with the money it received, it was to build a college that would specialize in education for agriculture and mechanical arts. Some states created new universities, and some funded colleges in universities that were already established. The University of Illinois and the University of California are two well known universities that were founded on land-grant money.

The experiment stations conduct research on farming techniques to develop the most effective methods of farming for each region. Scientists work with soil, crops, feed, animals, variations and genetic strains to devise the best method for the climate and the zone they work in. Some states have more than one station working in different areas to compensate for regional differences.

The stations are funded through state and federal programs. Scientists are state employees, working with university instructors and researchers. They also work with the extension agents who work for the government, distributing information and services to the farmers of the area.

According to the American Farm Bureau Federation, farmers spend over $140 billion to run their farms and ranches each year. Expenditures in 1986 included $9.5 billion for fuel and machinery, $6.4 billion for tractors and other equipment, $19 billion for feed and seed, and $5.8 billion for fertilizer and soil conditioners.

Half of the land in the United States is used for farming, but only about 4 percent of the population works in agriculture. The United States provides the world with 25 percent of the beef and 15 percent of the grain produced each year. The farming industry is incredibly important both at home and abroad. The jobs involved are diverse and wide ranging.

Careers

About twenty-three million workers in the United States earn their living from the agriculture industry. One out of every five jobs in private employment is related to agriculture. Specific jobs in the agricultural industry usually fall within one of the nine groups listed below.

Researchers: American farm production has advanced more in the last fifty years than in all preceding years; research is the big reason. Agriculture looks to research for new machinery and equipment; for improvements in nutrition, genetics (improving plants and animals), and disease control; and for the latest agricultural applications in such areas as radioactive elements, radiation electronics, solar energy, and computers.

New facts are found and unknown horizons of knowledge are explored in the Agricultural Experiment Stations in each state and in the U.S. Department of Agriculture. Thousands of professionals are employed as researchers. These professionals are supported by thousands of technicians and other assistants. The agricultural industry employs many thousands more. Candidates for these well-paid jobs must have acceptable educational qualifications (see Volume 1: Biological Sciences, Chemistry; Volume 2: Biochemists, Chemists, Geologists).

Business managers: The business staff engage in the wholesale and retail marketing of agricultural products. They manage private and co-operative businesses that sell to the farmer or move products to the consumer.

Commercial firms today are employing young people who have combined agricultural education with studies in economics and business administration. Job opportunities exist in agricultural finance, insurance, transportation, storage, grading, and sales. Banks, insurance companies, farm credit agencies, public utilities, and food chains are examples of business firms hiring people with specialized agricultural knowledge (see Volume 1: Business Administration).

Industrial and engineering scientists: The vast operations of agriculture require engineers, scientists, technologists, production workers, and salespeople with specialized knowledge. Farmers turn to scientists and engineers for machinery and equipment, feeds, fertilizer, lime, pesticides, and herbicides.

When crops are harvested and livestock is ready for market, specialized agricultural industries process them, package them, and bring them to the consumer. Included in such industries are dairy plants, food freezing plants, drying and canning operations, meat packing plants, poultry processing plants, and grain storage and processing operations (see Volume 2: Engineers, Industrial designers).

Educators: Each year, thousands of new teachers go to positions in high-school departments of vocational agriculture, agricultural colleges, and the Agricultural Extension Service (see Volume 1: Education).

Agricultural extension workers: Extension workers are employees of the Department of Agriculture and their state agricultural colleges. They live and work primarily in farming communities to bring new ideas and technology in agriculture to farmers and farm families. A minimum of a bachelor's degree is required for appointment to a position in the Extension Service at the county level. In most states, additional study in a particular line of work beyond the bachelor's degree will be required as a part of the Extension Service's in-service training program. It is common for a county extension worker to possess the master's degree and many hold the doctorate degree. Educational positions with governmental and industrial agencies or farm organizations require a mini-

A soil scientist records some topographical information on an aerial photograph of Saline County, Nebraska.

mum of the bachelor's degree, with some specifying advanced degrees (see Volume 3: Agricultural extension service workers).

Public information and public service workers: Government agencies, state departments of agriculture, and various departments in the foreign service hire agricultural employees in increasingly large numbers. The largest employer among these agencies is the federal government, which includes the Agricultural Marketing Service, Farmers Home Administration, Forest Service, Bureau of Land Management, and various regulatory agencies extending into every state (see Volume 1: Civil Service).

Each state has its department of agriculture. Many are charged with regulatory work to protect farmers in their purchases, and also to safeguard the health of the public, as in food inspection and grading. Nursery inspection requires particular specialists in entomology, pathology, botany, and horticulture.

There are also opportunities in community planning, recreation agencies, and private consulting services.

Foreign service has opened new fields of opportunity in recent years. Again, the principal employer is the federal government, which includes the Foreign Agricultural Service of the U.S. Department of Agriculture, the Agency for International Development of the State Department, and the Food and Agriculture Organization of the United Nations. In addition, several private foundations, church organizations, and world banks have employed consultants to help underdeveloped countries. More experienced personnel, many with advanced degrees, are sought. Land grant colleges participate in development efforts in many lesser developed countries of the world.

Another branch of international service needing people with a technical knowledge of agriculture is the Peace Corps. Members of the Corps teach, build, and work in newly developing areas of the world (see Volume 1: Foreign Service).

Veterinary medicine: Those wishing to serve as a veterinarian must earn the doctor of veterinary medicine degree (D.V.M.). This requires a minimum of six years of study, two years in a pre-veterinary program and four years in a professional program offered by one of the colleges of veterinary medicine. Veterinarians work on farms, labs, and any place where animals are kept or raised. Zoos frequently have a full time veterinarian (see Volume 2: Veterinarians).

Farm and ranch workers: Farm and ranch workers are employed in all types of farms. These include: dairy farms; beef farms; grain farms; fruit farms; fish farms; tree farms; and tobacco farms (see Volume 3: Dairy farmers, Farm operatives and managers, Farmers, Fishers, commercial). Aspects of engineering, automation, chemistry, pathology, entomology, genetics, nutrition, economics, and financial management are all important in the life of the successful farmer today.

For a young person, the main disadvantage of a career in farming or ranching is the enormous financial outlay necessary to become established on a competitive basis with the large commercial farms. Many farmers who can not compete are leaving the rural areas of the country in the hope of finding a more stable life in the cities.

The successful farmer, however, will continue to be a key person in the U.S. economy, with the opportunity of outdoor living and working independently that few others are privileged to enjoy.

Conservationists: The people who direct conservation projects, and others who plan and care for recreation areas, are graduates of agricultural colleges. They study agronomy, horticulture, landscape architecture, zoology, forestry, fish and wildlife management, agricultural engineering, botany, plant pathology, range management, or turf management. They find careers with federal, state, and local agencies charged with the responsibility for conservation and recreation programs. Some accept opportunities with private developments, such as golf courses or game preserves. Still others are employed in commercial nurseries or landscape firms (see Volume 1: Recreation and Park Services).

Soil, water, and forest conservation problems are now the concern of a number of agencies, both state and federal. Several states have set up commissions to advise and regulate water use for industry, domestic use, and irrigation. These and others are concerned with flood control, drainage, pollution, and the development of lakes and streams for recreation. The management of fish and wildlife resources is increasingly a task for highly trained personnel.

Education

As agriculture expands and becomes more complex, technical and educational requirements increase. Jobs of the future will require people with more education and training, more imagination, and more technical capacity.

The educational requirements for farming and ranching vary from a minimum of a high-school education or less for farm hands to a doctorate degree for managerial positions on many commercial and institutional farms. Many high schools have chapters of the Future Farmers of America (FFA), an organization set up to aid young people who plan to enter farming. With the trend toward bigger farms that require more investment, managerial ability, and technical knowledge, educational requirements will increase. A person planning to enter the modern business of farming or ranching as an owner or manager will find that a bachelor's degree is a minimum and that additional education is most helpful.

The technological explosion in agriculture and the rapid expansion of the off-the-farm phase of the agricultural industry have brought on an increasing need for semiprofessional workers. Many phases of the agricultural industry will require an increasing number of workers who have had one or two years of technical education beyond high school. The agricultural industry needs individuals with a good understanding of farming who can exercise sound judgment and can competently perform such activities as servicing, supervising,

A microbiologist prepares to inject antibodies into poultry. He is testing the effectiveness of vaccines that may eventually be used for commercial development.

controlling, building, and operating, in specialized situations.

Since the basic sciences are so important to modern agriculture, courses in biology, economics, chemistry, mathematics, and physics should be taken in high school.

Short-course or one-to-two year programs are specialized. Technical information and skills for a specific vocation are emphasized. Courses vary in length and content within an institution as well as from institution to institution. Some courses are as short as two weeks in duration and are designed to develop a specific skill. Other courses are two years in length, placing more emphasis on a technical knowledge of agriculture and providing on-the-job experience. New courses are continually being introduced as the need for new specialized training in agriculture becomes evident.

Short-course and technical programs can be taken at many community, junior, and four-year colleges. Many short courses are offered through the Agricultural Extension Service of the land grant universities. In some areas, spe-

An agricultural advisor from the Cooperative Extension Service answers a farmer's questions concerning the corn crop. The advisor visits several farms in the area to suggest new agricultural methods and help increase crop production.

cialized training programs in agriculture are available under the Rural Area Development Act or the Manpower Development Act.

College programs in agriculture can help provide an understanding of the basic physical, biological, and social sciences so important for a professional career in agriculture.

A young person interested in scientific research can explore the area of agriculture research to some extent in high school. Chemistry, biology, and mathematics courses are especially helpful. A number of high-school students have won Science Achievement Awards for research activities designed to improve agricultural techniques.

Generally, a doctorate degree is required as a minimum educational preparation for a career in research. Students obtaining a doctorate degree in agriculture must specialize in some area. Students with a B.A. or M.A. degree can qualify for a number of agricultural research jobs as technical workers and scientific aides. These jobs are generally concerned with assisting research specialists in their particular area of work, such as doing routine testing and recording of results on reports, charts, and drafts.

Engineering and scientific positions require various educational requirements. For example, certain technical positions with a feed or fertilizer plant may require the completion of a short course or technical program. On the other hand, a managerial position in the development program of an agricultural chemical company may require a doctorate degree. Most positions in the engineering and scientific field have a minimum educational requirement of a bachelor's degree.

Educational requirements for work in the conservation and ecology area vary considerably with the type of career selected. Most positions with the Soil Conservation Service, Forest Service, the Fisheries and Wildlife Service, and state Departments of Conservation require a bachelor's degree. Colleges and universities that hire personnel for teaching, research, and extension service may require graduate degrees. Many positions within private organizations also require graduate degrees.

The range in educational requirements for people working in agricultural information services varies from a short course of two weeks for a milk tester, to a Ph.D. degree for certain positions with the agricultural chemical industry. Vocational and technical positions that require a two-year to a four-year degree program are available in the agricultural services area. Professional positions in this area require a minimum of a bachelor's degree. Many overseas positions require a master's or doctorate degree.

Industry outlook

Employment of farm operators and managers was declining in the late 1980s and is expected to continue to decline, though at a slower rate. Increasing productivity made it possible to meet rising domestic and export demands for expanding populations with less labor, and the trend toward fewer and larger farms should continue. High costs of farm land and equipment, rising operating costs, and the complexity of modern farm management pose challenges for future farmers. Most openings on farms will result from the need to replace farmers who retire or leave farming.

Farms will become larger, more capital will be invested per farm, and farming operations will become more specialized. The farmer will become more efficient, thus forcing the percentage of the labor force working on farms to decrease. The off-the-farm segment of agriculture will expand, scientific knowledge will be applied to agriculture to an even greater extent, and educational requirements for careers in agriculture will increase.

In the future, the importance of other countries and their development to U.S. agriculture will increase. Each year billions of dollars worth of agricultural commodities are exported to foreign countries. The exportation of farm products will be greater in the future. With this expansion there will be more overseas careers for young people educated in agriculture and international trade.

The population of the United States will continue to grow. Since the agricultural industry has the responsibility of providing food, much of our clothing, and the materials used to build and furnish homes, it must expand to keep pace with the population growth.

The future of agriculture depends upon well-trained and well-educated young people. They must be able to apply the principles of fundamental sciences to all aspects of the agriculture industry. Thus, production of higher quality, lower priced food and fiber for the consumer will be assured.

◇ SOURCES OF ADDITIONAL INFORMATION

For information concerning availability of agricultural programs in a given area, write to the dean of agriculture at that specific school. Land grant colleges in each state are also good sources of information on education in agriculture.

Other organizations that can provide information include:

American Farm Bureau Federation
225 Touhy Avenue
Park Ridge, IL 60068

Future Farmers of America
National FFA Center
Box 15160
5632 Mount Vernon Memorial Highway
Alexandria, VA 22309

U.S. Department of Agriculture
Washington, DC 20250

American Society of Farm Managers and Rural Appraisers
950 South Cherry Street
Suite 106
Denver, CO 80222

American Agricultural Marketing Association
225 West Touhy
Park Ridge, IL 60068

Society for Agricultural Training through Integrated Voluntary Activities
Route 2
PO Box 242W
Viola, WI 54664

For those interested in the soil sciences, contact:

American Society of Agronomy
677 South Segoe Road
Madison, WI 53711

American Society for Horticultural Science
701 North St. Asaph Street
Alexandria, VA 22314

Soil Science Society of America
677 South Segoe Road
Madison, WI 53711

Regenerative Agriculture Association
222 Main Street
Emmaus, PA 18098

◇ **RELATED ARTICLES**

Volume 1: Accounting; Biological Sciences; Business Administration; Chemistry; Civil Service; Foreign Service; Machining and Machinery; Packaging; Recreation and Park Services

Volume 2: Accountants and auditors; Biochemists; Biologists; Biomedical engineers; Chemists; Engineers; Food technologists; Geologists; Groundwater professionals; Health and regulatory inspectors; Industrial designers; Packaging engineers; Veterinarians

Volume 3: Agricultural extension service workers; Agricultural scientists; Canning and preserving industry workers; Dairy farmers; Dairy products manufacturing workers; Farm operatives and managers; Farm-equipment mechanics; Farmers; Farriers; Fishers, commercial; Grain merchants; Meat packing production workers; Meatcutters; Pest control workers; Soil scientists; Tobacco products industry workers

Volume 4: Agribusiness technicians; Agricultural equipment technicians; Animal health technicians; Animal production technicians; Biological specimen technicians; Biological technicians; Biomedical engineering technicians; Farm crop production technicians; Fish-production technicians; Geological technicians; Hydrological technicians; Industrial engineering technicians; Industrial safety-and-health technicians; Ornamental horticulture technicians; Soil conservation technicians

Apparel

General information

Archaeologists have found no clothing from early periods before the Stone Age. Part of this may be because of the fragility of the garments; they may not have survived the weathering of the centuries, even if they were buried. It is assumed that prehistoric people made clothing for warmth from the skins of animals killed for food. The clothes may have been unfitted and tied or wrapped around the body.

Toward the end of the Stone Age (about 10,000 years ago) the first sewn clothing was made. In the southern regions, needles were made from carved bone. The thin needles were believed to have been used for stitching garments and weaving. In the northern regions of Europe, the tribes used leather straps to sew together skins. Holes were made in the garment and a hook was used to pull the leather thong through the skins.

From pottery and wall paintings, archaeologists have clues to the clothing of the ancient Egyptians. Material was woven from spun thread. Spinning thread was done on a spindle. The spindle is a long smooth stick with a notch at one end for catching the thread or yarn. Spinning the spindle against a bowl, called a whorl, produced a fairly even, continuous fiber. Weaving was the process used to form a fabric from the fibers. Weaving had been done to grass earlier by the Egyptians and other tropical people. Baskets, mats, and some clothing had been made by weaving and drying thin or thick grass blades or leaves.

In Egypt, The first clothing worn by men was a band around the waist. This narrow piece of fabric was primarily decorative, with pendants and religious objects hanging from the band. The first clothing worn by Egyptian women were white linen skirts worn down to the ankles.

The type of clothing worn in a certain location was often influenced by the climate. In warmer climates, both men and women tended to wear dresses and other loose-fitting apparel that did not wrap around the leg. Those in colder climates were more likely to wear pants.

Religious customs also influenced the type of apparel worn. For example, in the 12th century when the Muslims conquered north and central India, dramatic changes were made in the dress code so as to conform with Muslim practice. Up until the conquest, the warm climate had dictated that dress styles leave some of the body uncovered. But the Muslim practice of covering as much of the body as possible led to a change. Men began to wear wide trousers and long-sleeved coats that reached to the knees or below. Women wore long trousers, a long shirt-like garment, and an outer jacket.

In the Americas around A.D. 700, Indian tribes were weaving spun cotton threads into material for clothing. Cloth dyes were made from berries, ores such as iron, and plants such as the indigo. Patterns could be woven into the material or painted on the material. Weaving a pattern into the material was complicated. The Chinese had begun to weave complex patterns with silk threads between 2500 and 1000 B.C. The Persians imported Chinese silk during these centuries and developed a lucrative trade in silk brocade and fabrics.

The spinning wheel increased the speed at which threads and yarns could be produced. In use by the 12th century, the origin of the spinning wheel is unknown. About the same time the two-bar loom was invented, increasing the speed at which the threads could be woven. For the next few centuries the art of fabric making would increase in beauty and clothes would become much more widely available.

The next wave of inventions to assist fabric makers in their art came during the 18th century. The spinning jenny, a machine that spun more than one thread at a time, was invented by James Hargreaves around 1764. The water frame cotton spinning machine invented by Ri-

Two apparel managers inspect the quality of the textiles that have just been woven.

chard Arkwright made hard twisted thread from cotton instead of linen, the fiber used until then for the threads that ran the length of the fabric. In 1785, Edmund Cartwright developed a power loom that ran on steam. He opened a factory in England that used the machine for rapid production of fabric. Eli Whitney, an American inventor, developed the cotton gin in 1793. The cotton gin reduced the time and number of people required to clean the seeds from cotton.

In 1830, Barthelemy Thimonnier patented a sewing machine in Paris. However, Thimonnier's machines befell the same fate as Cartwright's factory. As the mass production of material became more likely, weavers and tailors destroyed the factories where the work was taking place. Their fear of being driven out of business led to may instances of destruction and violence across Europe.

In the United States, Elias Howe was working on a sewing machine as well. The machine was rapid and used two threads in a lock-stitch pattern, as the sewing machines use today. However, the Howe sewing machine was no more accepted in the United States than Thimonnier's invention had been accepted in Paris. Howe sold part of the patent rights in England.

In 1851, Isaac Singer build the sewing machine that would survive the objections of the

tailors. The machine only made simple stitches and the tailors would still be required for much of the work on clothing. The machine would speed production of the basic elements of garments.

As the Industrial Revolution progressed, the sewing machine was joined by a cutting machine that cut several layers of fabric. Buttonhole sewers were invented by the Reese Machinery Company. Factories were replacing craft shops. Workers were required to purchase their own sewing machines.

In the early part of the 20th century, New York City's East Side became the largest producer of clothing in the world. The conditions in the small factories that had sprung up were miserable. The ventilation and lighting were terrible. The rooms were packed with workers, who had twelve or fourteen hour workdays. The term "sweatshop" was developed as a description of the apparel factories.

On March 25, 1911, in New York City, one of the worst fires ever to burn in a building swept through the Triangle Waist Factory. It killed 145 people, most of them young girls employed in the factory. The fire burned for only a half hour. The building only had one fire escape and the exit doors were blocked. The factory had just been approved by the city inspectors for fire safety. The tragedy forced the city to revise its building codes and labor laws. Union membership increased dramatically for the unions working in the apparel industry. The International Ladies Garment Workers Union, founded in 1900, developed enough support after the fire to force labor laws to be enacted and enforced. The Amalgamated Clothing Workers of America was established in 1914, and soon became one of the largest unions for the apparel industry.

The era of the sweatshop was coming to an end. The World Wars increased the need for clothes production and kept the United States as the leader in the apparel producing industry. The industry was starting to specialize and departmentalize. Jobbers bought raw materials such as cotton and sold it to contractors. Contractors made materials—fabrics, threads, or even garments. Manufacturers bought materials and threads and made clothes to sell to wholesalers. They also had the option of selling to distributors who owned their own stores. Wholesalers sold finished products to retail stores. Shops, however, still existed that produced finished garments from raw materials; they were called vertical mills and vertical mill distributors.

The biggest change in the last fifty years has been the migration of manufacturing jobs to Asia. A substantial number of garments are made abroad because of the reduced cost of labor. The quantity of clothing imported has increased by more than 300 percent in the last decade. Employment in the apparel industry has risen slightly in the last few years, following years of declining employment. Small shops producing garments has helped to reestablish clothes production in the United States.

The limited investment required to cut and sew garments, and the tendency of firms to specialize in one operation, such as cutting, allow small firms to enter this industry with relative ease. Most manufacturers have small factories, employing fewer than 100 workers. The relatively few companies employing more than 100 workers, however, account for more than 60 percent of the apparel work force.

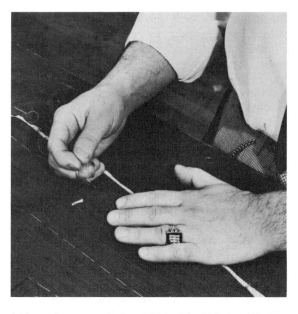

A tailor performs canvas basting, which involves distributing cloth over a canvas foundation. Such a task requires a steady hand.

The structure of the apparel industry

The apparel industry is made up of thousands of apparel manufacturing establishments, where garments are made. It includes almost all types of clothing, except for hats, shoes, hosiery, and fur. Excluded garments are not considered because of the fundamental differences in materials and in methods of manufacture.

Because the term apparel includes so many items of clothing, this general category is usually subdivided into male and female apparel. Male apparel, which includes men's and boys' clothing, includes such items as suits, overcoats, other outer garments, slacks, shirts, ties, and underwear. Female apparel, which includes women's and girl's clothing, includes such items as coats, suits, other outer garments, dresses, blouses, skirts, underwear, and nightwear.

The U.S. apparel industry began in the Middle Atlantic region, where it is still centered. The pool of experienced workers in the Mid-Atlantic states is far greater than in any other area of the country, and the largest concentration of factories producing men's apparel is located there. These plants are usually larger than those making women's garments because men's clothing undergoes fewer design and style changes, and thus is better suited to mass production methods.

In the women's and misses' outerwear sector of the apparel industry, for instance, the majority of the cut and sewn garments originate in New York City, but much of the sewing is contracted out to firms throughout the world. In addition, some relatively low-priced women's and children's garments, such as low-end cotton dresses, for which highly skilled opera-

tors are less essential, are made throughout the country.

While the majority of apparel factories are located in the Mid- Atlantic states, there are factories on the Pacific Coast as well. Other parts of the apparel industry are spread evenly throughout all parts of the United States, including large factories in the South and West.

The major operations in clothes making are designing the garment, cutting the cloth, sewing the pieces together, pressing the assembled garment, and merchandising.

A designer creates the look of a piece of clothing. The designer draws a picture of what the clothing should look like and then works with seamstresses and other workers to make a sample of the clothing. The designer might then make modifications on the design based on suggestions from apparel executives and other management personnel.

Once an item of clothing has been designed, the proposed item is sent to the merchandising department. Merchandising represents the "know-how" of preparing and presenting any garment line for successful sale to retailers. It can be subdivided into the buying of piece goods used in the manufacture of the garments and the proper pricing of the garments after the clothing has been styled by the designer.

Because the apparel industry covers such a wide variety of garments and uses practically every type of textile manufactured, merchandising problems vary from one segment of the industry to another.

When the garment style has been produced, been shown to retail buyers, and accepted by the merchandising department, the manufacturer gives the orders to the cutting department of the factory. There are five basic operations in the cutting department: spreading, marking, cutting, assembling, and ticketing. Small shops may combine two or more of these operations into a single job.

By traditional practice, spreaders lay out bolts of cloth into exact lengths on the cutting table. Markers trace the pattern pieces on large sheets of paper. In some cases, they trace the pattern with chalk directly on the cloth itself. A machine cutter follows the pattern outline on the cloth and cuts various garment pieces from layers of cloth. Using an electrical cutting machine, the cutter slices through all the layers at once.

Newer technology has been developed, so that computer-controlled cutters are often used. Computers allow for more precise information to be programmed into set patterns and more uniform shapes to be cut.

After the garment has been cut, it is sent to the sewing-machine operators. The cut pieces of cloth are prepared for the sewing room by assemblers who bring together various pieces needed, including lining, tapers, and trimmings, to make a complete garment. They match color, size, and fabric design and use chalk or thread to mark locations of pockets, buttonholes, buttons, and other trimmings. They identify each bundle with a ticket. (This ticket is also used to figure the earnings of workers who are paid according to the number of pieces they produce.) The bundles are then sent to the sewing room.

In the sewing room, seamstresses put the material together into its finished form. Seamstresses and other production workers must be careful to follow design patterns supplied by the designers.

The finished clothing is then inspected and sent to the shipping room. From there, the material is sent to the markets the manufacturer has created for the product. Manufacturers must have a good sales staff so that an interest is created in the product and stores will choose to carry the newly-created clothing line. Marketing plays a very important part in the success or failure of a line of clothing.

In the women's dress industry, the type of fabric used, particularly its color and pattern, is as important to the marketability of the clothing as the cut of the garment itself. In cotton and machine-made materials, the print or the weave may be an important selling factor. The undyed goods are then sold to wholesalers or converters who dye them or perhaps have them printed as ordered by the garment manufacturer.

With the fabrics purchased and prices for each garment established, the sellers travel to New York and other merchandising centers to show their goods. A great deal of selling in the women's wear field is done in the showrooms of New York.

The menswear division also has its semiannual buying periods, and the large retailers go to the New York market to purchase a substantial proportion of their seasonal requirements. The orders are usually larger than in the women's wear field, for a retailer can make more long-term commitments without fear that the garments will be out of style within a short time.

Executive offices are usually found in the states where the factories are located, but practically every important apparel manufacturer has a sales office in New York City. This is where large retailers usually do their buying and where industry-wide sales meetings are held each new season. Stores at some distance from New York employ New York residents to comb the market for merchandise and advise their clients on the placing of orders. Some stores have organized cooperative buying offices. The location of such New York resident buying offices has enhanced the importance of the New York market as a selling and buying center where fashion ideas originate and where buyers and sellers congregate.

More than 80 percent of the workers in the apparel industry are women (the highest percentage in U.S. manufacturing), and minorities account for about 27 percent of the work force. About half of the workers belong to unions. The two major unions are the International Ladies' Garment Workers Union and the Amalgamated Clothing and Textile Workers Union.

Careers

The career opportunities for young people entering the apparel industry vary widely. There are opportunities for skilled personnel in design, selling, management, or in the other departments of company operations. There are a large number of apparel companies nationwide, leading to a number of opportunities for employment and advancement. Opportunities in the apparel industry include those listed below:

Designers: A designer is a highly trained production technician who not only knows style but who fully understands methods of production. A designer creates garment patterns so that the garment may be efficiently produced with a minimum of fabric and a maximum of style.

The largest center of employment for designers is New York, because in New York designers can meet with retail buyers and note the consumer trends best. Often, in the better lines, designers go to Europe to attend the Parisian and Italian openings of the seasonal fashion designs.

Designers are also employed wherever manufacturing plants are located. Therefore, designers can find some employment opportunities in all parts of the United States.

Merchandisers: Merchandisers are responsible for purchasing the materials needing in production and pricing garments according to the manufacturing costs. A merchandiser's job requires a great deal of coordination and analysis. Intuition for future trends is also essential since manufacturers purchase their piece goods six months or a year in advance to allow the cotton and woolen mills time to weave the fabric well before the start of each new season.

Sellers: A salesperson's job is to sell garments to buyers. This requires a great deal of traveling. Many buyers and retailers reside in New York. Other sales representatives live in another part of the United States and travel to New York to sell products or collect information about new clothing styles.

Because the high fashion industries stress style and rapid change, and because there is such a great concentration of manufacturers in the New York area, buyers tend to go to the market frequently to see what's new, even though every segment of the industry has its regular semiannual seasonal openings. Beyond the semiannual buying conventions, salespeople are active in the market year-round.

Cutters: Cutters have a variety of responsibilities that include spreading fabric, machine cutting, and grading master patterns for sizing. These are skilled operations, and it takes some years to advance and become an experienced all-around cutter. However, the advantages of having acquired these skills are great, for a cutter can, without too much difficulty, transfer his or her cutting skill from one branch of the apparel industry to another. Cutters are usually the highest paid factory workers.

Sewers: Sewers are responsible for attaching the cut pieces of fabric through the use of a sewing machine. In menswear, these people are called tailors.

Pressers: Pressers operate the automatic pressing machines. Some pressing is done as a garment is assembled; sometimes it is done at the completion of all sewing. Delicate garments must be pressed by hand.

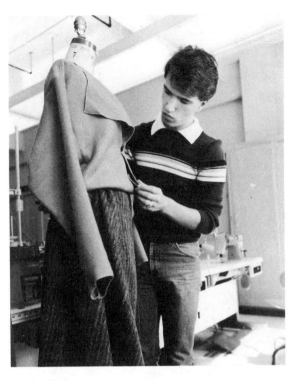

A fashion designer pins an unfinished garment on a model for sizing. After inspecting the lay of the fabric and the general appearance of the garment, he will make adjustments to the pattern.

Auxiliary workers: The average factory employs a wide variety of auxiliary workers. These workers include machinists who service the machines, receiving clerks, and shipping clerks.

Factory managers: Factory managers oversee the entire manufacturing process. In small factories, the owner might fulfill this function. But in large operations, the owner usually hires a factory manager to direct the day-to-day activities of a manufacturing plant. Factory managers usually also play a large part in the production and marketing decisions.

Section supervisors: Section supervisors oversee a specific group of workers engaged in a particular step in the production process. For example, one section supervisor will oversee the seamstresses on a particular project while another section supervisor will oversee the work of the assemblers.

Since the production of any garment is broken up into many operations (up to eighty operations are utilized in the manufacture of a man's coat), medium sized and large factories employ a large number of section supervisors.

Section supervisors are often experienced operators who have been selected by management to supervise the group because of their experience and because of their ability to handle personnel.

A model walks down a runway during a fashion show at an apparel center. The retailers who are attending the event will order garments after the show.

Shop supervisors: Shop supervisors are responsible for various stages in the production process, such as sewing and assembling. If a section supervisor has leadership ability and has acquired the proper experience in the production of a garment, he or she may be promoted to shop supervisor. In time the shop supervisor may become the factory manager.

Education

It is a combination of ambition, work, and education that seems to be the most successful formula in attaining advancement in the apparel industry. For factory management, training in industrial engineering is becoming increasingly important. Manufacturers with large factories are most interested in hiring people with engineering experience.

Graduates from regular engineering colleges or community colleges with applied engineering programs also have advantages for securing employment in the apparel industry. Such people may start their training as junior engineers or production assistants, but their

advancement is usually rapid. Within a few years, they can achieve secure status in the industry and earnings at an executive level.

Outside technical engineering training is so valuable in factory management that people holding full-time employment in the apparel industry are advised, whenever possible, to supplement their practical experience by taking courses at night in appropriate schools or colleges. Familiarity with the theories in factory layout, time and motion study, and other related subjects can be of immeasurable aid to a person who desires to advance further than factory experience alone will allow.

Highly technical knowledge is also necessary to become a qualified buyer of piece goods in the apparel industry. Those who have received good academic training will find the best opportunities in the industry. Although starting salaries may be relatively modest, the skilled apprentice can rise rapidly and earn an extremely high income.

Merchandisers need a thorough knowledge of textiles to understand how piece goods are to be made into garments. This type of knowledge can be gained at schools and colleges that provide textile courses.

A salesperson usually begins a career by serving as an assistant to a regular salesperson. The assistant, perhaps a graduate from a business school or college, will carry the sample merchandise and even act as a model to show the retailer how the various garments fit and look. The assistant will also learn selling techniques.

After some time, sales apprentices will have acquired experience and will probably be promoted by their companies to regular sales positions. If not, they will be in a position to use their experience to seek another job.

Aspiring designers may attend one of the schools located in various sections of the United States that teach pattern making and design. It should be stressed that a good designer must not merely have an innate style sense, but must acquire experience regarding methods of production, textiles, and all phases of manufacturing. Upon graduation from school, the aspiring designer can become an apprentice or assistant designer, helping the head of the de- signing department cut patterns. As the apprentice acquires practical experience, advancement is steady, and in time, he or she may become recognized as a full designer. Very few designers, however, work under their own label.

To enter the cutting department, a person usually starts as a fabric spreader and then advances to machine cutting. After further experience is acquired, the worker may grade the master pattern for the sizes, lay out the patterns on the fabric, and mark the cutting of the fabric.

A relatively short time is necessary to acquire the skill of an experienced operator in most branches of the apparel industry. Though it takes many different operations to complete a garment, each individual step is usually relatively simple and only a short training period is required for each one.

In the men's clothing field and in the women's coat and suit field, however, more tailoring is necessary, and the learning period is longer to become an experienced tailor or operator.

A number of schools offer programs specifically designed for a career in the apparel industry. These include the Fashion Institute of Technology in New York City, the George Brown College of Applied Arts and Technology in Toronto, Canada, and the Philadelphia College of Textiles and Science, in Philadelphia.

Industry outlook

In the face of foreign competition, the future of the apparel industry is unclear. Imports from foreign countries have deeply affected the U.S. apparel industry. Foreign imports have taken increasingly larger shares of such markets as blouses, coats, shirts, and sweaters. As a result, employment in U.S. plants has declined.

In addition, the value of apparel imports to the U.S. increased more than 85 percent between 1982 and 1985, while the value of the U.S. apparel industry increased only 3.3 percent over the same period. At the end of the 1980s, the apparel industry production had begun to increase again. The value of shipments had risen more than 6 percent from 1988 to 1989. One of the factors affecting this was the Free Trade Agreement with Canada and the United States. This allowed for gradual reduction of import duties between the two countries until import duty elimination in 1999. The other major factor affecting the market is the demand for higher wages by the employees of the Asian countries where most of the clothing is produced. As the wages begin to approach the U.S. wage level, the cost of production abroad will even out with the cost of producing clothing domestically.

With more than 21,000 plants in all 50 states, the industry is highly competitive, and low profits and wages are characteristic. Most firms are small. One-quarter employ fewer than five workers and more than seventy percent fewer than fifty workers.

Salespeople in the apparel industry spend much of their time traveling from one client to another. As representatives of the industry, salespeople must be well-dressed when visiting clients.

Employment has increased slightly after a ten year decline in the 1980s. In 1990 more than one million people worked in the apparel industry. Because of the average low wages in apparel, the industry is facing an employee shortage. It is likely that the apparel industry will undergo substantial organization changes in the next decade. Those changes will most likely be in increased computerization of the tasks in clothes manufacturing.

◇ **SOURCES OF ADDITIONAL INFORMATION**

Clothing Manufacturers Association of the USA
1290 Avenue of the Americas
Suite 1061
New York, NY 10104

American Apparel Manufacturers Association
2500 Wilson Boulevard, Suite 301
Arlington, VA 22201

Bureau of Wholesale Representatives
1718 Peachtree Street, NW, Suite 600
Atlanta, GA 30309

International Association of Clothing Designers
240 Madison Avenue, 12 Floor
New York, NY 10016

International Fashion Group
9 Rockefeller Plaza
New York, NY 10020

◇ **RELATED ARTICLES**

Volume 1: Design; Foreign Trade; Retailing; Textiles; Wholesaling
Volume 2: Buyers, wholesale and retail; Commercial artists; Designers; Export- import specialists; Fashion designers; Retail business owners; Retail managers
Volume 3: Knit goods industry workers; Leather tanning and finishing workers; Models; Retail sales workers; Shipping and receiving clerks; Shoe and leather workers and repairers; Stock clerks; Textile manufacturing occupations; Wholesale trade sales workers
Volume 4: CAD/CAM technicians; Robotics technicians; Textile technicians

Automotives

General information

The automobile industry is involved in the production of cars, trucks, buses, and other vehicles. As such, it is one of the most important manufacturing industries in the United States and a major consumer of steel, rubber, plastic, and plate glass. The industry as a whole employs people at all levels of the occupational spectrum, from professional engineers and scientists to semiskilled assemblers.

There are relatively few firms that manufacture vehicles, and much of the work is contracted to smaller firms that supply parts to the major assemblers. This network makes the industry a substantial player in the national economy.

Until the 1800s, the invention of a self-powered vehicle was viewed as little more than fantasy. Most people traveled by horse and buggy and saw no future in the development of a "horseless" carriage.

The first self-propelled power vehicle was invented in 1769 by Nicolas Joseph Cugnot in France. The machine was steam powered. It had three wheels and moved at less than five miles an hour. The tractor, as it was to be used, was wrecked on its very first run.

In 1801, Richard Trevithick build a four wheel vehicle with a steam powered engine. Sir Goldsworthy Gurney built a six wheel vehicle in the 1830s which could reach a speed of fifteen miles an hour. Steam vehicles became fairly common for public transportation in England during the middle of the nineteenth century.

The American, Thomas Davenport, made one of the first electric powered automobile in the 1890s. William Morrison, also an American, built one as well in the 1890s. Electric cars were more popular in the United States than in Britain.

Karl Benz and Gottlieb Daimler manufactured the first gasoline powered automobiles.

The production began in Europe in the last fifteen years of the nineteenth century. Armand Peugeot also became an early manufacturer of automobiles, and Louis Renault developed a drive shaft system, which replaced a chain drive, in 1898. Daimler-Benz still produces Mercedes-Benz automobiles, and Peugeot and Renault remain well-known car manufacturers to this day as well.

In the United States, Charles and Frank Duryea built a gasoline powered auto in the early 1890s. They began manufacturing autos for sale soon after.

Assembly line work was developed in the United States in 1901 at the Olds Motor Works in Detroit, after a fire gutted the production shop. Olds was able to produce 425 new cars in its first year on the assembly line, a big increase over the number of hand–built cars that were generated the year before.

Henry Ford set a goal that mass produced cars should be affordable to the average person. He built the Model T, a car that sold for $850, a fairly expensive purchase, but it still became the most popular car sold in the United States for the 20 years following its production in 1908. Ford developed a moving conveyor belt for the production line in an attempt to speed production and efficiency of car manufacturing. The moving assembly line was the foundation for the system that is still used today in most car factories.

By 1916, the Model T cost only $400, and other manufacturers had built their own conveyor systems of production. In Europe, gasoline powered vehicles were used in the war effort, and this accelerated the production rate and acceptability of such transportation.

As technology advanced so did car design. The cars became bigger, faster, sturdier, and more dependable. Roads were paved, and in 1921 Congress passed an act allowing for federal assistance in funding for a public highway system.

Workers at an automotive plant inspect the outer panel of a hood that is set on a sheet metal die. Large stamping presses are in the background.

In the late 1980s, some of the domestic firms formed partnerships with foreign companies, manufacturing vehicles as joint projects. In addition, several foreign companies have opened their own plants in the United States, generating new jobs.

Detroit remains the headquarters of the major automobile companies, but many of the manufacturing plants are located throughout the country. The majority of the industry's employees work in the Great Lakes region, including Michigan, Ohio, Indiana, Illinois, Wisconsin, and western New York. The single largest concentration of industry employees is found in the Detroit metropolitan area. While aspects of motor vehicle manufacturing take place in nearly every state in the country, most of the remaining workers are found in California, Pennsylvania, Kentucky, Tennessee, Georgia, and Texas.

According to the *U.S. Industrial Outlook*, in the late 1980s the U.S. automobile industry employed about 285,000 people. Approximately 28 percent of the automobiles sold in the United States are imported. Compact cars accounted for the biggest percentage of the market for imports, with more than 35 percent of the sales.

Wages and salaries in the automobile industry are among the highest paid in all industries. Plans for tuition payment to those taking approved education courses are growing in number in the industry, and merit scholarships for children of employees are another feature of most corporations. The majority of production and maintenance workers in the automobile assembly plants and in the parts plants belong to the International Union, United Automobile, Aerospace, and Agricultural Implement Workers of America.

The manufacture of a motor vehicle is such a complex task that it requires a wide range of occupations. Newer fields of electronics and a wider diversity of products make the industry even more complex in its output and thus in its opportunities for employment. Hundreds of jobs exist in the production category alone, to say nothing of the rest of the industry.

The latest refinements in mass production are called automation. Automation refers to processes that automatically transfer work from one operation to another. Automated processes use precise electronic and hydraulic controls to measure work in progress, to receive feedback on adjustments that may be necessary, and to adjust the machines to limits as small as one ten-thousandth of an inch.

The past few decades have seen a decline in the U.S. automobile industry due to foreign competition and recurring energy crises. The U.S. auto industry invested $84 billion in plant facilities, equipment, and special tooling between 1978 and 1985. After the 1979 energy crisis, the industry suffered from economic recession and from shifts in buyer preferences toward imported vehicles. Japan imposed voluntary restraints on its exports in 1981 through 1985, and the industry weathered its crisis, although it lost money in 1980 and 1981. By 1983 the industry again enjoyed strong profitability, and in the mid-1980s it reported healthy balance sheets.

The structure of the automotives industry

The task of taking a car from concept to production involves the skills of many people and the development of a plan or program. It involves the intricate coordination of the plan among four operations: styling, which must create a theme acceptable to the market and to design engineers; engineering, which must release a design from which a quality car can be constructed at a previously established cost; manufacturing, which must make the finished product according to prescribed quality standards; and sales, which must sell the final product.

The effect of a product program on the manufacturing operations varies with its scope. The new car may require completely new plans and equipment to accommodate the car's new materials and designs, or it may require only minor retooling.

Once program approval is received, interior stylists create new fabrics, colors, instrument panels, controls, and seat configurations, tailoring their work to the approved plan.

After stylists receive drawings and blueprints from drafters defining major exterior dimensions of the new model and the seat configurations, they can begin the pre-production styling phase. With a fairly precise definition of the new car's exterior now available, full-size models, finished in minute detail and painted to resemble production cars, are prepared by a team of skilled model makers.

These models are made of a special type of warmed clay that hardens as it cools. The clay is applied by hand to a wooden structure in the rough shape of a car. Stylists then sculpt and mold the desired final exterior. Chrome is simulated by use of high-gloss foil. Even moldings are extruded from clay and covered with foil to represent production parts. Fabrication shops create lines and scripts in plastic, while other ornamentation is hand-carved to resemble finished pieces. Clear plexiglass is used for windows. From a distance, a completed clay model could be (and sometimes is) mistaken for a production vehicle.

Cost estimators, personnel from manufacturing, and body engineering experts make certain that the car represented by the clay model can be manufactured according to cost and quality standards. They also determine whether the new model can be built with existing equipment.

After final approval of the full-size clay model, engineers translate the three-dimensional shapes of the model into two-dimensional, full-size body drawings. The clay model represents only the exterior surface of the car. Inner panel supports, brackets, and the joints and flanges for assembly of adjacent panels must be designed and engineered. Proposals for such items as door thickness and sheet metal and die specifications must be examined in detail.

Manufacturing engineers must work with design engineers and outside suppliers to set

In the chassis build area of an automotive plant, a worker makes a final torque check on an engine. An automated guided vehicle transports the chassis sections, engine transmissions, and cradles to the final assembly line.

standards that meet engineering requirements and manufacturing capabilities. Problems encountered on past models must be evaluated to assure that similar problems will not recur in the new model.

The approved exterior design of the clay model must be translated into blueprints and tools for production. Manufacturing and assembly facilities must be reworked to handle the new models while production continues on current models. Throughout this operation, quality control and safety experts ensure that their respective standards will be met.

Much of the early design, engineering, fabrication, and testing of chassis and engine components occurs in mechanical prototypes, independent of the styling portion of the program. As soon as possible, these mechanical prototypes are followed by operational prototypes, built as close as possible to the appearance and mechanism of the final car. These prototypes are specially built for final evaluation and are tested for safety, durability, and serviceability.

Car assembly procedures for new models are tested in a pilot plant. Here pre-production car assembly is carried on to check assembly tooling and to orient assembly personnel, as well as to test the fit of components according to specifications. Assembly plant managers, supervisors, and local representatives of the manufacturing and product engineering staffs visit the pilot plant to learn the production techniques required by the new model.

Before an auto body is painted, an automobile worker must smooth out the car's surface and apply the finishing touches.

Once the model car has been tested and approved, the company proceeds to manufacture these cars in mass quantities. Mass production is based on precision manufacture of identical parts (each one interchangeable with every other one like it). It also requires processes that automatically move parts to the worker in a carefully timed sequence, so that the final product is built up from its simplest parts to a complete unit.

Thousands of different operations must be performed before a car is put together on the final assembly line. Each part must be shaped accurately by one or more different forming operations. Nearly all these operations can be divided into four basic operational groups: foundry, machining, forging, and stamping.

In foundry operations, workers pour molten metal into a mold where it cools and hardens into a casting. Castings are made for such parts as the engine block, cylinder head, or camshaft. Before the metal is poured, patternmakers make patterns in wood or metal in the exact shape desired for the final casting. In preparing the molds, coremakers shape cores or bodies of sand that are placed in the molds to form the hollow spaces needed. When the casting cools, it is removed from the mold and trimmed to remove excess metal.

Machining operations consist of further shaping the castings with tools that cut away unwanted metal. This work is done by machine tool operators, who comprise one of the largest metalworking groups in the industry. Tool and die makers also work in machining operations and are highly skilled workers. Tool makers make the jigs, fixtures, and other accessories that hold the work being machined in place. Die makers construct the dies used in stamping, pressing, forging, and other kinds of metal-forming operations.

In the forge shop, automobile parts such as crankshafts and connecting rods are shaped with forge hammers and presses. Heaters heat the metal stock to be forged in a furnace and then pass it to hammer operators who pound the metal into various shapes between closed dies with drop hammers. Other workers in a forge shop clean, finish, and inspect forgings.

In the stamping process, the part is formed by being pressed between two matching forms under great pressure. As mounted in the press, the lower form is the die, the upper form is the punch. The sheet metal to be formed is placed between the punch and the die.

Three basic stamping operations are blanking, piercing, and forming. Blanking and piercing are often done at the same time. Blanking cuts the excess metal off the flat stock, leaving the piece from which the part will be formed. Piercing punches holes as needed.

In forming, the part is given its final shape. This sometimes requires a series of operations that may be performed progressively by a row of presses, each one bringing the part one step closer to its finished form.

The engine block must be constructed before it reaches the final assembly line. This is a process that involves numerous steps. When the engine block arrives in a manufacturing plant it is a metal case containing a series of holes or cylinder bores. Hundreds of separate operations must be performed by various machinists to turn it into the final product. One machine alone can do more than 100 operations in thirty-eight seconds. In some plants there are machines that work on seventeen engine blocks at the same time, finishing them to perfection.

The machines that cut and drill the engine castings are aligned so that progressive operations may be performed as the engines move automatically from one group of machines to the next.

In a typical plant, as the engine block is carried down an assembly line by overhead mechanical arms, workers install pistons, connecting rods, the crankshaft, the camshaft, flywheel, oil pump, and all other major parts.

Once the metal parts and engine block have been manufactured, the car is ready to be fully assembled. The first step in assembling a car is building the body. The various parts of the car body, such as the floor, roof, and side panels are put together on the longest feeder line in the assembly plant. Special framing fixtures hold the parts in place while they are welded or bolted together. Welders use electric welding machines to join parts together. Welded joints are much stronger than joints fastened together by bolts and nuts, but parts attached by nuts and bolts are easier to remove for repair or replacement.

The car doors and deck lid are then added. All metal surfaces are ground smooth and the body thoroughly cleaned. The body is now moved to the paint department.

After certain joints are sealed, protective layers of primer coating are applied. The body is then sanded and washed to provide a good surface for the finish color. At the color spray booth, multiple coats are applied. Next, the body moves to an oven where the paint is baked to a hard, bright luster. Then trimming and sewing operations begin to provide the motor vehicle with interior parts.

Although the front end is part of the body, it is built up on another feeder assembly line. It consists of the front fenders, radiator, grille, headlights, and fender aprons at the sides of the engine compartment. This subassembly is trimmed and moved to the final assembly area, where it is added after the main body structure is secured to the frame, or chassis.

Trimming an automobile body means more than installing upholstery and applying ornamental chrome. It also means installing the instrument panel, electrical wiring, glass, interior hardware, heater, radio, and other accessories.

Particular care is exercised during this stage of car assembly. Paint, trim, and upholstery are easily scratched, torn, or soiled, and handling large glass pieces without breakage is an art in itself. Trim crews at assembly plants have installed as many as 15,000 windshields consecutively without breaking a single one.

Through careful planning and split-second timing, parts and subassemblies for all body styles meet on the final line at just the right moment to make each car exactly as ordered.

When the car reaches the end of the assembly line, more than 13,000 parts have been put together, and the new car is started and driven away.

Just how well the finished automobile will operate depends to a great extent upon the precision and care with which all the parts are made and assembled. Tolerances (exact dimensions) must be made to assure that the pieces fit

Once an automobile has gone through an entire assembly line, a team of workers install the bumpers, fascias, splash guards, and body side moldings.

as planned. The machine tools must be made precisely to produce identical parts.

Inspection and testing continues throughout the entire manufacturing process. A rigid system of inspection is employed to catch any flaws that may develop in either the tools or the manufactured parts themselves. Engineers determine how many hours each tool can be safely used before it will begin to wear, and each is changed in time so that it maintains rigid tolerances.

At many stages during the manufacture of a part, as well as after its completion, all its physical characteristics are checked to be sure it will measure up to quality standards. Specialists use many ingenious checking and inspection devices. Among these are delicate scales, height and depth gauges, oscillographs, reflectometers, chemical baths, and X ray gauges.

Even before a car is manufactured, the sales and marketing departments are planning a promotional strategy. Sales and marketing must distribute information on the new cars well in advance of public introduction of the cars. The vehicles built in pre-production assembly line tests are used to introduce the new models to dealers and for other advertising and promotional activities. Along with the preparation of mass media advertising, large quantities of product brochures are made ready for distribution. Signs, posters, and displays for use in dealership showrooms must also be designed and printed long before the first car is built.

In addition, sales representatives must be able to suggest to dealers a variety of sales campaigns built around the engineering and pro-

A group of managers and automotive workers inspect a newly manufactured car.

duction features of the new models. The service personnel in the dealerships must be briefed in advance of any new service and maintenance techniques.

Careers

Stylists: During the preliminary planning stage, stylists create ideas in exterior and interior forms and proportions to be used in the new model. They draw heavily upon the most promising ideas developed in "dream cars" designed to test public receptivity to departures in styling themes and concepts. They also work with engineers and other technical personnel on problems of improving mechanical operation, design, and safety.

Model makers: Model makers construct clay models of the cars that have been designed by stylists.

Engineers: Engineers design, develop, and test all automotive parts. Engineers work on the body of the car, the electrical system of the car, the brakes of the car, and all other areas. They may be further assigned as a motor engineer, a transmission engineer, or a suspension or chassis engineer.

Drafters: There are many specific types of work in drafting, ranging from drawings of parts and assemblies to the drawings of tools needed to produce those parts. These drawings are prepared by a drafter or generated by a computer.

Technicians: Automobile makers use many technicians with skills and training in electronics, engineering, and maintenance fields to as-

sist scientists and engineers in the practical application of their work.

Craft workers: Craft workers help put the various parts of an automobile together. They may be machinists, tool makers, millwrights, die makers, patternmakers, sheet metal workers, electricians, or machine repairers.

Office workers: For an industry as large and varied as the automobile industry, office work of many types is necessary. The industry employs secretaries, bookkeepers, shipping clerks, keypunch and business machine operators, typists, and other clerical employees.

Because inventories and multiple facts are needed all the time, computers and various office machines are a vital part of automobile manufacturing, as are those trained to operate them. Whether coding and classifying, tabulating or storing, these machines and their technicians perform tasks that make better production possible.

Financial workers: Accountants and auditors help keep production costs under control and supervise the record-keeping procedures. Financial experts work in such areas as general accounting, cost accounting, auditing, and tax accounting.

Managerial and supervisory personnel: Managerial personnel supervise craft workers and others engaged in the manufacturing of automobiles. All aspects of the production process must be carefully monitored to ensure compliance with safety guidelines.

Marketers and *Salespeople:* Behind all of this work lies the marketing and distribution operation that brings models to dealers, provides sales information and training, and keeps the whole process of production in line.

Service technicians: The automobile, once tested and sold, requires a large and skilled force to maintain it. Service technicians have this responsibility. These workers are employed by dealers and perform a variety of jobs. Annual sales of automotive parts and labor amount to more than the cost of all the cars sold in a year. Many mechanics become service managers, parts managers, or teachers. In addition, many may become automobile dealers or owners of service stations because of the knowledge and experience gained in their initial work.

Education

A high-school education is basic to any employment in the automobile industry. And in many of the areas, specialized training in office practice or production skills is helpful. Tool and die makers, patternmakers, electricians, and some craft workers need at least four years of training. Apprentice training is the best way to learn a skilled trade. Applicants for apprenticeship usually must be at least high-school graduates. Training should include mathematics, science, mechanical drawing, and shop courses.

Apprenticeship includes both classroom and on-the-job instruction. For most craft jobs, apprentices must complete 8,000 hours of on-the-job instruction, although some apprentices receive credit for service in the Armed Forces or for other relevant experience.

Most engineers, laboratory assistants, drafters, and technicians are graduates of technical institutes or junior colleges. Engineers, scientists, and most automotive designers must have at least a bachelor's degree with an appropriate major, including automotive engineering, industrial design, architecture, or a related field. Advanced degrees are required for research-and-development jobs. Designers should have a background in practical application, such as model building, as well as design theory and techniques.

In addition to the apprentice training opportunities, most manufacturers have on-the-job training programs. Many technicians, for instance, are trained at company schools or at company expense at local technical schools or junior colleges. There are also training programs for engineers, scientists, and administrative personnel. Manufacturers usually have special training programs for supervisors.

Most companies also offer their employees grants, loans, or tuition refund plans for advanced study.

Administrative jobs are usually filled by people with degrees in business administration, engineering, marketing, accounting, industrial relations, and related fields.

Industry outlook

It is difficult to forecast with certainty the labor needs of the industry in the coming decades. Even if conditions improve, employment will probably not keep pace with output, as the industry comes to rely more on labor-saving technology, namely robots. Many assembly operations, however, are difficult to automate, and if conditions in the marketplace improve, workers capable of carrying out complex assemblies should be in demand.

Little employment growth is expected for machinists and tool and die makers. However, other skilled occupations should grow.

The increasing use of computers in design, engineering, and production operations should create more employment opportunities for programmers, systems analysts, and other computer personnel. More engineers, scientists, and technicians will be employed to meet the industry's research-and-development needs, especially to design new engines, exhaust systems, and safety equipment.

In the 1990s, the automobile industry must find innovative ways to adjust to changing public tastes, meet foreign competition, and satisfy government regulations regarding fuel economy and public safety. These are factors that affect everyone in the industry, from the largest car maker to the smallest parts supplier.

As the European markets open up, a reduced restriction on imports and the increasing profits abroad, may help the automobile industry expand abroad.

◇ SOURCES OF ADDITIONAL INFORMATION

In addition to the sources listed below, the personnel offices of the automobile manufacturing companies can supply information on opportunities for apprentice programs, industry educational programs, and employment prospects.

Motor Vehicles Manufacturers Association of the United States
7430 Second Avenue, Suite 300
Detroit, MI 48202

Motor and Equipment Manufacturers Association
300 Sylvan Avenue
PO Box 1638
Englewood Cliffs, NJ 07632

Automotive Service Association
1901 Airport Freeway
Suite 100
PO Box 929
Bedford, TX 76095

National Automobile Dealers Association
8400 Westpark Drive
McLean, VA 22102

United Auto Workers
8000 East Jefferson Avenue
Detroit, MI 48214

AFL-CIO
815 16th Street, NW
Washington, DC 20006

Automotives

◇ **RELATED ARTICLES**

Volume 1: Design; Engineering; Transportation

Volume 2: Designers; Drafters; Engineers; Industrial designers; Industrial traffic managers

Volume 3: Assemblers; Automobile mechanics; Automobile sales workers; Automobile-body repairers; Automobile-repair- service estimators; Automotive painters; Coremakers; Diesel mechanics; Electroplating workers; Forge shop occupations; Industrial machinery mechanics; Job and die setters; Machine tool operators; Machinists; Tool makers and die makers; Traffic agents and clerks; Welders

Volume 4: Automotive cooling system technicians; Automotive, diesel, and gas turbine technicians; Automotive exhaust technicians; Drafting and design technicians; Industrial engineering technicians; Industrial safety-and-health technicians; Mechanical technicians; Quality-control technicians; Tap-and-die-maker technicians; Welding technicians

Aviation and Aerospace

General information

Orville Wright took off at Kitty Hawk, North Carolina, on December 17, 1903 in the first successful engine-driven airplane. By noon of that historic day, four flights had been completed successfully—two each by Wilbur and Orville Wright. Their account of what happened next struck notes of simplicity and prophetic certainty when they wrote: "We at once packed our goods and returned home, knowing that the age of the flying machine had come at last."

By 1906, the Wright brothers had improved the design on the plane so that the craft was fully maneuverable. They were able to keep the plane aloft for more than half an hour. By 1908 they were making public flights for demonstration purposes.

The French engineer Louis Bleriot built a monoplane (one set of wings), with a tail for balance and an enclosed body. In 1909, he flew his plane, the *Bleriot XI*, across the English Channel for the first international airplane flight. Two years later a Bleriot plane was used to make the first United States airmail delivery, on a route from Garden City to Mineola in New York.

World War I established a military need for airplanes. Their effectiveness in surveillance and bombing was apparent from the onset of the war. Governments set out to build the fastest, most efficient aerial fighters they could. Germany started in 1914 with about 260 planes, France had around 150 planes, and England had fewer than 100. Planes could fly 60 to 70 miles an hour for up to three hours. By the end of the war, planes could move as fast as 200 miles an hour and fly as high as 15,000 feet.

Anthony Fokker developed a plane that fired front-mounted machine guns on a timing system that allowed the bullets to shoot between the rotating blades of the propellers. Used by the Germans, this gave them superiority in air combat. The other major contribu-tion of Fokker was the tri-plane DVII. Flown by Baron von Richtofen, the Fokker tri-plane was considered one of the finest flying machines of the war, and the baron (known as the Red Baron) was one of the finest pilots.

After World War I ended, pilots used the gains in technology to set new records for speed and distance in flight. Charles Lindbergh was the first to cross the Atlantic in a non-stop trip. He flew from Long Island, New York, to Paris, France, in May 1927.

The altitude record was officially recognized by the Federation Aeronautique Internationale in 1927. The record was first held by C.C. Champion, who achieved an altitude of 38,419 feet. The record was regularly broken every couple years by gains of at least 2,000 feet. In 1977, Russian flyer Alexander Fedotov set the standing record in a E-226M with an altitude of 123,523 feet.

Air speed records were registered in 1906, with Alberto Santos-Dumont setting the first official record at 25.66 miles an hour. The record, like the altitude record, was regularly broken as technology improved. The biggest leap in the record came in 1956, when L. Peter Twiss of Great Britain broke the previous record of 822.27 mph with a new record of 1,132.14 mph. Eventually records would top 2,000 mph.

While speeds of planes were being tested, so were the territories planes could cover. In 1926 Admiral Richard Byrd and Floyd Bennett flew across the North Pole. By 1928 solo flights were being completed from London to Australia. Flights across the Pacific were difficult but the U.S. Army had two pilots successfully navigate a non-stop flight from California to Hawaii in 1927. In 1931, Amelia Earhart was the first woman to fly solo across the Atlantic on a non-stop journey.

Pressurized cabins were developed for airplanes in the 1930s. This allowed pilots and passengers to tolerate the thin air at higher altitudes.

This huge airplane manufacturing plant assembles several airplanes at once. Given the expense of constructing planes, the manufacturer produces them only after they have been ordered by an airline company.

The leap in technology that allowed for major advances in flight capabilities was made in 1942. With World War II dominating the investment of all the western world's research, the improvement in aircraft was seen as an important edge by both sides. The motivation was dominance in air power for the warring countries, but the development of jet power had astounding influence on commercial aviation after the war. Germany was the first to build a jet plane, in 1939. The jet was a more powerful engine, fueled by gas turbines. It allowed planes to climb higher and fly faster than ever before. England had a jet plane in service by 1941; the United States had a model in 1942.

Jet aircraft made air transportation feasible for moving large numbers of people long distances. Travel times for domestic and international flights dropped, and refueling was needed much less frequently. By 1950, airlines in the United States were moving more than

sixteen million people a year. In 1989 the nation's airlines transported more than 450 million passengers.

One of the other major advances to come out of the development of the jet engine was the ability to travel out of the Earth's orbit into outer space. During World War II the Germans were able to successfully launch rockets that were directed from Germany to London and other enemy territories. The V-2, the first true rocket, burned a fuel of alcohol and liquid oxygen. It used gyroscopes for directional guidance and stabilization in flight. The rocket design had outer fins on the tail end for stabilization in the lower atmosphere, but had internal vanes for control in the thinner, higher atmosphere.

After the war, scientists continued to develop rocket technology, concentrating on multi-stage rockets that would allow for a powerful enough initial blast to carry the rocket out of the atmosphere, but shed the extra weight to allow enough fuel to remain to direct the rocket to the target in outer space.

The first to accomplish a space launch of any vehicle was the Soviet Union. *Sputnik I* was launched on October 4, 1957, sending a satellite into outer orbit. The satellite orbited the Earth 560 miles high, with a speed of 18,000 miles per hour. The second launch from the Soviets came a month later with *Sputnik II* which sent a dog, Laika, into orbit. The United States followed with *Explorer I* on January 31, 1958, sending a satellite into space.

In 1959, four more launches were successful. The Soviet Union launched *Luna I*, the first craft to break free of the Earth's orbit. It passed within 5,000 miles of the moon. The second Soviet launch that year was *Luna II*, which landed a probe on the moon. The third Soviet craft to successfully go up was *Luna III*, which signaled back the first photos of the far side of the moon. The United States launched *Pioneer 4*, which also successfully broke free of the Earth's gravity.

Several more launches followed, with animals sent up into space to determine the pressures placed on a living being in outer atmosphere conditions.

In 1961, the Soviet Union successfully launched the first man into orbit. Yuri Gagarin orbited once around the Earth on April 12. On May 5, 1961, Alan Shephard became the first American to go into space. On August 6 and 7, 1961, the Soviet cosmonaut Gherman Titov orbited the Earth sixteen times. On February 20, 1962, the American John Glenn orbited the Earth three times.

During the intensely competitive space race between the Soviet Union and the United States, the race for records in such areas as the first woman in space (Russian Valentina Tereshkova, 1963), the first multi-manned launch (*Vostok I*, 1962), the first satellite to Venus (U.S. *Mariner 2*, 1963) led to several tragedies. The United States lost three astronauts on a launch pad fire in the Apollo, in 1967. Virgil Grissom, Edward White, and Roger Chaffee were killed by a fire in the cabin that burned on the pure oxygen atmosphere. The flight was to be the first Apollo spacecraft in orbit. The fire delayed the space program for twenty months while scientists and engineers redesigned the vehicle. By 1971, the Soviets would lose four cosmonauts in space accidents as well.

The United States took the lead in space exploration with the first successful landing of man on the moon. In a nine-day flight starting July 16, 1969, Neil Armstrong, Edwin Aldrin, and Michael Collins successfully completed the first voyage to the moon and back. Neil Armstrong was the first man to set foot on the lunar surface. The landing was seen live on television by millions of viewers around the world. Armstrong broadcast back to the Earth one of the most famous lines from this century: "That's one small step for man, one giant leap for mankind." He and Edwin Aldrin spent two hours on the moon's surface taking photographs and rock samples and setting up experimental equipment, while Collins orbited above in the Command Module. The United States would send a total of seven missions to the moon before retiring the lunar exploration program.

Following the lunar exploration program, both the United States and the Soviet Union began a program to develop a reusable launch vehicle. The Space Shuttle program in the United States established a series of vehicles that would launch like a rocket and land on hard ground like an airplane. The program would have twenty-four successful flights before the first shuttle disaster took place. On January 28, 1986, *Challenger* exploded in air before leaving the Earth's atmosphere, killing all the astronauts on board. Again disaster set back the National Air and Space Administration's agenda until a safer design could be established.

The last of the projects to come out of the space programs of the 1980s were the space laboratories. The Soviets established the *Soyuz* in 1971, with a successful rendezvous between a rocket ship and the space station. By 1988, the Soviets would have a cosmonaut in space for a record 211 days.

In the 1920s, the pilot sat in an open cockpit, watching the ground to tell where he was going. By the 1990s, pilots were sitting in front of complex banks of controls, guiding long- and short-range jets around the world. The success of both the space program and the commercial air industry would pose both great opportunity and great problems for the government and the industry itself.

The increase in the numbers of flights and the number of people on commercial flights continued to increase throughout the 1960s and 1970s. In 1978, Congress voted to eliminate the controls that had been placed on airlines in the United States.

After deregulation of U.S. airlines under the Deregulation Act of 1978, there were a number of mergers and bankruptcies. Wages were depressed in some areas of the industry. With deregulation, ticket prices were expected to drop with open competition among the airlines for passengers. What happened was a decrease in the cost of tickets for trips between frequently traveled destinations, such as New York, Los Angeles, and Chicago. Smaller re-

An airline pilot inspects the reparations of an engine before he embarks on another flight.

gions found the price of tickets to their airports increasing dramatically. Services to smaller communities was reduced or curtailed by many larger airlines. It had been anticipated by the government that smaller airlines would move in to fill the gap. Several tried to do so, but the increased cost of fuel, equipment, maintenance, and staff salaries eliminated the profit on low priority travel routes. As different companies began to file for bankruptcy or were merged with larger, more profitable corporations, the federal government stepped up discussion of re-regulation of the industry to provide more efficient, cost-effective service to all regions of the states.

The other major concern for regulators of the airline industry was the overuse of several airports and the strain that the transportation was causing on air traffic control. For O'Hare airport in Chicago, the number of flights during peak travel hours was restricted by the Federal Aviation Administration (FAA). With more than fifty-five million people landing at O'Hare each year, the airport was the world's busiest, and the traffic control problems were mounting. By limiting the number of flights allowed to take off and land during the rush hours, the FAA hoped to ease the strain on the traffic controllers at the O'Hare tower and at the satellite control centers for the O'Hare flight paths. Discussions were also initiated between airline officials and the FAA for a long-term solution to the overcrowding of the skies over major cities.

In 1989 ten airlines in the United States had revenues of more than one billion dollars. An-

other eleven airlines brought in close to 75 million dollars. Of those twenty-one airlines, however, three have failed and filed for bankruptcy in 1989-90, and speculation about the future of other airlines remains unsure. More than 600,000 people were employed with airlines in the United States in 1990 and that represented an increase of 3.9 percent over the employment figures from the previous year.

The structure of the aviation and aerospace industry

The aviation and aerospace industry is involved in basic and applied research and the development and production of safe, efficient equipment. The work includes studies of the atmosphere and space; the improvement of the usefulness, performance, speed, safety, and efficiency of aeronautical and space vehicles; and the development and operation of vehicles capable of carrying instruments, equipment, supplies, and living organisms through space and through the atmosphere.

Aeronautics challenges the frontiers of higher speeds and safer, more economic operations. The results of these challenges are seen in bigger, better, faster aircraft. Space flight's challenge is the unknown. Questions that researchers try to answer through experimentation involve a variety of aspects of space exploration and travel. Some fundamental questions are: How long can humans live in a weightless condition? Is there other life in our galaxy? Practical questions concerning both the research scientists and the engineers are: Will the engine fire as planned? Will the power source continue to produce electricity?

When there is a failure, as in the Challenger shuttle disaster, a whole program may be set back for months or years while investigations and testing proceed to ensure safer operations in the future.

The aerospace industry includes many widely diverse areas of research and development, manufacture, and end use or operation. Included in the aerospace industry are airplane manufacture, parts of the electronics industry, research both in the university and in industry, and missile and space vehicle manufacture. Some companies specialize in manufacturing or managing the manufacturing of the entire system, usually by subcontracting various phases of the entire operation. Other companies specialize in components, thus becoming subcontractors. Huge plants and small companies manufacture entire units or small parts.

Aircraft for military use, passenger ships and freight airplanes comprise the largest portion of industry sales. Aerospace manufacturers also produce missiles for the armed forces and spacecraft for use by the National Aeronautics and Space Administration (NASA) and the U.S. Department of Defense. NASA has launched satellites for private communications companies and for other countries. Thousands of subcontractors provide parts, supplies, and subassemblies to the principal contractors who build aerospace vehicles for government use or for private business.

More than 10 percent of airline traffic consists of freight and mail, and use in this area continues to grow. Airlines now transport nine out of every ten intercity first-class letters and millions of parcel post packages. The annual volume of air freight, consisting of some of the world's most valuable goods and many commonplace items, saw a twelve-fold increase in the first two decades of the jet age (see Volume 1: Transportation).

Virtually all flights operated daily by the nation's airlines carry some type of cargo—mail or freight and usually a combination of the two. The freight and mail often are transported in the cargo compartments of aircraft also carrying passengers and their baggage. The combined use of air and truck extends the reach of air freight far beyond the cities served directly by the airlines.

The regularly scheduled shipment of goods by air began with an auto manufacturer with the foresight to use air transportation to ensure a timely supply of parts for production lines. Auto parts remain among the major commodities moving in air freight, but they have been joined by a long list of other commodities, ranging from household appliances, plastics, and electronic equipment to photographic equipment, newspapers, and other printed matter. Substantial quantities of fresh seafood, fruit, and vegetables also move regularly by air freight.

Wide-body jet freighters offer the capacity to airlift cargoes that could not have been accommodated as single air shipments a decade ago. These big freighters have carried as single shipments such things as two printing presses weighing 50,000 pounds, a complete chemical production line, all of the sections of a seventy-ton oil-well tower, and heavy construction equipment.

At the other end of the size scale, air freight moves millions of small packages. Often these packages are brought to airport ticket counters for movement on the next flight out. Moving that way nearly every day are such things as news films, television videotapes, blueprints,

Two astronauts undergo slidewire training during the Terminal Countdown Demonstration Test (TCDT). The TCDT is a mock countdown that allows the astronauts to practice emergency procedures.

computer tapes and disks, cancelled checks, and legal documents.

Of course much of air transportation is used to move business and commercial passengers. Millions of passengers a year travel by air.

Careers

The aviation and aerospace industry has a wide variety of career opportunities. A sample of those careers follows below:

Space scientists: Space scientists conduct research and make observations concerning the physical and chemical composition of the earth's atmosphere and outer space.

Fluid and flight mechanics engineers: Fluid and flight engineers investigate the dynamics of aeronautical or space vehicles and establish criteria for vehicle design based on the dynamics of flight.

Materials and structures scientists: Materials and structures scientists research, design, manufacture, test, and evaluate aeronautical and space flight vehicle structures and systems.

Flight systems engineers: Flight systems engineers design, manufacture, and evaluate aeronautical and space flight systems and subsystems. The flight engineer's chief concern is with systems integration, reliability, and quality assurance.

Measurement and instrumentation systems engineers: Measurement and instrumentation systems engineers research, develop, design, manufacture, test, and evaluate equipment and systems to measure physical phenomena and to control environments by means of tracking systems, telemetry, radio, optical, and mechanical systems.

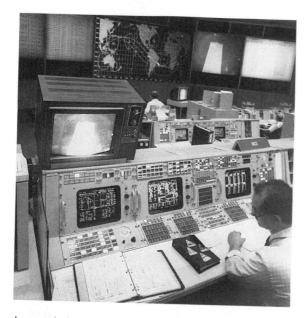

A communications expert operates the integrated communications console (INCO) at the Johnson Space Center in Houston, Texas.

Data systems engineers: Through the use of mathematics and numerical techniques, data systems engineers work on all phases of development, design, and testing and evaluation of equipment and systems for recording, handling, and computing aeronautical and space data.

Managers: Managers oversee the entire manufacturing process. Because of the complexity of the projects involved, the ability for management to understand the technical elements of each program is fundamental to the success of the project. Because of this, the management team is often comprised of those with management and scientific backgrounds.

Research pilots: Research pilots fly aircraft and/or space vehicles to determine equipment feasibility and to make recommendations for new equipment selection.

Life studies scientists: Life studies scientists conduct theoretical and experimental research on the effects of flight in the atmosphere and in space on living organisms and systems. For example, human-machine systems scientists work on theoretical and experimental research on the effects of aerospace environmental stresses on a human's functioning.

Ground crew: These workers are the mechanics, inspectors, and ground service people who make certain that aircraft are completely airworthy and fully prepared for passengers and cargo. Some ground operations people are responsible for loading of the aircraft and fueling. Precise records must be kept to make cer-

tain that the load is properly distributed in the aircraft.

Air traffic controllers: Air traffic controllers give landing and take-off instructions to all flights, using radar screens to track all airplane movement in the vicinity. Weather experts, communications people, and flight dispatchers must plan the flight and provide all necessary information about conditions likely to be encountered along the route.

Flight crew: The flight crew, headed by the captain, must operate the aircraft, while flight attendants look after safety requirements and cabin service for the passengers.

Sales staff: The sales staff of each airline promote the passenger and cargo services that airlines offer. Reservation specialists help people plan their trips. Agents issue tickets, handle baggage, and then check both at flight time.

Maintenance personnel: Among the important and highly specialized jobs in airline maintenance departments are those of airline maintenance inspector and the mechanics working on airframes and engines. Machinists, sheet metal workers, carpenters, electricians, painters, electroplaters, drill press operators, and upholsterers are all involved in the construction, repair, and maintenance of all commercial aircraft.

Airline offices also have the range of jobs usually found in any modern industry. These include research analysts, computer programmers, business machine operators, teletypists, and secretaries.

Education

Aerospace technology includes almost all scientific and technical specialties. Many different scientific and technical college majors are represented in sizable numbers in the aerospace industry. Those involved in design, testing, and other scientific endeavors usually have a graduate degree in engineering or a related field.

A career in aerospace manufacturing promises an opportunity for excitement and also creativity. But people looking to the aerospace field must keep in touch with the changing demands of the industry in relation to their own skills and ambitions.

Aviation and aerospace manufacturing plants employ various workers, including mechanics, sheet-metal workers, inspectors, assemblers, and metal processors. Skilled craft workers usually complete an apprenticeship program in which they learn blueprint reading, engineering, drawing, shop mathematics, elementary physics, and other subjects related to their specialty. These apprenticeship programs are run by manufacturers. Some programs include outside training at nearby schools with tuition paid by the employer. Smaller companies having no formal apprenticeship program rely on on-the-job training or select their employees from vocational or trade schools.

Some jobs for the airlines—pilots, dispatchers, and inspectors are examples—require a license from the federal government. There are a number of privately owned schools where one may obtain the training needed to qualify for federal certificates.

Airlines employ graduate engineers who work closely with aircraft manufacturers to develop equipment most suitable for the type of operation of a given carrier. Often, such an engineer is deeply involved in the design of aircraft and aircraft accessories and in improving maintenance and overhaul procedures.

Dozens of areas of aerospace technology require the skills of the technician. In research and development, it is the technician who develops the idea and plan into a testable device or a prototype. It is the technician who runs the tests and evaluates and operates the equipment such as wind tunnels, flight simulators, computers, and other highly complex units that give the scientist and engineer the information they need. It is the technician who lays out the complicated electronic device or develops the techniques for microminiaturization. The airplane and the space vehicle are complicated pieces of equipment. The research, development, manufacture, testing, and evaluation of this equipment and the devices used in these programs require a fundamental knowledge of science and mathematics and a practical skill in making things work.

Technicians are often educated in technical institutes or junior colleges. They are taught the fundamentals of science, technology, and mathematics and how to apply these to specific problems. Technicians become laboratory aides, drafters, tool designers, electronics aides, mathematics aides, production planners, technical writers or illustrators, and computer programmers.

Industry outlook

Accommodating growth in demand for airline service presents a number of challenges. Many of these challenges boil down to making better use of limited resources. One of the resource challenges is raising the capital to buy the more productive aircraft to replace older jets and to

Seconds after ignition, the space shuttle Atlantis heads out into orbit for a four-day mission. Shuttle launches can only occur during perfect weather conditions.

handle expected traffic growth. Another challenge is the need to make more productive use of the nation's system of airports. A third involves getting more work out of each gallon of fuel.

Aircraft are available that are more fuel efficient. These aircraft have the added advantage of being quieter. Airlines are ordering these advanced-technology aircraft and introducing them into service. Some will still be flying in airline fleets in the twenty-first century.

The space program will continue to depend on budget priorities. If the government is willing to spend large amounts of money on research and development, the space industry will flourish. However, if the government decides not to invest heavily in the space program, job opportunities will become scare.

In the space program, there has always been a high ratio of professional and skilled workers to those in unskilled or low-level administrative positions, and the space program will continue to demand highly trained employees who are flexible enough to move from one specialized job to another. The demand for professional and skilled personnel continues to grow even as the total employment in the aerospace industry decreases.

Aviation and Aerospace

About half of all workers in the aerospace industry work in plants on jobs directly related to manufacturing production.

◇ SOURCES OF ADDITIONAL INFORMATION

Aerospace Industries Association of America
1250 I Street, NW
Washington, DC 20005

American Institute of Aeronautics and Astronautics
370 L'Enfant Promenade, SW
Washington, DC 20024

Aerospace Education Association
1501 Lee Highway
Arlington, VA 22209

Air Transport Association of America
1709 New York Avenue, NW
Washington, DC 20006

Future Aviation Professionals of America
4959 Massachusetts Boulevard
Atlanta, GA 30337

The FAA offers pamphlets in its Aviation Career Series under the following categories: (1) Pilots and Flight Engineers; (2) Aviation Maintenance; (3) Airport Careers; (4) Aircraft Manufacturing Careers; (5) Airline Careers; (6) Flight Attendants; (7) Government Careers. They may be obtained by sending a self-addressed mail label to:

Federal Aviation Administration
Superintendent of Documents
Retail Distribution Division
8610 Cherry Lane
Laurel, MD 20707

◇ RELATED ARTICLES

Volume 1: Engineering; Mathematics; Military Services; Physical Sciences; Transportation; Travel and Tourism
Volume 2: Air traffic controllers; Astronauts; Astronomers; Biologists; Chemists; Drafters; Engineers; Industrial designers; Mathematicians; Meteorologists; Pilots
Volume 3: Aircraft mechanics and engine specialists; Airplane dispatchers; Communications equipment mechanics; Flight attendants; Flight engineers; Reservation and transportation ticket agents; Travel agents
Volume 4: Aeronautical and aerospace technicians; Avionics technicians; CAD/CAM technicians; Chemical technicians; Computer-service technicians; Drafting and design technicians; Industrial engineering technicians; Instrumentation technicians; Mechanical technicians; Robotics technicians; Solar collector technicians

Baking

General information

The baking industry is concerned with the production and marketing of perishable baked goods (breads, pies, cakes, and doughnuts) and dry baked goods (cookies, crackers, pretzels, and ice cream cones). Baking establishments include small retail bake shops, multi-unit bakeries, wholesale bakeries, and grocery chain bakeries. Because bread is a basic staple in the human diet, this U.S. industry provides steady, year-round employment for several hundred thousand workers.

Breads have been fundamental in the human diet for thousands of years. Bread has always been the major product in our diet and therefore has been called the staff of life. Ancient people made bread by mixing grain meal with water and baking the resulting dough on heated rocks. The ancient Egyptians baked bread in clay ovens heated with burning wood or charcoal. The ancient Greeks learned bread making from the Egyptians and later taught it to the Romans. During the Middle Ages (approximately between the years 400 and 1500), baking techniques spread throughout Europe. Most towns had public ovens because many people did not have ovens in their homes.

Baking techniques became more efficient as methods of cooking the bread improved. For example, during the 1600s and 1700s many people cooked bread in fireplaces. By the early 1800s, iron cookstoves became popular.

The baking industry in the United States started as early as 1640 in Plymouth and in 1645 in New York. The baking methods employed in Europe at the time were brought to the new shores by the colonists. Until the 1900's, most bread was still baked at home. The end of the nineteenth century saw the greatest immigration of workers from Europe. With it came skilled bakers from Germany, Poland, and other countries. In 1886 those workers formed their first union, the Journeymen Bakers Union

of North America. The union was formed in response to the low pay and poor working conditions.

Tremendous growth of the industry occurred in the first three decades of the twentieth century. By 1930, baking was a major food industry, exceeded in dollar volume only by meat packing. Baking ranked first in total wage earners employed, in number of establishments, and in value added by manufacturers.

The industry is divided into several segments, the classifications determined, for the most part, by their methods of distribution. Everyone is familiar with the corner baker, or the individual bake shop where baking is done on the premises. These bake shops are sometimes located in the larger shopping centers. Usually they are owned by one or two people who employ experienced bakers.

These small shops are places where most, if not all, products are produced by hand. Some baking methods are partially mechanized. The successful operators must be all-around bakers, that is, they must be skilled in making bread, various pastries, cakes, pies, cookies, and doughnuts. Many of these persons are either trained in Europe or are the sons or daughters of such people. Their bakery products display their artistry as bakers. Some of that artistry is lost in the mass production carried on by other segments of the industry.

A second classification is known as the "multi-unit" producers. They make the products at a central location and transport them, sometimes by several deliveries per day, to their own stores or to outlets in the supermarkets. They retain some of the artistry and individuality of the corner baker but produce larger amounts of goods. They employ mechanization when it will not affect the quality of the product adversely. It is important to note that since they control their sales outlets, multi-unit producers are able to give their customers fresher products. The multi-unit segment of the industry

Often, a baker must prepare certain foods according to the fruits in season. After making several strawberry cheesecakes, a baker prepares three strawberry shortcakes.

has continued to grow in both the number and size of establishments.

A third segment of the industry is known as wholesalers. These are the large mechanized bakeries. They have regular routes for delivering their bakery products to independent grocers and to supermarkets. This is by far the largest group, both in percentage of total volume of consumed bakery products, by size of establishments, by number of employees, and by added value of manufacturing. Many thousands of people are employed in this segment. Many of the companies identified with this group are national in character and use the same brand identification in all their market areas, even though their individual plants are located throughout the country.

Wholesalers range in size from a few bakeries to upward of fifty bakeries owned by a single company. Many are highly automated, mass producing and packaging their products at high speeds. They have large central offices employing specialists in production, engineering, research, food chemistry, packaging, transportation, purchasing, and advertising.

Another group is the grocery chain or in-store bakers. While fewer in number than the wholesalers, their impact on the bakery product market is growing. These are bakeries owned and operated by some of the large corporate supermarket chains. They use their own brand names (as opposed to the national advertised names used by the large wholesalers) and ordinarily give display preference in their stores to their own products.

The last, but by no means the smallest, segment in the baking industry is that which manufactures and distributes biscuits, crackers, pretzels, ice cream cones, and cookies. These are known in the trade as dry bakery products because of their longer shelf life or keeping qualities. Everyone is familiar with this class of baked goods, usually displayed separately and apart from the soft bakery products such as bread or other perishable goods. Recently, the number of manufacturing plants in this group has grown markedly.

By far the largest percentage of gross production in the soft bakeries is in white pan bread. Of the shipments of all types of bread in 1985 (valued at $5.4 billion), white pan bread accounted for $2.9 billion. Since the latter 1970s, however, per capita consumption of white bread has declined three percent annually; 26.8 pounds per person were consumed in 1985. Consumption of what is known in the trade as variety breads such as whole wheat and various dark whole grain breads, rye, raisin, diet, and other specialty types rose annually in the late 1970s and first half of the 1980s, though per capita consumption was still far below white bread (8.9 pounds per person for wheat breads in 1985; 2 pounds per person for rye and pumpernickel).

Statistics on the so-called soft bakeries show that multi-unit, wholesale, and grocery chain bakeries account for billions of dollars in total sales of products. The baking industry employs hundreds of thousands of workers in large U.S. industrial bakeries. Although there are many small bakeries, the larger plants account for most of the employment. Approximately three-quarters of the industry's workers are in plants with more than 100 employees.

Workers in the baking industry are represented primarily by two unions, the Bakery, Confectionery and Tobacco Workers International Union for production workers and The International Brotherhood of Teamsters for driver-salespersons. About 60 percent of the workers in the industry belong to unions (see Volume 1: Trade Unions).

Through their unions, bakery workers bargain collectively with the employers in the baking industry, and today the great majority of workers enjoy good wages and benefits, training opportunities for more challenging tasks, better-paying jobs, and safe and healthy workplaces.

Salaries and wages are comparable to those in most manufacturing industries. The average hourly wage from data reported in the late-1980s was roughly comparable to the average hourly wage of the manufacturing industry as a whole.

The structure of the baking industry

The production of different types of bread is quite similar. From the very start of the use of leavening agents to make bread, the same basic process has been used. This consists of making a "sponge" that contains part of the flour, yeast, and water. These are mixed and the resulting mixture is permitted to ferment and rise. The chemistry of this process, known as fermentation, is a study in itself. When the sponge reaches the proper stage of development, it is returned to the mixing machine and the remainder of the flour, the milk, the sugar, and other ingredients are added and mixed.

The resulting dough is then divided or weighed, allowed to sit for awhile, put in pans, and permitted to rise in the pans. The dough is then baked in an oven, after which it is cooled, sliced, and wrapped. This process is now known as the conventional method in the trade.

By far the most popular bread in America is white pan bread. A significant change in white pan bread is associated with processing the dough. After much experimentation, a process known as "continuous mix" was introduced. Essentially, this process was a change in equipment rather than changes in the ingredients. As its name implies, continuous mix starts with a "brew" made from the yeast, and the other ingredients are added in stages. The mixture is put through a pre-mixer that produces a finished dough which is put into the pans.

There are significant differences between the conventional and continuous mix processes. The continual mix process is more automated and the bread produced is a more even-textured and softer loaf.

Several significant developments in the manufacture of white pan bread occurred during the last several decades. The one that affects the nutritional content of the loaf was the introduction of enrichment to the bread formula. Enrichment means the addition of vitamins and minerals. This important step was taken in 1941 by agreement between the federal government, bakers, and millers. Most white breads are now labelled "enriched" and the packaging explains which essential vitamins and minerals are contained in a measured weight of the bread. Through enrichment, *beriberi* and other diseases linked to vitamin deficiencies have been minimized.

There are many types of nationality breads, such as Italian, French, and other European varieties. Most of these are baked directly on the oven hearth without pans. The loaves must be eaten when fresh, since the keeping quality is not as good as in pan bread.

A worker at a large bakery slides a pan of raw dough into an oven for baking. He is also responsible for removing the bread when it has finished baking.

Many other familiar products are made by the baking industry. Some, such as sweet rolls, Danish pastry, and sandwich buns, are made from yeast-fermented dough. Sweet cakes are leavened by baking powder or a combination of acids such as that in buttermilk, to which soda is added. Whereas these products all contain flour, the proportion of flour to the whole is not nearly as great as in bread. Eggs and sugar, shortening and butter, make up the difference.

In the production of cake products, for which formulation and mixing are very important, training is essential. The mixing times, the mixing temperatures, and the baking time and temperature impact the eventual quality of the finished products.

Great skill is involved in placing the finishing touches on the icing and frosting of cake products. When the art of baking is mentioned, it is here that one frequently finds the inspiration to become a specialist. In this line of bakery products, real artisanship is most important and the corner baker and the multi-unit retailers usually excel in it. With exactly the same ingredients, same formulation, and identical facilities, one baker (not unlike a cook in the home) may produce a distinctive product while the other may turn out a second-rate item. Even in mass production, differences in quality are discernible.

Frozen bakery products take two forms: one in which the product is completely baked, finished, and packaged; and one in which the product is unbaked or partially baked and then finished in the home by the consumer. It is only necessary to defrost the fully baked products or after defrosting to heat them for serving. However, in the case of partially baked or unbaked products, oven temperatures from 300 degrees to 450 degrees must be used to finish the baking process in the home.

A baked goods distributor places several trays of bread onto the shelves of a grocery store. He will visit many stores in the course of one day.

The marketing of frozen bakery products, one of the new and inviting fields in the industry, is following the development of frozen foods generally. Frozen bakery foods can remain in the frozen food cases in supermarkets or in the home for extended periods of time. Huge capital investments have been made by bakers in the expanding field of frozen bakery products.

Another product activity is the establishment of what are known as "bake-off" units. Frozen bakery products are delivered to the store where an oven has been installed. The frozen products are then baked off in the supermarket. They are, therefore, really freshly baked and the odor of baking in the store attracts customers, just as it invites a person to buy in a corner bakery. This is a rapidly developing segment of the industry.

Careers

Whether a young person decides to work in a corner bakery or chooses to work in a mass-producing type of bakery, career opportunities are many and varied. There are opportunities in all fields of endeavor, including management, administration, marketing, advertising, research and product development, engineering, packaging, sales management, production, law, and public relations. A sampling of career opportunities follows below.

Production: In production there are mixers, oven tenders, wrappers, and shippers, just to name a few. Approximately six out of each ten persons employed in the industry are production workers. These are the people who handle the raw materials, blend the flour, mix the dough, and attend the machines that scale the loaves.

Production supervisors: These people oversee the intermediate steps of "proofing" the bread after it is placed in the pans. These steps include baking, cooling, and packaging the bread before it is delivered to the shipping room.

Shippers: Shippers sort and select the loaves and direct deliveries to stores or to individual salespeople.

Decorators: Decorators embellish cakes and sweet rolls with fancy icings and frostings. Even with highly mechanized or automated production lines, skillful operators are required.

Maintenance workers: Maintenance people are specially skilled in fixing bakery machinery. These employees serve an important function because any mechanical breakdown could affect the quality of the product or its prompt delivery to the customers.

Housekeepers: Not least in importance in bakeries are the jobs done by the people responsible for housekeeping. Machines, utensils, and the bakery premises must be kept immaculately clean at all times. Specially trained monitors supervise these operations to meet the strict inspections and regulations of city, state, and federal authorities.

Marketing and *salespeople:* In marketing and sales there are the sales planners, sales managers, sales supervisors, and the route drivers themselves. As in most industries, the selling of the product is the all-important function without which production would be unnecessary. Good performance may lead to the position of a sales supervisor, who may supervise eight to ten salespeople. This position is normally the testing ground for future bakery sales managers, plant managers, and executives. Many of the top executives in the industry have risen through the sales departments of their companies.

Distributors: The distribution systems employed by the baking industry offer many job opportunities. For the most part, these are not just delivery functions, except for the grocery chain bakers. At the level of the route driver, a true sales job, there are many opportunities for persons who enjoy dealing with people. For the most part, employees in this classification are paid salary plus commission. The potential for high earnings may be inviting for those who are sales-minded.

Researchers and *product developers:* One of the most interesting vocations in the industry is in the field of research and product development. The larger companies in the field have their own laboratories where they employ chemists, technicians, and very skilled bakers in laboratories and experimental bake shops. These are pilot bakeries that develop new products. Laboratories also test ingredients for purity and workability.

Numerous companies allied to the baking industry have similar laboratories and experimental bake shops. Such firms sell raw materials to bakers and suggest formulations for their use in finished products. They carry on a continuous search for qualified technicians and practical, skilled bakers to work in their laboratories and also as field men and women to call on and demonstrate their products in the customers' bakery. The large flour manufacturers are especially active in this field.

Education

Specific training depends on what area of the baking industry is of interest. Those wishing to pursue managerial positions should have some training in business administration. The baking industry maintains its own school of baking, the American Institute of Baking in Manhattan, Kansas (address listed at the end of the article). Most students have had practical baking experience in a bakery and want to add technical training through classes at the Institute.

At the college level, Kansas State University, at Manhattan, Kansas, offers a four-year course leading to a college degree in Bakery Science and Management. Oklahoma State University offers a one-year course. An intensive four-month course is available for experienced bakery and allied trades employees. Some home-study courses for practical bakers are also available through correspondence schools and the American Institute of Baking.

Industry outlook

It is said of bread that it is humanity's cheapest and best food. Its use persists during highs and lows in the economic cycle. The daily demand for bread products assures steady employment for those who enjoy working in the baking industry. Unlike many industries whose production output can be stockpiled, most bakery products are still made fresh daily.

As for the future, even modest population growth assures a continuous and growing need for the industry's products, to say nothing of new products and new methods of distribution. Bread is so vital to humans that long after

A woman presents a tray of freshly-baked doughnuts in a shop. In most cases, doughnuts are baked on the premises.

many modern industries have failed, bakeries will continue to operate.

◇ **SOURCES OF ADDITIONAL INFORMATION**

American Institute of Baking
1213 Bakers Way
Manhattan, KS 66502

American Bakers Association
1111 14th Street, NW, Suite 300
Washington, DC 20005

Independent Bakers Association
3222 N Street, NW, Suite 32
Washington, DC 20007

Retail Bakers of America
Presidential Building, Suite 250
6525 Belcrest Road
Hyattsville, MD 20782

◇ **RELATED ARTICLES**

Volume 1: Agriculture; Food Processing
Volume 2: Home economists
Volume 3: Bakery product workers; Cooks, chefs, and bakers; Food service workers; Route drivers

Banking and Financial Services

General information

Banking in the United States started right after the Revolutionary War. The First Bank of the United States was a federally chartered bank, established to print money, purchase securities (stocks and bonds) in companies, and lend money. It was also responsible for establishing lending rules that state banks would have to follow. At the end of the twenty year charter, Congress refused to renew the First Bank's charter because of concern about the power that the bank held. The bank was subsequently closed.

Another federal bank followed, but only remained operational for four years before it suffered the same fate of the First Bank. With the demise of the federal banks, state banks quickly grew in power and size. Each bank was allowed to issue its own currency, which created an enormous fluctuation of the number of dollars actually in existence. This, in turn, influenced the value of each dollar.

If the bank produced too much money, or lent money and did not receive enough of it back, the bank would close and depositors would lose everything they had invested. This was a continual problem throughout the 1800s, but particularly during 1800 to 1863, an era known as the Wildcat Period.

In 1863-64, the government began steps that would eventually drive the banks' currency out of use. They established the National Banks Act to charter state banks, issue national currency and eventually tax the usage of bank currency. The taxation effectively killed all but the national currency.

In 1913 the Congress established the Federal Reserve. In response to a series of financial panics set off by the limited number of dollars being printed, the Federal Reserve was established to act as the government's central bank. It was divided into twelve districts, with a board of governors to determine policy, super-

vise the fluctuation of currency reserves for banks, and print currency.

In 1792, the forerunner of the New York Stock Exchange was started, allowing investors to buy stocks (a portion or share of the company) and bonds (a loan note from a company or the government to an individual lending money). With few controls on the purchase of stocks and bonds, investors in the stock market were able to receive great profits from companies who did very well. Investors were able to buy stocks and bonds with as little as 10 percent down.

From 1919 until 1929 more than $50 billion of new stocks and bonds were sold to the public. By 1932 almost one-half were worthless. Stock purchases had overinflated the value of the company stocks. When panic set in, the prices collapsed. The market crash of 1929 led to the passage of the Securities Acts of 1933 and 1934, which greatly strengthened previously established patterns of self-regulation and public disclosure. Each provision in these acts was directed at a previous abuse. The far-reaching Securities Act of 1933 provides for the full disclosure of all facts relating to new issues and is known as "the truth in securities" act. Because of the market crash, the government and industry representatives jointly acted to restore investor confidence in the securities markets.

In February 1933, banks in Detroit failed. They had lent too much money, without maintaining enough in reserves. The loans were risky and the amount paid back was too small to allow the banks to continue functioning. When news of this spread, people across the country lined up to withdraw their money from the banks before those banks failed as well. This created a "bank run," where more people tried to withdraw money than there was available. There was not enough money in the banks to return every investment to the investor. President Franklin Roosevelt shut down the banks on March 3 of that year, declaring a

Traders feverishly buy and sell stocks, bonds, commercial paper, and other financial options. They use a special sign language that determines the number of options and price at which they wish to purchase or sell. They will continue to operate in this fashion until the market closes at the end of the day.

bank holiday. The banks were not allowed to reopen until government inspectors had evaluated their books. The FDIC (Federal Deposit Insurance Corporation) was created in 1933 to establish government guarantees of the money deposited in banks.

Under the 1934 Securities Act the Securities and Exchange Commission (SEC), a federal agency, was created to supervise the trading of securities and to make sure that self-regulation functioned properly. Under reform legislation, misrepresentation and manipulation of the financial markets were made federal offenses. The securities industry itself accepted more fully and completely the basic obligations and responsibilities for self-regulation. The 1938 amendments to the Securities Exchange Act of 1934 established the National Association of Securities Dealers (NASD). It was organized as the self-regulatory organization responsible for the over-the-counter securities market. The SEC oversees the self-regulation of NASD dealers, as well as members of the New York, American, and regional stock exchanges. Through these legislative measures, a new era in the stock and bond business began.

There is little doubt that the growth of this industry since 1939 would not have been possible without the reforms achieved in the pre-

ceding years. Other difficulties arose in time, however, as many inexperienced people entered the stock market and the market itself began to grow rapidly. A lack of sophistication on the part of new investors and a lack of qualifications among many new brokers combined to create problems. A small stock boom erupted in 1961, with the prices of many obscure electronics and space-age stocks bid up to unreasonable heights and sometimes promoted by a few unscrupulous salespeople.

The speculative boom of 1961 collapsed dramatically in the sharp market break of May 28, 1962. Unlike the crash of 1929, however, this decline did not have a similar deadening impact upon overall business conditions. Also, many more individuals had purchased their stocks for long-term investment and were not overly concerned with the decline, which later proved only temporary.

In addition, a year before, Congress, realizing that important changes had taken place in the markets, ordered what became known as the Special Study of Securities Markets. This review was undertaken by a group of economists, lawyers, and brokers charged with taking a comprehensive look at the industry and suggesting ways in which investors might be better protected.

By the time the several volumes of the monumental Special Study report were issued by the SEC, the brokerage community had already taken many important steps to improve standards and operations. The Special Study with its 176 recommendations did not uncover abuses such as were prevalent in the 1920s. Some of the findings, however, became the basis for new federal legislation. The 1964 Securities Acts extended disclosure requirements to thousands of companies not previously covered by federal and exchange regulations. Most of the important and large companies throughout the nation must now regularly publicize the pertinent facts about their sales and earnings. Previously, only those companies that listed their securities on the exchanges were required to disclose and publish such information regularly. In addition, stricter standards were formally established for new persons entering the securities business. One continuing problem for Wall Street in the mid-1980s was stock manipulation based on insider information (information not known to the investment public). The SEC, however, conducted well-publicized investigations of violations of its rules, applying a system of safeguards that had been made more sophisticated and strengthened since the SEC's beginning in 1934. The SEC is the key federal agency devoted to discouraging and rooting out certain gross abusers and financial frauds.

On October 19, 1987, the New York Stock Exchange experienced a drop in stock prices far greater than the one in 1929. The Dow Jones Industrial Average had risen to an all-time high level of 2,722 on August 25, having climbed almost 1000 points in eight months. September saw a slight drop in the average, but nothing close to the drop that hit in October.

Over a three day period from October 14–16, 1987, the Dow Jones lost more than 261 points. On October 19, this downward spiral reached almost panic proportions, as the Dow Jones Average dropped 508 points. This reduced the overall value of the stock market by more than 22 percent. In actual cash value, the loss was estimated at more than $500 billion.

Two government investigations and a New York Stock Exchange investigation looked into the causes of the crash and determined that, although no single flaw in the system was responsible, more safeguards against market fluctuations were needed. As a result of the investigations, the limit on movement of stock prices was set at 100 points. If prices move in a range greater than that, trading will be shut down for an hour. If there is larger fluctuation after trading restarts, then other time restrictions apply

on trading. Also, the restrictions on electronic trading (where machines are programmed to trade automatically) have to shut off after a fifty point movement either up or down. The market built back up in value after the crash, but the overall effects of the largest market crash in history are yet to be established.

Unless a high level of trust existed between brokers and their customers and among brokers themselves, it would not be possible for millions of dollars to change hands as rapidly and as efficiently as they do. Thousands of binding transactions take place daily without signatures or even the formality of a handshake.

The structure of the banking and financial industry

The New York Stock Exchange, the American Stock Exchange, and the regional exchanges (for example, the Midwest Stock Exchange in Chicago and the Pacific Stock Exchange in San Francisco) provide central meetings places and supervised auction markets where member brokers may buy and sell securities for their clients. The exchanges as such do not buy or sell securities nor do they set prices. Instead, they provide the facilities for trading and enforce a variety of rules and regulations designed to maintain fair and orderly markets. The exchanges require the companies that are listed to meet certain specified standards of size and earnings, and to publicize important basic financial information regularly. Shares in companies that offer stocks are traded, along with other types of securities, every business day around the world.

The Over-the-Counter Market (OTC) is, after the New York Stock Exchange, the second largest U.S. market for stocks. It is served by a network of brokers; they are not in one specific place, as are exchange members. The electronic NASDAQ (National Association of Security Dealers Automatic Quote System) offers shares of new or smaller companies traded on the OTC.

The business practices of the member brokers are governed by rules requiring certain amounts of financial backing and strict standards of business conduct in their dealings with clients and with each other. Most exchanges are limited membership associations and admission is by election. Rules are established by a constitution and bylaws, and are enforced by an elected governing board with the aid of officers and committees. At the New York and the

American Exchanges, the supervisory work is carried out by a paid professional staff.

Specialists are those member brokers who deal only with other brokers and act for those brokers who cannot remain at a post on the Exchange floor until prices specified by their customers' buy and sell orders are reached. Part of the regular brokerage commission is paid to them when they act as a "broker's broker." The specialists also act as dealers, buying and selling shares for their own accounts. It is their job to sell stock when nobody wants to sell and to buy when there are no buyers. In this way they keep a continuous market and try to restrain wide fluctuations in price.

The American Stock Exchange (AMEX) trades in the shares of smaller, growing companies. Formerly known as the Curb Exchange because trading used to be done out-of-doors on the street, AMEX served as the proving ground for trading in the shares of such companies as Du Pont, General Motors, and RCA, all of which subsequently transferred to the New York Stock Exchange. The regional stock exchanges trade many of the same stocks that are listed on the two major exchanges. The regional exchanges also trade the shares of many smaller local companies.

The American Stock Exchange is also a membership organization. The New York and American Stock Exchanges operate in a similar fashion. The president, selected by the board of governors, is charged with administrative responsibility and under the president's direction a staff of several hundred people implement policy. The Surveillance Department follows the action of market prices, studies financial news, investment advisory service reports, and brokerage recommendations, watching for any signs of unusual activity.

Commodity exchanges in various parts of the country provide facilities and equipment for commodity futures trading. Formed as membership organizations like the major stock exchanges, they fall under the regulatory authority of the federal Commodity Futures Trading Commission. They have trading floors with "trading pits" or "rings," where futures contracts may be bought or sold. Five are in New York City, three in Chicago, and others are in Minneapolis and Kansas City, Missouri.

Organized in 1848, the Chicago Board of Trade (CBOT) is the nation's oldest and largest commodity futures exchange. It accounts for about half of all the futures trading volume in the United States. It provides facilities for trading in futures contracts (agreements to buy or sell commodities such as agricultural products, silver, gold, plywood, and energy sources) for its more than 1,400 members. The CBOT also

A bank teller offers assistance to a customer. In this case, she is processing a money order.

has about 700 associate members and over 900 members in special categories, for a total membership of more than 3,000 people. Millions of futures contracts are traded on its two trading floors every year.

The CBOT and another Chicago exchange, the Chicago Mercantile Exchange, account for most of all U.S. futures trading. Indirectly the two account for thousands of jobs in support and ancillary positions, from telecommunications specialists to brokerage house personnel.

Other American futures exchanges include the Commodity Exchange of New York, the Kansas City Board of Trade, the MidAmerica Commodity Exchange of Chicago, the Minneapolis Grain Exchange, and the New York Cotton Exchange. Some exchanges specialize. For example, the New York Cotton Exchange focuses on cotton contracts, while the Minneapolis Grain Exchange specializes in wheat. Other exchanges may offer facilities for futures trading in live and feeder cattle, coffee, copper, and other commodities.

Futures trading has been described as a means of providing protection against changeable prices in the cash markets. Users of the futures market (buyers of grain, for example, or the farmers who grow grain) hedge against rises or declines in the market by buying or selling futures contracts at prices immediately available. They thus minimize the risk of adverse price changes.

Self-regulation has characterized the securities markets in this country since their inception in the latter part of the eighteenth century. The exchanges have always, in varying de-

Computerized bank tellers are becoming increasingly popular, offering 24-hour service to its memebers.They can provide a variety of services such as withdrawals, deposits, and account transfers.

grees, imposed upon their members certain rules of conduct. These self-governing activities were officially endorsed and strengthened by the first federal Securities Acts of 1933 and 1934, which set the current pattern of self-regulation supervised by the government.

Before the passage of the legislation that created the Securities and Exchange Commission, the individual states had enacted a number of contradictory laws purporting to regulate the sale of securities. These varied greatly and only a few provided for effective enforcement. Today, however, each state has some legislation governing issuance and sale of securities. Some have created smaller and somewhat similar versions of the Securities and Exchange Commission. They all require securities and brokers to be registered and some have established qualification standards for salespeople. Certain selling practices are prohibited in some states, and the public sale of securities that do not meet strict standards can be prohibited by several state administrators.

It is the federal agency, the Securities and Exchange Commission, however, that bears the main burden of overseeing the operations of the securities industry. The SEC, an independent governmental organization located in Washington, D.C., enforces the laws passed by Congress in the interest of protecting the investing public. It is composed of five commissioners, appointed by the President, with no more than three commissioners belonging to one political party. The staff carries out the registration, supervisory, and investigatory functions that are its basic responsibility.

At the SEC headquarters in Washington, D.C., the Division of Corporation Finance examines the many detailed financial statements that must be submitted by companies that sell their stock to the public. If any statements seems misleading, inaccurate, or incomplete, the company is so informed and given an opportunity to file corrections or clarifications before the securities can be sold. The Commission can prohibit the sale of securities if all the facts are not presented or if they appear misleading.

The SEC, however, has no power to pass on the merits of a security. It cannot pass judgment on value or price. A company that might want to dig for green cheese on the moon could be permitted to sell its stock by the SEC, as long as all the facts about this venture were truthfully and completely stated. Congress left to individual investors the responsibility for appraising the actual value of particular securities offered for sale.

Two out of three SEC employees are located in Washington while the others work in the regional and branch offices. College training is a virtual necessity, the more important jobs requiring more specialized training. The SEC has been a noted training ground for many young lawyers who have subsequently gone into private practice.

While the individual exchanges supervise the trading on the floor and many of the activities of their members, the main responsibility for self-regulation of the over-the-counter markets rests with the National Association of Securities Dealers (NASD). This self-policing organization is a private, nonprofit organization headquartered in Washington, D.C., with fourteen district offices. It enforces the rules of fair practice that govern the professional conduct of its member firms and a uniform practice code that deals with technical methods for executing transactions and conducting a securities business. The bulk of its work is done by committees composed of brokers who serve without pay, acting on the principle that ethical standards can best be adopted and enforced by self-governing bodies of individuals rather than by direct government controls and regulations.

Surprise examinations are made of all member offices at least once every three years. Salespeople's backgrounds are reviewed and all must take special examinations, in addition to those required by the major stock exchanges. Underwriting practices are watched, and excessive price changes are reported and analyzed. Disciplinary actions such as fines, suspensions, and expulsion from the association are taken against those who violate the various rules.

Banks and savings institutions in the United States are financial businesses, chartered and supervised by either state or federal government agencies to provide financial services for the public. In the late 1980s banks collectively administered hundreds of billions in resources and millions of dollars more in trust funds and other accounts. There are thousands of commercial banks, which are sometimes described as "financial department stores" because they offer all kinds of financial services, such as checking and savings accounts, loans, and trust services for the administration of estates, endowments, and pension funds. There are also several hundred savings and loans institutions in various states that specialize in savings and time accounts and the making of mortgage loans.

In addition to large banks and savings and loan institutions, there are scores of private and specialized banks, such as investment banks and land banks. Under federal law, banks cannot underwrite stock or bond issues. They cannot engage in underwriting or investment banking. But they can take and fill orders, and in 1982 the government began approving requests from banks and bank holding companies to acquire or establish brokerages. These limited service firms either perform their own market operations or contract with carrying firms to handle stock and bond trades, registration and billing, and dividends and margin accounts. The SEC extended its regulatory scope over the stock-brokerage activities of about 2,000 banks in 1985.

Credit unions and other institutions not legally defined as banks offer some comparable services, such as savings accounts and consumer loans. In the aggregate, banks operate thousands of offices located in practically every neighborhood and community in the country. Many of the larger banks maintain offices in principal foreign cities of the world. The banks are organized so that through correspondent relationships they perform services for other banks or for individual customers both in this country and abroad.

Traditionally, the concept of working in a bank has been of record keeping and accounting. Of course most people know about bank

A broker on the Foreign Exchange Trading Floor of the Chase Manhattan Bank discusses the benefits of purchasing some stock at a certain price.

tellers who stand at windows cashing checks, accepting deposits, and performing other duties. But tellers must also exercise initiative, as do bank clerks who keep records and do accounting.

The major service areas of banking are commercial banking, including corporate lending; consumer, or retail, banking; and trust administration and estate planning. Business banking is the major service center for the industry. Business bankers are involved in making loans to businesses and corporations. Satisfying credit needs includes such things as accounts receivable financing, leasing, energy financing, and equipment financing. Bank loans to commerce and industry total hundreds of billions of dollars.

Corporate services also include foreign currency exchange and other trade-related requirements for companies that export their products. Such companies use special financing techniques, such as cross-currency loans and commercial letters of credit. International banking is one of the newer and interesting specialties within the industry.

Retail banking offers consumers not only lending services, but also savings, investment, and payment services. Mortgage loans are made for the purchase of homes, and smaller amounts are lent for appliances, cars, vacations, and the like through traditional installment loans or even a line of credit activated by a checking account or other means.

Bank cards represent the fastest growing type of consumer credit in America. Commercial credit cards, as well as individual bank cards, offer customers both flexibility in money management and convenient credit availability.

Payment services for bank customers range from regular checking accounts to bill-paying services, 24-hour a day automated teller machines, and direct deposit of Social Security checks and other dividend checks. Savings services include statement and passbook accounts, as well as a variety of long-term deposits offering higher rates of interest.

Bank trust services, which were originally for the administration and conservation of large estates, are now growing to include pension and retirement funds and a wide variety of smaller funds to meet the needs of people of moderate means. Through trust departments customers may arrange for professional administration of their assets, estate planning, and a variety of personal financial services.

Careers

A wide variety of career options are available to those interested in the banking and financial services industry. A sampling of career opportunities follows below.

Securities brokers: Securities brokers representing brokerage firms handle orders to buy and sell securities. They often counsel people as to what stocks to buy and sell, and also how to handle their overall financial situation. The salespeople who work for a firm that is a member of one or more of the major stock exchanges are known as registered representatives or account executives. They must pass a series of examinations (including aptitude and psychological tests), undergo at least a six-month training period, and are subsequently subjected to continuous supervision.

The salespeople who are with non-exchange-member firms or the smaller firms also are screened and tested by their employers and by the National Association of Securities Dealers, the self-regulatory association of all brokers who do business with the public. The NASD offers a six-hour examination for candidates for Registered Representatives (see Volume 3: Securities and financial services sales representatives).

Securities analysts: The largest and most important single group of employees in the investment advisory category are the security analysts. Their work underlies the advice given by brokerage firms and counseling firms. They are employed not only by the investment advisers and brokerage firms, but also by banks, insurance companies, pension funds, foundations,

mutual funds, and other large financial institutions.

The typical analyst is usually a college graduate who has majored in economics and, increasingly, graduate work is considered a necessity for further advancement (see Volume 2: Economists).

Securities sales staff: Securities sales representatives have many different kinds of duties. They open accounts for new customers, obtaining from them all the information required to permit the customer to buy and sell securities through the brokerage firm. They execute buy and sell orders for customers by relaying the information to the floor of the exchange where the order is actually put into effect. They obtain information on a company's prospects from their research department and are often called upon to advise a customer on the wisdom of a purchase or sale. They must be prepared to answer all questions on the technical aspects of stock market operations as well as be informed on current economic conditions. They are expected to have sufficient knowledge to anticipate certain trends and to counsel customers accordingly in terms of their particular stock holdings.

Some securities salespeople specialize in specific areas such as handling only institutional accounts or specializing in bond issues or mutual funds. Whatever the area in which they operate, securities salespeople must keep abreast of all significant political and economic conditions, maintain very accurate records of all transactions, and continually solicit new customers.

Mutual fund sales staff: Fund salespeople are essentially selling a professionally managed product. Neither they nor the selling organization has anything to say about the investment policies of the funds. Fund salespeople are primarily concerned with questions such as the suitability of the fund for their clients' needs and whether their clients should invest in securities at all. Unlike the regular security salespeople, they are not expected to be fully familiar with techniques of security analysis nor do they need the support of a large research department since they are not recommending the purchase or sale of individual securities. Instead, separate professional analysts and large research departments help formulate the fund decisions as to which individual securities to buy and sell. Those who buy shares of mutual funds are buying the expertise of the fund's investment advisers rather than the expertise of the salesperson.

Those who sell mutual fund shares are also subject to the federal securities laws designed to prevent fraud and deceit in the purchase and

Traders at the Chicago Board of Trade attend buying and selling sessions. The floor is divided into separate pits where different items are traded, such as soy beans, wheat, and other agricultural products.

sale of securities and to assure that only persons of financial responsibility and basic honesty engage in the business of selling securities. They must become familiar with the many strict regulations, industry and federal, governing the sale of mutual funds.

Bank managers: Bank managers are the heads of their financial institutions. They are responsible for overseeing the operations and regulations of the bank, making sure that their practices comply with the law and do not jeopardize the investments of the money their clients hold in the bank. They supply the financial statements to the government agencies that review their status, such as the FDIC. They answer directly to the board of directors of their association (see Volume 2: Financial institution officers and managers).

Operations managers: Operations managers must adapt new technologies to the business of dealing with individual bank customers. To help people in financial matters, operations managers are responsible for creating new ways to use machines like computers, lasers, and a host of other complex technologies that will make personal financial matters easier.

Bank trust officers: Bank trust departments serve as executors and administrators of the assets of deceased persons by assembling their assets, paying their debts, and distributing the remaining assets to the beneficiaries. Trust officers also act as financial guardians for minors and incompetent persons and perform a variety of property management functions.

Investment bankers/investment counselors: Investment bankers/counselors select appropriate investment vehicles, including stocks, bonds, money market instruments, and real estate. Their decisions are based on extensive research and analysis of the individual trust account. In a typical investment counseling firm, accounts are handled by an individual investment counselor or an account supervisor. The counselor usually has background experience in securities, and devotes full time to the management of the portfolios under his or her supervision.

It is the investment counselor's job to be familiar with the individual personal and financial needs of the investor and to make suitable recommendations regarding the purchase and sale of securities.

A customer service representative at a bank verifies a customer's account before providing information and discussing the status of the account.

Loan officers: The loan officer handles the customers who are looking to borrow money for a home, car, or other personal need. They also work with companies that require a loan for building expansion or other need. The officer evaluates the request by looking at the borrower's credit background and financial ability to repay the loan. The officer negotiates the loan contract, approves or rejects the application, and arranges the repayment schedule (see Volume 3: Financial institution clerks and related workers).

Tellers: Tellers handle many routine bank transactions. They receive and pay out money on accounts, enter the transactions into the computer records, cash checks, and fulfill other day-to-day responsibilities. (see Volume 3: Financial institution tellers).

Clerks: Clerks, often with the use of computer systems, verify the total cost of the stock purchased, including the taxes and the amount of commission to be charged to the customer. They see that the stock, the number of shares, and price paid are correct. They receive and deliver the stock certificates that have been bought for clients to see that they are acceptable for transfer of ownership. The same is done for certificates that have been sold for clients and are being delivered to other buyers.

Margin clerks keep track of stock purchases made on credit. Margin clerks must check the changing regulations on such purchases and be particularly alert to any downward price changes that would require additional cash or collateral from the customers.

Professional marketing officers: Marketing officers determine who the bank's customers are and who they should be. They identify customer needs and wants and evaluate bank locations and the need for new facilities. Specifically, they are involved in such things as attitude research, test marketing, and advertising effectiveness research.

Security officers: Security officers protect financial institutions from robbery, theft, and fraud. The bank's security officers are charged with doing everything possible to reduce threats, including computer fraud.

Legal advisors: People with legal training advise the banks on laws and regulations affecting the operations of the institution and are employed in the trust department to pass on wills and contracts or to draw up trust instruments (see Volume 1: Law).

Education

A college education with a degree in finance, business administration, or economics is the best foundation for a career in the banking and financial services industry. Because of the continual need for comprehensive understanding of the economy and financial rules and regulations, it is almost impossible to find employment as a broker or upper level officer in a bank without at least an undergraduate degree.

Knowledge of French, German, Japanese or other foreign language used in commercial transactions is very helpful because banks do a lot of business in the international arena. Courses in geography and history should be included wherever possible. It would also be useful for high-school students to take courses in basic economics.

High-school students, where possible, should consider summer and vacation employment in banks. Banks often employ part-time help and may be in touch with school employment and academic advisers in their communities.

A bachelor's degree in a field related to banking, such as business administration, economics, law, or accounting, is helpful for promotion to a bank officer position.

Following employment in a bank, young people will usually have an opportunity to further their education through short courses, conferences, seminars, or correspondence courses.

Most larger banks have middle-management training programs. With one out of every five bank employees an officer, most larger banks find it wise to train their own employees and generally follow a policy of promotion from within.

Most large brokerage firms conduct training programs of varying length and intensity, although at least a six-month period is a mandatory requirement for exchange-member firms. During the initial training program the trainees are on salary and do no selling. Usually, the larger the firm the longer the training period and the greater the number of trainees. The longer training includes classroom work in accounting, securities laws, exchange rules, market analysis, and on-the-job training in research and portfolio analysis.

The firms that are not members of the New York or American Stock Exchanges usually adjust their training programs to the particular type of securities that they sell, usually over-the-counter or mutual funds. The representatives of firms that are not members of the New York or American Stock Exchanges, however, must take the same six-hour exam that representatives of exchange members take to qualify as Registered Representatives.

The training given those who sell only mutual funds differs from that given to those who intend to sell a wide variety of securities. Some of the organizations that specialize in mutual funds give intensive two- or three-week courses in the special characteristics of mutual funds.

houses are bought through bank consumer loans. Inventories, equipment, and machinery for business and industry are financed by term loans made through bank commercial departments.

According to the *Occupational Outlook Handbook*, the growth of automatic teller machines and other electronic equipment indicated that the number of bank tellers would increase more slowly through the mid-1990s than the average for all occupations. However, officers and managers in banks and related institutions could anticipate that employment would increase faster than the average for all occupations through the mid-1990s.

For brokers and securities industry employees, the job outlook is less bright. After the 1987 stock market crash, most major brokerage firms reduced their staff. Many people have had to find employment in other industries. The staff reductions will probably remain in effect for some time, with only a gradual increase in the staff size as the quantity of stocks traded warrants it.

The fastest area of growth are in the specialty fields, such as international finances, corporate investment, or financial marketing. As the competition increases, the candidate with a college degree, some experience in the field, and a good overall education in finances and economics will have the strongest employment opportunities.

Industry outlook

Banking has been going through many changes. The application of electronic machines to bank operations, the expansion of banking services, and the growing need for bank facilities in connection with nationwide and international trade have all contributed to changes in the banking environment. There are more than 70,000 automatic teller machines (ATMs) in the United States, with more than 160 million automatic teller cards in use. These changes have resulted in a general upgrading of banking jobs, calling for more people with technical expertise.

Basically, individual banks act as intermediaries for the movement of money, credit, and capital to wherever they are needed within the economy. It is estimated that 90 percent of all payments in the United States are made by bank checks. In the late 1980s, there were billions of checks written in the United States each year, and the number is increasing steadily. Today, most automobiles, home appliances, and

⬦ **SOURCES OF ADDITIONAL INFORMATION**

American Bankers Association
1120 Connecticut Avenue, NW
Washington, DC 20036

Bank Administration Institute
60 Gould Center
Rolling Meadows, IL 60008

National Association of Bank Women
500 North Michigan Avenue, Suite 1400
Chicago, IL 60611

The Institute of Financial Education
111 East Wacker Drive
Chicago, IL 60601

Independent Bankers Association of America
One Thomas Circle, NW, Suite 950
Washington, DC 20005

◇ **RELATED ARTICLES**

Volume 1: Accounting; Law
Volume 2: Accountants and auditors; Economists; Financial institution officers and managers
Volume 3: Financial institutions clerks and related workers; Financial institutions tellers; Securities and financial services sales representatives
Volume 4: Computer-Service technicians; Data-processing technicians; Scientific and business data-processing technicians

Biological Sciences

General information

The biological sciences are concerned with living matter in all its forms. Biologists study anything that is or has been alive—animals, microbes, plants, insects, fossils, bones, cells, and genetic material. In addition to these studies, biologists also examine the effects of changes in the environment on living matter. The number and variety of life processes and evolutionary developments in living things are so vast and complex that the biological sciences encompass many areas of specialization. Nearly any field concerned with living things, either directly or indirectly, requires the services and talents of a biologist. Biologists develop medicine to combat disease, conservation measures to protect the environment, agricultural products to enhance and increase production, and even support systems for life in space.

The biological sciences developed slowly in the course of human history. With the dawn of civilization, people began to structure their approach to science. Aside from simply observing the world around them, early humans used what they could learn to further their basic needs. For example, the establishment of agriculture incorporated some scientific knowledge. The basic information was the understanding that from one type of seed one type of plant would grow. The more complex biological knowledge involved when to plant, when to water, and how to harvest seeds for the next season.

It was only with modern man that biology developed into what we may term an exact science. As primitive biologists of sorts, our ancestors learned to differentiate between desirable and undesirable plants (taxonomy), to live in the more habitable environments (ecology), to domesticate plants (agronomy and horticulture) and animals (animal husbandry), and to utilize the living matter about them for shelter, clothing, and food (economic biology).

Eventually plants were classified as herbs, shrubs, and trees and animals were classified as land, water, or flying organisms. Later on, beginnings were made in the study of how the organism functioned and how it was related to the other organisms about it. Thus, we had the beginnings of zoology (animal science) and botany (plant science).

The ancient Egyptians had substantial knowledge of the human body and its organs. During the process of mummification, important body organs were removed and preserved. Some written records indicate the awareness that the heart was of major importance in the maintenance of life.

Around 500 B.C., Alcmaeon, a student of natural philosophy under Pythagoras, conducted research on the difference between arteries and veins. He studied embryos and documented his findings, including the discovery of the optic nerve.

Aristotle, known mainly for his philosophical writings, also set about to form one of the first documented taxonomic systems for classifying animals. He categorized animals into two types: blooded (mammals, birds, amphibians, reptiles, and fishes); and bloodless (crustaceans, insects, and other lower animals). He also studied forms of reproduction and was able to identify and document asexual and sexual forms of reproduction among animals. Aristotle also proposed theories that have since been proven wrong, but which demonstrated some understanding of how embryos develop into animals.

From the 2nd century to the 11th century A.D., the Arabs made important advances in biological understanding. Unlike the European continent, the Arabians continued to study from the base of knowledge attained by the Greeks. Avicenna, a Persian born in A.D. 980, wrote *Canon of Medicine,* one of the most influential and important publications on medical knowledge of its time in both the East and

Two biological scientists prepare several types of solutions for an experiment.

West. Avicenna studied and wrote on the natural sciences, psychology, astronomy, and numerous other subjects. His publications on medicine were the most influential, although his writings on theology, philosophy, and astronomy also endured. *Canon on Medicine* remained the single authoritative work in medical knowledge for seven centuries.

Albertus Magnus, a German scholar from the 13th century, wrote thirty-three books on botany, with descriptions of plant anatomy and propagation. Albert the Great, as he was known, taught natural science; one of his students was Thomas Aquinas.

During the sixteenth and seventeenth centuries, gigantic strides were made in Europe in biological studies. Andreas Vesalius (1514–1564) described the anatomical structure of the human body, William Harvey (1578–1657) discovered the circulation of blood, Robert Hooke (1635–1703) discovered and named cells from the bark of a cork oak, and Antony von Leeuwenhoek (1632–1723) discovered microscopic life.

In the book *The Origins of Species*, Charles Darwin (1809–1882) generated the theory of evolution by means of natural selection, coining the term "survival of the fittest." The famous French doctor Louis Pasteur (1822–1895) developed the field of immunology. Many of the achievements that were gained in the 19th century were done specifically because of improvements in the microscope, allowing scientists to see much smaller structures than they have ever been able to isolate before. The 19th century is considered the age of cellular biology because of the advances made in cell study. Matthias Schleiden (1804–1881) and Theodar Schwann, (1810–1882) formulated the theory that the cell is the fundamental unit of all organisms; and Gregor Mendel, (1812–1884) discovered the principles of heredity through the study of corn.

The 20th century was dominated by studies and breakthroughs in molecular biology. Once knowledge of atomic structure was discovered, the fundamental building blocks for all of nature became open to study and categorization. A periodic table of elements was established in the late 1800s by Dmitri Mendeleev and Julius Meyer, assigning an atomic weight and molecular count to all known molecules. Because of the predictability of chemical properties, they were able to assign spaces for chemicals which were still undiscovered, but whose existence was determined by the logic and order of the table. They were later proven right when the chemicals were discovered.

At the turn of the 20th century, several scientists from around the globe were making discoveries in cellular biology that would establish how information was transmitted from one organism to its progeny. When chromosomes were recognized as the carrier of information, studies went on to discover the method of information transmission. In 1944, Oswald Avery and a team of scientists were able to isolate and identify DNA (deoxyribonucleic acid) as the transmitter of genetic information. James Watson and Francis Crick, in 1953, deciphered the complex structure of DNA as the genetic code for all living matter. Crick and Watson were the recipients of the Nobel Prize in 1962 for their achievement in physiology with the discovery of the Watson-Crick DNA model.

Nearly a third of the total number of biological scientists work in private industry for pharmaceutical, chemical, and food companies and for research laboratories. Roughly the same number hold appointments in colleges and universities. About one-tenth work in nonteaching jobs in academic institutions, and some work for hospitals, foundations, or nonprofit research institutions.

More than 25 percent of all biologists work for the federal government. By and large, the largest number of biologists is employed by the Department of Agriculture in its Agricultural Research Service, Forest Service, and Soil Conservation Service. Many are foresters, forestry researchers, and forestry aides. Others work as agricultural inspectors, in agronomy, plant pathology, and pest control.

The structure of the biological sciences

Biology includes broad fields such as agronomy, animal husbandry, biochemistry, forestry, horticulture, fish and wildlife conservation, and range management. Along with the traditional fields such as zoology and physiology, new careers have opened in oceanography, high-altitude biology, radiation biology, and environmental biology. Other new areas of specialization include bioengineering, biophysics bioinstrumentation, cryobiology, bionics, and biotechnology.

Biotechnology—the use of biological systems to produce new goods and services—is not a new field. Microorganisms have long been used to produce fermented substances and various foods. But applications arising out of new knowledge about recombinant DNA and RNA (sometimes called genetic engineering) promise to open many opportunities for commercial applications, especially in healthcare and pharmaceutical fields.

Experimentation and observation are the two key building blocks to scientific discovery. Rarely is a discovery made spontaneously. Most scientists build on the work of others, both past and present.

In developing a research approach, the biologist will determine an appropriate area of study, such as the influence of a chemical or compound on the human body. The arrangements for experiments can be quite varied. The number of participants involved, the time frame, and the number of outside influences on the results vary widely. The biologist judges all of these factors in setting up the experiment. Previous research done on related experiments is reviewed. Then the parameters of the test are set.

Funding for research projects may come from the institution where the biologist is employed. For university professors and researchers, the funding may be through the university or it may be through grants from the government or private corporations. For private research firms, projects frequently require approval from a board of directors. The biologist needs to have most of the details of the re-

An ecologist tests beet leaves for the effects of gaseous emissions from a nearby geothermal power facility.

search planned out before funding will granted. This planning includes determining what the potential results may show and how the research would benefit the funding organization.

In government labs, research ideas may be internally developed or they may be established by an outside group calling for investigation into some area of concern, such as the safety of pesticides used on crops or the effects of exposure to high intensity electric power lines. Investigations of this type may be related to pressure from outside organizations or it may come from statistics that the government has compiled and believes requires further observation and study.

Theories in biology, like any others, must be tested. Testing is accomplished generally in the laboratory by using all the tools of modern science including those of physics, chemistry, and mathematics. Theories shown to be true are then used to formulate other theories or are used with other facts to broaden knowledge in a particular field.

One should not think that overly complex apparatus is needed for study. Excellent research can be with basic scientific equipment: microscopes, glass slides, simple chemicals, rubber tubing, culture plates, incubators and ovens, and readily available tools.

For projects that involve testing on humans, the biologist will locate people willing to agree to the parameters of the test for the duration of the testing time. A few of the largest scale tests were conducted by the medical community on itself. For example, more than 100,000 doctors agreed to take one aspirin a day for several years to determine the effects of aspirin in reducing heart attacks. In another experiment, more than 115,000 nurses between the ages of thirty and fifty-five were tracked for eight years, covering data such as their weight and smoking habits, to determine the increase in chance of heart attacks in women who were obese. In both tests the results showed a much stronger link than had been originally anticipated. Aspirin was found to be more helpful in preventing heart attacks, and obesity was determined to create a much greater chance of heart attack.

Such wide scale testing is rare. Most experiments involve a few dozen subjects or less. Large group testing is both more expensive and more difficult to administer.

When the results are in, the biologist will prepare some form of analysis. This may be in the form of a presentation to the funding source, or it may be a printed article in a scientific journal. Publishing results of studies is one of the key elements of a research project. It is through shared data and evaluations that the scientific community is able to gain the most from research.

In areas of research that are heavily competitive, however, some results may be considered privileged or confidential information. In creating a chemical compound that is more effective at lowering blood pressure, for example, the key to success in sales is the ability to hold the only method of manufacturing the product. If one product is considered the best, and only one company produces that product, their sales will be enhanced by maintaining their control on the product.

For scientists working under certain types of contracts, their discoveries may remain the property of the company for whom they work. For other scientists, their discoveries may remain their own property with the right to patent and charge others for the use of the discovery.

For most biologists, the role of researcher and evaluator is shared with a team of scientists. There will be staff conducting various aspects of the research, and registering and evaluating results.

In general, biologists may be classified into four groups or areas of work: basic research, applied research, teaching, and supporting roles.

In basic research, biologists strive to uncover fundamental truths. In other words, they attempt to transfer the unknown into the known. Basic research is often done at universities and encompasses all areas of biology, including biochemistry, botany, and physiology.

Biologists engaged in applied research translate basic knowledge into practical, useful products and processes. In addition, these research scientists work closely with agricultural and medical scientists who are most aware of the impact of biology on human needs. Specialties in applied research and development might include agronomy, forestry, horticulture, and wildlife management.

Research biologists who work at universities, colleges, and medical schools may also perform as teachers or professors. However, some biologists may teach without doing research. Teaching can be a stimulating and rewarding experience at both the secondary and college levels.

Supporting biologists work closely with research and development scientists. The complexity of modern biological research requires a team approach to solve the many problems. Supporting biologists include laboratory technicians, instrument specialists, plant and animal caretakers, photographers, illustrators, writers, and clerical assistants. All of these should combine a thorough knowledge of biology with their other skills.

Careers

Biologists work in laboratories and offices, in fields and on farms, in administrative posts and in classrooms. Some work in academic institutions, others in industry and government. Some work for private foundations, others for botanic gardens and zoos. All of these individuals share some basic characteristics including curiosity, a capacity for problem-solving and independent thought, aptitude for the use of tools, an interest in contributing to basic knowledge, and an interest in living things.

Since biologists cannot cover the entire field of life, they must specialize; hence the large number of biologists. Listed below are many of the choices of biological occupations.

Agronomists: Agronomists study soils and relationships of soils with crop plants.

Anatomists: These scientists examine the structure and form of plants and animals.

Bacteriologists: Bacteriologists investigate the forms, processes, and structure of bacteria.

Biochemists: Biochemists study the chemistry and chemical processes of living matter.

Biophysicists: Biophysicists research the biological structures and processes in terms of the physical sciences.

Biotechnologists: Also called genetic engineers, these scientists apply genetic materials and biological systems to create new products and services for medicine and other fields.

Botanists: Botanists study all aspects of plants and their environment.

Bryologists: Bryologists deal with the portion of botany that examines mosses and related plants.

Cytologists: Cytologists look at cells, particularly their structure and function.

Ecologists: These scientists are involved with the study of organisms, their distribution, their abundance, and their relationship with and impact on the environment.

Evolutionists: Evolutionists are concerned with the development of plants or animals from the origins of the earth to the present.

Entomologists: These scientists specialize in the branch of zoology that examines insects.

Foresters: Foresters specialize in the planting and managing of forests.

Geneticists: Geneticists study the characteristics of heredity.

Herpetologists: These zoologists specialize in the study of reptiles and amphibians.

Histologists: Histologists examine plant and animal tissues.

Horticulturists: Horticulturists are botanist who specialize in fruit and vegetable crops.

Ichthyologists: Ichthyologists are zoologists that deal with the study of fish.

Limnologists: Limnologists study the physical, chemical, meteorological, and biological conditions in fresh waters (lakes, ponds, etc).

Mammalogists: These zoologists are concerned with the study of mammals.

Marine biologists: Marine biologists study life forms in the oceans.

Microbiologists: Microbiologists investigate microscopic life, including protozoa, bacteria, and viruses.

Morphologists: Morphologists study the form and structure of plants and animals.

Mycologists: Mycologists study fungi. Their work is related to studies in botany.

Nematologists: These zoologists specialize in the study of round worms.

Oceanographers: Oceanographers study tides, currents, topography, and the properties of sea water.

Paleontologists prepare recovered bones for transportation to a museum. Burlap bags are dipped in plaster and then applied to the bones, giving the specimens maximum protection.

Ornithologists: Ornithologists examine birds.

Paleontologists: Paleontologists study the fossilized remains of plants and animals that existed in former geologic periods.

Parasitologists: Parasitologists examine animals or plants that derive nourishment while living in or on another organism.

Pathologists: These scientists study the diseases of plants and animals.

Pharmacologists: Pharmacologists create drugs and study their effects on cellular, molecular, and biological levels.

Phycologists: Phycologists are botanists who specialize in the study of algae.

Physiologists: Physiologists are concerned with the functions of organisms and/or their parts.

Phytopathologists: Phytopathologists examine the causes and treatments of plant diseases.

Protozoologists: These are zoologists that deal specifically with protozoa—animals consisting of a single cell or a colony composed of single cells.

69

A biochemist tests for pesticide residue in serum samples. He uses a technique called "ELISA" or Enzyme Linked-Immunosolvent Assay that analyzes the pesticide concentrations.

Taxonomists: Taxonomists study the classification of animals and plants. They create systems that categorize living organisms.

Toxicologists: These biologists study the effects of toxic substances on living organisms and the environment. They determine which substances are toxic, or harmful, to either.

Zoologists: Zoologists study all aspects of animal life. They are concerned with the anatomy of animals, their lifestyles, and their interaction with the environment. This excludes the study of humans.

Almost all of these titles have the four basic levels of position: researcher; applied research; educator; and support staff. For each title there will be some variation of the type of research involved. The conditions under which the scientist works will vary according to the specialty, place of occupation, and specific goals of the employer.

Education

All biologists have earned undergraduate degrees in the sciences. This level of education is sufficient for those who are interested in becoming technicians. Most, however, go on to complete master's or doctorate degrees in their area of interest. A master's degree and a doctorate are essential for any budding biologist to conduct serious research, publish in scholarly journals, and obtain a faculty position at a college or university.

Research biologists are usually required to hold doctorate degrees for appointment and advancement in most academic and research posts. A master's degree may qualify applicants for some applied research jobs, depending on the area of specialty and the degree of research involved in the specific job in question. However, a doctorate is usually expected of applied research scientists. To direct a project or program, a doctorate is essential.

A bachelor's degree related to the field of research may be necessary in jobs for supporting biologists. Biologists who do most of the labor involved in biological experiments (bench work) normally have a degree in the area of study the research covers. Some bench work jobs have a broad enough application, though, that the experience can translate into other fields of study.

Industry outlook

Universities and colleges, once the leading employers of biologists, are currently suffering from decreased enrollments and are no longer seeking biologists in large numbers. Nevertheless as tenured professors retire, biologists with doctorates will be needed to fill the open positions. Opportunities still exist in selected specialties, and employment of biological scientists is expected to increase about as fast as the average for all occupations through the mid-1990s.

The growing concern for the protection of the environment and human health has created many new opportunities for ecologists in government, industry, and business. In addition, the growing support for health-related research continues to provide opportunities for microbiologists, biochemists, physiologists, and other biologists in health-related areas in government and industry.

Some areas currently gaining prominence for future employment are concerned with biological problems of aging, overcrowding in cities, disease, food supply, air, water, and soil pollution, waste disposal, use of drugs and medicines, human genetics, human ecology, resource conservation, and wildlife management.

American universities and colleges have about 50,000 posts for professors; a fifth of all registered biologists hold non-faculty positions at universities and colleges. A third of all biologists work in private industry, with that number expecting to increase through the 1990s. The number of government posts is growing slowing, but rapid increases are possible if large projects are approved by Congress. Much of this depends on future government funding, which provides essential money to zoos, industries, and educational institutions.

◇ SOURCES OF ADDITIONAL INFORMATION

For more detailed information on one or more of the specialties in biology, contact the organizations listed below:

Agronomy:

American Society of Agronomy
677 South Segoe Road
Madison, WI 53711

Anatomy:

American Association of Anatomists
Tulane Medical Center
1430 Tulane Avenue
New Orleans, LA 70112

Bacteriology:

American Society for Microbiology
1931 I Street, NW
Washington, DC 20006

Biology:

American Institute of Biological Sciences
730 11th Street, NW
Washington, DC 20001

Federation of American Societies for Experimental Biology
9650 Rockville Pike
Bethesda, MD 20814

Biochemistry:

American Society for Biochemistry and Molecular Biology
9650 Rockville Pike
Bethesda, MD 20814

Biophysics:

Biophysical Society
Biophysical Society Office
9650 Rockville Pike, Room 2505
Bethesda, MD 20814

Botany:

Botanical Society of America
Ecology and Evolutionary Biology
75 North Eagleville Road
U–43 University of Connecticut
Storrs, CT 06268

Bryology:

American Bryological and Lichenological Society
Department of Biology

Texas A & M University
College Station, TX 77843

Cytology:

American Society for Cell Biology
9650 Rockville Pike
Bethesda, MD 20814

Ecology:

Ecological Society of America
Center for Environmental Studies
Arizona State University
Tempe, AZ 85287

Entomology:

Entomological Society of America
9301 Annapolis Road
Lanham, MD 20706

Evolution:

Society for the Study of Evolution
Department of Biology
Washington University
St. Louis, MO 63130

Genetics:

Genetics Society of America
9650 Rockville Pike
Bethesda, MD 20814

Herpetology and Ichthyology:

American Society of Ichthyologists and Herpetologists
Florida State Museum
University of Florida
Gainesville, FL 32611

Limnology:

American Society of Limnology and Oceanography
Virginia Institute of Marine Science
College of William and Mary
Gloucester Point, VA 23062

Microbiology:

Society for Industrial Microbiology
Information Officer
PO Box 12534
Arlington, VA 22209

Mycology:

Mycological Society of America
Harvard University Herbaria
22 Divinity Avenue
Cambridge, MA 02138

Nematology:

Society of Nematologists
Department of Nematology
University of California
Riverside, CA 92521

Paleontology:

Paleontology Society
US Geological Survey
National Center MS970
Reston, VA 22092

Parasitology:

American Society of Parasitologists
Department of Biological Sciences
University of Texas
500 West University Avenue
El Paso, TX 79968

Pharmacology:

**American Society for Pharmacology and
Experimental Therapeutics**
9650 Rockville Pike
Bethesda, MD 20814

Photobiology:

American Society for Photobiology
8000 Westpark Drive, Suite 400
McLean, VA 22102

Phycology:

Phycological Society of America
Department of Botany
Louisiana State University
Baton Rouge, LA 70803

Physiology:

American Physiological Society
9650 Rockville Pike
Bethesda, MD 20814

Phytopathology:

American Phytopathological Society
3340 Pilot Knob Road
St. Paul, MN 55121

Taxonomy:

Society of Systematic Zoology
Information Officer
Smithsonian Institution
Washington, DC 20560

American Society of Plant Taxonomists
Department of Botany
University of Georgia
Athens, GA 30602

Zoology:

American Society of Zoologists
104 Sirius Circle
Thousand Oaks, CA 91360

**American Association of Zoological Parks
and Aquariums**
Route 88
Oglebay Park
Wheeling, WV 26003

◇ **RELATED ARTICLES**

Volume 1: Agriculture; Chemicals and Drugs; Chemistry; Energy; Engineering; Health Care; Physical Sciences; Recreation and Park Management; Waste Management

Volume 2: Biochemists; Biologists; Biomedical engineers; Chemists; College and university faculty; Geophysicists; Groundwater professionals; Medical technologists; Oceanographers; Petrologists; Pharmacologists; Veterinarians; Wood science and technology careers

Volume 3: Agricultural scientists; Foresters; Park rangers; Pharmaceutical industry workers; Range managers; Soil scientists

Volume 4: Agribusiness technicians; Biological specimen technicians; Biological technicians; Biomedical equipment technicians; Forestry technicians; Laboratory technicians; Medical laboratory technicians; Ornamental horticulture technicians; Pharmaceutical technicians

Book Publishing

General information

The earliest known books were the clay tablets of Mesopotamia and the papyrus rolls of Egypt. Examples of both date from about 3000 B.C. The Chinese also developed books quite early, with archeological findings indicating that the Chinese had books about 1300 B.C. Early Chinese books were made of wood or bamboo strips bound together with cords.

With the spread of Greek culture in the third century B.C., the Greek alphabet helped make books accessible to more people. For the first time, the general public began to read on a wide range of topics. Up until that point, books had primarily been produced for scholarly research or for use by royalty.

The Greeks gathered data from the many lands that they conquered and collected this information in book form. Although large libraries were established in Alexandria and other cities, very few Greek books survive to this day. As the Greek Empire was destroyed by the Romans, many of the books (written on rolls of papyrus) were also destroyed.

The Romans developed the book trade on a large scale. Private libraries became a mark of distinction and each Roman ruler established his own library. As with the Greeks, books were copied by having a reader dictate material to slave copyists.

A major advance in book publishing occurred with the substitution of codex for the roll. Instead of having leaves fastened together on alternate edges, as was the case with papyrus rolls, the codex was made from folded leaves attached together on one side. With the codex form, a pile of pages could be opened to any point in the text. This did away with the rolling and unrolling of text. The codex also made possible writing on both sides of a page. The codex form could contain much longer texts and permit much quicker access to information than papyrus rolls.

Another important advance was the use of vellum and parchment in place of papyrus. Vellum and parchment are prepared from the skins of animals. A sheet of parchment could be cut in larger sizes than a sheet of papyrus. In addition, parchment was flexible and durable and could better receive writing on both sides. Papyrus was brittle and therefore was more difficult to use in large volumes.

Mass production of books became possible in the mid-1400s with the invention of printing. In the 1450s in Germany, Johannes Gutenberg invented moveable metallic type for making printing plates. Chinese and Koreans had developed the same sort of printing system—moveable type with porcelain and metal pieces—but it had proved impractical because the number of characters needed was so high. They opted instead to carve the page into a wooden block to use for muliple printings. Gutenberg designed a moveable type for Roman letters that proved to be practical enough to be swiftly imitated.

The Gutenberg Bible was printed in 1456. The printing process spread rapidly throughout Europe, and by the year 1500 almost every major European country had a printing press. Before the development of the printing press, there were only thousands of books in Europe, all hand written. Within fifty years of the Gutenberg invention, there were millions of books.

The printing press revolutionized book publishing. The key to the printing press lay in its capacity to produce multiply copies of a book quickly and at a relatively low cost. Books were now available to everyone who could read. Ideas and opinions could be spread without the support of the king or other ruler. Not surprisingly, the rise of printing was matched by a rise in literacy.

By the middle of the 15th century, printers were incorporating illustrations into the text. They made use of woodcut blocks and copper

An editor reads over a manuscript to determine whether it is well-written and interesting. If he believes that the manuscript is marketable, he will agree to publish it. Most manuscripts need extensive editing before publication.

engravings. The copper engravings kept a fine crisp line in the illustration, allowing printers to produce maps in quantity.

Although the number of books printed would continue to rise, few changes were made in the method of book production until the beginning of the Industrial Revolution. With the advent of the power motor, paper was able to be machine run through the presses. Mechanical methods of typecasting and typesetting were developed that allowed the type to be produced and displayed faster. The cost of paper declined as the speed with which it could be made accelerated.

In 1905, Ira Rubel ran the inked block of type through the press so that the ink would print on the rubber impression cylinder. He did this accidentally, but when running paper through the press afterward found that the images printed from ink on the impression cylinder were sharp. Printing from the rubber cylinder was named *off-set* lithography.

In the 20th century, off-set printing and other technological advances enabled book publishing to reached all segments of society. Major changes, such as the advent of the pa-

perback book, have also occurred in book design and book distribution.

After World War II the lithography method of printing pages became the most widely used. Lithographic work had existed since the 1700s when it was discovered that chemically processed stones would repeatedly reproduce images burnished into the stone. Lithographic plates, usually metallic, are still used today. The image is set onto the plate chemically and a rubber cylinder inks the plate. The treated surface picks up the ink, the non-treated surface repels ink and is wiped off before printing. The offset method of printing allows for a more refined, more detailed print, and less water touches the paper being printed.

The structure of the book publishing industry

Publishing begins with authors and their ideas. To get a manuscript published, an author must usually hire a literary agent to present the manuscript or idea to an interested editor. The editorial department of the average book publisher is headed by an editor-in-chief or editorial director.

The editorial department is involved with accepting manuscripts, revising written material with the author, and preparing the manuscript for the production staff. They also maintain contact with major authors and their literary agents.

If more than one house is interested in publishing a manuscript, a bidding process among editors ensues. Bidding for a book can be a tense and competitive situation. Publishers and editors have to estimate their sales, convert this into a royalty figure, and then decide if the amount is sufficient to get the title. Frequently, guarantees are paid that are out of proportion to the potential sales, but are offered to make certain of obtaining rights to a major work and subsidiary benefits associated with those rights. This is especially true for paperback reprint rights.

Unlike trade publishers, textbook houses come up their own ideas for textbooks. They do not use literary agent. Editors decide to publish a book or a series in a particular topic. This decision may be prompted by a lack of books on the proposed subject, by some new developments in subject matter, or by an introduction of a teaching technique that makes existing texts obsolete. Once the proposed topic has been approved, editors seek worthy authors. The authors are usually respected academicians, anxious to publish their works. This situation is mutually satisfying for both the publisher and the author. The publisher is able to print a textbook by a leader in a given field, and the author is able to enhance his or her career through publication of a major work.

Frequently, textbooks are put together by a team composed of authorities on the subject matter, a specialist on the teaching technique, and possibly a reading-level specialist, who will make certain that the vocabulary used is appropriate for the grade toward which the text is directed.

Once a manuscript is revised and approved by an editor, it is turned over to the production department. Depending on the size of the company, the production department may be comprised of a single person who farms out the copy edited manuscript to a printing house, or it may be an extensive staff that not only performs editing duties but actually produces the books.

The production department provides artwork, maps, photographs, and other materials used in book production. All production costs must conform to a preestablished cost struc-

A proofreader must read a printed text for consistency in style and grammatical accuracy. Such work requires intense concentration.

ture. Outside specialists (such as artists and designers) may be called in even by the very large publishers to augment the regular staff.

The printing and binding of the book may take place at a small press or in a large factory printing shop. There are various technologies used to manufacture and produce books today. The use of computers has greatly enhanced the quality of printing while reducing the cost of prepress work.

Prepress is the set-up of pages and film for the press. Page makeup is the production of the type onto a page in the form the editors want it printed. After all editorial changes are made and the correct pages are finished, the type is set on a layout board with the page lines marked. This is called the mechanical.

The type is then photographed in film either in negative, (where the type is clear and the background opaque) or positive (where the type is opaque and the background clear). The method of page makeup from computers now allows some printers to skip the film stage of production.

Plastic or electrotype plates are made photochemically and then plate proofs are printed to check the quality of the plates for the final printing. Once the plate proof pages are okayed, the presses are ready to run. The book will normally be printed in one run with one or more presses turning out pages in *signatures*. A signature is a large sheet of paper that will fold in to several pages. Signatures can be in 12, 16, 24, 32, 36, or 64 page sections. For a color press, the colors will print consecutively, with a red, blue, yellow, and black plate. Fifth colors can be added, or some colors can be eliminated, depending on the need of the publisher.

The other method of publishing, commonly used in newspaper printing is called web press. A web press prints on a continuous roll of paper, and the paper is then cut and folded after the press run (see Volume 1: Newspapers; Printing.)

Once the ink is dry and the pages all printed, the paper is then stacked and bound into books. Binding can be sewn, glued with adhesive (perfect-bound), or stapled. Smaller publications normally use stapling since it is less expensive.

While a book is in production, the promotion department hires advertisers to schedule space in magazines and newspapers, works out cooperative advertising with retailers, produces point-of-purchase material for use in stores, and arranges for direct mailings to promote or sell the books. In these activities the promotions manager is generally assisted by a staff and by an outside advertising agency.

Promotion for textbooks is directed primarily toward teachers, principals, heads of academic departments, and school boards and curriculum committees. Supplementary or enrichment titles may be promoted in the same way, but rather than being purchased by a school authority, these books are frequently purchased from discretionary funds by teachers and principals. At the college and graduate levels, textbooks are purchased by the individual students, but the promotion is generally directed to the heads of departments and professors. Advertisements may be placed in professional journals. Exhibits, frequently elaborate and expensive, may be set up at conventions and meetings.

Academic presses usually advertise in professional journals, although books for a less specialized market may be advertised in book reviews and other more general media. Some academic presses publish books that have potential to sell in the trade market.

The importance of effective publicity is recognized in the book publishing industry. Promotional responsibilities are usually handled by a public relations staff that arranges for newspaper, radio, and television releases, sets up interviews with authors, and generally tries to keep the authors in the public eye.

Sales responsibilities involves selling to wholesalers, who arrange for further distribution. Salespeople also sell to retailers, schools and libraries, and occasionally directly to the consumer. A publishing house may have sales to both domestic and foreign markets. This can involve separate or combined staffs of salespeople paid a salary, a commission on sales, or a combination of the two (see Volume 1: Marketing).

With subscription publications, distribution is accomplished by salespeople who personally contact and demonstrate to prospective purchasers. Sales may be initiated by coupon advertising in magazines and newspapers and by direct mail promotions followed up by a call from a salesperson. The salesperson represents only one company and therefore becomes highly specialized and very knowledgeable about its products.

Orders for books are completed via computerized systems, often tied to the International Standard Book Number (ISBN) system. This system has significantly helped publishers control inventory and process orders, including handling returns and credits.

In addition to the sale and distribution of books, a trade book publisher is vitally concerned with the sale of subsidiary rights. Included are newspaper and magazine rights for serials or excerpts, motion picture rights, book club rights, reprint and paperback rights, and translation rights. To do an effective job selling in these fields requires a detailed knowledge of book publishing markets.

A large book publishing company will have the same support departments that would be found in any other large company, including a personnel department, office services, and an accounting staff.

In the United States, publishing companies vary in size from offices with only a handful of employees to corporate giants, employing hundreds of people.

The smallest firms employ from one to thirty people. Employees often take part in every publishing function: contacting authors, negotiating for manuscripts, editing, writing jacket copy, designing, styling, production, promotion, distribution, and negotiating the sale of subsidiary rights. Free-lancers are used for copy editing, proofreading, indexing, and designing. For sales and distribution, small firms either employ independent salesmen or participate in a joint venture with other publishing companies.

There is a growing trend toward public ownership and amalgamation of small publishers, giving small houses the resources of larger publishers.

A mid-size book publisher issues between 30 and 125 titles each year and has a permanent staff of approximately fifty employees. Houses of this size still use free-lancers for much of their work.

The larger book publishers, with separate departments for manuscript editing, sales, and the other publishing activities, employ hundreds of people.

There are many types of books published, including trade books, textbooks, and academic books. A publishing house may be print books in all these categories or may publish only one type of book.

Trade books are those publications that one expects to find in a book store. Trade books include both fiction and nonfiction material on subjects including history, religion, contemporary problems, science, politics, art, and children's literature. This classification includes hard bound and paperback volumes and features new releases and reprints. A publishing house may restrict its output to one subclassification: religious books, sports books, children's books, or even garden books; most, however, embrace a larger spectrum.

Textbook publishing is generally broken down into elementary, high-school, and college textbook publishing. A publishing house may attempt to cover all three fields or may specialize in one. A high percentage of textbook publishing is performed in large, well-integrated companies. One major consideration is the regular need to update textbooks. Five years is about as long as a book can go without revision. To compete with the popular used-book market, it has become common for new editions of college textbooks to come out every two years.

Another type of publication, the subscription book, relies on sales made in the customer's home and by direct-mail promotion. The encyclopedia publishers are predominant in this field, selling supplementary yearbooks. Other kinds of reference books and multivolume sets are commonly sold this way as well. Encyclopedia publishers employ extensive editorial staffs to revise their material. Dictionary publishers compile and validate usage, and atlas publishers must contend with everchanging boundaries.

To make the purchase of encyclopedias and other reference sets as affordable and appealing as possible, the buyer may pay in installments. This means that the subscription publisher must become involved in the financing of the sales, including checking credit and maintaining sales accounts.

Once a picture editor has selected the illustrations and photographs for a text, she must crop them to fit into the designated space.

University presses and other academic publishers disseminate knowledge through the publication of scholarly books and journals. Many private and state universities maintain their own book publishing facilities. They usually concentrate in highly specialized nonfiction publications, generally directed toward small but academically significant markets. Trade and textbook publishing houses cannot pinpoint their market so precisely and could not profitably publish such books because the print runs are comparatively small. The price of an individual volume is usually higher than a trade book or textbook.

As nonprofit organizations, university presses do not pay corporate income taxes, but they have the same staff and promotion costs as other publishers and seldom realize much profit.

Book clubs are the source of a large part of the total book sales in the United States. They acquire limited rights in the distribution of certain titles or they buy books for distribution to their members. Typically, a book club purchases the right from the trade publisher to manufacture copies of a book for distribution to

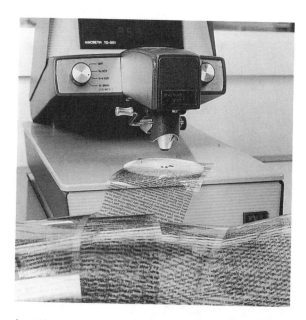

A machine scans a transparency of text to determine the printing thickness.

its members. Therefore, book clubs need not have an editorial department. Instead, they employ reviewers who read published works and try to determine what would be most appealing to their members. Book clubs are valuable to trade publishers. Not only do the clubs pay a royalty fees to the publishers and authors, but they also provide additional publicity at no cost to the publishing company.

The larger book clubs distribute books of all types. Others specialize in particular subjects such as detective novels, gardening manuals, children's literature, or romance novels. While some book clubs are independent of trade book publishers, others are operated by magazine and trade book publishing houses. Members are enrolled in the clubs through print advertising, direct mail promotions, and occasionally through other media.

Club memberships may be sold on a yearly basis. Memberships may require the purchase of a minimum number of books in a one-year period, or the member may be free to quit at any time. Generally, book clubs distribute books free or at nominal charge upon joining, and then offer price reductions on books throughout the year.

Paperbacks have grown to become a major segment of the book publishing industry, serving a vast market. The books are comparatively inexpensive, making them affordable to a large part of the population. In most cases, they are printed in a convenient size, fitting into pockets, backpacks, luggage, or briefcases without concern for loss or damage.

Unlike trade publishers, paperback publishers keep titles in print long after the volume of sale would have forced the hardback distributor to discontinue the title. They provide a relatively inexpensive format for the publication of specialized original books that otherwise would probably never be published.

Royalties from paperback distribution are always given to the author. In some cases the original hardcover publishers may also receive royalties. It is more common, however, that the paperback rights are sold exclusively to the paperback publishers at a high price.

Careers

Book publishing is a billion dollar industry, responsible for the output of more than 50,000 titles annually.

The pathway to publishing careers are open not only to experienced editors, but also to college graduates and people experienced in other facets of book publishing (production, promotion, and distribution). Many make the transition into editorial roles. Others may begin in editorial work and find later they are more comfortable in production, manufacturing, or promotion jobs.

Literary agents: Literary agents present manuscripts to publishing houses. Before they choose to represent an author, agents review writing samples, and in some cases, read an entire manuscript. In general, they function as intermediaries between authors and publishers. Once an manuscript is accepted, they negotiate royalties and contracts for the authors, taking a percentage of the author's profit.

Editors-in-Chief: Editors-in-Chief or Editorial Directors ensure that the publishing house's editorial policy is maintained with respect to the number of titles published each year, the content, the variety, and the general price range. They supervise the entire editorial staff and ultimately decide what shall be published.

Managing editors: Managing editors are responsible for the flow of editorial materials to the production department in time to meet sales objectives. They schedule assignments to the other editors.

Editors: It is the duty of the editor to seek out authors, help them formulate their ideas into publishable material, and encourage them to set those ideas down on paper.

Editorial staff: The editorial staff is made up of editors, associate editors, and assistant editors who read incoming manuscripts, develop editorial ideas, and hunt for authors. Editorial staff also report on the adequacy of manuscripts and the manuscript's potential for special markets.

Production managers: A production manager receives the manuscript and establishes the production schedule. The production manager's key responsibility is to ensure the timely and economical manufacture of the books. He or she coordinates the efforts of copy editors, proofreaders, indexers, researchers, typesetters, page layout designers, graphic artists, and photo and picture editors.

Copy editors: Copy editors read manuscripts for correct grammatical usage and spelling. They edit the manuscripts to conform with the publisher's style, which includes such points as capitalization, abbreviations, and the use of numbers.

Proofreaders: Proofreaders check the printed manuscripts for any typographical errors.

Indexers: Indexers create a list of topics for publications that require them. This involves scrutinizing a typeset manuscript and identifying key words, events, names, and places that warrant a reference in the index.

Researchers: Otherwise known as fact checkers, researchers ensure that the information published is accurate.

Typesetters: Typesetters commit a manuscript to type. Such work involves placing the text on a page in accordance with strict design specifications.

Page layout designers: It is the responsibility of page layout designers to ensure that the text and illustrations from a book will fit on to a page according to a given format.

Graphic artists: Graphic artists design the covers and general layout of books.

Photograph and art editors: Photograph and art editors select the illustrative materials that appear in a publication.

Publicity and promotions managers: Publicity and promotions managers are responsible for creating public awareness of the books they publish. They manage a team of staff members that concentrate on this goal.

Publicity promotions staff: The promotions staff assists the managers in all aspects of publicity, including press releases, promotional tours, and point-of-purchase displays.

Salespeople: Salespeople visit potential buyers in a given area, trying to receive orders on books.

Subsidiary rights managers: Subsidiary rights managers are involved with selling rights to toys or other products that are related to a book they publish.

Fulfillment workers: The distribution or fulfillment department fills orders and supervises warehousing, shipping, and, in some organizations, credit and collections.

Education

To enter the book publishing field, a candidate should have at least a college degree. Proficiency in writing is essential for those interested in editing. If one's interest is other than writing or editing, the liberal arts background should be augmented with advertising, sales, public relations, and other business experience.

University presses and scholarly publications normally require a higher degree in the field that the publications cover. For a science editor of scholarly or professional books, a master's or doctorate is normally expected.

For those who wish to learn more about publishing, various programs are offered by colleges and universities throughout the country. Radcliffe College, Rice University, and the University of Colorado in Denver hold summer-long sessions on all aspects of publishing. While these courses tend to be expensive, scholarships are available. Other institutions, such as the Chicago Book Clinic, offer courses throughout the year. There are publishing associations in every city that can direct a person to local publishing courses and associations.

Industry outlook

As long as people continue to read, there will be a future in book publishing. In the editorial department, some book subjects may become more prevalent as lifestyles and trends change. At present, there is an influx of computer and health-related publications.

Recent technological improvements have had a large impact on the publishing industry. Desktop publishing has made editing and page make-up simpler and more efficient, allowing for a greater output of titles. While CD-ROM (Compact Disk-Read Only Memory). publications are still in their early stages, the CD-ROM business is projected to expand as consumers continue to purchase computers and computer accessories.

Another area of development for the book publishing industry is in the relatively new market of books-on-cassette. The books are edited to fit in a one, two, or three hour presentation and are normally read by actors, broadcasters, or by the authors.

Computerized ordering systems have made the publishing business much more cost-effective. These systems allow for more accurate inventory maintenance and more efficient distribution networks.

Sales of books have increased in the past couple years. Sales were estimated to reach $15 billion for the U.S. book market in 1990. Staffing has increased approximately three percent from 1989 to 1990 to keep up with the renewed demand for books. That rise in employment and sales is expected to continue through the mid-1990s.

◇ SOURCES OF ADDITIONAL INFORMATION

The Literary Market Place publishes current addresses of publishing companies in the United States and Canada. In addition, it lists associations, significant individuals, literary agents, and other publishing-related organizations. The periodical Publishers Weekly contains current information on the book publishing industry as well as listings of job openings primarily in the New York area. For more information on book publishing contact:

Association of American Publishers
220 East 23rd Street
New York, NY 10010

American Book Producers Association
211 East 51st Street, Suite 11D
New York, NY 10022

National Association of Independent Publishers
2299 Riverside Drive, Box 850
Moore Haven, FL 33471

◇ RELATED ARTICLES

Volume 1: Design; Magazine Publishing; Newspaper Publishing; Printing; Public Relations
Volume 2: Advertising workers; Commercial artists; Designers; Photographers and camera operators; Writers and editors
Volume 3: Compositors and typesetters; Printing press operators and assistants
Volume 4: Graphics arts technicians

Broadcasting

General information

Humans have sought for centuries to improve methods of communicating with one another over long distances. In 1895, when an Italian engineer, Guglielmo Marconi, demonstrated how to send communication signals without the use of wires, instantaneous worldwide communication became a reality.

In the early 1900s, the transmitting and receiving devices were relatively simple, and hundreds of amateurs constructed transmitters and receivers on their own and experimented with radio. Ships were rapidly equipped with radios so they could communicate with each other and with shore bases while at sea. In 1906, human voice was transmitted for the first time by Reginald A. Fessenden. Small radio shows started in 1910, with commercial radio stations developing in 1920. By 1921, a dozen local stations were broadcasting. By 1926, stations across the country were linked together to form the first national network, the National Broadcasting Company (NBC). Four years later, the first radio broadcast was made around the world.

There has been a steady growth in the number of radio stations in the United States. Now nearly every large town has at least one radio station, and the larger cities have as many as twenty or more, with programming diversified to suit all tastes. The United States alone has 10,000 radio stations, both commercial and public.

The development of the iconoscope tube in 1923, which turned optical energy into electrical energy, made television possible. A few years later, the first experimental television program was sent by wire from New York to Washington, D.C., but it was not until 1939, when Franklin D. Roosevelt used television to open the New York World's Fair, that the public realized that television as a standard appliance for communication was just around the corner. Several stations went on the air shortly after this demonstration and successfully televised professional baseball, college football, and the Republican and Democratic conventions of 1940. The onset of World War II limited the further development of television until after the war was over.

Since television's strength is the immediacy with which it can present information, news programs started the foundation of regular programming. "Meet the Press" arrived in 1947, and nightly newscasts in 1948.

Television began to expand rapidly during the 1950s, following the lifting of the Federal Communications Commission freeze on the processing of station applications. In 1953, there were 120 commercial stations. By the end of the 1980s, there were over 1000 commercial television stations, and more than 300 public stations. Approximately 60 percent of the families with TVs also own video cassette recorders, from which they can record or watch motion pictures and television shows. About 50 percent of the households in the United States are also equipped to receive cable programs, with that percentage expected to rise even further during the 1990s.

With the vast potential audience for both radio and television, the broadcast medium has become a powerful industry, influencing people's opinions, buying habits, political views, and awareness on a variety of topics from health to the problems of drinking and driving.

The structure of the broadcasting industry

The radio and television industry is made up of a large number of relatively small and independent stations individually owned and operated. Over 200,000 people are employed in the

Many people are involved in the production of a news broadcast. There are camera operators, broadcast engineers, program directors, and producers that coordinate several tasks to generate these shows.

broadcasting industry. Commercial radio employs about half, and commercial television about one-third of the total. The others are employed by industry headquarters, such as network offices and public broadcasting stations.

In television, large stations located in metropolitan centers employ up to several hundred people, whereas a very small station in a small city may employ as few as thirty-five people. In radio, the smallest station may employ only four or five full-time people, whereas National Public Radio has around 350 permanent staff members. Most television stations and many radio stations are affiliated with one of the national networks. An affiliate station is not owned by the network, but merely has a business contract under which it is supplied by its network with a considerable amount of programming, usually produced in New York or Los Angeles and transmitted to the station through the airwaves on special frequencies. Networks provide programs that would be too expensive and elaborate for an individual station to produce. The network produces these programs, sells the advertising associated with them, and shares the revenues with the stations that carry the programs.

In television, the typical affiliate is supplied with programs during a portion of the morning hours, a portion of the afternoon hours, and a portion of the evening hours. During the remaining time, the station develops its own programming. This programming may be locally developed and presented live, or it may be videotaped for later showing. Stations also purchase programs from various organizations that produce programs for general sale or that have acquired the rights to programs. Each station develops the particular program format that in its judgment will best serve its market.

Cable television stations work under some of the same arrangements as commercial television stations. There are cable stations that broadcast commercials for most of their revenue, and run either original programming or purchase rights to rebroadcast shows that originally aired on network television. Other cable stations function on a basis of monthly payments by viewers. These stations tend to run motion pictures, special broadcasts of sports or entertainment events, and movies produced specifically for the cable station.

Cable stations may also broadcast material that is not limited by the restrictions of language, subject matter, or motion picture audience ratings that affect commercial television broadcasts. Pay-per-view cable programming is also being developed to cover special events that the viewer can opt to pay for on an event-by-event basis.

In radio, a structure somewhat similar to television networks exists, but with some significant differences. With the rise of television, radio networking was reduced in the amount and variety of programs offered. In the 1980s, however, satellite radio networks have increasingly provided music programming on audiotape. Still, many small radio stations came to rely entirely on their own resources for their programming.

In radio, the network's major responsibility is to supply national news and feature programs of national interest that would be difficult for the individual station to produce. There has been considerable interest in reviving the variety of programs offered by the national networks in such categories as drama, sports, and special features.

Radio and television depend on electromagnetic waves to carry signals from the transmitting tower to the receiver in the individual's home. Each broadcast requires a certain amount of air space for a certain amount of time; otherwise interference would occur. Thus each user of space is assigned an area of the spectrum, which is referred to as a channel in television and a frequency in radio.

There are many users of the spectrum besides radio and television stations, including the federal government (particularly the armed forces), state and municipal governments for police and similar types of communications, and private users of all types. Private users include airlines, private communication concerns, and amateurs. Without the assignment of spectrum space by a central authority, communications would be chaotic because of signal interference.

Because of the need of regulation in the broadcast industry, Congress established the 1927 Federal Radio Commission, which in 1934 became the Federal Communications Commission (FCC). The FCC became an independent agency of the federal government composed of five commissioners appointed for terms of five years by the President. It supervises and allocates spectrum space, makes channel assignments, and licenses radio and television stations for periods of three years to applicants who must be legally, technically, and financially qualified.

The FCC determines whether the operation of each station will be "in the public interest, convenience, and necessity." If there is more than one applicant for a station frequency, the FCC decides which should receive the license. At the end of the three-year license period, the FCC reviews the overall operation of the station and determines whether its license shall be renewed.

The commission also sets limits on the number of broadcasting stations that a single individual or organization can control. Further, the FCC has issued regulations for broadcasting stations concerning engineering and operating standards and certain other matters, such as the treatment of controversial issues, political broadcasts, and editorializing. To protect free broadcasting, however, the Communications Act states that the FCC shall not exercise cen-

A television producer must be present during all telecasts to take care of any problems that may arise.

sorship over station licenses. By the mid-1980s, deregulation policies had eased many of the restrictions placed on broadcasters and cable operators.

Broadcasting is a business in the usual sense, dependent on sales and profits for its continued existence. Radio and television stations cover all forms of entertainment, such as comedy, drama, music, sports, as well as with reporting the local, national, and world news.

Although broadcasting is a business, it operates under certain unique constraints. Broadcasting is show business with a stopwatch. Programming is timed down to the second, and precision and speed are important for both taped and live broadcasts. Broadcasting relies on the creativity of its employees to develop and hold the interest of its listening and viewing audiences. Yet, because of the unremitting pressures of deadlines, broadcasting must be geared to quick decisions and quick action.

Careers

An individual interested in broadcasting as a career should bring into it a balanced temperament and a willingness to work hard, often with irregular hours. This is necessary because broadcasting stations are on the air for seven days a week and many stations, particularly radio, are on the air for twenty-four hours a day.

Creative people are the mainstay of the industry, with the staff working in teams. Broadcasting programs are usually a synthesis of many talents (the writer or journalist, the actors

A field technician adjusts a camera before using it in a live news broadcast.

or newscasters, the directors, the producer, and others) and the final product is the result of cooperative activity by several people.

Reliability is very important in broadcasting. The broadcaster sells time. Once gone, it is gone forever; it cannot be warehoused and sold next year. Meeting deadlines is vital to the operation of any station or network. No network would function without the staff that arranges the scheduling of programs. Since advertisers purchase the air time for the commercials, thus paying for the programming on commercial television, the sales force in broadcasting is essential to the operations of the company (see Volume 3: Radio, television, and print advertising sales workers).

Almost all stations, large or small, have four divisions of activity—programming, engineering, sales, and general administration. Most stations have similar jobs within the four divisions, although there are substantial differences in job content, working conditions, and compensation between large and small stations. In many small stations, jobs may be combined; an announcer may shoot news film, a secretary may write copy, a salesperson may serve as an on-the-air sportscaster. Flexibility becomes the essential element of the employee's skills, and helps make the worker more valuable to the company, and more marketable when moving to another company.

All stations produce a variety of local shows such as children's shows, religious programs, and interview programs with local politicians and other leading citizens. Stations also cover sports events such as baseball and football games and public events such as parades, fairs, and other local celebrations. News also forms an important part of a station's local programming. Many stations have reporters covering events that take place throughout the city. Larger local stations are now branching

out into national news coverage of certain events, such as political party conventions, and presidential elections.

If the station is a network affiliate, the network supplies many programs. In addition, the station may purchase programs on film, videotape, or recordings from outside sources.

Many organizations in broadcasting own several stations. Frequently, these group owners have an administrative staff that generally oversees the activities of the stations in the group.

The broadcast industry has many different types of career opportunities, such as those described below:

Program Directors: It is the job of the program department to plan a program schedule and integrate programs to give the station a broad audience appeal, while at the same time offering specialized programs for segments of the population. The programming department maintains contact with the sales department to ascertain the commercial appeal of various types of programs to potential sponsors.

The program director of a station, in collaboration with the general manager, determines and administers the station's programming policies and plans the most effective program schedule for the station. He or she works with the producers, directors, talent, and other members of the department in developing new programs or improving old ones. The program director also supervises the activities of the program department's personnel. Most program directors have worked their way up through the programming department, and quite a few are former directors or announcers who have acquired experience and demonstrated ability for supervision and administration (see Volume 2: Radio and television program directors).

Producers and directors: Producers and directors plan and supervise the production of programs, both in rehearsal and during on-the-air presentations. They coordinate the various elements of the programs, including the selection of performers, scripts, and music; participate in the planning of the sets, lighting, and stage properties; and determine the sequence and angle of camera shots. For the particular show, the producer-director is the boss of the performers, studio technicians, production workers, and others who are involved in that show.

In larger stations and at the networks, the jobs of producer and director are separated. Generally, the producer handles the business and financial aspects of the show and maintains overall supervision. The director is the creative head of the program, responsible for supervising casting, rehearsal, and performance.

The job of producer-director is one of the most demanding in television. It requires a sense of dramatics combined with the ability to weld together into a smooth and artistic production the creative talents of performers and other personnel under pressure of time. Imagination is important and the ability to improvise is most helpful. The producer-director is the focal point of the production effort and must be simultaneously a supervisor, an administrator, and a creative artist.

Announcers: One of the basic jobs in broadcasting is staff announcer. Announcers are the people that the public is the most familiar with. Announcers, newscasters, sportscasters, reporters, and disk jockeys are the names and voices that will be associated with the station. Their work, and their personalities, are how a station develops its reputation and audience (see Volume 2: Radio and television announcers and newscasters).

News and public affairs staff: Radio and television news and public affairs departments have grown in number and importance. The news director determines the overall news policy of the station and supervises the reporters, making assignments and overseeing the preparation of news and special events shows.

Reporters and correspondents: In both radio and television, reporters collect local news, often working with tape recorder and a camera crew or operator. Many TV stations are now transmitting live news reports from remote locations via microwave and satellite. Reporters cover politics, consumer news, farm news, health, business, crime, local events, and all other newsworthy happenings. They may specialize in a particular field, such as economics, science, or foreign affairs. News writers select and write copy for newscasters to read on the air. In many stations, these jobs are combined (see Volume 2: Reporters and correspondents).

Editorializing on local and national issues is an important broadcasting activity. News personnel often participate in the research, writing, and delivery of these editorials. Some stations center this activity with one person; others rotate the work among various news department people.

Video directors: A number of jobs in the programming department are peculiar to television. The videotape director supervises the video editors who time, cut, splice, and clean tape. This person also supervises the advance screening of the videotape to determine its suitability for broadcast and participates in the decisions involving the purchase of taped shows.

Floor managers: The floor manager directs the performers on the studio floor in accordance with the producer-director's instructions by relaying stage directions and cues. Using a headset, he or she is in touch with the director in the control room at all times. Program assistants coordinate the various parts of the show by assisting the producer-director. They arrange for props and makeup service, prepare cue cards, and scripts, and usually time rehearsal and on-the-air shows. Floor staff work on the studio floor arranging sets, backdrops, and lighting, and handle the various movable properties used on the show.

Art staff: Many stations employ graphic artists or scenic designers who plan set designs, construct scenery, paint backdrops, and handle lettering and artwork. Some larger stations have makeup artists and costumers who work with the art staff.

Music librarians: In radio stations, a music librarian is occasionally employed because of the heavy reliance on recorded music. This individual evaluates and often selects the music to be used for a particular show, as well as cataloging and storing the records.

Promotions staff: Most stations have promotion departments that publicize the station's programs, image, and activities. Headed by a promotion manager, such a department typically plans and directs advertising campaigns, arranges for public appearances of on-air personalities, and designs other promotional activities aimed at the station audience. The promotion department may also develop sales promotions that include the planning and layout of advertising for trade journals and production of sales brochures and other material used by the sales department (see Volume 1: Marketing; Public Relations).

Community affairs directors: Local stations closely identify with their communities. Community affairs directors plan and execute a station's services and programs that are meant to respond to the needs of the community. These include public service announcements (PSAs), public affairs programming (often undertaken in conjunction with the news department), and special events and public service campaigns that deal with community-related issues.

Sales staff: The entire productive effort of most radio or television stations is supported by the money it charges for commercial announcements and programs. The sales department is charged with the responsibility of securing these advertising revenues. The typical station is supported by revenues from three sources. If it is a network affiliate, it receives a certain amount of money under a contractual agreement as network compensation for carrying programs originated by the network. The network salespeople actually sell the commer-

An engineer operates the sound controls during the broadcast of a television show.

cial time on these programs, and the network passes along to each affiliate a certain portion of the revenues. Thus, in a sense, salespeople employed by the network with which the station is affiliated also serve as salespeople for the station.

A second source of revenue is for those advertisers who do not require national coverage for their advertising. They prefer, often because their product is not nationally distributed or because they need to strengthen sales in a particular area, to "spot" their advertising in certain markets. For the purpose of reaching advertisers or advertising agencies located in distant cities who may desire to purchase this type of spot advertising, many stations employ a national sales representative on a commission basis. This "sales rep" functions as an out-of-town sales force for the station. Most stations have a national sales manager who works closely with the sales representative in handling these sales.

Sales to local merchants in the station's coverage area are the third source of revenue and are handled by its local sales force. The station sells time in the form of full programs, portions of programs, or commercial announcements to local advertisers or their advertising agencies. Local sales are the responsibility of the sales manager, who sets the general sales policy for the station and supervises the daily activities of the sales force. The sales manager develops sales plans that will appeal to sponsors and plans special campaigns to tie in with seasons of the year, special events, and so on.

In the late 1980s, the cost of an average 30-second television commercial in prime time was about $100,000; a 30-second announcement on radio cost about $1,000 in major cities, but much less in smaller markets.

Traffic department: The traffic department is a little understood but vital function in a broadcasting station. It is the heart of the station's administrative operations, through which all instructions regarding sales and programming must be cleared. The department maintains the logs of the station's daily program activities, which are used by the programming, sales, and accounting department. This job is generally the responsibility of a traffic manager who may be assisted by one or more traffic clerks.

Continuity writers: These writers script commercial announcements, public service announcements, and station promotional announcements. On occasion, continuity writers are called on to create program material.

Broadcast engineers: In the technical nerve center of a station, surrounded by racks of electronic equipment, the broadcast engineer brings together the various elements of the show, switching from the camera in the studio to a slide projector, then to a videotape player or a live remote, and finally to the network program usually originating in New York or Los Angeles. Broadcast engineers are supervised by the program director.

Engineers: On the studio floor, other engineers handle the camera and microphones as the show progresses. At the transmitter, often miles away, the transmitter engineers, who have final technical control over the program, monitor and adjust the complex electronic gear to assure the strength, clarity, and reliability of the signal sent from the transmitter.

In some stations, engineers are capable of handling the full range of technical work. In others, particularly the larger stations, responsibilities may be specialized so that an engineer serves only as a camera operator, switcher, or transmitter operator. All of this technical work is supervised by the chief engineer, a fully qualified engineer with considerable experience as a working technician. In radio, this person may be the only engineer; in television, he or she may supervise as many as forty people.

The work of the chief engineer is to plan and coordinate the engineering requirements of shows, including the scheduling and assignment of crews. The chief engineer is responsible for the operation and maintenance of the equipment, makes decisions about purchasing new equipment, and often designs and develops special equipment for the station's needs.

General managers: The job of general manager requires a unique combination of business ability and creativity. General managers are almost always people who have had successful experience in sales, programming, or engineering. Their responsibilities include the handling of the daily problems of station operations in consultation with program managers, sales managers, and chief engineers. They determine the general policies for the station's operations and supervise carrying out those policies. They normally handle the station's relations with the FCC and other government bodies and participate in many community activities on behalf of the station.

Network programmers and staff: Network jobs appear glamorous because they appear part of the captivating world of show business. Basically, however, the network is involved in the same activities as an individual station—producing and distributing programs and selling time to advertisers. Thus networks have all of the basic jobs found at the station level and described in this article. But they also have other jobs unique to network operations because of the network's size and programming efforts.

In programming, most network activity is centered around the purchase and production of the individual show. When networks produce their own shows, the production team includes producers, directors, writers, announcers, costumers, scenic designers, and production assistants. Performers, such as actors, singers, dancers, and comedians, are usually hired on a free-lance or contract basis for a particular show or a series of shows.

The technical and stage crew, along with all the other supporting personnel, are assigned by the network programming or engineering departments. News and public affairs form a large and important part of network activity, and the networks have considerable numbers of news writers, anchorpersons, researchers, commentators, and foreign and domestic correspondents. To reach the top rank at a network normally demands considerable experience as well as talent and determination.

Education

As the broadcasting industry has matured, it has been marked by a growing professionalism. College training has become more important in both securing a first job and in moving ahead. Because of the large number of small stations scattered throughout the country, it has been possible to get beginning jobs in radio and television with a high-school diploma, and those with initiative and intelligence can sometimes

A camera operator must undergo training to learn how to operate such a complex device.

progress to the top ranks of the industry. But, as in most industries, there is a high correlation between long-range job success and education. The individual who is interested in broadcasting as a career should carefully consider the value of college training, which will provide a breadth and depth that should substantially contribute to a more successful career.

People already employed in broadcasting recommend that the prospective broadcaster get as much hands-on experience while in school. This type of experience means getting involved in the school paper, radio station, and small productions in the community. Courses often teach theory, but practical experience is also a necessity in the ever tightening broadcasting job market. Since most entry level positions involve working in a range of areas, from technical production assistance to writing and editing, it is important that the student gain some experience in all areas while in school.

For broadcast news positions, a journalism degree is recommended but not necessarily required. Broadcasting and communications are also increasingly acceptable areas of study. For technical jobs, degrees in engineering are recommended.

Industry outlook

The best place for a beginner to look for a job in radio and television is in one of the many smaller stations throughout the country. Large stations will normally require a considerable amount of broadcasting experience for nearly all jobs in programming, engineering, and sales, but smaller stations, particularly those in smaller communities, are often willing to hire individuals with training in broadcasting but without experience if they seem to be particularly suited to a specific job that is open. Thus, generally speaking, the small station is the best place to break in to the broadcasting industry.

Many people establish roots in smaller communities and develop highly satisfactory careers. Others, after they have acquired an understanding of radio and television operations and a skill at their particular job, move on to larger stations in larger communities where the financial rewards are greater. It is, of course, possible to get a beginning job at a network, but networks have many more applications for jobs than openings. Although they may occasionally hire inexperienced people, it does not happen often.

The improvements in broadcast technology allow two or three people to accomplish the same things it took numerous people to do years ago. As technology continues to improve, it is likely that more jobs will be lost. With the intense competition among an increasing number of stations for audience, the ability to run a station efficiently will become essential. This will mean keeping employee hiring down, making sure that the employees hired are very qualified, and that they do their jobs well.

◇ **SOURCES OF ADDITIONAL INFORMATION**

For information on educational programs, consult the Broadcast Education Association, which rep-

resents schools and colleges offering degrees for radio and television:

Broadcast Education Association
1771 N Street, NW
Washington, DC 20036

Other associations that are good sources for general industry information include:

National Association of Broadcasters
1771 N Street, NW
Washington, DC 20036

Association of Independent Television Stations
1200 18th Street, NW, Suite 502
Washington, DC 20036

National Cable Television Association
1724 Massachusetts Avenue, NW
Washington, DC 20036

◇ **RELATED ARTICLES**

Volume 1: Advertising; Marketing; Performing Arts; Public Relations
Volume 2: Actors and actresses; Cartoonists and animators; Commercial artists; Dancers and choreographers; Radio and television announcers and newscasters; Radio and television program directors; Recording industry workers; Reporters and correspondents; Writers and editors
Volume 3: Radio, television, and print advertising sales workers
Volume 4: Graphic arts technicians; Sound-effects technicians; Sound-recording technicians

Business Administration

General information

Businesses are as old as trade itself. As long as humans have engaged in trade, they have combined resources to give them a better position for bargaining. Greek merchants would join with others to raise enough money to build or charter a boat to pick up merchandise from abroad. These partnerships were established and maintained through private arrangements and gentlemen's agreements. It was very rare to have actual laws that established business procedures and practices.

The two main forms of early businesses were private ownership and partnership. In a privately owned company, the person who had established the business would be responsible for the services provided, the profits gained, and the employment of any help that may have been required. Most businesses evolved around the trade or skill that the owner possessed. For example, a person skilled in working with iron might develop an iron smith shop, while a person skilled at baking bread would open a bakery.

Partnerships were established as a temporary measure for situations such as Greek merchants renting a boat, or for permanent establishments of a business. Many families established businesses, with the younger family members trained to follow their parents into the business when they were old enough.

In the early Middle Ages, corporations were developed as a legal alternative to private business or partnership. The significant difference this established for the business world was that a corporation was independent of the controlling members. The financial viability of the company would not consume the finances of the individuals in charge. The first corporations were religious orders, universities, and town governments.

The major structural differences for the newly designated corporations were that no individual owned or held assets in the company. The movement of individuals in and out of an organization would not effect its financial status. In addition, these corporations were chartered, regulated, and legitimized by the government.

In 15th century England, a strong motivation for establishing a corporation was established by the courts. It was the laws pertaining to limited liability. This determined that no individual could be held financially responsible for the debts incurred by a company. If the corporation ran into financial trouble, it would not be the jurisdiction of the courts to pursue the personal earnings of any one member or members of the corporation. The only money that investors could lose was the money they had used to establish the company.

Between 1600 and the mid-1770s, corporations took on the added burden of establishing and maintaining law in territories where they held monopoly. The East India Company, a British firm in India, and the Hudson's Bay Company in America were two such firms that regulated what eventually developed into British colonies. The companies had to put forth in their applications for government incorporation what their goals would be in the advancement of the public welfare.

One of the changes that the American Revolution brought to the American concept of business was the rejection of the role of business as government regulator. Establishing charters in the United States continued to reflect a predisposition to public-service companies, however, until the early 1800s. Most of the companies formed until then were involved in construction, particularly of water routes, banking, and insurance. Eventually commerce and manufacturing firms would be the predominant applicants for charter in the United States.

With the burgeoning of the Industrial Revolution in the late eighteenth century, the need

An accountant discusses a proposed tax deduction with his client over the phone. With the use of computers, calculations can be made almost instantaneously.

for specialized roles in business became increasingly necessary. In the earlier forms of business, the roles, although specialized for some types of trade, normally involved a few people who executed all the tasks involved in producing a product or service. As the number of people involved in the execution of the tasks increased, the number of people required to manage the administrative and financial end of the company also increased. Departments were developed that would occupy themselves with only one element of the business. Departmentalization of business responsibilities became a significant factor in the modern corporation. For example, people educated in investment procedures were hired to oversee financial functions. People who specialized in publicity and advertising were brought in to improve a company's image. With each expansion of business, the need for specialized personnel also increased.

The modern business still ranges from a few individuals who fill several roles in the company to vast empires with thousands of employees with quite specific tasks.

The structure of business administration

All businesses have similar administrative functions. Management is not restricted to the world of commerce, though that is where much of management theory has developed. Managers are needed in areas such as hospital administration, the education system, and not-for-profit agencies. Of course, managers also are needed at all levels of government work.

It is difficult to define operations specific to any one industry because every industry's operations are different. Simply stated, operations are the processes that lead to an organization's finished product; the conversion of input into output. It is the series of functions that link a plan for a product to a market in the public. Coming up with a product plan is the responsibility of top management. Top management often relies on information from market researchers, who determine what the public wants, and technical specialists, who figure out how to produce what the public wants. Developing and producing the product is the responsibility of the various types of departments, depending on what the company makes. Production involves a creative staff, a manufacturing staff, a development staff, and other trained workers. Getting the product into the public's hands is the job of marketing and distribution specialists, supported by advertising, public relations, and sales personnel. The term "operations" covers the whole production process, from start to finish.

Visualize the operations of a goods-producing industry, such as automobile manufacturing. This will involve an assembly line, with workers fitting the various parts of a car together. The input is the various components, such as the engine, the upholstered seats, the radio, and the headlights. The output is a ready-to-drive sedan. At every step along the assembly line, skill workers will have different tasks, such as putting in the radio or adjusting the steering wheel. The finished product (the car) will reflect the individual contributions of many different workers. A car manufacturer's operations are unique, although ship building and aerospace manufacturing certainly have some similar characteristics.

Service-producing industries also have unique production, or conversion, processes. Insurance companies convert a paid premium, the input, into a package of benefits that may or may not eventually be claimed, the output. Wholesalers convert unassembled or bulk items into smaller units that manufacturers can use to build or produce something or that retailers can sell to consumers. Transportation companies convert the combination of vehicles, vehicle operators, and terminal facilities into transportation for a traveler from New York to Los Angeles, for example, or into a freight junket down the Mississippi River.

When many people hear the word management, they are likely to picture the president of a huge manufacturing corporation making million-dollar decisions in an oak-paneled office. But this is only one kind of management. By the time students have reached high school, most of them have already been actively engaged in the practice of management. The person who organizes a camping trip with some friends, for example, may ask one to get the firewood, two others to set up the tent, another to stow the food, and another to scout for the water supply. That person is acting as a manager. The high school newspaper editor who makes assignments to reporters, layout people, and circulation staff is also managing.

One of the simplest and most accurate definitions of management is that is it the art of getting things done through other people. In today's complicated world, the overwhelming majority of jobs must be carried out by groups of people. This requires organization and direction. Without proper management, even the simplest tasks could be not successfully performed.

Large corporations will employ both top and middle managers; smaller companies may not make this distinction. General managers and top executives direct the policies and operations of private corporations and government agencies. Top managers include the chief executive officer and the president, with the executive vice president or general manager directly following. Vice presidents are in charge of various corporate functions: manufacturing, marketing, finance, human resources, international trade, research and development, and so on (see Volume 2: General managers and top executives).

Middle management includes such positions as plant manager, controller, accountant, sales manager, advertising manager, promotion manager, director of public relations, office manager, director of engineering, production manager, and industrial relations manager. A third level of management is a supervisory one, also called first-line management, because this level is in the most direct contact with the work force. Jobs here are shift supervisor, office supervisor, head bookkeeper, district sales manager, copy chief, and the like. This is by no means an exhaustive list, since each kind of business or industry will have managerial positions peculiar to itself (see Volume 2: Management trainees).

Careers

The work of managers/administrators is very complex. It includes planning and forecasting, organizing, selecting staffs and equipment, controlling, motivating, researching, and communicating. Managers need two kinds of training: training in the specific industry they work

An administrator with impaired vision drafts a memo using an audiovisual device. Adaptive aids help handicapped people conduct business with few physical inhibitions.

in and general management training. For example, a manager of a supermarket must not only have management experience but also knowledge of the food-retailing field. A manager of a computer business should combine a comprehensive knowledge of the computer field with sound managerial skills.

Training in a specific trade or skill is a good first step toward a managerial position in that industry. There are, however, some important exceptions. Few top hospital administrators are themselves physicians. This is because the skills and interests necessary to coordinate the work of a 500-person staff are very different from those of a competent doctor. Also, once a person has achieved a top management position, like executive vice-president, of one company, his or her skills can usually be transferred to another business enterprise.

Specialists in the business administration field include the professions listed below:

Treasurers: Treasurers are top executives who direct the financial planning for their organizations. Treasurers forecast the future finances of their companies by analyzing records, and advising other managers on investments and loans for short- and long-range financial plans.

A new employee undergoes management training at her place of employment. She must become familiar with the company's computer software and administrative methods.

Economists: Economists compile and interpret statistical data regarding the production and distribution of goods and services. They work hand in hand with management and marketing specialists. The majority of economists are employed in private industry and government, but many are faculty members in colleges and universities.

Accountants and auditors: Tax accountants prepare federal, state, and local tax returns for their company. They advise management concerning the effects of business transactions on taxes, and may devise and install tax record systems. If necessary, tax accountants may represent their employers before governmental taxing bodies.

Internal auditors examine and analyze the establishment's accounting records and prepare reports concerning its financial status and operating procedures. They report to management concerning the scope of their audits and may make recommendations regarding improving operations and changing the financial position of the company.

Cost estimators: Cost estimators try to project how much it will cost their companies to manufacture a product, build a structure, or acquire a service. They conduct studies and use data such as labor and material costs to estimate how much a project will cost, and to help determine whether the project should be undertaken at all.

Purchasing agents: Purchasing agents determine the quantity and quality of the items to be purchased, and negotiate costs, delivery dates, and sources of supply. They keep records pertaining to items purchases, costs, delivery, product performance, and inventories. Purchasing agents may work under managers of procurement services, who coordinate all the activities of personnel involved in purchasing and distributing materials. Procurement services managers also analyze market conditions to determine present and future availability of desired materials.

Retail industries employ a special kind of purchaser called buyers, who purchases merchandise or commodities for resale. In addition to meeting with sales representatives to make selections, buyers arrange for the transportation of purchases to stores.

Contract administrators: Contract administrators examine estimates of production costs, performance requirements, and delivery schedules to ensure completeness and accuracy. They prepare bids and other exhibits that may be required.

Contract specialists negotiate, administer, extend, terminate, and renegotiate contracts with suppliers. They may approve or reject requests for deviations from contract specifications and delivery schedules, and may arbitrate claims or complaints occurring in performance of contracts.

Marketing Personnel: The Marketing department of a company comprises the occupations concerned with managing sales for a manufacturer or other establishment. These include market research and analysis, managing a sales program, and evaluating sales reports.

Sales managers develop and control sales programs. They coordinate distribution by establishing sales territories, quotas, and goals. Sales managers also direct staffing, training, and performance evaluations.

If a company operates its own sales dealerships, sale managers advise dealers and distributors about sales and advertising techniques. They assess customer needs by reviewing market analyses, and help determine price schedules, discount rates, and sales campaigns. Sales managers may get actively involved in production of their companies' products to ensure that only the most desirable products stay on the sales line.

An export manager directs foreign sales and service outlets of an organization.

Statisticians: Statisticians collect, analyze, and interpret numerical data to help business professionals determine the best way to produce results in their work.

Personnel and labor-relations specialists: These administrators formulate employee policies and conduct programs relating to all phases of personnel activity, such as recruitment, selection, training, development, retention, promotion, compensation, benefits, labor relations, and occupational safety.

Ergonomists: Ergonomists study the workplace to determine the effects of the work environment on the activities of individuals and groups. They conduct research and analyze data about such factors as noise and temperature of the workplace, and evaluate the design of machines to see that they are safe, usable, and conducive to productive work.

Information systems personnel: Highly trained computer specialists are playing a larger and larger role in business administration. For example, computer-records managers plan, develop, and administer records-management policies to facilitate effective and efficient handing of business information. They are especially concerned with the protection and retrieval of records and reports contained on microfilm, computer disks, and other media.

Systems analysts plan, schedule, and coordinate the activities required to process data on electronic computer systems.

Computer programmers write and code the instructions that control the work of a computer.

Data base managers create data processing systems to collect, analyze, store, and transmit computer information.

Communications Personnel: This group includes occupations concerned with the development and distribution of favorable material in order to promote goodwill, develop credibility, or create a favorable public image for an organization.

Public relations managers plan and direct the development and communications of information designed to keep the public informed of their organization's programs, accomplishments, or point of view. A public relations manager for a retail operation, for example, will enlist media coverage for the opening of a new store.

Public relations specialists write publicity releases, catalogs, and brochures. They prepare speeches and articles.

Writers and editors research and write material for company newsletters, trade journals, and technical studies and reports.

Education

The educational requirements for people involved in business administration are varied. There are some people in managerial positions who did not receive formal training in business administration, but the majority of administrators hired today have at least an undergraduate college degree in business administration, marketing, or a related field. For those students who concentrated in the liberal arts in college, it is possible to supplement the education by

After printing out several charts, two cost estimators discuss the prospects of purchasing more equipment for their firm.

obtaining a graduate degree. Most administrators also have experience in their particular line of work. Most entry-level positions also includes extensive on-the-job training, because each company runs its operations somewhat differently.

A basic grounding in communications and mathematics is indispensable in every field of management.

Industry outlook

Opportunities in business administration are, to some degree, tied to the economy. If the economy is growing at a healthy rate, there figures to be more businesses opening and therefore more opportunities for administrators/managers. However, even in slow periods of growth, there will always be an opportunity for someone with skill, experience, and a little bit of creativity. All companies, whether large or small, need organized, thoughtful people who can manage other workers. The larger and more complicated an enterprise, the more managers it will need to carry on the work effectively.

◇ **SOURCES OF ADDITIONAL INFORMATION**

Administrative Management Society
4622 Street Road
Trevose, PA 19047

Association of Master of Business Administration Executives
AMBA Center
227 Commerce Street
East Haven, CT 06512

American Association of Industrial Management
Stearns Building
Suite 324
293 Bridge Street
Springfield, MA 01103

American Business Association
292 Madison Avenue
New York, NY 10017

American Management Association
135 West 50th Street
New York, NY 10020

Financial Management Association
Education Information
University of South Florida School of Business
Tampa, FL 33620

National Management Association
2210 Arbor Boulevard
Dayton, OH 45439

◇ **RELATED ARTICLES**

Volume 1: Accounting; Franchising; Human Resources; Retailing; Wholesaling
Volume 2: Accountants and auditors; Computer programmers; Cost estimators; Data base managers; Economists; General managers and top executives; Management analysts and consultants; Management trainees; Marketing, advertising, and public relations managers; Purchasing agents; Systems analysts; Technical writers; Writers and editors
Volume 3: Billing clerks; Bookkeeping and accounting clerks; Clerical supervisors and managers; Computer and peripheral equipment operators; File clerks

Ceramics

General information

Ceramics is an ancient art, an old industry, and a young science. Over eight thousand years ago people made non-metallic articles from earthen materials, usually clay hardened by heat. From these ancient beginnings ceramists have learned how to make a great variety of products from the clay and other materials in the earth's crust. They have learned how to use high temperature processing to blend ingredients and create new and useful products such as brick, tile, cements, glass, dinnerware, sanitary ware, and enamels.

Ceramics have been around since the dawn of civilization. From as early as 6500 B.C., the ancient Sumerians made bricks and pottery. Egyptians made crude glass from sand, powdered limestone, and potash in 1600 B.C. The Chinese produced high-quality ceramic articles from 1500 to 1000 B.C. The Romans developed natural cement materials to build many of their public structures and aqueducts. Glass art flourished in Venice during the Renaissance and later in France and Czechoslovakia. When earthenware and porcelain were developed in the 1700s using the deposits of English China Clay mixed with other earthen minerals (feldspar, flint, talc, and quartz), dinnerware achieved considerable refinement in England and Germany. In 1815 Josiah Spode experimented by adding cattle-bone ashes to clay and developed a translucent porcelain or bone china. About this same time the English found that by mixing clay and limestone and heating the mixture, a new material resulted, now called Portland Cement.

With the technological advances that have occurred within the past 150 years, ceramic engineers and scientists have been better able to understand the nature of clay and other earthen materials. The discovery and application of X rays, for example, enabled ceramists to understand the crystal structure of materials.

In the late 1800s scientists learned more about the nature of chemical bonding, providing explanations for the difference in properties between metals and ceramics, especially the high-temperature properties for which ceramic materials are known.

The understanding of these fundamental principles of bonding mechanisms (how the atoms or ions are held together in a solid) and the relationship between this structure and the resulting properties of the material spurred the development of vastly improved clay and sand-based materials—refractories, cements, and especially glass. In addition, the relatively new industry of ceramics science developed.

Many industries depend on ceramic materials: brick, cement, and glass in construction; insulation, heat generators, and nuclear fuels in the production and transmission of energy; appliances, dinnerware, glass containers, and lighting in consumer goods; and memory devices, micro-circuits, and a multitude of other electronic devices.

Pressure to develop new ceramic materials unknown in nature has come from various sources, such as the manufacturers of jet aircraft, automobiles, space missiles, nuclear power plants, electronics, and communications equipment. In addition, industries that require heat resistant materials such as steel and electricity need tougher materials such as porcelain and glass.

As the ceramics industry has developed, so have new products such as glass with very low thermal expansion that can withstand sudden changes in temperature. Other new products include glass that by proper control of composition and heat treatment becomes crystalline and has unusual strength; unbreakable dinnerware; and glass fibers that are used to transmit light and telephone messages. A bundle of these glass fibers the size of a little finger will replace a copper wire cable four inches in diameter.

95

A ceramics engineer tests a newly developed type of ceramic that is designed to be used for electrical devices.

In the electronics industry the ceramist and physicist have learned how to produce very pure crystals of silicon, the basis of the entire transistor industry. This has allowed miniaturization of all electronic circuitry resulting in low-cost pocket calculators, digital watches, and small computers.

The material in the emission-control system of a modern automobile is a ceramic material that must withstand sudden changes in temperature as well as a very corrosive environment.

Many of the breakthroughs in ceramics sciences have occurred in the past twenty or thirty years. Now that the concept of using ceramics in so many products has been established, the field is more than likely to change and grow even more rapidly through the year 2000.

The structure of the ceramics industry

Ceramic products are made from natural minerals and artificially manufactured minerals that ceramists have developed in the laboratory. The twelve elements that make up 99 percent of the earth's crust form the basis of the raw materials in the ceramics industry. In order of abundance these are oxygen, silicon, aluminum, iron, calcium, sodium, potassium, magnesium, titanium, phosphorous, hydrogen, and manganese. The oxygen content of the earth's atmosphere has caused these elements to occur as oxides, widely distributed and available. Most of the more common ceramic products are made from these oxides.

Many companies are in the business of supplying raw materials to the ceramic industry—materials such as clays, silica, alumina, feldspar, metallic oxides, special glasses for enamels, ferrites for ceramic magnets, and a multitude of other materials for various special applications.

Today it is essential that suppliers be knowledgeable about the materials they sell. Many suppliers hire ceramic engineers who oversee the development of their materials and ceramic products. The raw materials industry is highly competitive, demanding close control over material composition and properties. The material supplier must always be ready and willing to assist the customer with technical problems related to the use of the material.

The modern definition of ceramics is the use of inorganic, non-metallic materials to create new solids by the application of heat. In general, these products are made from powders that are formed into the desired shape prior to heat treatment—at temperatures as high as 540 °C (1000 °F) and above—or formed into shape after complete or partial melting. Ceramic products include tableware, decorative ware, insulators, pottery, glass, cement, building materials, and ceramic magnets.

Ceramic products are made by the melting and forming of viscous liquid (glass) or by the mixing and consolidation of particles into a shape, followed by a high-temperature treatment to densify the particles into a final product having durability, low maintenance, aesthetic appeal, or specific physical, electrical, or chemical characteristics. The durability of ceramic products assures their longevity and minimizes the need for replacement.

Due to the physical properties of ceramic products, they may be recycled, if necessary, by crushing and reblending with the starting materials. Furthermore, the ceramic process can be used to convert waste products from other industries into usable products.

Before raw materials can be sold, the buyer must have a product in mind. It is at this stage that development and research begin creating new ceramic products. A new product is conceived by a ceramic engineer who conveys the idea to researchers and developers. The engineer tells the researcher what is required on the production line, what new products a customer needs, and what current problems the customer or industry is encountering.

The research ceramist then examines the raw materials with the most sophisticated types of analytical equipment such as the electron microscope, the mass spectrometer, X ray diffraction, many types of spectrographic, differential thermal analysis, thermo-gravimetric analysis equipment, and sophisticated high-temperature furnaces.

Next, development ceramists work with production personnel to produce finished articles. Ceramists utilize exactly timed processing and operating equipment such as grinders, milling machines, sieves, mixing equipment, presses, and spray driers to aid in this process.

When a product is completed, the salespeople work on creating or expanding the market for the item and selling it to clients. The salesperson is active in the development aspect, providing consumer feedback and other marketing information.

Another type of ceramist is the artist or potter, who uses clay to produce works of art by hand. Potters shape, process, fire and glaze ware, continually experimenting with coloring oxides, firing, and other techniques to enhance the appeal of their pieces. Some ceramists create art for pleasure, while others make a living working with clay. Professional ceramists may be self-employed artists or they may work for a manufacturer that produces fine china.

There are generally two ways a potter makes a pot: by hand building or by using a potter's wheel. Hand building allows a potter to build free-form art, while the potter's wheel aids in making symmetrically-shaped works. In both cases, one must prepare the clay by wedging, which involves throwing the clay body down hard against a flat surface or simply kneading it. Wedging removes the bubbles and provides a consistent level of moisture throughout the clay.

In hand building, an artist uses either the coil or the slab method to make pots. The coil method entails forming long rods of clay, coiling the rods into a desired shape, and blending the coils to create a smooth surface. With slabs, one simply joins pieces of clay together to make a pot. Before actually joining the slabs or coiling, the potters must score the adjoining edges (*i.e.* lightly nick them to create a rough surface) and add watery clay known as slip. This process helps the adjoining pieces of clay to stick together.

When using a potter's wheel, one places a wedged piece of clay in the middle of the wheel, centers the clay body so that a symmetrical shape can be formed, and pushes down the center of the solid clay body to begin forming walls. Shaping a pot involves skilled hand movements that cause the clay to bend and constrict as desired.

Once a pot is taken off the wheel, it is left to dry until it is leather hard. At that time, the potter places the clay body back on the wheel to trim off any uneven edges and form a base. The ceramist can paint the pot or apply slip to add texture at this point. When the pot is bone dry, it is placed into a kiln for approximately six hours. Afterwards, the potter applies glaze and fires the pot again in a kiln for twelve to fourteen hours.

Tile technicians at the Kennedy Space Center prepare the space shuttle Columbia for a mission. They are applying specially-designed ceramic tiles that protect the astronauts from intense heat and radiation.

Careers

The ceramist is found in a wide variety of careers. Those mentioned below are representative of the many job opportunities in this field.

Ceramic engineers: Ceramic engineers have the responsibility of developing better and more efficient methods of mining, beneficiation (removal of ore impurities), and processing of materials. They suggest research and development projects and assist in outlining appropriate research programs. They utilize their knowledge of economic geography, materials, flow of materials, structures, power, and cost factors. They may become specialists in the manufacture of specific types of equipment used in the industry, for example, the kilns and furnaces used in the brick, dinnerware, refractories, or glass industries.

Modelers/mold makers: These workers construct the plaster molds required in most ceramic ware processes. While building the plaster molds, they work with the designer's plans.

Kiln firers: Kiln firers supervise the kiln operations. They make sure that the temperature remains at the correct level as the clay or other material moves through the kiln tunnel.

Brushers: Brushers clean all the pieces after they have gone through the kiln. Flat pieces are clean by mechanical brushes, but many pieces have to be cleaned by hand.

Handlers: Handlers attach ornamental parts to ceramic pieces. They do their work by hand.

Clay puggers: Clay puggers mix clay with water and then beat the mixture so that it has the consistency of bread dough. They then feed the mixture through machines that separates it into blocks of clay.

A ceramist creates a vase on a potter's wheel. It takes a great deal of practice to keep a clay body centered on the wheel.

be used by the purchaser. The outstanding sales engineer is energetic, knowledgeable, congenial, imaginative, and creative. The sales engineer is a privileged person, having access to processes within a company that no other person outside the organization sees. A technical salesperson must exercise good judgment regarding disclosure of such privileged information.

Artists/designers: Ceramic artists or ceramic designers work directly with clays, clay mixtures, and with glass. Though they understand and appreciate the important properties of these materials, they do not concern themselves with fundamental structures and behaviors as do scientists.

Many graduates of a program in ceramic art find satisfaction in teaching at the secondary school or college level, and an appreciable number of those who go into teaching manage to operate small studio shops where they can continue to develop and utilize their creative abilities. Others may concentrate on work in their own studios and while doing so take on minor teaching assignments. Some find important positions in industry and direct the production of novel, attractive, and commercially profitable products. Positions of this sort in industry require a knowledge of the principles of production and cost and a sensitivity to changes in taste and designs.

Research ceramists: The research ceramist searches out reasons why ceramic materials behave as they do and develops an understanding of the basic characteristics of the materials. They test new theories, new techniques, new operations, new processes, and new products. They also run many sophisticated experiments to determine the suitability of the materials for use in the ceramic industry.

Development ceramists: The development ceramist interprets the work of scientists and researchers, translating their findings directly to the production of new or improved products.

Engineering supervisors: Engineering supervisors usually direct the manufacturing process in a ceramics plant. Advancement to more responsible managerial positions depends on the ability to work with others, apply correct engineering and scientific judgment to the solving of production problems, and awareness of the economic factors of the process.

Technical salespeople: Technical salespeople find clients for finished ceramic wares. The ceramist who becomes a sales engineer or sales manager must know the basic principles involved in the manufacture of a product, and be familiar with the ways in which the product can

Education

For ceramic engineers, it is necessary that a person obtain a solid background in mathematics, physics, and inorganic chemistry. Students should learn about inorganic materials, their crystal structure and properties, how they behave when subjected to high temperatures, how they are blended, formed, and heated, and the resulting products and their properties. Supplementary laboratory experimentation is essential.

All ceramic engineers possess master's degrees in their fields, and many continue their studies to earn doctorates.

As in any profession, both oral and written communication skills are important. In addition, courses in history, philosophy, social sciences, and art are an important segment of the education of engineers in order that their interests be broadened and an appreciation developed for the surrounding community. Finally, a knowledge of computer technology is a necessity in today's industrial world.

Ceramists may be employed by engineering organizations whose operations involve the design, construction, and equipping of many types of industrial plants. In most cases, the ceramic graduate finds employment in ceramic plants. The first assignment may be in the laboratory, where the graduate becomes acquainted with the new products being developed and the production problems that can be solved by laboratory research. After becoming acquainted with the materials used, the quality control of materials, and customer demands, the new employee may be transferred to the production facility and assume responsibility for supervision of a segment of the production process.

For a ceramic artist, a bachelor's degree in fine arts or ceramics is not required but is extremely helpful in providing the artist with the skills in ceramics required. Particularly in glazing and construction, practice is essential. Some shops that produce hand-made pottery may offer apprenticeships, but this is rare because apprenticeships are expensive to coordinate and profits are not extremely high on hand produced items.

Production workers can often learn their jobs with several weeks of on-the-job training. These employees should be comfortable working around large equipment and have mechanical ability and manual dexterity.

Two technicians create a ceramic piece that is heat-resistant and durable.

Industry outlook

Ceramic materials have been touted as miraculous substances, having potential to solve many of the world's industrial and environmental problems. Scientists are developing many uses for ceramic materials; yet the development of new ceramic materials is still in its infancy.

Because of the widespread availability of ceramic raw materials, the adaptability of ceramic products and ceramic processes to recycling problems, and the economics of substitution, the ceramic industry will grow.

Regardless of the type of future energy system being considered, ceramic materials will play a key role. Ceramic materials provide the only solution to the problems posed by the high-temperature, corrosive environments involved in solar heating, nuclear reactors, coal gasification, geothermal heat production, coal slurry pipelines, and gas turbines, for example.

Solutions to environmental problems also require ceramic materials. Porous ceramic plates are used in the aeration of sewage systems. Various types of glass are being developed that will incorporate nuclear waste, allowing for its safe disposal. Large garbage-disposal plants will require special high-temperature re-

fractories for their incinerators. Better emission-control systems are required for all types of power plants.

Other potential consumers of ceramics include new power plants and automobile manufacturers. The efficiency of any engine depends on the difference in temperature between the inside of the engine and the surrounding atmosphere. Metals begin to fail around 1900° F. One of the big promises for ceramic materials is in a 2500° F high-temperature range. New materials are being developed, new design techniques are required, and thus, ceramic engineers will be required to develop unusual production techniques to provide sophisticated and reliable materials.

According to the *U.S. Industrial Outlook*, it is anticipated that the ceramic industry will grow faster than many other industries in the coming decade. As companies continue to search for methods of creating flawless ceramic materials and as demand grows for new products, opportunities should expand in this field. Even as the ceramics industry grows, however, employment opportunities will be somewhat limited. This is because mechanized processes limit the number of workers needed.

◇ **SOURCES OF ADDITIONAL INFORMATION**

American Association of Cermamic Industries
1100-H Brandywine Boulevard
PO Box 2188
Zanesville, OH 43702

American Ceramics Society
757 Brooksedge Plaza Drive
Westerville, OH 43081

National Institute of Ceramic Engineers
757 Brooksedge Plaza Drive
Westerville, OH 43081

United States Advanced Ceramics Association
1440 New York Avenue, NW, Suite 300
Washington, DC 20005

United States Potters Association
518 Market Street
East Liverpool, OH 43920

◇ **RELATED ARTICLES**

Volume 1: Automotives; Aviation and Aerospace; Chemistry; Design; Electronics; Glass; Plastics
Volume 2: Biochemists; Chemists; College and university faculty; Engineers; Geologists; Painters and sculptors
Volume 3: Aircraft mechanics and engine specialists; Bricklayers and stonemasons; Cement masons; Coremakers; Glass manufacturing workers; Heat treaters; Marble setters, tile setters, and terrazzo workers
Volume 4: Chemical technicians; Product test technicians

Chemicals and Drugs

General information

One of the earliest ventures made into processing chemicals was in the prehistoric use of paints and dyes. The cave paintings in Lascaux, France, are dated between 15,000 and 10,000 B.C. The compound used to create the red and black paints were from iron oxide. Other prehistoric peoples from Africa, the Americas, and Australia were also using decorative paints and dyes.

For Egyptian and Asian cultures, the use of paints can be dated back to 2000 to 1000 B.C. There were dyes produced from soil, berries, and plants. One of the brightest colors came from the indigo plant. The plant, when crushed, would produce a dark blue dye that proved to be fairly permanent on brick, wood, and textiles.

Another element that the Egyptians used to prolong the life of the wall paintings was a gum arabic coating that worked as varnish does in sealing the paint onto the surface and protecting it from wear. In China, during the 10th century B.C., a varnish was used on buildings, weapons, and carriages. The varnish was also made from gum arabic, but wax, and egg white were also mixed in to give the lacquer a clear, shiny surface.

Another early chemical was tallow, a solid made from animal fat that had been heated then cooled. Soap was made from tallow and ash. It is believed that soap was used only for medicinal purposes until the 2nd century A.D. when Galen, a Greek physician, wrote about its use as a cleanser. Tallow was also used for illumination. By soaking a wick in the processed animal fat, the oil on the wick burned slowly, providing a fairly even light.

For medicinal purposes, prehistoric humans discovered that certain plants were effective on injuries and fevers through the use of trial and error. Once a plant was recognized as having medicinal qualities, the information was usually passed on from generation to generation. Eventually early tribes developed a medicine man in their group. The medicine man (known by different names such as shaman, witch doctor, and obeah doctor) was frequently thought to have magical or religious powers.

Healing was considered an extremely powerful skill and could be used against someone as well as for someone. Many of the treatments may have been ineffective chemically, but some of the plants used for healing had chemical healing powers. In the regions where traditional tribal doctors still practice, bio-ethnologists study plants used for cures to extract any potential pharmaceutical benefit.

As the effects of chemicals became better understood, the process of purifying, isolating, and utilizing them became more effective. In the late 1700s, Nicolas Leblanc developed a chemical process that converted common salt to sodium carbonate. Sodium carbonate was in heavy demand for the manufacturing of soap and glass. Leblanc developed a process that was eventually named after him, which used treatment with sulfuric acid and heating.

Leblanc also developed a process known as the chamber process in which a corrosive gas mix was processed in a lead container. This process enabled mass production of sulfuric acid. Sulfuric acid was the largest selling product of chemical producing companies, and remains the top seller today.

In the 19th century, it was discovered that an electric current passing through a chemical may cause chemical breakdown, producing two chemical elements from a chemical compound. For example, electrolysis of sodium chloride (common salt) in solution produces chlorine and sodium hydroxide. Sodium hydroxide was substituted for sodium carbonate for certain manufacturing needs.

Discoveries of different chemicals and their effects continued through the next century. The development of high powered microscopes, the

Two biochemical engineers study computer-generated models of a complex kidney enzyme. They are searching for inhibitors that act as potential antihypertensive agents. Hopefully, they will be able to synthesize the enzyme into a drug.

antihistamine. He started working with iminodibenzyl, a compound that had been synthesized around 1900 but never used. In his laboratory in Basel, Switzerland, he began building up a number of new compounds, all based on the fifty-year-old iminodibenzyl compound.

As he tested his first series of compounds, Dr. Haefliger found some acted generally as antihistamines. Some also looked like potential sedatives and analgesics. However, he kept building up new compounds until he found one that appeared to produce a tranquilizing effect. Then, by still another rearrangement of the basic molecule, Dr. Haefliger synthesized a compound that achieved the opposite effect of a tranquilizer. His new compound acted as an antidepressant.

A tranquilizer depresses the central nervous system and has highly selective action on brain function. Obviously, it seldom helps the patient suffering from mental depression, one of the most common and disabling of all mental illnesses. But Dr. Haefliger's new compound, in the majority of clinical tests, dispelled the symptoms of depression without producing signs of over stimulation. Today, his discovery ranks among one of medicine's most effective drugs for aiding the depressed patient.

New drugs have been a major factor in the remarkable reduction in mortality rates from pneumonia, influenza, tuberculosis, syphilis, and other diseases. Drugs have saved millions who otherwise would have died or been incapacitated. By preventing illness and returning people to work earlier, it has been estimated that new prescription drugs add billions of dollars to worker's income each year.

The drug industry is notable for employing the highest proportion of technically trained people of any industry. Research expenditures for products prescribed by physicians have increased steadily.

The structure of the chemical and drug industries

The chemical industry makes products ranging from dyes and explosives to plastics, paints, and paper. The drug industry, one large section of the overall chemical industry, produces goods that ease pain, fight or prevent disease, and help the body to function better.

Unlike single product industries or those that have diversified into subsidiary lines, chemical manufacturing plays a role in virtually all industries. With more than 10,000 different products in regular commercial production, it is

periodic table, and atomic structure model allowed for better prediction and understanding of how chemical reactions worked. However, experimentation still plays a big role in chemical development.

Before 1945, there were a number of chemical firms in the United States that did practically all the chemical manufacturing. But with the growth of the chemical processing industries—textiles, paper, glass, leather, and petroleum refining—a number of manufacturers in these industries began to engage in chemical manufacturing on a large scale. It was not long before electrical companies, distillers, and other production houses entered the expanding field of chemical manufacturing.

Attracted by somewhat higher profit margins, new or outside companies began to enter chemical manufacturing—particularly in the fastest growing areas of chemicals: plastics, synthetic fibers, agricultural and medicinal chemicals.

The process of developing a drug for use by the public may be best illustrated by an account of the discovery of a distinctive antidepressant drug. In 1948, a Swiss pharmaceutical chemist, Dr. Haefliger, was striving to develop a new difficult to describe or limit the extent of the industry.

One economist has described the chemical field as an everlasting juggling of personnel and materials as companies merge and introduce new products. All the while, there is intense competition for patents, engineering know-how, marketing techniques, and technically trained workers. No single company makes all needed chemicals even for its own operations, so, in a very real sense, the industry is its own best customer.

For a chemical company, the integration of a concept into a usable product begins with applied research. Applied research concerns itself with product development—finding suitable uses for new products, improving products, and finding new uses for existing products.

A look at how silicone was developed will illustrate how research plays a vital role in the chemical industry. Most of the basic research in silicone (polymeric organic silicon) chemistry dates from 1900, nearly fifty years after the first organic compounds of silicon were made in the laboratory. Silicon is a nonmetallic substance found in the earth's crust. Researchers sought to show that silicon compounds could by used in place of hydrocarbon compounds by replacing the carbon atoms with atoms of silicon. It was when the chemists learned to link chemical groups into long chain molecules that the basic research could be turned to practical uses.

It required more than eight years to develop a silicone magnet-wire enamel for a miniature motor and other devices. Masonry paints now are made water-repellent by the addition of silicones. Today, in addition to a variety of military uses, silicones are used by the aeronautic, automobile, tire, steel, electric, glass, paper, textile, and plastics industries.

After scientific application of a discovery has brought about a usable product or procedure, research is done by the marketing department into the potential sales of the product. Before manufacturing of almost any chemical begins, the market is checked to make sure the product is needed and wanted by the potential consumers. If there is no market for a product, the company may lose money if sales do not cover the manufacturing costs.

The chemical and drug industry also must submit their product to government testing. The Food and Drug Administration (FDA) tests all pharmaceutical products that are sold. Chemicals that have routine exposure for humans and animals must also be tested for toxicity. This testing process can take years. A new medication may take as long as ten years in government testing before approval is given to the company to manufacture the chemical.

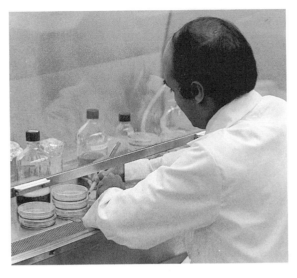

A chemist prepares and labels several petri dishes for a drug test.

It is important for chemical and drug companies to request patents on all new inventions and products. Patents are the legal method of restricting anyone from copying or duplicating a product without permission from the company that holds the patent.

If all goes well for the company, market research shows an interest in the product, testing by the company shows that the product does what it is intended to do, and the government approves the product for sale to the public. It may cost one to two million dollars for the research and development of a new product. For every product that finally reaches the stores, ten will be abandoned at some stage of the production process.

The manufacturing of one product to substitute for another product, such as cellophane replacing paper in certain packaging applications, has become one the largest areas of competition for chemical companies. If a cheaper product or method of production can be found for almost any chemical produced, some of the savings will be passed on to the consumer, and the product becomes more desirable because it is more cost effective. In other areas, substitute chemicals and compounds may be used to replace diminishing supplies of another chemical. In the petroleum industry, for example, the development of another energy source in place of gas or oil could save an industry where supplies are increasingly limited.

Another area of growth is the development of chemicals to accomplish something that may not have been done before or may have been done by another means. For example, cleaning up an oil spill on water has been done through slow and costly efforts with suction, net drag-

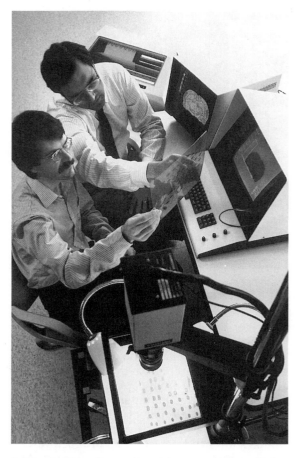

Studying the effects of an experimental drug, two doctors use computer-based images to analyze the activity of specific brain areas.

ging, and some chemical breakdown of the oil. If a chemical can be found that would convert the oil to a floating solid without threatening the environment, the cost of oil clean-up would be greatly reduced.

Manufacturing products for consumer convenience is another area of growth for chemical companies. Products such as household cleansers, detergents, spot removers, and specialty products like anti-static spray for clothes, are all goods developed for the consumer. Other recent developments include artifical sweeteners and fat substitutes.

Development of new materials to meet extreme physical requirements is the fourth of the major areas of development for the chemical and drug industry. Fluorocarbon resins for use in missile fuel systems are one example of a chemical developed specifically for its value in withstanding tremendous heat and change in atmosphere. Other materials are being created in chemical laboratories to meet physical standards from the extreme colds of the arctic to the extreme pressures of deep sea exploration.

Careers

The chemicals and drugs industry offers a wide range of professional opportunities. A sampling of career options follows below.

Research chemists: Research chemists extend the knowledge of the chemical world by studying chemicals, their structure, and the changes under different situations. These chemists decipher and discover elements and compounds through laboratory work and research analysis (see Volume 2: Chemists).

Applied research chemists: After a chemical has been found and analyzed, applied research chemists determine practical applications for the new chemical.

Chemical engineers: Following the discoveries of the researchers, chemical engineers develop and improve the process of developing the chemicals needed. For example, when a new synthetic fiber is developed, the engineer finds a way to mass produce the fiber in a form that is usable to the consumer (see Volume 2: Engineers).

Chemist specialists: Because of the vast number of chemicals and chemical compounds that are studied, specialists have developed in all the major areas of research. For the water treatment industry, for example, water-purification specialists analyze the chemical content of water used for drinking to make sure it meets required standards. Other specialists exist for the perfume, cosmetic, food, and drug industries as well.

Pharmacologists: Pharmacologists study the effects of a drug on humans and animals. They may be working with an experimental compound, a drug with uses other than its original intention, or reinvestigating the effects of a known compound. The pharmacology department of a pharmaceutical manufacturer may work concurrently with a government analysis before approval of a chemical, or it may be developing data before the company approaches the government for FDA evaluation (see Volume 2: Pharmacologists).

Toxicologists: In addition to evaluating drugs for their toxic effect, toxicologists are responsible for evaluating most chemicals for toxicity. If a drug is accidentally ingested, or provokes burns or adverse reactions, it is important that the information be available to treat the ailment. Toxicologists provide that information and continue to build the level of data available on chemicals that may be harmful (see Volume 2: Toxicologists).

Chemical laboratory technicians: Chemical laboratory technicians assist the chemist in experiments that evaluate chemicals and compounds (see Volume 4: Chemical technicians).

Chemical engineering technicians: The manufacturing and production aspects of chemical development are the areas that chemical engineering technicians cover. They assist the work of the chemical engineers.

Laboratory technicians: Conducting the bench work of the laboratory experiments, lab technicians follow the directions of the laboratory supervisors to ensure that all elements of any experiment or research are conducted exactly as specified.

Education

Constant scientific advancement gives rise to many problems and opportunities, creating an ever-increasing demand for trained professionals. Corporations, associations, professional societies, and government institutions are engaged in guidance programs with certain schools. These programs help identify and encourage qualified students to prepare for careers in science, engineering, and health professions.

Students interested in pursuing a career in chemistry are usually curious individuals with an ability to concentrate on details. They must also enjoy working with groups and on their own.

On the college level, it is wise to concentrate in the sciences with continual exposure to laboratory procedures. Course work should include classes in subjects such as biology, chemistry, and chemical engineering.

Many students continue their education on the graduate level, obtaining masters degrees or doctorates. In general, a masters degree is required to conduct any substantial research in the chemical industries. To work in the drug industry, most people attend graduate schools of pharmaceutical sciences.

Industry outlook

From its beginning as an industry shortly after World War I, chemical manufacturing in the United States has grown at a rate that has outpaced even the most optimistic estimates. Sales for the twenty-two largest manufacturers of chemicals and allied products more than doubled during the 1970s, with annual sales for these corporations reaching over $200 billion during the 1980s. The drug producing industry in the United States employed more than 175,000 employees in 1989, according to the *U.S. Industrial Outlook.* Overall the United

An employee at a drug company packages newly-manufactured drugs for shipment to various pharmacies.

States has the largest production of pharmaceutical chemicals in the world.

Employment in the industry is expected to continue to climb, although mergers of companies which are taking place tend to slow the number of job openings as consolidation of jobs takes place. The outlook is for continuing gains because the industry invests heavily in research and development. No other industry spends more of its own money for research. Many companies, particularly those manufacturing pharmaceutical products, consistently allocate more than 5 percent of their sales dollar each year for research and development programs.

Sales of chemicals and allied products should continue to grow as research opens up new marketing possibilities. Areas that hold out particular promise are: (1) replacement by synthetic polymeric materials of large volumes of glass, paper, wood, leather, and metals; (2) further replacement of natural fibers by synthetics, and the development of techniques that will replace the still cumbersome procedures of converting fibers into textile products; (3) chemical control of still-unconquered diseases; (4) provision of adequate food supplies for a rapidly expanding world population, and further increases in labor-productivity of agriculture by pest control and yield improvements.

In the pharmaceutical industry, diagnostic products research and development is the fastest growing field. Pharmaceuticals and pharmaceutical preparations are likely to increase as the average age of the population increases.

105

Chemicals and Drugs

◇ **SOURCES OF ADDITIONAL INFORMATION**

American Pharmaceutical Association
2215 Constitution Avenue, NW
Washington, DC 20037

National Association of Pharmaceutical Manufacturers
747 Third Avenue
New York, NY 10017

National Pharmaceutical Council
1894 Preston White Drive
Reston, VA 22091

Chemical Manufacturers Association
2501 M Street, NW
Washington, DC 20037

Chemical Specialties Manufacturers Association
1001 Connecticut Avenue, NW
Washington, DC 20036

Drug, Chemical and Allied Trades Association
2 Roosevelt Avenue
Syosset, NY 11791

Fragrance Materials Association of the U.S.
1620 I Street, NW, Suite 925
Washington, DC 20006

Synthetic Organic Chemical Manufacturers Association
1330 Connecticut Avenue, NW
Suite 300
Washington, DC 20036

Chemical Marketing Research Association
139 Chestnut Avenue
Staten Island, NY 10305

◇ **RELATED ARTICLES**

Volume 1: Chemistry; Energy; Engineering; Health Care; Physical Sciences; Plastics; Pulp and Paper; Rubber
Volume 2: Biochemists; Biologists; Biomedical engineers; Chemists; Pharmacists; Pharmacologists
Volume 3: Industrial chemical workers; Paint and coatings industry workers; Pharmaceutical industry workers; Plastics products manufacturing workers
Volume 4: Biological specimen technicians; Biological technicians; Chemical technicians; Dietetic technicians; Farm crop production technicians; Laboratory technicians; Petroleum technicians; Pharmaceutical technicians; Pharmacy technicians; Plastics technicians

Chemistry

General information

Chemistry is the scientific study of substances. It is concerned with the composition of matter, its changes, reactions, and transformations. Chemists often work in laboratories and investigate the characteristics of physical substances, both natural and manufactured. For example, a chemist might investigate the impact of raindrops as they fall on certain types of soils. Similarly, a chemist might conduct research into plastics as they burn and become ashes and gases. Chemists may specialize in organic, analytical, physical, biological, or organic chemistry. They are frequently employed in industry, educational institutions, and government.

In the broadest sense, chemists have existed as far back as the first human beings who observed the world around them and noticed how it changed. Like physics, biology, and geology, chemistry looks at the physical world in terms of matter. However, it is chemistry's concern with the composition of matter and its changes, reactions, and transformations that distinguishes it from the other sciences.

The modern science of chemistry traces its beginnings to very practical roots. Fire, first used by humans over one million years ago, was the earliest chemical reaction that prehistoric people learned to generate and control. Through the use of fire, ancient people were able to change the properties of other substances. For example, fire enabled the Egyptians and others to harden clay and create pottery. Great strides were made when it was discovered that by melting copper and tin together, bronze was made. Early records also show that chemical techniques were applied toward extracting medicinal juices from plants. In this manner, chemistry became increasingly important in everyday life.

The science of chemistry continued to develop despite the fact that most early peoples believed that gods or spirits caused natural occurrences. This kept many people from seeking to understand the forces that drive the universe. Between 700 and 600 B.C., Greek philosophers began to postulate that nature worked according to a set of laws that people could determine through observation and logic.

About two thousand years ago, the Egyptians gave an impetus to the field of chemistry, gathering knowledge about matter and attempting to organize this knowledge into systems. Egyptian scholars and practitioners developed a chemical practice that came to be known as alchemy, a term referring to a power or process of transforming something common into something precious. The motivation behind this chemical practice centered around the desire to change lead and other metals into gold.

Alchemy itself was a colorful chapter in the history of chemistry. It was a mixture of science and superstition, existing simultaneously as fact and fiction. Alchemy flourished in Europe during the Middle Ages and dominated chemical thinking well into the seventeenth century, when the modern science of chemistry finally displaced it.

Alchemists tried for hundreds of years to produce gold from other materials, but they never succeeded. Despite this failure, they did acquire wide knowledge of chemical substances and invented many tools and techniques still used today by chemists.

Chemistry was established as a modern scientific discipline by the great work and brilliant minds of such scientists as Antoine Lavoisier, Dmitri Mendeleev, and Julius Meyer. These scientists used carefully planned experiments, objective observations, and logical reasoning to back up each conclusion they presented. Although this work was important for the facts they discovered, of much greater significance were the theoretical foundations given to chemistry by the studies of these early modern chemists.

A chemist prepares equipment before conducting an experiment. Since measurements must be precise in the field of chemistry, he must ensure that the equipment is assembled properly.

The French chemist Antoine Lavoisier made important contributions to the field of chemistry in the late 1700s. He discovered that the weight of the product that resulted from a chemical reaction equaled that of the original ingredients. This discovery became known as the *law of the conservation of matter.*

Theory was a powerful tool. It enabled workers to make certain types of predictions and to organize facts within a more universal, but still working, system. With both practical knowledge and theory, chemistry developed rapidly. The cycle was self-perpetuating. Needs demanded new discoveries, and discoveries found new uses.

A periodic table of chemical elements assigning an atomic weight and molecular count to all known molecules was established in 1869 independently by the Russian chemist Dmitri Mendeleev and the German chemist Julius Meyer. The periodic table was based on their discovery that when elements are arranged in a table according to their atomic weights, elements with similar properties appear at regular intervals, or periods, within the table. Because of the predictability of chemical properties, Mendeleev and Meyer were able to assign spaces for chemicals which were still undiscovered, but whose existence was determined by the logic and order of the table. They were later proven right when those predicted chemicals were discovered. The *periodic law* discovered by Mendeleev and Meyer summarizes the chemistry of all known elements and gives chemists a structure in which to operate.

The technological advances generated by the Industrial Revolution provided both the means and the demand to put chemical knowledge to widespread use. In the present day, innumerable applications of chemistry can be found in all types of manufacturing processes. The number and variety of consumer products directly or indirectly dependent on chemical technology and know-how cover the whole spectrum.

The chemical industry itself contributes a good deal in this respect. By providing bulk quantities of industrial chemicals, it makes available the raw materials that other industries use to produce consumer products. Manufacturing industries that depend on chemistry or one of its many applications include petroleum, rubber, plastics, foods, metals and machinery, textiles, soap, paper, automobiles, fuels, paints, drugs, and agricultural products. These industries, in turn, provide consumers with products related to all aspects of their lives.

Nearly all useful items contain chemicals, have somehow been affected by chemicals, or are a result of an application of chemical knowledge. Just consider a small part of the list: table salt, detergents, drugs and pharmaceuticals, antifreeze, gasoline, moth-proofing, water repellent, weed killer, meat tenderizer, and furniture finishes (see Volume 1: Chemicals and Drugs).

Unfortunately, the success of the chemical industry has led to safety and environmental hazards. Many chemical waste sites have leaked, creating problems for neighboring communities. In addition, pesticides and other chemically-produced products have generated soil and water pollution. In response to these problems, chemical companies have developed methods to minimize health risks and they are continually seeking safer ways of producing chemical products and disposing or chemical wastes (see Volume 1: Waste Management).

The structure of the chemistry industry

More than 50 percent of all chemists work in research and development. Much of the research is performed in laboratories, but research and development chemists may also work in offices, where they do theoretical research or report on research results.

Research and development can be broken into two major areas: basic research and applied research. In basic research, chemists try to uncover new knowledge about substances and new ways to combine substances. They investigate the properties (characteristics) of substances and the laws governing the elements and reactions of substances. Much of the knowledge acquired in basic research is used in applied research.

In applied research, chemists are concerned with finding new products or improving old ones, and then putting the products into a form designed for use by the consumer. For example, a chemist involved with applied research may help develop a new type of synthetic rubber. New drugs and more effective drugs, such as the polio vaccines, may also be the result of applied research.

Chemists also work in production and quality control in chemical manufacturing plants. They work with plant engineers to develop specific mixing instructions and temperatures for specific products and then prepare instructions for plant workers to ensure that these instructions are carried out (see Volume 3: Pharmaceutical industry works).

Chemists involved with marketing and sales are responsible for determining what products are in demand and then helping to sell the products. They also provide customers with technical advice on the chemical products.

Chemists also may be involved with teaching in high schools or universities. It is common for university chemistry professors to be involved with research. Chemists may also work as consultants to private companies (see Volume 1: Personal and Consulting Services).

Specialized instruments help chemists in their work. For example, a mass spectrometer permits chemists to determine the mass and atomic makeup of molecules. Utilizing a research method known as chromatography, chemists are able to detect and measure extremely low concentrations of substances. This helps, for example, in detecting low concentrations of pollutants in the soil, water, and air.

Careers

Chemistry has progressed to such a point that chemists today are generally specialists, highly trained and working in one specific area. As a result of this specialization, chemists frequently work in teams to solve a particular problem,

A chemistry professor discusses the results of a graduate student's experiments and suggests new methods of procuring data.

each contributing in his or her particular area of expertise.

The field of chemistry has more than twenty-four branches and sub-branches. The positions available demand a wide range of skills, talents, and educational backgrounds. There are many avenues that one can explore in the field of chemistry and many careers that one can choose from. The general careers are as follows:

Organic chemists: Organic chemists study chemical substances that contain carbon compounds. These substances include plastics, drugs, and fertilizers. Much of the work involves preparing compounds and studying their characteristics.

Inorganic chemists: Inorganic chemists study chemical substances that do not contain carbon compounds, such as electronic components.

Analytical chemists: Analytical chemists study the composition and nature of rocks, soils, and other substances. They also identify the presence of pollutants in soil, water, and air.

Physical chemists: Physical chemists study how chemical reactions work. A physical chemist working with nuclear power, for example, will study the chemical techniques in nuclear reactions.

Biochemists: Biochemists study the action of chemicals both as a part of and in living organisms.

Chemical technicians: Chemical technicians work with chemists in the operation of research equipment necessary to conduct experiments.

Technical librarians: Technical librarians handle the wealth of technical scientific information currently available. They must be knowl-

Using a complex computer system to organize data, a chemist analyzes the results of his work.

edgeable in the sciences in order to maintain an up-to-date research library.

Patent attorneys: Patent attorneys work with chemists in securing the legal rights to their discoveries. Legal matters have become so complex in the chemical industry that the patent attorney specializing in this area often finds it necessary to have a comprehensive background in chemistry.

Teachers and professors: Teaching today spans all levels. While most teachers are employed by educational institutions, others may hire chemists for special teaching positions. The teacher should combine strong interests in chemistry and teaching. Chemistry is now not only being taught in the colleges and universities but also in grade schools and junior and senior high schools. (see Volume 1: Education).

A background in chemistry is a good foundation for many other occupations. Many chemists find jobs that are outside the laboratory but nevertheless require a strong background in chemistry. For instance, chemists have found employment as museum specialists, industrial hygienists, insurance investigators, and editors and staff of technical journals.

Chemists also work for state, local, and federal agencies and for nonprofit research institutions.

Education

Although there are excellent positions for chemists with bachelor's or master's degrees, a good number of the positions available in research and development are filled by chemists with a doctorate degree in chemistry. Almost without exception, those positions with great responsibility, such as researcher, college and university teacher, and manager, demand the doctorate degree. The bachelor's degree takes four years; the doctorate, three to five additional years of graduate work. Courses should include inorganic, organic, and physical chemistry. In addition to these required courses, students usually study biology, mathematics, physics, and the liberal arts.

Decisions concerning an area of specialization, degrees, work activities, and so on are not usually made until at least the last two years of college. Even then, some chemists are employed for a time until they determine their field of special interest. Then they may go back to graduate school or go to night school to earn advanced degrees.

Industry outlook

The technological progress of society is reflected by chemistry in its growth as a theoretical science and its expansion in providing a wide variety of needed goods. Both the theoretical and practical levels of chemistry have created a need for chemists. Not only is this trend expected to continue, but also many new areas and demands for entirely new kinds of chemists will very likely arise in the future.

According to the U.S. Department of Labor's *Occupational Outlook Handbook*, employment opportunities for chemists are expected to grow more slowly than the average for all occupations through the year 2000. This is because improvements in production techniques will allow fewer chemists to be hired.

Many new openings will occur as established chemists leave the field for a variety of reasons. New product development in private industry and biotechnology research and development also promise to offer good employment opportunities. Little growth in faculty positions in colleges and universities is anticipated.

Chemists filled more than 86,000 jobs in the late 1980s. Over half of them worked for manufacturing firms, and about one-half of these worked in the chemical manufacturing industry. Colleges and universities employed about 19,000 chemists during this same time period.

◇ SOURCES OF ADDITIONAL INFORMATION

American Chemical Society
1155 16th Street, NW
Washington, DC 20036

Chemical Manufacturers Association, Inc.
2501 M Street, NW
Washington, DC 20037

American Institute of Chemical Engineers
345 East 47th Street
New York, NY 10017

Sales Association of the Chemical Industry
287 Lackawanna Avenue
Suite A7
PO Box 2148
West Paterson, NJ 07424

◇ RELATED ARTICLES

Volume 1: Biological Sciences; Chemicals and Drugs; Engineering; Health Care; Physical Sciences
Volume 2: Biochemists; Biologists; Biomedical engineers; Chemists; College and university faculty; Librarians; Pharmacists; Pharmacologists; Physicians; Teachers, secondary school; Toxicologists
Volume 3: Agricultural scientists; Industrial chemical workers; Paint and coatings industry workers; Pharmaceutical industry workers; Plastics products manufacturing workers; Soil scientists
Volume 4: Chemical-radiation technicians; Chemical technicians; Farm crop production technicians; Laboratory technicians; Medical laboratory technicians; Pharmaceutical technicians; Pharmacy technicians; Soil conservation technicians

Civil Service

General information

In the early 1700s, before the founding of the United States, governments were established for each of the thirteen relatively independent colonies. Each colony had a governor and representatives elected from each of the regional divisions. States developed constitutions before the federal government had one.

In 1781, the federal government was designed under the Articles of Confederation. Although limited in its powers, the federal government was able to develop leadership with the Congress. As the deficiency of a weak federal government became increasingly apparent, the country's leaders organized the Constitutional Convention of 1787. This gave the government the basic structure and powers that it holds to this day.

The structure of power for the government has been divided and shared between federal, state, and local levels. The battle over the constitution was centered on the argument of how much power the states should have and how much power the federal government should have. The federal government was given the right to tax, create an army, and rule directly on federal law.

Hiring for non-elected government positions was done on a "spoils system," where the winning candidate was able to put his supporters on the staff. Many of the people who were hired had little or no qualification for the job they had been assigned. This led to serious problems in corruption and organization in the government.

Reforms began to develop in the Congress, with regulations established for giving exams to potential employees. To run the government programs, in 1883 Congress established a Civil Service Commission and assigned it the task of recruiting and evaluating the people needed. The system stayed in effect until 1978, when the Commission was abolished and replaced by an Office of Personnel Management (OPM) and a Merit Systems Protection Board. This system of hiring is explained later in this article.

State governments were developing along with the federal government. As the population increased in the country, it became necessary to share the burden of cost and staffing on state controlled areas, such as education and housing. By the mid-1900s, all of the states except Nebraska had developed two-house legislatures that resembled the Congress in style. Nebraska chose to use a one-house structure. With the growth of government, the states developed departments that would supervise and legislate on different areas. Departments of housing, health, education, and welfare were used to work with the federal government to develop effective methods of legislation.

Different forms of city government were developed in the United States. The first was the mayor-council government, developed in the late 1700s. Depending on the structure of power in the city, the mayor may have a strong role in running the city, or the mayor may have a weak role. The weak mayor was the first style of city government and developed from the British system, with a city council and a mayor who presides over the council. In the weak mayor structure, the council chooses the heads of departments and develops legislation.

In the late 1800s, a stronger mayoral structure emerged. Particularly popular and workable in the larger cities, the strong mayoral system allowed for a mayor with veto power over legislation, appointment privileges in department hiring, and responsibility over the city budget.

Another style of city government emerged in the 1900s and was developed from the need for a more professional approach to political administration. It was apparent that the task of running a city required a specialist, someone with a background and education in effective methods of operations for city government.

Members of the House of Representatives for the state of Texas prepare for a meeting. It is their job as public servants to keep the best interests of their constituents in mind when voting.

This led to the creation of the council-manager approach.

The council-manager approach to local government was started in Staunton, Virginia, in 1908 when the city council appointed a general manager to be in charge of day-to-day municipal business. Within a few years the basic form of the plan had taken shape: a council elected by the people to set policies and to adopt programs and a trained manager to supervise and coordinate the process. The council-manager plan had a particularly rapid growth after World War II. A majority of cities with more than 25,000 people now use the plan.

The government was structured to assist people in improving the quality of their lives, with education, safety, and health being primary concerns of the government. As the structure of the U.S. government became more professional, the desire to work on improvement elsewhere also advanced.

Working to improve people's lives through government programs was moved beyond the U.S. borders. The Peace Corps was founded for interested Americans to work abroad at improving the conditions in lesser developed na-

tions. The law authorizing the Peace Corps was signed by President John F. Kennedy on September 22, 1961.

The Peace Corps Act set forth three goals: to help the people of the developing nations, especially the poor, meet their needs for trained personnel; to help promote a better understanding of the American people on the part of the peoples served; to help promote a better understanding of other peoples by Americans.

The structure of the civil service

The federal government has three branches in which people can work: the executive branch, for those who work under the direction of the President's office; the legislative branch, for those who work under the direction of Congress; and the judicial branch, for those who work under the direction of the courts.

State governments are led by a governor. In all states except Nebraska, there is a two-house legislature . This branch may be referred to as

A township manager discusses a newly-approved ordinance with her assistant.

the general assembly, legislative assembly, assembly, or general court.

Local governments normally have a mayor with a city council and perhaps a city manager. There will also be heads of departments for a city and such positions as the school board are often filled by city employees.

More than fourteen million people work for state and local governments. Another three million work for the federal government. The federal government hires thousands of people each year. It does so through the use of merit system principles first adopted in 1883. A change was made to separate the recruiting and hiring programs from the protection of employee rights, assigning each of these functions to a separate agency.

Local and state governments are concerned with the administration of all services below the federal level. Due to the many responsibilities shouldered by these governmental units, there are numerous opportunities available for people interested in careers in public administration. Many of these same occupations are also found in private businesses; others, such as city manager, city planner, and traffic engineer, are unique to local government.

State government has a unique role in the federal system. Many programs that have been supported by the federal government such as public assistance, unemployment compensation, employment services, and public health are guided by strong state government departments.

There are many places in state service for people aspiring to broad careers as administrators and as specialists in such fields as public health, highway engineering, forestry, labor relations, and social welfare.

Public administrative staff work as city and county managers, department and agency heads, and their chief assistants. The states employ similar administrative personnel. In the United States, there are more than 82,000 local governments in addition to the fifty state governments. Most employ full- and part-time staff for education, technical and administrative duties, public health, safety, recreation, and other services important in daily life.

More than 2,600 cities and counties have managers who are appointed by the elected city and county governing bodies. Hundreds of other cities and counties have chief administrative officers whose duties are similar to those of managers. These local governments employ several thousand assistants ranging from interns to assistant administrators.

Hiring in the federal government follows a rigid and specific structure. Unless a position in the executive branch is exempted by law or by action of the Office of Personnel Management, it is in the competitive service and subject to examinations or other means of determining the individual best qualified for the position.

Not all job examinations are open all of the time. The number of people hired in any given field will vary periodically depending on the demand for the particular services, the launching of new programs, or other changing circumstances. Applications will not even be accepted unless there is the likelihood that job openings will be developing in the near future. When jobs are anticipated, examinations are announced and applications are accepted at job information centers throughout the nation.

Examination announcements give the job title and tell about the responsibilities, pay, qualifications, and whether a written test is required.

There are many different kinds of examinations designed to measure the ability and aptitude of men and women who apply for jobs in the wide range of occupations found in the government. Some positions are filled through special examinations announced under specific job titles. Among these are the examinations for engineers, physical scientists, and such related professions as mathematicians and architects. Men and women working in these occupational fields have unprecedented opportunities to engage in activities vitally important to the nation's economy, security, and future strength.

For trainees and experienced people for professional accounting and auditing positions, selections are made through the accountant and auditor examinations, and no written test is required for college graduates. Pay scales range from GS-5 for trainees to GS-15 for top-level jobs. Highly qualified trainees may be hired at grade GS-7.

For many positions, the examinations are not written tests. Those who apply for examinations that do not involve written tests have their grades assigned on the basis of experience and training described in the application and on the basis of any additional evidence secured by the Office of Personnel Management. This is called an unassembled examination. Applicants who pass examinations are put on a "list of eligibles." When a job in a federal agency is to be filled, the agency may choose to promote an employee, hire an employee from another federal agency, reinstate a former federal employee, or turn to the list of eligibles. If the decision is made to hire from the list, the employing agency is required to make a selection from among the three people heading the appropriate list, and the names of those not selected for a particular job are returned to the list so that they may be considered for future jobs.

The merit system of employment has replaced patronage arrangements for most jobs in local governments, especially those served by appointed professional chief administrators. The goal of reforms and policy changes is to improve the efficiency and effectiveness of government through merit pay, performance appraisals, and other programs, while at the same time striking a proper balance between management rights and employee protection.

Appointments to jobs in federal service are either temporary, career-conditional, or career. When a person is hired on a temporary basis, there is no promise of continued employment. This type of appointment generally lasts no more than one year. A temporary worker has no promotion or transfer rights and is not under the retirement system.

When it is believed that a job is of a continuing nature, the new employee is given a career-conditional appointment. For the first year, the employee serves a probationary period, which is part of the examination. If ability to do a satisfactory job is not evident by the end of the probationary period, the employee may be dismissed. If the employee satisfactorily serves three years, the word conditional is dropped and the career appointment begins. A career employee has promotion privileges and can transfer from one agency to another, and is entitled to all the rights and benefits granted to those who earn career-service appointments.

Hiring is usually done at the lowest step in a grade. Employees below grade GS-13 whose work is at an acceptable level of competence receive within-grade increases. Employees may qualify for these increases every year for three years and then less frequently until the top of the grade is reached. These within-grade raises

Tax assessors reevaluate property within the area of Teaneck, New Jersey.

are for employees who stay within the same grade.

Government employees have good advancement opportunities. Agency officials are expected to provide employees with training and career development assistance to provide a reservoir of capable personnel to fill key positions in the future.

Training activities vary from one agency to another, but all agencies seek to develop promising employees and train them for positions of increased responsibility. Many men and women in top jobs in the government began their careers in jobs in the lower grades and worked their way up the career ladder.

The government does not expect new employees to know everything about the work as soon as they step into new jobs. All agencies have orientation programs in some form or another for new employees. Through these programs, employees learn about the agency's mission and the way it is organized and operated. New employees may be trained within their own agencies, under cooperative interagency programs, or outside the government, such as at a university setting.

Although federal employees retain the rights to vote in elections and express opinions on political subjects, they are barred from active participation in partisan politics. They cannot be required to contribute to a political fund or to render any form of political service.

The Peace Corps offers an opportunity to work for the government abroad and is now a possible path of entry into civil and foreign service work.

The Peace Corps is the official international volunteer program of the United States. Peace Corps serves in 60 countries in Africa, Asia, the Pacific, Latin America, and the Caribbean. Volunteers work on projects designed by host country governments in agriculture, forestry, fish culture, health and nutrition, education, skilled trades, community and small-business development, and many other fields.

Peace Corps volunteers are not technically employees of the United States government, so they enjoy no diplomatic privileges or immunities. They make a commitment to serve for two years and serve only in countries that have invited them. They work for the host government, serving under host country supervisors and usually with host country coworkers. One Peace Corps aim is to train local workers to take over the volunteers' jobs when they leave.

Careers

A sampling of civil service career opportunities follows below.

Managers: Managers exercise general supervision over the personnel and facilities of the local government unit. In a small city, the work of relatively few city employees will be involved. In big cities, thousands of professional, skilled, and semiskilled people will work under their general direction. Managers are also responsible for long-range planning, particularly in the use of fiscal resources. Preparing the budget is one of their major responsibilities.

City managers: City managers bring the city's problems before the city council and suggest solutions for consideration. City managers keep the city council and public informed about plans for the future and about what is happening in the community. They manage the city's business and usually appoint the administrative and other employees. The position also entails carrying out the will of the people as reflected in the policies adopted by the city council.

Public works staff: The public works department is in charge of much of the city's equipment and the streets, sewage treatment facilities, water system, and other service operations. It is one of the largest users of city workers. People with engineering and construction backgrounds are needed for the design, maintenance, and inspection tasks this department performs.

Personnel officers: People trained as personnel officers are needed in medium- and large-sized cities. Those with public administration or business training are needed to devise ways to recruit employees, to set up training programs, and to devise and administer retirement, safety, and other similar programs.

Budgeting and finance staff: The finance department is one of the city's major divisions. Finance officers, many of whom are trained in public administration, are valuable aides to the manager in budgeting financial resources and assigning workers.

City planners: City planning draws people of many backgrounds. Public administrators, engineers, architects, and landscape architects are all employed as city planners. Planning, one of the most rapidly growing branches of local government, attempts to anticipate the problems of the future in such areas as recreation, public safety, police work, and urban renewal (see Volume 2: Architects; Landscape architects).

Transportation: Specialists are also needed who know traffic patterns and problems and can help control the enormous flow of cars, trucks, and public transportation in large cities. Plans for developing faster and more efficient public transportation systems need to be made by specialists with the right education and training.

School board: Local governments need well-qualified people to handle the increasing demands of the public education system. Many school systems are having managerial problems trying to stretch limited budgets to provide adequate schools and qualified teachers for high-quality education. Teachers, business administrators, and social workers are regularly active on school boards. The job varies with the size of the school and the control of the board over the school system.

International operations: International Operations is responsible for volunteer and overseas staff training, program development, and overseas activities. The latter are administered by three regional divisions: Africa; Inter-America; and North Africa, Near East, Asia, and the Pacific (known as the NANEAP region). The Office of Recruitment, Placement, and Staging is responsible for training qualified candidates for volunteer service.

The Office of Management is responsible for personnel, budget, accounting, contracting, auditing and investigation, and the provision of medical and administrative support service to volunteers and staff.

Education

Specific educational requirements depend on the job specifications of the particular job. Although not all civil service jobs require a college education, more and more positions are only open to those with an undergraduate or graduate degree. In a general sense, those with a college degree are more likely to be promoted.

While professional training was first provided decades ago for school superintendents, librarians, engineers, and others, it was not until the early 1920s that several universities established graduate programs leading to a master's degree in public administration (MPA). Now about 200 colleges and universities provide such training. Often specialists, such as planners, engineers, or police officials, recognize the need for training in administration and seek a master's degrees in public policy or public administration as a step toward advancing in their careers.

There recently has been a trend toward professional training for general city management. Whereas many educational patterns may lead to city or county employment, one path would be to study liberal arts in college with some concentration in public administration or political science. The student then might earn a master's degree in public administration and serve as intern for about a year in a manager's office. After that, he or she might serve as an administrative assistant, either in the same or a different city, for another two or three years. Then the person typically would seek a manager's job in a small city. A variation of this career pattern is for a person, after completing formal education, to rise to head of a municipal department before moving on to head the administration of a city. People have become managers in large cities by both routes: serving as manager of two or three cities of increasing size or by transferring from a leadership position in a department to that of manager.

Some agencies offer summer employment and work-study programs that enable students to gain experience in their field before they graduate. Most summer job opportunities result from the need for temporary replacements for vacationing employees and temporary project work. Most jobs are in clerical and related office work, sub-technical or subprofessional work, or as laborers and helpers. Summer job opportunities are limited, however, and there

A judge hands a piece of correspondence to his clerk. As an elected official of his county, he must abide by the rules of conduct of all civil servants.

are usually many more applicants than jobs to be filled.

Prior knowledge of a foreign language or other subjects usually is not required for Peace Corps service but a college degree is helpful. During training, volunteers learn to speak the language of their host country, understand the country's customs and culture, and train in the skills they will need during their service.

Industry outlook

Since Congress defines the needs of government programs and international responsibilities, it is difficult to predict future trends in federal employment. The need for replacements, as well as changes in programs, technology, and methods of operation are reflected in the different kinds of jobs available at any one time.

Engineering jobs in the government have greatly increased in recent years. The greatest demands are for electronics, mechanical, civil, chemical, and petroleum engineers. Government occupations in the health field are growing also.

The introduction of different kinds of machines in government offices has caused many changes in opportunities for office workers in federal jobs. For example, the expanding use of computers and advanced data-processing equipment is providing new jobs such as systems analyst, computer programmer, and computer operator.

Over the past several years, the growth of state and local government hiring has slowed to a one or two percent annual increase. The federal government is also at a point where staffing has come close to stabilizing. However, the types of jobs that are available may vary. Some departments are expanding while others are reduced or merged with other areas. The fluctuation depends on the technology available and the funds and public interest in an area of government work.

Thousands of administrative assistants, assistant managers, and department heads are helping city and county managers and chief administrative officers to make the best use of financial and human resources in order to make the government more effective.

It takes a lot of people working together to provide the many varied services the public expects from its government. Practically every occupation in the private sector is now represented by a similar occupation in government. New kinds of jobs are being created each day as the government adjusts to information processing and other technological advances.

◇ **SOURCES OF ADDITIONAL INFORMATION**

Information about federal job opportunities may be obtained from the central or regional offices of the Office of Personnel Management, federal job information centers, and state employment offices. OPM's central office is at:

Office of Personnel Management
1900 E Street, NW
Washington, DC 20415

For information on school programs and internships, write to:

In the Public Interest
National Association of Schools of Public Affairs and Public Administration
Suite 520, 1120 G Street, NW
Washington, DC 20005

For information on careers in urban and regional planning and educational programs, consult:

American Planning Association
1776 Massachusetts Avenue, NW
Washington, DC 20036

For general information on urban and county affairs, including salary and other statistics, see:

The Municipal Year Book
International City Management Association
1120 G Street, NW
Suite 300
Washington, DC 20005

Council of State Governments
Iron Works Pike
PO Box 11910
Lexington, KY 40578

National Association of Counties
440 First Street, NW
Washington, DC 20001

The Peace Corps application forms are available from their regional offices or by writing:

Peace Corps
Office of Recruitment
1990 K Street
Washington, DC 20526

◇ **RELATED ARTICLES**

Volume 1: Business Administration; Foreign Service; Law; Military Services; Politics and Public Service
Volume 2: City managers; Lawyers and judges; Political scientists
Volume 3: Court reporters; FBI agents; Police officers; Postal clerks; State police officers; Toll collectors

Computer Hardware

General information

Computer *hardware* is the physical equipment that makes up a computer system. *Software* refers to the programs that tell the various parts of the computer what to do. This article will deal primarily with the hardware industry. Please see the Computer Software article in this volume for information concerning that part of the computer industry.

The origin of modern computing devices may be traced to the abacus. The abacus, which was developed in the Orient and widely used in the Middle Ages, is a calculating device in which beads or blocks strung on lines represent units of numerical value. The abacus has been used in Japan since the sixteenth century.

At the age of seventeen, French philosopher and physical scientist Blaise Pascal (1623–1662) had already attracted the admiration of scholars for a treatise on mathematics. Shortly thereafter, at the age of nineteen, he invented the world's first digital calculator. This invention, intended to help his father administer his tax office in Rouen, was based on rotating drums controlled with a ratchet linkage. The principle of his "adding wheel" is still applied in automobile speedometers for recording mileage. (In the early 1970s, a computer programming language that was developed to detect coding errors more efficiently was named after Pascal.)

Gottfried Wilhelm von Leibniz (1646–1716), a German philosopher who contributed to many disciplines, including information science, later improved upon Pascal's machine and created a forerunner of today's hand-held calculators. His calculator was never commercially available, however.

The first significant automated data processing techniques were applied to fabric pattern making, not to numbers. They were incorporated in a weaving loom developed by Joseph Marie Jacquard (1752–1834) and introduced at the 1801 World's Fair in Paris. The machine used punched cards to control the pattern of the color threads as the cloth was being woven.

Punched cards were also put to use by U.S. inventor and statistician Herman Hollerith for the 1890 Census. Perforated cards could be read electrically for the data. Hollerith was a founder of an enterprise that eventually became International Business Machines Corporation (IBM), a leading company in the computer industry.

In 1939 John V. Atanasoff, with Clifford Berry, built a prototype computer at Iowa State University and later—after patent infringement legal action—won recognition as one of the founders of the modern digital computer. At Harvard, in the same year, Howard Aiken began work with IBM on what became the Mark I (1944), a large electro-mechanical machine fifty feet long and eight feet high.

In the mid-1940s, punched cards also were applied in work on ENIAC (Electronic Numerical Integrator and Calculator) at the Moore School of Electrical Engineering at the University of Pennsylvania. For the U.S. Army, J. Presper Eikert, Jr., and John W. Mauchy, ENIAC's inventors, developed the world's first all-electronic, general-purpose digital computer, which used some 18,000 vacuum tubes. They ushered in the first generation of general-purpose computers and the modern computer age. In 1949, they produced BINAC (Binary Automatic Computer), which used magnetic tape. Univac I (Universal Automatic Computer), which followed, was designed for the U.S. Bureau of the Census. It was the first digital computer to handle both numerical data and alphabetical information with speed and a high degree of efficiency. In 1954, the first commercial computer built by IBM, the 650, was installed in Boston. Other first-generation computers, which used vacuum tubes and were programmed by symbolic notation or in machine language, included the RCA 501, Burroughs 220, and IBM 701.

119

A technician at a manufacturing plant uses a huge computer system to test and regulate the items that come off of the assembly line.

By the late 1950s, the transistor (invented in the late 1940s) had made the second generation possible. Transistors performed most of the functions of vacuum tubes and many beyond vacuum tube capabilities. Transistors, moreover, require much less power, are lighter, smaller, sturdier, and more efficient in most applications than vacuum tubes.

Examples of second-generation computers built from the late 1950s to the mid-1960s included the IBM 1401 for business applications and the IBM 1620 for scientific applications. Others were produced by Honeywell and RCA, which later withdrew from computer manufacturing.

The integrated circuits of the later 1960s introduced the solid-state technology that made it possible to carry transistors, diodes, and resistors on tiny silicon chips. These advancements further reduced operating costs and enhanced speed, capacity, and accuracy. Minicomputers of much smaller size than mainframe (large-scale) machines but of comparable power and capacity were developed.

The next important advances were large-scale integration (LSI) and the microprocessor on a chip. Such microprocessors made possible microcomputer systems no larger than portable TV's and remote terminals. Microchips brought the cost of computer production down, and the storage capacity of the computer up. The speed with which a computer could process, calculate, retrieve, and store data was increased tremendously. The decrease in cost and the in-

creased capacity allowed for new markets to bloom.

Computer systems are now used in almost every business or profession. They help physicians diagnose and treat patients, they help engineers design bridges and buildings, and they help guide spaceships. Electronic data processing systems record sales, compute sales tax, validate credit cards, and issue customized sales receipts in retail stores. Computers have made automation possible in manufacturing plants, they control the amount of energy buildings consume, and they assist in forecasting the weather. Information processing manufacturers provide users with such equipment as computers, optical scanners, graphic display units, control systems, and advanced communications systems.

The structure of the computer hardware industry

The two most important components of computer hardware are the primary memory and the processor. The primary memory stores data and programs in the computer. The processor carries out programs and transforms data. A computer's ability to produce text is an example of the processor at work.

Computer components other than the primary memory and processor are called peripheral hardware. This hardware includes input equipment, output equipment, secondary memories, and communications devices.

Input devices, such as a keyboard, are used for entering programs and other data into the computer. Input devices convert the language of instructions into electrical signals. These signals are then processed by the computer.

Output devices, such as a television-like display screen, allow a person to get information from a computer. Video display terminals (VDTs) are the name for the computer screen. They are designed for monochromatic, or one-color, displays, or multi-color displays. A printer for producing copies of data is another type of output device.

Secondary memory devices, such as floppy disks or diskettes, are used to store information. A floppy disk is inserted into the computer's disk drive and data is stored from the computer onto the disk. Magnetic tape can also be used to store information. Another type of secondary memory device is the *hard disc*. The hard disc is actually installed in the computer, so the user can gain access to it without having to change discs. The hard disc can store millions of characters (many more than a floppy disk). Most computer users install their software into their hard disc. Hard discs are more expensive than floppy discs or magnetic tape.

Communication devices, such as modems, enable the computer to transmit data to other computers. Modems often connect computers via telephone lines. The modem allows data to be picked up from other computer systems or from computer systems with the same storage base as the computer being worked. Some computer systems rent use of their memory banks and customers can retrieve a variety of information from recent magazine articles to news-show transcripts.

Programming is a vital part of the computer hardware industry. Programmers write instructions to enable a computer to do a particular job. The programmer starts with the statement of a problem, studies and analyzes it, then organizes the information into a step-by-step procedure. This procedure becomes a program that can be "understood" by the computer.

There are two distinct types of programmers—applications and systems—and they may overlap. The applications programmer is usually employed by computer users, while the systems programmer often works for computer manufacturers.

The applications programmer primarily writes computer instructions to do specific jobs that run the gamut from analyzing traffic congestion problems to guiding astronauts (see Volume 1: Computer Software).

Whether a program is used once or many times, the job of writing it is tremendously simplified by the programming languages and program packages prepared by the manufacturer's programmers—the systems programmers. In essence, they write programs that make it easier to operate and program computers. Their programs operate input/output equipment such as disk drives and printers.

A women produces parts of a computer hardware system in a manufacturing laboratory. Given the toxicity of the chemicals, she must wear protective clothing.

Careers

The computer hardware industry offers a variety of career opportunities, ranging from design engineers to manufacturing workers. A sampling of careers follows below.

Computer manufacturers: Computer manufacturers design and develop new computer systems. To keep up with developments in the information-processing field, a computer manufacturer needs a knowledge of engineering and technology. This knowledge includes awareness of new materials and techniques for computer design, and developing and testing the new products.

Computer researchers: Computer researchers develop new computer applications. The researcher may initiate a change many years before it actually appears in the form of new components or techniques. A researcher may work in a laboratory doing basic research or in an office developing new mathematical approaches to problems in science and business. No matter what the environment, researchers have considerable freedom to explore promising scientific ideas.

Development engineers: While the researcher usually develops a theory or idea, the development engineer takes those ideas and translates them into working products. Engineers and scientists in this area—men and women with backgrounds in such fields as electrical or mechanical engineering, physics, chemistry, or mathematics—are often called the architects of new computer systems. They may focus on new components, subassemblies, or units; or be involved with entirely new systems. In any

After a computer system is installed, it must be tested to ensure that all parts are working properly.

case, they are in the forefront of producing new technology.

Product engineers: Product engineers plan engineering changes in computer hardware systems.

Systems development engineers: Systems development engineers put components together into a working computer. They also devise ways to analyze new-product capability.

Manufacturing workers: Manufacturing workers help build computer hardware systems. They may be concerned with the analysis of tools, materials and production costs, or problems in developing computer controls for manufacturing processes. Industrial engineers, chemists, metallurgists, and mathematicians are all manufacturing workers.

Computer programmers: Computer programmers write and code the instructions that control the work of the computer. They must be able to develop carefully prepared instructions for each assignment.

Quality control engineers: Quality control engineers assure that final products meet company and customer requirements. They plan, design, build, and maintain measuring systems and automated test equipment.

Computer sales representatives: Computer sales representatives assist potential clients in the selection of appropriate hardware equipment. They must have a thorough knowledge of the equipment so that they can actually develop computer applications for a customer's business-management problems.

Electronic-computer-subassembly supervisors: Electronic-computer-subassembly supervisors read schematic diagrams and written proce-

dures to determine fabrication specifications. They train workers in wiring computer chassis, soldering connections, testing wiring continuity, assembling switch and relay panels, and assembling and tying wiring cables.

Semiconductor-development technicians: Semiconductor-development technicians assist in the development of transistors, diodes, rectifiers, and other semiconductor devices. They conduct tests on experimental and prototype semiconductor devices and collect data for engineers to use in evaluating new designs or production techniques.

System engineers: The systems engineer, or SE, provides technical knowledge to solve a wide range of business and scientific problems. The SE discusses a problem with a customer, determines what machines are needed to get the desired results, may use other computers to test ideas, and finally comes up with a system designed specifically for a given customer. The systems engineer must be able to analyze problems logically and develop solutions.

Field engineers: Field engineers install and maintain computers in customer offices. On visits to customer installations, the field engineer examines the computer and maintains it in peak working condition. In case of a malfunction, this individual not only locates the malfunction but, relying on a knowledge of the machine's structure, replaces or repairs the inoperative part.

Systems analysts: Systems analysts devise ways of using the computer equipment. They do the planning, scheduling, and coordination of activities required to develop methods of data processing.

Education

Educational requirements vary as to the specific nature of the job. Some research and development positions are highly technical, requiring a graduate degree in one of the scientific disciplines. Other positions, particularly those for computer operators, are open to high-school and technical school graduates. In any case, a certain amount of on-the-job training and a desire to continue learning are required once you enter the field. This applies to skilled engineers as well as to beginning data-entry and computer operators.

Those involved with designing or manufacturing computer hardware systems usually have at least a bachelor's degree in engineering. Many have graduate degrees, and those involved with research and development often have doctorate degrees.

Computer programmers usually have a college degree in computer science. Employers usually send new programmers to specialized training programs to familiarize the new worker with the specific computer system being used at the company. The training period may last several weeks to several months. It often takes at least a year before a computer programmer is trained to write complicated programs.

Many of the technician positions require at least two years of electronic or electro-mechanical training or equivalent experience in these areas. In all cases, technicians are carefully evaluated for mechanical aptitude.

Most manufacturers provide extensive training programs to help their sales representatives understand computers and the needs of the customers.

Industry outlook

The computer industry is a growing industry. As computer usage expands and advances in technology spur the development of new computer applications, opportunities for computer programmers, systems analysts, and others will rise faster than the average for all occupations through the year 2000. Computer systems are sure to get faster and more efficient, and trained personnel will be needed in all areas of design, engineering, manufacturing, and programming.

The strong job potential has brought more people into the field, and therefore competition should be great for many positions, especially those with large firms. Analysts say that the best way to get a top job in the industry is to specialize in a particular hardware application.

The increased use of computers has led to growing concerns about maintaining individual privacy. Computers are the driving force behind the "information explosion," and a great number of people are concerned that those in business and the government can learn a great deal about someone's personal life simply by gaining access to a number of information files. Congress has already instituted some legislation designed to minimize the danger of the misuse of data files.

There is also the danger of computer crimes and other breaches of security. Those involved with research are continually looking for new methods to minimize the risk of a "hacker" entering a system illegally and committing fraud or stealing information.

◇ SOURCES OF ADDITIONAL INFORMATION

Data Processing Management Association
505 Busse Highway
Park Ridge, IL 60068

Association for Systems Management
24587 Bagley Road
Cleveland, OH 44138

American Society for Information Science
1424 16th Street, NW, Suite 404
Washington, DC 20036

Associated Information Managers
3821-F South George Mason Drive
Falls Church, VA 22041

◇ RELATED ARTICLES

Volume 1: Computer Software; Electronics
Volume 2: Computer programmers; Data base managers; Drafters; Engineers; Graphics programmers; Industrial designers; Management analysts and consultants; Mathematicians; Numerical control tool programmers; Operations-research analysts; Systems analysts; Technical writers
Volume 3: Assemblers; Communications equipment mechanics; Computer and peripheral equipment operators; Data entry clerks; Instrument makers; Office-machine servicers
Volume 4: Aeronautical and aerospace technicians; CAD/CAM technicians; Computer-service technicians; Data-processing technicians; Electronic sales and service technicians; Electronics technicians; Industrial engineering technicians; Mathematical technicians; Robotics technicians; Semiconductor-development technicians; Software technicians

Computer Software

General information

Computer *hardware* is the physical equipment that makes up a computer system. *Software* refers to the programs that tell the various parts of the computer what to do. This article will deal primarily with the software industry. Please see the Computer Hardware article in this volume for information concerning that part of the computer industry.

The origin of modern computing devices may be traced to the abacus. The abacus, which was developed in the Orient and widely used in the Middle Ages, is a calculating device in which beads or blocks strung on lines represent units of numerical value. The abacus has been used in Japan since the sixteenth century.

The first significant automated data processing techniques were applied to fabric pattern making, not to numbers. They were incorporated in a weaving loom developed by Joseph Marie Jacquard (1752–1834) and introduced at the 1801 World's Fair in Paris. The machine used punched cards to control the pattern on the cloth as it was being woven.

The punched card, which the International Business Machines Corporation (IBM) was to make so familiar, was the input medium used by the English mathematician Charles Babbage (1792–1871). At Cambridge University in the early 1880s, Babbage conceived the idea of calculating numerical tables by machinery. He came up with a "method of differences" and later designed Analytical and Difference Machines that foreshadowed the elements of a modern computer. The limits of the technology of machine manufacture during his time did not allow for commercial production, however. He was aided and supported by the daughter of the poet Lord Byron, Lady Ada Lovelace. *The Whole Computer Catalog* calls her "the world's first programmer" because she "wrote several of the operating instructions... ...[and] helped clarify and improve several of the internal op-

erations of the machine." (The U.S. Department of Defense named a new computer language ADA in her honor.)

Punched cards were also put to use by U.S. inventor and statistician Herman Hollerith (1860–1929). For the 1890 U.S. Census, Hollerith provided a mechanized system for processing data. Holes in perforated cards, he showed, could be read electrically for sorting and manipulation of the data. Hollerith was a founder of an enterprise that eventually became IBM.

In the mid-1940s, punched cards also were applied in work on ENIAC (Electronic Numerical Integrator and Calculator) at the Moore School of Electrical Engineering at the University of Pennsylvania. For the U.S. Army, J. Presper Eikert, Jr., and John W. Mauchy, ENIAC's inventors, developed the world's first all-electronic, general-purpose digital computer, which used some 18,000 vacuum tubes. They ushered in the first generation of general-purpose computers and the modern computer age. In 1949 they produced BINAC (Binary Automatic Computer), which used magnetic tape. Univac I (Universal Automatic Computer), which followed, was designed for the U.S. Bureau of the Census. It was the first digital computer to handle both numerical data and alphabetical information with speed and a high degree of efficiency.

In 1954 the first commercial computer built by IBM used vacuum tubes and were programmed by symbolic notation or in machine language.

By the late 1950s, the transistor (invented in the late 1940s) performed most of the functions of vacuum tubes and many beyond vacuum tube capabilities. Transistors, moreover, require much less power, are lighter, smaller, sturdier, and more efficient in most applications than the older devices.

The integrated circuits of the later 1960s introduced the solid-state technology that made it possible to carry transistors, diodes, and resistors on tiny silicon chips. These advancements further reduced operating costs and enhanced speed, capacity, and accuracy.

The next important advances were large-scale integration (LSI) and the microprocessor on a chip, which brought the storage capacity of the computer up. The speed with which a computer could process, calculate, retrieve, and store data was increased tremendously. The decrease in cost and the increased capacity allowed for new markets to bloom.

Apple Corporation was started in the mid-1970s out of a garage by two young computer entrepreneurs, Steve Wozniak and Steve Jobs. The MacIntosh computers produced by Apple in the 1980s developed a new market for home computers. "User- friendly" computers allowed people who were untrained in computer skills to adapt to the computer's style and learn from instructions on the screen. They introduced the instrument known as a "mouse" that allowed a user to operate a program at the touch of a button. Many consumers found this method easier than typing directions on the keyboard. For this reason and several others, Apple Computer Corporation became one of the leading manufacturers of home, or personal, computers.

After IBM entered the personal computer market, software options increased as sales of computers were counted in the millions and as IBM-compatible "clones" were developed for expanding markets in the United States and other countries.

Very large-scale integration (VLSI) allows for simultaneous operation of different computer functions. Supercomputers (50,000,000 instructions per second) are able to store information gained from one action and use it as source information on the next action. For example, a computer playing chess is able to retain lessons from previous games and use them to plan moves in following games. It is a form of learning, but the computer is not capable of thought processes attributed to humans.

Further advances in microcomputers may be anticipated, and even smaller and more compact computers will continue to offer more powerful and offer increasingly complex options to users.

After annual growth rates of as much as 50 percent in the early 1980s, sales growth of personal computers had moderated by the late-1980s. Many computer magazines folded, and the number of software producers dropped significantly. Yet, as the demand of the home market for personal computers softened, business professional sales continued to be strong. Among the more popular programs are stand-alone packages for word processing, spreadsheets, and databases.

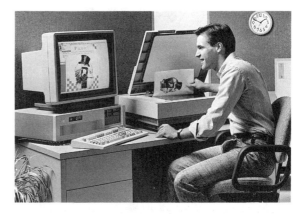

Computer software is progressing at an inexhaustible rate. In this desktop publishing program, a machine scans an image and transmits the information to a computer. This saves a person time from using a graphics program to draw the image.

The structure of the software industry

A computer needs to be told how to do what it does. A human being has to instruct the computer how to become a word processor, an automatic dialer, or a timer, for example. In fact, the only thing that a computer can do by itself is accept instructions and carry them out.

Giving instructions to a computer is called programming. Programs are written in systems of coding and organization called computer languages. There are many computer languages, including machine language, assembly language, and higher level languages. Higher level languages allow the user to instruct the computer to print a letter or complete similar tasks. Specific computers accept specific languages.

One of the simplest languages is called BASIC. It is elementary and new computer users learn programming with it. For business data processing, the most common language is COBOL, which means "Common Business Oriented Language." For scientific data processing, a very common language is FORTRAN, whose name is derived from "Formula Translation."

When used to program a computer, all of these computer languages must be translated to the computer's basic machine language. This is done by a compiler, which is simply a separate program that accepts the program written in COBOL, FORTRAN, or whatever language is used to solve the problem. The compiler translates the language or converts it step-by-step into the computer's own language.

A computer program starts with the definition of a problem. This phase is entered upon jointly by a senior programmer and analyst who define the problem in detail and identify the relationships between all factors to be con-

Computer software is an invaluable educational tool for students of all ages. These children are listening to instructions on an audio system while operating a computer.

sidered. For example, if the problem deals with cost accounting or large inventory control, the analyst and senior programmer must identify aspects of accounting, operational procedures, file maintenance techniques, and related subjects.

No matter what the size or complexity of a problem, the programmer's method of solving it is almost always the same. First, a programmer must understand the problem and be able to break it down into its component parts. Second, the programmer must know the capabilities and limitations of the machines that are going to process the data. Finally, the programmer must know precisely what results a program is expected to produce.

To do all this, the programmer may spend weeks, and sometimes months, studying a problem in depth. A programmer who is writing instructions for a railroad scheduling system, for example, will have to become familiar with railway scheduling. And a programmer doing an order-inventory system for a chemical company will need to learn a great deal about how a chemical company fills its orders, how long various chemicals can last on the shelf, and other similar information.

Once a programmer understands the problem, he or she starts drawing a step-by-step flow chart that contains the significant logical steps needed to solve it from beginning to end. A programmer may use standard symbols to represent some of these steps and English words for others. These words and symbols are then translated into the simplified instruction of the computer language and punched into cards or entered by other media or by keyboard into the system. Finally, the input is processed through a computer to discover any "bugs" or errors in the program.

In computer systems, the input—that is, the raw information to be entered into the machine for processing—may be first punched onto cards or tape or entered directly via keyboard. This is done either by keypunch operators, typists, or other workers.

Among the most popular software programs are those devoted to word processing. Word processing entails the use of the computer to compose, format, edit, and print out text. Software programs have the capacity to check spelling, rearrange sections of text, format tables, justify margins, and a host of other functions. Since the text stored in the word processors can be reused repeatedly, word processors have become enormously popular with businesses. Businesses often use word processors to send out form letters, tabulate financial tables, and develop sales literature. Of course, word processors have also proven immensely popular with individual; personal computers have changed the way hundreds of thousands of people do their taxes, write their letters, and a variety of other tasks.

A few large companies, such as IBM and Apple Computer produce many of the software programs.

Careers

There are a number of career opportunities in the software industry. Not all of these workers are involved directly with the creation of software programs, yet all work in affiliated positions.

Graphics programmers: Graphics programmers design the software necessary to allow computers to generate charts, illustrations and other types of graphic arts. They can be employed either by software manufacturing companies or by the companies that buy and use the software, known as the "end user."

Computer programmers: Computer programmers write and code the instructions that control the work of the computer. They must be able to develop carefully prepared instructions for each assignment.

Software sales representatives: Software sales representatives assist potential clients in the selection of appropriate software programs. They must have a thorough knowledge of the programs so that they can actually develop computer applications for a customer's business or management problems.

Computer researchers: Computer researchers develop new computer applications. The researcher may initiate a change many years before it actually appears in the form of new components or techniques. A researcher may work in a laboratory doing basic research or in an office developing new mathematical approaches to problems in science and business. No matter what the environment, researchers have considerable freedom to explore promising scientific ideas.

Development engineers: While the researcher usually develops a theory or idea, the development engineer takes those ideas and translates them into working products. Engineers and scientists in this area—men and women with backgrounds in such fields as electrical or mechanical engineering, physics, chemistry, or mathematics—are often called the architects of new computer systems. They may focus on new components, subassemblies, or units; or be involved with entirely new systems. In any case, they are in the forefront of developing new technology.

Data base managers: Data base managers implement and coordinate data processing systems. They assist in the purchase of new computer equipment and allocate access to the computer system.

Computer operators: Computer operators put the programmer's instructions to work on the computer. They load the computer with the disk or magnetic tape containing the operating instructions, and then monitor the program as it is processed by the computer.

Information scientists: Information scientists design systems for collecting, organizing, interpreting, classifying, and retrieving information stored in a computer. They often use mathematical models to help design these systems.

Computer-service technicians: Computer-service technicians install, program, maintain, and repair computer systems. They also diagnose problems that are caused by mechanical or electrical malfunctions in computer units and systems.

Education

Educational requirements vary as to the specific nature of the job. Some research and development positions are highly technical, requiring a graduate degree in one of the scientific disciplines. Other positions, particularly those for computer operators, are open to high-school and technical school graduates.

For those wishing to enter graphics programming, a college degree in computer science or related subject is most helpful.

Computer programmers usually have a college degree in computer science. Employers usually send new programmers to specialized

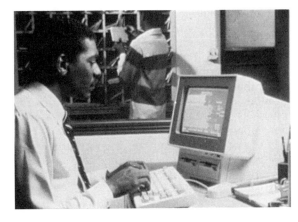

Computer software has innumerable uses for the office. This man is incorporating text into his spreadsheet that he will use in a business presentation. Computers aid in making such work presentable and flawless.

training programs to familiarize the new worker with the specific computer system being used at the company. The training period may last several weeks to several months. It often takes at least a year before a computer programmer is trained to write complicated programs.

Most manufacturers provide extensive training programs to help their sales representatives understand computers and the needs of the customers.

Those involved in management positions may have a college degree in business administration or related field. Ideally, these candidates will also have a background in computer sciences.

Industry outlook

Already a multi-billion dollar industry, the computer software industry is still rapidly growing. While perhaps not as "hot" as it was in the early 1980s, the software industry will continue to create new applications for home and business computer use.

There should be strong employment opportunities in all sectors of the computer industry, although the increased use of software programs may limit somewhat the need for computer programmers.

A growing number of computer firms are specializing in artificial intelligence, the effort to get computers to think like people. There has been significant progress in this field, with computers now able to help doctors diagnose illnesses and complete other highly complicated tasks. The artificial intelligence field is expected to provide a growing number of employment opportunities in the future.

The increased use of computers has led to growing concerns about maintaining individual privacy. Computers are the driving force behind the "information explosion," and a great number of people are concerned that those in business and the government can learn a great deal about someone's personal life simply by gaining access to a number of information files. Congress has already instituted some legislation designed to minimize the danger of the misuse of data files.

◇ SOURCES OF ADDITIONAL INFORMATION

Association for Systems Management
24587 Bagley Road
Cleveland, OH 44138

Data Processing Management Association
505 Busse Highway
Park Ridge, IL 60068

American Society for Information Science
1424 16th Street, NW, Suite 404
Washington, DC 20036

Association of the Institute for Certification of Computer Professionals
2200 East Devon Avenue, Suite 268
Des Plaines, IL 60018

National Computer Graphics Association
2722 Merrilee Drive
Suite 200
Fairfax, VA 22031

◇ RELATED ARTICLES

Volume 1: Computer Hardware; Electronics; Engineering
Volume 2: Computer programmers; Data base managers; Drafters; Engineers; Graphics programmers; Industrial designers; Management analysts and consultants; Mathematicians; Numerical control tool programmers; Operations-research analysts; Systems analysts; Technical writers
Volume 3: Assemblers; Communications equipment mechanics; Computer and peripheral equipment operators; Data entry clerks; Instrument makers; Office-machine servicers; Retail sales workers
Volume 4: Aeronautical and aerospace technicians; CAD/CAM technicians; Computer-service technicians; Data-processing technicians; Electronic sales and service technicians; Electronics technicians; Industrial engineering technicians; Mathematical technicians; Microelectronics technicians; Robotics technicians; Semiconductor-development technicians; Software technicians

Construction

General information

Construction covers the erection, maintenance, and repair of buildings and other immobile structures, together with the building of roads and other service facilities that become integral parts of structures and are essential to their use for any general purpose. Construction includes structural additions and alterations. It does not include the building of mobile structures such as trailer houses, trailer offices, and ships.

People have always attempted to improve upon their environment by developing more efficient types of shelter. Most early attempts were crude, but there are examples of wonderful achievements by people who lived centuries ago—the Egyptians pyramids, the Roman amphitheaters, and the Mayan temples.

Craft training in the building trades came to the United States in colonial days with the European settlers. It reflected then, as it does today, a traditional apprenticeship period wherein individuals were indentured to a skilled artisan or organization until such time as they became proficient enough to attain the status of a skilled craft worker. Skills were developed through on-the-job training.

It was not until the invention of the steam engine in the mid-1800s that Western Europe and the United States made rapid progress in constructing public buildings, roads, and water and sewage systems.

The construction industry in the United States offers a great number and variety of useful, interesting, and rewarding career opportunities located in all parts of the country. It is the nation's largest industry and its operations extend from border to border and coast to coast. It provides employment for more workers, directly and indirectly, than any other single industry, requires many different kinds of highly developed skills, and pays some of the highest wage rates.

The structure of the construction industry

Construction is a detailed and complex industry, dealing with all aspects of building a structure. This includes the clearing of the site and the development of the structure. Construction also covers service equipment that, when installed, becomes an integral part of the structure, such as plumbing, heating, central air-conditioning, electrical wiring, lighting equipment, elevators, and escalators.

In general, the first step in construction involves bidding for a project. The contractor that bids the lowest price is usually awarded the contract. He or she then hires subcontractors to perform selective projects such as laying the foundation, fireproofing the structure, and installing the ventilation system. After all of the tasks have been coordinated with the subcontractors, the structure is ready to be built.

Construction takes many forms and its products vary widely in size, appearance, composition, character, and purpose. These products are divided into major groups or categories, according to their principal characteristics, and each of these is further divided into subcategories.

One group includes structures ranging from small homes to huge housing developments, and these are part of what is called residential building construction. It is the largest single category of construction, usually amounting to about one-third of the total annual dollar volume.

Another major category is nonresidential building construction, or general building construction. It includes industrial buildings such as plants and factories; commercial structures ranging from small stores to great skyscrapers; and institutional and other kinds of nonresidential structures such as schools, churches, and hospitals.

This worker is assisting in the construction of a high-rise office building. He is trained to perform a number of tasks. In this case he places wooden boards that are used to shape the reinforced concrete. Such work requires stamina and strength.

Highway and heavy construction is another principal category. Highway work embraces not only networks of interstate highways, but also bridges, local roads, and streets. Airport runway construction is largely done by highway contractors also, since runways and highways involve much the same methods, materials, machines, and skills. Typical heavy projects include dams, big bridges, tunnels, railroads, missile bases, refineries, and waterways such as the Panama Canal, the St. Lawrence Seaway, and river channels. Similar equipment and construction methods are employed for highway and heavy construction. Earthmoving, for example, may be done for a highway project or for an earth-fill dam.

Finally, municipal-utilities contractors construct the essential services for counties, towns, and cities. Such projects include sewage treatment plants, water purification projects, water and sewer lines, underground utilities, street resurfacing, park and playground construction, and sidewalk construction and maintenance.

New construction activity is divided into two broad classifications—private construction and public construction. Private construction is construction work performed for private owners, whether individuals, corporations, or other business firms, organizations or institutions of a nongovernmental character. It is usually paid for out of private funds.

Public construction is construction work performed for federal, state, or local agencies of government and usually paid for out of tax money, bonds, or other public funds.

The governing distinction between private and public construction, however, is the ownership of the project at the time of construction and not the source of funds used to pay for the project.

Construction work has a strong natural attraction for active people. It requires physical vigor, hardiness, dexterity, and ingenuity. It employs many kinds of tools and mechanical equipment. It is primarily an outdoor occupation. It offers opportunities for travel and change of scenery as workers complete one project and move on to another, sometimes hundreds or even thousands of miles away. It is a dynamic industry, offering many opportunities for quick advancement.

There is also a great deal of personal satisfaction to be found in construction work. People in construction have a creative nature. They take much pride in their work and in the completed projects that they helped to build.

The life of a construction worker naturally has its disadvantages, too. The advantage, to some workers, of opportunities for travel, is a distinct disadvantage to others who wish to settle down. On this point, however, job opportunities in construction are usually sufficient to allow a worker to have a choice.

Another disadvantage is that construction is a seasonal industry and workers are subject to periods of unemployment. This, however, is not the disadvantage it was in the past, because technological improvements in winter construction methods have made many kinds of construction work virtually a year-round operation.

Finally, an unfortunate disadvantage is that construction work is one of the more hazardous occupations. While this remains a serious problem, there has been marked improvement in construction safety in recent years, and the industry is striving earnestly to make working conditions safer. Thanks to the efforts of both management and labor, construction safety has shown substantial improvement and can confidently be expected to continue improving.

Most building trades workers are employed by contractors in the contract construction industry or by home builders and developers in speculative residential building. Many small contractors employ ten or fewer workers. Others are employed by business firms or government agencies that do work with their own construction forces. Many building trades workers are self-employed, performing maintenance and repair work directly for property owners or operating as contractors on small jobs.

The total number of contract construction firms in the United States, according to the Department of Commerce, numbered in the hundreds of thousands. The great majority of these firms are small, employing only a few workers, or often none other than the self-employed proprietor.

Careers

The work of the construction industry, from first blueprint to the finished building, encompasses an enormous range of talents and educational backgrounds: architects, engineers, contractors, drafters, skilled workers such as cement masons, carpenters, bricklayers, and heavy-equipment operators, and semiskilled and unskilled workers such as laborers and hod carriers. It is an industry that affects many others, either as suppliers or consumers. It is currently the largest employer of skilled workers in the United States. A sample of the career op-

A lift operator moves heavy materials at a construction site.

portunities in the construction industry follows below.

Special trade contractors: Special trade contractors usually do specialized work on a project, such as electrical work, roofing, or painting. These contractors may also work on two or more related tasks, such as plumbing and heating, or lathing and plastering.

General contractors: General contractors coordinate and manage an entire construction project and assume full responsibility for its completion at a time and cost specified in the contract. They may sometimes subcontract to special trade contractors to do some of the work, but they retain overall responsibility. General contractors fall into four main groupings according to the type of construction work in which they engage: building contractors, highway contractors, heavy-industrial construction, and municipal-utilities contractors.

Project managers: The project manager coordinates all construction functions on very large projects and performs administrative duties.

General superintendents: The general superintendent directs all construction functions and large projects according to established schedules, specifications, methods, and procedures.

Job superintendents: The job superintendent directs all construction functions on small or medium-sized projects, or on specific phases of large projects.

Estimators: The estimator obtains basic data on a proposed construction project, usually from architectural/engineering plans and site inspections, and computes cost of construction plus overhead and profit.

Expediters: The expediter maintains construction schedules by reviewing deliveries,

A subcontractor reviews a work order with the general contractor to confirm his assigned task.

scheduling arrival of materials and personnel at job sites, establishing priorities, and obtaining clearances.

Purchasing agents: The purchasing agent determines the most economical sources of materials and makes purchases at the lowest prices consistent with specifications and required delivery schedules.

Marketing managers: The marketing manager maintains contacts with owners, architects, engineers, public officials, and businesspeople seeking opportunities for obtaining construction contracts.

Drafters: The drafter prepares working plans, drawings, and diagrams for engineering and construction purposes and computes strength of materials.

Safety directors: The safety director plans and executes a program for instructing supervisors and workers in safe construction practices, maintains a continuing study of each job site and prepares a safety program for each project designed to safeguard workers and the public from any special hazards of conditions encountered.

Office managers: The office manager performs, or supervises office personnel in performing, various services such as keeping books and records, making up payrolls, and billing clients. About one-sixth of the employ-

ees in contract construction are office workers. Construction firms employ accountants, bookkeepers, clerks, stenographers, and telephone operators. They also require special kinds of executives and office personnel.

Foremen/forewomen: The foreman or forewoman supervises all craft workers of a particular trade on a project, plans work, maintains schedules, assures proper procedures, and maintains close contact with the job superintendent.

Craft or trade occupations in construction fall into three broad work classifications—structural, finishing, and mechanical.

Structural workers: These workers include carpenters, bricklayers, stonemasons, cement masons, ornamental iron workers, reinforcing iron workers, rod workers, riggers, boilermakers, operating engineers, and welders.

Finishing workers: These workers include lathers, marble setters, tile setters, terrazzo workers, painters, glaziers, roofers, floor layers, and insulating workers.

Mechanical workers: Those with responsibility in this area include plumbers, pipe fitters, air-conditioning and refrigeration mechanics, millwrights, construction electricians, sheet-metal workers, and elevator constructors.

Education

A person generally enters the construction industry at one of three levels: from high school as an apprentice or trainee; from a technical school into a contractor's office as a technician; or from a college of construction or engineering into a contractor's office as a professional engineer or management trainee.

A person can usually advance according to his or her level of education. There is no set path of advancement. However, through hard work and years of experience, a high school graduate can advance to the position of job superintendent, while a college graduate studying engineering and finance may rise to the position of partner.

Schools of construction that offer undergraduate and graduate degrees in the general disciplines of construction provide a major avenue to mid-level management positions. These schools may offer a combination of finance, construction marketing, basic engineering and architecture, personnel management, labor relations, and other construction-related courses.

There are opportunities for construction employees to improve their skills and their knowledge of industry operations through special courses of study in night schools, correspondence courses, and industry-sponsored supervisory training programs. This has been the road taken to success by many ambitious workers.

Opportunities for construction workers to advance also include the possibility of becoming independent contractors. Opportunities for workers with the necessary ability to form their own firms are greater in construction than in most other lines of business because contractors customarily hire workers and rent equipment only as needed for specific projects. These factors make entry into the construction industry relatively easy. It is, however, a business involving much risk, and the failure rate is high in comparison to most other industries.

Construction workers customarily enter the industry soon after completing high school, beginning as apprentices or trainees in one or another of the numerous building trades. Mathematics, English, and the sciences are especially important subjects for the prospective construction worker to study in high school. Manual training courses, like mechanical drawing and woodworking, can also be helpful.

The typical apprentice training program ranges from two to five years for the different trades. Apprentices must usually be at least 18 years old and in good physical condition. They are generally paid 50 percent of the experienced worker's rate at the beginning, and are advanced at intervals until they receive about 90 percent of the experienced worker's rate toward the end of the training period.

Industry outlook

The construction industry traditionally adds more to the nation's wealth each year than any other industry. With annual dollar volume estimated in the early 1990s at over $342 billion, construction accounts for approximately one tenth of the U.S. annual gross national product. The largest repository for the savings of individuals and the capital investments of businesses is in the physical facilities built by the construction industry—homes, stores and buildings, mills and factories, highways and streets, bridges, railroads, airports, wharves and docks, pipelines, tunnels, dams, power plants, irrigation projects, public works, and defense installations.

Whether it is the life savings of one family buying a home or the investments of many used, for instance, by an insurance company to finance the erection of a skyscraper for a business corporation, it all adds up to a substantial

Cement masons prepare a work area before they pour the concrete to form the sidewalks and entrance ways.

yearly increase in national wealth. The nation's banks, insurance companies, pension plans, and other financial institutions have a big stake in construction, for they finance most of it.

Construction requirements continue to rise year after year because of such factors as gains in the number of households, the increasing shift of families from the cities to the suburbs, and, at the same time, the revitalization of urban centers.

Traffic congestion has brought demands almost everywhere for more and wider expressways, on the one hand, and on the other, for modernized mass-transit systems. Urban renewal projects, expressways, and mass-transit systems all involve construction on an extensive scale. So do all other community needs for physical facilities.

In addition, demands for modern industrial and commercial structures continue to rise. Continuing technological advancements in commerce and industry necessitate periodic modernization.

All these factors point to a continuation of the steady expansion of the market for construction services for many years to come. Although further technological improvements in construction methods and equipment may be expected to raise the productivity of workers, the volume of activity will require substantial numbers of craft workers in the various building trades, mostly as replacements for those who retire or leave the labor force for other reasons.

Although prospects look promising, the construction industry is very sensitive to the fluctuations in the national economy. Therefore, a downturn in the nation's economy could adversely affect job opportunities.

Bureau of Labor Statistics studies indicate that, on the average, construction activity creates more demand for employment off-site. Such off-site work consists of all the tasks required to produce and fabricate materials and supplies and to transport these items from the producers to the distributors and then to the job sites. In considering the importance of construction to employment, it is essential to take into account the number of workers for whose jobs the industry is indirectly responsible, as well as direct employment. The overall industry was responsible for around four million jobs, as of the late-1980s.

◇ SOURCES OF ADDITIONAL INFORMATION

People contemplating careers in construction may obtain information on trainee and/or apprenticeship programs from local construction contractors, building trades' unions, or high-school vocational counselors. A person who has decided on the particular trade he or she would like to enter should consult a contractor who performs that type of construction, a contractor association, or the appropriate local union.

Prospective apprentices or trainees wishing to become bricklayers, carpenters, cement masons, iron workers, or equipment operators should consult a general contractor or the appropriate union. These five trades are associated with general contractors and are known in the industry as the "basic trades," along with two other trades—the construction laborers and the teamsters.

Other sources of information on craft training include local employer associations, offices of the Bureau of Apprenticeship and Training of the Department of Labor, and state employment service offices. Also consult:

Associated General Contractors of America
1957 E Street, NW
Washington, DC 20006

American Subcontactors Association
1004 Duke Street
Alexandria, VA 22314

National Association of Home Builders of the U.S.
15th and M Streets, NW
Washington, DC 20005

American Institute of Constructors
20 South Front Street
Columbus, OH 43215

Construction Specifications Institute
601 Madison Street
Alexandria, VA 22314

AFL-CIO
Building and Construction Trades Department
815 16th Street, NW, Suite 603
Washington, DC 20006

◇ RELATED ARTICLES

Volume 1: Engineering; Mining; Real Estate; Trade Unions
Volume 2: Architects; Construction inspectors, government; Drafters; Engineers; Surveyors
Volume 3: Air-conditioning, refrigeration, and heating mechanics; Blue-collar worker supervisors; Boilermaking occupations; Bricklayers and stone masons; Carpenters; Cement masons; Construction workers; Drywall installers and finishers; Electrical repairers; Electricians; Elevator installers and repairers; Floor covering installers; Glaziers; Iron and steel industry workers; Lathers; Marble setters, tile setters, and terrazzo workers; Operating engineers (construction machinery operators); Painters and paperhangers; Pipe fitters and steam fitters; Plasterers; Plumbers; Roofers; Structural-steel workers; Welders
Volume 4: Architectural and building construction technicians; Civil engineering technicians; Drafting and design technicians; Electrical technicians; Electromechanical technicians; Electronics technicians; Poured concrete technicians; Surveying and mapping technicians; Welding technicians

Design

General information

Decorative elements on furniture, walls, and clothing can be traced back thousands of years. The purpose of the wall paintings by cave dwellers in Lascaux, France, made between 15,000 and 13,000 B.C. is unknown, but it marks an example of how early humans integrated the concept of design into their culture.

Furniture design was common by 3000 B.C., when Egyptians, Assyrians, Mesopotamians, and other Mediterranean cultures flourished. By the rise of the Greek Empire about twenty-five hundred years ago, decorations were a common part of homes, furniture, and clothing. Pottery was painted and shaped to be attractive as well as functional. Mosaics in front of houses in Pompeii, for example, were well designed, depicting dogs on chains. The dogs bore the warning "Mean Dog" in Latin.

From the earliest times, building design was a fundamental element of religious structures. The design of these buildings was as important as their function. Cathedrals and temples have been the central focus of most cities for centuries, and their designs were, and still are, considered some of the finest displays of architecture in existence. Stonehenge, located in England, is widely believed to have some religious significance, as well as astrological functions to the ancient people who created it. The Parthenon in Athens was a monument to one of the Greek gods.

The strides made in architectural design were matched by designs being used on clothes, pottery, windows, furniture, and all sorts of objects used in daily life. Each was open to design and redesign as the styles changed. Some designers became well known in their day, and some names are still held in esteem today. Paul Revere, for example, was well known for his role as a patriot in the American Revolution, but he is also highly regarded for the beauty of his designs as a sil-versmith. Louis Comfort Tiffany, a stained glass designer from the turn of the century, popularized the use of stained glass for lamps, home windows and doors.

Often, entire regions became known for their design skills. The glass blowers of Venice were considered the top glassmakers for more than a hundred years during the Middle Ages. Their glassmaking industry is still strong today.

The rise of design as an modern industry was not solidified until the great upsurge in advertising about fifty years ago. Before the advent of advertising, most designers worked in their chosen craft. Once a market was established for free-lance designers, one could design objects as different as lamps and automobiles. Advertising created a need for artists with an eye for the practical elements of the object, and advertising artists had to appreciate the aim of the advertisement as well as the beauty of the design.

The structure of the design industry

Design plays an important role in almost every aspect of our daily lives. The homes we live in, the clothes we wear, the furniture and appliances we use, the newspapers and books we read, all were produced with the input of designers.

To understand exactly what design is, it is helpful to take a moment to think about fine arts, engineering, and science. Many universities have a college of Arts and Sciences, and while at first glance arts and sciences may seem to have nothing to do with one another, at their most basic level they are both ways of understanding the world. Artists arrive at understanding by creating images, sometimes beautiful, sometimes disturbing, that help them and others make sense of their lives. They express these images in such art forms as paintings,

135

The interior of the Johnson Wax Company administration building in Racine, Wisconsin, was designed by the famous architect Frank Lloyd Wright in 1936–1939. He was one of the few architects that insisted on designing the furnishings within his buildings.

sculpture, literature, music, and dance. Scientists gain knowledge of the world and life by studying natural phenomena and drawing conclusions from the patterns they observe.

Some artists and scientists make careers of discovering these universal principals. Other artists and scientists make careers of applying these principles. The artists that apply these principles are called designers, and such scientists are called engineers. The main thing that separates design from fine arts like painting and sculpture is that the designer's freedom of choice is limited. Designers cannot simply create something to please themselves; they must create something that is pleasing but that also serves a purpose.

Both design and engineering involve a highly organized mental process. Designers and engineers must be able to blend many kinds of information into a coherent set of ideas, which can then be transformed into a product. Generally speaking, design has to do with the creation of objects for which appearance and use are both important, whereas engineering tends to focus on use alone. The fields of design and engineering often overlap when a design requires considerable technical expertise, as with electrical appliances and other machines.

There are many different kinds of designers. Different designers deal with different materials and different technologies, but the overall process is the same.

Design is the arrangement of details, form, and color into useful objects. As design is applied to specific projects, it falls into one of two categories: structural design and decorative design.

Structural design comprises what something is supposed to do, what it looks like, and what it is made of. These three elements are known as function, form, and material.

Function is the most important consideration in any kind of design, whether the design is for a kitchen appliance, a printed form such as a job application, or a bridge. The object is supposed to fulfill some role or need. A building may be needed as a school, a private home, or a factory. Each requires a much different design to serve its purpose. Obviously, a school that resembles a factory, with one huge room, will be a failure; it would be hard to separate students by grade-level, and the environment would be too noisy in which to learn.

Form is the second consideration in structural design. The architect Louis Sullivan set forth a motto: form follows function. What something looks like should reflect what purpose it serves. But this is not to suggest that form is not important in design; it merely cannot come before function. For example, a designer might come up with an attractive design for a clothes iron. The iron is sleek, lightweight, and can be folded up for easy storage. But what if the designer fails to design the iron so that it can press the wrinkles out of clothes? It may be lovely to look at, but it must fulfil the purpose it was designed for.

A third consideration in structural design is material. A designer must choose materials that are available and that make sense for the object. Returning to our earlier example, what if the iron is easily handled, but is designed to be made entirely of plastic? The iron would melt, the clothes would be ruined, and the consumer would have to buy a new iron. Of course, nobody would be foolish enough to design a plastic iron. That is just an extreme example of the importance of materials in design. Often manufacturers are surprised to discover, only after their products are returned by consumers, that a material they have used is inadequate.

Decorative elements are often looked upon as something that is not essential to the form of an object, but this attitude underestimates its value. Decorative elements are more than ornamentation; true decorative design is something that cannot be removed without spoiling the effectiveness of the object. Once the practical elements of a product are determined to be equal, it is usually the appearance of an object that attracts the buyer. For example, all lamps light a room to some extent, but the beauty of the lamp is what sells one particular design over another. So for the manufacturer, an attractive design is what makes a product marketable. The decorative element sells the object, if the object is something that is needed or wanted by the consumer.

Designers are employed in some capacity in almost every industry. Graphic artists, for instance, design brochures for marketing and ad-

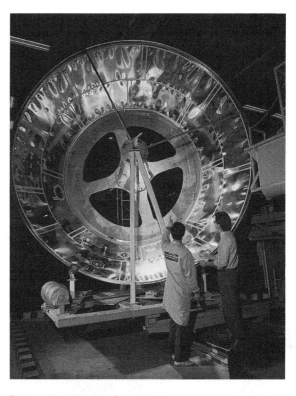

This "transition skin" of the Centaur's upper stage booster was specially designed for the Air Force's Titan IV program.

vertising companies, business forms for banks, containers for the packaging industry, and even menus for the food-service industry. Industrial designers design aircraft for the aerospace industry, cars and trucks for the automotive industries, computers and peripheral equipment for the computer hardware industry, stereos and televisions for the electronics industries, as well as toys and games.

Architects design buildings for the construction industry and plan urban spaces for cities. Textile designers come up with patterns for fabrics, and fashion designers plan clothes using those fabrics. The ceramics, glass, metals, plastics, rubber, and woods industries all need attractive, functional designs for their products.

Designers usually find employment in one of three arenas. In one instance, they may serve on the full-time staff of a company whose main business is not design, but which needs design services on an on-going basis for ads and promotional materials. Toy manufacturers, for example, have permanent staff members who work solely on toy design. In the automotive industry, design is one of the most important elements in car sales, and designs are considered secret and confidential by the company. The designs are closely-guarded secrets until the car is produced and ready for sale.

An architectural illustrator uses computer software to make her renditions as accurate and as detailed as possible.

Designers may also work for companies whose main purpose is design. Design companies can be highly specialized or they can offer a wide range of design services. They may provide commercial art or graphic design services for advertising agencies, publishers, and other businesses and industrial users. These designers determine the need behind a design of an object and then they try to come up with a workable plan. The plan includes steps in research, conceptualization, choosing materials, preliminary drafts, trial, and revision.

Designers may also be self-employed. Because so many companies need designers on an irregular basis, there are many opportunities for free-lance design work.

In the past, the very first step in design would be a meeting between a client and a designer in which the client would tell the designer what he or she wanted, leaving the designer to figure out how to do it. Now, research often precedes this first meeting.

Research is a growing area in design. Rather than rely solely on a designer's ideas, many companies are recognizing that it pays to spend time, effort, and money to find out what consumers really like before starting the design process. Often, firms will hire design consult-

ants to conduct research rather than retain full-time staff for this purpose.

One example of the practicality of design research is related to the world of work. People who sit all day at desks have a tendency to have back problems, and back problems may decrease their productivity. To design the best possible product, furniture designers may conduct research to find out what conditions put the least physical stress on people. They may discover that the standard desk height makes people hunch over too much, and so they will design higher desks. They may discover that armrests on chairs relieve strain on the back and neck, and then design affordable armchairs that companies can buy for every employee, not just for a few employees who have already encountered problems. This is just one example of design research, but it can be applied in almost every realm of manufacturing.

Another element of design research deals with something less objective than how an item performs, and that is how it is perceived by consumers. In trying to find out how an item communicates its purpose and desirability, design research resembles some advertising and marketing functions.

After research is completed, designers begin conceptualizing a design. Whatever their specialty, all designers take a similar approach to a project. They begin by determining the needs and preferences of the clients and potential users. Once they assemble a list of requirements, they must come up with a solution to a whole cluster of problems. For example, the kinds of concerns that the architect must consider when designing new windows for a house are that the windows should provide insulation and ventilation and yet not conflict with the original style of the house. Also, they must keep the house structurally sound. Using those parameters, the architect envisions a number of possible designs, only one of which will ultimately be determined the best solution.

Logotypes provide another example. Logotypes, or logos for short, are the visual images that represent corporations or products. For many businesses, coming up with a corporate logo is not taken lightly. A conservative banking firm wants to make sure that the symbol that represents it does not communicate "fun," in the way that a surf-board manufacturer might. Instead, the bank wants to project an image of stability and trustworthiness so that people will feel confident placing their money in its hands. These are the kinds of design considerations that come into play in the conceptualization process.

A number of factors affect choice of materials. One of them is the availability of materials. Eskimos originally designed igloos because ice was available and other building materials were not. In this day and age, just about any material can be transported to any site, but the element of cost determines the sales of an object. Shipping redwood from California to Massachusetts, for instance, when another wood is more readily accessible, will unnecessarily increase the cost of the object and perhaps reduce sales.

In addition to practicality and availability, other factors determining material choice include cost and personal preference. If a client insists on a silk evening gown because she likes silk, then silk is what the designer will use.

Different designers choose different materials. Fashion designers pick fabrics, package designers pick cardboard and plastics, and graphics designers pick papers and typefaces. One fashion designer may specialize in imported materials and styles, another may design functional work clothes. Each fulfills the specific needs and desires of their clientele.

Once a design has been conceived and materials chosen, a designer prepares a sketch for approval. This gives both the client and the designer a chance to visualize the final product and to anticipate potential problems. For a two-dimensional design such as magazine layout, a designer can proceed directly from approved sketch to working art board. For designs of buildings and appliances, the next step is to construct a three-dimensional model to aid in visualization. Drafting is a step that is never bypassed because otherwise a designer might complete a project only to discover that the client does not like the concept. Designers often prepare their own drafts and models, but sometimes they delegate that responsibility to other workers, who prepare drafts both manually and with the aid of computers.

As mentioned before, design problems are not always apparent. Something that seems like it should work may not work after all, or at least not as well as it should. Trial and revision is the process of testing and correcting designs before putting them to their final use. This is easier in some instances than in others. It is simple enough to build one chair to make sure it can support a heavy adult before mass-producing hundreds of such chairs; it is less simple to test an architectural design by building a trial house. Therefore, each design discipline has its own systems for double-checking and fine-tuning designs. This first step in manufacturing operations is the last step in the design operations. Once a design is determined to be attractive, practical, and without any apparent flaws, the production of the object begins and the designer moves on to another project.

This ophthalmic device, the Coopervision Surgical Footswitch, controls surgical hand piece functions. It won the 1989 Industrial Design Excellence Award for Equipment from the Industrial Designers Society of America.

Careers

There are many different kinds of designers employed in many industries. These include:

Architects: Architects plan, design, and supervise the construction of all types of buildings (see Volume 2: Architects).

Civil engineers: Civil engineers design and supervise the construction of highways, airstrips, bridges, dams, buildings, and many other types of structures (see Volume 2: Engineers).

Landscape architects: Landscape architects plan outdoor areas for people to use, with a special emphasis toward protecting the natural environment. They make recommendations for new housing communities, commercial centers, parks and plazas, recreation facilities, parkways, and highways (see Volume 2: Landscape architects).

Commercial artists: Commercial artists create artwork to attract the attention of readers and viewers and stimulate their interest in products or ideas found in publications, television, or advertising. Commercial artists design everything from the cartoon characters that sell cereal on television to the book cover of a best selling novel (see Volume 2: Commercial artists).

Design

Fashion designers: Fashion designers create original designs for new types and styles of apparel. Fashion design is one of the few arenas where designers become celebrities in their own right. The names of fashion designers are included in the advertisements for their clothes. Christian Dior, Perry Ellis, and Coco Chanel all became so popular that their names continue to be marketed on a line of clothes even years after their deaths (see Volume 2: Fashion designers).

Industrial designers: Industrial designers combine technical knowledge of materials, machines, and production with artistic talent to improve the appearance and function of machine-made products (see Volume 2: Industrial designers).

Interior designers: Interior designers plan and organize the furnishings of residential, commercial, and industrial buildings. Interior designers rely on other designers to create the individual pieces of furniture, carpeting, and wall and window coverings, that they use in combination to create an attractive interior (see Volume 2: Interior designers).

Display workers: Display workers design and install displays of clothing, accessories, furniture, and other merchandise in windows, showcases, and on the sales floors of retail stores to attract the attention of prospective customers (see Volume 3: Display workers).

Miscellaneous designers: Miscellaneous designers include banknote designers, exhibit designers, floral designers, fur designers, furniture designers, memorial designers, ornamental-metalwork designers, package designers, stained-glass artists, and textile designers (see Volume 2: Designers).

Drafters: Drafters prepare clear, complete, and accurate working plans and detailed drawings from rough sketches, specifications, and calculations of engineers, architects, and designers (see Volume 2: Drafters).

Drafting and design technicians: Drafting and design technicians assist drafters and architects in the completion of design projects. Their responsibilities include handling specific details of a design element, such as stairs or windows. They may create final copies of blueprints from the architect's originals, or they may be asked to carry out some other implementation of the drafting process. For example, the technician may build a scale model of the building or park under construction to give the client a good visual idea of what is being recommended (see Volume 4: Drafting and design technicians).

CAD/CAM technicians: CAD/CAM technicians use computer-controlled systems to assist industrial designers and engineers in designing products and carry-out automated industrial processes. CAD is an abbreviation for "computer-aided design" or, less frequently, "computer-aided drafting." CAM is an abbreviation for "computer-aided manufacturing" (see Volume 4: CAD/CAM technicians).

Education

Educational requirements vary according to the area of interest. For example, floral designers may not need graduate college whereas a designer in the architectural field would need at least an undergraduate degree, with some course work in design and architecture.

In general, designers must be disciplined workers who pay close attention to detail. They should be creative, yet also be able to make sure their ideas are practical enough to help sell a product.

Industry outlook

Because design plays an integral part in so many different industries, there will always be a need for designers. However, non-corporate designers may find themselves vulnerable to recessions, when other businesses have to cut back on production.

◇ SOURCES OF ADDITIONAL INFORMATION

American Institute for Design and Drafting
966 Hungerford Drive, Suite 10-B
Rockville, MD 20854

American Institute of Graphic Arts
1059 Third Avenue
New York, NY 10021

Association of Professional Design Firms
621 West Randolph
Chicago, IL 60606

Center for Design Planning
1208 North McKinley Street
Albany, GA 31701

Design International
3748 22nd Street
San Francisco, CA 94114

Design Management Institute
777 Boylston Street
Boston, MA 02116

National Academy of Design
1083 Fifth Avenue
New York, NY 10128

American Society of Interior Designers
1430 Broadway
New York, NY 10018

◇ **RELATED ARTICLES**

Volume 1: Advertising; Engineering; Packaging
Volume 2: Architects; Commercial artists; Designers; Drafters; Engineers; Fashion designers; Industrial designers; Landscape architects
Volume 3: Display workers
Volume 4: CAD/CAM technicians; Drafting and design technicians

Education

General information

Millions of professional personnel are engaged in teaching or supporting activities in education. The teaching field covers a broad area of occupations: teachers in public and private elementary and secondary schools; school administrators, supervisors, consultants, researchers, and other specialists in elementary and secondary schools; professors and other personnel in colleges and universities; those involved in continuing education; and professional staff members in professional organizations, government offices of education, and private agencies with educational programs.

Teaching is in a state of revolution. The ferment of revolution comes from both the internal self-examinations of the profession and the critical opinion of those outside it. Widespread public discussion, for example, followed release of "A Nation at Risk" (1983), a report whose title suggests the deep concern of the National Commission on Excellence in Education, established in 1981 by T. H. Bell, U.S. Secretary of Education, to address "the widespread public perception that something is seriously remiss in our educational system." The commission found that the educational system falls far short of the goal of cultivating "the learning society" and made a series of recommendations for improvements.

In many ways, criticism has proven healthy. Standards for teaching, particularly in the elementary and secondary schools, have advanced dramatically.

The commitment and idealism of educators have been sobered by such problems as violence in urban schools, poorly motivated or disruptive students, and uninvolved or highly critical parents. Added to that has been uncertainty about continued employment as enrollments decline and budgets tighten, reducing the number of positions that the school can support. Many people still see the challenge and possible satisfaction of a teaching career, but they approach it with more skepticism, and they search for employment in more deliberate ways.

Despite its problems, teaching has a broad appeal and offers varied opportunities. It attracts people who have a keen interest in a particular subject area, a desire to work with young people, a commitment to social service, a wish for a life of scholarship and study, and a need for a secure professional career.

Many people see teaching as a way to preserve a humanistic spirit and to avoid the competition and authoritarianism that they attribute to the business world. But some would argue that these negative qualities of the working world are as prevalent in teaching as in other careers.

Some women have traditionally viewed teaching as a secure path toward independence. Others have seen it as a source of a second income for their families. The equal rights movement has significantly altered perspectives. Many women see teaching now less of a second income and more as a rewarding career.

Teaching has become popular as a second career. Women have entered teaching after raising a family or pursuing other career goals, and men have become teachers after successful careers or retirement from other vocations or professions.

The structure of education

The great majority of people involved in education are engaged in teaching, and most of the expenditure in education is for instruction. The diversity of teaching responsibilities is great in terms of the subjects, schedules, and assigned duties. For example, elementary school teachers typically work with one group of youngsters, while secondary school teachers (junior and senior high school), meet four, five, or more groups of youngsters each day.

Teachers of younger children perform many of the roles of a parent, so the job of the elementary school teacher includes the personal–social responsibilities that are assumed by parents outside of school. The job, of course, also includes the full gamut of responsibilities for the social, emotional, and intellectual growth of children. These responsibilities include the actual job of teaching, reading professional literature, selecting and arranging materials, planning appropriate procedures, observing, reading, and evaluating student achievement. Participation in conferences with parents, meetings with other teachers and administrators on problems of curriculum, instruction, and guidance, and overseeing other out-of-class activities are also part of the elementary teacher's job.

Increasingly, schools provide in-service education for teachers. Teacher centers, relatively new to American education, are among the agencies to which elementary teachers can turn for in-service education. Often, teacher centers can assist them on the job, rather than after hours in a distant lecture hall.

High-school teachers have similar basic responsibilities as elementary school teachers, but they act less as parent substitutes. Traditionally, their concerns are more academic. But even at the high-school level, the teacher will be concerned about more than the student's academic progress.

The college teacher shares with the high-school teacher the commitment to a specific field of knowledge, except that such commitment is more intense. Participation in the activities of a learned society or professional association is more clearly expected of college professors than of their counterparts in the lower schools. Increasingly, the professor is sought out as a consultant in business, government, and public service. It is not unusual for the college teacher to have temporary part- or full-time assignments to serve in a consultant or advisory capacity.

With the competition of many non-teaching attractions, college teachers may find difficulty in spending as much time as they would like in the classroom. As college professors become more specialized, they are more apt to be attracted to teaching graduate students. Professors in graduate schools spend more time in research activities and in a close working relationship with a small number of graduate students.

At all levels of the profession, American teachers are often better educated than they were a few years ago. All states require a bach-

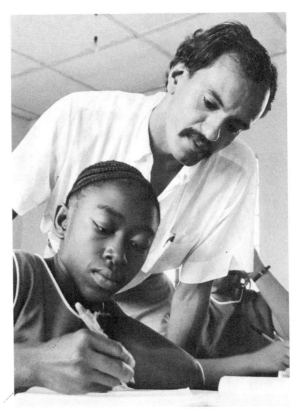

A high-school teacher helps a student with an algebra problem. He gives each student his undivided attention during independent work periods.

elor's degree for a beginning teacher, with many teachers having a graduate degree. Most teachers today are educated in the mainstream of higher education alongside students who are preparing for other positions that demand college degrees.

New developments in elementary and secondary schooling—such as team teaching and new staffing patterns—promise to alter present concepts of teaching. Plans for the future envisage compensating teachers in proportion to the responsibilities they assume; some teachers will make salaries that are equal to, or more than, the salaries earned by principals.

A variety of new teaching jobs will develop. Already there are many teaching jobs in non-school agencies such as recreation departments, drug and alcohol abuse programs, planned parenthood units, and others. Education has become much broader than school or college. Almost daily, new non-school positions that require teaching are being created.

As elementary and secondary school teaching evolves further, radical changes will probably occur, bringing more status and greater rewards to teachers. Changes can be expected in college teaching also. The campus turmoil of

A chemistry teacher prepares an experiment before the class begins. Much work goes into planning each classroom session.

vate agencies with educational programs, and government offices of education. Every state in the United States has an office of education, which monitors local educational policies and practices and makes recommendations or policy decisions for the schools in its state. Most of these workers are former teachers or persons trained as teachers.

The federal government also employs many professionals in education to ensure that any national legislative mandates from Congress are carried out at the state and local level. Federal education officials are concerned with such areas as bilingual education, busing, and school health.

Many professional positions in education that are outside the classroom require public school teaching experience. For example, there are hundreds of thousands of public school administrators, most, if not all, of whom have been teachers. Many professional association staff members, and educators in government offices of education began their careers as teachers. Most of these people have completed graduate study to qualify for these jobs, and in this respect they may be little different from the teacher who continues graduate study but chooses to remain in the classroom. The point is, however, that initial preparation for teaching can lead to numerous other positions, such as supervisors, guidance counselors, or administrators in schools. Most educational publishing houses prefer to hire textbook editors with teaching experience.

Most teachers belong to a professional union. Of those who do, a majority belong to the National Education Association and its state and local affiliates; a smaller number belong to the American Federation of Teachers. These professional organizations grew steadily after World War II. Most teachers also join other associations or learned societies that represent their own subject field or area of specialization. The activities of teachers to improve their professional circumstances have already resulted in reduced teaching loads, more time for planning and evaluating teaching, research in the public schools, written personnel policies, and budgets to permit teachers to attend professional meetings. These improvements are not widespread as yet, but they are gradually being accepted. Teachers have also effected changes in conditions of employment guaranteeing them due process, establishing grievance procedures, ensuring fair dismissal procedures, protecting their rights, and protecting their academic freedom.

A job description of teaching is easy to provide. More difficult is the task of conveying the essence of teaching, what teaching is all about,

the 1960s resulted in many concessions to students, including greater opportunity to choose their course work and a wider range of choices. Colleges later began to reconsider those concessions, asking what constitutes a liberal education and whether greater discipline should guide student choice. Some colleges placed more emphasis on core curricula that convey the elements of a liberal education. Reviews of curricula and programs with an eye toward suitability for the years to come promised change and exciting times ahead. Teaching could become a very different and more challenging profession.

The federal government has contributed to the improvements in the professional stature, performance, and conditions of public school teachers through such federal programs as the Trainers of Teacher Trainers, Urban/Rural School Development, the Education Professions Development Act, and the Teacher Corps. The government has also helped through such state programs as standards and licensure commissions, comprehensive plans for in-service education, and collective bargaining legislation.

Thousands of professional personnel are employed by professional organizations, pri-

As students display their works of art after completing an assignment, the teacher assesses the art and discusses the techniques involved. In such an unstructured environment, other students are welcome to contribute to the discussion.

how it feels to be a teacher. The latter is important to the person who is considering teaching as a career, to the teacher, and to others who should understand more than the superficial facts, legends, and folklore about what teaching is.

Bel Kaufman's fictional *Up the Down Staircase* presents a graphic picture of one high-school teaching situation in a large city. Nonfiction too can communicate the essence of teaching. *Teacher* by Sylvia Ashton-Warner describes the author's creative work with Maori children in her native New Zealand. *Conrack* portrays a young white male teacher's memorable sojourn with black youngsters on an island off the coast of South Carolina. *Teacher in America* by Jacques Barzun of Columbia University treats the life of a college teacher–scholar.

Careers

The teaching profession includes many different kinds of teachers and many supporting professional personnel who work with or supervise teachers. Many teachers work in elementary schools, secondary schools, or colleges and universities. Administration is another large category of personnel in education.

School principals, assistant principals, deans, and assistant deans total hundreds of thousands of persons, and they are often assisted by consultants and researchers. Elementary and secondary schools typically employ a number of supporting personnel—some on a part-time basis—such as physicians, nurses, audiologists, speech therapists, guidance counselors, athletic coaches, and band directors. A sample of education career opportunities follows below.

Kindergarten teachers: Kindergarten teachers use games, music, and artwork to teach basic skills to young children. They introduce children to numbers, language, and social studies, and play an important role in the development of their students.

Elementary school teachers: Elementary school teachers usually instruct one class of children in several subjects, such as mathematics and social studies. They are occupied directly with children for most of the school day, although they also prepare lessons, meet with parents, attend faculty meetings, and supervise activities after school.

Secondary school teachers: Secondary school teachers specialize in specific subjects, such as history, mathematics, or languages. They lecture and design classroom presentations to meet the needs of their students. Secondary school teachers also prepare tests, meet with parents, and supervise extracurricular activities. In addition to teaching responsibilities, these teachers also help students with other concerns as the students become young adults.

Elementary and secondary school teachers are only beginning to achieve the conditions and status of upper level educators. Compared with their college counterparts, elementary and secondary school teachers have considerably less control over their time, their schedules, even their physical whereabouts, and they participate less in decision making. They face behavior and discipline problems that college teachers do not, because their students are compelled to attend school whereas college students enroll voluntarily. They have less status and smaller rewards. And their sense of professional self is different—their first loyalties are usually to their students and their institution rather than to their field and their colleagues. But impressive progress in achieving a more professional climate and posture has been made.

College/university professor: The college teacher's responsibilities include teaching four or five classes or sections of students. Although in four-year colleges this may be the actual teaching load, in the university it often includes committee assignments, research, and other duties. College teachers are also expected to keep office hours for student conferences.

In addition to classroom responsibilities, college and particularly university teachers are expected to write scholarly articles and books, and do research.

In some fields, college teachers serve as consultants to agencies outside their employing institutions. Some confine their consulting to nearby agencies, others range more widely; some receive payment from the agency, others serve as part of a collaborative arrangement between their institution and the agency. Usually, college teachers are also members of one or more faculty committee. They are expected to do scholarly work in their teaching field, plus engage in individual study, attend conferences and scholarly meetings, and participate in the professional associations of their discipline or area of specialization. It is often inaccurate to say that the primary job of college teachers is teaching, even though it may be their most important responsibility. The college teacher is usually several of the following: teacher, author, researcher, student, consultant, and authority in a field.

Adult and vocational education teachers: Adult and vocational education teachers help prepare adults for specific careers or provide for personal enrichment. They may instruct adults in subjects such as computers or automotive me-

chanics, or early U.S. history or cooking. Adult and vocational education teachers may lecture in a classroom or conduct classes or in another location.

School administrators: School administrators supervise teachers and other personnel. They provide leadership and day-to-day management of different types of education facilities, such as religious schools, elementary and secondary schools, technical schools, and colleges and universities. This group of professionals includes principals, assistant principals, college deans, provosts, and directors of student activities.

Education

All states require a bachelor's degree, including appropriate work in education, to begin teaching in elementary or secondary schools. Requirements for specialization in a teaching field vary greatly from subject to subject, from state to state, and from institution to institution.

Precise specification of time to be spent in the three major aspects of teacher education (general education, specialization in a field, and professional education) often vary from student to student. In general, a reasonable balance in a teacher education program is 40 to 50 percent for general education, 30 to 40 percent in a field of specialization, and 15 to 25 percent in professional education. The purpose of the three-part program in teacher education is to assure that teachers are well educated in the general or liberal sense, adequately prepared in depth in a major area, knowledgeable and skillful in procedures of teaching, and aware of the importance and place of the school in society.

Concentration in a major area or teaching field varies for elementary and secondary school teachers. Typically, prospective secondary school teachers have major and minor teaching fields—the subjects they will teach. The prospective elementary school teacher is expected to teach many subjects and thus is expected to have general knowledge in many areas as well as in-depth knowledge in one or two. Some states and colleges require a major for elementary school teachers. Some recommend a major similar to that expected of other liberal arts students. Others suggest an area of concentration, such as social sciences, humanities, arts, or the sciences.

Student teaching and other field experience are an important part of a teacher education program. A small percentage of teachers are prepared by way of the liberal arts degree plus an internship, with appropriate work in professional education (the fifth year of master of arts in teaching).

Student teaching and internships are widely recognized as important aspects of teacher education programs because they bring the new teacher in direct contact, under supervision, with the complex problems of teaching. The prospect of increased attention to quality field experience is a promising development.

In all states, minimum requirements for teacher education are set by the state department of education. If a college is approved by the state department, it determines its own requirements for prospective teachers. As a rule, college-imposed requirements are greater than the minimums set by the state. Under this system, which is called an "approved program approach," colleges recommend their graduates to the state licensing or certification agency for a teaching certificate. Under almost all circumstances, graduates recommended by a college are granted a certificate.

College and university teachers rank among the nation's most highly educated citizens; the vast majority of full-time teaching faculty have earned a doctorate degree. College teachers are usually required to have at least a master's degree. A Ph.D. is almost always an essential degree for a college teacher who hopes to reach the rank of full professor.

Many college teachers acquire teaching experience as graduate students while they are completing their degree programs. These teaching sessions help pay for a graduate student's education while he or she works on a dissertation. It takes some students up to eight or ten years to complete a dissertation, though the average span of time is four or five years. Some may teach at the high-school level while they study for a Ph.D., and still others return for graduate study after a period of work in an occupation or profession following college graduation.

College teaching often does not occur to an individual as a career until the possibility is opened by work experience. Many college teachers enter the profession after successful careers in business or government work. Some college professors continue to work in another profession during the day, and teach in the evenings.

Many education administrators begin their careers as teachers. In almost all cases, they have graduate degrees in education and many years of teaching experience. College and university administrators usually have doctorate degrees, and increasingly elementary and secondary school administrators, especially those working in large school districts, also have doctorate degrees.

A special education teacher carefully guides a student through a speech exercise.

Industry outlook

A shortage of elementary and secondary school teachers that grew more critical over a twenty-year duration turned into a surplus in the 1970s and first half of the 1980s. The chief cause of the surplus was a decline in school enrollment as the large number of babies born shortly after World War II reached adolescence and then maturity. Another cause was hard economic times, which diminished the number of jobs available outside teaching and at higher levels within teaching, and hence reduced teacher turnover.

By the mid-1980s, prospects for elementary school teachers' employment had changed. The job market was expected to improve, in part because of rising enrollments and in part because of job openings caused by teachers leaving the profession. School enrollments by 1995 were projected to increase to more than 32 million (compared with about 27.2 million in the mid-1980s), reflecting a rise in the elementary-school-age population.

Salaries of elementary and secondary teachers vary, chiefly according to education, experience, geographic region, size of system, and grade level. As a general rule, high school teachers within a district are paid slightly more than elementary school teachers in the same area. Salaries are often paid on a twelve-month basis for nine or ten months' work. Thus there is the potential for additional earnings during the summer. There is also the potential for extra school work. About half of all elementary and secondary teachers have additional income from such sources.

147

Nine out of ten of the approximately one million U.S. secondary school teachers taught in public schools. A decline in job opportunities was foreseen until the early 1990s. By 1995, employment was expected to be slightly higher because of population trends and lower pupil-teacher ratios. Most job openings will result from teachers leaving the profession.

Continued competition for government and private industry for science, mathematics, and computer specialists indicate that persons qualified to teach in those fields would remain much in demand.

Employment for college teachers is available in a number of kinds of colleges. The typical breakdown of types of institutions includes universities, liberal arts colleges, state colleges, teachers colleges, and junior or community colleges. The openings for college teachers in the late-1980s were limited, and the number was likely to decline through the mid-1990s with a decreasing college-age population. Many of the science-related and technical fields of study are dependent upon government funds. Given the current political turmoil and changes of the 1990s, it is unclear how much money the government will supply to universities for defense research.

The supply of prospective college teachers, on the other hand, was more than adequate. In most fields, there were far more doctorates than suitable positions available. Demand was greater in two-year colleges, which increased their enrollment substantially, but that demand reached a plateau.

Employment opportunities for school administrators will vary according to the area of specialization. Those involved with primary and secondary schools should have increased job opportunities as the population of young people continues to grow. Those involved with higher education can expect to find stiff competition through the 1990s for the small number of jobs available.

◇ **SOURCES OF ADDITIONAL INFORMATION**

National Association of Professional Educators
412 First Street, SE
Washington, DC 20003

National Council for the Accreditation of Teacher Education
1919 Pennsylvania Avenue, NW, Suite 202
Washington, DC 20006

American Federation of Teachers
555 New Jersey Avenue, NW
Washington, DC 20001

National Education Association
1201 16th Street, NW
Washington, DC 20036

◇ **RELATED ARTICLES**

Electronics

General information

The electronics industry is composed of industrial organizations that are involved in the manufacture, design and development, assembly, and servicing of electronic equipment and components. The electronics industry offers a wide variety of products, which frequently have only one thing in common—their dependence on electronic technology for operation. Great importance is placed on the research and development of new products, and the industry offers good employment opportunities for scientists, engineers, technicians, and skilled craft workers.

Electronics is the branch of science and technology that deals with the study, application, and control of the phenomena of conduction of electricity in a vacuum, in gases, in liquids, in semiconductors, and in conducting and superconducting materials. Such a variety of outlets for electricity allows for thousands of electronic products with countless applications.

Electronic products consist of materials, parts, components, subassemblies, and equipment that employ the principles of electronics in performing their major functions. These products may be used as instruments and controls in communication, inspection, detection, amplification, computation, testing, measurement, operation, recording, analysis, and other functions employing electronic principles.

The electronic industries emerged from the radio industry of the early 1920s. Until World War II, their chief output was radio receivers and broadcasting equipment. The war revealed many new applications of electronics to modern warfare and suggested many more. Consequently, when the United States began to rearm during the wars in Korea and Vietnam, the military services turned first and foremost to the electronics industry. Electronic instruments were used to guide unmanned missiles and control the flights of spacecraft. Other devices made it possible to communicate over vast distances, often by satellite. Electronic devices directed, controlled, and tested production processes in the steel and chemical industries. In homes, television and radio receivers provided information and entertainment.

New uses for electronics in industry and commerce, especially uses associated with the computer, also served to stimulate the industry's rapid growth. The first computers were gigantic in size and very expensive. Only the federal government and giant industries could afford them. Today, they are being installed in increasing numbers in department stores, banks, and even in many homes.

Total U.S. shipments of electronic equipment, components, and systems grew steadily in the 1970s and early 1980s, totaling many billions of dollars in sales. Exports comprise about 25 percent of the electronic industries' business.

Today, electronics manufacturing is national in scope, with plants in all parts of the United States. However, there are heavy concentrations of manufacturing plants along the Atlantic Coast from Baltimore northward, in the Midwest centering around Chicago, and on the Pacific Coast, with the greatest production center in southern California. In recent years new plants have been established in many other areas, particularly in the vicinity of defense or space installations, and in the South.

Few industries offer the exciting opportunities and the intellectual challenges that may be found in electronics manufacturing and associated service operations. New applications are being discovered in such areas as space exploration, national defense, and industrial and commercial automation. In addition, electronic devices are being developed for home-use.

As society becomes increasingly automated at home and at work, the electronics industry will continue to be a promising field of employment.

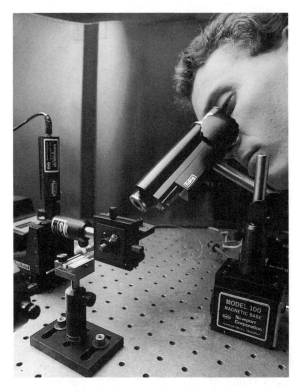

An electrical engineer analyzes the power in the cavity of a one-millimeter glass fiber by aligning it with a thinner fiber that is the size of a human hair.

The structure of the electronics industry

Industrial and communications products together account for over two-thirds of total electronic sales. Industrial products include computers, testing and measuring instruments, industrial control and processing equipment, electronic instruments for nuclear work, and radiation detection devices.

Communications products include television and radio broadcasting equipment, microwave devices, navigational instruments, and television systems. Also included in this category are electronic systems that are vital parts of missiles, spacecraft, aircraft, tanks, ships, and other items used in national defense and space programs. Representative examples of these include guidance and checkout systems; ground, tracking, and support equipment; radar, sonar, infrared, and other detection systems and devices; and different types of high-speed communication equipment.

Consumer products include some of the most familiar kinds of electronic equipment and also some of the newest. Examples are television and radio sets; phonographs and stereo sound equipment; tape recorders; electronic ov-

ens; home intercommunication systems; video recorders and players; and video games.

Electronic components are usually classified in three broad groups: electron tubes, semiconductors, and passive components. Tubes include receiving, television picture, and various power and special-purpose tubes. Principal semiconductor devices are transistors, diodes, and rectifiers. Passive components include capacitors, resistors, transformers, relays, connectors, and switches.

Because of its dependence on technology and the need to keep abreast of technical progress, electronics manufacturing provides a large number of opportunities for engineers and scientists. However, the proportion varies widely within the industry. Manufacturers heavily involved in defense and space programs or in developing industrial markets employ the greatest share of engineers, while producers of established consumer goods employ the fewest.

Probably no other major industry offers a greater opportunity for engineers to move into management positions. In fact, many engineers have become presidents of companies in which they worked as engineers. Substantial technical knowledge is necessary in the management of most electronic manufacturing companies, and the engineer has become an essential member of the management team.

Some engineers find their way profitably into sales or marketing jobs because many complex electronic products can be sold only by a salesperson who understands and can demonstrate the products. Today, the engineer is the indispensable partner in electronics manufacturing.

New electronic products and devices combining the functions of older components are constantly being developed. For example, an amplifier that used to require about a square foot of space can now be made no larger than a dime. Manufacturers who fail to anticipate these changes and do not adapt their products to the changing markets usually lose out to more alert competitors.

Sales and marketing of electronic equipment requires an exceptionally high level of competence, and manufacturers provide intensive training programs for persons who qualify. Whereas a generation ago an electronics sales manager frequently relied on instincts, observations, and sales ability, the marketing of complex electronic equipment nowadays depends on accurate and timely statistical data.

The principal unions involved in electronics manufacturing are the International Union of Electrical, Radio and Machine Workers; International Brotherhood of Electrical Workers; International Association of Machinists and Aerospace Workers; and the United Electrical, Radio and Machine Workers of America.

Careers

Electronics manufacturing plants provide a wide variety of occupations, requiring a broad range of training and skills. About three out of five employees are plant workers engaged in production, maintenance, transportation, and service. The others are either highly skilled professionals such as engineers, scientists, and technicians, or in administrative, sales, and clerical jobs.

While there are numerous job opportunities in electronics manufacturing, the most attractive careers fall into three categories: engineers and scientists; technicians; and marketing and sales workers. There are, of course, also the usual opportunities found in any manufacturing industry for administrative personnel, managers, and executives. A sampling of career opportunities follows below.

Electronics engineers: The largest group of engineers employed in electronics manufacturing are electrical or electronics engineers. Electronics engineers may work on a highly sensitive instrument designed to land a spacecraft on the moon or send signals back to earth from one of the planets. They may also be engaged in work on radio or television receivers, mobile communications equipment, or a variety of new component designs such as those found in microminiaturized devices.

Electronics engineers are specialists in given areas of knowledge and training. These specialties include radar engineers, airborne electronics engineers, data systems engineers, or systems engineers.

Mechanical engineers: Mechanical engineers often work as design engineers in developing tools, equipment, or other products.

Industrial engineers: Industrial engineers work chiefly in the production of electronic equipment, but also are concerned with plant efficiency and operating methods.

Scientists: Scientists are members of the engineering team, but their chief concern is usually research and development work in connection with such products as microwave tubes or microelectronic components and circuits. Often they are managers of research programs. Most of the scientists in electronics manufacturing are physicists, although many are chemists and metallurgists.

Electronic technicians, along with scientists and engineers, are advancing the frontiers of future technology, and their importance and

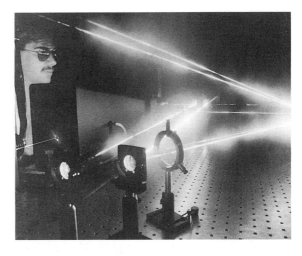

An engineer operates an electro-optics system that he devised for the U.S. Army. The system is designed to help tank crews identify enemy tanks.

recognition is continually growing. Technicians who work with engineers and physical scientists are among the fastest growing occupational groups in the United States.

The technicians listed below illustrate the varied, interesting, and challenging work of technicians in electronics manufacturing.

Electronics technicians: Electronic technicians are part engineer, part artisan. They must be able to use both theoretical knowledge and manual skills, working with engineers at times and with skilled craft workers at others. In short, they help to change ideas into accomplishments. Technicians may make suggestions for improvement in design of the device, adjusting or modifying it as required to produce a practical operation capability. They may also have to construct, install, modify, and troubleshoot laboratory test equipment. Laboratory technicians may work under a minimum of supervision, and may direct other personnel. They are, in fact, assistant engineers.

Laboratory assistants: Laboratory assistants (or laboratory technicians) are at the highest level among electronic technicians. They assist design and development engineers (or scientists) by wiring and testing engineering models of electronic devices conceived by the engineers. To do so, they perform mechanical and assembly work, using hand tools and light machine tools; make complex parts, components, or subassemblies; and conduct physical and electrical tests (such as humidity, temperature, vibration, and life test), using complicated instruments and test equipment.

Quality control technicians: Quality control technicians help ensure the quality of the electronics product. They compare the wiring and

A scientist controls a hard-wired reliability safety system for the TREAT reactor at the Argonne National Laboratory.

assembly details and general quality of sample products from the assembly line to ensure compliance with specification requirements. They determine the causes for rejection of parts or equipment by assembly line inspectors and analyze field and manufacturing reports to ascertain cause of failure. They make specific recommendations and submit reports to their supervisor and may even suggest design, manufacturing, and process changes. Their job, in short, is that of detective and constructive critic; they are the watchdogs of the company's quality control.

Electronic drafters: Electronic drafters must have technical knowledge. They must understand technical language and the "how" and "why" of electronic circuits to convert rough sketches and written or verbal information into easily understandable schematic, layout, and wiring diagrams. Usually, they also prepare lists of parts and bills of material of the component parts of the equipment. They prepare "road maps" by which the manufacturing department can make the ideas of the engineers available for use by customers.

Technical writer-editors: Technical writer-editors are technicians who compile, write, and edit a wide variety of technical information. This includes instructional leaflets, operating manuals, books, and installation and service manuals having to do with the products of the company. To do this, they must confer with design and development engineers, production personnel, salespeople, drafters, and others to obtain the necessary information to prepare the text, drawings, diagrams, parts, lists, and illustrations. They must understand thoroughly how and why the equipment works to be able to tell the customer how to use it and the service technician how to install and service it.

Cost estimators: Cost estimators are required to prepare estimates of the cost of manufacturing a new product with sufficient accuracy to allow the sales department to determine in advance of manufacture the price at which it can be sold. After the engineers have prepared drawings, engineering specifications, an engineering model, and other information on the new product, cost estimators will use this engineering data to estimate all labor and material costs involved in assembling the product. They then lay out the assembly processes, plan the type of tools required and the cost of such tools, and determine whether the component parts and tubes, transistors, or microprocessors should be manufactured or purchased. They may even find it advisable to review the design with the engineering department and suggest changes to lower costs or facilitate manufacture.

There are also equally challenging and rewarding electronic technician occupations outside the factory—in the "field" (but closely allied to electronics manufacturing). Typical examples include:

Broadcast technicians: The glamour and excitement associated with radio and television make careers in broadcasting attractive to many. The basic job in the engineering department of stations is that of the broadcast technician. These technicians control the operation of the transmitter to keep the output level and frequency of the outgoing broadcast within legal requirements. They also set up, operate, and maintain equipment in the studio and in locations from which remote broadcasts are to be made. In addition to thorough technical training in communication electronics, the broadcast technician must have a license from the Federal Communications Commission.

Instrumentation technicians: During the past twenty-five years, the field of industrial instrumentation, machine controls, and processing (automation) has expanded at a fantastic rate. This field includes such equipment as electrical and electronic recorders and controllers, electrical and electronic test equipment, electronic sensing elements and transducers, and electronic computers used in automation. Instrumentation technicians are engaged in the design, installation, operation, maintenance, and repair of instrumentation and automatic control systems. They are employed in many industries such as aeronautical, chemical, petroleum, food, paper and pulp, electric power, and textiles. The increasing number and complexity of electronic instruments and automation equipment require great numbers of instrumentation technicians to install and keep them operating efficiently.

Programmers: Every problem that is processed in a computer must first be carefully analyzed so that plans can be made for processing the data in the most efficient manner. Once the general plans have been completed, the programmer prepares a detailed plan for processing the data on the computer.

The exact plan depends on the kind of computer used and the nature of the problem being programmed. The calculations involved in preparing a payroll, for example, are very different from those required in scientific and engineering work, and the programming techniques are also very different. In any case, after preparing the plan, the programmer makes a flow chart showing the order in which the computer must perform each operation. For each operation, detailed instructions or routines are prepared. These routines are transferred into a sort of code to which the computer can respond. The final step is to check on whether the instructions have been correctly written and will produce the desired information. The programmer must be a combination of mathematician, analyst, and technician who understands not only the computer but also the scientific or business problems that need to be handled on the computer.

Television and radio service technicians: These skilled workers use their knowledge of electrical and electronic circuits to install and repair a growing number of electronic products. Of these, television receivers are by far the most prominent. Other major electronics entertainment and home products are radios, phonographs, high fidelity sound equipment, tape recorders, and video recorders (see Volume 1: Broadcasting).

Service technicians: Most of the skilled work done by service technicians involves diagnosing troubles in equipment and making necessary repairs and adjustments. They use complicated electronic test equipment, tracing the flow of the electronic impulses and electricity through wires, or transistors, and other parts. Service technicians must also be adept in the use of small tools and basic mechanical skills. Much time is spent talking with customers, particularly in their homes, where most servicing is done.

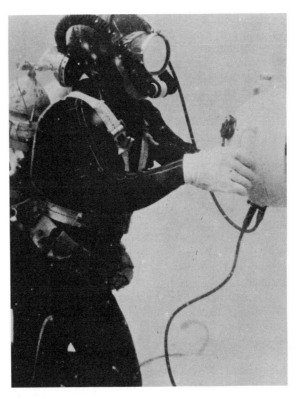

An electronics engineer conducts sonar equipment tests under water.

Marketing workers: Manufacturers in recent years have relied heavily on marketing workers, who are a combination salesperson, product planner, and market research specialist. The work is more creative than that of a salesperson. The primary functions are to uncover and create new products and markets for the company.

Marketing managers: The marketing manager can both point to the opportunities for new markets and warn the manufacturer of probable changes in existing markets.

Statisticians and economists: Behind the marketing manager is usually a staff of statisticians and economists whose responsibility it is to chart trends in sales and production.

Education

There are many effective things you can do while still in high school to prepare for a career in electronics. You can learn to develop orderly study habits and the ability to express yourself effectively. These qualities are important for progress in electronics.

Build up your reading skills. Learn as much as you can about use of the English language and how to use it logically in the solution and explanation of problems. Go heavily into mathematics and science. Courses in physics, chemistry, algebra (a "must"), geometry, and trigonometry are most important. Drafting and shop courses are good preparation for a precision assembler or technician. Understanding technical drawings, knowing how to use your hands, and acquiring experience with machine tools will prove invaluable in such a career.

Join your school science or computer club. Participate in science fairs. Get interested in electronics kit-building (a vast variety of low-cost project kits are available). Collect tools, books, electronic components, and instruments and work with them to acquire an understanding of basic electronics theory. Consider becoming an amateur radio operator. It is a rewarding hobby and a good way to prepare for a career in electronics.

Educational and training requirements for positions in electronics manufacturing vary widely from high-school or vocational school degrees to doctorate degrees. Scientists and engineers require the most formal education and most have advanced degrees. A few workers are able to reach professional engineering classifications by taking advanced electronic courses in night school or in plant training programs, but they seldom qualify for the higher professional positions.

Many of the marketing specialists have college degrees, often in economics. Management executives generally are also graduates of college or business schools, and many take periodic training courses.

Technicians generally require specialized training to qualify for their jobs. They should have a high-school or vocational school diploma and at least two years of post–high-school training, or equivalent apprenticeship training. Study should be concentrated on mathematics, English, electronics theory, physical sciences, and related laboratory experiments. There is no quick and easy method for obtaining the necessary background knowledge and experience in mathematics and electronics theory to reach the higher grades of electronic technicians.

Technical writers must have a flair for writing and enough technical training to be able to understand and interpret complicated engineering or scientific documents. Some have engineering degrees, and others have degrees in English composition and journalism and have obtained their technical training and knowledge on the job.

Manufacturers heavily involved in military and space contracts not only require high-grade engineers of special skills but often provide training facilities to train them for completely new responsibilities. For exceptional or promising engineers, manufacturers sometimes finance graduate studies so workers can improve their knowledge and skills.

Industry outlook

More than one million Americans were employed in electronics manufacturing in the late 1980s. Employment in U.S. electronics industries grew steadily in the late 1980s, especially compared to the growth rate for overall U.S. nonagricultural employment.

A large share of the available openings were professional, chiefly in the engineering and scientific field. However, there were many career opportunities in marketing, sales, and management as well, and many more openings for skilled technicians who provide the necessary support for the creative engineer. Thousands of additional jobs were available in the electronics servicing area. In addition, thousands of electronics workers were employed by the federal government in activities such as research, development, and the negotiation and administration of contracts. A relatively small number of electronics workers were employed by colleges, universities, and nonprofit research centers.

In the mid-1980s, despite a strong U.S. economy, the electronic components industry suffered a sharp downturn. Intense foreign competition and offshore operations by American companies contributed to a trade deficit. But high levels of research and development and of capital expenditures were sustained in the late 1980s. Economic recovery is anticipated in the 1990s. Automated production will be increasingly seen in the industry.

Electronics manufacturing probably has created more jobs outside production plants if one takes into account such activities as television broadcasting, equipment servicing, merchandising, and operation of countless electronic devices. For these reasons, the electronics industry still offers promising employment opportunities.

◇ **SOURCES OF ADDITIONAL INFORMATION**

Electronic Industries Association
1722 I Street, NW, Suite 300
Washington, DC 20006

Institute of Electrical and Electronics Engineers Board
345 East 47th Street
New York, NY 10017

International Society of Certified Electronics Technicians
2708 West Berry
Suite 3
Ft. Worth, TX 76109

JETS, Inc. (Junior Engineering Technical Society)
1420 King Street
Suite 405
Alexandria, VA 22314

American Electronics Association
5201 Great America Parkway
Suite 520
Santa Clara, CA 95054

National Electronic Sales and Service Dealers Association
2708 West Berry Street
Ft. Worth, TX 76109

◇ **RELATED ARTICLES**

Volume 1: Engineering; Mathematics; Physical Sciences
Volume 2: Chemists; Computer programmers; Drafters; Engineers; Industrial designers; Marketing research personnel; Physicists; Systems analysts; Writers and editors
Volume 3: Assemblers; Communications equipment mechanics; Computer and peripheral equipment operators; Electricians; Instrument makers; Instrument repairers; Manufacturers' sales workers
Volume 4: Avionics technicians; Biomedical equipment technicians; Computer-service technicians; Drafting and design technicians; Electroencephalographic technicians; Electronic organ technicians; Electronics sales and service technicians; Electronics technicians; Electronics test technicians; Instrumentation technicians; Laboratory technicians; Nuclear instrumentation technicians; Quality-control technicians; Semiconductor-development technicians; Software technicians; Telecommunications technicians; Video technicians

Energy

General information

Throughout history, various sources of energy has been used to power industrial development and provide humans with the energy they need in other areas. The source of energy was fire for most of the history of modern man. Wood, charcoal, then coal were the main sources of fuel for fire. As people developed more scientific knowledge on fuels and energy, they developed the ability to manufacture, store, and utilize fuels as needed.

The first gas company was founded in Britain in 1812. The first gas company in the United States was developed in Baltimore in 1817. When the oil rush started in 1859, the development of natural gas stopped. Another barrier to the natural gas industry came with the development of the electric light. Gas lights had been more effective and easier than kerosene, but electric lighting was far more popular. Cooking gas was the one area where popularity increased over the early years of the industry.

When huge reserves of natural gas were discovered in the southwest in the early 1900s, the production of natural gas increased to 800 billion cubic feet a year. Further increases in the quantity of natural gas produced were dependent on the development of pipelines that could carry the gas to potential market areas.

Production of natural gas reached a plateau by the mid-1980s at almost eighteen quadrillion BTUs (British thermal units); production totaled more than sixteen quadrillion BTUs in 1987.

While the natural gas industry continued to change, other energy sources were also being developed. When the internal combustion engine was patented in 1838, the beginning had been set for gasoline to come into use as a fuel.

Jean Joseph Etienne Lenoir built a single cylinder engine in 1860, which, by 1865, had 400 copies in use in Paris for such machines as printing presses and water pumps. German inventors developed the two- and four-cylinder combustion engine that would be used to burn gasoline and power moving vehicles.

With the development of the automobile, the demand for gasoline grew dramatically as the popularity of the auto increased. World War II increased the demand and the development of petroleum products. Fuel for tanks, ships and other wartime vehicles allowed the industry to develop a large quantity of oil wells across the country. After the war, the surplus was used in development of gas powered farm vehicles and machinery. Refineries also developed petroleum products that would be used for synthetic rubber, medicinal oils, and explosives.

In the early 1950s, petroleum became the largest energy source in the United States. Coal had been the largest until then, but it would begin a decline that only began to reverse itself in the mid-1960s.

In the 1970s, the Middle Eastern countries began to export huge quantities of oil to the developed nations. Demand for oil had increased to the point where western nations could not meet their own needs for oil. They had to import the oil from outside nations. When the Middle Eastern countries were able to control the quantity and the price of the oil being sold, the countries formed a cartel, the Organization of Petroleum Exporting Countries (OPEC), which became one of the major influences on world economy.

To combat the influence of OPEC, Great Britain, the United States, and other oil producing countries, increased domestic production in order to reduce the percentage of oil the world depended on from the OPEC nations. The increased production forced OPEC to reduce prices and broke the control that OPEC had held.

Because of the continual increase in demand for petroleum, extensive developments of new drilling areas and increasing the speed and quantity shipped from existing oil fields be-

Offshore drilling rigs are becoming increasingly popular as a cost-effective means of obtaining petroleum. At present, they supply over 20 percent of the oil produced in the world. They are located primarily along the coast of the North Sea and the Arctic Ocean.

came the primary goal of the industry. In the 1950s, plans called for extension of the U.S. pipeline system to link Alaska with the lower 48 states through a new 5,000-mile pipeline from the fuel-rich North Slope to the West Coast and the Great Lakes regions. The pipeline would be the largest single construction project ever undertaken by private industry and would provide a large source of oil and natural gas to the United States.

The structure of the energy industry

The U.S. energy industry comprises thousands of companies engaged in one or more of the five principal categories: exploration, production, refining, transportation, and marketing. Companies that are active in all five are known as "integrated" companies.

Practically every field of science and engineering is used somewhere in the oil industry. Among the key employees are geologists, geophysicists, petroleum engineers, chemists, and chemical engineers. Together, these highly skilled men and women carry much of the responsibility for finding oil, producing it, processing it in the refinery, and doing petroleum research.

Mineralogists and paleontologists who study fossil remains in the earth as a clue to oil-bearing sands are among the scientists who do exploration research. As one expert has said: "In an area where oil has not yet been found but which is believed to hold oil, the chances of striking any oil when a well is drilled average one in nine; the other eight are only dry holes." Only one in 144 wells drilled in new fields finds commercially significant quantities of oil and natural gas.

Geologists use a variety of sources to help find petroleum. A geologist will, for instance, use background information on the previous uses of land to hunt for signs of certain kinds of underground rock formations in which research has shown oil is most likely to collect. For example, oil may be found where layers of certain kinds of rocks have slipped or tilted in a particular way, or where the layers have been pushed up to form a kind of underground "dome." Sometimes geologists can find places

157

An industrial engineer checks the equipment at an oil refinery. He must make sure that all stations are running smoothly.

where the tilted layers stick out of the earth. They frequently drill holes to get core samples of the underground layers.

Geophysicists rely on another important type of exploration method. Geophysicists work with tools, such as the gravimeter, the magnetometer, and the seismograph that use the principles of physics. With these instruments, underground rock formations can be charted, and the geophysicist can also calculate the composition, depth, thickness, and slope of the rock structures underground. In the past, these calculations were arrived at through use of explosives, set off at several different points.

Later developments in seismic land surveys include the use of vibratory or percussion devices that do away with the drilling of holes and the use of explosives. With vibratory devices, the geophysicist can get accurate information and minimize environmental damage. In water, these devices send out pulses in the form of electrical discharges or contained explosions of propane gas or air so that there will be no harm to marine animal life.

When the geologist and the geophysicist have turned in their reports and recommendations, the company makes the decision whether to drill. Petroleum and natural gas are often found in the same fields. Because of this, the petroleum engineer takes over at this point in the exploration of the area, recommending the type of derrick and drilling equipment to be used and supervising the work of drilling. If the well strikes oil, a petroleum engineer oversees its production.

The petroleum engineer must be an expert on conservation. The primary goal is not the immediate production of large quantities of oil. Rather, the goal is to recover the greatest total amount of oil over a long period of time. With careful management, wells may still produce oil after more than thirty years of operation.

Petroleum exploration involves the out-of-doors to a large degree. The geologist, geophysicist, surveyor, and other members of exploration parties do most of their work out-of-doors. So do some teams carrying out exploration research. On a field trip, they may be away from home several weeks or months, living in a trailer or camping out in the woods. Petroleum engineers also spend most of their time out-of-doors, although some of their work is done in an office, particularly if they are supervising the production of oil in one or more fields. Usually, they do much less traveling than the geologists, and sometimes they stay in one area for several years.

Preparing the site for drilling is an important part of the oil-production process. Rig builders put up the tall, open towers called rigs or derricks. Drillers bore holes in the ground, often two or three miles deep, and then they bring up new oil or gas.

The rig houses the hoisting equipment that lifts and lowers the heavy tools, pipe, and casing that are used in drilling a well. Many rigs are portable, so they can be moved more easily from one drilling site to another. For deep drilling, a permanent rig is usually built. It is made of structural steel parts fastened together.

The rig-builder supervisor directs work on the rig. Crews vary in size according to the job. A small rig may require only three or four workers, whereas a rig for a large drilling project may need twenty-five workers.

Most wells are drilled by the rotary method. The rotary drilling crew bores a hole in the ground, much as a hole is bored in a wooden plank. They use a steel bit with sharp teeth, called the drill stem. Power applied to the drill stem at the surface of the well rotates the bit and its teeth, chewing a hole down through the earth's layers. As the hole is bored deeper, new pipe lengths are put on at the top.

A typical rotary drilling crew consists of a rotary driller and four or five helpers, often called "roughnecks." An engine operator runs the engine that keeps the pipe and bit rotating. A derrick operator works on a platform high up on the rig and is busiest when a drilling bit grows dull and must be replaced. Then the whole string of pipe has to be pulled up out of the hole. As each pipe section comes up, the roughnecks disconnect it; the derrick operator snares the upper end and pulls the pipe over to a rack beside the platform. Several miles of pipe are often racked up in the derrick before the worn bit is brought to the surface.

An average-sized rig-building or drilling job has another group of workers called "roust-abouts." They clean the derrick floor, clean pipe, and help in other ways.

Offshore, where there is an increasing amount of petroleum industry activity, well-trained and experienced divers handle much of the work that must be done. In exploration work, they frequently dive for observation purposes or to retrieve lost cables or other equipment. Divers also do underwater construction work, put up platforms, and complete underwater pipelines. Such divers must be skilled in welding, cutting, pile driving, and riveting.

A variety of other skilled workers are also needed at drilling sites. For example, the tractor driver operates the tractor, rooting out tree stumps, leveling the ground, and preparing a rough path. The ditching-machine operator cuts a trench through the earth for the pipeline. The spacer sees that the pipe lengths are spaced end to end with precision, so they can be joined together by the welder. If the pipe has not already been coated at the mill with material to limit corrosion, a crew applies it on the job.

More than half of all refinery workers are maintenance workers. Their job is to keep the complex equipment running smoothly. Maintenance workers are also employed in exploration, production, transportation, and even in marketing, where they repair service station gasoline pumps, home oil burners, and other types of mechanical equipment.

Refining occurs when crude oil is heated in a fractionating tower at the refinery. The lightest elements of the oil, gases and gasoline fractions, vaporize first and are carried off at the top of the tower. Other fractions such as those of kerosene and lubricating oil are separated from the crude oil and drawn off through pipes farther down in the column. In later, more complex refining operations, these various fractions are processed into such products as gasoline, kerosene, jet fuels, diesel oil, home heating oil, motor oil and other lubricants, waxes, asphalt, and basic ingredients for thousands of petrochemicals.

In the oil field, almost all the work in mechanical trades is out-of-doors. Since drilling goes on around the clock, drillers work in three shifts, with three complete crews. Most oil

An inorganic chemist uses sophisticated equipment to devise new ways of removing sulfur and nitrogen from heavy crude oil.

fields are in isolated regions, and crews live in quarters furnished by the company.

Oil wells, pipelines, and refineries are in operation twenty-four hours a day, seven days a week. Control workers are usually assigned on a rotating basis to one of three shifts, and they take their turn on weekends and holidays.

Transportation of crude oil and refined products is carried out by pipeline, barge and ship, railroad tank car, and highway tank truck. Most of the crude oil and oil products move through a great network of pipelines totaling about 174,000 miles.

Tank-truck drivers deliver oil products to service stations and other outlets, to dealers and homes, to farms and factories, and to airlines and surface transportation companies. Drivers of trailer trucks haul gasoline and other products from refineries to distributing points, particularly in regions not served by pipelines.

Marketing is the sale and distribution of petroleum products. The largest portion of these products is sold through more than 135,000 service stations in the country. Thousands of other outlets, such as garages, auto repair shops, and parking lots, also sell gasoline and lubricants. Large volumes of these and other products are sold directly to trucking fleets, air-

Roughnecks on an offshore drilling rig pull up a rotary drill in order to replace the bit. The drill may be over a mile long.

line companies, bus lines, federal, state, and municipal governments, public utilities, steamship companies, and other large users.

Although much of the gas energy that is needed will come from domestic natural gas wells, gas production has been bolstered by pipeline imports from Canada, by domestic production of synthetic natural gas from petroleum, and by delivery of liquefied natural gas by ship from overseas. Potential sources for future use include natural gas by pipeline from Alaska and Mexico, natural gas from coal, and gas from renewable organic and other unconventional sources. By the twenty-first century, advancing technology may allow us to draw energy from seawater and from pools of superheated brine.

Careers

An outline of some of the careers involved in the energy industry are provided below:

Geologists: Through research, geologists locate oil, gas and other natural resources. They collect the samples from the area of study, oversee the laboratory studies on the data, and report to the commissioning company on their findings of potential quantity and accessibility of the resources present.

Geophysicists: Like geologists, geophysicists are used to locate natural resources. Their investigations use physics, mathematics, engineering and other sciences to determine the likelihood of oil or gas reserves. They study the land formation with seismic testing, using sound waves to record echoes that would point to the presence of natural energy resources. They study the cause of land formations such as mountains and faults to see if the changes in the earth's structure would give rise to oil or gas reserves.

Chemists: A chemist may develop a new product and devise a laboratory process for making it. He or she then tries out this new process in a pilot plant to find out if it will work in actual production. The chemist is the watchdog of the refiner's reputation, devising tests to assure that all products shipped from the refinery are of the required quality. Laboratory technicians assist in routine testing and sample taking.

Petroleum engineers: Since petroleum and natural gas are often produced in the same fields, much of the petroleum engineering graduate's training can be applied to the gas industry. Petroleum engineers contribute to the development of other energy sources. In this capacity, they seek to develop processes to turn coal, oil shale, and tar sands into gas or oil. They are working to make energy from the sun, the winds, and the tides a commercial reality.

Gas engineers: These engineers may work with diverse engineering problems such as designing new transmission or distribution systems. Their other responsibilities include helping to plan changes in the degree of company automation, dealing with problems of the effects of weather on gas flow, and helping to solve the difficulties of natural gas liquefaction.

Chemical engineers: The chemical engineer designs and operates refineries, putting to work the research findings of the chemist. If the findings are favorable, the chemical engineer designs equipment to handle the new process.

Chemical engineering is also needed in many phases of oil and gas conditioning, transmission, storage, and liquefaction. When these energy products reach the point of actual use, particularly in specialized industrial applications, the chemical engineer is employed to ensure safety and quality of the product being used.

Civil engineers: The gas industry's growth created excellent career opportunities for its civil engineers. Civil engineers construct refineries and terminals, and plan water and sanitation systems for them. They also build roads and pipelines.

Much of the construction is done under challenging conditions. Pipelines are laid through swamps, across waterways, over mountains, under highways, wherever gas is needed. Difficult civil engineering problems are also encountered in increasing the capacity of gas systems in highly populated urban communities.

Electrical engineers: Electrical and electronics engineers supervise telephone, telegraphy, and radio communications systems. Radio is extensively used because of the remote location of many exploration and production operations. Electrical engineers also help geophysical engineers design, operate, and maintain geophysical exploration equipment. Research projects by electrical and electronics engineers developed the complicated measuring instruments used in fundamental research on the hydrocarbons in petroleum.

Mechanical engineers: The gas industry needs more qualified mechanical engineering graduates than any other type. The gas and oil industry has tremendous investments in plants and equipment. Mechanical engineers design pumping stations, pipelines, and storage tanks for oil products. Together with electrical engineers, they design and operate power plants and transmission lines, because many refineries supply their own electrical power.

Industrial engineers: Industrial engineering graduates perform many functions in gas companies. Among the most typical are methods analysis; work standards development and control; planning, scheduling, and budgeting techniques; and economic analysis of operating practices and facility investment.

Marine engineers: Increasing emphasis on offshore exploration and production has created many opportunities for marine engineers. Their work involves design, operation, and maintenance of drilling equipment, underwater gathering lines, and similar facilities.

General engineers: The complex nature of energy operations draws on diverse fields of engineering. As a result, general engineering students can find many career positions that make use of their broad knowledge. These positions often lead to responsible posts in gas company engineering management.

The chief engineer in a gas company has charge of the utility's mechanical operations.

Pumps are placed in wells where oil will not readily emerge. The pumps come in various sizes, depending on the speculated amount of oil present.

This person is generally responsible for the operation and maintenance of compressors, pumps, turbines, and similar equipment. An engineering assistant performs responsible work such as drafting, preparing dimension drawings of gas systems, machinery, and structural parts, assisting in engineering calculations, and preparing estimated cost data. A drafter prepares accurate working plans and detail drawings from sketches and makes the finished designs.

Metallurgists: Energy companies rely heavily on the specialized technology of the metallurgist and the welding engineer. Metallurgical engineers not only study the uses of metal in new installations and test and inspect metals already in service, but they also develop new metals for special purposes. The design, construction, maintenance, and improvement of pipelines, mains, and other facilities are typical assignments.

Research staff: Larger companies in the energy industry usually have research operations exploring areas that may be of special interest to the individual company. In addition, national research programs are also seeking answers to matters of general interest, usually under the sponsorship of such organizations as the American Gas Association and the Institute of Gas Technology.

Many petroleum scientists are engaged in exploration research. By finding out more about the nature of oil (how it was formed and in what kind of areas and underground rock structures it is most likely to collect) they hope to take at least some of the guesswork out of drilling for oil in a new location.

General operating personnel: Jobs for skilled operating personnel cover a broad range in all phases of the energy industry. For instance, a supervisor is responsible for the operation and maintenance of some part of a gas system and coordinates those operations with the other groups. A shift boss is responsible for assisting and directing operating and maintenance workers in the proper use of all equipment. A lease buyer negotiates for the leasing or purchase of possible oil-bearing land on which a company wishes to drill a well. Another important job is that of a scout who reports to a firm on the activity of other companies in exploring, leasing, drilling, and producing in an area.

Pipeline workers: The district supervisor oversees pipeline maintenance crews in construction, installation, and repair projects needed for a given area or section of the pipeline system. Machinists repair and rebuild all types of mechanical equipment needed for plant operation and maintenance. They have to know how to operate equipment such as engine lathes, milling machines, grinders, and drill presses in order to machine rings, grind compressor rods, and thread stud bolts and similar items.

Compressor operators run compressor engines and other related equipment. They load and unload compressors, start and stop engines, and control the speed of the engines to maintain designated operating pressures.

An oiler assists the compressor operator with the compressor engines and related equipment by operating bypass valves and loading and unloading compressors. Oilers lubricate all moving parts and clean the engines, periodically checking bearings, lubricating systems, and water temperatures. A laborer performs various manual duties required for the construction, operation, and maintenance of the gas system.

A pipeline repairer with a transmission company repairs and services main-line valves and assists in installing and maintaining the main line, feeder line, and dehydration equipment. This person may act as a welder's helper or as an assistant in repairing pipeline heavy-duty equipment.

Along the pipelines, pumping stations are set up at intervals to push the oil along, since friction and gravity must be overcome as the oil travels over mountains and across long, level stretches. Operational control people regulate the pumps and keep watch on these underground rivers of oil. In the oil fields and on the pipelines, they are helped by automatic equipment operated by electronic devices.

Distributors: For distributing companies, the distribution superintendent is responsible for many of the functions of the gas distribution system, including such things as the performance of metering equipment, the design and installation of house piping and customer appliances, and preparation of cost estimates.

A service supervisor directs service people and gas fitters who set and remove house meters, install house piping and appliances, and adjust and repair electrical appliances.

The street supervisor has responsibility for the smooth operation of the gas distribution system from the point where the various gas mains leave the plant up to the metering equipment installed on the customer's premises.

A meter repairer's duties include testing all types of meters and accessory equipment; removing and reinstalling valves; and reassembling and adjusting meters.

Dispatchers: For gas distribution companies, dispatchers control the volume of gas needed to maintain specified requirements. They analyze fluctuating supply and demand factors and accordingly issue instructions to regulate pressure and approve the opening or closing of any valve affecting the flow of gas.

Communications staff: Communications supervisors direct the installation, operation, and maintenance of the radio and telephone communications equipment. They plan and organize work, review progress reports, and assign job duties. A radio technician is responsible for installing, repairing, and maintaining base and mobile radio and telephone communication equipment.

Corrosion experts: The corrosion inspector reviews corrosion progress reports, determines the locations having the greatest need for preventive installations or tests, and makes work assignments. A corrosion technician assists the inspector by conducting surface potential and pipe-to-soil surveys on the main lines, feeder lines, and dehydration equipment within the assigned area. The technician may install and maintain electrical equipment associated with the prevention of corrosion.

Conservationists: Environmental conservation experts are called on throughout almost the whole process of finding, extracting, refining, transporting, and marketing oil and natural gas. The industry has invested billions of dollars to abate pollution.

Education

Although a bachelor's degree is ordinarily sufficient for many starting jobs in scientific applications and engineering, postgraduate training is a valuable asset, particularly for research positions. For any advanced level engineering position, a master's degree is the minimum requirement, and a doctorate is the standard level of education for people filling the post. It is very rare that upper-level researchers find employment with less than a doctorate.

A geology major will probably be hired as a junior geologist and after several years of experience may be promoted to geologist. Later he or she might become a division or district geologist in charge of surveys in one area of the country. A person of exceptional ability may step up to chief geologist of an oil company or may become a consulting or research geologist.

A chemistry major may start in the analytical and control laboratory of a refinery, where the first assignment is apt to be testing of petroleum products. With experience, he or she is eligible for the position of chemist, possibly then moving into a research laboratory. A chemistry major may also get a starting job in a research assignment, working at first under supervision.

Engineers, geologists, chemists, and other scientists who have leadership qualities may advance to top managerial posts in refineries or other branches of the industry.

Several areas of specialization may attract the graduate with a law degree. One is regulatory proceedings before the various governmental bodies that have jurisdiction over gas industry matters. Another is the intricate area of right-of-way leases and royalty rights. Still others are contract preparation for various company departments and responsibilities in claims and suits.

The high-school student looking toward a science or engineering career will want to emphasize chemistry, physics, biology, mathematics, and English. The ability to write clearly and simply will not only help in college courses but also will be valuable later on, since people in scientific and engineering positions must compile many reports.

There are various opportunities for high-school and vocational school students in petroleum exploration. Science and mathematics ma-

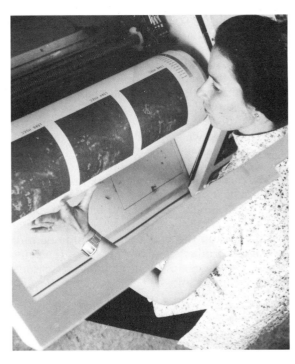

A technician operates a color plotter that is used to develop three-dimensional graphic displays of underground formations. Such information helps reduce the odds of drilling a dry hole.

jors have found good jobs as laboratory assistants. High-school and trade school graduates have become surveyors, computer and radio operators, and technicians of other kinds. Men and women who combine a science–math interest with some drawing ability make excellent drafters.

Beginners on a drilling crew usually start as roustabouts, rig-builder helpers, or rotary driller helpers, As they gain skill and experience, they can work up to better-paying jobs. For example, the roustabout may advance to rotary driller helper, to engine operator, to derrick operator, to driller. Next step up is tool pusher (drilling supervisor), who oversees the operations of one or more drilling rigs and has the responsibility of supplying the crews with materials and equipment.

Maintenance workers might start as laborers. If their educational records show interest and ability in the mechanical field, they might begin as apprentices and work into more responsible jobs.

High-school preparation is important. Courses in shop (wood, electrical, and metal), drafting, shop mathematics, and blueprint reading are useful for a mechanical job. General science, physics, and chemistry courses provide good background. On-the-job training will help advancement.

Most of the control personnel work in refineries. A modern refinery is a vast complex of pipes and processing equipment costing millions of dollars. It is operated by remote controls, and the people in the control room have a heavy responsibility. They are faced by banks of gauges and levers that operate valves, motors, pumps, and other control equipment. They must be well trained, alert, accurate, and cool-headed at all times.

A high-school or vocational school education is normally required for work in refineries. Mathematics will help develop skill and accuracy in instrument reading and record keeping. Courses in chemistry and physics will give background on the processing of crude oil into petroleum products and on the use of the principles of science in the operation of various types of equipment.

Industry outlook

U.S. energy consumption was expected to increase at an annual compound rate of about one percent between 1990 and the early part of the next decade. Much of the increased demand will probably be met by imports with average energy imports increasing around 5 percent, according to the Energy Information Administration. (EIA is an independent statistical agency within the U.S. Department of Energy). Uncertainties that could affect any predictions include possible interruptions of supply from the Middle East, future decisions by OPEC, American legislation on off-shore drilling facilities, increases in energy efficiency by users, and changes in assumptions about the rate of economic growth and the relation of energy consumption to it.

The number of oil refineries in the United States is gradually declining, along with the overall production capacity of the refineries. Refining and marketing energy is as important economically as crude oil production and can bring in as much money as oil production can.

Natural gas is gradually increasing in use, with some industries switching from coal and oil operations to gas for their power. Production of natural gas sources is expected to rise slightly, according to the *U.S. Industrial Outlook.*

The demand for engineers is expected to be about average to that of all occupations through the mid-1990s, assuming moderate economic growth. In 1989, petroleum engineers filled about 38,000 jobs in the industry and related fields.

◇ SOURCES OF ADDITIONAL INFORMATION

American Petroleum Institute
1220 L Street, NW
Washington, DC 20005

The Society of Exploration Geophysicists
PO Box 702740
Tulsa, OK 74170

American Gas Association
1515 Wilson Boulevard
Arlington, VA 22209

A source of information about the technical aspects of natural gas production is:

Institute of Gas Technology
3424 South State Street
Chicago, IL 60616

◇ RELATED ARTICLES

Volume 1: Chemistry; Construction; Electronics; Engineering; Mining; Nuclear Sciences; Physical Sciences
Volume 2: Engineers; Geologists; Geophysicists; Groundwater professionals; Petrologists
Volume 3: Gasoline service station attendants; Operating engineers; Petroleum drilling occupations; Petroleum refining workers; Roustabouts
Volume 4: Chemical technicians; Coal mining technicians; Geological technicians; Hydrological technicians; Metallurgical technicians; Petroleum technicians; Pollution-control technicians; Solar collector technicians

Engineering

General information

The field of engineering combines an understanding of the mathematical and natural sciences and applies them to develop effective ways to utilize the materials and forces of nature. To an engineer, knowledge is not an end in itself but is simply the raw material from which may be fashioned structures, machines, and processes.

Building things has always been one of humanity's basic activities. The development of civilization is marked by the building of pyramids, bridges, roadways, aqueducts, walls and fortifications, canals, and many other structures. These projects were designed and supervised by master builders. We know that those builders had a sound understanding of many of the structural principles—the masonry arch, for example—which are used in engineering today.

But the master builders of antiquity could not construct a modern skyscraper, tunnel under the sea, put a single-span bridge across New York Harbor, or design structures to be transported to the moon. All of these things can be done by engineers today.

Engineers help rebuild and change the face of the earth according to the needs of society. They apply scientific knowledge to bring us to the threshold of such things as mining the seas, setting up interplanetary communications systems, and probing with powerful radio telescopes to the outer limits of the universe.

Engineers are often identified with spectacular technological adventures, but they are also key figures in some of the major problems faced right here on earth. Shortages of fresh water, for example, are causing many problems for farmers and industrial firms in the western and southwestern United States. We know there is enough water in the seas to meet all our needs. Getting the salt out of this seawater at a reasonable cost, however, is not a simple matter.

Engineers put scientific knowledge to work on this problem, as they are putting science to work on a broad range of unsolved technological problems all over the world. For instance, in the underdeveloped areas of Africa and Asia, the people are in need of modern roads, bridges, dams, transportation and port facilities, local industry, adequate housing, and training in fundamental construction and industrial skills—all things that cannot be achieved today without engineering knowledge and skill.

The scientist and the engineer form the team that paces today's technology. If science is basically analytical, engineering is basically creative. The engineer is concerned with machines, the environment in which they operate, and with the people who affect their control. The engineer must be recognized as a person of action with a high order of versatility in application of new knowledge to practical problems. The scientist makes it known. The engineer makes it work.

The structure of the engineering sciences

Engineers utilize the principles of mathematics and science to discover practical solutions to problems in all industries. Engineers develop methods of producing less expensive electric power and devise more effective waste disposal systems. They design construction machinery and develop equipment to explore outer space and the ocean floor. Engineers also design and help produce consumer products, such as telephones, televisions, and automobiles. Engineers work in both the public and private sector and are instrumental in the smooth functioning of society.

Two aerospace engineers inspect an Atlas booster which will launch a U.S. Navy communications satellite. Given the delicate nature of the project, the equipment must meet precise design specifications.

Engineers are intricately involved in the development of new products. They must design and test all new components and fit them together into an overall plan. Engineers also make sure the product can be manufactured safely and economically. The product may be as simple as a child's toy or as complex as a missile launcher or a spacecraft. For example, making a synthetic fiber like nylon or uranium fuel elements is the job of the engineer. To accomplish this production, industrial know-how must go beyond the specific formulas for making each of these things. Quantity and cost factors demand that intricate processes and systems be set up if industrial plants are to achieve any production and profit goals. Engineers devise these intricate processes and systems.

Engineers are also involved in constructing large-scale projects. At a nuclear power station, for example, the contributions of the engineer include helping select the site for the power sta-

tion and developing excavation plans and the blueprints for all structural details of the reactor building. Engineers are called on to provide analyses of stress and load factors for the floors, walls, and other structural parts of the building itself. These engineers, traditionally listed under the grouping of civil engineers, are joined by other engineers in such specialties as mechanical, electrical, ceramic, and nuclear engineering. Each specialist would be using a mathematics and science background to solve design problems. The complexity of a nuclear power station is such that these design problems could not be solved without drawing upon a body of scientific and mathematical knowledge embracing nuclear physics, metallurgy, chemistry, radiation, and electronics.

Communications satellites are now weaving the first strands of what will ultimately be a planet-wide radio and TV network. These satellites, primitive as they will undoubtedly seem by the year 2000, nevertheless represent a massive reservoir of engineering knowledge and skill ranging from microwave transmission and amplification through tracking and telemetry.

Like their colleagues in large-scale construction, the engineers in communications must be thoroughly grounded in mathematics and the fundamentals of the physical sciences. They must work daily with equations that describe electromagnetic fields, electrical resistance and capacitance, current flow, carrier wave modulation, antenna design, voltage, and equivalent circuits.

The advances in construction and communications are inconceivable outside the framework of engineering. Each is an example of creative engineering problem-solving and design in response to a vital human need.

The large and growing field of petroleum products offers many examples of the engineering role in systems and processes. Oil, coal, and gas are the main sources of power today, and they are also important basic raw materials. Petroleum is actually a combination of hydrogen and carbon atoms, and engineering application to the rearranging of these atoms gives us a variety of new types of hydrocarbon molecules; which in turn give us products ranging from synthetic fibers to cosmetics.

Engineering opportunities in petroleum are duplicated in the larger field of mining. Mining engineers are involved in the extraction of all of the basic metals, coal, and a large number of other raw materials and chemicals. The mining engineer takes the physical sciences down into the earth and brings up valuable raw materials and sources of power.

Already the computer has become the indispensable partner in laboratories, defense plants, university research departments, industrial firms, and banks. It has also greatly affected the practice of engineering. Many engineering problems can be reduced to computer language and, consequently, to computer solutions. Computers are able to handle differential equations, hold millions of facts in their memories, and solve complicated problems in a fraction of a second.

It is now clear that the twin problems of fresh water sources and air pollution will provide some of the greatest challenges in the next several decades. Problems such as those associated with acid rain are coming into sharper focus as more people realize how many toxic substances are spewed out into the atmosphere by the very technology that makes a modern industrial nation. Engineers help find solutions to these problems. Mammoth engineering programs are under way to develop economical desalting processes. Nuclear energy will be har-

A design engineer demonstrates the use of a gate array chip for the Adaptive Interference Blanker Unit. The chip will be carried aboard the F-14D and the A-6F aircraft.

nessed in one such process. All branches of engineering from structural to electronic are engaged in this research and development. Many new and original approaches have been tried and more will be developed in the future.

There would appear to be limitless opportunity for creative engineering contributions to economically practical techniques for solving pollution problems. Engineers design and supervise the construction and operation of water and waste treatment plants and waste collection systems. They survey and investigate water in rivers, lakes, wells, and off-shore areas to determine the nature and amount of pollution. Engineers work with other specialists in locating sources of clean water for home and industry use. They advise government and industry officials on methods of treating, controlling, and eliminating waste products from manufacturing processes.

When they turn to the air we breathe, engineers design and use such things as filters, exposure meters, and densitometers to measure, analyze, identify, and eliminate polluting substances. Air quality has become a key issue in the 1990s, making it a promising area of concentration for budding engineers.

Engineers also help find solutions to problems in medicine, agriculture, and space exploration. Clearly, as civilization marches into the twenty-first century, engineers will play an increasingly important role in developing practical solutions to a myriad of problems.

Careers

The number and variety of engineering career possibilities in processes and systems will expand as the calendar moves us toward the end of this century. As our goods and services become more complicated, methods of making and performing these things must reflect this increased complexity. Engineers in all the specialties have a part in developing and perfecting these processes and systems.

Responsibilities within a specific engineering specialty will vary from job to job. For example, an engineering career in communications could range from designing original circuit boards to a position as sales representative for radio and telephone equipment.

A sampling of career opportunities in engineering follows below.

Aerospace engineers: Aerospace engineers are involved in the development, design, and assembly of all types of aircraft. Such structures include missiles, space capsules, airplanes, engines, and other related equipment.

Agricultural engineers: Agricultural engineers are concerned with improving farming methods and increasing food production. They design farm equipment, develop irrigation systems, coordinate food processing systems, and install land reclamation projects.

Ceramic engineers: Ceramic engineers work with nonmetallic minerals, clay, and silicates to create ceramic products. Such products range from light bulbs to exterior tiles on space shuttles. Ceramic engineers study the properties of the materials they use and design heat-resistant products such as porcelain, glass, bricks, and coatings for industrial equipment. Ceramics is an expanding field of study.

Chemical engineers: Chemical engineers develop, research, and produce a variety of substances for commercial sale such as detergents, plastics, and medicine. They are also involved in the design of chemical plants.

Civil engineers: Civil engineers design and supervise the construction of bridges, highways, dams, waste management systems, and other large projects. Major specialties within the field of civil engineering include transportation, hydraulic, and construction.

Electrical engineers: Electrical engineers concentrate on the generation, transmission, and distribution of electricity. In addition, they develop and improve electrical equipment and appliances. They may also consult in the planning of electric power plants.

Electronics engineers: Electronics engineers are electrical engineers that have specialized in electronic equipment. They design, develop, and test products such as computers, stereo components, medical devices, and communications equipment.

Fire-protection engineers: Fire-protection engineers develop ways to prevent fires in all types of structures. They often work as consultants during the construction of buildings and industrial plants, designing fire prevention methods. In addition to prevention, they also devise plans for disposing of post-fire refuse, particularly with chemical fires.

Industrial engineers: Industrial engineers are responsible for plant layout and design, quality and production control, cost analysis, sales engineering, and other industrial concerns.

Logistics engineers: Logistics engineers ensure that a project is carried out smoothly, from its conception to the final phase in production. They coordinate all facets of production, trying to complete a project in the most efficient way possible.

Marine engineers: Marine engineers are involved in the construction of maritime vessels. With naval architects, they try to design the most fuel-efficient and cost-effective ships.

Materials engineers: Materials engineers develop and test materials for specific products. They study plans for new products and recommend the appropriate materials to be used, such as metals, ceramics, polymers, fibers, or other appropriate substances.

Mechanical engineers: In general, mechanical engineers design motors and machines that generate power. Such products include automobiles and their engines, refrigerators, machine tools, presses, and nuclear reactors. Due to the all-encompassing nature of their tasks, mechanical engineers are involved in nearly all types of industry.

Metallurgical engineers: There are two types of metallurgical engineers: extractive metallurgists and physical metallurgists. Extractive metallurgists are involved with the removal of ore, the separation of metal from the ore, and the processing of the extracted metals. Physical metallurgists study metals and related alloys, finding more efficient means of converting them into final products.

Mining engineers: Mining engineers work on mining projects from surveying the land to designing shafts. They study the cost-effectiveness of mining projects and design means of transporting the mined ore to the surface.

Nuclear engineers: Nuclear engineers develop products that either create or use nuclear energy. They design and monitor the operation of nuclear power plants, ensuring their efficiency and safety. In addition, they develop new uses for nuclear technology in industry and in medicine.

Engineers inspect a fuel tank that has been designed for the space shuttle. The tanks holds up to 500,000 gallons of fuel.

Optical engineers: Optical engineers design equipment for such instruments as cameras and telescopes. Their work requires great precision.

Ordnance engineers: Ordnance engineers are involved with the design and development of explosives for military purposes. They are knowledgeable in other related fields of engineering such as metallurgy, electronics, and materials.

Petroleum engineers: Once an oil or gas field has been discovered, it is up to the petroleum engineer to choose a drilling method and supervise the drilling operation. Petroleum engineers are always looking for ways to recover oil reserves from remote locations and to increase oil output.

Photographic engineers: Photographic engineers design photographic equipment for industrial, individual, and scientific pursuits.

Pollution control engineers: Pollution control engineers design systems that curb pollution. These systems include solid waste management, noise abatement, water quality control, and air filtering. Pollution control engineers

who work for the government set standards for allowable pollutants in the environment.

Project engineers: Project engineers are in charge of entire engineering projects. They are responsible for scheduling and overseeing every stage of a project, ensuring that each stage is completed in an efficient and timely fashion. They must also make sure that the project is completed according to standard procedures and regulations.

Resource-recovery engineers: Resource recovery engineers find ways of converting solid waste into usable products.

Soils engineers: Soils engineers study the grounds on which proposed buildings will be constructed to determine whether the ground is suitable for construction. Soils engineers must take into account any environmental problems that may occur such as strong winds, earthquakes, or heavy rains.

Engineering technicians: Engineering technicians assist engineers in all areas of work. They are highly trained individuals with strong backgrounds in some specialized technological field. They do not have degrees in engineering, nor

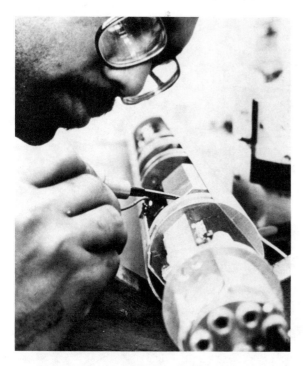

This genetic engineer is trying to develop new biological techniques for increasing oil and natural gas production.

do they do engineering analysis or design. Many of them have completed two- or four-year programs leading to degrees in engineering technology.

The challenges of the new technology have made heavy demands on our engineering labor resources. Good utilization of this personnel has become one of the most urgent problems faced by industry and federal officials in recent years. Engineering technicians have helped greatly in this utilization.

Education

Some young people are attracted to engineering because of their interest and ability in mechanics and takings things apart. Engineers may well have such interests and abilities. But engineering is centered upon mathematical and analytical solutions to problems in mechanical, electronic, chemical, and nuclear relationships.

One of the most serious handicaps for high-school students interested in careers in engineering is that they get no real contact with engineering applications as part of their formal educational experience. They get courses in mathematics and courses in science, but they get no course or specific instruction in how engineers actually apply science to solve human problems and to satisfy human needs. There-

fore, high-school students interested in engineering should consider participating in such extracurricular activities as those offered by JETS (Junior Engineering Technical Society) and other engineering groups.

The trend in engineering education is toward a strong preparation in the fundamentals of mathematics and science for all engineering students, with specialized subjects coming later in the program or at the graduate level. This trend in education has come about because of the great growth in scientific knowledge in recent years. A strong foundation in mathematics and the basic physical sciences is necessary if the engineer is to be able to assimilate and use new scientific knowledge correctly. Thus, the four-year engineering school program will cover basic mathematics, extensive lab and lecture courses in chemistry and physics, a variety of engineering application courses in which the student must use mathematics to solve engineering problems, and an assortment of liberal arts courses.

Many engineering schools offer scholastic aptitude tests for prospective students. Students should write to the registrars of schools of their choice for detailed, specific entrance requirements.

More and more engineers find it necessary to earn degrees beyond the bachelor's degree to meet the challenges of modern technology. Postgraduate education through the master's degree is becoming more necessary for the engineer as technology moves into the space and nuclear age. A growing number of engineers now pursue their formal education through the doctoral level.

It should be kept in mind that the impact of the new science and technology is such that it is becoming quite difficult to identify any particular area of engineering activity with the traditional branches such as civil, mechanical, electrical, and chemical. Education for engineering is undergoing deep changes in response to the new demands in science application with which the engineer of the future will be faced.

The initials "P.E." used after an engineer's name signify that he or she is established as a qualified engineer by passing an examination administered by an examining board of one of the states. All the states and the District of Columbia now have license or registration laws for professional engineers. It is illegal for a person to use the title "professional engineer" if he or she has not qualified under state law. These laws generally require graduation from an accredited engineering college with a minimum of four years of responsible engineering experience.

Industry outlook

While no one can predict future economic changes that will influence engineering personnel requirements, it is safe to say that continuing concern with the quality of life, the need for economic growth and productivity, and the increasing limitations on energy and natural resources will challenge engineering personnel well into the future. Those trained in the applications of science and mathematics through engineering will have challenging opportunities in the years ahead.

There is a growing body of evidence that suggests that science and technology will advance more from now to the year 2000 than in all recorded history. The young person just beginning high school today who chooses engineering as a career will be at work as we pass into the twenty-first century. Everyone will look out on a fantastically different world on New Year's Day in the year 2000. But today's high-school freshmen and sophomores who choose engineering will be living in a world that they will have helped to bring about. The engineer's special contribution to the world of 2000 will be the practical application of the knowledge generated by those mighty engines of our times—the physical sciences.

Engineering is the second largest U.S. profession (teaching is larger) in the United States, and engineers filled more than 1.3 million jobs in the late 1980s. Opportunities for graduates with engineering degrees are expected to be good through the mid-1990s and employment is expected to increase faster than average for all occupations. Many engineers move on to management or sales positions, creating openings for new workers. In certain fields, such as the aerospace industry, cutbacks in research and development or defense expenditures may lead to layoffs. More than half of all engineering jobs were in manufacturing industries.

By the year 2000, we will have made large gains in the amount of control we have over our physical environment. An engineering career decision made in high school today could bring a person into the intellectual mainstream of one of the great creative eras in human history. Of course, many areas of specialized training will make specific contributions to human welfare in the years ahead. But most, if not all, of the solutions to major human problems must be implemented by the applications of science through engineering.

◇ **SOURCES OF ADDITIONAL INFORMATION**

American Association of Engineering Societies
415 Second Street, NW
Suite 200
Washington, DC 20002

National Society of Professional Engineers
1420 King Street
Alexandria, VA 22314

Accreditation Board for Engineering and Technology
345 East 47th Street
New York, NY 10017

Junior Engineering Technical Society— JETS
1420 King Street
Suite 405
Alexandria, VA 22314

Food Processing

General information

Advances in the food processing industry allow us to eat foods that were grown thousands of miles away and produced days and weeks earlier. Food processing prevents food from spoiling as quickly as it would otherwise. It also provides greater convenience, variety, color, taste, and, in many cases, monetary savings. Food is processed and preserved by cold storage, canning, freezing, drying, freeze-drying, curing, and most recently by the use of antibiotics and ultraviolet rays.

The food processing industry is constantly changing and adapting its products to the tastes and needs of its consumers. Such work involves the research and development of new processing techniques, market studies to determine what customers want, package design, and actual food processing. Many people are employed in this enormous and important industry, from the farmer or livestock owner to the checker in a supermarket.

As a fundamental human need, food has always played a central part in our life. Our ancestors lived or died according to their ability to grow food, to hunt for food, or to fight for food. The first colonists in America aided their survival by discoveries of such food products as corn and turkeys.

Years ago there were relatively few food products and even fewer of them were processed and packaged. People bought their foods mostly in bulk out of barrels, bins, sacks, and jugs. These bulk products were sold in small stores; the self-service supermarket did not exist.

Food manufacturers observed that consumers wanted tasty foods and insisted on clean products. They saw that consumers wanted foods of dependable, high, uniform quality. Consumers also wanted seasonal items year-round, and a wider variety of products which were easier to prepare and easier to store.

With this knowledge to guide them, food manufacturers began the processing and packaging revolution that transformed the food industry from a "bulk" to a "packaged" goods industry. They fulfilled consumer desires by developing new and improved processing methods and varieties of new products. They also developed the containers and packages for suitable and safe handling of these products.

Americans are eating the benefits of a revolution in new foods. The supermarket—a world symbol of the age of plenty—was made possible by the implementation of improved methods of processing and packaging food. Today's supermarket is filled with products that were unavailable not long ago. The development of new processed foods has not only broadened the eating horizons of millions of Americans but also has increased the sale of raw farm commodities.

U.S. consumers select groceries from an assortment of some 10,000 to 12,000 items instead of a limited selection of about 1,000 items that were available not too many years ago. Two-thirds of today's grocery store items are either new or have been materially improved within the past few decades. Today's new household items include many time-savers that have materially lightened the homemaker's chores. In addition, there are often cost savings in convenience foods, too. Frozen vegetables may cost less than fresh vegetables, frozen orange juice may be less expensive than juice squeezed at home from fresh oranges, and a cake made from scratch may cost more than one made using a mix.

Food products today are, in many instances, far superior in nutritional value, tastiness, safety, variety, and reliability than they were thirty years ago. All of this has helped make the industry grow. The food processing industry has moved ahead because of forward-looking management, new scientific devices, new foods, new packages. Indeed, it is an ever-changing, dynamic industry.

The structure of the food processing industry

In the United States, food manufacturers stand in the middle of the food industry production line. They work with the farmers who supply the raw crops, with the research laboratories, with the wholesalers and retailers who distribute their finished products, and with the consumers who buy them. For that reason, there is a great variety of jobs in food manufacturing companies.

Most food manufacturers, large or small, divide their companies into areas responsible for manufacturing, purchasing, and packaging. They also divide their companies into areas for marketing, engineering, finance, and research and development. Depending on the size of the company, there may be special departments for traffic, distribution, law, public relations, and personnel. Within each of these departments there are subdivisions.

Manufacturers perform the obvious functions of processing, packaging, and physically distributing the food to the warehouses of distributors. But their role goes far beyond that. They are the innovators, the creators, the marketers, and the risk-takers who provide the vehicle for the continuing expansion of the food industry.

The contributions of manufacturers extend to include creating thousands of new products and developing consumer markets for them; improving their old products; promoting greater public understanding and appreciation of nutritious foods and good eating; offering their advertised brands in safe, attractive, and convenient packages; and making products available at reasonable prices.

The industry tries to provide consumers with a flow of new and improved products. These products come out of the research laboratories of manufacturers who invest millions of dollars annually in research on new products and on new uses and improvements of old ones. They employ thousands of scientists and other specially trained people for this purpose.

Food research has become so complex that a battery of scientists does constant work in many areas. Organic chemists, biochemists, analytical chemists, food technologists, and chemical engineers each have special roles.

Before a new product is introduced, its potential market is carefully surveyed by market researchers who must be consistently alert to changes in consumers' attitudes, needs, and shopping habits. Market researchers plan and conduct studies and surveys to get the facts on the performance and acceptance of existing

Workers at an ice cream manufacturing plant prepare strawberries for processing. They must make sure that all of the strawberries are of uniform color and size.

products or to define the potential market for a new product. Prices, brand image, distribution, size and appearance of packages, advertising and promotion are some of the areas in which market researchers work. Market researchers provide information used in major food production decisions.

The term "marketing" in the food industry defines all the important functions between the factory door and the consumer's kitchen—distribution, selling, packaging, and all forms of promotion directed to the consumer. Marketing considerations, for example, led to the creation of the mythical Betty Crocker, identified with the kitchens of General Mills in Minneapolis.

Those who supply and process food must be constantly aware of changing consumer tastes and demands. In the mid-1980s, for example, consumers turned increasingly toward natural foods, as additives came under growing scrutiny and criticism by consumers and the Federal Drug Administration. Consumers' concerns with their health led to the introduction of products emphasizing high-fiber or low-sodium content. Aspartame, a low-calorie sweetener, was introduced in many drinks.

The processing of foods is a modern technological accomplishment and a highly complex business. It is also a high-cost operation with narrow quality limits. Consequently, food and grocery manufacturers have relied on sophisticated processes to aid in the production and marketing of food items.

Dehydration is one such process. A stepchild of wartime necessity during World War II, dehydration became a highly respected contender in the field of convenience foods. A key word that has helped sell dehydration to the American consumer is "instant," which is now

An employee at a candy factory oversees the panning operation where jelly beans are coated.

used with products such as instant coffee, instant tea, instant cocoa, instant potatoes and cereals, milk powders, and dozens of other packaged dry products that are ready in a wink simply by adding water.

Freeze-dry is another process consumers have become accustomed to. It involves first freezing the food so that the moisture is transformed into ice crystals. Then it is dehydrated under vacuum at low temperature. The ice sublimates so that the crystals pass off as vapor without going through an immediate liquid state. Freeze-dry foods retain bulk but lose water weight. For example, three freeze-dry pork chops weigh no more than a single fresh pork chop. After preparation, however, freeze-dry chops regain normal weight and retain original flavor and texture.

Among the first consumer packages containing freeze-dry ingredients were soups. Other freeze-dry products include beef steaks, precooked scrambled eggs, ham patty mix, chicken stew, shrimp, pot roast of beef, and Swiss steak, with the promise of many more to come, including fruits and vegetables.

Processes that relatively recently were only laboratory terms are becoming household words. In the United States, for example, more than 40 percent of the homes have microwave ovens, and the industry provides many products suited for microwave preparation.

Another modern processing method is irradiation, which can keep seafood, meats, fruits, and vegetables fresh. Irradiated food is not frozen, rather it tastes and looks fresh. Like freeze-dry foods these foods can be stored on the shelf. When ready for use, they can be cooked just as fresh foods are.

New processes are continually being developed that will continue the ever-broadening revolution in eating for the American consumer.

Careers

There are fine career opportunities in all segments of the food industry, from the farm to the supermarket. Some of the most challenging of these opportunities are to be found in companies that manufacture or process food products. Opportunities in the food industry exist for people with general skills and for those trained in nutrition, pharmacology, bacteriology, toxicology, and packaging technology and methodology. A sampling of career opportunities follows below.

Product managers: Product managers are the coordinators of all aspects of the food product to which they are assigned. Product managers and their assistants are responsible for marketing plans, product and package improvements, the coordination of production with distribution, and the appraisal of competition. They oversee the production of the food at the manufacturing plant and plan the marketing strategy and consumer advertising for each grocery item produced. In general, they are responsible for promoting a product and ensuring that it is on the shelves as scheduled.

Food technologists: Food technologists study the chemical, physical, and biological composition of food to learn how to safely preserve, package, and market it.

Food inspectors: Food inspectors ensure that foods are produced according to state or federal regulations. They look for inaccurate food labeling, and for any contamination that could result in a product becoming unhealthy. Food inspectors may work as part of a team or on their own.

Salespeople: The salesperson is the link between the distributor and the manufacturer. He or she is really the eyes, ears, and voice of the food manufacturing industry. Since the first objective is to get the order, today's salespeople use more than charm and persistence; they draw on a sure knowledge of their markets as well as their products. Besides work in field sales operations, there are many opportunities in sales planning, sales promotion, and sales management.

Engineers: At the manufacturing plant, every process from receiving the raw materials to packaging and distributing the finished product is the concern of engineers with many and varied degrees and titles. For example, a chemical engineer translates the basic information provided by chemists and food technologists into the fundamental data required for the design of profitable commercial processes. The engineer is involved in planning, constructing, and operating plants.

An engineering degree has proven to be an effective first step toward managerial responsibilities. On the headquarters staff, an engineer may reach supervisory and administrative levels—planning assignments, assessing projects, establishing goals, and directing and serving in important liaison capacities with many company departments and division operations.

Organic chemists and *biochemists:* The organic chemist is responsible for solving the problems of how various raw materials can be processed into food, while the biochemist is concerned with the changes that occur in raw materials during food processing, particularly to flavor, texture, and storage quality.

Analytical chemists: Analytical chemists use knowledge of science and engineering in developing new products or improving existing food products and processes.

Accountants: Accountants are responsible for keeping complete, consistent records of the company's assets, liabilities, and operations. Accountants also provide the facts and figures on which top-level decisions are based. Auditing is another area that calls for a good background in accounting, and a job in auditing offers an excellent opportunity to learn firsthand all of a food company's essential operations.

Budget analysts: The budget and analysis staff is responsible for continually evaluating present and future operating plans and for providing corporate and division management with independent financial counsel on running the food business.

Administrative systems analysts: Administrative systems analysts are another group of problem solvers who work closely with all departments and divisions to develop and install systems and techniques for planning and control. A typical project for a systems analyst would be the investigation of food sales patterns to develop a method of reliable sales forecasts. Operations research and computer systems people help apply the latest analytical and data processing systems to the manufacturer's operating problems.

Many of the jobs cited can be found at both the plant and company headquarters since in many food companies the two parallel each other. There are many jobs directly in the man-

A food processing lab technician measures the amount of broccoli that may be added to each bag of a new frozen vegetable medley.

ufacturing process such as production supervision, quality control, and production planning and control. All offer professional training and advancement toward managerial posts.

At headquarters there are careers for those trained in and interested in law, public relations, and personnel as well as purchasing and package development, traffic, and distribution.

In fact, every department or subdivision of a food company, large or small, is ready to hire the young graduate who sees a bright future in one of the country's biggest businesses: the food industry.

Education

An education for a career in the food industry depends on the particular job. Some jobs require specific academic preparation at the college or university level; for others a high-school diploma is sufficient. In almost all grocery manufacturing companies, a high-school diploma is essential for any job.

The food industry wants people who are technically well-grounded and are able to grasp the rudiments of a business quickly; can communicate with scientists and engineers as well as nontechnical people quickly and with under-

Workers at a food processing company unload frozen fish on the receiving dock. The fish will be boned, cleaned, and packaged for retailers.

standing; and can apply their formal education effectively to company problems. The production jobs filled by workers with limited formal education are being automated, and the worker with a skill and better academic background, and especially with a college degree, will have a more certain future.

The opportunities and the challenges in the food industry to reduce costs, improve product performance, and develop new products are almost beyond imagination. Most opportunities are not in the area of pure research, however, but result from mixing a basic technical knowledge with the right amount of practical application. The properly trained food scientists or food technologists should have the advantage in the matter of job placement within the food industry but must nevertheless compete with many other disciplines.

In many jobs, it does not matter whether a person bears the title of physicist, chemist, food scientist, chemical engineer, mechanical engineer, or pharmacist. Grocery manufacturers are primarily interested in the person who can do the job. At the same time, for many technical jobs in the food industry a person trained in a particular basic discipline is preferred.

Because financial administration is at the very heart of a successful enterprise, many highly trained people are needed. Courses in statistics and economics are prerequisites and familiarity with computers and data processing is equally helpful. Given the consumer-based nature of the food processing industry, executives must be familiar with marketing trends.

The scope of the industry with its diverse opportunities makes it unlikely that food science students will learn all the required skills in school. The needs of small companies are not always the same as those of large companies. A production job does not demand the same talents and abilities as a research and development job or a technical service job. Yet the common denominator of all these jobs is a technically sound training in the basic sciences, with emphasis on foods.

Industry outlook

The total food industry, including all the processes from farm to table, is one of America's biggest businesses. In fact, it is perhaps the biggest business in the world. More than one-fourth of all working people in the United States are employed in some part of it. They may work on farms, or for food processing companies, food research laboratories, food wholesalers, food retailers, restaurants, railroads and trucks that transport food, or agencies that prepare food advertising. Or they may work in hundreds of other companies that supply goods or services vital in converting a raw farm crop into a ready-to-use food.

The food industry has changed dramatically in only one generation. Frozen foods were a novelty in the early 1950s. Now, we are preparing food in tubes, capsules, and in other ways to eat in space. All this in just a few years. It is difficult to predict what the dynamic food industry will be doing in another thirty years, but for the next decade, the food processing industry is assured of some growth.

The food industry grew from a $46 billion a year business in 1950 to about $280 billion in the early 1980s. By the early 1990s, the value of the U.S. food and beverage industry's shipments totaled more than $366 billion a year. This did not happen simply because people have to eat or because of the population increase. This extra growth resulted from many things—good management at all levels, fine teamwork among all segments of the food industry, heavy investment in research, new and improved products, modernization of plants, new equipment, automation, and a great deal of advertising and promotion. The combination of these many factors helped to promote this extra growth, and the industry is moving right ahead spending more dollars for advertising, research, and new buildings and equipment.

◇ **SOURCES OF ADDITIONAL INFORMATION**

National Food Processors Association
1401 New York, NW
4th Floor
Washington, DC 20005

Associated Food Industries
177 Main Street
PO Box 776
Matawan, NJ 07747

National Frozen Food Association
PO Box 398
Hershey, PA 17033

Snack Food Association
1711 King Street
Suite 1
Alexandria, VA 22314

◇ **RELATED ARTICLES**

Volume 1: Agriculture; Baking; Food Service; Packaging; Wholesaling
Volume 2: Biochemists; Biologists; Chemists; Dietitians; Economists; Engineers; Food technologists; Health and regulatory inspectors; Home economists; Packaging engineers; Physicists; Purchasing agents; Restaurant and food service managers; Systems analysts; Toxicologists
Volume 3: Agricultural scientists; Bakery product workers; Canning and preserving industry workers; Confectionery industry workers; Cooks, chefs and bakers; Farmers; Fishers, commercial; Food service workers; Meat-packing production workers; Meatcutters; Route drivers; Stock clerks
Volume 4: Agribusiness technicians; Dietetic technicians; Farm crop production technicians; Packaging and paper products technicians

Food Service

General information

The food service industry includes all types of establishments that prepare, supply, and serve food outside the home. This includes restaurants, carry-out operations, cafeterias, school and college dining rooms, catering and vending companies, hotels and motels, and retirement centers.

Food service operations primarily serve food to their customers, but they may also provide entertainment, group accommodations, and other services. They range in size from modest neighborhood establishments to luxurious restaurants and nightclubs. Whatever their size, they must pay careful attention to food purchasing, preparation, and serving, and a host of other activities to ensure that they meet the expectations of their clientele.

Inns with food service and dining halls are traced back to the Roman Empire. These establishments offered meals to travelers who stayed at the inn, and may have provided meals to outside guests as well.

With the development of roads and the increase in travelers abroad, such as pilgrims to the Holy Land, the number of dining halls and inns began to increase throughout Europe and Asia. Places where one could stop to have a meal were founded in England in the 1500s. Taverns also sprang up to provide travelers with food and drink.

Sometime during the 17th century, coffee was introduced in Europe from Turkey. The beverage became quite popular, and public establishments that specialized in coffee began to develop. The first coffeehouse was believed to have been opened in Vienna in 1645. London had one by 1652. They became regular meeting places for local residents.

The origin of the term *restaurant* and the history of the modern eating establishment may be traced to France. In 1765, a Paris soup vendor, A. Boulanger, advertised *restaurants* ("restoratives") and offered choices from a menu of dishes at his modest establishment. Previously, inns and other public rooms had served paying guests, but Boulanger, the soup entrepreneur, is credited with making the restaurant the first public place where any person might choose from a menu from a variety of food dishes.

When the French Revolution brought down the aristocratic houses, the kitchen staff from those fine dining halls began to open their own restaurants. Fine dining halls and restaurants began to flourish during the late 1700s, and by the early 1800s Paris had more than 500 restaurants.

During the 1849 gold rush in San Francisco, California, a cafeteria styled restaurant opened for gold miners. The cafeteria offered the miners an opportunity to pick out the food from the counter and then pay for what they had chosen before sitting down to eat.

By the beginning of the 1900s, the United States had also developed diners and the beginning of fast-food restaurants. Fast food offered quick service and a limited menu.

The first true fast-food restaurants began in the 1920s. In 1955 in Des Plaines, Illinois, the first McDonald's opened. McDonald's was to become the most extensive fast-food franchise in the world. McDonald's expanded from one restaurant in 1955 to more than 6,000 by 1990. Now almost every town in the United States has at least one McDonald's and a host of other fast-food restaurants that cater to those people who want to eat cheaply and quickly.

In the late 1980s, there were more than 625,000 restaurants and lunchrooms in the United States and sales totaled more than $200 billion, excluding alcoholic beverages. Almost one million chefs and cooks were employed. Restaurants employed nearly 80 percent of the approximately two million waiters and waitresses (10 percent worked in hotels and others in clubs and other institutions).

The structure of the food service industry

The food service industry is composed of two important parts—operations that prepare and serve food, and organizations that produce and distribute the food, equipment, and services that the food providers require.

The establishments that prepare and supply food to customers, such as restaurants, coffee shops, fast-food chains, food outlets in hotels, catering firms, and a host of other establishments all have specific methods of preparing and serving food. Each fulfills a vital role in providing alternatives to the hungry consumer. For patrons who want a nice leisurely meal, for example, a traditional, sit-down restaurant is often the best bet. For those who need to eat in a hurry, a fast-food eatery provides a good option.

Other food service establishments provide dining accommodations in a variety of settings. A caterer, for example, can provide food in a large hall or in the privacy of a client's home. Hotels can serve food in a banquet hall or in a cozier setting. Hospitals and other institutions often provide food in a cafeteria setting.

Perhaps the simplest way to divide food service work would be into "front of the house" and "back of the house." Employees working in the front of the restaurant, for example, have the important responsibility of dealing with the public. Those in the kitchen have the equally important responsibility of producing quality food so that the customers will want to return. Throughout the food service industry there is a close working relationship between the preparers and the servers that makes the ability to get along with others very important.

For those who work directly with customers, it is important to have a natural liking and tolerance for the almost infinite variety of customers' temperaments. In the food service industry, the customer is almost always right because if the customer is not happy, business suffers.

For those who work in the kitchen—the dishwasher, salad and sandwich maker, the cooks at different levels, the dietician, and manager—restaurant work depends a great deal on close teamwork. If the dining room attendant does not sort the dishes properly, for instance, the busperson may have to do extra work, and the waitresses may not have clean tables ready to seat customers.

Food service usually begins with menu selection. For caterers who are selecting the items for a single evening's affair to restaurants that are picking specialties that will remain with them for years, the selection of the menu is the

Cooks, food preparers, and chefs at hotels must be equipped to provide meals at all times of the day. They are also responsible for creating complimentary food baskets and bedtime snacks for the patrons of the hotel.

single most important factor in distinguishing one facility from another.

A menu is decided by owners, managers, dieticians, caterers, and others who have an understanding and idea for the type of food service they will be offering. The combination of foods will be selected for ease in purchase, preparation, variety, nutritional value, and beauty. Gourmet restaurants will be more likely to select items that require patience, expensive ingredients and great skill in preparation. Hospital food services will focus on nutritional content and dietary concerns. Fast-food restaurants will be most concerned with speed of preparation and cost. Freshly delivered Maine lobster is unlikely to be found in fast-food restaurants in the mid-West, for example.

Modern operating methods are becoming essential in today's food service industry. Restaurant companies that have devised better systems for using labor and cutting costs will prosper. But this certainly does not mean that the food service worker is going to be replaced by machinery. Whatever automation may be achieved in the future, the need will remain for personal service to the customer, and for skill and imagination in the kitchen.

Cooks, chefs, bakers, and other food preparers are then trained to fix the meals that will be offered. They may be responsible for stocking and purchasing the items, or another staff member may be the buyer. They then determine assignments and roles in the kitchen to establish the most efficient method of food preparation. For one kitchen, it may be best to have one chef who makes the main dishes and other heated foods. For another kitchen, it may

In the food service industry, waitresses function as the liaisons between the food preparers and the customers. They must maintain congenial dispositions at all times.

be better to have a sauce maker, a dessert maker, and a entree preparer at three different stoves. It is up to the managers and owners to determine the best method of staff and kitchen organization.

The service side of the food industry is also quite varied. Large restaurants rely on waiters and waitresses to take orders, bring food to the table and assist the customers in ordering from the menu. Fast-food restaurants have counter help that takes orders, receives money, and either bags the food or has another helper deliver the food to the customer. Cafeteria-style restaurants have customers take the food from display counters so the need for table waiting staff is minimal. Clearing the tables of dirty plates may be the only table help hired.

The organization of the staff is determined by the style, size, and service goals of the organization. The types of restaurants are plentiful. They may fall into one category exactly or they may provide a few types of service. It is not unusual for restaurants to also offer take-out and delivery of food. Some restaurants have counters and tables.

Owners of restaurants must take all this into consideration when designing the format of the new establishment. There are a number of methods to consider for establishing a new restaurant.

Chain operations, which have grown in size and numbers, offer excellent opportunities for success in the food service industry. A chain, and also a franchise operation, has certain advantages over an individual operation. It may make better use of a menu item, a promotion piece, an equipment arrangement, or a way of doing things that has been carefully worked out and proved successful. The idea can be transferred to other similar operations without the cost of developing and testing it all over again.

Then, too, the chain has the advantage of headquarters specialists, which an individual operator usually cannot afford. A small restaurant may not be able to justify the cost of an elaborate advertising campaign or a series of radio and television commercials. Other opportunities in chain organizations lie in accounting, in purchasing, and in the supervision of food and food service by dietitians and managers.

Franchise restaurant operations have been growing rapidly and profitably. Its chief appeal is to people who can invest in their own businesses. Franchisees have the advantage of support from nationwide chains, while at the same time they exercise some individual control over food products (see Volume 1: Franchising, for further information).

Purchasing is a specialized function in any sizable food service operation. It involves detailed knowledge of hundreds of food products, their suppliers, and the specifications needed to get the right product at the lowest price.

Today's management problems are complicated. Financing is more complex, and necessary paperwork has multiplied. As in many industries, computers are playing an increasingly important role in administrative functions. Computer programs are available, for example, which help monitor food inventories, thus making it easier to know when to reorder supplies.

Those in the food service industry must be alert to changes in society. Now that the population in the United States is aging, more restaurants are catering to older customers. They have introduced senior citizen discounts and special menu choices for such patrons. There are health-food restaurants featuring salads and fresh fruits and vegetables, ethnic restaurants, which continue to grow in popularity, and restaurants that specialize in omelettes, crepes, or other foods.

The low pay and demanding hours of the food service industry has created a situation where there is a high turnover rate among employees. This is especially pronounced in the fast-food segment of the industry, where it is estimated that a fast-food position is filled about twice a year.

Equipment suppliers are an integral part of the food service industry. Salespeople are needed to inform food service establishments of the latest ovens, kitchen utensils, and other types of supplies. With the latest equipment, food service establishments are able to enlist the latest technology in the age-old quest of providing quality food to customers.

All kinds of sources exist for the restaurant worker to find out information about new equipment, new trends, and education opportunities. Magazines, books, seminars, and associations that specialize in every aspect of the food industry are available to anyone interested in finding out more about food service. At the end of this article is a short list of some of the places to write for more information.

Careers

Food service is a vast, expanding field which embraces hundreds of career opportunities. A sampling of career options follows below.

Chefs and cooks: Chefs and cooks prepare meals for customers. These meals should be attractive and tasty. Chefs and cooks also often supervise all food preparation in the kitchen. In large establishments, there may be one or more cooks responsible for specific foods, such as soups and meats.

Kitchen assistants: Kitchen assistants help cooks, chefs, and bakers prepare foods. Often, kitchen assistants quickly become cooks, chefs, or bakers.

Bakers: Bakers prepare cakes, cookies, and other desserts, as well as breads and rolls.

Dietitians: Dietitians plan nutritious meals for hospitals and other institutions. They may also work directly with individuals. Dietitians also purchase food and other supplies, and supervise cooks and other food service workers.

Waiters and waitresses: Waiters and waitresses take customers' orders, serve food and beverages, and prepare itemized checks. They also often accept payment. Waiters and waitresses must be quick and efficient, but also must be patient with customers. They often explain to customers' how certain foods are prepared and may explain special items on the menu.

Hosts and hostesses: Hosts and hostesses welcome guests. They also escort guests to suitable tables.

Caterers: Caterers plan, coordinate, and supervise food service at parties and other social functions. They work closely with customers to make sure that large or small parties are enjoyable.

Pantry supervisors: Pantry supervisors oversee the preparation of sales, sandwiches, and beverages. They may also supervise cleaning crews and be responsible for ordering supplies.

Dietetic technicians analyze data that they collected from recent food tests. Their findings are helpful to the food service industry.

Food service sales personnel: Food service sales personnel sell a particular company's product line. They may work for food suppliers, equipment manufacturers, or other organizations.

Purchasing agents: Purchasing agents order, receive, and inspect all goods shipped by suppliers. They ensure that food items are always available when needed.

Food service managers: Food service managers supervise all phases of a food service operation. The manager's responsibilities include supervising the hostesses, head waiters, waiters, and waitresses as well as the kitchen staff. He or she may also arrange for banquets and other festive meals.

Food and beverage managers: Food and beverage managers purchase, receive, and store food and related non-food products—a task that requires both integrity and an interest in safety and security. This work may be delegated to receiving clerks or, in smaller operations, to various other employees.

Head bartenders: The head bartender, who reports to the food and beverage manager, often takes charge of storing and issuing wines and liquors, preparing mixed drinks and serving the patrons of the bar. Bartenders also often order liquor, and (frequently) help to purchase liquor supplies. This work requires good judgment and a keen sense of integrity.

Executive chefs: Executive chefs plan menus and supervise their preparation. They usually work in large restaurants or larger hotels and motels. The executive chef, who typically

To create healthy and palatable meals, chefs must use the freshest foods available. This accounts for the seasonality of many dishes in restaurants.

brings years of training to this work, commands wide respect and is often granted near autonomy in the kitchen and pantry areas.

Food technologists: Food technologists study the physical, chemical, and biological composition of food. They use this information to develop methods for safely processing, preserving, and packaging the food.

Fast-food workers: Fast-food workers take orders from patrons at fast-food restaurants. They usually gather the ordered items from food waiting to be sold, serve them to the customer, and accept payment. Workers also often help prepare drinks, french fries, and other items.

Education

Generally speaking, the food service industry does not require a college degree for employment or promotion. All segments of the food service industry emphasize the importance of on-the-job training. Many workers begin in entry level jobs (such as waiters or waitresses) and through a series of promotions become managers.

Although college training is not always a guarantee of success, many food service establishments now look to college graduates to fill upper-level managerial positions.

Management training can be obtained in several ways. For those going into the food service industry directly from school, an excellent idea is to choose one of the larger restaurant organizations that has a training program. This does not necessarily need to be a management training program. Some of the chains and individual operators, for instance, have waiter and waitress training programs that in a few weeks can give people excellent experience that will serve them in good stead, not only working for the company, but also as a reference in applying for jobs in other restaurants.

The graduates of trade schools, junior colleges, and colleges who specialize in the field of food planning, preparation, and service are in demand. Chef's training schools, such as the Culinary Institute of America, concentrate on teaching all aspects of food preparation. For most gourmet and fine food restaurants, a degree from a cooking school is becoming more important. For those who are beginning as chefs, it is one of the fastest ways to achieve credentials as a top quality chef. Experience in other kitchens is also a method of training but may take longer to achieve the same status as a cooking school graduate. Talent for cooking, baking, and actual food preparation is an art. Skills can be learned to prepare anyone to be an adequate chef, but the finest cuisine, like the finest pottery, comes from someone with an affinity to the art form.

Many colleges and universities offer four-year courses in the food service field. A student may choose to take a degree in restaurant administration, institutional management, dietetics, home economics, or business administration.

In addition, there is a three-year apprenticeship administered by the American Culinary Federation which combines on-the-job training with related course work at a post-secondary institution. This prepares individuals to enter the food service field at the management level.

More colleges and universities are suggesting that their students devote their summers to working in restaurants or other food service establishments.

Successful food service managers are constantly learning because the business changes from year to year. Customers' eating habits and food preferences change; new competition comes in to challenge successful operations; food prices may soar or drop and menus have to be changed. For this reason, restaurant managers and owners must continually search for ways to keep people coming. And all restauranteurs must be able to develop effective advertising and promotion programs if they are to continue to attract customers.

Industry outlook

Food service is a rapidly growing industry. Currently restaurants and other components of the food service industry employ about eight million people, and the Educational Foundation of the National Restaurant Association estimates that 250,000 new employees will be needed each year to keep up with the growing demand for services. Many of these workers will be needed at fast-food establishments. Jobs for chefs and for waiters and waitresses should remain plentiful.

Because food is such a vital commodity, and eating out has become such a part of the American way of life, the food service industry should continue to grow even during downturns in the economy.

Unfortunately the increased need for workers is not expected to change the fact that food service employees remain among the lowest paid workers in the United States. Many workers earn close to the minimum wage and even experienced workers often earn very low salaries. Waiters, waitresses, and some other employees usually earn tips to supplement their earnings. Many food service workers also receive free meals while on duty.

Certain parts of the food service industry should grow faster than others. The fast-food segment (with sales in the United States already exceeding $50 billion a year) should continue to grow at a healthy clip. Traditional, sit-down restaurants, on the other hand, should experience slower growth.

Some analysts predict that robots and other forms of automation will be widely used in the future to prepare food and mix drinks. These technological changes will be most pronounced in areas where it is hard to attract food service workers due to the availability of higher-paying jobs.

◇ SOURCES OF ADDITIONAL INFORMATION

American Culinary Federation
10 San Bartola Road
St. Augustine, FL 32084

Council on Hotel, Restaurant, and Institutional Education
1200 17th Street, NW
Washington, DC 20036

Educational Foundation of the National Restaurant Association
250 South Wacker Drive, 14th Floor
Chicago, IL 60606

International Food Service Executive's Association
3017 West Charleston Boulevard, Suite 50
Las Vegas, NV 89102

National Restaurant Association
1200 17th Street, NW
Washington, DC 20036

Programs in Hotel, Restaurant, and Institutional Management in the United States: Junior/Community Colleges and Culinary Schools
American Hotel & Motel Association
1201 New York Avenue, NW
Washington, DC 20005

◇ RELATED ARTICLES

Volume 1: Agriculture; Food Processing; Franchising; Hospitality; Marketing; Wholesaling
Volume 2: Caterers; Dietitians; Food technologists; Home economists; Hotel and motel managers; Management trainees; Restaurant and food service managers; Retail business owners; Retail managers
Volume 3: Bakery products workers; Bartenders; Cashiers; Cooks, chefs and bakers; Fast food workers; Food service workers; Meatcutters
Volume 4: Agribusiness technicians

Foreign Service

General information

The Foreign Service, an arm of the Department of State, includes the men and women who represent the United States government, through its embassies and consulates, to the governments of other nations all over the world. Foreign Service officers and their staffs keep the Secretary of State advised on conditions and situations in other nations and on the plans and actions of their governments. In turn, they keep those governments informed of the United States' foreign policies. In addition, members of the Foreign Service advise and help U.S. citizens living or traveling abroad.

The Foreign Service traces its origins to the secret agents sent abroad by the Continental Congress in 1775. The foreign service of that time was studded with illustrious Americans—Benjamin Franklin, John Adams, John Jay, and Thomas Jefferson. Although the original Constitution of 1789 provided the legal basis for a foreign service, it was many years before an organized system developed to select and train diplomats. Diplomatic salaries were modest and consular salaries almost nonexistent. Many of the early envoys served their country at great personal sacrifice.

By the beginning of the nineteenth century the United States was turning inward toward the task of developing the vast resources of the continent. It was a period in which foreign relations languished. The Foreign Service suffered from both neglect and excessive political interference. A proposal by a congressional committee for severe cuts in the number of posts abroad was typical of congressional attitudes toward the Service during this era. Fortunately the Congress refrained from making these cuts. The inadequately paid members of the consular service were expected to live on fees they charged for the services that they performed or to depend on private incomes that they generated through other ventures.

After World War I, the United States was considered among one of the few great world powers; however, its Foreign Service was inadequate to handle the many new foreign-relations problems facing the nation. This situation led to the adoption of the Rogers Act of 1924—the most important piece of reform legislation in the history of the Foreign Service. It merged the personnel of the diplomatic and consular services—formerly separate—into a single Foreign Service; it adopted a new and uniform salary scale and, by eliminating the need for private incomes, made it possible to select candidates on the basis of merit alone. The Rogers Act also granted allowances that lessened the demands upon the personal fortunes of ambassadors and ministers and made possible promotion of trained officers to those positions and it established a retirement system.

The Foreign Service today is broadly representative of the entire nation. It includes all the major ethnic and cultural groups and as many different national backgrounds as have gone into the making of the nation. As of January 1985, the United States maintained representatives at 140 embassies, 11 missions, 73 consulates general, 34 consulates, 3 branch offices, and 30 consular agencies throughout the world. To staff these posts the Department of State can call on thousands of Foreign Service officers, on reserve officers, and on staff officers. Of the approximately 14,000 officers and staff members, about 8,000 are on duty in Washington, D.C.

The structure of the foreign service

Under the U.S. Constitution, the President has primary responsibility for deciding and implementing foreign policy. The President's chief adviser on matters of foreign policy and the person responsible for seeing that these decisions are put into action is the Secretary of State. The Department of State and the Foreign Service of the United States are the organizations that the Secretary, in turn, depends upon for advice and for action. This means that the Foreign Service is charged with tremendous responsibilities for the safety and welfare of the country.

The primary mission of the Department of State and the Foreign Service of the United States is to promote the welfare and guard the security of the country and its citizens. But the work of the Department and the Foreign Service touches on nearly every aspect of human endeavor, and it is almost impossible to catalog all the varied jobs an officer may be called upon to perform during a career. The tasks assigned, however, will correspond to both experience and rank. On the other hand, the work performed by our diplomatic corps is of such importance that virtually all assignments will call on an officer's resources of maturity, judgment, discretion, originality, and initiative.

Despite the great variety of individual tasks to be performed, both consular and diplomatic work abroad are generally grouped in the following categories: consular functions, negotiation, observing and reporting, administration, and representation.

The most important job of a consul is to protect the welfare and interests of American citizens living or traveling in the country of assignment. When Americans are in a foreign country, they come under the jurisdiction and law of that country. If they break the law they will be subject to the penalties imposed under the foreign system. Usually the consul can only make sure that the American citizen receives just and equal treatment under the foreign law and gets competent legal aid. Consuls can be most effective when they have established good relations with local authorities.

A consul may be called upon to help an American who is ill or injured abroad. This help may take the form of providing the names of competent physicians or of arranging for hospitalization or for the patient's return to the United States. A consul will also seek to aid destitute Americans, either through a local American charitable organization or by helping to arrange for transportation home.

Perhaps the grimmest and saddest task of an American consul is to dispose of the body and property of an American who dies abroad. Usually a consul arranges to ship the remains to the United States. The consul takes charge of, inventories, and protects any personal property of the dead person and returns it to the survivors. Sometimes this duty becomes hazardous and arduous. For example, when a

Given the technological advances in communications, the newsroom of a Voice of America office in Europe receives reports continuously. It must be manned at all times of the day.

Royal Nepal Airlines DC-3 crashed at 11,000 feet in an inaccessible mountain region of Nepal, it took the American consul six days of dangerous climbing up slippery mountain trails before he could arrange to cremate the remains of four passengers and fly the ashes back to Katmandu.

The single largest task of the American consul is the issuance of visas to foreigners who want to go to the United States as immigrants, students, tourists, or businesspeople. There is a great body of law that applies to the granting of visas, and one of the first tasks of a new consul is to become thoroughly familiar with the rules that have to be applied.

Among the many other varied duties, an American consular officer may issue or renew passports, distribute Social Security and veterans' pension checks, provide notarial services, help Americans vote by absentee ballot, give information on income taxes and customs regulations, act as a witness to the marriage of Americans, document the birth of children to Americans abroad, furnish the names of reputable attorneys, and perform a myriad of minor services for both Americans and local nationals.

Along with consular responsibilities, another important part of a Foreign Service officer's work is diplomatic negotiation. It consists of finding ways of reaching agreements on various matters with the representatives of other governments.

Negotiating is part of the work of an officer at every level. It may involve matters of the highest importance, such as the negotiation of the Austrian State Treaty, which was carried on over the period of a decade and through more

Negotiations form an integral part of a foreign service officer's job. Treaties and agreements on commerce and navigation are among the topics most frequently discussed.

than 375 separate sessions. Negotiations of that importance usually involve officers at the ambassadorial level. Middle-level officers will often negotiate simpler treaties or agreements such as the more standard treaties of friendship, commerce, and navigation, which must, however, be finally agreed upon through the ambassador's office.

Most negotiations, however, have little to do with treaties and agreements. They consist of the many talks, social chats, telephone conversations, and other communications that officers engage in to work out the numerous everyday problems that crop up between governments. They may include such matters as establishing the U.S. citizenship status of a resident of the host country, setting the pay scale for embassy chauffeurs, or arranging space for a trade or cultural exhibit.

Because economic work is an important phase of the embassy's activity, there are frequent negotiations in this field. Foreign Service officers act as economic officers and commercial attaches for the embassy and may negotiate with foreign officials on the conditions under which American businesses operate in a foreign country. They may negotiate treaties that guarantee U.S. businesspeople the same rights as local businesspeople, or they may work out ways to avoid the imposition on U.S. business of certain import restrictions or taxes. The final agreement is made through the ambassador's office.

In addition to negotiating, the Foreign Service is also involved with observing and reporting information. The Foreign Service of the United States has often been called "the eyes and ears of the United States abroad." In the early days of the nation, communications were poor and slow and reporting was haphazard. Today, many thousands of words are funneled daily into the Department of State from posts abroad, reporting regularly on virtually every aspect of the life of other countries.

The subjects of an officer's reporting depend upon the embassy or consular assignment. In a large embassy, officers will probably specialize as political, economic, consular, or administrative officers. In a small consulate, on the other hand, they may be engaged in a great variety of work and thus report in many areas.

A political officer may submit reports on such matters as expected changes in the local government, discussions held with members of the host government, or factors in an upcoming local election. Officers also send in biographic information about prominent individuals in foreign countries, to inform officials in Washington about persons with whom they may have to deal.

Reporting may be a routine procedure of gathering information from local press and similar sources, or it may be an exciting and even dangerous job. In the world's less developed regions, reporting is particularly difficult since there is often very little statistical material regarding the economy prepared by the local government. An economic officer may, for example, have to go into the countryside and estimate the yield of a certain crop, visit mines, petroleum refineries, ports, or other economic centers where firsthand information can be obtained.

To be effective as a reporter, an officer must develop wide personal contacts in the country of assignment, not only with host-government officials, but with politicians, businesspeople, reporters, importers and exporters, diplomatic representatives of other nations, and many members of the American community.

At all foreign posts someone must do the "housekeeping," or administrative tasks necessary to keep a post running. In a new country, for example, arrangements must be made to obtain an embassy or chancery building, an ambassador's residence, and quarters for Foreign Service personnel. Local employees must be hired, payrolls and budgets figured, commissaries stocked, motor pools operated, supplies purchased and maintained, the security of the mission assured, and many other jobs performed that are connected with running an office abroad.

All Americans overseas are in a sense representatives of the United States. But because of their official standing, Foreign Service members have responsibilities that require them to be particularly careful in all they say and do abroad. Whether they are stamping visas or meeting with a head of state, Foreign Service personnel will be judged by other people abroad as typical of all Americans. In addition, Foreign Service officers have certain formal representation duties, which may include making public speeches or attending a variety of formal functions.

The embassy or consulate abroad also represents the United States to Americans working in or visiting that country, and much of a Foreign Service officer's time, particularly that of ambassadors, is taken up with escorting official visitors and entertaining both American businesspeople and local officials.

If Foreign Service officers spent their entire career abroad, they would before long get out of touch with American life and might become poor representatives of the country. For this reason officers are periodically returned from abroad to serve in the Department of State in Washington for periods of from two to four years. Working in the Department, officers learn how the many reports prepared in the field are finally utilized by the Department of State and other agencies of government and by American business. It becomes their turn to draft instructions to be carried out by other officers in our missions abroad. They relay to the missions policies developed by the Secretary of State and the President. In preparing instructions for the field, the Foreign Service officer often works closely with officials in many other agencies of the government.

The Foreign Service officer in Washington may be assigned to a policy-making position in the Department. It may range from desk officer for a middle-grade officer to Assistant Secretary of State for an officer who has been serving as ambassador. A "desk" for a particular country or area is the office in which all matters relating to that country or area are channeled and coordinated, and the officer in charge exercises a great deal of responsibility.

Officers returning from abroad also may be assigned to any of a number of other government agencies, including the Departments of Defense, Agriculture, Commerce, and Labor. They may be sent to various American universities, the Defense colleges, or the Department's Foreign Service Institute for advanced training. The training is part of a career-development plan carefully worked out for each officer and designed to bring out his or her greatest potential.

In the Foreign Service, as in military service, an employee serves wherever and when-

Support staff in foreign service offices are often local residents that have been carefully screened by the U.S. Government.

ever the Service sees fit. While some consideration is given to an employee's preference, the final determining factor is the need of the government. The Foreign Service is not a nine-to-five job; officers are expected to get their job done irrespective of any regular schedule, and many officers serve hundreds of uncompensated overtime hours annually.

Foreign Service officers rarely spend more than four years at the same post. They are subject to periodic transfers, which may shuttle them and their families from a frigid to a tropical climate, from a small town in Africa to a cosmopolitan European capital—with all the attendant problems of adjusting to new language, customs, and living conditions.

The needs of the Service determine the type of work an officer performs. In making assignments, however, the Department takes into account training, experience, language competence, career-development needs, and similar factors, as well as the desires and aspirations of the officer.

All these elements are part of the discipline of a Foreign Service career. In fact, self-discipline is an essential ingredient of a Foreign Service officer's makeup. Officers must, for example, subordinate their own personal desires and the use of their time to the needs of their posts. They learn that the rounds of social events—which they are required to attend regardless of their own preferences—are mainly work sessions in which they make contacts that help them do their daily jobs. At such gatherings, and in fact in all their public appearances, officers exert tight discipline over what they say and do, to ensure that they neither reveal information that could injure American interests nor, by a careless phrase or action, inadvertently offend a representative of another nation.

There is, in fact, a built-in discipline that governs these social events, and it is called pro-

An employee of the U.S. Information Service shows an audio-visual program about American culture to citizens of Lagos, Nigeria.

tocol. Protocol is nothing more than a detailed set of rules regulating the conduct of diplomatic personnel. To the new officer some aspects of protocol may seem petty or cumbersome, for they include such details as determining who has the right to sit on a sofa, who enters and leaves a room first, and how to turn down the edge of a calling card. But an experienced officer recognizes that protocol provides an extremely useful method of conducting diplomatic business. Official calls, for instance, give the officer at a new post an accepted and easy way to meet people and make friends. Protocol furnishes a guide to conduct in official relations with people of other countries, no matter how diverse their customs may be.

Careers

Each officer also has a title, which is determined by assignment as well as class. An officer's title establishes his or her status at a post. Among the more common diplomatic titles are: ambassador, minister-counselor, first (second, third) secretary, and attache. Unusual consular titles include consul general, consul, and vice-consul. Generally, the higher an officer's class, the higher the title he or she will hold at a post.

There are four categories of U.S. Foreign Service personnel: chiefs of mission, Foreign Service officers, Foreign Service reserve officers, and Foreign Service staff employees. For-

eign personnel employed at missions abroad are known as Foreign Service "locals."

Ambassador: An embassy is headed by an ambassador, who is a personal representative of the President of the United States and must be accorded the same respect and consideration due the President. Ambassadors are the highest-ranking Americans in any country, and the officials of all other agencies of government overseas, with the exception of the commanders of military forces, are under the ambassador's jurisdiction. Ambassadors may be appointed by the President, with the advice and consent of the Senate, from the ranks of the Foreign Service officer corps or from outside the Service. Today, more than three-fourths of the mission chiefs are career officers. Embassies are known as diplomatic posts, and they are usually located in the capital city of the foreign country.

Consular posts: The other broad category of Foreign Service posts is the consulate. Consular posts are established in various important industrial and maritime cities in a country according to the need and in agreement with the host government. Consular officers do not have diplomatic status and are not authorized to represent the President in negotiations with other governments.

Foreign Service officers: Foreign Service officers make up the professional corps that performs the main work of the Service. Foreign Service officers (FSOs) are ranked in eight classes, plus the top classes of career minister and career ambassador. They are commissioned by the President, by and with the advice and consent of the Senate. New officers serve a probation period of three to four years as FSOs of the junior class and then are commissioned as FSOs, as secretaries in the diplomatic service, and as vice-consuls.

Foreign Service reserve officers: Foreign Service reserve officers constitute a corps of men and women on active duty; they are not reserves in the military sense. Unlike Foreign Service officers, who enter the service primarily through an examination process, Foreign Service reserve officers are recruited from among specialists who have some particular skill needed by the Service.

Foreign Service Staff Corps: The Foreign Service Staff Corps, the third American branch of the Service, is made up of thousands of American officers and employees. The Staff Corps supplies many of the technical skills needed to run posts overseas. The middle and upper ranks consist of technical and administrative personnel, while the lower ranks include clerks, stenographers, and code clerks. Many Staff Corps members make the Foreign Service their career, some eventually joining the Foreign Service officer corps through Civil Service examinations.

Foreign Service nationals: Foreign Service nationals are citizens of the countries in which posts are located. The jobs they hold range from janitors, messengers, and chauffeurs to clerks, accountants, translators, and political and economic analysts. Because of their knowledge of the local language and conditions, and the continuity of their work, they make an indispensable contribution to the operation of Foreign Service posts.

Attaches: Attaches are officers assigned to a post to do a specialized job. Labor and commercial attaches are Foreign Service personnel. Agricultural, mineral, military, and other attaches are not usually career members of the Foreign Service but are assigned to an embassy from other government agencies, and are recruited for their specialties.

Retirement is required at age sixty for all Foreign Service officers. An officer with twenty years' experience may retire at age fifty with the Secretary's approval. On retirement, officers receive a lifetime annuity based on their salaries.

Education

To be eligible to take the Foreign Service officer examination, applicants must be American citizens and be between the ages of twenty and fifty-four. Candidates must be willing to serve at any post to which they are assigned.

There are no formal educational or job-experience requirements for becoming a Foreign Service officer, but it has been found that most successful candidates possess at least a bachelor's degree and many have earned or worked toward advanced degrees. Students planning a career in the Foreign Service should acquire a good general education, including the ability to speak and write well in English; some facility in a foreign language; and a good background in history, government, geography, commerce, economics, and management.

The Department of State does not recommend any particular educational institutions or courses of study in preparation for a career in the Foreign Service. Schools throughout the country offer the kind of well-balanced curriculum that provides a candidate with the varied knowledge and ability he or she will need in this career.

Foreign Service officers are not exempt from military service and during times of selec-

tive service are subject to draft as are any other citizens.

The examination for entrance into the Foreign Service consists of five parts: a written examination, a one-day assessment examination, a physical examination, a background examination, and a final review. The written examination is usually given in December of each year in cities throughout the United States and at U.S. diplomatic or consular posts abroad.

Those who pass the written examination will be further evaluated by a series of techniques lasting one day. This will include a variety of observations and measures involving trained observers, simulation techniques, interviews, and inventories. All candidates will participate in all exercises with no decision made until all the results are in. The assessment procedures are based on current job analysis of Foreign Service work and the knowledge, skills, abilities, and personal characteristics judged to be important in the performance of that work.

Candidates who pass this examination, as well as any dependents who are to accompany them abroad, are required to pass a thorough physical examination. However, an Employment Review Committee has the responsibility of making a recommendation to the Director General of the Foreign Service as to whether or not applicants for employment in the Foreign Service have the potential to be successful Foreign Service employees, even though these applicants or their dependents have not been able to meet current Foreign Service medical standards.

While knowledge of a foreign language is not required in order to take the examination, a foreign-language test is given after an officer begins duty, and language skill contributes to an officer's advancement. Passing a speaking and reading test in any of more than a score of languages will entitle an officer to a salary increase.

All successful candidates are subject to a thorough examination of their character, reliability, and loyalty to the United States. And lastly, there is a final review of the preceding four steps to determine which candidates are eligible for appointment.

Candidates who pass all the foregoing examinations have their names placed on a rank-order registration of eligibles. The eligibility of candidates expires eighteen months after their names have been entered on the register. Appointments are made from these registers from time to time, depending upon the officers required by the Department and the availability of openings in the training classes at the Department's Foreign Service Institute.

Generally, new members of the Staff Corps are assigned to serve in the Department in Washington for periods of up to nine months. During this time the new employee learns the routines of government business in general and Department of State procedures in particular. Then, just before going overseas, Staff Corps members attend the Foreign Service Institute to learn about the work they will do abroad.

Industry outlook

There are only a few thousand officer positions in the Foreign Service, and in any one year rarely more than a few hundred new officers are appointed. Yet, the Foreign Service is such an attractive way of life that it draws many applicants for every available position.

Although officer positions are very competitive, the Foreign Service is continually recruiting young men and women to serve as secretaries, stenographers, and communications and records clerks. From time to time there is also need for diplomatic couriers, nurses, clerks, telecommunications specialists, budget and fiscal personnel, and others.

Among the attractions of Foreign Service work is the satisfaction of knowing that one's job is important to the welfare of the country. In addition, the Foreign Service offers prestige, good pay, and the opportunity to live in a number of different countries for long periods of time.

As in other professions, there are some disadvantages. The Foreign Service has its share of hazards and inconveniences. For example, raising and educating a family abroad in a number of different countries presents problems of language, availability of schools, and adaptability.

A Foreign Service officer's salary is determined by classification. An officer who performs competently may be expected to be promoted periodically and to receive periodic salary increases. Selection Boards meet annually to consider each officer for promotion in competition with all other officers in his or her same class. The Board's decisions will be based on reports by an officer's supervisor and on those of the Foreign Service inspection corps. If an officer fails to receive a promotion within a set time limit, or if it is officially established that his or her performance is unsatisfactory, that officer is "selected out" of the Service.

Living and traveling abroad entail certain expenses for which Foreign Service officers, both career and reserve, receive allowances. In those countries where government living quarters are not provided, an allowance is paid to compensate for the cost of rental and maintenance of private quarters. A cost-of-living allowance is provided when an officer is assigned to a post where living costs are substantially higher than in Washington, D.C. Other allowances to provide for special circumstances include: a temporary lodging allowance to pay the cost of living quarters for employees and their families upon arrival at, or just before leaving, a foreign post; a post differential of from 10 to 25 percent for serving at a post where extraordinarily difficult living conditions or health hazards prevail; a per-diem allowance to cover official travel costs; and an educational allowance to help officers provide elementary and secondary education for their children when they are stationed abroad.

◇ **SOURCES OF ADDITIONAL INFORMATION**

General information is available from:

U.S. Department of State
c/o Recruitment Division
Box 12209
Rosslyn Station
Arlington, VA 22209

Applications to take the examination for Foreign Service officer can be obtained from:

Board of Examiners for the Foreign Service
U.S. Department of State
Washington, DC 20520

For information on films and videotapes, write to:

Bureau of Public Affairs
c/o Special Projects Staff
Room 4827A, Department of State
Washington, DC 20520

◇ **RELATED ARTICLES**

Volume 1: Civil Service; Foreign Trade; Politics and Public Service
Volume 2: Foreign-Service officers; Political scientists; Sociologists

Foreign Trade

General information

Foreign trade was one of the major resources for the Roman Empire. Rome expanded its territories and the countries with which it traded as the wealth of goods came in from overseas. Spices from India, silk from China, and food, clothing, and gems from other countries were shipped to Rome along the trade routes. The Roman Empire built roads from Rome through Europe as far as northern France, Germany, and across the Alps to Switzerland. They sailed the southern shores of Africa and had camel routes to the Orient.

Trade gave each culture something new and different. Tea was unknown to Europeans until the Middle Ages. Tobacco was first discovered in America, and was shipped back by the Colonialists. Spaghetti noodles were supposedly brought back from China by Marco Polo.

Along with the great trading routes, large markets were built for people who had traveled to one central region to buy things from all over the world. Istanbul had an ideal central location, between Asia and Europe, off of the Mediterranean Ocean and the Black Sea. It became the capital of the Roman Empire in 330 A.D. and was then named after the ruling Roman emperor Constantine. The city became known as Constantinople.

International trade developed and has continued to be practiced by countries for two basic reasons. The first was that another country could supply something that the buying country may not have or may not be able to produce. For example, Hawaii has no metals on the islands. In order to construct something out of a material stronger than wood, metals had to be brought in.

The other reason for international trade is cost. Although one country may be able to produce an item, it may be cheaper to make it somewhere else and have it brought in. Tea can

be grown with some difficulty in a northern climate, but most tea for the world market is still supplied by India. They have a climate and soil well suited to the production of tea, and everything is in place to grow enough tea leaves to meet the demands of the world market.

With the establishment of standard trade routes and fairly constant governments in the western countries, international trade became regulated and controlled. Taxes were levied against some import items to allow local producers to compete economically against foreign producers. (Import taxes are labeled tariffs.)

Trade limits were set on other items to keep the local market from being flooded with foreign goods. Europe traded with the United States from the first settlements in the 1600s. As the American economy and industry expanded, European countries found themselves competing against each other on several commercial products sold at home and abroad.

Meanwhile America was developing its own industries at home and abroad. Directly after World War II, American international business had quickly expanded its manufacturing and distribution facilities overseas. Many of these facilities were and still are controlled or completely owned by the parent company. In other instances, they have been established under licensing arrangements or were established as joint ventures with a foreign company.

Direct foreign investments have increased substantially since 1946. Exports of U.S. goods and services, in 1987, were at $252 billion. Imports totaled $424 billion in 1987. Most economists believe that imports and exports should be equal in value, or exports should be higher. When exports shipments are smaller than imports, it means that money is being spend in other countries that will not be returned to the first country. Because of this imbalance, the United States is keenly interested in either expanding the export of American goods, or controlling the import of foreign goods. The

A dock worker at the Port of Indiana loads carefully-weighed packages of corn on a ship that is bound for Eastern Europe.

growth of foreign business and its importance to the national economy has created a great need for the individual who is prepared to handle the complex problems of international business.

The structure of foreign trade

About one out of every seven persons in private employment is engaged in activities linked to foreign trade. Foreign trade today affects almost every person in the world. It enables each country to make the best use of its most abundant resources. By selling its surplus—be it a raw material such as coal, a semifinished product like cotton stuffs, or finished products such as computers or a banking or engineering service—a country earns the money to import another nation's surplus. Foreign trade involves the building of offices or plants in foreign countries, sending technical or other specialists abroad, or expanding the distribution of a product into the international market.

Four basic types of structures exist in international trade. The most basic arrangement is the single trade transaction. For example, someone in Florida has a shipment of orange juice to sell abroad. That person, the seller, either hires someone to find a buyer or personally finds someone that would like to purchase his shipment. A buyer is found in France, a contract is signed after legal matters are settled, and the orange juice is shipped abroad. There is only one contract and one shipment.

The second type of arrangement concerns installment sales. More than one transaction will take place between the seller and the buyer. A series of contracts for shipments may be signed, or one contract may be signed that outlines a series of sales over time. Either way an extended relationship is developed between the seller and the buyer for continued supplies across the border. Both the multiple contract and the single contract arrangements will have multiple deliveries and payments. Many products are bought with such regularity that a continued supply of an item can be counted on to sell, and allows the importer to develop regular customers who rely on the continual receiving of goods from abroad. Wine, cheese, and many other food items are shipped on installment contracts.

License arrangements are more complex because they involve the production of the item in the country where it is to be sold, but the rights to produce the item remain with the country that originally produced the items. Products made under patents are licensed to other companies for manufacturing, as long as the company manufacturing the product pays royalties on each item sold. For example, books may be produced in another country, or in another language, under a license agreement. If an American author has a book published in Germany, the German publisher has to get a legal agreement allowing him to publish, and he would normally pay the author a set fee for each book sold.

The joint venture is the fourth type of arrangement for foreign trade. Two companies, one from each country, will agree to produce something in a cooperative effort. They may choose to produce the item under one company's name, under the two names combined, or they may choose to create a third company with an independent function from the two parent companies. Both parent companies get benefits from the sales of the items produced by the joint venture.

Subsidiary companies are branches set up in foreign countries. Many Fortune 500 countries have branches all over the world. Oil companies commonly have branches abroad, as do large banks and investment firms, and automobile manufacturers. Multinational corporations, of which there are more than 7,000, are companies that have operations in two or more countries. It is estimated that at least half of the multinational corporations have branches in more than two countries and at least 300 companies operate in six or more countries. These companies may operate production branches out of countries where it is cheaper to manufacture the product, or the raw materials may be close at hand. They may also produce the item in one or two locations and then use the other operations for sales and administration.

With each of the types of trade contacts and arrangements, there are a number of jobs needed to organize, develop, and maintain the agreement. The jobs vary with the product or service offered and with the company's goals for the product abroad.

Careers

Foreign trade careers are basically those that involve jobs at home and abroad with America's growing number of international business concerns. In the United States, thousands of companies are engaged to some extent in the export business, including small manufacturers that sell overseas under the impetus of the Export Trading Companies Act, as well as large corporations that have substantial investments in foreign plants and facilities in addition to their export business. Millions of jobs in the United States are linked to the export of goods and services.

Approximately 500 large companies employ most of the American personnel abroad. These include the major petroleum companies, large manufacturing firms, contract-engineering firms, banking and other services, and a scattering of other operations. The trend to replace Americans with qualified local nationals is especially strong in the larger corporations and particularly those operating in Europe; fewer than one percent of their overseas employees are likely to be Americans.

Opportunities for U.S. citizens fall generally in these categories:

Technical specialists: Most of the people currently being sent abroad by large companies are technical specialists whose assignments are often for only limited periods of one to two years. These specialists are repatriated when a specific job is done or a local national has been trained to handle it. Engineers and chemists have good chances because of the scarcity of suitable technical training overseas, particularly in the developing countries. Those who are highly competent in such areas as merchandising, financial management, and advertising, however, may well be sent to areas where there is a shortage of local nationals with advanced management skills.

Senior executives: Many U.S. companies assign senior executives such as the general manager and treasure to the top jobs in foreign subsidiaries. These are mature executives who are well versed in company operations and management skill.

Organizers: When new plants are established overseas, those people with middle-

Philippine wheat buyers inspect the Idaho wheat crop with an American grain merchant. If they are satisfied with the quality of the wheat, they will negotiate the price with the merchant.

management organizing skills may be assigned temporarily. The ideal candidate would be a person knowledgeable in company operations, having previous experience in other foreign units (see Volume 2: Management analysts and consultants).

In smaller companies, there is likely to be a higher proportion of American executives with overseas assignments. Although local nationals may fill some of the management positions in these companies, the American managers hold important responsibilities that necessitate their being permanently assigned. The Americans who handle these assignments usually have established their value to the company either in the domestic operation or in other foreign assignments.

Accountants: With the establishment of a company or contract abroad, it is important to have someone with strong a international finance background. Since the company will be dealing with two or more currencies, the accountants' job will be more complicated than his or her job was at home. Accountants are responsible for trade and tariff payments, investments, currency exchange, and sales and other taxes required by both the home country and the host country. It may be required to hire accountants from both countries for the work.

Economists: Economists are hired to work with market fluctuations and aid the company in warding off any surprises in their foreign transactions. For example, if a devaluation occurs for one of the two currencies involved in the international agreement, then the cost of production or sales could force the product off the market.

Ship workers unload imported goods from Switzerland. The packages must be inspected before being allowed into the country.

Marketers: Sales of a product or service abroad will require the skills of someone who has some awareness of the cultural differences between the original country and the country where the product is to be marketed. International marketing relies on the talents of someone who can make the transition between one culture and another (see Volume 1: Marketing).

Consultants: For a smaller company, it may not be feasible to hire a permanent staff member to handle one or more aspects of foreign trade. Many companies and individuals offer their services on a free-lance basis to companies wishing to enter into international trade agreements. The consultant is free to work when or where he or she wants, as long as the market is open. Typically, the consultant has some corporate experience in international trade, and a high degree of expertise in the legal, financial, or marketing area.

Translators and interpreters: Translators will be needed for contracts, hiring, training, sales, and almost every other aspect of the work. Business in the foreign country is normally done in their language, although most other countries have many people who speak English. Large corporations will need fluent translators for many different languages (see Volume 2: Interpreters).

Lawyers: International law is a specialized field with lawyers required to negotiate legal contracts for two countries' sets of laws. Familiarity with U.S. trade laws and tariffs is important, and some background education in international trade consultation and contract negotiation is necessary. Lawyers may be permanent counsel for a company, or hired on a single contract arrangement. They may work in private practice or with firms specializing in world trade (see Volume 1: Law).

International affairs specialists: International affairs specialists give advice and counsel to a company on the political and business climate in which the company will work. They are the experts on the stability of a country's government and are responsible for determining the relative safety of the company's employees and investments abroad. Advanced education in international affairs, along with work experience abroad, is the typical background for specialists (see Volume 2: Political scientists).

Management: Of the more than 25,000 companies in the United States engaged in exporting, many maintain small export departments for handling foreign orders. This department is likely to be under the supervision of an export manager, whose duties might include working with the domestic sales, credit, and production managers. In larger operations, he or she may have a staff including an assistant export manager, export credit manager, export shipping clerk, export traffic manager, translators, documentation clerk, and other assistants. Foreign language skills are helpful in these jobs, as well as knowledge of documentation procedures for overseas shipments.

Large organizations may employ foreign branch managers and resident sales representatives abroad, as well as staffing a home office department divided up by region. Such a department may be headed by a vice-president-international, or vice-president in charge of foreign sales, and may include an international advertising manager and other specialists. The international divisions of a few of the largest companies include international public relations managers as well.

Independent exporters: Some American manufacturers prefer to turn over the responsibility for export sales to an outside agent specializing in foreign trade. This may be an individual export manager or an export commission house, which represents several lines of products on a contractual basis, often receiving a retainer as well as a commission. Other specialists are the manufacturers' export agents, who operate on a straight commission basis, and export merchants, who buy and sell on their own accounts.

Separate import departments are maintained by companies in some fields, notably by large retailing organizations. The staff would include foreign buyers, import sales managers, customs clerks, and other administrative experts concerned with tariff rates and the entry of foreign goods through U.S. customs. Commodity experts who act as import managers also have to be familiar with the intricacies of world trade in cotton, wool, silk, hides, spices, coffee, or other commodities in which they specialize (see Volume 2: Export-import specialists).

Sales representatives: The traveling export sales representative best epitomizes American foreign trade, spanning the world to maintain personal contact with agents, distributors, and customers in overseas markets. Even in an age of specialization and internationalization in production and marketing, the international traveling sales representative is a vital cog in the machinery of foreign trade.

Despite the rigors of travel, there is a certain glamour attached to foreign trade. There are relatively few international sales jobs, and there is keen competition for those that exist. Base salaries on the international side of business are generally the same or somewhat higher than comparable jobs with a domestic company.

The typical foreign trade career will start in the United States, involve a transfer to one or two foreign locations, and perhaps be capped by a return to the home office in an international management capacity. It is the foreign service phase of such a career that typically calls for the broad spectrum of qualifications implied in the term international business person.

In addition to having technical competence, basic managerial competence, a flair for teaching and leadership, the ideal overseas salesperson should also have special capabilities in cultural relations. Some of these capabilities are a genuine desire to go abroad and a willingness to live in a different social, cultural, or business environment; an ability to adapt to new living and working conditions and to integrate into a new kind of community; independence and the ability to achieve results with limited resources; and a facility for foreign languages and an interest in learning the customs, history, and culture of foreign peoples.

The whole family must be able to adjust to living abroad. The concerns of spouses and children are important considerations for business people working abroad. The need to prematurely end an assignment because of family difficulties can be costly.

The expanding international side of business offers a world of career opportunities to the resourceful person who likes travel, is self-

Foreign traders must keep abreast on the latest economic changes in certain countries. There are many periodicals that cater to the specific needs of these merchants.

reliant, imaginative, adaptable, and possesses an instinct for cultural empathy. Many presidents and corporate directors of the largest corporations have come up on the international side. This trend may well intensify as world trade becomes more important.

Education

Formal education for international business can begin in high school, with such fundamentals as science, mathematics, foreign languages, history, and English. The high-school student should make an effort to achieve economic literacy, that is to understand the relation of the American economy to the world economy.

At the college level, the requirements for international business generally parallel those for domestic business careers. A liberal arts curriculum plus essential business courses will provide the broad background for the person who most often succeeds in international business. Extracurricular reading would be helpful in such subjects as international trade, banking and foreign exchange, tariffs and other trade barriers, the balance of payments, and economic development and growth.

A graduate school of business can then provide theoretical management skills that will be of long-range value to the future executive. International companies generally look for individuals with a background in marketing, financing, and other broad elements of modern management. Special language skills and economic knowledge of particular countries are also helpful.

In addition to many graduate schools of business that offer courses in foreign trade, certain institutions specialize in preparing individuals for overseas work. Some of these, such as the American Institute for Foreign Trade in Phoenix, and Georgetown University in Washington, D.C., offer special courses for people preparing for new foreign assignments.

For specialists, advanced degrees in the areas of specialty is normally require. For example, a law degree with a background in international law is usually necessary for overseas legal work. Accountants and economists should also have a background in international economy to work in foreign trade.

A company seeking candidates for foreign assignments ordinarily looks first within the company itself for people who know the organization and who have demonstrated their ability on the job. Those who have the motivation and other qualities that would indicate success overseas may be offered foreign assignments. An intensive orientation program would follow: language training, orientation in the cultural, political, and social factors of the area of assignment, and orientation in the international division's policies and practices.

Major companies also scout schools regularly for new people who may qualify for eventual assignment to international operations. Many of these are assigned initially to home office staff jobs involving occasional trips abroad, usually on special assignments.

Direct employment is also possible with smaller companies, which may prefer to go outside their own organizations for overseas employees.

Industry outlook

The trend in recent years has been to send abroad only those U.S. employees who have skills and abilities not available locally. Americans go abroad to train local nationals in technical know-how and management techniques or as engineers or contractors on a project. After two or three years, perhaps longer, they are replaced by the local nationals they have trained. The Americans may then move on to help establish another foreign operation. Yet the number of jobs for Americans abroad is not decreasing. As more and more companies enter foreign markets, new employment opportunities are created.

This fact applies particularly in the less developed regions. U.S. firms are supplying technical and managerial experience to the developing nations of the world. The work of the American abroad can be pioneering, challenging, and may be deeply satisfying.

With smaller businesses becoming involved in foreign trade, the expansion of the field is rapid. The jobs are still fairly undefined because the industry is new to most companies. Mid-size companies are looking for individuals with background and desire for foreign trade. Self-motivation and creativity are essential to the employee who will be breaking new territory for a company.

The large companies that have been abroad for many years have well established programs, and hiring practices. They may have programs that train within the company for work abroad, or they may be able to rely on the local nationals to run most of the organization. It is not easy to break into the international field in the large corporations, although students have been recruited occasionally for overseas service. Usually, a number of years must be spent in the domestic office, learning the business and the company and often specializing in one aspect of it. Maturity and experience in decision making ordinarily must be gained in the United States before a person is sent overseas.

◇ SOURCES OF ADDITIONAL INFORMATION

General information about international business may be obtained from:

American Association of Exporters and Importers
11 West 42nd Street
New York, NY 10036

Council for Export Trading Companies
1225 Connecticut Avenue, NW, Suite 415
Washington, DC 20036

International Traders Association
c/o The Mellinger Company
6100 Variel Avenue
Woodland Hills, CA 91367

International Trade Administration
U.S. Department of Commerce
Constitution and 14th Street, NW
Washington, DC 20230

Commerce Business Daily, published by the U.S. and Foreign Commercial Service, is available from:

The Superintendent of Documents
U.S. Government Printing Office
Washington, DC 20402

For organizations concerned with international trade and a bibliography of periodicals and indexes, consult Foreign Commerce Handbook provided by:

Chamber of Commerce of the United States
1615 H Street, NW
Washington, DC 20062

For information on training to become a translator or interpreter, contact:

American Translators Association
109 Croton Avenue
Ossining, NY 10562

◇ **RELATED ARTICLES**

Volume 1: Accounting; Banking and Financial Services; Business Administration; Marketing; Retailing; Wholesaling
Volume 2: Accountants and auditors; Buyers, wholesale and retail; Economists; Export-import specialists; Financial institution officers and managers; Interpreters; Lawyers and judges; Management analysts and consultants; Merchant marine occupations; Political scientists; Purchasing agents
Volume 3: Stevedoring occupations; Traffic agents and clerks

Franchising

General information

Franchising began in the late 19th century when the Singer Company first allowed individuals to sell its sewing machines in particular regions. Soon afterward, General Motors started doing the same with its cars, as did Coca Cola with its soft drinks.

Dairy Queen, one of the oldest fast-food franchises, started in 1940, and began selling franchises in 1944. The line of products were limited to cones and the occasional sundae. Each franchisee set the product line on the basis of what he or she thought would sell. The contracts were short and did not restrict the franchisee to a particular product line or store style. The basis of the contract was a royalty arrangement based on sales of the product and the use of the name.

It was during the 1950s that franchising really took off. Among the most well-known franchisors to emerge at that time were McDonalds, Dunkin Donuts, and Aamco Transmission. McDonald's was one of the first franchisors to establish rules for what the store would look like, what products would be sold, and what types of promotions could be run. The organization held strict control over product line, guaranteeing consistency from franchisee to franchisee.

Originally, most franchises were offshoots of goods-producing companies, like Singer sewing machines. Franchising has adapted however, to almost every kind of industry. Today, the trend is toward service-industry franchises, such as real-estate offices and cleaning services. In the early 1990s, more than 2,000 companies sponsored more than 500,000 franchises, and this number increases by more than 25,000 per year. Sales generated in the average store from any of the top ten franchising companies are more than $400,000 a year and can be as high as $1,600,000. It is predicted that one half of all sales will be generated by franchises by the year 2000. In the early 1990s, franchising provided employment for more than eight million people.

The structure of the franchising industry

Owning one's own business is, for many people, the realization of the American dream. But, today, as transportation and communication networks have made it easier for big companies to expand their markets, the small businessperson is finding it harder and harder to survive. How can an individual with a shop in one town compete against a company that has outlets across the country and that advertises its product on prime-time television? Franchising is a system whereby manufacturers can get their products to new markets at a relatively low cost, and individuals can own and manage their own businesses. Franchising is a viable and lucrative alternative to starting from the ground up.

A multi-billion-dollar industry, franchising has become an important way of doing business, and it is projected to continue to be well into the future.

The word *franchise* literally means a privilege or right. *Enfranchisement* commonly means the right to vote. In the world of business, however, a franchise is the privilege of providing a parent company's goods or services in a given area. The formula is simple: A business with a product or service offers territories or product lines to individuals in exchange for an up-front fee and a percentage of their future profits. The company offering the franchise is the *franchisor*; the person or partnership buying the franchise is the *franchisee*.

To understand franchising, it is helpful to remember that it is simply a method of distribution, like retailing or direct mail. There are

This interior view of an Ace Hardware store shows the wide variety of items and brands that it sells. Such a business is an example of a trade name franchise. The owner of the store has purchased the right to associate his goods with the established name of Ace Hardware.

two ways for a company to increase profits: decrease expenses or expand revenues, preferably both. In order to increase revenues, a company must expand its distribution channels. Retailing and direct mail, however, are not practical ways of distributing many products.

Does it make sense for a donut company to sell its products in a grocery store? Some do, and yet most people do not want to stand in line in a supermarket just to buy a donut and a cup of coffee. Besides, you rarely find grocery stores on downtown blocks, next to the office buildings where people work. Obviously, the best way to sell donuts is to set up small shops in areas of heavy pedestrian traffic.

Clearly, the best way to distribute many goods and services is through specialty outlets, like fast-food restaurants, automotive centers, and travel agencies. In addition, the best way to ensure the profitability of these outlets to increase their numbers. The common logic is that when a customer sees the same restaurant in several locations, he or she will figure that their food must be good, and it increases the chances that the customer will try that restaurant.

So, not only do many companies need specialty outlets to distribute their products, it is in their best interest to have many outlets. And yet, opening up stores is expensive, and managing the personnel to run them can be beyond the capabilities of many organizations. If the

parent company were going to operate their own additional outlets, it would require loans, leases, and staff on their payrolls, and investment in more equipment, among other things. The expenses involved with expansion are prohibitive for many. Franchisors also would have to take on additional management responsibilities. The solution for many companies is to sell franchises.

Franchising offers additional benefits as well. Franchisors usually are successful because their franchises are well managed, stemming from the franchise managers who have made an investment in their success. The financial investment a franchisee makes gives that person the added incentive of making sure that the operation runs smoothly and economically. This financial incentive is not a part of chain-store management.

An added advantage to franchising is the collective buying power it generates. If 100 franchisees chip in for one television ad, all 100 and their parent company will benefit, but it will only cost them a tiny fraction of what the ad would have cost them on their own.

Each year the number and variety of franchisors grows. Franchising opportunities can be found in dozens of categories, with food franchises still in the lead. Food franchises include hamburger, chicken, and pizza restaurants, waffle houses, ice cream shops, and popcorn

199

Franchisees of the sporting goods store The Athlete's Foot meet annually to discuss store policies and other franchise changes.

stores. Automotive franchises include muffler shops, car-wash systems, tune-up operations, and car-rental services. Beauty and health franchises include diet and weight-loss centers, fitness clubs, and hair-care salons. Some franchises perform such services for other businesses as accounting, advertising, direct-mail marketing, training, and executive-searches. Other franchising opportunities include building and decorating services, home and office maintenance products and services, children's products, real estate agencies, and travel agencies.

There are two main kinds of franchises: product franchises and trade name franchises. In product franchising, independent retailers purchase brand-name products, such as gasoline or soft drinks, from a parent company and distribute them in their territories. The quality of the product is the responsibility of the franchisor; getting the product to customers is the responsibility of the franchisee.

In trade name franchising, franchisees do not necessarily distribute particular brand-name products, but they buy the right to be associated with an established company. Trade name franchises are common among hardware stores, which sell a variety of merchandise from different manufacturers, but which have the advantage of name-recognition when customers try to decide where to shop. Trade name franchises are also frequently purchased for maintenance services, such as pest control and lawn-care companies.

Currently, product and trade name franchising dominate the industry, in part because they are the simplest kinds of franchises for companies to offer. Business-format franchising, however, is the fastest-growing segment of the franchising industry. Business-format franchising is a combination of sales training, dis-tribution, and marketing that creates a potentially successful franchise. Entrepreneurs receive training and formal procedures in addition to products and names. One advantage of business-format franchising is its incredible flexibility. Some can be set up in vans and buses, or in booths in the lobbies of buildings.

A fourth kind of franchisee includes those who hold the rights to a franchise for a specific territory and subcontract individual outlets; this is also called franchise-within-a-franchise.

Some franchisees merely run their businesses as any retail business owner would, hiring employees to carry out actual tasks (see Volume 2: Retail business owners). Others, operating smaller franchises may perform the labor as well as manage the business.

As franchising continues to expand, there are literally thousands of franchises to choose from. Franchisors that have been in business for a longer period of time tend to be larger and better established and, as such, offer greater promise of success. Their up-front fees, however, tend to be high, and often the best territories have already been taken by other franchisees. Newer franchisors tend to be smaller and less stable, but they offer the greatest potential for short-term growth because prime locations are usually still available.

Investing in a franchise is a decision that entails considerable financial risk if the franchisee does not choose a reputable franchisor. One way to make sure that a franchisor is worthy is to read its Uniform Franchise Offering Circular (UFOC), which details the company's history, principles, experience, and franchise program. Developed by the North American Securities Administration in the 1970s, the UFOC is now required by federal law so that franchisees know what the type of business they are getting involved with.

In addition to information about the franchisor's business activities, experience, and current franchises, the Uniform Franchise Offering Circular requires disclosure of biographical and professional information about all the franchisor's principle officers, its legal history, its fiscal history, its start-up fees and royalty formula, and any additional fees. The UFOC further includes all obligations on the part of the franchisee to buy goods, services, supplies, equipment, inventory, or real estate from the franchisor.

Terms and conditions of financing arrangements, the obligations of the franchisor, territory agreements, and information about trademarks, logotypes, patents and copyrights are also included in the UFOC. Finally, the UFOC provides projections regarding earnings and information about other franchises already sold by the company, such as where they are and how they are doing.

While the Uniform Franchise Offering Circular may seem to help the prospective franchisee make a sound investment decision, it also benefits franchisors by giving them the opportunity to document their procedures and expectations. Many prospective franchisees, however, make the mistake of never reading UFOCs thoroughly. In order to be assured of a sound investment, one should read the UFOC carefully. No one should assume that a franchise is a good investment just because a form is filled out, even when it is filled out accurately.

In addition to the UFOC, a franchisor should provide a franchise agreement, which details the terms of the business arrangement. After reviewing the UFOC and other documents, a prospective franchisee should arrange for an in-person interview with a representative of the franchisor. Sometimes franchisors hire independent franchise brokers to conduct interviews, but it is preferable to talk directly to someone on the franchisor's staff, preferably the president or the franchise sales manager. Future franchisees should know more things about franchisors than are included in the UFOC. They should learn about the franchisor's operations and what is its main source of revenue. They should make sure that the franchisor has a vested interest in seeing franchises succeed, and that it is not just looking for someone to sell its products to.

Questions to ask when looking to invest include: Does the franchisor provide training, advertising, and other services that will help franchisees succeed? How much money does a franchisee need to cover rent, wages, utilities, and other expenses during the start-up months? A reputable franchisor will refer prospects to established franchisees to get this information.

Potential franchisees should be wary of any franchisor that tries to rush them into a decision; if a franchise is really so desirable that it is going to be snapped up, why should the franchisor care whether it is you or someone else that purchases it? Sometimes franchisors operate their own outlets, so franchisees should find out whether they will be competing against company stores that franchisors make more profit from, and that they are more likely to support.

Finally, what qualifications does a franchisor demand of its franchisees? Franchisees should be suspicious of franchisors who are willing to grant franchises to just anyone: They may only be interested in collecting start-up fees and have no long-term investment in the venture.

Franchises reward their stores for exceptional service. In this case, the founder of Ziebart poses with the franchisee that serviced the 10 millionth car to receive Ziebart rust-proofing.

The Better Business Bureau in any community collects criticism and complaints that have been filed with their bureau about any business in the area. Requests made for information about a company may be informative about the reputation the company has earned.

As stated before, franchising is not only good for franchisees; it is also good for franchisors. Not every entrepreneur starts out by buying a franchise. Sometimes they inherit a family business, or start a company from the ground up, the "old-fashioned" way. If their companies are doing well, they may choose to sell franchises as a way to expand their markets and increase their profits.

There are several basic rules that businesspeople should follow to help ensure the success of their franchising operations. First of all, the franchisor should have been thriving for at least three years; this suggests that its success has not been a passing fad. Second, the business should not be peculiar to one specific geographical area. For example, a surfboard rental shop may be doing great in California, but it's not likely to survive in most other locations. Third, the business should be simple enough to be duplicated easily. If a concept is too complex, it will be difficult for franchisees and their employees to learn it. Also, the simpler the concept, the greater potential to make money, because more franchises will be able to be sold. These standards of profitability, adaptability, and simplicity should be met before a business person decides to open a franchise.

New franchisors should know in advance that it can take many years to refine a franchising format until it runs smoothly and profit-

Franchises come in all forms, from fast-food restaurants to cleaning services. It provides an opportunity for entrepreneurs to establish their own businesses.

ably. They should not expect overnight success. Once the optimum format is achieved, however, franchisors must work fast to sell franchises in every desirable market before their formats are copied by competitors. Also, franchisors should understand that operating a franchise network requires additional personnel at headquarters. Franchisors needs skilled financial managers, information-systems specialists, marketing experts, human-resource managers, and technological staff. They also need lawyers to interpret the regulations that govern the industry. If they do not have the resources to manage a franchising system, prospective franchisors should reconsider.

Careers

A sampling of career opportunities follows below.

Franchisors: Franchisors are the owners of the business concept or goods or services, and grantor of the franchise to the franchisee. The franchisor may provide initial equipment, goods, and other necessities required in founding a new branch of the business. Franchisors stipulate to the lessees where supplies will be bought, what goods will be offered, and, in some instances even, what the building and store space will look like where the franchise is set up.

They are responsible for establishing the contract that binds the franchisee to the parent business. In addition, the franchisor categorizes the structure of the franchise and the limitations and expectations of the parent company and of the franchise.

Franchisee: The franchisee is the person who is granted the franchise from the franchisor. The franchisee is the business manager of the franchise and is responsible for the success of that particular branch of the business.

Store managers: In charge of the franchise, but not necessarily the owner, the store manager is responsible for the day-to-day business of the franchise, including working with, hiring, and firing staff.

District managers: Frequently hired by the franchisor, district managers oversee a large area with several franchises. They make sure that marketing is done properly, that stock is current, and that staff are trained correctly and kept up on all new developments in the business. They serve as the link between the parent company and the franchisee.

Regional managers: Usually promoted from the position of district manager, the regional manager covers a broader territory than the district manager, and heads promotion and training for new franchisees.

Vice presidents of operations: The vice president of operations is the senior executive for the franchisees. Along with the vice presidents of finance, sales, marketing, and other divisions, the vice president of operations is responsible for the major decisions that establish the direction and goals of the company.

Franchise development officers: When a prospective franchisee applies for a franchise, the franchise development department reviews the application, and, if accepted, will proceed with all the necessary instructions and information to establish the new franchisee in his or her business. This will include training the new owner in operations procedures.

Trainers: Trainers direct the educational programs that new owners attend. They also conduct continuing education courses to update and upgrade the staff of the franchises as well as the staff of the parent company. Trainers may either be employees with experience in managing and marketing or they may be professional educators in training programs.

Education

An individual's preparation for a job in franchising depends on what side of the industry he or she wishes to work in, as a franchisor or as a franchisee. Persons interested in handling operations for a franchisor should have a strong business background, acquired either in school or through practical experience. Some colleges have started offering programs in franchising, including the University of Nebraska at Lincoln, which has an International Center for Franchise Studies at its College of Business Administration. A few universities even confer masters of business administration degrees (MBAs) with a concentration in franchising.

Prospective franchisees need not have a college education, but some academic background in business or accounting is helpful. Also, some managerial experience, perhaps with a chain store, is a plus, as that will help earn the confidence of franchisors. Students who think they may be interested in franchising might want to get part-time jobs with franchises such as fast-food restaurants. The jobs they will perform will not necessarily give them managerial experience, but at least they will get some idea of how a franchise is run.

Many franchisors offer training programs for their new franchisees. During these sessions, which run from several days to several weeks, franchisors instruct franchisees on how to operate the business, how to keep books, and how to hire and train the staff. Often, franchisors will pay the franchisees' travel, food, and lodging expenses for these training sessions.

Other areas of education that are frequently used in franchising enterprises are law, marketing, and advertising. People with degrees in any of these areas will be sought by the franchisors to handle broad aspects of the business, its contracts, and its promotion.

Industry outlook

While 65 percent of all new businesses fail within five years, the failure rate for franchises is less than 4 percent. Some franchisees become millionaires, but they are the exception, not the rule. Franchisees who are willing to work hard, however, have great potential to make more money than they would working for someone else.

Categories that show higher than average growth include franchises that market in building materials and hardware, apparel and accessories, and home furnishings.

In addition to large franchisors like McDonalds, numerous small companies are selling franchises to distribute their goods and services.

Furniture

General information

Furniture can be seen from four different perspectives: from the functional view, as serving a purpose; from the view of status, representing a monetary or class status; from the technological viewpoint, showing craftsmanship and construction; or it can be seen as making a statement about the owner's personality and taste. Furniture reflects the culture in its design, function, and quality. Most furniture today is designed to be practical and comfortable, allowing for easy maintenance.

The first furniture dates back to the Stone Age. A neolithic house was discovered at Skara Brae, Orkney, off the northwestern coast of Scotland. This prehistoric house had built-in benches and sleeping spaces. Ironically, built-in furniture is a concept associated now with modern furniture.

Furniture was part of the treasures stored in Egyptian tombs, giving archaeologists great insight into the character of Egyptian culture.

Egyptian furniture featured side chairs and arm chairs with carved and shaped legs that frequently resembled a hoof or paw. Low three-legged stools, folding seats with pivotal x-shaped legs and small stands are samples of other furniture found in the tombs. The woods that Egyptians favored were cedar, sycamore, olive wood, yew, and ebony.

Furniture pieces from the royal tombs in Ur (once Sumer, in the kingdom of Mesopotamia), Iraq, has been uncovered. Made of bronze and ivory, furniture mounts for chairs and beds survived the ages.

Knowledge of classical Greek furniture was obtained from their writings and the decorations on their fine vases. Although some Greek furniture may have been modeled after Egyptian furniture, Greek furniture was consistently lighter and more delicate. The woods used by the Greeks were olive wood, box, cedar, yew, and ebony. Types of Greek furniture included chairs, stools, large and small tables, and various couches. Greeks used different types of couches for reclining while eating, drinking, reading, or sleeping.

Roman furniture was first copied from the Greeks, but as the Roman Empire expanded, so did the function and decoration of its furniture. Their furniture was lavishly carved and had intricate inlays of ivory, cherry, holly, ebony, gold, silver, precious stones, and fancy colored marble. Furniture made in bronze or stone has also survived, with pieces such as buffets for displaying silver showing the Roman interest in furniture as an art and a symbol of wealth.

Comparatively little is known about the furniture of other ancient civilizations because it was probably made of wood, bricks, or cloth that deteriorated over time.

Actual specimens from pre-14th century Europe are scarce. The period from about 1000 to 1200 A.D. was known as Romanesque and was characterized by simplified interpretations of the Greco-Roman designs. Furniture was simple and mainly made from wood. Most of the pieces of furniture were designed for sleeping and eating.

Gothic architecture, starting in the 12th century, was also simple and basic to needs of the household. Chairs from this period are extremely rare. Chairs were reserved for the most important members of the house and their important guests. Less important people were given stools for seating. Beds were quite spacious because they were frequently occupied by several people. One bed on display in the Victoria and Albert Museum could sleep twelve people.

Gothic architecture influenced furniture design as it became more ornate. The ornamental arched carved on the panels of chairs, chests, and tables became popular during the 1500s. Sideboards were also introduced at this time. Gothic styles remained significant in furniture design into the early 16th century.

Renaissance furniture featured ebony and tortoiseshell inlay, rich decoration, and simpler designs. Tables had columnar legs, and chairs had solid panels for support. Renaissance design remained an influence until the middle of the 17th century.

Baroque design was most prominent in the later part of the 17th century. Throughout Europe, the Baroque influence brought about the use of scroll-shaped and spiral-turned legs, and carved furniture fronts on large pieces such as chests and wardrobes. Rich carvings and the embellishment of metal (pewter, gold, bronze, and silver) and ebony inlays were popular across Europe.

In America, the Pilgrim style of furniture, which was popular from 1650 to 1690, naturally reflected the style of the immigrants' English roots. Some of its function and design traced back to the Renaissance style that was popular in rural, middle class England. The Pilgrims brought few pieces of furniture over to America with them. The only furniture brought over were chests holding personal and household items. As a result, furniture making was an early and flourishing industry in the colonies.

In the Dutch settlements, the furniture was designed with built-in beds, large cupboards, and tiles to give the settlements their own flavor of design. The style of the Dutch furniture remained unchanged until the 1700s.

Between 1725 and 1760, the Queen Anne period of furniture was popular. The period was characterized by a change in the leg forms. The legs changed from the familiar columnar style to a curved one, and were of animal or bird forms copied from the Rococo style that was beginning to wane in Europe. These carved legs were known as cabriole legs.

Replacing Rococo styles were the Neoclassical styles that had begun to sweep Europe in 1760 and would last until almost the turn of the century. Once again the influence of the Greek and Roman design would change the look of furnishings.

Thomas Chippendale was an English cabinetmaker who published several design books. His style of furniture became popular between 1760 and 1780. It was lighter in scale than that of the Queen Anne period but the design became more complex by the addition of elaborately carved ornaments. The legs are characterized by a tapered shape set in metal mounts that resemble animal feet. Chippendale furniture used mahogany and walnut but, after 1770, native cherry was used as a substitute for the mahogany.

Inlaid patterns of light woods and precisely carved details are characteristic of the neoclassical period from 1780 to 1815, as were ta-

This furniture was designed by the architect Ludwig Mies van der Rohe over fifty years ago. While simple in style, its construction is complex.

pering legs. The linear motifs of this period were based on ancient Greco-Roman art.

American craftsmen often used English design books for inspiration, and the designs of George Hepplewhite and Thomas Sheraton were popular between 1790 and 1815. This period was also influenced by Greco-Roman art in the ornamentation used. Hepplewhite favored the use of mahogany with panels of satinwood veneer, while Sheraton favored the use of mahogany or cherry with satinwood or bird's eye maple veneer. In the United States, a distinctive touch of simplicity was introduced into the reproduction of the Hepplewhite and Sheraton designs.

Furniture making in America was considered a craft until the late 1700s and early 1800s, as furniture was still being produced in small woodworking shops. During the early part of the Victorian period, furniture making in the United States gradually shifted from individual craftsmen in small shops to the factory system and mass production as steam powered tools became widely used.

Furniture manufacturing became an important industry. Large factories were built to offer a variety of furniture. The midwestern states became the chief furniture manufacturing region for the United States because they had an abundant supply of hardwoods and were near the water transportation routes. Grand Rapids, Michigan, became the most famous furniture center in the United States. The first furniture factory in Grand Rapids was opened in 1848 by cabinetmaker William Haldane. Other factories soon opened in that city, and artisans and designers from Europe were drawn there, bringing their ideas and expertise and adding to the quality of the furniture produced.

Mass production greatly influenced the furniture of the early 20th century. Mission furni-

Furniture

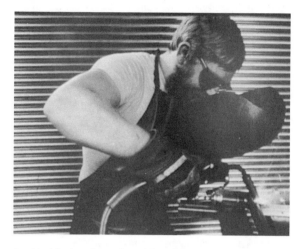

A welder joins two pieces of metal that will form the legs of a chair.

ture, mainly made of oak, was plain and functional. Architect Frank Lloyd Wright designed furniture with an emphasis on the geometrical format. His furniture was designed to complement the houses that he designed. Art Deco furniture reflected Wright's innovations in geometric design and machine forms, but tended to be more exaggerated in length and sinewy line. At points the design of the furniture enhanced the beauty of the piece but adversely affected the functionality.

The Bauhaus School, founded in 1919 in Weimar, Germany, set out to unify architecture and furniture and relate them to the techniques of mass production. Mies van der Rohe's Barcelona chair, with elegantly curved steel strips, was one of the more notable pieces of furniture to come from the Bauhaus School. Another noteworthy design was Marcel Breuer's chairs that were supported on S-curved chrome plated tubing.

The Bauhaus perspective on mass production techniques did much to change the focus of American designers. In the United States, in the 1940s, Eero Saarinen and Charles Eames developed an upholstered chair formed by a molded plywood shell. Saarinen also designed chairs and tables with space saving pedestal bases.

Modern furniture uses a wide array of materials. Wood is used in the form of molded or shaped plywood. Steel tubing is bent and shaped to form chair frames and table legs. Tabletops, handles, and ornaments are made out of synthetic plastic. Other metals, such as aluminum, chromium, and stainless steel are used for their structural strength and simplicity. Upholstery materials now include many synthetic yarns and fibers.

The midwest remained the main furniture manufacturing region in the United States until the end of World War II, when the southern states replaced it. The midwest now produces about 20 percent of the American furniture market, while the south manufactures over 50 percent.

The structure of the furniture industry

Furniture manufacturing is the mass production of furniture from wood, metal, plastics, marble, glass, fabrics, and other related materials, such as rattan (palm leaves). It is a complex process that involves skillful crafts workers.

The wood furniture manufacturing process has four main operations: woodworking, assembling, finishing, and upholstering. The jobs vary with the size of the plant and with the kind of furniture that is being made. In large factories, there is specialization and division of labor, and job categories range from the skilled and semi-skilled to the unskilled.

Most furniture is made out of wood. There are two basic types of wood furniture: case goods and upholstered furniture. Case goods are not upholstered and include such items as tables, bookcases, cabinets, and dressers. Upholstered furniture is padded and covered with fabric and includes some kinds of chairs, sofas, and other pieces.

Small manufacturing plants that specialize in custom work need skilled craftsmen who can do detailed handwork. Large factories need skilled workers to run woodworking machines or to upholster furniture, and they need semi-skilled workers in both the woodworking and the assembly operations. Factories that mass produce furniture run production lines where workers do one or two tasks repeatedly.

The first step in the manufacturing of any piece of furniture is the design. Furniture designers use their knowledge of design trends, of production costs, and of the capabilities of their companies' facilities to draw up blueprints for furniture designs. Some furniture designers are classified as fixture designers and create only fixtures and equipment, such as counters and display cases. Designers also take into account the furniture market and what the competitors are offering. Designers confer with sales personnel to get an idea of what customers are looking for, and then they determine the feasibility of producing the suggested item. They submit simple sketches for approval.

After the design has been approved, the piece of furniture is constructed and tested. The designer draws blueprints for the production department. The blueprints contain manufacturing specifications that include the dimensions and the materials to be used.

Patternmakers make sketches from the blueprints to create the different patterns for the parts needed to build the furniture. They trace the outline of the patterns on to the building materials. The patternmakers then cut the pieces out of the wood, metal, glass, or other material, using hand and power tools. If the pieces are divided into sections, they will put them together before sending the pieces on for further assembly.

Highly skilled model builders then make the prototypes of the new furniture to test the practicality of the new designs. They cut and form the parts using lathes, power saws, and hand tools, and then join the parts using screwdrivers, wrenches, glue, and welding torches. As specifications and measurements are revised, model makers may alter the design of the finished model. The model is then approved for production and the engineers then plan for its mass production.

Mass producing furniture begins in the woodworking operation. Factories receive lumber in the form of rough planks which must be seasoned (dried) for months to prevent warping. First the planks are placed in kiln tanks, which are special structures used for outdoor drying. After several months of the outdoor drying, the wood is then placed in drying kilns for further seasoning.

When the seasoning is complete, machine operators cut the wood into different sizes and shapes using planers, crosscut saws, ripsaws, and other kinds of machinery. The wood is then brought to the planing and jointing shops where it can undergo routing, doweling, boring, carving, shaping, and dovetailing. Eventually the wood will be shaped into furniture arms, legs, and other pieces. The shaped wood is then sent to the machine sanders who smooth the pieces. Some wood receives a layer of veneer, which is a very thin layer of fine wood glued and pressed on to a less expensive wood. Veneer can also be used in decorative patterns of different colors or stains. The sanded or veneered wood is then ready for assembly.

The assembly line is usually a series of loose rollers over which the assemblers can push the work as they finish their part of the assembly. There are clamps positioned along the way to hold the assembled units for gluing. A slight push from an assembler sends the wood over the rollers to the next section.

Workers assemble the frames and fit the doors and drawers using screwdrivers and

A woodworker sands the surface of a round tabletop before drilling holes for the dowels.

other tools. To glue and press small parts together, they use special machines in which radio-frequency heating sets the glue in less than a minute.

After all the pieces of wood are assembled, the furniture piece is ready for the finishing department. Furniture finishers sand, stain, varnish, and paint the furniture. Finishers apply many separate finishing coats to color and seal the wood. Hardwood assemblers add any of the hardware or metal pieces to the finished wood. Mirrors, handles, decorative metal plates are the last touches on a finished piece. Before going to the stockrooms or to storage, each piece of furniture is inspected for flaws.

Upholstering consists of four operations: upholstery workers make the chair and sofa frames out of wood; the springers put in springs; the cushion padders add the polyester, foam, or cotton padding; and the cover assemblers cover the units with fabric. Upholstering does not adapt well to mass production and remains largely a craft.

Larger factories are departmentalized and employ cutters, sewers, and cushion makers. The cutters lay out and mark the patterns. They may cut the fabrics by hand or may use cutting machines to clip several layers of fabric at once. Springers attach the spring coils to burlap webbing that is installed separately. They may tie the springs to each other and then to the frame to keep the springs from shifting.

The padding and fabric is installed over the springs and to the inside of the arms and the back. Other upholsterers will install the fabric over the outside of the arms and back of the frame. They staple, glue, or sew on the fabrics and trim.

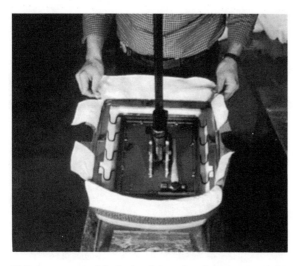

While many aspects of the furniture industry have become automatized, it is necessary for people to perform the more complex tasks.

In metal furniture production, there is the preparation of the metals and materials for fabrication of the pieces and parts required for assembly. The assembly of the parts is the next step, with the metal pieces being attached to other metal pieces or to parts of another type of material. Finishing operations follow.

Wicker, rattan, and plastic furniture manufacturers have many operations that are similar to wood and metal furniture manufacturing, but differ in the raw and assembly materials being used. There is a preparation or fabrication of the assembly materials and pieces, the assembly itself, and then the finishing. The jobs are similar to those in wood and metal manufacturing.

Furniture workers should have manual dexterity and good coordination, and should like working with their hands. They should also have mechanical aptitude. Woodworkers have to follow the manufacturing specifications on the blueprints when working on the different elements of the furniture. This requires strict attention to detail and precision, so patience, persistence, and accuracy are important for the production of quality work.

Wages in the furniture industry vary depending on the specific job, the location of the plant, and the plant's wage policies. In general the wages in this industry are lower than in other manufacturing industries.

Many workers have jobs that pay piecework rates, so their earnings depend on how fast they work and how much they produce. Workers in large plants that make upholstery furniture for home use earn a higher pay than machine operators in wood furniture plants.

Furniture manufacturing workers usually work a forty hour week. While there are occasions for overtime during high volume periods of production, there may be layoffs during slack periods of production. Benefits vary, but they usually include paid holidays and vacations, health insurance and pensions.

Working conditions vary according to the job and the size of the factory. Modern plants have good lighting, ventilation, and heating systems, while older plants may have less comfortable temperatures and poorer lighting. There is a great deal of work that requires the use of machines, conveyors, and other equipment, and therefore the workplace may be very noisy.

Although woodworking produces sawdust and other particles and the finishing work gives off paint and chemical fumes, modern ventilation systems relieve a lot of problems connected with this situation. The work is not dangerous, but workers must be careful when using machines and tools. Workers have to stand much of the time, and they may have to stoop, bend, and reach for parts. Safety rules may require the use of protective gear and masks.

Careers

A sampling of careers in furniture manufacturing follows below.

Designers: The architects of furniture, designers create the blueprints and the style of the pieces that will be manufactured for sale. Designs include the color, materials, sizes and measurements, and all other information that will be needed to begin the manufacturing process.

Patternmakers: Patternmakers are responsible for creating the first pieces from the material that will be used in the mass production of the furniture. Wood patternmakers mark the design pattern onto the original material, cut the pieces, and then assemble the pieces into a finished work to make sure that the specifications of the blueprint actually translate into a workable design.

Supervisors: Supervisors of fabrication and assembly should have a thorough knowledge of layout, product design, and machine functions. They supervise machine operators in the fabrication of the metal furniture and train new workers. They also are often responsible for ordering the necessary materials to meet production goals.

Cabinetmakers: Cabinetmakers make custom furniture for their clients in small shops. Cabinetmakers not only need many years of experience to develop excellent woodworking skills, but they also need the ability to conceptualize what a piece of furniture will look like from a blueprint or from a client's description. There are schools where the basics can be learned but it takes actual work experience and perseverance to rise from apprentice to craftsman.

Chair, table or frame assemblers: Assemblers may work in groups or in lines and may assemble single pieces or sections of a product.

Cabinet assemblers: Cabinet assemblers are highly skilled and do the more difficult assembly jobs because of their experience and fine handwork.

Hardwood assemblers: Hardwood assemblers put on the mirrors, door hinges, handles, and other hardware.

Handcarvers: Skilled craftsmen, the handcarvers carve the designs into furniture. The design is roughed out by hand or by cutting along tracings using a chisel and mallet, a router, or a jigsaw. Then hand tools are used to finish the design.

Metal furniture assemblers: Assemblers perform a combination of tasks in putting the metal furniture pieces together. These tasks include drilling holes in parts, and fitting parts together with clamps, bolts, staples, screws, and rivets. The assemblers fit interlocking parts together and join upholstery and cushions to the metal frames. Adjusters bend or shape the doors and drawers so that they fit snugly and work smoothly in the assembled metal furniture.

Cleaners: Furniture cleaners employ various methods to remove dirt, grease, rust, nicks, and scratches from the furniture. They may immerse metal pieces into chemical baths or rub the pieces with sandpaper. They may also guide a steam iron covered with a damp cloth across laminated tabletops. Inspectors look for defects and either return the pieces to the proper department for repairs or make the minor alterations themselves.

Finishers: Sanders, stainers, and painters are all furniture finishers. They give the furniture a final covering that seals the wood and gives it the best presentation.

Education

Any furniture store will offer the opportunity to see the end products of the furniture manufacturing industry. Most furniture stores can provide listings of furniture manufacturers. Writing to these furniture manufacturers will prove helpful in gaining answers to all kinds of questions concerning furniture production.

A furniture manufacturer sprays a coating of resin on a finished table for protection from everyday use.

It must be taken into consideration that only thirty-five states have plants that manufacture furniture. The states that have a greater share of the plants are Michigan, Indiana, California, New York, Virginia, North Carolina, Mississippi, and Tennessee.

Most furniture manufacturing workers learn their skills on the job. The high-school courses that are helpful in this kind of work are architecture or drafting (for blueprint skills), woodworking, metal shop, and mathematics. There are many community colleges and technical schools that offer one- and two- year programs in furniture manufacturing. The programs include courses covering furniture design, woodwork, drafting, production technology, and upholstery cutting and sewing.

Cabinetmakers should have a high-school diploma, or the equivalent, and enter into an apprenticeship program. Apprentices learn to use saws molders, mortisers, and other tools. Apprentices become skilled in the art of woodworking and can eventually become master cabinetmakers.

Some woodworking machine operators may be able to learn their jobs with a few weeks of training, while other workers with more complex jobs may need several months of training. Some skilled jobs may take a year or more to learn proficiently. New employees start as helpers, and these trainees may learn to read blueprints, set up machines, and plan the sequencing of operations. New employees usually advance to other jobs as openings occur.

Most assembly workers require only a few months of training to learn their tasks and acquire the necessary skills. Some jobs may be learned in a few days, but much practice is needed to build up speed. Finishers begin as helpers or begin in easy jobs in the finishing department. Their on-the-job training may take from a few weeks to several months and they can advance to more difficult work as job openings allow.

Those workers who are skilled in all phases of finishing work need three or more years to learn all their skills. Some upholstery jobs in large factories require only a few weeks of on-the-job training, while cutters may need as much as two years of training to become fully proficient.

Industry outlook

Toward the end of the 1980s, increased construction of hotels, motels, office buildings, and nursing homes had increased the sales of commercial and contract furniture. However, with the downward turn in the number of houses constructed, the furniture manufacturing industry has also experienced a decline.

Along with the influence of the construction industry, the influence of bank interest rates and percentage of personal savings determine the purchase rate of large household items such as tables, sofas, and such. With a low current savings rate, the purchasing rate of the average family is lower than it was in the mid-1980s.

Exports from the United States are increasing slightly, according to the Department of Commerce, but the rise is at a slower rate than in previous years. The plateau in production will set a plateau in hiring.

As more companies computerize tasks, the number of employees required to produce a piece of furniture will decrease. The increasing use of computerized and mechanical equipment will require workers educated on such machinery. Overall, the number of employees in furniture manufacturing will probably continue to decline, as it has over the past decade.

Most of the labor will involve fewer people, and the furniture that is still labor-intensive will be imported because labor can be found cheaper abroad.

◇ **SOURCES OF ADDITIONAL INFORMATION**

American Furniture Manufacturers Association
Box HP—7
High Point, NC 27261

Contract Furniture Council
1190 Merchandise Mart
Chicago, IL 60654

National Association of Professional Upholsterers
PO Box 2754
200 South Main
High Point, NC 27261

American Society of Furniture Designers
PO Box 2688
200 South Main
High Point, NC 27261

◇ **RELATED ARTICLES**

Volume 1: Design; Metals; Plastics; Wood
Volume 2: Designers; Drafters; Industrial designers; Interior designers and decorators
Volume 3: Assemblers; Carpenters; Furniture manufacturing occupations; Furniture upholsterers; Lathers; Leather tanning and finishing workers; Machine tool operators; Machinists; Molders; Paint and coatings industry workers; Patternmakers; Plastics products manufacturing workers; Wholesale trade sales workers

Glass

General information

Nature has been making glass since the beginning of time. Glass is made naturally by lightning and volcanic eruptions. When lightning strikes sand, the heat from the lightning can fuse the sand into long, slender tubes that are called fulgurites or petrified lightning. And when volcanoes erupt, their terrific heat can fuse rocks and sand into a glass called obsidian. Obsidian was used by primitive people for arrowheads, tools, knives, and decoration.

The oldest piece of man-made glass dates back to about 7000 B.C. Around 4000 B.C., Egyptians were using glass mainly as a colored glaze on stone or pottery beads and vessels. By 1500 B.C., the Egyptians were making colored beads and vessels entirely out of glass, with glass objects becoming as valuable as jewels. The glass industry flourished in Egypt for the next 300 years. Around 500 B.C. Syria, and other Mediterranean countries also became glass manufacturing centers.

Early glassmaking was slow, costly, and required hard work. Furnaces were small, the heating was barely sufficient, and the clay pots used to heat the sand mixture were of poor quality.

It is speculated that glass blowing was invented in Syria around 50 B.C. by the Phoenicians, who were famous glassmakers. Glass blowing revolutionized glassmaking because it greatly extended the types of objects that could be made of glass. Glass objects were no longer the luxury items that they once had been. The art of glass blowing flourished under the Roman Empire, creating the first golden age of glass from A.D. 100 to 400.

Glassmakers could make transparent glass by blowing. They did glass blowing, painting, and gilding to create color patterns in the glass. They would build up layers of colored glass and crystal glass, called casing, and then cut out designs in high relief. Many of these cutting techniques, including casing, are still in use today.

After the fall of the Roman Empire, the skill and techniques perfected under the Romans were lost, although crude glass bottles were continuing to be made, By the 12th century, the European glassmakers were creating works of art in their stained-glass windows in gothic churches. About the year 1200, returning Crusaders brought some of the best glassmakers to settle in Venice, where there were large quantities of good quality sand and other necessary raw materials.

The second golden age of glass began. Making use of many ancient and medieval decorative techniques to produce richly colored and ornamental glass pieces brought Venetian glassmakers fame. The Venetians perfected a nearly colorless glass called cristallo, which could be blown to extreme thinness into almost any shape.

Glassmaking again became an art. The Venetians also developed a design called latticino, where a mold was covered with different colored bands of glass, covered with yet a different color of glass, and then blown. A second bubble of glass was blown inside the first to produce a rectangular mesh of colored bands lying inside. Another Venetian technique was rolling a bubble of glass over broken pieces of a different kind of colored glass to create ice glass. To keep the skills of their craft secret, the Venetian glassmakers were forbidden to leave Venice and forbidden to tell anyone of their techniques, except to pass them down to their children or apprentices. But Venetians did leave and spread the wealth of their knowledge.

In France, glassmakers had developed several different techniques for making flat glass. One method was a method that had been developed by the Romans hundreds of years earlier. This dangerous and difficult method made flat glass by pouring molten glass on to large

Producing glass is a delicate process. Finished glass must be carefully stacked to avoid any breakage.

tables with tops that were braced by moveable iron bars to shape the glass. The glass would then be spread to the right thickness.

Another method, called crown, was an ingenious process where a cylindrical bubble of glass had a punty (an enlarged head of an iron rod) attached to it. The punty rod was then spun, flaring the bubble into a flat piece of glass. The punty rod would leave a bull's eye in the middle of the glass, which can be seen in the center of some old windows.

Larger pieces of glass were blown by the cylinder process. With this process, blown glass is swung out into a long cylinder, which is then cut lengthwise and then pressed into a flat shape.

Venetian glassmakers brought their knowledge of mirror manufacturing techniques to France. They coated one side of a large piece of French glass with tin and mercury and created the art of mirror-making. Mirrors required great skill because the glass had to be very clear and flat. Flaws diminished the quality of the reflection. Before the glass mirror, polished metal had been used.

By the late 1400s and early 1500s, glassmaking had become an important industry in Germany and other northern European countries for manufacturing containers and drinking vessels. In the 1500s, a new type of glass was perfected in Bohemia (now Czechoslovakia) that worked well for copper wheel engraving. Bohemia became an important glass producer until early in the 20th century.

In the 17th century, English glassmakers were making glass in the Venetian tradition. In 1673, George Ravenscroft added lead oxide to glass, making glass not only sparkle, but making the material softer and easier to cut. This type of glass became known as lead crystal. The invention marked the beginning of modern glassmaking.

English glassmaking flourished. English craftsmen added more and more lead to the crystal, making it even heavier to allow deeper geometric patterns to be gut into the glass. The famous Irish Waterford crystal goblets are an example of this kind of lead crystal.

Glassmaking was the first American industry. In 1608, the first American glass factory was established. The colonists had come to America in hope of finding gold, but found forests and sandy seashores. A glass production house was built at Jamestown because of the availability of raw materials and fuels. Captain John Smith had brought European glassmakers to Virginia, and the colonists were able to make glass to export to England. But famine and Indian attacks thwarted the glass industry there. In the 1700s, a pair of colonists from Germany brought over their talents in glass blowing, They refined American glass blowing to an art, producing beautiful blown-glass objects until the start of the Revolutionary War.

Production of glass in the United States continued to grow and mature. The growth of America's glass manufacturing was greatly increased in 1827 by the invention of a machine that molded glass. A popular American pressed glass, called sandwich glass, got its name from the Boston and Sandwich Glass Company, founded in 1825 by Deming Jarves. In the early 1800s, the greatest demand on the glass producers was for window glass. Until Jarves' invention, flat glass was produced by crown and cylinder processes that had been popular in France. Plate glass was developed for mirrors and other products needing high quality flat glass. The sandwich glass allowed for cheaper and faster production of glass in different sizes and shapes.

The screw-top Mason jar for home canning was invented in 1858, and, by 1880, commercial food packers had begun using glass containers. Use of glass tableware was also increasing in use. The kerosene lamp created a demand for millions of glass lamp chimneys. All these developments helped expand the market for glass.

Coal had become the primary fuel in manufacturing glass, but after 1890 natural gas had replaced it. This meant that glass factories no longer needed to be located near a fuel source, and could now relocate closer to their markets.

After 1890, the development, manufacturing, and use of glass advanced rapidly.

In 1904, Michael J. Owens invented an automatic bottle making machine that helped to meet the ever-increasing demand of commercial food packers. In 1908, I.W. Colburn invented a process for drawing window sheet glass directly from the glass melt. But it took until 1917 to perfect the process. Colburn's process was developed to be used in conjunction with a continuous glass-melting furnace to produce large quantities of flat glass.

Specialized glass was developed as needs arose or changed. Heat resistant glass, insulated glass, and shatterproof glass all became part of the manufacturers' list of products for use in the home, car, or workplace.

Fiberglass was developed between 1931 and 1938 by the Corning Glass Works and Owens-Illinois Glass Company (now Owens-Illinois, Inc.). Fiberglass is actually glass threads—tiny, solid glass rods—usually much finer than human hair. When fiberglass is coarse, it is called glass wool. Fiberglass is heat-resistant, incombustible, and a non-conductor of electricity. Prior to World War II, fiberglass was used as a filtering material. But World War II saw diversification in its use, and the fiberglass industry grew rapidly. The application of fiberglass ranges from aircraft parts to insulation to fiber optics.

It was in 1970 that fused silica glass fibers were fabricated by Corning Glass Works as a light wave conduit, and fiber optics came into its own. Fused silica glass was used because of its high optical clarity. Now, fiber optics are creating revolutions in computers, data transmissions and storage, and in telephone and radio communications.

The glass manufacturing industry continues to grow, not only in volume, but also in the many different types and uses of glass. It is one of America's larger manufacturing industries.

The structure of the glass industry

Glass can be as light as cork or as heavy as iron. It can be as soft as cotton or almost as hard as diamonds. Glass can be as flexible as a ribbon, as fragile as an eggshell, or as strong as steel. Glass can be laminated, colored, tempered, etched, and chemically coated. It can also be bulletproof, heat-absorbent, photo-sensitive, radiation-sensitive, radiation- absorbent, conducting, non-conducting, tensile, and refractory. This flexibility of glass allows for countless products to be made.

A glass manufacturer finishes large panels of glass that will be used as windows on a high-rise.

The glass manufacturing industry is highly diversified, and each year it grows in scope and market penetration. The expansion of the glass industry not only lies in increased production, but also in the impact its versatility and innovation have on other industries, such as space travel, telecommunications, food chemistry, and medical research. One glass manufacturer alone has developed more than 65,000 different variations of glass.

Making glass involves four basic steps: melting the raw materials; forming the molten glass to the desired shape; cooling the formed glass; and finishing the glass by polishing, edging, engraving, decorating, or coating it.

The basic raw materials used in making glass; sand, soda, ash, and limestone, are stored at the glass factory in huge bins called silos. Mixers carefully weigh the raw materials and various additives, such as lead oxide for lead glass. Then they mechanically mix the raw materials in the right proportions. Workers operate machines that crush and wash waste glass. This waste glass is call cullet. The cullet is then melted with the raw ingredients to make new batches of molten glass. Between 5 and 40 percent of a new batch will be cullet. Cullet is recycled waste glass that would not otherwise be used; it reduces the amount of heat necessary to melt all the ingredients. These ingredients are then dumped into batch-mixing equipment.

After the batch is mixed together, it goes into a hopper that feeds a gigantic furnace, where the materials are melted. Workers must adjust the air, fuel, and water pressure inside the furnace and determine when the tempera-

An automatic braiding machine spins a shell of fiberglass yarn on part of an engine air duct for F-16 fighters. After curing, the braided material provides a high-temperature composite insulation jacket for ducts on the plane's engine.

ture is correct for melting the glass (about 2700 degrees Fahrenheit). In early times, the ingredients were melted in small clay pots, called refractory pots, that were heated by wood fires. Today, special refractory pots hold 500 to 3,000 pounds (230 to 1,400 kilograms) of batch and are used for making optical glass, art glass and specialty glass. Furnaces can hold from six to twenty refractory pots. Larger glass quantities of special glass are melted in furnaces that are called day tanks. They are called day tanks because it takes twenty-four hours to complete the process and empty the tank. These day tanks can hold one to four short tons (0.9 to 3.6 metric tons) of glass.

Most of the glass made in factories is flat, or sheet, glass which is melted in large furnaces called continuous tanks. These continuous tanks can melt 400 to 600 short tons (360 to 540 metric tons) daily. Most other kinds of glass are produced in smaller continuous tanks and day tanks. The production of flat glass is a continuous process, as raw materials are fed into the loading end as fast as the molten glass is drawn off.

After the glass is melted, it passes into a chamber known as the forehearth, or drawing pot. Flat glass can be formed using the drawing off process or the float process. In the drawing off process, kiln workers operate machines that draw molten glass through a kiln between rollers, which the workers adjust according to the desired thickness of the glass sheet. The kiln operators observe the glass through a peephole and watch for defects, such as stones in the sheet. If they see a defect, they signal a balcony operator to lift the rollers, letting the defect pass through to keep the sheet from breaking.

The rollers do mar the glass, so the glass is then moved on a long conveyor to be ground and polished on both sides to restore the luster.

Layers and joiners feed and position the sheets of glass onto plaster-covered tables, which hold the glass while it is being ground and polished. Workers use polished wheels or electric hand buffers to polish the edges of the flat glass, while blockers use a polishing compound and felt-covered polishing heads to polish the top of the glass. Strippers then remove the glass from the plaster tables for shipping or storage.

The float process is used to make high quality glass, and it is a more expensive way to produce glass than the drawing off method. In this process, a large sheet of molten glass is drawn into a tank holding molten tin. This tank is often called a float because the glass floats in an even layer over the perfectly smooth molten tin. By carefully controlling the heating of the float bath, any roughness is melted out of the glass which gives it a smooth, undistorted surface as it cools in sheets. Glass turns solid at higher temperatures than the tin so it is able to be moved along for further cooling. Flat glass produced in a float bath can be formed at high speeds and has such a brilliant finish that no polishing is required.

Glass is formed or manufactured by being drawn, blown, cast, or pressed into molds. The float process is considered a drawing process, but fiberglass and tubing is also drawn. Glass tubing is made by drawing a stream of molten glass from the furnace around a rotating ceramic cylinder or cone (called a mandrel). If air is blown through the mandrel, the drawn glass will form a hollow tube. If no air is blown, then the drawn glass will form a rod. The tubing or rod can be drawn over the mandrel at a rate of about forty miles an hour, and a single machine can draw many miles in a day. The temperature of the glass and the rate of pull determine the size of the tubing or rod. Highly efficient machinery draws, anneals (heats and cools), cuts, and grades the diameter of the glass. For the fiberglass the manufacturing principles are the same but the machinery is different.

Glass blowing, also called offhand glass blowing, uses a hollow iron blowpipe, four to five feet long. The pear-shaped end of the pipe is dipped into the molten glass. The glass blower, or gaffer, blows into the pipe while gently rotating it to form a hollow bulb. It is the pressure of the breath that determines the bulb's size and shape. The glass bulb can then be squeezed, compressed, elongated, or even cut. During the process, the glass is reheated many times to keep it soft, until it is finally ready to be broken from the blowpipe. When production is rapid, a gatherer puts a gob of molten glass on the blowpipe and hands it to the glass blower. Workers will finish the hand-made glassware by forming and attaching secondary pieces such as handles, stems, or pedestals. Glass can also be blown into iron molds by a glass blower or by machine.

Workers set up and operate automatic machines that either press, blow, or spin molten glass to form bottles, containers, cathode ray tubes, and other objects. To blow-mold glass, a machine with arms fanning out from the center picks up a gob of glass on each arm from the forehearth. A puff of air then blows the glass into a mold to form the object. Glassware is formed by pressing molten glass into a mold. Molders change the dies and adjust the press to form the glass blanks used in the molding presses. Many workers are employed to take care of the molds used in this process. They remove residue, blemishes and other defects from inside the molds, using files, buffing wheels, emery paper, and steel wool. Cleaning the molds insures that the glass coming out of them will be smooth and strong.

Cast glass is poured, not blown or pressed into molds. The glass is either poured from ladles or poured directly from the furnace. It can also be poured from the bottom of the furnace. The glass is poured into molds to form one or more pieces, or poured around decorative objects into what are called forming molds. The molds are usually made of plaster or clay and are destroyed by the removal of the glass. The casting method is used in the production of architectural glass pieces, art glass, and laser glass. One example of cast glass is the 200 inch mirror disk made for the Palomar Observatory in California. It is the largest piece of man-made glass in the world, weighing twenty tons.

Some glass undergoes reheating to remove defects or to strengthen the material. Workers tend "lehr" machines that heat and cool flat or molded glass slowly to relieve internal stresses. Machine operators reheat and fire-polish glass to remove chips, air bubbles, and rough surfaces. The heating also makes it malleable for further processing and working. Workers remove any rough edges and surface convexities using belt or disk grinders. They also use grinding wheels to bend the edges of irregularly shaped glass. Some of the defects in glass objects can be repaired by using acetylene torches and molds.

Glass objects are often decorated by etching, sandblasting, cutting, or painting. Mark-up designers lay out and cut stencils for the designs. They also trace designs directly onto the glassware. The design is etched into

A technician operates a computer-regulated optical surfacing machine.

the glass using hydrofluoric acid and sandblasting.

In etching with acid, the glass is painted with an acid-resistant chemical to protect all the areas that are to remain smooth. The glass is then either dipped in or sprayed with acid that eats away the unprotected design marks that have been put onto the surface, exposing the glass. Depending on the composition of the glass, the concentration of the acid, and the amount of time the acid is left on the glass, the etched glass surface can be rough, frosted, or almost opaque. It can be made to appear soft, satiny, or translucent. Frosted light bulbs, for example, are light bulbs etched with a satin finish on the inside.

Sandblasting gives glass a translucent surface that is rougher than etching. Plate and window glass are often made translucent by sandblasting. Sandblasting uses compressed air to blow coarse sand against the glass. When sandblasting a design, a rubber stencil is used in order to protect the section of glass that is not to be decorated.

The only major change in glass cutting techniques since the time of the Romans has been the replacement of the early sandstone wheels with synthetic carborundum cutting wheels. Spotters locate and ink the points for cutting. Even with marked guide points, cutters must still use their trained eyes and experience to reproduce a design. The piece of glass is held against the cutting wheel and the cut is made instantly. It is the cutter's judgment and expertise that creates the design. The cuts may be quite deep or they may be shallow, depending on the design and the desired effect. Edgers pencil-edge the glass by machine and by hand. The original luster of the glass is restored to the rough cut surfaces by etching with acids or by polishing with a very fine abrasive.

Using special paints, designs, logos, labels, and pictures are painted on glassware. Some processes fuse the paint onto the glass by using the lehr machines that heat and cool the glass slowly.

Many workers are employed as supervisors of the different departments involved in the glassmaking processes. Receiving and processing supervisors are in charge of buying and receiving raw materials and delivering them to the furnaces for mixing and melting. Glass and glassware also undergo inspection before leaving the factory, and different inspection workers have different titles depending on the product that they inspect.

Since glass is made by many machines, glass factories depend on skilled mechanics to keep the factories running. Upkeep mechanics help maintain the equipment. Glass manufacturing also requires unskilled labor. Floor attendants haul molds, machine parts, and graphite solutions. They sweep floors and do whatever else is required to keep the factory clean and running smoothly.

The glass industry offers different kinds of advancement opportunities for workers. Workers who learn to operate several different kinds of machines may become supervisors or crew leaders. Experienced workers may receive higher pay and may earn the right to work the shifts they prefer or they may transfer to more desirable jobs within the production process.

Glassmaking plants stay open and operating at full crew twenty-four hours a day, every day of the year. This is to keep the glass furnaces at the constant high temperature that they require. As a result of the continual operations, shift work is required, as is holiday scheduling. The average work week is forty hours, and some overtime may be required. Overtime pay is common for employees. Some plants have shift rotation so that everyone has a turn working night shifts.

Workers who make glass using the float process must sometimes work in high temperatures, but the vast majority are not exposed to uncomfortable conditions. Heat and sharp glass are dangerous, but workers are protected by safety measures, equipment, and clothing. The many chemicals which are used to manufacture glass can produce fumes and dust but their hazards are minimized by exhaust systems and modern machinery.

There are many more workers involved in making pressed and blown glass products than in making flat glass. Wages and salaries for glassmakers vary with their job descriptions, but as a whole, these workers have pay scales somewhat higher than most manufacturing industries.

Careers

The workers are categorized primarily by the machines they operate:

Blow-pipe workers: Blow-pipe workers use blow-pipes, pincers, forks and paddles to manipulate, remove, and carry hot glass pieces to cooling areas. Glass containers such as bottles are made through the blow molding process. Gobs of molten glass, called "gather," are dropped on spindles of a machine that works similarly to a carousel. The spindles are attached to a center hub, and gather is placed on each spindle. The machine shoots a puff of air through the spindle into the gather, forming the bottle shape. The final forming is accomplished through heating the objects. When the finished bottle has cooled, it is released from the spindle and the process is repeated.

Glass blowers: Glass blowers set a gob of glass on a charred woodblock and begin to shape it. They then blow into the glass with a blowpipe refining the final shape and contour to each piece. Glassblowers usually require more intense training than factory workers.

Pressworkers: Pressworkers set and monitor heating controls and timers on furnaces, glazing machines, or lehrs.

Glass manufacturer workers: Glass manufacturer workers remove excess glass by using various tools. Workers make a variety of products including windshields, tableware, and art objects. Glass is comprised of soda ash, limestone, silica sand, and other raw materials. The heating and forming processes performed by glass workers utilize its malleable quality.

Machine operators and tenders: Machine operators and tenders comprise the majority of glass manufacturer workers. The industry has become increasingly more reliant on automatization to be able to meet the demand for glass products.

Forming machine operators, furnace operators, and *lehr tenders:* These workers monitor special ovens that heat and cool glass. Forming machine operators often manufacture items such as glass containers and tableware, products that are primarily made from molding or formation processes. Forming machine operators control and monitor the entire process of controlling the heat and release of the formed bottle.

Press mold operators: Mold operators utilize a related process to the forming process, where gobs of glass are manipulated by plungers that imprint and form the gather into specific shapes. Many common items are manufactured through this process, such as automobile headlights, ashtrays, and certain glass cookware. Press mold operators are also known as molders.

Molding glass has increased the varieties of shapes and designs available, as well as assisting productivity. Machines that form glass tubing can dispense hot glass from the furnace at high speeds; the float glass process, used for flat glass, can dispense a ribbon of glass up to ten or twelve feet wide at the rate of 1,500 feet per hour.

Education

The amount of training and education required for employment in the glass manufacturing industry depends upon the specific job performed. Applicants for positions such as mold maker, machine operator, and furnace tender need to have a high-school background in subjects such as physics, chemistry, mathematics, and machine shop. Glass blowers and workers who create and execute designs for glass need a background in art and design, especially commercial art.

Skilled machine operators and other crafts people must go through apprenticeship programs, which are normally about three years of training. Through laboratory work, on-the-job training, and classroom lectures on glassmaking theory, apprentices learn glassmaking skills. Apprentices learning to make containers may obtain a journeyman's card after 4,000 hours of glassmaking work.

Apprenticeships offer training and experience for glass workers, and unions can provide the information about these programs. Unions are strong in the glassmaking industry. Most of the workers in the factories that make flat glass belong to the Aluminum, Brick, and Glassworkers International Union. Container workers and pressed or mold glassmakers may belong to either the Glass, Pottery, Plastics, and Allied Workers International Union or the American Flint Glass Workers Union of North America.

Signing up for an apprenticeship program is a practical way to enter the field. Otherwise,

Hand-blown glass is an age-old craft that is still practiced in many parts of the world, particularly in Europe. Such work requires extensive training.

job seekers should apply at the personnel offices of glass manufacturing plants. Applicants should contact state employment agencies for information about openings.

Like most production workers, glass workers must often perform repetitive tasks. Glass workers should have physical stamina and have the ability to concentrate on machine operations. Both machine work and handwork require speed, precision, and skill. Skilled workers exercise a lot of responsibility and control over production. An artistic background as well as a mechanical background are important for glass workers. Workers with mechanical aptitude and concentration are well suited for this type of work.

Industry outlook

Glass is considered so versatile that its uses seem almost endless. As new technologies develop so do innovations in glass manufacturing and production. New ways of using glass as well as new forms of glass are constantly being invented. Glass is now used to replace various metals and building materials. Glass is even replacing some textiles. As new products create new markets, the demand for skilled and specialized glass makers increases. Employment in this field should grow along with the areas that use glass, such as construction, transportation, telecommunications, nuclear energy, solar energy, fiber optics, aerospace, and electronics.

For certain products, such as glass containers, the current market is tightening. With the increased usage of plastics as a replacement for glass containers, the demand for glass containers is decreasing currently at about one percent a year. If the demand for recyclable products grows as is anticipated, however, people may return to the use of glass containers.

Associated Glass and Pottery Manufacturers
2800 East Military Road
Zanesville, OH 43701

Society for Glass Science and Practice
PO Box 166
Clarksburg, WI 26301

Glass Technical Institute
12653 Portada Place
San Diego, CA 92130

◇ SOURCES OF ADDITIONAL INFORMATION

National Glass Association
8200 Greensboro Drive, Suite 302
McLean, VA 22102

American Scientific Glassblowers Society
1507 Hagley Road
Toledo, OH 43612

◇ RELATED ARTICLES

Volume 1: Design; Energy; Engineering; Metals; Plastics
Volume 2: Engineers
Volume 3: Assemblers; Glass manufacturing workers; Glaziers; Machinists; Welders
Volume 4: Industrial engineering technicians

Health Care

General information

The origins of medicine began with prehistoric people who believed that diseases were derived from supernatural powers. To destroy the evil spirits, they performed trephining. Trephining involved cutting a hole in the victim's skull to release the spirit. The first doctors, known as medicine men, used herbal concoctions to heal their patients. The herbal treatment was often accompanied by a ritual such as a dance or incantation. Skulls have been found in which the trephine hole has healed, demonstrating that people did survive the ritual.

In about 3000 B.C., the ancient Egyptians made considerable medical progress, developing a systematic method of treating illnesses. This system introduced the notion of specialization within the field of medicine. The famous physician Imhotep was so respected that the Egyptians regarded him as the god of healing.

The Greek physician Hippocrates was the first person to declare that disease was caused by natural, not supernatural, phenomena. He introduced a method of conduct and ethics for the practice of medicine. To this day, each physician pledges the Hippocratic oath on the day of his or her graduation from medical school.

Galen of Pergamum was a Greek physician who studied in Rome during the second century A.D. He worked as physician to the emperor Marcus Aurelius and lectured to physicians on dissections and experimental physiology. He conducted anatomical studies of animals, particularly apes, because the dissection of humans was illegal. He is credited with the discoveries of blood transport by arteries, the pumping mechanism of the heart, and the function of the kidneys. His written work remained influential for hundreds of years, and during the fifteenth and sixteenth centuries many physicians repeated his experiments to gain further insight into the mechanism of human anatomy.

Avicenna (980-1037), from Persia, was another major contributor to the early development of western medicine. His single largest contribution was the book *The Canon of Medicine*. The book compiled the information of Greek and Arabic physicians that had been gathered from many generations, as well as some of his own findings. The book remained the most important publication for medicine through the sixteenth century. It served as a major resource of information for eastern and western countries.

When dissection of human corpses was accepted in the 1500s, Andreas Vesalius was able to conduct his own examinations and correct many of the errors that Galen had made. Vesalius published *On the Structure of the Human Body* in 1543, detailing the findings of his dissections.

William Harvey (1578-1657) made the most important contribution to medicine in the seventeenth century. Using the observations Hieronymus Fabricius made on the valves in veins, Harvey conducted physical tests to prove in his book *On the Motion of the Heart and Blood in Animals (1628)* that blood circulates through the body and through the veins and arteries.

It was the development of the microscope that moved medical study into the next plane of understanding. Zacharias Janssen, a Dutch eyeglass maker, discovered the benefits of combining magnifying lenses. He is credited with developing the first compound lens microscope around 1590.

Another Dutch scientist, Anton Van Leeuwenhoek, used microscopes to study the microscopic contents of water, blood, and other body fluids and tissues. He described bacteria from his observations, becoming the first person to recognize the presence of foreign bodies in human fluids.

Discoveries were made more rapidly once the concept of germ infection became recog-

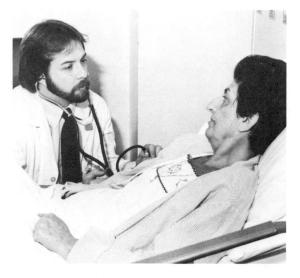

Before a hospitalized patient undergoes surgery, a physician checks her heart rate and overall condition.

nized and accepted. The awareness of bacteria, fungi, and viruses led to concepts—taken for granted today—which proved to be a major boon to the medical profession. Washing hands before surgery, examinations, and deliveries of newborns led to a decrease in cases of infections and death. Joseph Lister developed the concept of an antiseptic environment that promoted sterilized equipment and surroundings in medical work.

Louis Pasteur successfully produced vaccinations that battled diseases. In the mid-1800s, Pasteur inoculated sheep against a common animal disease called anthrax. He went on to develop a vaccination against rabies, demonstrating that vaccinations were as successful in preventing disease in humans as they were in animals.

Another discovery that the modern world relies on every day was the development of anesthesia. Surgery had been performed without it for hundreds of years, but it was hazardous and extraordinarily painful. In 1846, a surgery by William Morton in Boston before a group of physicians proved to the medical world that the use of anesthesia freed the patient from surgical pain and allowed the physician to work more accurately, more thoroughly, and more extensively than ever before. Early anesthetics were nitrous oxide, ether, and chloroform.

Drugs were discovered that battled and killed some bacteria and infections. Penicillin was discovered by Alexander Fleming in 1928. Howard Florey and Ernst Chain were able to isolate the penicillin compound in pure enough quantities to use it to combat infections such as staph. That discovery in 1938 led to mass pro-

duction which allowed the British and American armies to use it on wounded soldiers through World War II. The number of lives saved by penicillin is beyond calculation.

Immunologists and bacteriologists experimented with methods of inoculating soldiers against viral infections. Tetanus antitoxin was developed by Emil von Behring and Shibasaburo Kitasato in 1890. The two also worked on diphtheria antitoxin which, only after the vaccinations had a combination of toxins and antitoxins, would produce an immune response in humans.

During the 1930s technology was developed that allowed immunologists to isolate and cultivate viruses for study and experimentation. As viruses were isolated, the proper vaccinations could be developed that would trigger immunization in humans. The most heralded of the vaccines was the one developed by Jonas Salk for poliomyelitis (polio). Albert Sabin developed an oral vaccine soon after, which also immunized against polio. Polio had infected hundreds of thousands of people in the United States between 1940 and 1959 and had killed 26,635 people, according to the National Center for Health Statistics. Initial use of the vaccination began in 1954. In 1960, thanks to the vaccination, only 3,190 Americans developed the disease.

Viruses still plague the population and therefore impact on the medical community. Acquired Immunodeficiency Syndrome (AIDS) has become the latest deadly virus to affect the population. By 1989, 63,159 people had died from AIDS in the United States, according to the Centers for Disease Control. Researchers are attempting to find a preventive vaccination and a cure, but the process is expected to take years.

The medical and health field has become one of the largest and most varied occupational areas. More than eight million people are employed in some aspect of the U.S. health care system. Health care workers are employed as physicians, nurses, nursing aides, technicians, technologists, therapists, and a host of other occupations.

The structure of the health care industry

The single most familiar element of the medical industry is the physician. For many years the main health consultant was the family physician. General practitioners still serve the role of the family doctor to many families in the

United States but the role and the method of medical care delivery by the family doctor has changed.

According to the U.S. Department of Labor, less than 12 percent of the physicians in the United States are general or family practitioners. This means that most people who require medical consultation are seeing specialists. General practitioners will handle most medical problems, but when an emergency or problem arises that the family doctor may not have the equipment or capability to handle, the patient is referred to a specialist.

If the patient is relying on his or her generalist to recommend a specialist, then the selection of the specialist is made by an attending physician who is trained in such matters. However, patients may be able to determine the specialist they require without assistance. For skin problems, for example, most patients would go to a dermatologist. Often the choice may depend on health insurance restrictions.

Physicians in internal medicine are frequently used as general practitioners. They are capable of handling most medical concerns that are presented to them by their patients, and will send referrals to specialists as needed. There are at least forty different specialties for the physician to choose from while in medical school. They range from anesthesiologist to urology. About one quarter of the practicing physicians specialize in some aspect of surgery. The rest work in either one specific area of the body, one specific element of treatment, or with one specific clientele. For example, pediatricians work with children; neurologists work with problems of the nervous system; and anesthesiologists handle anesthetization during surgical procedures. About 7 percent of the physicians are psychiatrists.

Physicians have several employment options. Private practice is one structure of employment for physicians. Private practice includes independent partnership, and group arrangements. Normally an office space is rented or purchased for the physician. Diagnostic equipment is also purchased. The doctor will employ a staff, usually consisting of a receptionist and secretary, a nurse, and perhaps an x-ray technician or lab assistant. In group practice, three or more doctors will share the work space and schedule hours that allow each some time off from emergency calls. In group practices, the doctors also share the cost of staffing, overhead, and insurance. Partnerships are the same arrangement as the group practice, with only two attending physicians. Determining the number of physicians is done by cost benefit analysis, number of patients, and need of the community.

A doctor consults with his office staff between patient visits. He must have competent staff members to take care of the scheduling and bill processing.

In the decade between 1979 and 1989, the cost of expenses for physicians in private practice rose more than 50 percent. Two of the major expenses for private practice are medical malpractice insurance and salaries for administrative staff trained to file insurance paperwork. The arrangement of sharing office costs has helped to alleviate the rising expense of medical practice.

Another medical office arrangement is the managed–care office. This is the structure that is sponsored by health maintenance organizations (HMOs) and preferred provider organizations (PPOs). The basic concept behind this structural arrangement is that patients pay a monthly fee instead of a fee-for-service arrangement. The treatments, within the limits of the provider package, are completely covered. So, for a regular monthly payment, basic health care is provided. PPOs may be arranged as a fee-for-service, which offer a reduced fee to patients signed up to use one (preferred) facility for their medical treatment.

Clinics, or group medical facilities, are utilized by HMOs and PPOs for the provision of medical services. Other groups may also have clinics. A clinic functions like a group practice. The clinic is usually privately owned and is a profit making organization. The number of employees may be quite large. The Mayo Clinic in Minnesota is one of the best known clinics in the United States.

Clinics provide many of the services that a hospital provides as well as the general health care that a private practice physician provides. They may be equipped to do outpatient surgery (surgery which does not require overnight stay), technical examinations and tests, and other complex procedures that the private office may not be able to do. Clinics may provide general care, with several different specialists on staff to handle the different aspects of health care, or they may specialize, with most of the physicians working in the same area of treatment.

Clinics may be affiliated with hospital facilities, universities, teaching centers, nonprofit organizations such as Planned Parenthood, or profit-making companies or partnerships. They are located all over the country.

Hospitals provide extended-stay health care for the ill or injured. They provide the broadest range of health care to the public. Hospitals may be run by private investors and owners, or they may be affiliated with an outside institution or organization. Universities, churches, and the federal government sponsor hospitals. Community hospitals are normally nonprofit institutions. They provide service to the community at large, but they have become the most common treatment center for patients without medical insurance and those covered under Medicaid. Most hospitals in the United States are nonprofit institutions.

Hospitals, like clinics, may cover general care or specialized care. Some hospitals have emergency wards where any emergency condition can be treated by emergency room physicians and surgeons. Other hospitals may specialize in maternity care, psychiatric treatment, drug dependency, or some other category of health concern. Long-term care is provided in nursing homes, psychiatric hospitals, hospices for the terminally ill, and general and special long-term facilities.

In most large cities, there is at least one general care hospital. The cost of maintaining emergency room facilities, however, has brought down the number of hospitals that have sufficient staff to adequately handle emergency situations.

The number of hospitals in the United States peaked in the 1970s. There are fewer hospitals today because of hospital closings and consolidation of facilities. With the difficulty in maintaining a manageable budget, many hospitals have not been able to survive the rising cost of health care. For hospitals that service uninsured patients, the lack of reimbursement has eroded the profitability of the institution. Federal, state, and locally sponsored hospitals have been the most likely to close. Rural hospitals are also harder hit by the rising cost of insurance and health care. The loss of a rural hospital also may affect a larger area than the loss of an urban hospital, where the closest facility may be a few miles away. The rural patient may have a hundred miles to travel to find the nearest open hospital.

The structure of medical care insurance has influenced the structure of medicine more than almost any other single element of the industry. The cost of reimbursement by Medicare for services provided by a medical facility is determined by the federal government. The rising cost of medical treatment is not always matched by the maximum rate the government will pay for treatment. This puts the physician in the position of receiving lower rates for treatment or reevaluating the treatment provided in order to lower costs. The trend to release patients from the hospital earlier than in the past has become one common method of lowering costs. Medicare and many private insurance companies will review procedures or charges and may, if they choose, refuse to pay for some procedures on the grounds that the procedures are excessive, overpriced, unwarranted, or redundant. The purpose of refusal to pay is to eliminate abuses, waste, and over-treatment of patients, and to keep the cost to insurance companies down.

The HMO and PPO insurance system has attempted to stress preventive care instead of curative treatment. By designing a system that requires the patient to see the same physician whenever possible, the programs strive to reintroduce the family doctor. With one primary care physician, the patient is more likely to have early warning signs for medical problems recognized. The consistency in treatment is emphasized because the same doctor is consulted for all illnesses, allowing one trained medical person to know all the aspects of the medical treatment being given to a patient.

The problems with the HMO and PPO are normally in the size of the staff. Because of the large number of patients seeking care, many doctors have less time to consult with each patient than they would want. The appointment schedule to see a doctor may be filled for several weeks from the time the patient calls. The patient may be inclined to skip a doctor's visit because of the length of wait before a visit can be scheduled. However, the HMO and the PPO are becoming one of the more common forms of medical coverage, despite any current structural problems, and they are likely to become more popular as medical insurance costs continue to rise. By 1990, it was estimated that half of the practicing physicians in the United States were active members in a managed-care program, according to the American Medical Association.

Most of the medical practitioners work in private practice. Of those who do not, most are involved in teaching, research, or the administration of schools, hospitals, or research institutes.

The largest group of workers in the health field are those in the nursing occupations: physician assistants, nurse practitioners, registered nurses, licensed practical nurses, nursing aides, orderlies, and attendants. Depending on training and work setting, the nurse's job may include a wide range of duties related to caring for the sick or educating those who are well.

Registered nurses (RNs) are graduates of an associate (two-year), diploma (three-year), or bachelor degree (four-year) program. Each level allows for a different career path (see Volume 2: Registered nurses).

Licensed practical nurses and licensed vocational nurses are graduates of nursing programs that are normally one year long (see Volume 2: Licensed practical nurses).

Physician assistants normally have two years of undergraduate work in science or health and then complete specialized training, which may be a two to three year program (see Volume 2: Physician assistants).

In hospitals and other inpatient institutions such as nursing homes, staff nurses frequently work with patients who are grouped together on the basis of some common characteristic—for example, pediatric patients or patients undergoing surgery. Nurses in some specialties, such as those working in intensive care units, are required to complete extra courses in addition to their basic education. Many nursing schools now provide training in certain specialties as part of their regular curriculum, for example, preparing students to work with elderly patients.

Registered nurses may opt for other work arrangements. Private-duty nurses are RNs who are hired directly by patients and work in a variety of settings, including hospitals and nursing homes. Occupational health nurses oversee the health needs of business and government employees in their workplaces. Public health nurses specialize in promoting good health practices to prevent illness and restore health; they may provide care and counseling in schools, clinics, or other settings. Office nurses generally assist physicians, surgeons, and sometimes dentists in private practice or in clinics, often performing routine office and laboratory work in addition to nursing services. Other registered nurses teach, staff nursing organizations, act as administrators, or are engaged in research.

Licensed practical nurses (LPNs) observe and record information about patients, including temperature, blood pressure, and respiration rates. They assist patients with their per-

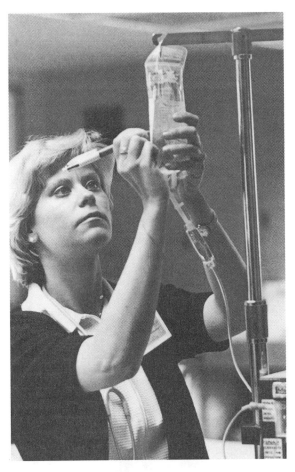

A registered nurse labels an intravenous bag filled with water and nutrients so that other hospital staff members are aware of its contents.

sonal hygiene and prepare them for medical examinations. In addition, they may give injections, change surgical dressings, and administer prescribed medicines.

Some LPNs specialize in pediatrics (care of children), coronary care (care of heart attack victims), hemodialysis (operating an artificial kidney machine), or work principally in the operating room or recovery room.

Most LPNs work in hospitals. Others work in nursing homes, extended-care facilities, day care centers, physicians' or dentists' offices, clinics, private homes, schools, camps, industrial establishments, public and home health agencies, correctional institutions, or other settings.

In addition to providing nursing care, LPNs who work in private homes may prepare meals, see to the comfort and morale of their patients, and instruct family members in simple nursing tasks. In physicians' offices, LPNs may make appointments, maintain records, and counsel patients.

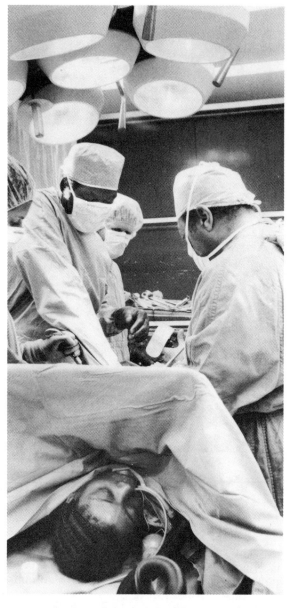

Most surgeries require a large medical staff including an anesthesiologist, a surgeon, and several surgical technicians.

Most nursing aides, orderlies, and attendants work in hospitals, but substantial numbers are also employed in nursing homes and other extended-care facilities.

One of the most distinctive features of modern medicine is its increasing reliance on new and sophisticated pieces of medical machinery. New technology aids in making diagnoses, providing effective treatments, and taking over body functions when organs fail or patients are undergoing surgery. Because these new machines require special skills from the people who attend them, they provide opportunities for many new jobs.

One of the areas in which technology has made particularly dramatic breakthroughs is in the area of heart disease. There are a number of tests that have made the discovery of heart disease much more likely. These include tests that pick up heart sounds and murmurs (phonocardiology), tests that record the heart's electrical activity (vector cardiography), stress testing, ultrasound testing (echocardiography), as well as more complicated testing procedures in which technicians may assist a physician in performing cardiac catheterization (inserting a tube through veins into a patient's heart).

People working in therapy or rehabilitation help injured, disabled, or emotionally disturbed people regain their strength to the fullest extent possible. There are many different kinds of therapists, each with special knowledge and special skills. Some therapists, for instance, use dance, art, and music to help resolve patients' physical, emotional, and social problems.

Research is one the most publicized areas of medical work. Research teams looking for cures to diseases, studying drugs for treatment, and working on preventive measures for disease and disabilities are regularly in the news with breakthrough discoveries. Nobel prizes are awarded to medical teams for their work. It is also one of the most frustrating and difficult aspects of medicine because one may work for years on a disease and never find a cure.

Biomedical research concentrates on eliminating specific diseases and health hazards such as cancer, heart disease, radiation contamination, and studying other environmental hazards that are damaging to human health.

Biomedical research is funded by a variety of institutions including manufacturers of pharmaceutical, electronic, chemical, and medical supply products; by private health agencies, such as the American Cancer Society and the American Heart Association; by endowments from philanthropic organizations; by federal, state, and local governments; and by hospitals, universities, and research organizations.

Medical research offers employment opportunities to individuals with varying amounts of training, ranging from the researcher who possesses an advanced degree to the technicians and assistants who may have high-school or community college diplomas or a certificate from a laboratory technical school.

Many health care professionals perform research work in pathology laboratories or other types of laboratories. Health professionals may also work with architects, city planners, government officials, law enforcement officers, and highway engineers to solve such health-related problems as traffic safety, drug abuse, rodent control, and the design of appropriate and adequate community health facilities.

Other health professionals research the problems concerned with the delivery of medical care services. They investigate such problems as why infant mortality and the incidence of tuberculosis is four times as great among some segments of the population as among others. They try to find the means to establish cooperative arrangements among various hospitals so that duplicate facilities for certain types of treatment do not exist where the area patient load requires only one facility. They may work out the logistics of an efficient system of evening and weekend medical coverage for a community or design an effective emergency team trained in the latest methods of cardiopulmonary resuscitation.

Closely allied to research is teaching. Opportunities for teaching exist at all levels in the health professions. There are opportunities in professional schools of medicine, nursing, dentistry, and veterinary medicine, and in the allied medical professions including therapy occupations and medical technology.

Overall, the structure of the medical world is enormously varied. There are many different jobs to choose from and many different facilities in which to work, once the job is chosen. The great variety of facilities and jobs is a direct reflection on the vast task that is assigned to the medical world. Preventing, curing, and repairing the diseases and injuries that affect the population is a major undertaking, requiring skill and training on every level.

Careers

An article of this length cannot describe all of the careers available in the field of medicine and health. This section covers the major categories of the medical and health industry.

Physicians: The principal medical practitioner is the physician, or doctor of medicine (M.D.). There are more M.D. physicians than all other medical practitioners combined, including optometrists, chiropractors, osteopathic physicians, and podiatrists. Medical practitioners work to diagnose and prevent disease and treat ill people with medications, surgery, and other accepted treatments.

Not all physicians provide direct care to patients. Physicians also teach, carry out research, hold administrative positions, write and edit medical books and magazines, or perform some combination of these activities.

Optometrists: Optometrists diagnose problems with vision, prescribe corrective lenses or other optical aids to correct vision, and may prescribe visual training aids and exercises. Optometrists do not perform surgery, nor do they ordinarily prescribe medicines, though in some states they are authorized to use drugs for diagnosis and other medical reasons. If they detect diseases requiring surgery, they refer the patient to an ophthalmologist (a doctor of medicine who has specialized in treating eye disorders).

Podiatrists: Podiatrists diagnose and treat diseases, injuries, and deformities of the feet. They prescribe drugs and corrective devices, set fractures, and perform surgery. Treatment sometimes consists of foot massages or special exercises. Foot problems can sometimes be signs of general illness, such as diabetes or heart disease. When podiatrists find signs of these illnesses, they refer the patient to a physician for treatment.

Most podiatrists treat all kinds of foot problems; however, some specialize in specific areas of foot care including surgery, orthopedics (the treatment of deformities of foot muscles, joints, or bones), and podogeriatrics (the care of elderly people's feet).

Chiropractors: Chiropractors practice a special system of health care that is based on the principle that a person's health is determined largely by the nervous system and that most disorders of the human body are due to interference with the nervous system. Chiropractors treat patients primarily by manual manipulation, especially of the spinal column. In addition to manipulation, most chiropractors also treat patients with light, heat, water, ultrasound, and various forms of physical exercise. Chiropractors use X rays to help in making diagnoses, but they do not prescribe drugs or perform surgery. If patients require that kind of treatment, they are referred to a physician.

Osteopathic physicians: Osteopathic physicians practice another special system of health care, based on the principle that a person's health is determined largely by the musculoskeletal structure of the body. Osteopaths prescribe drugs and perform surgery, but they stress a special treatment called manipulative therapy in which they use their hands to move parts of the patient's body, especially muscles and bones, into their proper places.

Registered nurses: Registered nurses, or RNs, play a vital role in the health care team. At various times, a nurse's activities may include comforting and instructing patients, making comprehensive assessments of patients' behavior, administering treatments and prescribed medicines, recording observations on physical and behavioral progress, preparing equipment, assisting in examinations and surgical proce-

Health Care

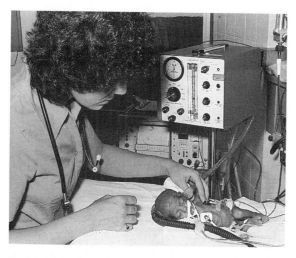

A pulmonary function technician monitors the breathing of a premature baby who is on a mechanical ventilation system.

dures, and supervising other personnel who perform more routine tasks.

Specialized registered nurses: Other RNs in institutional settings may be obstetrical nurses (who care for mothers and newborns from before birth to after delivery), operating room nurses (who perform various duties in the operating room), rehabilitation nurses (who help patients regain health and optimal functioning after serious illness or injury), and psychiatric nurses (who care for patients with mental disorders). Some nurses are less specialized: general medical-surgical nurses, for example, care for patients with a broad range of conditions.

Nurse practitioners: Nurse practitioners are RNs with specialized training beyond the bachelor's level who perform specified tasks otherwise performed only by physicians. In rural areas with few physicians, these health workers fill an important gap in availability of care and must constantly exercise judgment in ways consistent with good medical practice. In health maintenance organizations (HMOs), a nurse practitioner might screen patients' telephone calls, listening to a description of symptoms and making a judgment, for example, whether to suggest certain medical attention, refer the caller to a staff physician, arrange an appointment, or send the patient to a hospital emergency room.

The nurse practitioner performs some of the medical duties that do not require years of extensive training—treating common ailments, recommending standard medications, and, in some states, setting simple fractures or suturing minor wounds. They allow physicians to spend more time on duties that only the doctor can perform.

Physician assistants: Physician assistants work under the supervision of a physician and perform some of the duties that require different training than that of a registered nurse. Physician assistants' duties will vary from state to state according to local regulations. Their duties may range from interviewing patients and taking medical histories to suturing minor cuts, starting intravenous injections, and treating common ailments. Physician assistants are usually trained at colleges, schools of public health, or at medical schools that have allied health programs.

Nurse anesthetists: Nurse anesthetists are RNs with advanced training beyond the bachelor's level. They are trained to administer anesthesia to patients undergoing surgical procedures.

Nurse midwives: Nurse midwives are RNs with special training preparing them for obstetrics and the care of normal expectant mothers.

Licensed practical nurses: Licensed practical nurses (LPNs), sometimes called licensed vocational nurses (LVNs), provide most of the bedside nursing care in the United States. Working under the direction of a physician, RN, or dentist, they furnish routine care that requires technical competence but not extensive professional education.

Nursing aides: Known also as orderlies and attendants, nursing aides help nurses care for patients in hospitals. They carry meal trays to patients, answer call lights, assist in moving patients, and in general help to make the patient comfortable. They make beds, give baths and massages, and fill water pitchers and ice bags. They also set up medical and surgical equipment and take temperatures and pulse rates. The duties and responsibilities of nursing aides depend on the type of patient being cared for, the policies of the institution employing them, and the experience, training, and resourcefulness of the nursing aide or orderly.

Clinical chemists: Clinical chemists perform tests or direct other people who perform clinical tests. They also train people in clinical chemistry and carry out administrative tasks. They must have at least a bachelor's degree, but the majority have a master's, Ph.D., or M.D. degree. Clinical chemists may qualify for various kinds of certification by passing examinations conducted by professional organizations.

Medical laboratory technicians: Medical laboratory technicians perform the tests and laboratory procedures that are more complex than the routine procedures assigned to laboratory assistants. Medical laboratory technicians must have earned at least an associate degree from an accredited community college and have completed an accredited program of clinical education and laboratory experience.

Cytotechnologists: Cytotechnologists work with pathologists and perform procedures that detect cell changes caused by different disease processes.

Histological technicians: Histological technicians prepare tissue samples for diagnosis, research, or teaching purposes. They usually work with pathologists, but sometimes they also work with surgeons who give them samples to prepare for testing and evaluation while a patient's surgery is in progress.

Radiological technologists: In addition to taking diagnostic X rays, radiological technologists work in a number of specialized fields. For instance, radiological technologists in the field of computerized tomography use special X-ray equipment (CT scanners) linked to a computer to provide cross-section X rays of parts of the body. Thermography is a field related to radiology. It uses nonradioactive equipment and detects different bodily conditions by the heat given off from the affected part of the body.

Other medical technologists: This category includes electroencephalographic technologists and technicians who measure and record brain waves; nuclear medicine technologists who use radioactive materials and drugs in diagnosis of disease; diagnostic medical sonographers who use a sound-wave technique somewhat like sonar to determine internal bodily conditions; dialysis technicians who operate kidney machines; perfusionists who operate heart–lung machines; radiation therapy technologists who use radiation for the treatment of disease; and respiratory therapists and respiratory therapy technicians who operate respirators, oxygen tents, and other machinery that is used to treat patients with breathing difficulties.

Physical therapists: Physical therapists treat patients with fractures, sprains, nervous diseases, and heart trouble. Physical therapists prescribe exercises, administer massages, and perform body manipulations designed to correct muscle ailments. Physical therapists work as members of the medical team and participate in case conferences about patients' problems and progress.

Speech therapists: Speech therapists work with patients who have speech or voice disorders resulting from total or partial hearing loss, brain injury, cleft palate, mental retardation, or other disorders. Closely related to the work of the speech therapist, or speech pathologist, is the work of the *audiologist,* who assesses and treats hearing disorders.

Corrective therapists: Corrective therapists help patients strengthen and coordinate their body movements through programs of physical exercise.

Manual arts therapists: Manual arts therapists use mechanical, technical, and industrial activities to assist patients in improving work skills.

Occupational therapists: Occupational therapists help patients prepare for a return to work. They work with rehabilitative exercises and programs that develop physical and mental skills needed for the work place.

Public health educators: Public health educators work with the community as a whole and with special groups such as labor unions, civic organizations, and voluntary health and church groups. They may plan exhibits or health fairs, arrange forum discussions or prepare printed materials—whatever will motivate their audiences to accept health facts and act in their own best interests.

Emergency medical technicians: The occupation of emergency medical technician (EMT) has received increased attention. EMTs are often employed in ambulance services. They respond to medical emergencies, determine the nature and seriousness of injuries or illness, and decide on the sequence of emergency medical treatments. They may control bleeding, restore breathing, treat shock, apply splints, or assist in childbirth. EMTs may also have to free trapped victims or perform rescue maneuvers under hazardous conditions. A special grade of EMT, the paramedic, may also administer drugs intravenously and use complex medical equipment, such as a defibrillator (a device that uses electrical shock to restore beating in a stopped heart).

Biomedical engineers: Biomedical engineers are concerned with applying engineering concepts to all aspects of health care and research. They design and build medical instruments and devices such as artificial kidneys and heart valves, cardiac pacemakers and lasers for surgery, and computers to monitor patients in operating rooms and intensive-care units. Most biomedical engineers have a master's degree or doctorate.

Biomedical equipment technicians: Biomedical equipment technicians build, maintain, and repair various types of medical electronic equipment used to diagnose and treat disease. They work with physicians, nurses, and researchers to conduct experiments, plan medical procedures, and instruct medical staff members on the use of new devices. These technicians often have training or skills in electronics, glassblowing, or the use of plastics. In addition, they must be knowledgeable about the physiological principles that are related to their work. Biomedical equipment technicians must have completed a training program usually ranging from one to three years.

Many other careers in the health care industry are available in the field of health information and communication. Hospitals, public health agencies, and publishers of books and magazines require medical writers, medical illustrators, and medical photographers. Many interdisciplinary careers are available, such as medical sociologist and health economist. In the area of public health, there are careers for environmental engineers, who are concerned with the management of air, water, and land resources; industrial hygienists, who try to control risks in the workplace; and environmental and public health specialists, who are concerned with health and safety aspects of the environment.

Education

Medical school for doctors earning the degree "Doctor of Medicine," or M.D., is an extensive training. Following an undergraduate degree in any major, with a number of required science courses, the applicant must pass the Medical College Admission Test (MCAT). Medical school is normally a four-year program. Following graduation from medical school, licensing procedures in most states require some form of post-graduate training. This may include residency of at least one year in an accredited program, or internship at a hospital or other medical facility. Specialists may be required to serve up to three years in a residency program. A licensing examination is also required by every state. Re-examination may be required for certain specialties on a regular interval, depending on the specialty and the state in which the doctor is practicing. Doctors of osteopathy (D.O.s) fulfill similar requirements.

What sets optometrists, chiropractors, and podiatrists apart from the doctor of medicine is that these practitioners do not attend medical school or earn the M.D. degree. They attend specialized schools (schools of podiatry, osteopathic medicine, and so on). In general, these disciplines may require fewer years of training, and the academic requirements for entry into the respective schools are less demanding than for medical schools.

Registered nurses must be licensed in the state where they practice. Applicants must have graduated from state-approved nursing schools and have passed an examination. There are three kinds of nursing programs that may be suitable preparation: two-year associate degree programs offered in community colleges; two- or three-year diploma programs conducted by hospital schools of nursing; and four-year baccalaureate programs offered by colleges and universities. For some nursing specialties, at least a baccalaureate degree is required; thus the choice of program depends on the kind of practice the student anticipates.

Training programs for nurse practitioners are quite varied, but generally last from eighteen to twenty-four months. Evening classes are available at many schools.

Practical nurses are licensed and regulated throughout the United States. To qualify for a license, a person must complete a state-approved practical nursing course (usually lasting twelve to eighteen months) and pass a written examination. Educational requirements for admission to such programs range from having completed tenth grade to having earned a high-school diploma.

Nursing aides are usually trained after they are hired, although many employers still prefer to hire high-school graduates for these positions. Training consists of a combination of on-the-job supervised experience and classroom instruction and usually lasts from several days to several months.

The field of clinical laboratory services has a number of different specialties, each requiring different skills and varying levels of education. Certified laboratory assistants, for instance, perform routine tests and procedures under the supervision of medical technologists or physicians. They must be high-school graduates, complete a twelve-month course of classroom instruction and laboratory training, and pass a special examination.

Various kinds of certification are available for medical laboratory technicians, most requiring that a person pass an examination or complete an approved program of courses.

Teaching opportunities exist in the health care industry from the primary to collegiate level. Many school systems employ health educators who develop the necessary curriculum in such topics as personal hygiene, sex education and family living, scientific principles of disease prevention, first aid, and nutrition.

To acquire and maintain the most accurate and current knowledge about their health specialties, many health professionals must periodically take time off from their regular responsibilities to update their knowledge and skills. Computer-assisted programmed learning, seminars, short courses, and special lecture series and demonstration projects are available in almost all phases of the health field. Today more teachers are needed to organize and staff continuing education and in-service training programs for all health-related subjects.

Industry outlook

From 1970 to 1982, the number of workers in this field more than doubled. The increased number of physicians happened in response to the perceived need for an increase in the number of doctors for the increased population. Since 1982, however, the number of first-year students enrolled in medical school has reached a plateau at around 18,000. Through the mid-1980s the number of applicants to medical school rose tremendously, peaking at 37,000. The competition for medical school placement was well publicized and created a system that allowed only the very finest applicant to be accepted. As a result of that competition, the number of applicants to medical schools has fallen off sharply. By 1990, the number had fallen to around 26,000. The other element influencing the enrollment in medical schools may be the prediction that the market may soon have more physicians than are needed. There will continue to be a large need, however, for dentists, medical technicians, and all sections of nursing.

The employment outlook for all kinds of nursing appears to be favorable through the 1990s. Although some nurses working in hospitals can expect to earn salaries higher than the average for non-supervisory workers in the United States, most nursing personnel are not highly paid. This has created a shortage of staff in the field of nursing. Other factors have also aided the decrease in the number of people seeking nursing degrees. The fact that nursing has been a female dominated role for many years has led the position to be regarded in a less-than-positive light. As women's roles in the work force expanded, the options for positions in fields other than nursing drained many of the potential candidates. Other women, interested in the field of medicine, have chosen to pursue career paths that are more respected or higher paid, such as medical doctor or chiropractor. The nursing schools and many hospitals suffering from the shortage have attempted to remedy the situation by increasing pay, making hours more flexible, and providing a more significant role to the nurse in the overall arrangement of medical care. It is still undetermined whether the shortage will be alleviated before the year 2000. This means that openings for all levels of nurses should be plentiful, and that job opportunities will be abundant for many years to come.

One of the factors that will have a major impact on the entire health care industry is the aging of the American population. As modern American medicine enables more people to live longer, the elderly will make up a larger and

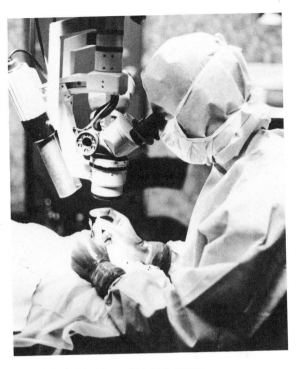

An ophthalmologist performs vitreous eye surgery.

larger portion of the population. Older people generally need more health services and somewhat different kinds of services than younger people. The shift in average age may stimulate changes in how the health care system is organized. For example, it may bring about more emphasis on home health care, different kinds of "walk-in" facilities, and the development of more nursing homes to furnish less intense care than that provided in hospitals.

Among other factors that are likely to affect the future of medical and health services are the growing public awareness about health questions, the costs of providing services, and the amount and kind of insurance coverage available to employee groups.

The uneven distribution of medical personnel in the United States is particularly evident in the case of physicians. The highest ratio of physicians to patients is in the northeastern states. Many rural areas and inner-city areas are seriously under served. Often rural areas make special efforts to attract physicians.

◇ **SOURCES OF ADDITIONAL INFORMATION**

American Medical Association
535 North Dearborn Street
Chicago, IL 60610

Health Care

American Health Care Association
1201 L Street, NW
Washington, DC 20005

American Hospital Association
840 North Lake Shore Drive
Chicago, IL 60611

American Nurses' Association
2420 Pershing Road
Kansas City, MO 64108

National League for Nursing
Ten Columbus Circle
New York, NY 10019

American College of Surgeons
55 East Erie Street
Chicago, IL 60611

American Dental Association
211 East Chicago Avenue
Chicago, IL 60611

American Academy of Family Physicians
8880 Ward Parkway
Kansas City, MO 64114

Healthcare Financial Management Association
2 Westbrook Corporate Center
Suite 700
Westchester, IL 60154

◇ **RELATED ARTICLES**

Volume 1: Biological Sciences; Chemicals and Drugs; Chemistry; Insurance; Social Science

Volume 2: Biochemists; Biologists; Biomedical engineers; Chemists; Chiropractors; Dental hygienists; Dentists; Dietitians; Health services administrators; Licensed practical nurses; Medical record administrators; Medical technologists; Occupational therapists; Optometrists; Perfusionists; Pharmacists; Pharmacologists; Physical therapists; Physician assistants; Physicians; Podiatrists; Prosthetists and orthotists; Psychiatrists; Psychologists; Registered nurses; Rehabilitation counselors; Respiratory therapists; Social workers; Speech- language pathologists and audiologists; Therapists, miscellaneous; Veterinarians

Volume 3: Dental assistants; Homemaker-home health aides; Medical assistants; Nursing and psychiatric aides; Occupational safety and health workers

Volume 4: Biological specimen technicians; Biological technicians; Biomedical equipment technicians; CAD/CAM technicians; Dental laboratory technicians; Dietetic technicians; Home health technicians; Medical laboratory technicians; Medical record technicians; Optometric technicians; Orthotic and prosthetic technicians; Pharmaceutical technicians; Pharmacy technicians; Physical therapist assistants; Psychiatric technicians; Radiological (X-ray) technologists; Surgical technicians

Hospitality

General information

The hospitality industry provides accommodations, meals, and personal services for both the traveling public and permanent residents. The range of employment opportunities in the industry includes positions in hotels and motels, restaurants, resorts, sports and recreation centers, condominiums, airlines and marinas, and such institutions as schools and colleges, hospitals, nursing homes, and correctional facilities. In its three major branches—lodging, restaurants, and institutions—hospitality is a people-oriented profession.

Inns have been in existence for as long as people have needed to travel long distances, requiring an overnight stay. Biblical stories recount the importance of receiving guests in a pleasant manner. As the Roman Empire expanded over two thousand years ago, inns sprang up to accommodate the large numbers of travelers going from town to town.

Pilgrimages to the Holy Lands also aided in the development of hotels and inns throughout Europe and the Middle East. Monasteries were accustomed to housing visitors for the night, throughout the Middle Ages. Eventually monasteries developed separate dormitory lodgings for such visitors, and it was the regular responsibility of some of the monks to tend to the guests' needs.

Hotels and inns began to flourish in England in the middle of the fourteenth century. By 1446, there were enough inns to warrant government regulation of the profession. The term *hotel* comes from the word used in England, during this period, for hotel workers—hostlers.

In England, some inns of the fifteenth and sixteenth centuries were noted for their lavish rooms. In America, the first public inn was built in Jamestown, Virginia in 1607. Most of the early American hotels were established on the East Coast, where travelers from Europe would disembark. As the country developed the western territories, farmhouse inns were maintained along the stagecoach routes. The railroad also created a demand for hotels and inns in both Europe and the United States. Having a railroad stop was usually a boon to small towns.

As lodgings developed, they began to offer more than a bed, a meal, and a roof over one's head. People began to have parties and meetings at inns. The size of the average hotel increased. The largest hotels would have hundreds of rooms. The biggest hotel in the United States in 1930 was the Stevens in Chicago. It had 3,000 rooms.

Free-standing (or self-contained) restaurants were once associated almost exclusively with hotels. But Prohibition and the 1920s dramatically altered that association. Before the Volstead Act, which outlawed the consumption of alcohol in the United States, hotel guests could relax with a drink in the downstairs bar or restaurant. Denied their drinks during Prohibition, they left their hotels in the evening to scout the neighborhood for one of the many speakeasies that served liquor illegally. Most of the speakeasies also provided food, both to cover their illegal activities and to please their customers. Thus, Prohibition helped drive a wedge between the hotel and the restaurant, two institutions that had traditionally coexisted for mutual profit.

Evidence of the spectacular growth of the hospitality profession was reflected in the numbers of motels built between 1948 and 1960. The establishment of the interstate highway system was as much a benefit to the industry as the stagecoach had been to the establishment of the industry in the United States. Chain hotels were beginning to take hold in the 1920s with Statler Hotels as one of the first large U.S. chains. Conrad Hilton also began his chain of hotels in the 1920s. He developed a corporation to support his business during the 1940s, just

With the advent of computerization in the hospitality industry, checking into hotels has become a quick process.

before the company launched their international branches of the Hilton Hotels. The Hilton chain, along with many others, have world-wide facilities. The number of motels, hotels, and inns in the United States has surpassed 30,000. Motels can be found virtually everywhere, many of them so elaborate that they resemble the multi-storied hotels that the early roadside motels originally replaced.

The greatest concentration of hospitality centers can be found in the trade-oriented and heavily populated cities like Boston, Los Angeles, Chicago, Atlanta, New York, and Washington, D.C. The other concentrations appear in the vacation cities like Miami Beach, San Francisco, and Orlando. However, hotels and motels are located everywhere in the United States from the smallest towns to the largest cities.

Until recently, inns and hotels were primarily set up to service the wealthy traveler or the person going from place to place. Once a large portion of the general public was able to afford leisure time, resorts appeared. These resorts and fancy hotels are no longer simply places to stay while visiting a certain location. They have become travel destinations in themselves.

Today, the efforts to appeal to specific markets of potential guests is creating significant change. Budget hotels and other types of accommodations continue to take a growing market share in the hospitality industry, forcing the large hotels to offer discounts and other incentives to travelers.

The structure of the hospitality industry

The traditional hospitality components centering on lodging and rental hall accommodations have always applied to hotels, resorts, recreation centers, convention centers, and other parts of the travel and tourism industry. The ingredients necessary for a successful hospitality operation have also always applied to the work carried out in such institutions as colleges and universities, hospitals, military installations, and a wide variety of other facilities where people live and eat away from home.

Hospitality establishments in the hotel and motel industry are usually classified as commercial or transient hotels; motels or motor inns (the latter, a more elaborate and elegant version of the former); the residential or live-in hotels; and resort hotels like those associated with the Atlantic Coast, the Bahamas, and Las Vegas. Some commercial and resort hotels specialize, often seasonally, in convention business.

An inn is a small building, perhaps an extension of somebody's home, that provides simple services such as a clean bed and bathroom. The number of rooms range from five to twenty. A growing branch of inns have become "bed and breakfast" places. They offer a homelike setting for a relaxing weekend in the country, with breakfast included in the room cost.

Motels are generally located near highways and airports and in small cities. The facilities range from simply a room with a bathroom, to motels with swimming pools and restaurants. Others rooms are designed as separated structures, each with a bed, bathroom, and kitchenette. These accommodations are referred to as suites. Some hotels are offering suites only, mainly housing business people who are on extended stays.

Hotels are larger structures that usually contain restaurants, bars, and at least fifty rooms. More elaborate hotels have swimming pools, saunas, exercise facilities, ballrooms, boutiques, conference rooms, and convention facilities.

While first-rate hotels have many of the same facilities as resorts, resorts are designed primarily for the pleasure and relaxation of its customers. Warm-weather resorts may offer a wide range of water sports such as sailing, wind-surfing, snorkeling, water skiing, and scuba diving. Winter resorts may cater to down-hill and cross-country skiers.

Every inn, motel, hotel, and resort has a general manager who oversees the entire operation. Depending on the size of the facility, there are seven branches of the hospitality industry that a manager may oversee: service, front office, housekeeping, food and beverage, engineering and facility maintenance, marketing and sales, and accounting and financial management.

The service branch is involved with making the guest feel welcome. This includes greeting guests, parking cars, opening doors, carrying baggage, and assisting with travel plans and entertainment.

The front office deals with all of the paperwork involved with checking in and out. The people that work in this department also run the reservation desk, switchboard, and mail room.

The housekeeping department is responsible for keeping the rooms clean. Along with the room attendants, there is a large support staff that cleans the bedding and supplies fresh linens and towels.

The food and beverage department is one of the largest and most lucrative sectors in the hospitality industry. It includes all of the services involved with the bars and restaurants of a hotel. The food and beverage director manages such people as the chefs, food preparers, waiters and waitresses, dishwashers, wine stewards, buspeople, and bartenders.

The engineering and maintenance department keeps the facilities of a hotel, motel, or other establishment in working order. The chores include plumbing, painting, electrical wiring, and general repairing.

The marketing and sales sector strive to attract potential customers to their place of business. The employees of this department try to find out what guests need and desire in order to make their establishment more appealing. Marketing and sales workers often use surveys or other research methods to gauge the feelings and opinions of guests and potential guests. The creative efforts of those in marketing and sales might be expressed in new programs to attract guests or a promotional campaign designed to inform potential guests of current services.

The accounting and financial management branch controls expenditures and projects future expenses. The staff includes accountants, cashiers, personnel, and controllers.

Hospitals, colleges and universities, and other establishments that provide hospitality services are set up in much the same way as hotels, resorts, and other private-sector operations. Each organization provides front office services, housekeeping, marketing and sales, and other services. However, the emphasis might be different. For example, a college cafeteria is not as dependent on attracting new

Large hotel chains offer services that allow a person to make reservations for any hotel in the chain by simply calling one toll-free telephone number.

customers as an expensive restaurant and so may not put as much emphasis on marketing and sales. Budgets are frequently smaller in the public sector of the industry.

Careers

All hospitality centers—the well-furnished motels, the metropolitan hotels, the country clubs and ski resorts, the modern trailer parks, the various styles of restaurants, and the extravagant amusement parks—need conscientious, well-trained employees. The people who offer the skills and services that the traveling public expects and depends on make up the hospitality professionals. These are the men and women who keep the comfort and security of these travelers uppermost in their minds and who have been trained and educated to do it efficiently.

One can seek employment in hotels, motels, and resorts, as well as in such associated areas as restaurants, nursing homes, colleges, hospitals, amusement parks, military bases, and airlines. Those with appropriate training often find careers as salespeople for hospitality products.

The hospitality industry requires a special kind of employee, one equipped with skills that have become firmly associated with the field over the centuries. The following list describes some of the many career opportunities in the hospitality industry.

General managers: General managers supervise the overall operations of a hotel or other hospitality establishment. They coordinate

The cleaning staff of hotels and motels follow strict guidelines for preparing each room.

front desk service, bell service, housekeeping, and other aspects of day-to-day operations.

Front office workers: Front office workers coordinate reservations and room assignments. They also greet guests as they enter the building. Front office workers also handle complaints and requests for special service. They are often the employee guests turn to most frequently for assistance.

Convention services managers: Convention services managers supervise meetings, conventions, and other special events. They usually work at large hotels or resorts.

Housekeepers: Housekeepers keep bedrooms clean. They also inspect rooms, stock linens and toiletries, and provide additional services, such as picking up and delivering dry cleaning for guests. In large hotels, housekeepers may supervise maids and other personnel.

Doorkeepers: Doorkeepers assist arriving and departing guests with their luggage. They often direct customers to the check-in counter.

Financial employees: Financial employees, such as controllers, accountants, and bookkeepers undertake the accounting and auditing duties. They are responsible for recording sales, controlling expenditures, and keeping track of overall profits or losses.

Sales and marketing staff: Sales and marketing people are found working mainly in the larger hotels and for franchise operations. They constantly strive to keep the name of the operation before the public by arranging for favorable radio, television, newspaper, and magazine publicity and by seeking additional business clientele. Sales and marketing workers also often conduct surveys designed to monitor the feelings and opinions of guests or potential guests.

Maintenance and engineering workers: Maintenance and engineering workers maintain and repair the operation's equipment. They keep the electrical wiring and appliances, the plumbing, and the numerous machines in good repair and working smoothly. They also clean the premises to attract customers, to improve safety, and to reduce the expense of wear and tear on the establishment.

Food and beverage managers: Food and beverage managers direct the activities in an establishment's cocktail lounge, restaurant, and banquet facilities. The manager supervises and schedules food preparation, deals with suppliers, and makes sure inventories are at their proper level.

Education

One way to learn the hospitality business is actually to work in it and to master the necessary skills. In fact, hospitality managers have traditionally hired people and then provided on-the-job training to teach employees specific skills. As the profession has become more automated and demanding, however, higher education has assumed an increasingly important role in determining who gets the jobs with the highest responsibility.

For those who desire management positions, a college degree is quickly becoming a prerequisite. While some employers prefer those who have degrees in hotel management, business administration, or similar programs, many employers will hire those with a more general college education.

Employment prospects in the field have encouraged more and more educational institutions to offer programs in the traditional branches of the profession—hotels, restaurants, and institutions. Most of the post-secondary schools address all three of these hospitality branches. Indeed, several universities have won national reputations for the excellence of their programs. Vocational schools, junior and community colleges, and other schools sometimes focus on only one aspect of the profession.

An educational program leading to employment in the hospitality industry should include courses in economics, food service management, marketing, hotel maintenance engineering, computer applications, housekeeping, and similar subjects.

In additional to educational requirements, it is helpful if those in the hospitality industry are able to move from place to place to secure employment. Often, certain sectors of the country will offer strong employment opportunities for a limited period of time. It may be necessary for those just starting in the industry to move around a bit to gain the necessary experience to become managers.

It is important not to underestimate the importance of on-the-job training. Many employees start as doorkeepers, maids, or other entry-level positions, and with several months or years of experience are promoted. It is not unusual for someone to start as a front desk clerk or waitress and work their way up to manager within a relatively short period of time.

The skills in the hospitality industry are fairly transferable. A person trained as a front desk clerk, for example, can readily switch to another clerk position in a hotel.

Industry outlook

As people have more and more leisure time, the hospitality industry is expected to grow rapidly in the future. The number of hotels and motels should greatly expand as individuals and families spend more time traveling.

The work force in food service (one indicative aspect of the hospitality field) is expected to grow almost three times as fast as the work force in general. While the largest number of employees will still be in the traditional skilled and semiskilled positions (clerks, maids, cooks, and waitresses), there will also be a growing need for managers.

Given the current predictions for strong growth in the industry, it will become increasingly important to recruit skilled workers to fill new openings. The problems of finding and keeping staff are expected to become more difficult as the pool of younger workers shrinks.

Another challenge for the industry will be how it integrates new technology. Already many hotels, airlines, resorts, and other organizations are establishing data processing terminals to process reservations, bookkeeping procedures, and other services. Other advances include security systems based on card-activated access, fax machines in rooms, and TV-based guest shopping. Those establishments that are able to provide these and other services should be able to attract a wide range of customers. As the labor force continues to shrink, the hospitality industry will increasingly automate.

While the prospects for growth in the hospitality industry are particularly bright, it should be remembered that the industry is directly tied to the amount of money people can spend on leisure and business activities. There-

At large resorts, the food and drink services extend to all areas of the establishment.

fore, any downturn in the economy could have a negative impact on industry growth.

The gross sales from hotels and other lodging places exceeded $50 billion in the late 1980s, and employment reached over one and a half million people. Although in some markets there was an oversupply of hotel rooms, new properties and opportunities for new jobs continued to reflect the industry's willingness and capacity to provide up-to-date accommodations for the traveling public.

Another trend seems to be the consolidation of hotels and other companies providing hospitality services. It is expected that the number of companies involved in the hospitality industry will shrink as mergers and acquisitions accelerate.

America is a country on the move. And travelers need a place to stay and friendly efficient people to make them feel welcome. The hospitality industry, which offers lodging, restaurant, and other services, has a promising future.

◇ SOURCES OF ADDITIONAL INFORMATION

For general information about careers in the hospitality profession, contact:

American Hotel & Motel Association
1201 New York Avenue
Washington, DC 20005

American Bed and Breakfast Association
16 Village Green, Suite 203
Crofton, MD 21114

Hotel Sales and Marketing Association International
1300 L Street, NW, Suite 800
Washington, DC 2005

Council on Hotel, Restaurant, and Institutional Education
1200 17th Street, NW
Washington, DC 20036

Educational Institute of the American Hotel & Motel Association
1407 South Harrison Road
PO Box 1240
East Lansing, MI 48826

◇ **RELATED ARTICLES**

Volume 1: Business Administration; Food Service; Marketing; Recreation and Park Services; Travel and Tourism

Volume 2: Advertising workers; Caterers; Dietitians; General managers and top executives; Hotel and motel managers; Management trainees; Marketing, advertising, and public relations managers; Musical occupations; Public relations specialists; Recreation workers; Restaurant and food service managers

Volume 3: Bartenders; Cooks, chefs, and bakers; Counter and retail clerks; Food service workers; Hotel and motel industry workers; Hotel clerks; Hotel housekeepers and assistants; Reservation and transportation ticket agents; Travel agents

Human Resources

General information

In the eighteenth century, the U.S. economy was primarily agricultural, dependent upon crops such as wheat and cotton. During the nineteenth century the United States underwent an industrial revolution, and the economy shifted largely towards production of raw materials, such as iron and steel, and finished products, such as cars and refrigerators. In both instances, agricultural and industrial, the economy was based on the goods produced.

Today, however, an increasingly large portion of the economy depends on service industries such as banking, accounting, health care, travel, and hospitality, among many others. A service industry is one in which the main product is not something that you can buy in a store, but rather a set of actions that someone performs for a client. For example, the travel agent who reviews all possible flight connections and prices and comes up with the best reservation for your schedule and budget is providing a service. The banker who helps arrange the best mortgage for the property you want to buy is providing a service. Similarly, the computer specialist who helps you choose the software package best suited for your needs is providing a service. Service is the "product" that they sell and you buy. This shift towards a service economy has contributed to the growth of a new industry: the Human Resources industry.

The success of any economy depends on its resources. The United States' agricultural and industrial economies thrived because of the nation's natural resources of rich farmland and substantial mineral deposits. The success of a service economy depends on the quality of its work force. The function of the human resources industry is to produce competent personnel and to keep employees productive.

The increased emphasis on human resources is not limited to service industries, however. High-tech goods-producing industries, such as the computer industry for example, are placing greater importance on the quality of their personnel. Such industries are more vulnerable to human error because the smallest error in a complex computer system can make the system unusable. The more technical skills that are involved in the design, manufacture, marketing, and sales of a product, the more competent a company's workers must be.

Human resources professionals, also known as personnel managers, are responsible for hiring skilled workers and helping to maintain a productive work environment. Personnel management is not a new field, but the nature of the field is changing. In the past, personnel specialists served primarily as technicians with such responsibilities as hiring and training workers, managing the payroll, and dealing with labor issues.

Today, human resource professionals are being entrusted with a broader, more conceptual and strategic set of responsibilities. They may set up job classifications, employee benefit systems, and training systems. In addition, they work with top management to devise plans for the optimal use of human resources. For example, human resource professionals often advise management on policies to reduce absenteeism and on methods to improve morale and productivity.

The essence of human resource management is transforming an input, which is an employee or group of employees, into an output, which is a job well done. The transformation processes are systems for acquiring, developing, allocating, conserving, utilizing, evaluating, and rewarding workers.

Human resources management comprises a number of job responsibilities, which may be carried out by one person or by a number of specialists. Different kinds of specialists include personnel managers, industrial-relation directors, recruiters, job-development specialists,

A prospective employee completes a brief form that provides information concerning past employment experiences and professional skills.

job analysts, compensation managers, training instructors, benefits managers, retirement officers, employee health-maintenance specialists, and mediators (see Volume 2: Personnel and labor-relations specialists). Other occupations in the human resources field include ergonomists and employment firm workers (see Volume 2: Ergonomists; and Employment firm workers).

The structure of the human resources industry

Human resources professionals are generally employed in one of two major arenas. First, they may work for large or medium-sized companies in any kind of industry. Any place where there are many employees, whether at a bank or a oil company, there is a need for personnel specialists.

The second major arena is companies whose business it is to help other companies find qualified personnel, both on a permanent and temporary bases. Such companies provide a service to employers and those seeking employment. These establishments include employment agencies, executive-placing services, temporary-help services, labor contractors, registries for chauffeurs, maids, models, nurses, ship crews, and teachers.

Before a company or organization can make any decisions about personnel, it must come up with a game plan for itself. What are its goals

for the future? Does it see itself developing new products? How much does it want to grow, and how quickly?

Once these basic questions are answered, an organization can start its human resource planning. A good first step is determining what needs to be done at every level of the organization to achieve its goals. It's important to take future needs into account. For example, if a company operates in only one city but plans to have offices in ten cities five years from now, in five years that company will need a manager with the skills to oversee the activities of ten regional offices.

Once a plan is in place, management should evaluate the capabilities of the people already on staff to see how they might fit into this plan. If they discover that they do not have the personnel they require, they need to figure out the best way to hire the appropriate workers.

An increasingly important part of planning is human resources accounting, a relatively new field. Generally speaking, human resources accounting is essentially a process of cost estimation, a mathematical way to determine the cost and value of people as resources. The role of the human resource accountant is to help management understand the monetary implications of business decisions.

When a company has to decide between hiring from within the company or hiring a new employee, human resource accounting can provide figures on the costs of acquiring and developing people for positions. When the person is already on staff, for example, the amount of money it will cost to retrain that person must be taken into account. If the person is an outsider, the cost to hire and integrate that worker into the company must be considered.

In another example, a company may save money by laying people off. But if those people get different jobs and don't come back, the company will have to spend money to train new people. This may not be a savings in the long run.

Human resource workers are also involved in helping a company acquire new workers. Acquisition involves recruiting, selecting, and hiring people. It is process of bringing the right people together to perform a job in the most effective way possible. Human resources professionals are responsible for finding the best workers to do a job. They do this by knowing the right places to look for workers, and by conducting good interviews with candidates.

But there is more to acquisition than finding the personnel a company wants; making the company attractive to prospective employees is equally important. To get the personnel it wants, a company might decide to make concessions to families by providing on-site day-care, flexible schedules, and job sharing. Human resources professionals devise proposals that balance the needs of employers and workers to come up with employment packages that benefit both.

Human resource professionals help increase productivity by making people into better workers. This involves various forms of training to enhance workers' technical, administrative, and interpersonal skills, either through formal programs or on-the-job training. Developing workers' skills costs money, but it is often a good investment. For example, sending an employee out of town for a seminar costs money, but what the worker can gain from the seminar may more than offset that investment. Similarly, reimbursing employees for tuition paid for college-level courses may be costly, but it makes the employee more valuable to the company.

Allocation is the process of assigning people to various roles and tasks. Ideally, people should be assigned to jobs to fulfill three basic requirements. First, the jobs should get done. Second, the employees should learn more skills. Third, the employee should be happy with the situation.

Sometimes assigning the most qualified person to a job may not be the right decision because it keeps someone else from learning the task. Incorrect allocation can be costly, because, in many industries, if workers don't develop skills, they become less valuable.

Utilization is the process of using human services to achieve a company's objectives. If the aim of human resource management is to increase the value of an organization's workers, then task design, selection, role assignment, development, performance appraisal, and compensation are more than just a set of functions to be performed—they are a set of strategies that can change the value of human assets.

Conservation is the process of maintaining the capabilities of workers and the effectiveness of the work team developed by an organization. This can save a business money in the long run. Unless monitored, human resources may deteriorate and an organization will have to incur retraining replacement costs.

Workers' productivity is often directly linked to their psychological well-being. A manager may put pressure on people temporarily to increase productivity or reduce costs. But it is important that the effects upon worker motivation and attitudes do not go unnoticed. Highly skilled employees may become dissatisfied and leave. Good human resources professionals are like good coaches: they keep work-

A personnel staff member looks up an employee's file on a computer to determine the health benefits available to the employee.

ers performing well and feeling good about themselves.

An important element of conservation and retention has to do with individual workers' professional ambitions. Not everybody wants the same thing out of a job. Some people want to climb the corporate ladder. Others want to be teachers, consultants, or entrepreneurs. Human resource workers need to develop different career paths and reward systems to deal with different types of people.

The areas of evaluation and compensation are important ones for human resources professionals. Evaluation is the process of assessing the value of people to an organization. It involves measuring the performance of workers and determining how much they should be paid for their contribution to a company. This is a very important function because it is directly related both to general productivity and to hard dollars. If a company pays an employee $30,000 a year and nobody notices that this employee is not doing a very good job, then the company is throwing its money away. On the other hand, if an employee's excellent work goes unnoticed and under compensated, he or she may leave the company, and not only will the company spend time and money training a replacement, but the replacement may not be as good as the original worker.

Clearly, accurate evaluation is an essential part of effective human resources management. Human resource professionals can facilitate evaluation by helping managers develop creative ways to assess their workers' skills, and by reminding them not to take their workers for granted. Perhaps one employee could do more if given the chance; maybe another is simply not equal to a task.

Compensation goes hand in hand with evaluation. Compensation is how workers are rewarded for their performance, and a savvy

239

An interviewer takes notes while asking a candidate questions concerning the responsibilities at her current place of employment.

human resources professional understands that there is more to compensation than salary. Some employees would prefer to have their entire reward concentrated in their salaries, but for others benefits such as insurance, pension plans, vacation time, profit sharing, and general job flexibility are equally if not more important. It is up to the human resources team to determine the best way to compensate workers in line with both the company's and individuals' needs.

Careers

A sampling of human resources career opportunities follows below.

Job analysts: Job analysts collect and examine information about job responsibilities to prepare job descriptions. These descriptions are used to recruit new workers. The descriptions explain the responsibilities, training, and skills each job requires.

Compensation managers: Compensation managers develop and maintain a company's pay system. In order to determine fair and equitable pay rates, compensation managers often conduct surveys to see how their rates compare with other companies.

Employee benefits managers: Employee benefits managers administer a company's employee benefits program, including its pension plan and health insurance policy. These workers must keep up to date on various methods of providing comprehensive health care at a reasonable cost.

Benefits analysts/benefits administrators: These workers administer insurance programs such as

dental insurance, accidental death insurance, and homeowners' insurance, for those companies that provide these benefits. Benefits analysts also oversee profit sharing and thrift/saving plans.

Training specialists: Training specialists conduct orientation sessions, arrange on-the-job training for new employees, and help employees prepare for future job responsibilities. Specialists may utilize classroom training, programmed instruction, or other techniques to prepare workers to do their jobs successfully. In addition, specialists also help supervisors deal effectively with employees.

Employee welfare managers: Employee welfare managers oversee programs designed to promote occupational safety and physical fitness. They coordinate first aid stations, food service and recreation activities, counseling services, and a variety of other programs. As health issues become more and more important, employee welfare managers have developed programs to deal with alcoholism, financial problems, and a vast array of other subjects.

Labor relations managers: Labor relations managers develop labor policy, coordinate labor relations, and negotiate agreements resulting from labor disputes. These managers must work closely with employee benefits managers and other personnel administrators because wages, employee welfare, and other issues all may be part of a labor dispute.

If a labor dispute becomes very controversial, a labor relations manager may call in a arbitrator to decide grievances and bind labor and management to specific conditions on a labor contract.

Ergonomists: Ergonomists study the workplace to determine the effects of the work environment on the activities of individuals and groups. They conduct research and analyze data concerning the physical factors of the workplace (noise, temperature, etc.) and evaluate the design of machines to see that they are safe, usable, and conducive to productive work.

Industrial-safety-and-health technicians: These technicians plan and carry out activities in industrial plants to evaluate and design controls for potential health and safety hazards. Using precision measuring instruments, they measure noise levels and air quality. They may also test employees for problems and instruct them in safety practices.

Occupational safety and health workers: These workers are responsible for preventing or minimizing work-related accidents and diseases, property losses from accidents and fires, and injuries from unsafe products. These workers include safety engineers, fire-protection engineers, industrial hygienists, and loss-control and occupational-health consultants.

Education

Individuals with all kinds of backgrounds can find job opportunities within the human resources industry, but a college degree is usually helpful. This degree can be any number of areas, but those most useful are business administration, communications, psychology, and liberal arts. Some colleges offer majors in human resources.

Graduate study in industrial or labor relations is important for those seeking employment in the labor policy area. Many of those involved with contract negotiations should have a law degree or some experience with legal issues.

In addition to academic credentials, human resource workers should speak and write effectively and be able to work with a wide variety of people. They must have the patience to train workers and be able to supervise employees under sometimes stressful conditions.

Depending on which occupation you choose, you may want to pursue certification from one of the industry's trade associations.

Industry outlook

Human resource professionals should continue to find good employment opportunities in the 1990s. Much of the growth will occur with personnel consulting firms, as more and more businesses hire human resource specialists on a contractual basis to meet the increasing demands of training and development programs.

There should also be good job possibilities with larger companies. Whenever there are a lot of employees, there will be a need for human resource professionals to integrate these workers into the company. The health care industry and other growing industries should offer good job prospects.

As training programs become more and more sophisticated, especially in high-technology industries, human resource workers will need to increase the complexity of training programs and other programs designed to improve the productivity of workers.

Personnel administrators must keep track of all employee information including health benefits, vacation days, and other absences.

◇ **SOURCES OF ADDITIONAL INFORMATION**

American Society for Personnel Administration
606 North Washington Street
Alexandria, VA 22314

National Association of Personnel Consultants
1432 Duke Street
Alexandria, VA 22314

National Employment Counselors Association
5999 Stevenson Avenue
Alexandria, VA 22304

International Personnel Management Association
1617 Duke Street
Alexandria, VA 22314

Human Resources Research Organization
1100 South Washington Street
Alexandria, VA 22314

Human Resources

Insurance

General information

The insurance industry provides protection for its customers against financial loss from many kinds of hazards. This protection is offered in the form of insurance policies. It is a giant, highly complex industry that has grown out of an ancient and very simple principle: The more people who share a financial risk, the smaller the risk is for each.

A crude but effective form of insurance based upon this principle was applied thousands of years ago in China. Boats often sank in the treacherous Yangtze River, and their cargoes were lost, sometimes bringing financial ruin to their owners. Then the shippers hit upon the idea of sharing the risk by having each person's goods distributed among many boats. That way, if one boat sank, a number of people lost a small part of their belongings, but no one person suffered a heavy loss.

The early Babylonians had a form of credit insurance. The Code of Hammurabi, a collection of Babylonian laws written about 1700 B.C., stipulated that a borrower did not have to repay a loan if personal misfortune made it a hardship to do so. The borrower paid an additional amount for this protection.

Another form of insurance made life a little less hazardous for American settlers in the early frontier days. If a family's cabin burned, the neighbors would get together and build them a new one, knowing that they would get the same kind of help if they suffered a similar misfortune. In a way, they too were sharing the risk.

Today, the population is much too large and life much too complicated for such simple means of sharing the risk to protect people against the many hazards that could cost them their property or their financial security. Instead, people share the risks by purchasing insurance policies. Customers pay a certain amount of money, called a premium, to an insurance company for coverage against possible loss.

When a person buys a fire insurance policy on a home, for example, he or she pays the insurance company only a small fraction of what it would cost to replace the house. If the house burns down, however, the insurance company is able to pay the owner for all or part of the loss by using the money that many other people have paid for their insurance policies. In that way, each person who buys an insurance policy is protected against financial loss by all of the others who have bought policies.

Employment opportunities in the insurance industry can be found anywhere in the country. In small communities, however, employment is usually limited to agents, brokers, and the clerical workers they employ. They account for roughly half of the people in insurance.

The other half work mostly in the larger cities, in home offices or regional offices of the insurance companies or industry organizations. These offices are in cities throughout the country, but the greatest number are concentrated in New York, New Jersey, Massachusetts, Connecticut, and Illinois.

The structure of the insurance industry

The insurance industry is divided into three main branches: life insurance, health insurance, and property and liability insurance. Companies may specialize in one or all three types of coverage.

Life insurance is basically a means by which one person provides for the financial security of others—usually other family members—in the event of that person's death. Using life insurance in its simplest form, a person pays an insurance company a small amount each month for a policy that guarantees that the family will receive a relatively large amount of

An insurance agent reviews the home and automobile insurance rates with a client.

money if the person dies while covered by the policy. However, many life insurance policies combine this form of protection with others. Some provide for the policyholder to receive a regular income after reaching retirement age. Some provide funds for a college education for the policyholder's children. Some will pay off the mortgage on a person's home if he or she dies or becomes unable to work.

Health insurance pays all or part of hospitalization, surgery, medicines, and other medical costs. This helps protect the policyholder against large medical bills in the case of an illness or accident.

In Canada and other countries, people are covered by government health insurance. In the United States, most of the health insurance is provided by insurance companies, medical service plans, or health maintenance organizations (HMO's). Often, an employer plays all or part of the insurance premiums for employees. The government provides health services for those unable to afford private health insurance.

Property and liability insurance comes in a wide variety of forms. It includes all of the different kinds of insurance that protect people from financial loss if their property is destroyed, damaged, or stolen. It also includes all forms of liability insurance—the insurance that protects people from financial loss if they are responsible for injury to another person or damage to another person's property.

Within the property and liability field, there are several specialized branches, or "lines" of insurance. Some companies write all lines, while others write only one. In addition to insurance on homes, business places, automobiles, and personal property, this field includes marine insurance, which covers boats and ships and their cargoes, and inland marine insurance, which covers almost anything capable

of being transported or which is used in transportation. Inland marine insurance covers everything from furs and paintings to locomotives and bridges.

Also included in the property and liability field is worker's compensation insurance, which pays a person for loss of wages and medical expenses if he or she is disabled because of an injury or illness connected with a job. Worker's compensation also provides death benefits for dependents if death is due to a work-connected injury or illness. Fidelity bonds, which protect an employer from loss due to dishonesty of an employee, and surety bonds, which guarantee that contracts will be carried out properly, are other forms of insurance written by property and liability companies.

Agents and brokers deal constantly with the public. In addition to selling insurance policies, they are responsible for advising each client about the particular kinds and amounts of insurance that will meet the client's individual needs. In some cases, they also help settle claims when a loss occurs by working out a payment agreeable both to the policyholder and the insurance company. Agents who sell certain types of life insurance may also collect premiums.

Some agents are employed by a single insurance company and are paid either a salary, commission, or a combination of both. (Commissions are a percentage of the premiums paid to the agent based on the value of the policies an agent sells). Many other agents are independent businesspeople who are under contract to represent several companies.

Insurance brokers are independent businesspeople who represent no particular companies but who may order policies from many. In other respects, the broker's work is the same as the agent's. They both are paid commissions on the policies they sell.

Like the insurance companies they represent, agents and brokers often specialize either in life insurance, health insurance, or property and liability insurance. Some specialize still further and handle only one line of liability insurance, such as automobile coverage. Others may handle a diversified firm's entire range of business.

Agents may work in large offices with a number of other agents or in small one-person agencies. Some work out of their homes. Many agents combine their insurance business with other types of business; it is not uncommon, for example, for a property insurance agent to be in the real estate business, too.

In addition to selling and performing services for their clients, insurance agents spend considerable time on paperwork, record keeping, and correspondence. Depending on the size of the agency, an agent may also supervise a number of clerical workers and sometimes a staff of salespeople.

Because an agent's income depends on the amount of insurance policies he or she sells, the agent devotes a lot of effort to finding new prospects and establishing contacts with people who might buy insurance. This frequently involves considerable activity in civic and social affairs.

Large insurance companies that use independent agents and brokers hire field representatives to promote their line of insurance. Field representatives make regular calls on each agent in their territory who handles their company's insurance. They instruct the agents on new types of insurance and changes in old policies. They help find new business and assist agents in examining their clients's insurance programs to make sure the clients have the right kind of coverage in sufficient amounts. They also encourage the agents to conduct vigorous sales campaigns.

Field representatives are, in effect, district sales managers, but they must be exceptionally good at getting along with people because the agents they manage are independent businesspeople and not employees of the company. Their job is to sell the local agents on selling more of the company's insurance.

Because their job is to instruct the agents about changes in the business, field representatives must keep themselves up to date on all policy changes and be able to explain them clearly and thoroughly. Field representatives frequently conduct educational meetings at which agents are informed about developments in insurance and sales methods.

After an agent fills out an insurance application for a client, the application goes to an underwriter. The underwriter considers all of the information available about the risk involved, and then decides whether it should be accepted. If, for one reason or another, an underwriter decides that the hazards involved in insuring a particular risk are far above average, he or she may turn down the application or may accept it, but reduce the company's risk by reinsuring part of it with another company. If the underwriter decides that the company should accept the risk, he or she then sees that the proper kind of policy is issued and the proper rates are charged.

In large companies, underwriters are usually specialists in a particular type of insurance. Life insurance actuaries, for example, study statistics on how long people live, what causes people to die, what kind of people live longer than others. From those statistics, they can project how long persons in certain statistical categories can be expected to live—"life expectancy" is the term they use. They cannot, of course, predict when a particular person will die, but they can predict with great accuracy how long an average person of a given age, sex, occupation, and so forth will live. With that knowledge, they can determine the amount of premiums that must be collected on each life insurance policy so that the insurance company will have enough to make payments when policyholders die and still earn a return for the company.

Actuaries in the property and liability field make many of the same kinds of studies and predictions. They can predict, for example, how many auto accidents will take place in a particular area and how much they will cost. That enables insurance companies to set rates that will bring them enough money to pay all their claims.

Not all actuaries work for insurance companies. Some are employed by industry associations that propose insurance rates for groups of companies. Others work for insurance departments of their states. Some are independent consultants who run their own businesses.

When an accident, death, or other loss has occurred, the adjuster examines the claim. An adjuster may work on a great many different kinds of claims. He or she may be required to estimate the amount of damage to a house that is struck by lightning, the cost of repairing a damaged fender on an automobile, the value of a stolen necklace, or how much income will be lost because a store owner's shop burned down.

The adjuster may also be a specialist on one particular kind of claim. The General Adjustment Bureau, an organization that handles much of the adjustment work for property and liability insurance companies, set up one group of adjusters to work only on losses caused by missile tests.

Many adjusters travel to all parts of the country and sometimes to foreign countries. Large numbers of adjusters travel to the scene of major disasters, such as hurricanes or tornadoes, which result in thousands of insurance claims. In such cases, the adjuster's job is to examine insurance policies to make sure each individual's loss is covered by insurance, to inspect the damaged property and estimate the cost of repairing or replacing it, and to work out a fair settlement with the policyholder.

With the pool of money insurance companies collect from premiums, they invest in the national economy. Insurance companies invest huge sums of money in government, transpor-

A group of independent agents meet annually to discuss sales techniques, new policy changes, and new legislation that may affect current rates.

tation, and utility bonds, thereby helping to finance many public improvements. In addition, they invest in stocks and insure many home mortgages.

Through research, safety engineering, and accident prevention and health programs, the industry helps to reduce illness, injuries, and hazards that cause property loss. By so doing, the insurance industry lessens the risks that must be shared and thereby helps control the amount of money that people must pay for premiums.

There are a number of organizations supported by the insurance companies for various purposes such as proposing rates to be charged for different kinds of insurance, advising companies on policy matters, conducting public information campaigns, and other services.

Careers

By far the largest numbers of people employed in the insurance industry are people whose skills and training could be used in many other industries. These include clerical personnel, en-

gineers, doctors, lawyers, technicians, accountants, investment analysts, computer analysts and programmers, statisticians, advertising and public relations personnel, and others.

There are also, however, many positions that require specialized knowledge in the insurance field. These include the positions of agent, actuary, underwriter, claims adjuster, and field representative. Descriptions of some of the more specialized positions follow.

Insurance agents: Insurance agents are primarily salespeople, offering insurance to prospective buyers. Some are independent, selling many brands of insurance; while others represent a single company. Either way, agents receive a commission on the insurance they sell. In addition to selling, however, insurance agents perform certain specialized tasks for their clients. They must be licensed by the state, and they must be able to pass a state examination on their knowledge of regulations that govern the insurance business.

Field representatives: Field representatives are salaried employees of insurance companies who work out of regional offices and spend much of their time traveling. The field representative is assigned to a territory and is primarily responsible for helping agents in the territory increase the amount of insurance they sell for the company.

Claims adjusters: Claims adjusters are responsible for determining whether losses are covered by insurance policies and how much the losses amount to. Adjusters may be employed by insurance companies or they may be independent businesspeople who make their services available to insurance companies.

Claims adjusters must have broad knowledge of the values of many different kinds of things, or know how to find out quickly what things are worth. They must also be able to interpret and explain insurance policies that are difficult for untrained people to understand. They must, in addition, know a good deal about the laws that govern insurance, because questions about whether an insurance policy covers a particular loss sometimes becomes a legal issue.

Underwriters: There is a saying in the insurance industry that a company's success depends upon the skill of its underwriters. That is because the underwriter is the person who decides whether the company should insure a given person or piece of property—a risk—and what rates should be charged. Certain life insurance agents are known as underwriters because they must judge whether the person involved is a good risk when they write policies that do not require physical examinations. Usually, however, the term underwriter refers to a person who works in the home office, or sometimes the regional field office, of an insurance company.

The term underwriter originated in London in the eighteenth century. Merchants and shippers would write the names of ships and descriptions of their cargoes on a blackboard. Persons who were willing to share the risk of a ship's voyage, in exchange for a share of the profits, would write their names under the name of the ship.

Actuaries: Actuaries are responsible for determining the rates that should be charged for different kinds of insurance policies. Actuaries must be skilled in applied mathematics. Their job is to study past incidents and predict what will happen in the future.

Insurance physicians: Doctors not only run employee health programs for insurance companies but also examine persons who apply for life insurance and persons who make insurance claims based on accidental injuries. Doctors employed by insurance companies also may be called upon to testify in court in personal injury cases.

Insurance attorneys: Attorneys draw up the wording of insurance policies and defend policyholders who are involved in lawsuits. In addition, they perform the legal work that is required in any large industry.

A claims adjuster inspects a car for damages and estimates the reparation costs.

Education

Some beginning positions in insurance are open to high-school graduates with no additional training or experience. Others require college degrees in specialized fields of study. Many require special knowledge or experience that can be obtained on the job or in special trainee positions.

Graduation from high school is generally regarded as sufficient preparation for beginning clerical positions. A person who starts at this level can often advance to more responsible positions. A clerk in an underwriting department, for example, can, with on-the-job training, become an assistant underwriter and then advance to underwriter.

Similarly, high-school graduates who start with clerical positions at local insurance agencies also can learn the business on the job and sometimes become agents. Generally, however, insurance companies and large agencies prefer trainees for the more responsible positions to have college degrees or at least some college training.

For persons who wish to enter the insurance field as agents, requirements vary widely.

Most companies prefer people with some college education, business experience, or both. Some companies require a college degree, and they prefer degrees in insurance or business administration. All states require insurance agents to be licensed. In most states, the agent must pass a written examination on the fundamentals of the business and the laws that cover it. Some states set certain educational requirements for agents.

The actuary enters the insurance industry as an actuarial trainee and must be a college graduate. An actuarial trainee does not necessarily need a degree in mathematics, but he or she must be proficient in differential and integral calculus.

To advance, the actuary must pass a series of written examinations. The first few of these examinations can be taken while the person is still in college, and insurance companies recommend that this be done.

Actuarial trainees receive on-the-job instruction that prepares them for the later examinations. In the life insurance field, examinations are given by the Society of Actuaries. In the property and liability field, examinations are given by the Casualty Actuarial Society. The actuary moves on to more responsible and better-paid positions as he or she proceeds successfully through the various examinations.

College education is generally considered essential for management positions. Persons who majored in many different fields in college fill important positions in the industry. However, the special courses in insurance that are offered at many colleges and universities, as well as courses in business administration, are helpful in obtaining insurance positions.

Independent insurance agents spend much of their time on the telephone keeping in contact with their clients and recruiting new ones.

In addition to on-the-job training, some insurance companies pay a large part of the tuition for employees who take college courses on their own time. The Insurance Institute of America furnishes a study guide on the property and liability business and awards certificates to persons who pass its examinations.

Industry outlook

In the late 1980s, there were 2,265 U.S. life insurance companies employing more than 590,200 people. The value of life insurance in active policies was estimated at about $8.8 billion (1989). There were more than 3,500 individual companies offering property and liability insurance (about 900 write most of the business). These companies employed more than 470,000 people. Assets of U.S. insurance companies reached a record 1.35 trillion dollars (three-fourths held by life and health insurers).

Salespersons selling insurance of all kinds held about 500,000 jobs in the late 1980s. Many work part-time. About one in three is self-employed.

There are many reasons for the steady growth of the insurance industry and the prospect that career opportunities will continue to grow. Probably the most important reason is that as the economy expands more people buy more insurance of all kinds—insurance on their lives, their health, their homes, their cars, and all their possessions. As other industries grow there are more stores, factories, merchandise, ships, and millions of other things to insure. Moreover, people are steadily becoming more

aware of their need for insurance. Changes in occupational safety, and other labor laws—for example, broadening of the workers' compensation system to cover more different kinds of workers—also creates more insurance business.

Even scientific advances help increase insurance business. New medical knowledge, for instance, makes it possible for insurance companies to write life insurance on some people who might not have been eligible in the past.

Advances in the insurance business itself also contribute to the growth of the industry. New forms of insurance coverage are constantly being devised and old forms revised, and the changes frequently open up new markets for insurance.

Faced with possible new competition, tax issues, and widespread underwriting losses in the early and mid-1980s, the industry confronted new challenges for the 1990s. Although many companies in the industry appeared likely to regain their strong financial positions, the United States Department of Labor predicts that the number of employment opportunities in insurance probably will not grow quite as fast as the amount of business done by the industry.

◇ **SOURCES OF ADDITIONAL INFORMATION**

American Council of Life Insurance
1001 Pennsylvania Avenue, NW
Washington, DC 20004

The National Association of Life Underwriters
1922 F Street, NW
Washington, DC 20006

Insurance Information Institute
110 William Street
New York, NY 10038

Independent Insurance Agents of America
100 Church Street, Suite 1901
New York, NY 10007

National Association of Independent Insurers
2600 River Road
Suite 845
Des Plaines, IL 60018

Professional Insurance Agents
400 North Washington Street
Alexandria, VA 22314

National Association of Insurance Brokers
1401 New York Avenue, NW
Suite 720
Washington, DC 20005

Health Insurance Association of America
1025 Connecticut Avenue, NW
Suite 1200
Washington, DC 20036

Society of Actuaries
475 North Martingale Road
Schaumburg, IL 60173

◇ **RELATED ARTICLES**

Volume 1: Banking and Financial Services; Health Care
Volume 2: Actuaries; Insurance claims representatives; Underwriters
Volume 3: Insurance agents and brokers, property and casualty; Insurance agents and brokers, life; Insurance policy processing occupations; Securities and financial services sales representatives
Volume 4: Data-processing technicians

Law

General information

The legal system largely provides the means by which our lives are organized. Embodied in statutes enacted by legislatures and decisions rendered by the courts, the law establishes rules that govern personal, social, and business activities and provide a mechanism for the resolution of disputes arising from them. It is based on democratic principles and has as its goal the protection of individual rights and the assurance of a just and free society.

Throughout history, societies have established systems of law to govern people. One of the earliest known laws is the Code of Hammurabi, developed about 1900 B.C. by the Sumerians. Roughly four hundred years later, Moses introduced the Ten Commandments, which have become the foundation of Judeo-Christian ethics and hence our current legal system.

The ancient Greeks and Romans set up schools for young boys to learn the many skills involved in pleading a case. To be an eloquent speaker was a great advantage.

In the late 1700s and early 1800s, European law was organized and refined under Napoleon in what came to be known as the Napoleonic Code.

The legal code for the American colonies was largely influenced by the English settlers who brought a long tradition of English common law with them. In areas of the United States that were heavily settled by Spanish colonists, there are traces of Spanish law. But in all cases, the laws of other countries and other times were adapted by lawyers and courts to fit the needs and customs of American society.

The legal profession has matured a lot since its earliest days. Today, whenever a person faces problems involving legal rights, buys or sells a house or other parcel of real estate, wants a divorce, starts a business, or decides to make a will or draw up a trust, that person needs a lawyer.

The structure of the legal profession

The legal profession in the United States is composed of lawyers and judges whose basic task is to interpret and apply the law. Given the large number of laws in society and the diverse situations in which they come into play, lawyers provide the critical role of helping avoid and settle legal disputes that may arise. They are supported by paralegals, legal secretaries, court reporters, and other specialists.

There is a tremendous variety of work available within the legal profession. The choice depends essentially on the subject matter a lawyer is interested in, the people he or she is interested in working for, and the place where he or she would like to live while doing that work. The possibilities include working for a private company, becoming a government employee, or working for a public interest law firm. In addition, lawyers may also serve as judges or assume teaching responsibilities.

Over the years, most lawyers have chosen to go into private practice—that is, devoting full time to the performance of legal services for private clients. These are the lawyers most commonly known to the public. A majority of lawyers engaged in private practice still work by themselves, without the immediate assistance of any partners (although they may have salaried associates). Others work together with colleagues in law firms that range in size from two lawyers to as many as several hundred attorneys. Typically, law firms are composed of partners, who own the practice and share expenses and earnings on an agreed basis, and associates, who are salaried lawyers working for the firm and usually expecting one day to become partners themselves.

Most lawyers, particularly private practitioners, spend very little time in court and handle few criminal cases. Most of their work hours are spent in their offices, consulting with clients, doing legal research, drafting various documents, and giving advice, much of which is designed to avoid a lawsuit or trial. The specific nature of the work a lawyer does depends on whether the lawyer (or the firm) has a general practice or one that is more specialized.

A general practitioner is a counselor, adviser, and at times, advocate, willing to accept employment in the broadest possible spectrum of legal problems. Of all the lawyers, it is the general practitioner who is most often called upon by individuals in times of personal distress or need.

As a general practitioner, a lawyer's work includes drafting wills, settling estates, preparing contracts and leases, arranging real estate transfers, negotiating the purchase or sale of businesses or homes, solving tax problems, and handling family matters (divorce, separation, adoption, and child custody). In addition to the trial practice, which it occasionally involves, a general practitioner's work may also include representing of workers before compensation boards and appearing for clients before other administrative bodies.

Specialized practitioners limit themselves to one area of law, whether it be taxation, criminal defense, estate work, trials of personal injury cases, or any of the many other specialties. More often than not their clients are referred to them by other lawyers rather than by previous clients. Frequently specialists are lawyers who were formerly engaged in a more general practice and found that they prefer to devote their time to the development of a particular specialty.

Specialists are likely to have their offices in metropolitan areas, state capitals, or county seats, since a less populous area generally does not provide sufficient demand for their services. Only in some jurisdictions can one become a certified specialist, and there are restrictions on designating oneself a specialist.

As a general rule, lawyers who work in firms are expected to specialize to some extent in the work that they do. One of the reasons for working with other lawyers rather than working alone is to save time and effort that results from taking the fullest advantage of the particular training or skill of each partner and associate. Although individual partners are likely to have certain clients for whom they are primarily responsible, each problem coming into the firm will usually be resolved by the person within the firm most qualified to treat it. Thus a partnership of half a dozen lawyers handling a general practice is likely to have one lawyer who concentrates on trial work, another who specializes in tax matters, a third who is primarily responsible for trust and estate work, and so on down the line.

To resolve a legal dispute, a judge shows a relevant passage in a book that delineates state laws.

This same division of labor is apparent in the very large firms as well. These firms, predominantly located in major cities, have the ability to offer a wide range of highly developed skills under one roof. They attract clients with diversified needs, who are likely to be the bigger businesses and wealthier individuals. They consequently develop particular facility in the areas of the law with which these clients are predominantly concerned, including antitrust, and financial matters, international transactions, the regulation of stocks and bonds, corporate tax problems, and the like. There are, in addition, whole firms devoted almost entirely to one specialty, particularly in such fields as patent law, trademark, and copyright work.

Other than private practice, lawyers can opt to work for the government, on the federal, state, or local levels. The difference between government work and private practice is primarily in the conditions of employment. In government service there is no such thing as a partnership, and government employment is always on the basis of salary, which at most stages of one's career is likely to be somewhat less than might be achieved in private practice. Further, the nature of government employment naturally implies somewhat less independence and greater adherence to regulations.

Government attorneys are often given greater responsibility at an earlier stage than is likely to occur in private practice. Government attorneys who have been out of law school only a few years, or even less, often handle trials against the most prominent and skillful attorneys in private practice. They acquire invaluable experience and are able to develop their resourcefulness to a far greater degree than they might have been able to had they gone directly into private practice. Indeed, one often finds young lawyers gaining valuable experi-

A lawyer offers legal advice to one of her clients.

ence in government and then leaving it to establish themselves successfully in private practice.

Almost every employment opportunity for a government attorney implies specialization because it is usually with a particular board, department, or bureau. A lawyer for the National Labor Relations Board, for example, is involved with labor law. An attorney in a state tax bureau will be occupied with tax matters. A lawyer in a city attorney's office will be primarily involved with municipal law. There are areas of government practice in which more general experience is needed, such as in the civil rights sections of the various state and federal attorneys' offices. But on the whole, specialization is far more probable in the government than it would be in private practice. These specialists often find themselves in high demand, if and when they do enter private practice.

Apart from the probability of increased responsibility and the opportunity for specialization, government service offers opportunities and rewards unavailable to the private practitioner. There are areas of the law in which government attorneys become involved that are closed to those in private practice. Private practitioners cannot prosecute persons accused of crime, for example. Neither can they engage in intergovernmental negotiations regarding treaties, consular agreements, and contracts. They

are likely to have little opportunity, if any, to practice in the fields of Indian affairs, nuclear energy problems, or military law. Virtually all lawyers, including private practitioners, will be called upon for some public service during their careers. The rewards gained by private practitioners from their occasional, part-time civic endeavors, however, are different from those derived from long careers of professional public service.

Lawyers may also work solely for a corporation. Lawyers on the legal staffs of these business corporations are usually referred to as corporate or house counsel. Sometimes, but not always, they assume business responsibilities as well. A business may have only one corporate attorney, usually designated as the general counsel, or it may have a large legal staff composed of the general counsel, associate general counsels, and lesser positions commonly called assistant general counsel, senior attorney, general attorney, or simply attorney. The larger the corporation, the larger its legal staff.

Since the job of a corporate attorney is to advise the corporation in legal matters that affect it, the nature of the job depends very much upon the business in which the particular company is engaged. If the corporation is an insurance company, for example, the chances are that its staff attorneys will be involved with seeing that the company complies with the applicable laws and government regulations and planning the defense of litigated cases in which the company's clients are involved. An attorney employed by an airline, railroad, or other transportation company, on the other hand, is likely to be heavily involved in work with the various federal and state administrative boards and commissions that govern those operations. The extent to which one becomes a specialist or has the opportunity to handle a more general series of problems depends entirely on the size of the company, the nature of its operations, and one's position with the company.

One might say that corporate law positions combine the advantages of private practice and the disadvantages of government service. Corporate legal positions traditionally offer one of the greatest opportunities for financial reward. This is partly because they also offer a great opportunity for the lawyer who is interested in business to enter into actual management. On the other hand, there are companies in which one is likely to feel the pinch of bureaucracy and experience the frustrations of work in any large organization.

Another type of law practice involves public interest work. Since the mid-1960s, the public interest component of the legal profession has enlarged considerably, even though the overall percentage of lawyers working in the area is still small. Public interest law refers to the representation of individuals, groups, and interests that have been underrepresented in the past. A major employer of public interest lawyers is the neighborhood Legal Services program, a federally funded organization that provides free legal help to the poor. The Legal Aid Society provides similar services.

Groups and interests not necessarily poverty-related are also represented by public interest lawyers. A number of law firms, largely funded by private foundations, direct substantially all of their efforts to public interest work. In addition, there are other private organizations that support large legal staffs devoted to special goals. The various civil rights groups, for example, employ a number of attorneys to bring or defend civil rights cases in courts throughout the country. The same is true for a great many of the special interest groups dedicated to preservation of the environment, conservation of energy, equal opportunity for women, and protection of minority rights, among dozens of other interests and sectors.

Probably the most essential segments of the legal system are the courts. After all, without courts and judges to preside over them, there would be no use for lawyers. On the federal level, the judicial system is made up of a series of courts. The Supreme Court is the highest court of the land and rules on issues related to the U.S. Constitution. The Supreme Court is made up of nine judges, appointed by the president with consent of the Senate, who review selected decisions made on the state level.

The Circuit court of appeals deals with decisions that have been appealed by the district courts, and reviews judgements of lower courts.

The District courts are the third level of federal court system, servicing approximately 100 areas across the country.

Careers

Lawyers may enter such fields as business, teaching, or government service. Many corporation executives, for example, have law degrees. Legal qualifications are especially valued for executives in the insurance and real estate industries. Legislators and state and local executives are often trained in the law. Even persons planning to enter business as sole proprietors find legal education useful.

There are many career opportunities in law from becoming a judge to working as support staff in law firms. A sampling of career opportunities follows below.

As with most modern businesses, law firms are highly computerized.

Probate lawyers: Probate lawyers specialize in planning and settling estates. They draw up wills, deeds of trust, and similar documents for clients.

Criminal attorneys: Criminal lawyers deal with offenses against society such as murder, rape, arson, and theft. They defend the accused suspects.

District attorneys: District attorneys, also called prosecuting attorneys, are elected officials, representing the people of a city, county, state, or federal government. They gather evidence that may incriminate a prospective criminal and try to convince a judge to grant an indictment. District attorneys have a large staff of lawyers working as assistants.

Judges: Judges can be elected or appointed to their positions. They preside over every type of case that appears in court. They are supposed to be nonpartisan and not associated with a political party.

Corporation lawyers: Corporation lawyers advise corporations concerning their legal rights, obligations, or privileges.

Tax attorneys: Tax attorneys handle cases resulting from problems such as income tax and estate tax issues.

Patent lawyers: Patent lawyers secure patents for inventors from the U.S. Patent Office and prosecute or defend cases of patent infringement.

Real estate lawyers: Real estate lawyers draw up legal documents and act as agents in various real estate transactions.

Title attorneys: Title attorneys deal with titles, leases, contracts, and other legal documents pertaining to the ownership of land and gas, oil, and mineral rights.

Law school students undergo rigorous training in order to fully understand laws and interpret their meaning.

Paralegals: Also called a legal assistant, a paralegal is a lawyer's assistant. Paralegals do things that lawyers would do themselves if they didn't have the help of an assistant. Whether it be interviewing witnesses, examining documents, preparing papers or conducting research, a paralegal's work saves a lawyer's time and energy and quickly becomes indispensable to the task of getting the job done.

Researchers and *editors:* Researchers and editors are responsible for preparing the thousands upon thousands of legal publications produced in the United States.

Law librarians: Law librarians organize and administer the numerous libraries of law books throughout the country.

Court reporters: Court reporters document the events in court.

Education

Most high-school students considering a career in law are understandably concerned about the educational background they should have in order to do well in law school and in the profession itself. There is no "prelaw" curriculum for undergraduates. A person is trained for the law only when he or she enters law school. Prior to that time, a law school candidate must complete a high-school and college education, keeping in mind that the best way to prepare for the law is to pursue a broad range of studies.

An education in the liberal arts is often the most satisfactory general preparation for practicing law. One reason is that lawyers generally spend a great deal of time writing briefs, contracts, opinions, and other materials. They also prepare numerous memoranda to colleagues, clients, clients' business associates, government agencies, and members of the court.

To specialize, such as in patent law, a degree in engineering or some other field may be desirable. Knowledge of basic accounting may be useful as lawyers should know how to read a financial statement and know how to prepare a tax return.

In addition, a law school candidate should participate in extracurricular activities throughout both high school and college. For the most part, the nature of the activities is of little importance, although work on a school newspaper or other publication or participating in debate is likely to improve one's ability to express oneself. In any event, what matters is that one is involved in organized activities that give one leadership skills.

Prospective law school student are required to take the Law School Admissions Test (LSAT). Upon completion of this standardized test a person can then apply to law school. Some schools are far more selective than others and are thus harder to get into. According to the Law School Admission Council, however, 80 percent of those who apply to ABA-accredited law schools get into at least one of those schools. Law school is a three year commitment.

A prospective student will want to look into as many schools in as many areas of the country as possible before deciding where to apply. Schools differ in size, expense, and quality of programs, and it is important to attend a school suited to one's own preferences. Generally speaking, accredited schools use the casebook and Socratic methods of teaching, thereby focusing on training students to think like lawyers rather than teaching them "the Law."

The approximately 175 law schools approved by the American Bar Association generally cover principles governing law in the United States. All ABA-approved law schools have a more or less standard core curriculum, teach from national casebooks, have adequate library holdings, and have faculties with a reasonably wide spectrum of academic and professional experience. A number of state law schools teach elective courses on specific jurisdictions; others use the home state's statutory system in courses in which code or statute law may be controlling. Law school catalogs usually spell out any specific orientation.

The law school that a person attends may have a good deal to do with what and where that person ends up practicing. There are a number of well-established big-city firms, for example, that recruit new lawyers principally from the nationally-renowned law schools. While law schools have similar core curriculums, many schools specialize in certain methods of study. Some concentrate on theoretical law, while others emphasize current legal methods.

Upon completion of three years of law school, students ordinarily study for and take the bar examination of the state in which they plan to practice, a grueling climax to years of legal studies. Upon passing the bar examination, lawyers are admitted to practice, and their careers begin. Lawyers must continue to study and learn to keep up with new developments and changes in the law. Continuing legal education programs are important for practicing attorneys.

A high moral character is essential to success because of the primary position that honest dealing has in the profession. Lawyers are bound to abide by the strictest of ethical standards, as promulgated in each state's Code of Professional Responsibility. Even aside from the Code, the public's faith in a lawyer's integrity is his or her greatest asset. Lawyers who are less than honest, or not quite fair, will lose cases, clients, and respect and confidence from other members of the profession.

Paralegal training has become available at many schools, colleges, and universities. Some programs require only a high-school diploma and last for a year, while others require a college diploma but take only three months. In some, the students specialize in an area of their choice, while others offer only general studies. Once trained, paralegals typically work for law firms or corporate legal departments, and assume responsibility over as wide a range of legal problems as the lawyers they assist delegate to them.

If a prospective paralegal receives a college degree, he or she may well become a paralegal even without attending a special training program. Many paralegals working in some of the larger firms are employed directly from college. They are trained on-the-job by the lawyers they work with and never receive any instructions more formal than that.

Industry outlook

As laws become more complex, taxes more complicated, and society more litigious, legal services will continue to expand. However, there are more young lawyers entering the field than the industry can absorb.

Demand for legal services was anticipated to increase in the 1990s and the number of persons in legal services was expected to top one million. The total number of practicing lawyers in all fields was about 700,00 in 1990.

Although there are more opportunities within the legal profession, it has become increasingly difficult to establish a new private practice, and in large metropolitan areas new graduates and experienced lawyers outnumbered salaried openings. An increasing number of lawyers will probably enter fields such as banking, real estate, and government.

◇ SOURCES OF ADDITIONAL INFORMATION

American Bar Association
750 North Lake Shore Drive
Chicago, IL 60611

National Lawyer's Guild
55 Sixth Avenue
New York, NY 10013

Law School Admissions Council/Law School Admissions Services
Box 40
Newtown, PA 18940

Association of American Law Schools
One Dupont Circle, NW, Suite 370
Washington, DC 20036

National Association for Law Placement
440 First Street, NW, Suite 302
Washington, DC 20001

◇ RELATED ARTICLES

Volume 1: Politics and Public Service
Volume 2: Crime laboratory technologists; Lawyers and judges; Legal assistants; Political scientists
Volume 3: Court reporters; FBI agents; Police officers; State police officers

Letter and Package Delivery

General information

Postal service touches the daily lives of everyone. Letter carriers and window clerks come in contact with millions of people, and few of society's activities do not rely on this essential service.

Postal service in some form has existed in America since early colonial times. Service throughout the colonies was greatly improved by Benjamin Franklin, who was Deputy Postmaster General of the colonies under the British from 1753 to 1774. Continuation of postal service was considered so important that one of the first acts of the 1775 Continental Congress was to appoint Franklin as Postmaster General as the uniting colonies began the Revolutionary War.

As the nation's prosperity increased, so did the work of the post office. In 1847, each person in the United States wrote about six letters a year. By the mid-1980s, the U.S. Post Office handled almost 600 pieces of mail annually for each person in the country.

Airmail began a few years after the Wright brothers inaugurated the age of aviation at the beginning of the twentieth century. The first regular airmail flight was established between New York City and Washington, D.C., in 1918. Among the pioneer pilots who flew for the post office was Charles A. Lindbergh, famous for his solo flight across the Atlantic in 1927.

There have been many individual heroes in U.S. postal history. One is Chester Noongwook, an Eskimo, who until 1963 delivered mail on remote Saint Lawrence Island, in the Bering Sea, 120 miles west of the Alaskan mainland. His route was 120 miles, round trip, and his transportation was dogsled. Noongwook's Alaskan huskies have surrendered to progress and now the route is serviced by airplane.

As the volume of mail skyrocketed during the early 1960s, the Postal Service was faced with the problem of handling the new load without a corresponding increase in staffing. It was apparent that hiring more clerks, supervisors, carriers, drivers, and other personnel would not permanently solve the problem. In addition, a large increase in post office employment would have created a problem with the postal budget, which was already running a deficit. It was obvious also that more mechanization was not the entire answer.

A breakthrough came when the ZIP system was devised. ZIP Code (Zoning Improvement Plan) is really the second generation of the zone numbers that were first used in the 1940s. It assigns a five-digit number to every postal address in the country. The first three digits identify the city of the nearest installation located at the junction of air, highway, and rail transportation. There are more than 500 of these sectional centers across the country. The last two digits identify the post office or delivery station, just as the old zone number did.

Before the use of ZIP Code, each envelope or package had to be read as many as ten different times before final delivery. Each reading consumed valuable time. Full use of ZIP eliminated many of the readings and reduced the chances of human error.

Using ZIP Code, mail could be sent from the sectional center nearest the point of origin directly to the sectional center nearest its destination. From there it would be dispatched to its ultimate delivery point. Mail processed in bulk according to ZIP Code often bypassed the post office in the city of origin and headed for the nearest transportation center.

An advance in the development of the ZIP Code was the installation of optical character readers (OCRs), which read the city, state, and ZIP Code at the rate of approximately 30,000 pieces of mail per hour, and sorted the mail by sections of the country. These OCRs also put a bar code on the envelope that represents the ZIP Code and enables subsequent sorts to be performed on a bar code sorter (BCS) machine.

Employees for an overnight mail service must work quickly and efficiently to ensure that packages are delivered promptly. Such operations require extensive tracking systems.

In the late-1980s, the Postal Service used approximately 700 OCR and BCS machines in the 211 largest post offices.

In September 1978, the Postal Service announced plans to add four digits to existing ZIP Codes. The "ZIP+" system applied primarily to business mailers, and the average citizen would not be required to use the add-on digits. The additional four numbers provide the potential for OCR/BCS sorting to each block of a street and to office buildings and companies receiving large volumes of mail.

Postal customer councils have been created to encourage major users of mail, such as businesses and government agencies to deposit their mail early and to cooperate with the Postal Service in the handling of mail. Before these councils were established, a huge glut of mail piled up in all large post offices at the end of the work day. Most large-volume mailers saved their mail for only one deposit, usually around 5 P.M. With a smoother flow of mail throughout the day, postmasters were able to reschedule some personnel from night to day shifts. Expensive machines that had been left idle in some post offices for as much as eighteen hours a day, waiting for the peak loads, could now be used more efficiently.

There is continued discussion in Congress of making the United States Postal Service a private enterprise. Discussions range from breaking up the divisions of mail (first, second, and third class) into different companies to selling the entire enterprise intact. However, the public's resistance to a private post office has restricted any major change in the post office. The biggest division to have competition from private delivery companies is in the overnight and package delivery business.

Two major competitors to the government postal service, Federal Express and United Parcel Service, developed systems for same-day, overnight, and two-day package and document delivery. Other, smaller companies also provide overnight and package delivery services either to some areas or to all of the United States and abroad. More than three quarters of the six billion packages in the United States are now sent through private delivery services.

Today, the postal system delivers more than 140 billion pieces of mail annually. There are over 30,000 post offices located in every section of the country.

The structure of letter and package delivery

Under the Postal Reorganization Act of 1970, the Postal Service began operations as an inde-

Letter and Package Delivery

The United States Postal Service uses optical scanning technology such as this bar code reader to process the nation's mail.

pendent establishment of the executive branch on July 1, 1971.

The U.S. Postal Service employs about 800,000 workers. About 80 percent are letter carriers or postal clerks. The two largest private firms are United Parcel Service (U.P.S.), with 220,000 employees, and Federal Express, with more than 80,000 employees.

U.P.S. delivers about 10 million parcels a day with the ground service, and another 600,000 parcels are delivered by air. They cover the entire United States and have direct service to another 41 countries, with 122 countries linked in to the delivery system. Federal Express delivers more than a million packages a day in the United States and 110 other countries.

Unseen by the general public, the giant workrooms in the post offices and private delivery companies are busy centers of activity. At all hours of the day and night, an endless flow of mail moves from unloading platforms through the workrooms and out to loading platforms. In the workrooms, the mail goes through a series of separations in which it is sorted according to type of mail and its destination.

Part-time employees make up a large percentage of the sorting staff because the time required for the rush period of package movement is less that the standard eight hour day. These employees can adjust their schedule around classes if they are in school, and at least 40,000 students find employment as sorters each year at U.P.S. alone.

For both the government Postal Service and the private companies, the sorting room is often the beginning for people who make a career

of letter and package delivery. Working in the sorting room is an ideal way to learn how the post office works, and work experience in this area aids in advancement in the company.

There are also highly developed merit promotion programs. With experience, knowledge, and common sense it is possible to secure positions of increasing responsibility and recognition. Promotion from within is favored.

A highly selective Management Associate program with the U.S. Post Office is open to those with an MBA degree or equivalent experience. It is a two- to four-year training program for individuals interested in management positions. In addition, the Postal Service has a two-year Postal Service Management Trainee program open to postal employees with a bachelor's degree or equivalent experience.

Members of the Postal Service staff have been responsible for the development of automated and mechanical mail-handling equipment and improved management techniques for coping with the avalanche of letters and packages that go through the system each day. Often, employees with ideas and talent work themselves up the employment ranks to planning and supervisory positions.

Because most mail is generated in larger urban areas, there is a concentration of employees in the big cities. Large centers of employment include New York, Chicago, Los Angeles, Boston, Philadelphia, and Dallas.

Four unions represent U.S. Post Office employees in national bargaining. The National Association of Letter Carriers is affiliated with the AFL-CIO. Other unions are the American Postal Workers Union, the National Post Office Handlers, and the National Rural Letters Carriers Association. U.P.S. is unionized by the International Brotherhood of Teamsters.

Most full-time postal employees work an eight-hour day, five days per week. Part-time employees work as scheduled. If a full-time employee works more than eight hours in a day or forty hours in a week, he or she is paid at one-and-a-half times the regular rate for the extra hours worked.

The post offices are under the supervision of a multiple-level field structure, beginning with five regional offices. Approximately 450 employees in these regional offices supervise operations, transportation, personnel, and other functions of the post offices. In addition, employees in Postal Data Centers perform centralized payroll, timekeeping, and other financial functions. There are other support installations, such as the Postal Service Management Academy, which trains supervisors and postmasters; the supply centers, which fill acquisitions for supplies; and the mail bag repair centers and mail equipment shops.

Post office employees perform a great many non-postal services too. Among other things, they distribute food coupons and alien address report cards, accept passport applications, and provide assistance to the Census Bureau.

Careers

Most jobs in postal employment are for clerks, letter carriers, and mail handlers. Employment is also available in the fields of automatic data processing, maintenance, transportation, research, engineering, design, and various other positions. A sampling of career opportunities follows below.

Postal supervisors and *postmasters:* These workers direct the work of clerks, carriers, and mail handlers. Supervisors are responsible for tracking the movement of trucks and packages.

With the aid of computer systems, packages are able to be tracked much more precisely than before. Computer strips on the packages and documents can be registered into computers with the destination point. Then with each transfer of the package, the computer can re-register the location so, if the package is lost, the manager can find the last point where the package was registered.

Letter carriers: Letter carriers collect much of the mail that flows into the city post office and deliver the mail after it has been sorted. The rural letter carriers collect and deliver mail in rural and suburban areas. Both city and rural carriers cover assigned routes on regular schedules. Some city carriers may work exclusively delivering parcel post or collecting mail.

Postal clerks: These workers, sometimes called window clerks, sell stamps, register and insure mail, and accept parcel post. The private firms hire counter staff to accept packages for delivery at numerous sites in both large cities and small.

Mail handlers/mail clerks: In large post offices, mail handlers load and unload large sacks of mail. In the smaller post offices, this work is performed by the clerks. In addition to handling sacked mail, the mail handlers make rough separations of the mail into parcel post and letter mail, and take the mail to distribution clerks for processing. They also pick up the processed mail and put it into sacks.

Distribution clerks and letter-sorting-machine (LSM) operators help organize the large volume of mail that comes into the post office on a daily basis.

While much of the United States Postal Service is automated, employees are hired to perform tasks that cannot be aided by the use of computers.

Service employees: These employees are concerned with the operation, maintenance, and protection of post office buildings and equipment. Some are janitors, building guards, elevator operators, and laborers. Others are mechanics, electricians, carpenters, and painters.

Motor vehicle operators: Vehicle operators drive trucks transporting bulk mail. For private firms, the drivers are responsible for delivering the packages to "hub" centers, picking up packages in the early morning from the hub, and moving them to a feeder center. From the feeder center, the packages and documents are loaded onto local delivery trucks for delivery to their final destination.

Fleet maintenance workers: Maintenance workers maintain the post office vehicle fleet. This group includes garage workers who do routine servicing of vehicles, automotive mechanics, body and fender repairers, and parts clerks. With the addition of overnight service, the U.S. Postal Service and the private firms are beginning to operate their own fleet of airplanes. Pilots, maintenance crews, and loading crews are now required for letter and package delivery.

Education

To qualify for a job in a post office, an applicant must be a citizen (or legal resident alien), pass

259

With the increasing number of services offered by the United States Postal Service, postal clerks must be trained to handle a number of requests.

an examination, and meet the minimum age requirements. Generally, the minimum age requirement for employment is eighteen years of age. For high-school graduates, the minimum age limit is sixteen, except for jobs that may be considered hazardous or may require operation of a motor vehicle. There are no residence requirements for post office examinations.

Formal education or special training, while highly recommended, is not required for most post office entry jobs. As in the case of other government examinations, honorably discharged military veterans have five extra points added to their passing grades, and a disabled veteran receives ten extra points. Veterans with compensable disabilities are placed at the top of the list. Certain jobs (guards, elevator operators, custodial laborers, janitors, and the like) are reserved for veterans whenever possible.

The names of applicants who pass an examination are placed on a register in the order of their scores. The appointing officer selects one of the top three available applicants to fill a job vacancy. Those not selected are put back on the list for consideration for the next job opening. Postal employees, as are all federal government workers, are subject to an investigation examining their characters and suitability for employment. Before an applicant may be appointed to any position, he or she must pass a physical examination. Specific physical requirements differ according to the nature of the work in each of the various jobs.

For private delivery companies, a college degree is also not required for entry-level positions. For some skill-specific posts, however,

training or college education may be required. Pilots, engineers, mechanics, etc, should have the appropriate background for these jobs. But most management positions are filled by people who have held jobs in the entry level at the company, and on-the-job experience counts heavily during promotion evaluation.

In general, most of the work in a post office requires considerable physical stamina. Some of the work requires considerable exertion, such as prolonged standing, walking, reaching, lifting, and carrying heavy sacks of mail.

Another important quality is a good memory. Clerks, for example, must be able to memorize the streets and numbers that make up a district so that they can sort mail rapidly. Both clerks and carriers must also remember many postal regulations, delivery routes, regular customers, and company schedules.

Industry outlook

There is job security and chances for advancement. Pay raises are offered on a liberal schedule to employees with satisfactory work records. New and useful ideas are sought, and those that are put into operation bring financial reward.

Although the majority of jobs are in the mail handler, carrier, and clerk classifications, many thousands of career workers have moved to other positions ranging from postal inspectors to postmasters.

Competition for jobs in the Postal Service is strong. Relatively few applicants under the age of twenty-five are hired. Temporary workers, many of whom may be younger, are hired for help at peak periods. They are not necessarily appointed later as career employees, however, though they may find the experience useful in considering whether to try for a permanent position.

Competition in the private delivery industry is not as tight. With the expansion of delivery services, staffing continues to rise. Private companies are also more likely to consider young people without work experience, or with summer job experience. It is easiest to move up from inside the company, rather than apply for a middle management position after gaining work experience elsewhere. Therefore, moving into the private delivery service becomes much more difficult as position rank increases.

As the private firms expand into international delivery, employment abroad becomes an option for management staff. Although ground delivery staff may be hired from the host country, the development and management staff may be selected from U.S. employees. The international market is increasing rapidly and will develop new opportunities for hiring.

The U.S. Postal Service does not have the expansion opportunities that the private industry has. Despite the increases in the volume of mail anticipated, from 141 billion pieces a year in 1985 to over 160 billion pieces annually by the early-1990s, jobs for postal clerks are expected to decline. This is due to improved automation systems. Employment of carriers is projected to remain about the same, however. Openings will result chiefly from retirements. Comparatively few postal employees leave their jobs for other occupations before normal retirement age.

Information about Inspection Service employment may be obtained from the Chief Postal Inspector.

Current information is summarized annually in the U.S. Government Manual.

Other associations not affiliated with the U.S. Postal Service are as follows:

American Package Express Carriers Association
2200 Mill Road
Alexandria, VA 22314

Messenger Courier Association of America
Information Officer
2200 Mill Road
Alexandria, VA 22314

◇ SOURCES OF ADDITIONAL INFORMATION

For information about eligibility and qualifying examinations, consult local post offices or state employment services.

U.S. Postal Service
Public and Employee Communications
Department
475 L'Enfant Plaza, SW
Washington, DC 20260

National Association of Letter Carriers of the U.S.A.
100 Indiana Avenue, NW
Washington, DC 20001

◇ RELATED ARTICLES

Volume 1: Aviation and Aerospace; Transportation
Volume 2: General managers and top executives; Pilots
Volume 3: Aircraft mechanics and engine specialists; Airplane dispatchers; Automobile mechanics; Blue-collar worker supervisors; Counter and retail clerks; Industrial-truck operators; Mail carriers; Postal clerks; Route drivers; Shipping and receiving clerks; Truck drivers, local and over-the-road

Library and Information Science

General information

Libraries provide far more than books to the public. They also offer audio and video recordings, various visual aids such as microfilm and film strips, lectures and other adult programming, puppet shows and reading hours for children, photocopying facilities, and a host of other services. In addition to public libraries, there are college and university libraries, school libraries, and other libraries that are located at such places as hospitals, military bases, and resorts. The largest library in the United States is the Library of Congress, which contains more than 83 million items, including about 21 million volumes, pamphlets, and other printed materials.

Ever since humans learned to write, libraries have been important in preserving the history of human civilization. No one really knows when the first library was established, but there are many remains of important libraries that existed in very early times. There are records of libraries in ancient Egypt as old of the pyramids, for example, and a large library existed at Nineveh in Assyria as early as the seventh century B.C.

One of the great libraries of ancient times was at Alexandria in Egypt, where scholars could study manuscripts in Greek, Ethiopian, Persian, Hebrew, and Hindi. In Rome, private libraries were common among educated citizens. There were twenty-eight public libraries in use in Rome by the beginning of the fourth century A.D.

During the Middle Ages, when knowledge of Greek and Latin classics was threatened with extinction, the libraries of the monasteries preserved copies of precious manuscripts. Later, when the monasteries and their libraries fell into disuse and ruin, collectors of the Renaissance such as Petrarch and Boccaccio preserved many important works of literature and philosophy in their libraries. Many of these libraries, together with book collections gathered by kings and noblemen, were the beginnings of some of the great scholarly libraries that still exist in Europe.

Before the invention of the printing press by Johannes Gutenberg in the mid-1440s, manuscripts were written by hand. The movable type press allowed for books to be printed more efficiently and inexpensively, thus providing a larger circulation of books.

All early libraries were intended for the use of small, elite groups. Few people had received enough education to be able to read well, and most people were too poor to have the leisure time to enjoy books. The Industrial Revolution and other social changes in the eighteenth and nineteenth centuries upset the old social order, and new generations of working people were able to acquire an education. Their desires called for a new kind of library, one that would not only preserve the best works of earlier times but would also be an educational facility for the common people.

Libraries were formed by associations of young mercantile workers, apprentices, mechanics, and clerks. In 1731 Benjamin Franklin and a group of his friends organized the Library Company of Philadelphia, the earliest library of this kind in the American colonies.

Public libraries, supported from public funds and open to all readers, were established in Manchester, England, in 1852 and in Boston in 1854, and additional public libraries were soon started in many other cities in both countries. By 1876 there were 342 public libraries in the United States; by 1920 the number had grown to more than 6,500, located in every state in the union. Today there are more than 33,000 libraries in the United States (excluding school libraries and media centers).

In the contemporary information society, libraries play an increasingly important role. Because the amount of information has increased enormously, libraries are needed to help citizens find their way through puzzling and often contradictory information. Whether there are students in a school or college, ordinary citizens of a community, or people engaged in business or one of the professions, there are libraries to help all citizens.

The structure of library and information science

The field of library and information science is made up of a variety of professionals that help meet the growing demands of our information-based society.

Perhaps the fastest-growing group of libraries in the United States is school libraries. There are about 74,000 libraries in the elementary, junior high, and high schools. A generation ago there were approximately 20,000 such libraries. This increase has come about partly because many more children are enrolled in schools. But a more important reason is that changes have been made in the methods of teaching and learning. A class of seventh-grade children studying how their state government works, for example, may continue their assignment by seeing a motion picture; some members of the class may study a film strip about the state constitution; some may watch a videotape of one of the governor's press conferences, or listen to a recording of the governor's inaugural address. All of these sources of information are available in a modern school library.

The school library, or media center, has become an indispensable part of education. In it, a carefully selected collection of books, magazines, newspapers, pictures, films, videotapes, recordings, and other materials are brought together, indexed, and arranged for convenient use. The school librarian is a part of the teaching team of the school and works with the other teachers in planning and determining what topics are most likely to be successful.

For the inquisitive student, the library provides materials for independent study. For the student with special interests, the library can supply information to help develop a hobby. For all students the library can provide a larger world of knowledge that will complement classroom instruction.

There are approximately 5,600 junior college, college, and university libraries of all types serving millions of student enrolled in institutions of higher education. These libraries range from a 10,000-volume library to the many millions of volumes in the large private and public university libraries. Their clientele

A reference librarian directs a person towards a relevant publication and shows him how to use it as effectively as possible.

ranges from beginning college freshmen to university professors engaged in research.

University libraries collect publications in many languages and develop highly specialized collections of books, periodicals, manuscripts, and other materials. They are equipped for scholars and for graduate students who are preparing themselves for scholarly careers. To make the library's collection useful, each university library needs a specialized staff to offer expert assistance in many subjects and in many languages.

The university library consists of a network of specialized libraries to serve the faculty and students. The library system may typically emphasize such subjects and professions as engineering, music, commerce, fine arts, agriculture, medicine, law, chemistry, education, sociology, architecture, and psychology. It must also serve the entire academic community. In recent years many universities have established undergraduate or "core" libraries—sometimes in separate buildings, with smaller, less specialized, and easier to use book collections.

College libraries have more modest goals than university libraries because they serve academic institutions primarily concerned with teaching, although some colleges offer graduate degrees and many college teachers spend part of their time in research and writing. The book collections are smaller—generally from 50,000 to 100,000 volumes, and most of the books are in the English language. College librarians, like school librarians, are able to work closely with members of the teaching faculty in selecting books that will be useful to undergraduate students.

Community college libraries serve the many two-year colleges. Frequently called Learning Resource Centers, these libraries emphasize the use of a wide variety of films, tapes, and other audiovisual materials, as well as books. Their collections are usually smaller than those of four-year college libraries, but they are carefully selected and organized to support the range of academic, paraprofessional, and technical courses offered.

Public libraries provide a variety of services for entire families—from the youngest toddlers who have just learned to enjoy picture books to the retired adults who have found time to renew their interest in subjects that they had little time for during their working years. Public libraries range in size from The New York Public Library with millions of volumes and more than 80 branch libraries to town libraries with 10,000 to 15,000 volumes. Regardless of size, they have a common goal of providing information and recreational reading to all people.

A typical public library will feature a children's room, where the natural curiosity of children can be stimulated by storytelling, puppet shows, and displays, as well as by the privilege of choosing a book to borrow with a minimum of advice from grown-ups. Teenage groups have their own part of the library, too, where the books of most interest to them are available.

Other parts of the library are usually arranged by the subjects that have been found to be interesting and useful to more readers. The Enoch Pratt Free Library in Baltimore, an example of a heavily used public library, established the following divisions: Business and Economics; Civics and Sociology; Education, Philosophy, and Religion; Fine Arts; History, Travel, and Biography; Industry and Science; and Literature.

In some public libraries, adult services includes an information and referral center for people who need help in using other community services. Information on voter registration, employment offices, health and family services, and other services are available, and individuals are guided to the appropriate agencies.

Branch libraries provide neighborhood library service to many parts of the city. Bookmobiles take smaller collections of books to communities where no branch libraries exist.

Library service to smaller towns and rural areas has greatly improved, thanks to the federal Library Services and Construction Act, which made money available for this purpose. The United States, however, is still short of its goal in providing good library service to all the people of the country.

Some libraries provide specialized information services to many trade organizations, research laboratories, manufacturing companies, government agencies, art museums, hospitals, newspapers, publishers, and others. Because these libraries are generally concerned with highly specialized subjects, they have relatively small collections—a few thousand volumes may be a large special library—and work very closely with the employees of the company. These libraries provide workers with access to esoteric materials. The librarians that work in these places often have supplemental training or previous academic experience in the subject of the special library.

The library of the Merck, Sharp & Dohme Research Laboratories, a pharmaceutical company in Rahway, New Jersey, for example, contains about 15,000 volumes carefully selected to aid the scientists who carry on research and testing of new medicines. Special librarians often assist in the research by pointing out likely sources or by searching through books and journals to compile bibliographies and summaries of previous research on the subjects being investigated by the researchers. They contribute to staff current awareness by circulating digests of the current acquisitions in the field.

In many special libraries the usual stock of books and periodicals is supplemented by technical reports, maps and charts, files of clippings and pamphlets, pictures, slides, disk and tape recordings, microfilm, and other forms of recorded information.

The rapid expansion of government services in many areas has stimulated the growth of library services and created new opportunities for librarians in federal and state governments. The libraries at the top of the federal-network are the Library of Congress, the National Library of Medicine, and the National Library of Agriculture. The Library of Congress contains all of the books that are published in the United States and other valuable materials. These three great libraries have developed extensive collections in their fields and provide services to the entire country.

Almost all departments of the executive branch of the government have specialized libraries that provide the information needed to carry on the work of these agencies. Outside Washington, D.C. are libraries serving all branches of the Armed Forces, Veterans Administration hospitals, federal research laboratories, and other field agencies. In state governments there are historical libraries and archives, legislative reference libraries, law libraries, public library extension agencies, and many smaller libraries that serve specialized branches of the state government.

Careers

A sampling of career opportunities follows below.

Library administrators: The Director, or Head Librarian, has the task of seeing that the talents of all staff members are brought together to provide the best possible library service. He or she must be able to plan a budget and present it to the library board or other authority that controls funds. Directors work with architects in planning new buildings and remodeling older ones. With the help and advice of other members of the staff they interview and select new staff members, and they seek to publicize the services of the library to the community by talking before local groups and seeing that radio, newspaper, and television publicity is prepared for the library.

Public service librarians: Librarians in the public service departments of the library meet the users of the library and help them find information. They receive the many requests for information that come to the library from telephone calls, letters, and from readers who visit the library. Their work requires a wide knowledge of books and sources, an outgoing personality, and a genuine interest in people.

Reference librarians: Reference librarians must be knowledgeable about many sources of specialized information that go beyond the general encyclopedias and dictionaries. They are called upon to find answers to difficult questions on subjects ranging from sports to philosophy.

Children's and Young Adult librarians: These librarians work primarily with young people and their parents. They must enjoy working with young children and be knowledgeable about books and other materials that will meet the interests and abilities of their patrons.

Circulation librarians: The circulation librarian supervises the clerical workers, who maintain the records of books that are borrowed and returned, and the stack attendants, who keep the shelves in order.

Bookmobile librarians: These librarians select books to be taken to outlying areas and ride with the bookmobile to learn more about the needs and interests of the readers who come to borrow from this kind of traveling public library.

Acquisitions librarians: Acquisitions librarians are busy selecting the best books from the 50,000 or more that are published in the United States each year. They must have a knowledge of many subjects and the bibliographical guides to those subjects. They also need to know a great deal about booksellers and publishers. A sense of business procedures is highly impor-

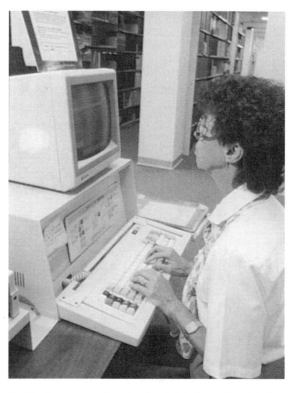

Most libraries use computerized systems to help them with such tasks as monitoring the availability of books and tracking their circulation. Computers also offer alternative catalogue systems and publications, such as encyclopedias, that are available for usage on CD-ROM systems.

tant because librarians, like business firms, must stretch their dollars to get as much for their money as possible. The cost of many reference books can add up very quickly.

Catalogers: Catalogers supervise the preparation of cards for the card catalog and they may input the information into a computerized library catalog system so that every book in the library can be located quickly by anyone searching for an author, a title, or a subject.

In most libraries, catalogers take advantage of the work already done by other libraries by using a computer-based network of data or cards prepared at the Library of Congress. But in every library some books must be cataloged from scratch and catalogers must be able to skim through a book to determine exactly what the book is about and assign a classification number that will make it more likely that all books on the same subject are placed together. They must be able to describe the book accurately and briefly so the readers can decide what books are most likely to be useful to them by consulting the card catalog or the particular terminal a library may use.

Conservation librarians: Many libraries have a conservation librarian in charge of a program to

This stack attendant reshelves books and ensures that the books on all shelves are placed in order.

lengthen the life of books. Larger public libraries and university libraries that have collections of rare books must have librarians who specialize in the history of printing and publishing and who are able to give valuable books the expert attention they deserve. The conservation of older books is becoming increasingly important, because most books published since about 1870 were printed on paper that contained acid and are now gradually turning brown and crumbling.

Archivists: Archivists collect, arrange, and prepare indexes to collections of manuscripts. They work primarily in specialized libraries.

Systems planners: In larger libraries the administration may include a systems planner who helps to plan the organization and the flow of work to see that the library system works efficiently and effectively.

Personnel librarians: A personnel librarian develops job descriptions for all positions in the library, arranges for interviews with individuals seeking employment, and sees that accurate records of vacations, promotions, and salaries are kept.

Other specialized librarians include *microfilm librarians, map librarians, record librarians,* and *film librarians.*

A number of vocations are closely related to librarianship. Larger libraries need staff mem-

bers who are skillful in preparing displays and exhibits, writing television and radio scripts, and preparing press releases. Some knowledge of librarianship is necessary to do such work, but artistic talent, creativity, and writing ability are even more important. Audiovisual specialists who work with films, audio recordings, videos, and similar materials are needed in public schools and colleges and in many public libraries.

Students with a strong interest in science may find a useful and interesting career in the newly emerging science information professions, a rather loosely knit group of specialties that draw upon many fields but have the common job of sifting, analyzing, interpreting, and disseminating the most important bits of scientific information from the large volume of published material. Careers in this field include the following:

Literature researchers: Literature researchers review all published sources and prepare reports on the current status of research on a specific topic.

Abstractors: Abstractors prepare brief summaries of articles in scientific journals so that experts are able to keep up-to-date with the current literature of their subject even though they do not have time to read all the books and articles.

Translators of scientific literature: Translators of scientific literature read important material in a variety of languages and translate it into a specified language. Translators are in demand because few scientists or engineers are able to read all the languages in which important work in their field is published. One must have a broad knowledge of science and know the scientific vocabulary in other languages in order to translate technical articles accurately.

Education

A librarian usually has obtained a fifth-year professional degree, the master's degree in Library Science (MLS); however, there are many technical and clerical jobs in a library for persons who are not library school graduates.

The best way to begin a career in librarianship is to work as a student assistant in a school or college library or as a assistant in a public or special library. This experience enables the student to see a part of librarianship from behind the counter so that the student can learn about the profession. Many of the leading librarians today were introduced to librarianship through a job of shelving books, typing and filing cards, operating office equipment, opening and sorting parcels of mail, and doing many other routine tasks.

College study may begin with a strong liberal arts curriculum leading to a bachelor's degree. There is no prescribed college course for preparation for library school. There are jobs for librarians with a background in biology, physics, chemistry, and other sciences, as well as for those who have specialized in history, literature, art, music, or other subjects in the humanities or the social sciences. Reading knowledge of foreign languages is helpful. Those interested in a school librarianship will want to enroll in the education courses recommended by their state department of education.

Beyond the bachelor's degree, most professional librarians study for at least a year in one of the approximately fifty-six accredited library schools in the United States. The American Library Association (ALA) evaluates and accredits the graduate education programs periodically. The ALA also grants accreditation to schools in Canada. Some sixty other schools (not accredited by ALA) also offer master's degrees in library science. Employers often specify that applicants should be graduates of ALA accredited programs.

In library school a student will learn the basic principles and methods of librarianship in a series of introductory courses in cataloging, reference and bibliography work, computer applications in libraries, and surveys of the literature of the sciences, the humanities, and the social sciences. These introductory courses are followed by specialized courses in school, college and university, public, or special librarianship; children's services; audiovisual materials; government publications; library administration; advanced cataloging; and reference services. Some library schools require their students to enroll in other departments for some courses related to the kind of library career the student desires.

The master's degree in librarianship, which usually comes after completion of at least one year of graduate work, is the minimum requirement for most professional library positions. Some schools offer graduate work leading to the doctorate degree. However, most doctoral candidates have considerable experience before admission to a doctoral program, and beginning librarians ordinarily put their library education to the practical test of full-time professional employment immediately after they complete their master's degree.

Training for work as an audiovisual technician can be gained by on-the-job experience and from courses offered in many community colleges; advanced courses for specialists are offered by most universities.

At the circulation desk, people check out materials that they can keep for a certain period of time.

Industry outlook

There are about 136,000 librarians employed in the libraries of the United States. About 63,200 (48 per cent) work in school libraries, 31,200 (23 per cent) in public libraries, 20,400 (15 per cent) in college and university libraries, and 19,000 (14 per cent) in special libraries. More than 150,000 technical and clerical staff members support the work of librarians.

Librarianship, like other professions, is affected by economic trends. Thus, the number of new positions decreased during the 1980s. All public libraries, most school libraries, and many college and university libraries receive their money from taxes, and voters have been reluctant to increase taxes; thus, libraries often find themselves in an economic squeeze. Generally speaking, employment is expected to increase slower than the average of all occupations through the mid-1990s. As school populations have decreased and the general population growth slows, so have job opportunities in libraries. In public libraries and college and university libraries, moderate increases in opportunities have resulted more often from replacements than from new positions.

Librarians with special qualifications—computerized systems, foreign languages, technical services, children's services—could anticipate a better job market. Computerized ordering, cataloging, information retrieval, and current awareness programs require specialized training. Professional librarians and information scientists continue to be necessary to direct, review, and coordinate such systems and to train and supervise operations.

Library and Information Science

A women monitors printers at the Online Computer Library Center in Dublin, Ohio. This bibliographic utility allows subscribing libraries access to other collections nationwide via computer.

In the future, libraries will seldom operate independently of one another but will become a part of a national network linking public, college and university, school, and special libraries into one information source. Each library will retain its own identity and serve its own clientele, of course, but information in any library can be made available to readers in any part of the country in a very short time. Many systems will be available, such as a central catalog of the resources of the libraries, perhaps supplemented by regional catalogs that will provide the location, and high-speed electronic communications.

Libraries will use more computers to perform most of the record keeping done in libraries, and thus free librarians to work directly with readers. Card catalogs will be replaced increasingly by computer terminals connected to a central storage unit. Terminals in the library will also cover indexes to periodicals and scientific journals. Information search will be accomplished in a few minutes, and many publications are appearing on CD-ROM computer systems.

There will be a continued increase in the quantity of publications that libraries must acquire and make available. The number of books published in the United States has increased from 6,000 in 1920 to about 50,000 in the latter 1980s, and the number of periodicals has grown to more than 60,000. Libraries will acquire films, recordings, videocassettes, and other audiovisual media as extensively as books.

Libraries will expand their collections to include the most important books that are published in all parts of the world. The world is unifying in intellectual matters, if not in political arrangements. Information about new developments must be available in libraries whether the discoveries are made in the U.S.S.R., China, Australia, or anywhere else.

◇ **SOURCES OF ADDITIONAL INFORMATION**

American Library Association
50 East Huron Street
Chicago, IL 60611

American Society for Information Science
1424 16th Street, NW, Suite 404
Washington, DC 20036

Special Libraries Association
1700 18th Street, NW
Washington, DC 20009

American Association of Law Libraries
53 West Jackson Boulevard, Suite 940
Chicago, IL 60604

Association of Research Libraries
1527 New Hampshire Avenue, NW
Washington, DC 20036

Medical Library Association
6 North Michigan Avenue, Suite 300
Chicago, IL 60602

◇ **RELATED ARTICLES**

Volume 1: Book Publishing; Magazine Publishing; Newspaper Publishing
Volume 2: Human services workers; Librarians; Medical record administrators; Statisticians; Writers and editors
Volume 3: Bookkeeping and accounting clerks; Statistical clerks
Volume 4: Audiovisual technicians; Library technicians; Medical records technicians

Machining and Machinery

General information

The machining and machinery industry manufactures metal parts that are used to make machines, tools, or other machine parts. In other words, the industry creates metal machines that make other machines. The machining and machinery industry also makes parts to such items as engines, tools, molds, and other machine pieces. It is, in effect, the first stage of the manufacturing process.

Machining is simply the process of producing something, using machine-operated cutting or finishing tools. This industry covers, for example, the manufacture of the boring or jig machine that produces nuts and bolts, as well as the production of the nuts and bolts themselves.

Although humans have used wheels and other tools since the dawn of history, the use of machine tools is relatively recent. When the Scottish inventor James Watt experimented with steam engines in the mid-1700s, he could not find anyone who could drill a perfect hole; thus his engines leaked steam. In 1775, John Wilkinson invented the boring machine.

Several years later, Matthew Murray, Joseph Clement, and Richard Murray developed the planer. Thus holes and flat surfaces could be smoothed to necessary degrees.

In the United States, the most rapid spurt in the use of machine tools came during World Wars I and II. It was necessary to build tanks, planes, jeeps, ships, and guns quickly and accurately, so machines had to be devised to turn out the thousands of pieces required. Since that time there has been a steady increase in the amount and types of consumer goods that Americans desire, so the mass production methods developed for the war periods have been converted and improved to make the countless products American manufactures produce today.

The structure of the machining and machinery industry

People often think of the metalworking industry as being limited to operating machine tools. A machine tool is a power-driven machine, not portable by hand, that is used to shape or form metal by cutting, impact, pressure, electrical techniques, or by a combination of these processes. The most common types of machine tools are drilling and boring, turning, milling, grinding, planing and shaping, forging, shearing, and pressing machines.

Operating a machine tool, however, is just one of the many occupations in the metalworking industry. To remain competitive, a metalworking company must invent, improve, and anticipate the future needs of its customers. To do this, the industry needs a variety of competent workers.

The machining and machinery industry begins with research engineers who analyze market needs and decide what new products are in demand. Once the researcher has envisioned a new product, the design and product engineers draft the method of its construction.

The engineers design the machines that construct the metal product. Such a product can be another machine or simply a tool. Once the product has been designed, the rest of the manufacturing process simply involves creating the item. Depending on the product, the item may follow a variety of production steps.

If the end-product is a machine, then molds and patterns must be cut according to very exact measurements, called tolerances. This process is completed by tool and die makers, who follow blueprints to cut the metal and press it into shape. After the metal has been cut, the parts are given to the machine builders for assembly.

The manufacturing of many items requires specialized tasks in the production process.

A machinist must work within very close tolerances, usually with an accuracy greater than .0001 of an inch.

Such tasks depend on the size and complexity of the product. For instance, in the mass production of tools, layout workers may first mark the metal castings before they are cut and pressed. In the product's assembly there may be several people performing repetitive, simple tasks like screwing in nuts and bolts or more complex tasks like welding. After the product has been assembled, the production painters spray the item with an industrial coating.

In the precision metalworking trade, most designers start as tool and die makers or mold makers and move to designer positions if they are so inclined. In manufacturing, a machine operator may become a machinist, then a supervisor, assistant superintendent, shift superintendent, general superintendent, works manager, and on to top management. Similar progressions occur in every area of the metalworking industry; an individual's success depends upon diligence, aptitude, ambition, and making contributions to the success of the company.

Careers

The metalworking industry offers a broad range of employment opportunities for almost every skill. Several of the occupations that are closely associated with the design and manufacture of products in the metalworking and machinery industry are listed below.

Research engineers: A research engineer is concerned with discovering new products and improving or developing new machines or new concepts for production. Researchers must make a systematic survey of current machine

applications, plan and execute experimental work, and be able to approve, reject, or modify ideas advanced by others. They also must be able to communicate and consult with various other engineers to get their ideas on a particular project. A research engineer must have a thorough knowledge of the company's products and its manufacturing techniques.

Product engineers: Product engineers are responsible for improving equipment usage. They may try to increase reliability, correct deficiencies, increase safety, reduce maintenance, or otherwise improve the performance of a product. They must know how the company's products are used and often are called upon to make modifications to meet specific production needs. Most product engineers work with a minimum of supervision, often in areas where modifications are desired but not completely defined.

Design engineers: Design engineers write specifications, give advice on construction and manufacture processes, and establish minimum acceptable standards of performance for new products. They must have a good mechanical engineering background, be creative, and possess knowledge of machinery and mechanical apparatus. They must know the company's manufacturing facilities and capabilities and must keep abreast of engineering developments.

Sales engineers: Sales engineers in the machine building and metalworking industries can either work for the manufacturer or the distributor of such equipment. It is their job to sell the company, its reputation, its products, and its services. For this reason, they must be completely familiar with the technical aspects of the product they sell, as well as its method of manufacture, its servicing needs, and the various uses to which it can be put. Sales engineers communicate data to both technical and nontechnical personnel. They use their knowledge to solve customers' problems concerning materials specifications, production rates, accuracy, and cost.

Machining workers: Machining workers is a broad term used to describe those people who operate the machines. They are generally classified into the following categories: tool and die makers, skilled machinists, machine builders, set-up operators, and machine tool operators.

Tool and die makers: Tool makers specialize in producing tooling needed for a machine operation. Die makers make dies for forming, stamping, or forging metal. Tool and die makers also repair the tools and dies. They must be able to operate any machine tool and use a wide variety of precision measuring instruments. They must have extensive knowledge of shop practice and metallurgy and must be able to work to extremely close tolerances.

Often tool or die makers specialize in a particular phase of tool making or die making. As specialists, they may be classified as cam makers, fixture makers, gauge makers, mold makers, tool or die repairers, die finishers, forging die makers, die polishers, or die sinkers. In general, tool makers and die makers are expected to have more mechanical skills than any of the other metalworking trades.

Skilled machinists: Skilled machinists are general craft workers who set up and operate a variety of machine tools. With their knowledge of shop practice and metallurgy, they select the proper equipment on which to manufacture a part, set the work up in the machine that will do the job most efficiently, and then complete the job. While skilled machinists do not have to work within the same close tolerances as the tool and die maker, they must be able to work from either a blueprint or written specifications and select and use the proper tools to make the desired part. They use precision measuring instruments to check their work and often use such hand tools as files, chisels, and scrapers to finish the piece to final specifications. Machinists are expected to have all-around skill in operating machine tools and in using hand tools and measuring devices.

Machine builders: Machine builders fit and assemble components from assembly blueprints and specifications. In general they check part measurements and layout and position subassemblies. They also connect electrical panels, electronic controls, and hydraulic lines. To complete their projects, they must use a variety of hand and powered tools and work to close tolerances of fits and alignment. They must also assemble, set up, and operate the new machine, often producing the customer's parts to verify the machine's performance. On large machines, they may then tear down the machine, prepare it for shipment, and reassemble and retest the machine in the customer's plant.

Machine set-up operators: Machine set-up operators perform work similar to machinists and while they may operate certain machines more skillfully than a machinist, they are not expected to be able to do so on all machines. Most production employees are machine set-up operators.

Machine tool operators: Machine tool operators specialize in the operation of one specific machine tool. The work is usually highly repetitive. They make only minor adjustments to the machine tool in operation; if trouble arises, a supervisor or job setter is called to make the necessary major adjustments. Special purpose

Much machining is done with the use of robots. This particular robot is welding a tube.

gauges, which simplify measurements, are often used instead of precision measuring instruments. Machine tool operators are classified by the type of machinery they operate, such as engine lathe operator, milling machine operator, or drill press operator.

Job setters: Job setters get machine tools ready for operation by machine operators. They may be required to explain the work functions to be performed and to show how to check the accuracy of the work. Job setters usually service a number of machine tools of a single type, such as drilling or milling machines. They set up the work from blueprints or operation sheets, select the feed and speed rates at which the material is to be machined, and determine the tooling and operation sequence. They may select and install the proper cutting tools, adjust guides, stops, cams, and other controls, and make trial runs until the parts produced conform to specifications.

Layout workers: Layout workers are highly skilled specialists who mark metal castings and forgings to indicate where, and how much, machining is needed. Layout workers use such measuring and layout tools as calipers, micrometers, height gauges, and center punches. They are familiar with standard machine tool operations and with the machining properties of metals. As with the job setters, layout workers work primarily in the mass production metalworking industries, where large numbers of machine tool operators are employed. Their work enables other workers to use machine tools simply by following lines, points, and other instructions marked on the part.

This patternmaker guides a sheet of metal through a drill that cuts the metal according to a specified design. Steady hands are required for this job.

Instrument makers: Instrument makers are often experimental machinists or model makers, producing various experimental models of special laboratory equipment and nonstandard instruments used in prototype work. The skills of instrument makers are similar in many respects to those of the tool and die maker or machinist. The instrument maker must operate a variety of machine tools, as well as hand tools and measuring instruments. Instrument makers, however, are seldom given such detailed instructions as blueprints. Rather, they often work from rough sketches, verbal instructions, or only from ideas. Instrument makers frequently may be found working with materials other than metal. The increased interest in research and development testing work has increased the importance of the instrument maker.

Assemblers: The assembler puts together parts or finished products that have been machined in previous operations. Semiskilled assemblers do relatively simple repetitive operations under close supervision. For example, in the automobile industry, one assembler may start nuts on bolts, and the next worker on the assembly line tightens the nuts with power-driven tools.

Skilled assemblers, on the other hand, work on the more complex parts of subassemblies with little or no supervision and are responsible for the final assembly of complex machines. These workers must be able to read blueprints and other engineering specifications and use a wide variety of tools and precision measuring instruments. In a machine tool plant, for example, skilled assemblers install and fit previously machined parts into subas-semblies and then into the final product. Assemblers are often classified as floor assemblers or bench assemblers, depending upon whether they put together large, heavy machinery and equipment on shop floors or work on smaller products or parts that can be assembled on a work bench.

Inspectors: The workers who make certain that various operations in a metalworking plant meet specifications are known as inspectors. Semiskilled inspectors may make visual checks for defects in products or parts. They use various gauges and special purpose measuring instruments to check size. Inspectors may use a limited number of simple hand tools, such as screwdrivers and pliers, in their work. They may be required to keep records of the number of parts accepted and rejected in inspections and to file special reports for quality control purposes. The skilled inspector usually works under general supervision and must be able to work from blueprints, interpret specifications, and use complex precision measuring instruments.

Material handlers: A material handler operates various types of cranes, hoists, and powered trucks that move raw materials and products in a metalworking factory. A typical truck has a hydraulic lifting mechanism with attachments such as forks to lift piles of cartons or scoops to lift loose material. Some power trucks are equipped with tow bars used to pull in-plant trailers. Besides operating these vehicles, material handlers may be required to keep records of material moved, do some manual loading and unloading of materials, and maintain their trucks in good working condition. They must be skilled drivers, often operating through narrow aisles where material is stored or around closely spaced operating machinery.

Production painters: The work done by production painters in factories is different from that performed by painters employed in construction and maintenance work. The production painter often uses a spray gun as well as brushes to apply paint, lacquer, varnish, or other finishes to parts or finished manufactured products. Painters who operate spray guns pour mixed paints into a spray gun container attached to a compressor. They adjust the nozzle of the spray gun and the compressor so that the paint will be applied uniformly. The objects being sprayed may be stationary or attached to moving conveyors. Production painters are often required to replace nozzles and maintain guns and other paint equipment.

Stationary engineers: Stationary engineers employed in manufacturing plants operate and maintain steam boilers used to power industrial machinery and to heat factories. A boiler tender may be responsible for inspecting boiler equipment, for lighting boilers, and building up steam pressure. In most plants, boiler tenders operate mechanical devices that control the flow of combustion air and fuel. Duties of these workers may include reading meters and other instruments to make sure the boilers are operating efficiently and in accordance with safety regulations. Qualified stationary engineers should be able to detect malfunctions and take appropriate action.

Welders: Welders join metal objects by means of an oxyacetylene torch or arc, and they repair broken or cracked metal objects. In addition to performing welding or brazing operations, welders also may cut metal with the cutting torch. Skilled welders often plan and lay out their work according to drawings, blueprints, or other written specifications. They also must have a knowledge of the welding properties of a variety of metals and alloys and be able to work under a variety of conditions.

A production painter uses a spray gun to apply an even coat of paint on a newly manufactured product.

Education

Whether the new employee has a degree from a university, a certificate from a technical institute, a diploma from a high school, or just the interest and aptitude to learn, a job in a metalworking company is just the beginning of a satisfying career. In most companies, the new employees are assigned to a training program. Many companies also provide additional education at nearby vocational schools or colleges, or specialized instruction conducted within the plant.

Apprenticeship training is required for many of the jobs in the machining industry. A machinist apprentice program, for instance, lasts four to five years and consists of a combination of on-the-job and in-shop training and considerable related classroom instruction. Shop training includes the learning of proper machine speeds and feeds and the operation of various machine tools. The apprentice is trained in the use of hand tools and assembly procedures. In the classroom, the apprentice studies blueprint reading, mechanical drawing, shop mathematics, and shop practices.

Most apprentices are hired right out of high school. Preference goes to students who have taken machine shop, drafting, or blueprint reading, and applied math (algebra through trigonometry) and know some electronics, computer applications, and physics.

After completion of the apprenticeship program, skill as a tool or die maker or machinist

requires many years of additional shop experience.

The completion of a new employee's training usually marks the beginning of a period of specialization. In several communities where the metalworking industry is essential to the local economy, cooperative courses are available that make it possible to alternate between working in the plant and going to technical schools or universities for further education. Full-time employment, with study toward a college degree at a night school, is a career path also followed by many.

Technical school graduates fill a major need in the metalworking industry. This type of educational background equips graduates, after a short orientation period, for employment in many phases of manufacturing, product design and development, quality control, plant engineering, supervision, and engineering technology. By further study, job rotation, and related courses in schools, technical school graduates may qualify themselves for advancement in both engineering and management jobs.

Industry outlook

Machines will continue to contribute to the progress of civilization in the future. Highly productive computer-controlled machining and turning centers that change their own tools; transfer machines that completely machine, assemble, and test mass-produced products; and innovative metal removal and forming systems have revolutionized America's manufacturing industry, producing goods and services un-

273

heard of just a few years ago. Robots are relieving workers of the tedious, dangerous, and repetitive aspects of shop work, freeing them for jobs where imagination, ingenuity, and judgment are required. And computers speed the design, manufacture, and distribution of almost everything we use.

There are currently more than 500 companies in the machine tool industry, employing over 65,000 people. This industry has a very promising outlook for the 1990s. The increase in sales has risen steadily for the past few years.

Advances in the science of metalworking will continue in the future. New methods, new techniques, new concepts, and new principles of metalworking are rapidly evolving. New families of machine tools, totally unlike conventional equipment, have been introduced. Throughout the industry, in every phase of metalworking, there is an acceleration of design and testing to develop the machines needed to make the products of tomorrow. And skilled people will be needed to design, manufacture, and operate these machines.

◇ **SOURCES OF ADDITIONAL INFORMATION**

NMTBA—Association for Manufacturing Technology
7901 Westpark Drive
McLean, VA 22102

National Tooling and Machining Association
9300 Livingston Road
Ft. Washington, MD 20744

Precision Metalforming Association
27027 Chardon Road
Richmond Heights, OH 44143

North American Die Casting Association
2000 North Fifth Avenue
River Grove, IL 60171

Machinery and Allied Products Institute
1200 18th Street, NW, Suite 400
Washington, DC 20036

◇ **RELATED ARTICLES**

Volume 1: Engineering; Metals
Volume 2: Computer programmers; Cost estimators; Drafters; Engineers; Industrial designers; Industrial traffic managers; Packaging engineers; Purchasing agents
Volume 3: Assemblers; Automobile mechanics; Boilermaking occupations; Electrical repairers; Forge shop occupations; Instrument makers; Instrument repairers; Job and die setters; Lathers; Layout workers; Machine tool operators; Machinists; Manufacturers' sales workers; Millwrights; Molders; Patternmakers; Sheet-metal workers; Tool makers and die makers; Welders
Volume 4: Drafting and design technicians; Electrical technicians; Electromechanical technicians; Electronics technicians; Engineering technicians; Industrial engineering technicians; Layout technicians; Metallurgical technicians; Quality-control technicians; Robotics technicians; Tap-and-die maker technicians; Welding technicians

Magazine Publishing

General information

Magazines exist to serve the interests of people who want to know more about certain subjects than they can learn from other, more general media. The magazine publishing industry produces over 11,000 magazines that provide information, entertainment, and instruction to people of all ages and interests. These magazines might be published weekly, bi-weekly, monthly, or at various other times throughout the year. Thousands of specialized trade magazines, professional journals, and other publications serve special interests. Most larger associations publish periodicals for their members, including timely newsletters to supplement news in regularly published media.

Henry R. Luce, founding editor and publisher of *Time*, once said of his publications: "We are in the teaching business [with] a touch of show business." To some extent the same thing is true of almost every magazine. The editorial job is to transmit information and knowledge from mind to mind. A magazine's purpose is to intrigue, attract, and hold the interest of its readers.

The advent of Johannes Guttenberg's printing press in the mid-1400s allowed printed matter to be produced quickly and relatively inexpensively. The earliest printed matter tended to be religious books, scholarly works, and pamphlets and filers. The earliest magazines appeared in Europe in the 1660s. They were specialized journals and compositions that appealed to academicians. A decade later, publications with a more general appeal emerged. Given the high level of illiteracy in Europe in the 17th century, the earliest magazines appealed to an educated and elite crowd.

As public interest grew to encompass more than just the news of the day and more people were able to read, the variety of magazines on the market increased. With the advent of photography in the mid-1800s, most general interest magazines and nonacademic publications carried photographs.

In the United States, magazines have played an important role in entertaining and informing people throughout the twentieth century. Some magazines such as *Life*, *Time*, and *Newsweek* have achieved a nationwide circulation of several million readers. Other, more specialized magazines have maintained a more limited circulation while appealing to those with an interest in a certain area, such as sports, economics, or theater.

Today there are more than 11,300 regularly produced periodicals listed by the Audit Bureau of Circulation. Many smaller professional journals and other special-purpose periodicals do not report to the Audit Bureau, and therefore the actual number of publications is much higher. The bulk of these magazines are produced by small staffs and are of modest size and limited circulation. Often, these smaller publications have little or no advertising revenue. Other publications have large staffs of writers, editors, and photographers. With large circulations, these magazines collect thousands of dollars for an advertisement and serve the interests of its readers while contributing revenue to a multi-million dollar industry.

The structure of the magazine publishing industry

The editorial staff is the core of a magazine; however, it represents a relatively small part of the publishing operation in terms of size. The prospective writer who looks for a staff job on a magazine where material is contributed primarily by outsiders or free-lancers may find the ratio of noneditorial to editorial jobs running as high as ten to one. On staff-written magazines the ratio may still be four business or technical

Many magazines use computers for page layout design. This allows designers to experiment with different layouts at little cost.

positions for every one editorial job. For most magazines, editorial departments account for only 9 percent of the typical budget, whereas manufacturing, distribution, and sales departments account for more than 60 percent of the budget.

There is a difference between magazines that are almost completely staff written such as *Newsweek, Time,* and *Business Week* and those that are composed largely of material contributed by outsiders, such as *Ladies' Home Journal, Atlantic, Harper's,* and *Playboy.* The former category has very few free-lance writers. Most work is done in-house. In the latter, the editorial function is basically one of editing, checking, and displaying the submitted or assigned material.

On magazines made up largely of material collected from outsiders, an editor usually requests a free-lance writer to submit material on a particular subject. The writer usually must have a particular expertise in the specified area. A very limited number of individuals—numbered only in the hundreds—make an adequate living on writing for magazines on a free-lance basis alone. Some mass circulation magazines occasionally pay writers very high fees for excerpts from especially controversial or high-interest books before book publication.

On staff-written magazines the staff conceives, researches, writes, edits, and checks the written copy. Magazine writers organize and present the information in a concise manner so that the vital elements will be absorbed by the reader, not merely listed on the page. Often writers interview large numbers of people to gain the facts and impressions necessary for a story. These writers also use published material

and other sources to conduct background research.

On some larger news magazines, such as *U.S. News and World Report,* correspondents in the field, as well as researchers, may do much of the interviewing and analysis of background material.

Some editorial positions require considerable amounts of travel, and correspondents spend extensive periods away from the home office. But others, such as those on a copy desk, generally do not travel. Editors, writers, and photographers have the opportunity to examine situations in depth, cover a wide variety of subjects, and meet a great variety of people.

The business and publishing departments include accounting, advertising and sales, circulation, promotion, and production. These departments place a high premium on initiative and ingenuity, and many require writing and presentation skills.

The accounting side of publishing presents a magazine staff with many possible economic strategies. Sophisticated business techniques are utilized to keep effective managerial control. Heavy fixed costs, such as operating a printing press, are typical of the financial picture of a consumer magazine, and the business or controller's office is responsible for keeping production costs under a specific budget.

A certain number of advertising pages is necessary to cover the fixed costs; beyond that number, additional pages of advertising produce the profit essential to continued publication and growth. Controllers and others in the accounting department help management officials decide how to best reinvest capital to ensure the continued success of the magazine.

With the fluctuations in the total national economy and the seasonal nature of some advertising expenditures, the income against the fixed costs of publishing is not even, and sensitivity to economic trends is a steady concern for the publisher.

The advertising and sales department solicits advertisements. This department is charged with the responsibility of providing the major source of revenue for most consumer magazines. The sale representatives must demonstrate to advertisers and their agencies that its magazine is a good medium for carrying a message about the advertiser's product or service. One magazine may try to reach only a small segment of the population, attempting to attract specialized advertising, while another may be aimed at the general public, looking for advertising aimed at the total market.

Sales representatives must be completely informed regarding both the magazine they represent and the company they sell to. They must know the magazine's page rates, editorial policies and procedures, and the size and character of audience reached. They must also know a great deal about their advertisers, the character of their business, the immediate and long-term situations of their industry, and their special needs and goals.

The circulation department is responsible for making sure that the magazine reaches the reader in the most efficient and cost effective way. Circulation workers handle subscription problems and other concerns. Here the employee is exposed to the marketing issues that are the key to the success of any publication. Most magazines distribute through subscriptions and newsstands, which means that the circulation department is involved with subscriptions, newsstand displays, and magazine distribution.

The promotion department helps ensure that potential advertisers know about a magazine. Messages are aimed at groups of advertisers in magazines, newspapers, direct mail, and through special event promotions. The objective is to pave the way for salespeople by stimulating interest and understanding on the part of the advertiser.

The promotion department also helps create an awareness on the part of potential readers. Promotion workers might help organize contests or other events to publicize a magazine. In promoting a magazine, magazine executives often utilize market research to determine who the target audience is. Market research can help determine the age and income of the average reader, as well as other important demographic information. Market research can also provide valuable information on the magazine's competition and other issues.

The production department coordinates the design, layout, and printing of the publication. Employees in this department make sure that all text and illustrations are properly marked and then sent to the printer. With large magazines, production may be done on the premises. For the majority of magazines, however, printing is done elsewhere. Production workers negotiate prices with the printer and inspect color quality. Close contact with the printer must be maintained to assure that quality is preserved despite tight production schedules.

Careers

Magazine publishing requires a remarkably wide variety of talents. Besides writers, editors, artists, and photographers, there are vital

During the binding process, magazines are prepared for shipping to subscribers.

places for accountants, financial analysts, and investment managers.

A sample of the variety of career opportunities available in magazine publishing follows below:

Editors-in-chief: The editor-in-chief is responsible for the overall editorial content of the publication. He or she is concerned with the image of the magazine, ensuring that the content appeals to the audience that the magazine is trying to reach. The position is managerial, overseeing the entire department and setting editorial guidelines.

Editors: The editor's job is to execute the editorial image of a magazine as it is set forth by the editor-in-chief. In general, editors envision an idea for an article, hire a person to write it, and edit the article according to the style of the publication. Editorial work, in addition to requiring the ability to write with style and substance, also demands responsibility. Editors must also be capable administrators, able to manage a staff of individuals. He or she must plan future issues, making sure that editorial excellence is continually maintained.

Editorial staff: The editorial staff writes and edits the written content of the publication. Creativity is basic to the functioning of an editorial staff. The staff includes such positions as features editor, contributing editor, copy edi-

The advent of desktop publishing has allowed many small institutions to write, design, and print magazines at a comparatively low cost.

tor, associate editor, assistant editor, and editorial assistant.

Free-lance writers: Some publishing companies hire free-lancers to write articles for their magazine. Often the free-lance writer solicits manuscripts to various publications in the hopes that his or her article will be accepted. Usually, only well-known writers are asked by the magazine editors to submit an article.

Researchers: Researchers ensure that the content of an article is factually correct. They spend their time checking facts to guarantee that what is written is accurate.

Art directors: Art directors are concerned with the general layout and look of the magazine. They select photographs, colors, and typefaces that give a publication the appropriate image.

Photographers: Photographers take the photographs for articles. They can be hired on a free-lance basis, or they may be part of the staff. In some cases, they may accompany the writer while the article is being researched and written. Some simply take pictures of events that they believe are worthy of a story and sell them to agencies that provide the photographs to magazines.

Publishers: Publishers are responsible for the business aspects of the publishing company. They oversee the advertising, circulation, promotion, and production of the magazine. Sometimes they also make editorial decisions.

Advertising manager: The advertising manager oversees the staff of sales representatives. He or she distributes advertising accounts to each sales representative and ensures that each account is being handled correctly.

Advertising sales representatives: Advertising sales representatives try to get companies to advertise in their publication. It is their job to convince prospective clients to advertise in their magazine. They solicit business by finding accounts themselves or by being assigned accounts through the advertising manager. Some work with national accounts (those businesses that sell products nation-wide), and others work with local accounts.

Circulation managers: Circulation managers keep track of subscribers. Much of their job entails analyses of income from subscriptions.

Promotions manager: Promotions managers try to stimulate interest in the magazine. They are responsible for maintaining or increasing subscription levels through some promotional devise. For instance, they may solicit subscriptions through direct mailings.

Production managers: The production manager works with the printer to publish the magazine. He or she spends most of the time setting up printing schedules, selecting the paper weight, size, and other physical properties of the magazine, and inspecting the quality of the printed matter while it is being produced.

Education

All magazines look for people with broad educational backgrounds. The magazine industry's most important future employees will be drawn from the ranks of college graduates, and especially from those who are interested in a wide variety of topics, such as history, language, and economics. Those who can communicate effectively through the written word and graphic devices are also suited for work in the magazine industry.

Most employers expect applicants to have college degrees, but there is little agreement as to the preferred major for most editing and writing jobs. Journalism schools offer courses in magazine production, and some employers may prefer to hire graduates in communications or journalism. Others prefer degrees in various academic fields. Evidence of ability may be shown by unpaid experience on school and community publications and projects. Some magazines offer students internships.

There are summer courses in magazine and book publishing that provide exposure to the industry. While these courses are most helpful in networking and ultimately finding a job, they do not offer a great deal of experience.

For editorial positions, an active interest in writing, as demonstrated by work on school and college publications, is helpful. Some part-time or summer work for newspapers and news services is also a plus. A student with an interest in both writing and an occupational field—for example, agriculture—might consider becoming a specialized journalist.

Industry outlook

The magazine industry is estimated to grow 2 to 3 percent in the upcoming years, provided that the economy continues to grow at a steady rate of about 3 percent. As more and more specialized publications are introduced to the marketplace, the competition for advertising dollars will remain great. It is estimated that the primary growth in the magazine industry will come from these new, specialized publications. Thus, the general interest magazines will have to develop advertising strategies and options that will satisfy potential advertisers. This means offering regional advertising and other options for their publication.

Throughout the mid-1990s, the outlook for writing and editing jobs is expected to be keenly competitive. Opportunities will be best in firms that prepare business and trade publications and in technical writing. Yet a growing demand for publications and the growth of advertising and public relations agencies should provide new jobs in the magazine industry.

◇ **SOURCES OF ADDITIONAL INFORMATION**

Magazine Publishers of America
575 Lexington Avenue
New York, NY 10022

Successful Magazine Publishers Group
PO Box 2029
Tuscaloosa, AL 34503

American Society of Magazine Photographers
419 Park Avenue South, #1407
New York, NY 10016

American Society of Business Press Editors
4445 Gilmer Lane
Cleveland, OH 44143

Association of Business Publishers
205 East 42nd Street
New York, NY 10017

◇ **RELATED ARTICLES**

Volume 1: Book Publishing; Newspaper Publishing; Printing; Pulp and Paper; Public Relations; Telecommunications
Volume 2: Advertising workers; Commercial artists; Designers; Literary agents and artists' managers; Marketing, advertising, and public relations managers; Marketing research personnel; Photographers and camera operators; Public relations specialists; Reporters and correspondents; Technical writers; Writers and editors
Volume 3: Bindery workers; Compositors and typesetters; Photoengravers; Photographic laboratory occupations; Printing press operators and assistants
Volume 4: Darkroom technicians; Graphic arts technicians; Photofinishing equipment technicians; Photographic equipment technicians

Marketing

General information

Marketing has come a long way since Henry Ford announced that you could have a Model T car in any color you wanted, as long as you wanted black. Marketing has become one of the most important elements of designing and selling a product. Knowing who the buyer is and what he or she wants guides most business decisions.

A combination of events led to marketing as an industry. The first influence was that the "roaring twenties" had developed an abundance of products. The idea that a good product will sell itself was no longer true. The competition for buyers became increasingly competitive, and producers needed to increase awareness of their products.

The second major influence was the Depression of the 1930s. As money became scarce, the increased number of producers were competing over an even smaller marketplace. Up until the crunch, producers had been willing to market anything with the assumption that someone out there somewhere would buy it. As P. T. Barnum once cynically put it, "there's a sucker born every minute."

Businesses soon found otherwise. If there was no interest or need in a product, an advertising campaign might carry the company through the first wave of purchases, but after that there would be little chance of improving sales. Producers had to develop a system of market research, where they could determine what the purchasing public wanted and needed. Once a company had that information, they could develop the product, and then direct sales at the targeted buyers.

The business of marketing took hold. If a group of potential buyers could be found for a product, the product could be better designed to suit the needs of the user. By locating a group of buyers before starting an advertising campaign, the advertising could be styled to reach that specific group and the producer would have a better chance of launching a successful product. Marketing would provide a service for both sides of the business world, the seller and the buyer.

Marketing is now a major part of business. Product development, manufacturing, and sales are all directly involved with marketing. Most large companies have their own marketing departments. Smaller companies may choose to use outside marketing services. In every case, companies with a product to sell will have someone with marketing skills helping them make decisions.

The structure of the marketing industry

Field interviewers start the work for the marketing department. Interviewers gather the data that will be used to determine information about a product. Using small-group interviewing techniques, interviewers ask potential buyers a series of questions designed to gather such information as whether people need a particular product, what people think of the product name, and if consumers have tried a similar product.

Secondary data is information provided by previously gathered polling. Government surveys or independent surveys by universities and such are all sources of secondary data. The big benefit to using statistics gathered by others is that it is much less expensive than gathering the information first hand. However, it will not provide insight into specific questions for a specific product, and that is when primary data research is required.

Given the vast number of products on the market today, research will normally start long before a product is developed. There is little sense in developing a product that no one wants. For example, the competition for the new product will be checked out to see if there is room in the market for another similar item. The difference that the new product will have over the current products will be examined as well. This will be done for a new brand of green beans, a textbook for schools, a car, a magazine, a television show, or a new opera company. If a product or service is going to be sold to the public, chances are a marketing team will look into the sales potential before the public even hears of the item.

In order to determine the potential sales and competition for a new product, the marketing department will talk to the producers about what they had in mind. Armed with information about what the market goal is, the marketing department goes to work compiling information about what already exists in the marketplace for that product. How much the other products cost, how well they sell, and how long they have been selling, are all questions to be answered.

For example, a new magazine will look at its competitors on the market. The marketing department will look at other similar magazines and determine such information as how many magazines they sell, how much that magazine costs, how long they have been in business, and is their business increasing or decreasing. The hardest question to answer is on the likelihood of sales: is there enough interest by the public to purchase a new magazine on this topic.

Once a product is deemed viable, meaning that there is some chance it will be able to make enough sales to pay back initial costs, the cost of launching the new product will be itemized and evaluated. Start-up costs will be determined for launching the new product with the staff required. For an existing large company with an extensive staff, this will often mean little hiring. Their staff may be able to handle the initial work on a product until it proves that it has a spot in the marketplace. They can choose to hire additional staff when the product is already making sales.

For a small company, or a company that is starting with a new product, there is a much larger start-up cost. Everything must be financed for the new product, from the people who design it to the people who sell it. All the work and all the materials must be accounted for in the cost of the first production. It is much easier to start a company with a product that is inexpensive to produce, although home computers are one example of a product that had a relatively high start-up cost yet did very well as a new product.

To promote new products, food manufacturers often offer free tastes at grocery stores. Such marketing techniques inspire people to taste products that they may not under ordinary circumstances.

The pricing of the object for sale is determined by the overall cost of production, plus the profit desired by the company. Marketing helps in pricing a product by determining what the public would be willing to pay. Certain materials may force the cost of the production beyond what the public will pay for a product.

The marketing department will also help develop a distribution plan for a product. If the sales of a product are expected to do well with a certain group, for example, then marketing must decide how to reach that group by determining where they shop, when they shop, and what kind of advertising is going to reach them.

Once the merchandise is designed, and the market evaluated, then the actual production begins. The marketing department is not finished yet. They must determine the methods that will get the new product as much exposure as possible. They will try to create an interest in the product through the use of the media.

If the new product is unique in some way, then the marketing department, along with the public relations department, will try to get the press to write stories about it. If a story is written about the product, then the company gets free promotion. People reading the story will receive information on the item to be sold. The risk, of course, is that the review might not be favorable. With some motion pictures, for example, if the producers fear negative reviews, they may not release a film for review before the opening date, because they wish to avoid negative information going out to the public.

The marketing department will also work with advertising to determine where they should advertise, how the advertisements should look, and when the advertising should

To successfully market a product, manufacturers must study the demographics of certain markets and conduct many market tests. This task involves the analysis of large amounts of data.

begin. Launching an advertising campaign too early may create a peak in interest before the product is available, and by the time the product is released, the public may be no longer interested.

Timing and design on advertising are extremely important to the success of the advertising campaign. The look of the ad will be researched by the advertising and the marketing departments to make sure that the ads effectively interest the audience they want. Some ads may not interest one group but another group may find the same ad funny or informative. Ads for children's products may target the children, or they may target the parent purchasing the product. The marketing department must know which target audience is the best one, because the ads are different for each group. How the product is marketed may determine the success or failure of the product.

Large companies will handle sales and distribution from inside the company. It is more cost effective to have a permanent sales staff for a large company than to use wholesalers or outside sales help. Smaller companies may sell through wholesalers, who supply retail stores with the products of many different manufacturers.

Once the product is released, the opening sales are evaluated. If they are not as strong as predicted, then marketing will probably go back to the researchers to get more data on why the product is not selling. If the problems are something that can be corrected easily, the company will decide if that is the route they want to take. If they realize that the target audience is not being reached, or that the audience they expected to be interested is not as strong as another audience, then they may re-

design the product or the advertising, or they may stop production of the product.

Failure rate for new products is very high. For example, about 80 percent of new magazines do not survive to the fourth year. A company must determine if what they are selling has a chance to make a break into the market or if the product will not make enough profit in the end. The company has to be sure they are not giving up a product that may do well after a slow start, or that the company is not backing a losing product long after they should have understood that the product was failing. The marketing department will continue to run evaluations on the sales, the advertising, and the direction of the product and its competition, until the product is no longer being produced.

Although it is not an exact science, marketing uses as much science and statistics as are fitting, so that companies can judge as well as possible on all the questions that arise when selling a product to the public.

Careers

A sampling of marketing career opportunities follows below.

Field interviewers: These workers gather the product information for the researchers. They solicit responses directly from the public with questionnaires given to them by the marketing department. The surveys can be long or short, depending on the need of the company. The interviewers will provide the marketing department with a variety of information, from what age, income, and sex the purchasing group is, to what the purchasing group thinks of the name, design, style, or advertisements of the product (see Volume 2: Marketing research personnel).

Analysts: These are the people who design the questionnaires and compile the answers into meaningful information for the company. They determine if the company has received an adequate amount of information to evaluate the product awareness of the target audience. Analysts find new trends in audience response to questionnaires and thereby provides companies with a continued assessment of the needs and interests of the marketplace.

Statisticians: The group that will be interviewed by the field researchers are selected by the statisticians. Their background in statistics gives them the ability to determine the group that will provide the best possible information for the company (see Volume 2: Statisticians).

Only with a clear understanding of demographics and statistics are statisticians able to determine the smallest group to be polled while still getting a response that is meaningful. For television shows, for example, 1800 families determine the percentage of population in the United States that watches every show. The Nielsen ratings, which are partly responsible for determining how much advertising will cost for a show, are national audience percentages that are based on the viewing habits of 1800 families selected to closely reflect families across the country.

Research director: This position is the highest in the research end of marketing. This is the job that pulls all of the other work together. The director assigns the project, decides on the scope of the research, and deals with the company or department that is requesting the information (see Volume 2: Marketing, advertising, and public relations managers).

Product manager: This position is normally held by someone in the company where the product is being made. The product manager is responsible for arranging the initial information gathering, the start-up cost estimates, and the evaluation of market and competition. Product managers usually present research findings to the president of the company or the financial backers for the new enterprise. For large companies, normally there will be product managers for each of the products. For smaller companies there may only be one manager for all the products handled.

Product marketing staff: Under the product manager are assistants, associates, and specialists all working to provide the necessary information and background needed to make decisions on product development and marketing. Depending on the product, the staff background may be general marketing, or may be quite specific to a particular product.

Marketing director: The marketing director is in charge of gathering all marketing information and presenting the information to groups interested in backing the product. He or she will work closely with the advertising department, the research department, product development staff, and the financial staff of the company.

Education

For managerial positions, a master's degree in marketing or business administration is standard. In either undergraduate or graduate work, courses in statistics, economics, advertising, sociology, and demography should be

REACH FOR THE POWER. TEACH.

Much of marketing involves the careful placement of advertisements in magazines. Marketers strive to give advertisements the greatest amount of exposure possible to their targeted audience.

taken to get a clear understanding of the job responsibilities in marketing. It is certainly possible to get a job without some of these courses, but a student becomes more qualified with the broader based education.

Market researchers normally have an undergraduate degree in business, although study in other areas, such as liberal arts, is also an acceptable path. Some businesses are more interested in employees with a strong liberal arts background, whom they can train in the technical areas of market research. There is also a range of part-time work to be found in market research conducting field interviews.

Given the scientific nature of high-level research positions, masters and doctoral degrees are frequently expected for people in these positions. Degree programs in statistics, demography, and marketing have been developed for research.

Conventions offer outlets for manufacturers to display their products for possible consumers. Such exposure allows manufacturers to meet their customers face to face and promote their products.

a higher degree has become much more important in the last ten years.

Hours can be quite long, with overtime a frequent requirement of every level of the marketing profession. Stress is a continual element of the job, since an inaccurate estimation on a product can be the difference between the survival and failure of a small company.

Employees who fare the best in marketing are detail oriented people who work well under pressure and enjoy the challenge of developing a new product for sale. Success and failure are continual elements of the job, since no one launches only successful projects. The worker who can learn from failure and continually strive for the successful project will enjoy marketing.

Product managers commonly have graduate degrees in business administration (MBAs) or Masters of Management (MMs). Managers have a strong background in marketing, which is needed to compile and understand the information used to make decisions about a product. As the number of people with MBAs increases, it will become difficult to compete if one has a bachelor's degree. Although the number of students registered for higher degrees in business is declining slightly, there are still a large number of people already through an MBA program who will make up the competition for higher-level jobs.

Industry outlook

Since marketing has become an integral part of manufacturing, production, and sales, the job outlook for those in marketing is very strong. More people are currently employed in marketing than in production. The costs of the marketing staff and operations makes up about half the cost of manufactured goods. Because marketing positions are often well paid, the competition for jobs is fairly stiff. The need for

◇ **SOURCES OF ADDITIONAL INFORMATION**

American Marketing Association
250 South Wacker Drive
Chicago, IL 60606

Society for Marketing Professional Services
801 North Fairfax Street, Suite 215
Alexandria, VA 22314

Women in Advertising and Marketing
4200 Wisconsin Avenue, NW, Suite 106-238
Washington, DC 20016

◇ **RELATED ARTICLES**

Volume 1: Advertising; Public Relations
Volume 2: Demographers; Marketing, advertising, and public relations managers; Marketing research personnel; Mathematicians; Media specialists; Statisticians
Volume 3: Public opinion researchers; Retail sales workers; Telemarketers

Mathematics

General information

Mathematics involves the use, manipulation, and interpretation of numbers. It forms the basis of nearly all studies and occupations. All jobs benefit from the results or use of mathematics. In addition, arithmetic is needed by all people for such tasks as making change, figuring costs, calculating real interest rates on loans, filling out income tax forms, balancing checkbooks, and preparing recipes.

The history of mathematics begins with counting. Prehistoric people most likely used their fingers to count, keeping track of numbers with pebbles, knots on a cord, or some other basic method. Approximately 3000 B.C., the Egyptians developed the decimal system, which has remained the basic form of counting today.

The ancient Greeks concentrated on pure math, specifically geometry. In about 300 B.C., Euclid wrote the influential book *Elements*, constructing a system of geometry that we use to this day. Other Greek contributions include Archimedes' discovery of the number *pi*, Ptolemy's work on the *Almagest*, and Pythagorus' formulation of his theorem.

The Arabs made substantial contributions to mathematics. Most of their work was done from A.D.825 to A.D.1100. During that time period, they introduced the study of algebra, discovered and applied the number zero, and made substantial contributions to trigonometry. So influential were the Arabs, that our number system today is based on Arabic numerals.

The Europeans continued to develop mathematical formulas during the Renaissance. It was not until the scientific revolution in the 1600s, however, that the study of mathematics blossomed. One of the greatest contributions to mathematics was Sir Isaac Newton's invention of calculus in the mid-1660s.

From the 1600s to the present day, such accomplishments as Rene Descartes's discovery of analytical geometry, Jakob Bernoulli's work with probability, George Boole's study of symbolic logic, and the manufacture of the computer have all turned mathematics into a fundamental part of our lives.

With the advent of computers, the progression of mathematics has accelerated. Great minds can now work on theory while computers deal with the dull computational tasks in a matter of minutes or seconds.

The structure of the mathematics professions

There are many varieties of mathematicians. Those who like to share their mathematical ideas with other people may find their niche in teaching or participating as members of a scientific research team. Those who prefer to work alone may find opportunities in private offices or libraries.

One occupational branch of mathematics is teaching. Mathematics teachers instruct students in all types of mathematics. It is a challenging profession, whose goal is to stimulate and develop young minds. Those who teach on the elementary and junior high school level may either be general teachers, instructing for all subjects, or they may specialize in mathematics. On the high-school level, teachers instruct students in more complex mathematics such as algebra, geometry, pre-calculus, and calculus.

The college mathematics professor is responsible for training future mathematicians and for giving basic instruction in mathematics to students in other scientific fields. Prospective professors should recognize that courses must be taught at various levels, remedial as well as advanced. University professors also provide guidance for doctoral candidates.

Typically, the college professor does not spend nearly as many hours in the classroom as the high-school teacher. One to three hours a day may be spent in teaching, whereas a considerable amount of time will be spent seeing individual students, reading student papers, preparing lectures, and reading mathematical books and journals. Service on university committees or committees of national mathematical organizations are still other ways that the college teacher's time is used.

Relatively few mathematicians are highly productive in creative research; those who are usually are in great demand and are ordinarily given every encouragement to develop their talents. If the college is part of a university with a graduate program, the professor may be expected to guide graduate students and make original contributions to the rapidly growing body of mathematical knowledge. This includes the preparation and submission of articles to mathematical journals.

Until a few years after World War II, relatively few people were employed as mathematicians in nonteaching jobs, and the few mathematicians who were employed in industry or government were generally called "engineers" or "physicists." Currently, many college graduates with mathematics majors accept well-paying jobs in industry or government. Estimates of the numbers of mathematicians employed in industry and government vary according to the definition of mathematician, but it is clear that industry and government are major employers. Although many of these mathematicians have duties connected with computer installations, a considerable number work as statisticians, operations researchers, classical applied mathematicians, and information scientists.

The majority of industrial, or applied mathematicians are hired because they can contribute to the solution of some current problem. Usually, these mathematicians are part of a team and thus a fundamental requirement is the ability to communicate with engineers, physicists, and other technical personnel, as well as with management.

Typically, a mathematician solves a problem in three major phases: formulating a mathematical model of the problem, finding its solution, and testing the agreement between the solution and the experimental evidence. First, the mathematician constructs one or more mathematical models that simulate the problem under study and embody its essential features. In dealing with problems that are too complex for complete analysis even with the aid of large computers, the construction of appropriate models is a function requiring the highest order of creativity. This is often the most rewarding activity of the applied mathematician.

The successful model maker must have a familiarity with the areas in which the problems arise, which may be, for example, fluid dynamics, solid mechanics, structural design, or electromagnetic theory. The model maker must also be able to communicate effectively with the people responsible for the project, both to be able to understand more than just the essential features of the problem and to explain the results of the completed work.

The second phase, the solution of the problem, may at times require only routine application of well-known formulas, but it may also tax the highest mathematical abilities and sometimes require the development of new, nonstandard methods.

The third phase, testing the solution against experience, also requires good mathematical work in the design of a meaningful experiment and the interpretation of the data obtained from the experiment. For this phase, statistical training is necessary.

In the federal government, many mathematicians perform duties very similar to those of the applied mathematician. Mathematicians, mathematical statisticians, survey statisticians, and actuaries are employed by local, state, and federal governments. Government agencies employing mathematicians include the National Aeronautics and Space Administration (NASA), the National Bureau of Standards, the National Security Agency, and many centers under the Department of Defense such as the Aberdeen Proving Ground, the Naval Ordnance Research Laboratory, and the Naval Ordnance Test Station.

Much that has already been said about mathematicians applies equally to statisticians. Statisticians are frequently trained in departments of mathematics, and are often classified as mathematicians. They have their own distinctive organizations, interests, and skills, and are very much in demand, both in college and university teaching and in industry and government. Mathematical statisticians have mathematical training at the doctoral level, including advanced analysis, matrix algebra, linear programming, and measure theory. They deal with general mathematical theory and estimating unknown quantities specified in terms of probability. They may be employed as teachers or as consultants in industry or government.

The applied statistician may work in such fields as industrial statistical quality control, industrial research and development, reliability analysis, information theory and communications, collection and analysis of government statistics, market research and commercial sam-

In our highly technical society, mathematics is an essential field of study for every person. This teacher instructs junior high-school students in division. It is important that the students learn the basics of mathematics without the aid of calculators.

ple surveys, psychological testing, and medical research.

The actuarial profession requires competent statistical and mathematical capacity, adequate computer science, economic, and financial knowledge, and wide social information. Actuaries design and plan insurance and pension programs. The work requires proficiency in probability and statistics.

About 60 percent of all actuaries work for insurance companies, determining how much a policy holder should pay for a given policy. Other actuaries are employed by large corporations, labor unions, and various government agencies; still others are employed in organizations offering computer or financial products and services.

Careers

The field of mathematics offers a wide range of career opportunities. Of course, many people who use mathematic formulas in their work are not known as "mathematicians." These include computer specialists, bank administrators, and scientists. A listing of some of the careers in mathematics follows below.

Applied mathematicians: Applied mathematicians use mathematical theories and techniques to solve practical problems in business, engineering, and the sciences. They may, for example, investigate the start-up costs of developing a new business or the mathematical aspects of drilling for oil.

Theoretical mathematicians: Theoretical mathematicians seek to develop new principles and new relationships between existing mathematical principals. In this way theoretical mathematicians help to advance mathematical science. Much of the basic knowledge discovered by theoretical mathematicians is later used by applied mathematicians.

Mathematics teachers: Mathematics teachers instruct students in elementary, junior high school, and high school. Depending on the grade level, a teacher will instruct students in arithmetic, algebra, geometry, precalculus, or calculus.

Mathematics professors: Mathematics professors work in colleges or universities, educating students in advanced mathematics. Many of the courses provide supplemental training in the sciences, while others prepare students for masters or doctorates in mathematics. Some professors are required to do their own research.

Mathematical consultants: Mathematics consultants are hired to assist scientists in projects that demand advanced knowledge in mathematics. The mathematical consultant must not

A mathematician discusses theoretical mathematics with his colleagues. This collaboration can result in new findings.

only know considerably more mathematics than the scientists who seek the advice but must also have an understanding of the scientific fields in which the problems arise. These fields may be, for example, mechanics, electromagnetic theory, plasticity, or economics. Mathematicians with lesser training will usually work under the supervision of senior mathematicians, but they also need some familiarity with the other sciences, both natural and social.

Statisticians: Statisticians perform surveys, collect large amounts of data, and interpret the results. Many of the calculations are done using statistical software packages; however, statisticians must determine the validity and accuracy of their findings.

Actuaries: Actuaries use sophisticated probability and statistical measures to determine the level of premiums policy holders should pay an insurance company. They try to predict the number of claims on particular policies, thereby keeping the company financially successful. They also design insurance and pension programs.

Education

Persons with the interests and aptitudes for a career in the mathematical sciences usually make a series of decisions that eventually lead them to their choice of career. The first decision is to take four years of mathematics in the ninth through twelfth grades. Those who enter col-

lege with less than two years of high-school algebra and one year of geometry may have difficulty in keeping up with the standard college sequence for a mathematics major. On the other hand, those who are able to qualify for advanced placement may be able to start their college mathematics with the second or third semester of the standard sequence and thus acquire additional skills that will give them preferred opportunities in employment.

Once in college, a prospective math major must decide whether to continue mathematics in the first two years in college. If so, then the student must decide whether to qualify for a teacher's certificate or take graduate work in mathematics. These decisions should be made early enough in the junior or senior year so that the necessary preparatory courses such as advanced calculus are included in the undergraduate program. About one-fifth of those with a bachelor's degree in mathematics later earn a master's degree.

After earning a masters degree, a student may want to continue beyond the master's degree for a Ph.D. This decision should be made in consultation with faculty members who know the student's abilities in mathematical work. Some students with excellent grades in course work do not have the creative ability to write an original thesis. The Ph.D. is required, with rare exceptions, for positions in a college or university. Most of the higher-level positions in college teaching and some of the better positions in research and development are open only to those with a Ph.D., so those with the ability should seriously consider earning the doctorate. Those who hold the Ph.D. in applied mathematics could anticipate more opportunities for employment than Ph.D.s whose studies are more theoretical.

Some actuaries major in mathematics in college, and all must pass preliminary examinations based heavily on calculus, linear algebra, and probability and statistics. Yet the actuarial profession does not require graduate work in mathematics, and in a sense is not primarily a mathematical profession.

A student attains professional status as an actuary by taking a series of difficult and exacting examinations over a period of years. The initial examinations are administered jointly by the Society of Actuaries and the Casualty Actuarial Society. After completing the first five examinations of the series, the student becomes an Associate of the Society of Actuaries or an Associate of the Casualty Actuarial Society. After all nine examinations are passed, the student becomes a Fellow.

All math teachers should be competent in the basic techniques. The Committee on the

Undergraduate Program in Mathematics (C.U.P.M.) of the Mathematical Association of America recommends that all elementary teachers take college courses including, the structure of the real numbers system, the basic concepts of algebra, and geometry. Recommendations of C.U.P.M. for the training of teachers for grades seven to nine include courses in analytic geometry, calculus, history of mathematics, and at least one upper-level course in algebra and geometry. Math teachers for grades seven through nine should also have some knowledge of elementary concepts in set theory, logic, matrix theory, and probability theory.

Higher levels of training are needed for teachers at the upper levels. Those who teach the senior courses in high-school should have a college major in mathematics, and those who teach at the junior college or community college level should have a master's degree in mathematics and preferably a year of additional training.

Mathematics is rapidly becoming the language of all the sciences, physical, biological, and social. No longer are two years of high-school mathematics an adequate preparation for majoring in economics, business administration, or psychology in college. These subjects are making increasing use of statistical methods, linear programming, and other mathematical techniques that require at least a year of college mathematics and at least three years of college preparatory mathematics. A wide variety of occupations, including those of the bank clerk, plumber, or medical technologist requires some knowledge of high-school mathematics. More than the usual high-school training in mathematics may be required of airplane pilots or flight engineers and of technicians and drafters.

College-level mathematics is also helpful to such professional people as biological scientists, physicians, dentists, veterinarians, pharmacists, economists, accountants, marketing researchers, purchasing agents, business administrators, bankers, psychologists, anthropologists, sociologists, social workers, political scientists, home economists, dietitians, geologists, geographers and meteorologists, agricultural economists and research workers, soil conservationists, and foresters.

Industry outlook

Opportunities for those with a background in mathematics will be best in selected areas. The computer science area, for example, has become the fastest growing mathematics-related

The use and knowledge of computers is essential in the field of mathematics.

field. A single high-speed digital computer may require dozens or even hundreds of mathematicians and scientists to direct its high-speed calculations.

According to the U.S. government, employment for mathematicians is expected to increase about as fast as the average for all occupations through the year 2000. Opportunities for applied mathematicians with doctorate degrees appear especially strong. Below the Ph.D. level, the prospects are closely tied to the economy and the demand for technically trained personnel. However, for the near future, the competition for college positions will be intense.

Demands are growing significantly for those in many fields who are not primarily mathematicians but are conversant with mathematical language and can apply it successfully in their own areas. Thus every high-school student whether or not he or she plans to major in a mathematical or physical science should acquire as strong a mathematics background as possible.

About half of the people receiving bachelor's degrees in mathematics in recent years earned teaching certificates, but only about three-quarters of those with certificates actually entered the field of secondary school teaching in the year after graduation. Increasing enrollments in mathematics and mathematics-related fields accentuate the need for mathematics teachers qualified to prepare students for the demanding requirements in many of the newer applications of mathematics.

◇ **SOURCES OF ADDITIONAL INFORMATION**

American Mathematical Society
PO Box 6248
Providence, RI 02940

Mathematical Association of America
1529 18th Street, NW
Washington, DC 20036

Institute of Mathematical Statistics
3401 Investment Boulevard, Suite 7
Hayward, CA 94545

Society for Industrial and Applied Mathematics
1400 Architects Building
117 South 17th Street
Philadelphia, PA 19103

National Council of Teachers of Mathematics
1906 Association Drive
Reston, VA 22091

◇ **RELATED ARTICLES**

Volume 1: Accounting; Banking and Financial Services; Biological Sciences; Chemistry; Computer Hardware; Computer Software; Education; Engineering; Insurance; Nuclear Sciences; Physical Sciences

Volume 2: Accountants and auditors; Actuaries; Biomedical engineers; Chemists; College and university faculty; Computer programmers; Credit analysts, banking; Economists; Engineers; Industrial designers; Mathematicians; Numerical control tool programmers; Physicists; Statisticians; Surveyors; Systems analysts; Teachers, secondary schools

Volume 3: Bookkeeping and accounting clerks; Insurance policy processing occupations; Statistical clerks

Volume 4: Calibration technicians; Civil engineering technicians; Data-processing technicians; Integrated circuit technicians; Mathematical technicians; Software technicians

Metals

General information

The first crude metal objects, knives for hunting and tools for farming, raised humanity out of the darkness of the Stone Age. Forging metal (heating, then hammering the metal into shape) was used to shape simple blades and hoes.

Available data indicates that metal casting was being done around 4,000 B.C. Forged copper weapons preceded castings and led directly to the discovery of the casting art.

Soon after metal castings were invented, the people of the Black Sea area swept down on Mesopotamia, conquering large areas as they went. Their victories were due primarily to their stronger weapons, made from forged copper. Liquid metal was discovered accidentally during the forging of hot metal. While heating the metal for shaping, some of the copper would reach a temperature hot enough to melt it. So, casting the melted metal into a shape was tried. Casting would be a faster way to form metal.

The first molds were made in sand and clay, but it was soon found that permanent open molds were more desirable. Molds were then cut in stone, or formed in limestone or sunbaked clay, facilitating faster reproduction of more or less identical objects.

The casting process grew during the Bronze Age and developed rapidly in the Orient, where the art first matured industrially. Development in Europe progressed with the casting of guns, bells, stoves, and ornamental iron.

Casting in America started during the development of the colonies. Massachusetts has the honor of being the birthplace of the first American casting—the famous "Saugus Pot" in 1642.

With the advent of the Industrial Revolution, the production of machines and engines increased dramatically with the rise in technology. Mining became an extremely important industry, supplying the world with the materials required to build the machines that transformed society. Manufacturing the metals that would be used to create strong, durable engine pieces led to the development of industrial complexes and mining towns centered on either the production or manufacturing of metal products.

Steel, a stronger metal than iron, is made from iron with other minerals added. Modern, large-scale production of steel in the United States is generally considered to have begun when the first commercial batch of steel made by the Bessemer process was produced at Wyandotte, Michigan in the mid-1800s. This pneumatic process, developed independently by an American named William Kelly and an Englishman named Henry Bessemer, made it possible for the first time to produce steel by the ton instead of by the pound. The Bessemer process eventually was displaced by the open hearth process, which in turn is now being displaced by the oxygen and electric furnace processes.

As the competition increased from abroad, steel production began to decline in the 1970s in the United States. World demand for steel has remained about the same since the mid-1970s, at 475 million tons a year, but with the increased import of cheaper steel from foreign countries, the demand for American produced steel decreased. This decrease had to do, in part, with the inefficient and obsolete steel factories in Indiana and Pennsylvania.

In the early 1980s, the American industry modernized with oxygen-fired furnaces, brought down the cost of production through streamlining staff, and reducing the average wage, and was able to regain some of the market that had been lost.

The demand new and different metals fluctuates with the needs of the industries using the products. With each discovery that involves metals comes a new turn in the demand and the processing of the metal industry.

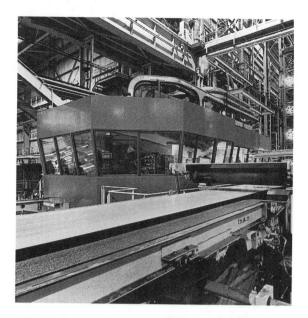

This highly automated control room operates an annealing production line that enhances the properties of steel sheets through precisely controlled heat treatment.

The structure of the metal industry

Metallurgy is the art and science of extracting metals from ores found in nature and preparing them for use by alloying, shaping, and heating treatment. Extractive metallurgy uses mineral processing operations to eliminate a great proportion of worthless rock by differences in density, magnetic susceptibility, or other properties. The resulting concentrate is then treated to produce the actual metal by processes that may use high temperatures, aqueous solutions, or electricity.

Nonferrous metallurgy is concerned with practically all metals except iron and steel. Ferrous metallurgy works with iron and steel. Metallurgy is the link between the mine and the finished product.

The extractive metallurgy industry receives raw material from the mines, removes the valuable metal minerals from the great preponderance of worthless rock, converts these minerals into metals, and then refines the metals to meet the demands of the market (see Volume 1: Mining). Some exceptions can be found to this general description, as, for example, when the raw material may be recovered scrap that has already served a useful purpose and now must be put through the system to be purified.

Physical metallurgy, in contrast, studies the structure and properties of metals and alloys for industrial use and for scientific purposes.

The nonferrous metals include eighty or more elements that are metallic, with the exception of iron and its alloys of steel. There is a fairly even division between the iron and steel industry and all of the other metals grouped together.

Copper, aluminum, gold, silver, zinc, and lead, as well as such comparative newcomers as tantalum, zirconium, uranium, and molybdenum have chemical and physical properties in the nonferrous metals that vary so greatly that the extractive and refining processes must also differ. In addition, the price and the final user will greatly dictate the size, type, and mode of operation of the plants.

The task of the workers in the extractive metallurgy business is to take a metal-bearing substance, convert the mineral or impure metal into a reasonably pure metal, and if need be, to refine it even further until it meets the most stringent requirements. The proverbial attempts to make a silk purse out of a sow's ear pale in comparison to the ability of the metallurgist to take the dull, rock-like ore as it is excavated from the earth's surface and, in a series of operations and processes, to convert it into usable metal for the forging, foundry, and casting procedures (see Volume 4: Metallurgical technicians).

The first step is assigning workers to obtain samples of an ore or mineral. The analytical laboratories will determine the amount of the desired metal in an area, the regularity of its distribution, and its mode of occurrence. These findings require not only chemical analysis but also more elaborate techniques, such as microscopy, spectroscopy, and X-ray diffraction.

With this basic information at hand, some decision must be made about possible processes of separating the metal from the surrounding elements. A preliminary step consists of reviewing the technical and patent literature to see what other companies have done in the past to recover this metal.

Another objective of the preliminary study is to determine what peculiar properties are possessed by the metal that might be the basis of a new separation process. Often, such studies can be made by technical librarians; computerized systems for searching databases and indexes have greatly enhanced speed and coverage.

Assuming that a new procedure is to be attempted, the first experiments will be made on a small scale, probably in a glass apparatus by technical personnel. Again, the results must be determined by analytical means.

If the small-scale investigations are encouraging, the next step is to enlarge the scale of operations. This will require special equipment, and now the skills of the carpenters, machinists, welders, electricians, and other trades are needed. When the experiments are scheduled, much of the work will be done by the workers under direction of the scientific staff. The analytical laboratory will receive more and more samples.

Now, if the results are favorable again, it is time to make a careful economic evaluation. Engineering studies are required to estimate the costs of installation and operation. Economic studies must be made on the production and consumption of the metal to determine whether the present market price is realistic and what new production will do to this price. Patent attorneys must try to obtain patents on the new process. Management must decide if it is prepared to embark on this new venture.

The whole development represents the cooperative efforts of a wide variety of employees, most of them having a specialized or technical skill.

After the mining of the unrefined metal, the next process is the conversion of the metal into a usable substance. With iron and other metals such as copper, the process is well established.

Steel making takes unprocessed iron ore and strengthens it with processing. It begins with the production of its raw materials, notably iron ore, coal, and limestone. Iron ore is mined and processed into pellets, which are loaded into ships and railroad cars for transport to steel mills (see Volume 3: Iron and steel industry workers).

Processing operations covers three major areas: the blast furnace, where iron ore is heated and combined with other elements to drive off impurities and leave only the iron itself; the steel furnaces, where steel is made by adding alloying agents such as silicon and manganese to give the steel added strength or other desired properties; and rolling and finishing, where the raw steel is shaped into finished and semifinished products.

At the steel mill, the iron is smelted (melted to separate the iron from the other elements) into pig iron in blast furnaces with the help of coke, an almost pure carbon material processed from coal. The molten iron is then transported to steel making furnaces, where it is further refined into raw steel, or cast into pigs (shapes used for storing steel) for use by foundries.

Liquid steel leaves the furnace through a tap hole and flows into a ladle. A hot-metal crane operator controls an overhead crane that picks up the ladle of liquid steel and moves it over a long row of iron molds that will shape the steel into ingots (cast blocks). A worker operates a stopper at the bottom of the ladle to let the steel flow into these molds. Finally, ingot strippers, operating overhead cranes, remove the molds from the ingots, which are sent on for rolling and finishing.

Where steel products are made from ingots, the heated ingots are squeezed between two cylinders or rolls. Before the ingots are rolled, they are heated to a specified temperature. The heating is done in large furnaces located in the plant floor called soaking pits.

A heater operates the soaking pits, assisted by helpers. The heater determines the exact time when the ingots are ready for rolling.

The ingots are placed in the soaking pits by the crane operator who controls an overhead crane. When the ingots are sufficiently heated, the crane operator removes them and maneuvers them onto the rolling machinery, where they are rolled into semifinished shapes, blooms, slabs, or billets.

The roller is in charge of the rolling mill. He works in a glass-enclosed control booth and operates levers and buttons that determine the speed at which the ingots are rolled and the width of the opening between the rollers. The roller is assisted by a manipulator operator, who runs the controls that position the ingots on the roller conveyor.

On leaving the rolling mill, the red-hot slab, billet, or bloom moves along a conveyor to a place where a shear operator controls a heavy hydraulic shear that cuts the steel into desired lengths.

Semifinished steel forms produced by continuous casters do not require this kind of primary rolling. Instead, after a certain amount of reheating, they can be rolled directly into finished products on finishing mills.

After the steel is rolled, most of it is put through finishing operations. Slabs, for example, can be reduced into sheets, and billets can be made into bars, rods, and pipe.

In recent years, the steel industry has increasingly employed continuous casting to make semifinished steel. This process, which now accounts for about 30 percent of total U.S. raw steel production, produces steel ready for final processing directly from liquid steel, bypassing the processing steps associated with ingot casting. This makes the steel production process more efficient.

In continuous casting, a ladle of molten steel is placed above the tundish, or reservoir, of a continuous caster. The steel is then released into the tundish, from which it flows into a long, curved, water-cooled mold at a controlled rate. The steel solidifies during its descent, and is solid when it emerges at the bottom of the caster. It is then cut to length by torches. Casters produce forms ready for final forming: slabs, blooms, billets, and tube rounds.

Metals

A forge shop inspector measures a completed product to determine whether it meets the exact specifications required.

Most steel made in the United States today is produced in basic oxygen furnaces. About 30 percent is made in electric furnaces that can use up to 100 percent ferrous scrap as raw material. Less than 5 percent of steel is still made in open hearths.

The raw steel is converted into basic products, such as billets, blooms, and slabs. Further processing is required to make other products, such as tinplate, pipe, wire, sheet, plates, bars, and structural shapes.

The three principal methods of shaping metal in plants are rolling, casting, and forging.

The forging process shapes metal by hammering or by tremendous pressure that forces the metal into cavities in a set of matching dies. This produces a metal part that is unusually strong and resistant to strain. Forging workers are employed by independent forging plants and in forging departments of such manufacturers as automobile, steel, and farm machinery (see Volume 3: Forge shop occupations).

The metals most commonly forged are iron, steel, nickel, titanium, aluminum, and bronze.

The hot metal, under enormous hammer blows or continuous press pressures, flows be-

tween two matching dies containing a cavity shaped exactly like the part desired. It flows in the pattern required for the best properties. Just as clay responds to pressure and takes on a particular shape when you work it in your hands, heated forging-quality metal responds to the shaping and sizing effect of the forging dies as they are pressed or struck against the metal by automatic equipment.

To best understand the beneficial effects of what the forging process does to metals, it is necessary to consider grain flow. In nature grain flow is found in trees. Wood grain grows in the way that best strengthens the tree. Forging, and only forging, creates the fiber-like flow lines that add so much to the strength of a metal part.

Forging press operators work on either huge mechanical or hydraulic forging presses that shape hot metal stock by squeezing it between either open or closed impression dies. The skills of operators in open die forging press work are similar to those of a hammer smith, because both groups of workers handle metal stock between two open or flat dies. Closed impression die press operators work to more exacting design specifications than open die press operators, but do not need the handling skill of the open die press operators.

Open and closed impression die press operators must know how to control the heating of metals, regulate the pressure of the machines they use, and position the work between the dies. Their duties may also include setting up the dies in the presses.

Casting, the activity of the foundry industry, is a method of metal forming in which molten metal is poured into a prepared mold, often having a core within the mold, to form a hollow cavity within the finished metal casting. Castings play a vital role in our national economy and daily life.

The largest tonnage of castings is produced in sand molds. Sand molds include green sand molds, which are a mixture of sand, clay, and water, and dry sand molds, which are baked or flame-dried before the mold is poured. Other molds are made of metal, plaster, ceramics, resin-bonded sands, and chemically bonded sands.

The foundry, or metal casting industry, uses the metal while it is liquid to shape it. Most solid materials have freezing or melting points. Metals, too, have freezing or melting points. The melting points of metals and alloys (two or more chemical elements, one of which is a metal) vary greatly. Pure metals such as tin, lead, zinc, and copper freeze at one constant temperature whereas alloys freeze over a range of temperatures. This is of prime importance to foundry workers who deal with the melting, pouring, and solidification of metal alloys.

A casting, then, is a metal object formed to a predetermined shape by pouring or injecting liquid metal into a mold. In making the mold, the molder places the pattern in a two-part box called the flask. The top half is called the cope, the lower half, the drag. Cope and drag parts of the mold are made with pattern molders in place and packing (ramming) sand firmly around the pattern and throughout the mold. A tapered sprue pin is included in the cope, through which the metal will be poured. If required, cores are placed in the drag cavity to allow a hollow shape to be made.

The mold is then checked, cleaned, vented, closed, clamped or weighted, and made ready for pouring. After pouring, the molds are allowed to cool to solidify the castings. The castings are then shaken out and cleaned.

Of the several forging methods and kinds of equipment available, those used in a given instance depend on factors such as number of parts to be made and characteristics of the material and shape to be forged. But in all cases, the process operates on the same principle and results in tough, uniform, and strong products that will have outstanding qualities as operating parts after processing and final assembly.

The larger forge plants and departments hire many engineers to work as a team on any one forging job. Crews, generally consisting of from two to ten people, operate the forging equipment used to pound or press metal parts into shape. In smaller plants, however, an engineer might be required to put to use the complete range of knowledge required to produce a given part.

Today's production demands require that castings be made much faster and more uniform than hand operations permit. High-production foundries and some jobbing foundries, therefore, use machines for molding, core making, and cleaning whenever possible. Automatic and semiautomatic equipment in modern foundries produce at high production rates. Hand operations are also minimized with power-driven tools. Recent developments use automatic pouring and mechanized handling and cleaning of castings. Molding machines are capable of producing hundreds of completed molds per hour, and the same is true in core making.

Throughout the United States and Europe, foundries exist primarily as jobbing foundries and captive foundries. Jobbing foundries are operated independently, and even though they may have machining, welding, and other facilities, final processing of finished products is not

Molten steel pours out of a tap and into a ladle where it is refined before it is molded into a designated shape.

their business. They produce casting for customers.

Captive foundries are owned and operated by manufacturing organizations who use them to produce castings for their own use. An automotive foundry, for example, produces thousands of brakes, engine blocks, housings, engine heads, manifolds, crankshafts, valves, and smaller castings.

Foundries may be ferrous (iron-base alloys) or nonferrous, pouring alloys such as aluminum, brass, bronze, or magnesium that contain no appreciable amounts of iron. Ferrous foundries produce the larger tonnage, with the greatest production in cast iron.

In 1970, the United States produced 131.5 million tons of raw steel, the highest production level in thirty years. By 1982, production had dropped to 74.5 million tons. In 1987, production had risen to more than 89 million tons, with the levels fluctuating in the intervening years.

In 1989, the United States produced as estimated 16.6 million tons of aluminum, 2 million tons of copper, and 1 million tons of lead.

A metallurgical technician uses an electron microscope to analyze the purity of the metals used at the foundry.

Careers

There are several areas of employment and training in the metal industry: research and development, production of raw materials, production of refined materials, and production of a finished product. A sampling of career opportunities follows below.

Metallurgists: These scientists and engineers are concerned with extracting metals from ores, refining them for use, producing and preparing alloying elements, and developing methods for using metals safely and economically. This is called metallurgical engineering. The terms metallurgist and metallurgical engineer are frequently used interchangeably.

Physical metallurgists: Physical metallurgists work for the producers of metallurgical products and are concerned with the specifications imposed on their products by the consumer industries. They set up and control the procedures that will be used to transform the raw materials into final products, so that the sizes, shapes, and properties will meet the specifications of the consumer industries. They are concerned with inspection procedures that ensure quality control in the production processes.

Blowers: Blowers oversee the operations of one or more blast furnaces. They coordinate the addition of raw materials by stock house workers and they supervise keepers and their helpers in tapping the liquid iron and the impurities from the furnace.

Stove tenders: Tenders operate gas-fired stoves that heat air for the blast furnaces. They also control the air entering the furnaces and keep the stove flues free of carbon and dirt.

Melters: The melting department is responsible for producing molten metal for the molds. Metal may be melted in such furnaces as crucible, cupola, electric (induction or direct arc), open-hearth, or air furnace. Melters make the steel according to desired specifications by varying the proportions of iron, scrap metal, lime, and other alloying elements in the furnace. A melter supervises the workers who load the furnace with raw materials, directs the taking of samples of liquid steel, and coordinates the loading and melting of raw materials with the steel molding and casting operations.

Metallurgists, melters, furnace operators, supervisors, and laboratory control personnel work in or for the melting department. New foundry workers often start in melting operations, where they are assigned a specific responsibility.

Molders: The molding department produces the metal molds, some by hand, but most by machine. Molders are responsible for their molds. They may or may not be responsible for their sand, including the mixing and control. Most foundries have a sand laboratory where sand technicians make laboratory tests and record data for proper sand control. Some careers in sand control today are highly specialized (see Volume 3: Molders).

Forge engineers: Forge engineers make the critical production decisions. They design the basic part to meet customer specifications regarding weight, strength, and cost. They select the best materials, processing methods, and equipment to meet these requirements and make final preparation of the dies, materials, and equipment for the production process. Finally, they must follow through on instructions for finishing operations such as trimming, grinding, chipping, and cleaning.

Die sinkers: Die sinkers are highly skilled craft workers with a broad knowledge of forging technology. They use a variety of machines and hand operations to transfer the shape of the product to be forged from blueprints to blocks of metal to be used as dies in forging equipment.

When the forging design has been completed and approved by the forge engineer, the die sinker, after consulting with the designer on any special details of the job, begins the process of sinking the desired shape or impression in die blocks of high alloy steel. Die sinkers are responsible for preparing exactly aligned matching upper and lower die blocks to make a die set.

Hammer smiths: Hammer smiths control steam-driven hammers, equipped with open or flat dies, that pound pieces of hot metal called blanks into particular shapes. They interpret blueprints, drawings, or sketches to determine how to work the metal under the steam-driven hammer.

Drop hammer operators: This position operates forging equipment that pounds heated metal into shape between closed impression dies, which have been grooved to make the metal flow into the desired location. They must use special care to position the metal under the hammer. The level of skill required increases with the size of the hammer and the metal stock and the complexity of the forging.

Upsetters: Another type of forging machine operator, an upsetter applies pressure to hot metal being shaped between closed impression dies.

Heaters: Heaters control the supply of fuel and air in furnaces that heat different metals to the most suitable temperatures for forging (see Volume 3: Heat treaters).

Inspectors: Inspectors check semifinished and finished forgings for size, shape, quality, and other specifications. Inspectors may use micrometers, calipers, or other measuring devices to determine whether forged parts meet the exact specifications required.

Metal cleaners and finishers: Many forge shop workers are employed in cleaning and finishing operations. For example, trimmers remove excess metals from hot or cold finished forge pieces with presses equipped with trimming dies. Chippers use pneumatic hammers to remove imperfections from stock. Grinders remove rough edges from completed forgings with mechanically powered abrasive wheels. Blasters operate sandblasting or shot-blasting equipment to clean and smooth forgings. Picklers dip forgings in an acid solution to remove scale. Heat treaters improve the physical properties of forgings by heating and cooling metals under controlled conditions.

Coremakers: In the coremaking department, coremakers, apprentices, supervisors, and semiskilled workers produce and bake the cores required by the foundry. Made by hand and also by machine, the core must be just as accurate and dependable as the mold (see Volume 3: Coremakers).

Patternmakers: Patternmaking is a highly skilled craft, one that requires specialized training and accurate workmanship. The patternmaker requires an exact replica of the casting to be produced, usually made of wood, metal, plaster, wax, or plastic (see Volume 3: Patternmakers).

Millwrights: Millwrights overhaul machinery and repair and replace defective parts (see Volume 3: Millwrights).

Die makers: Die makers use machine tools to form dies (see Volume 3: Tool makers and die

At the end of the production line, a metal finisher inspects steel sheets.

makers; and Volume 4: Tap-and-die maker technicians).

Education

All of these jobs require knowledge in the areas of design principles, properties of various alloys, die materials, grain flow and tolerances, forging equipment and techniques, and heating methods. Much of this knowledge can only be gained through on-the-job experience, but engineers and metallurgists can concentrate their efforts on these particular areas in college courses offered with a view to seeking employment in the forging industry upon graduation.

A college degree in engineering or science, with an emphasis on courses in design, metallurgy, and production, is essential to enter the engineering and science area in the metal industry. Postgraduate study is also recommended to assure advancement in this area.

The research and development phase of extractive metallurgy requires a technical staff of trained engineers and scientists. A large number of these technical employees must have a master's degree or doctorate as evidence of their familiarity with research procedures. At

From a control room, a supervisor operates the straightening, cutting, and piling of steel slabs.

one time, graduate engineers were used in analytical laboratories, but this is not as common today.

Most of the workers in the mechanical trades learn their skills through on-the-job training and work experience. As they acquire experience and skills they progress from the simple to the more difficult jobs. Advancement to the skilled job of hammer smith, for example, requires several years of on-the-job experience and training.

The basic entry job on hammer, upsetter, and press crews is that of helper. Employers usually require only basic education for helpers and other workers in entry occupations, but high-school graduates are given preference. After a worker has served as a helper on a hammer, upsetter, or press crew he or she may be graduated to one of the more skilled jobs, such as heater, hammer smith, hammer operator, or press operator.

A few companies offer apprenticeship training programs for the more skilled jobs such as die sinker, heat treater, hammer smith, hammer operator, and press operator.

There are a number of apprenticeship training programs to prepare beginners for skilled trades and crafts in steel work. These programs may require up to four years of work under the direction of an experienced craft worker. The apprentice usually receives shop training and classroom instruction in related subjects. This classroom work may be within the company or in local vocational schools. Companies have

different qualifications for apprentice applicants. A number of companies provide some form of financial assistance, through scholarships, fellowships, and loans, to help deserving students pursue higher education.

Education is often the key to advancement. Some companies operate their own schools in various subjects so that employees may attend one or two nights a week.

Due to the special nature of metal products, salespeople are often called upon to provide technical advice. Therefore, college graduation is practically a necessity to enter this area, although it is possible to take a major in any one of several fields. An engineering degree in design, metallurgy, or production, with a minor in sales and marketing subjects would greatly help a person's advancement in this field. The person who can combine the attributes of a salesperson with the technical knowledge of the experienced engineer has an outstanding opportunity to go far in the industry.

Emphasis on environmental quality control opened opportunities for qualified candidates with ecologically-oriented disciplines. Many of the industry's leaders began their careers in the engineering and production area. Graduates in law, business administration, and accounting also have the opportunity to enter and rise through the industry's executive ranks.

Industry outlook

The production of metals is a basic industry of enormous size. Yearly production is subject to some fluctuation, but the continuing trend is sharply upward in response to the ever-increasing demand of our complex, technologically based society. The United States is one of the foremost producers of many of the metals, such as copper, lead, and zinc. But even so, the domestic production must be augmented by imports to match domestic consumption.

Even though the total metal production in the United States increased, mineral deposits are a waning asset and some metal-producing localities are on the decline or will soon face such a decline. An example is the copper industry of the Upper Peninsula of Michigan, which was once the leading copper district in the United States, but which later produced only a fraction of its former output. A similar drop in metal production and corresponding decrease in employment occurred in the lead-zinc districts of Kansas, Missouri, and Oklahoma, known as the Tri-State area.

Although production-line opportunities will continue to open up as present steelworkers retire or leave the industry, total hourly employment is not expected to grow as rapidly as long-term production. One reason is that the introduction of new labor-saving technologies is increasing the potential output per worker. Production also varies from year to year, because of the steel industry's sensitivity to general economic conditions.

Continuing mechanization of the forging process may limit somewhat the growth of employment in forge shop occupations. Automation will primarily affect the employment of helpers and unskilled laborers, since the latest mechanical developments in the forging process are designed to reduce the amount of unskilled work in many forging operations. Nonetheless, mechanization means cheaper prices which leads to more steel orders and ultimately more jobs.

However, mechanization is creating new jobs in the science and engineering area of the forging industry, as well as placing increased demands on and expanding the need for office and administrative personnel. Automation has little effect upon the need for skilled hammersmiths, forge-press operators, and die sinkers who are all much in demand, because machines cannot be easily substituted for the training and experience of these workers. The increased competition from other processes, including newer metalworking processes, has stepped up requirements for sales and distribution personnel to publicize the advantages of the forging process over these other methods of making parts.

From time to time, an argument develops about the supply of engineers and scientists in the United States and whether shortages will become acute. As far as physical metallurgists are concerned, there is almost never any argument. The number of new graduates in metallurgy each year is much smaller than the number of available positions. Despite a growing need for physical metallurgists in industry and government, the number of professionals in this field has remained fairly constant.

The U.S. Bureau of Labor Statistics predicts that additional metallurgists will be needed in the future to help solve problems of nuclear energy production and solid waste disposal. They may also be called on to produce new methods for processing low-grade ores. Employment was expected to grow faster than the average for all occupations through the mid-1990s.

The metal industry is a diversified one. Changing needs for new materials often direct or redirect educational emphasis in the field. Metallurgists were able to find employment even during depressions and recessions in the past, and they are in especially short supply during periods of economic expansion.

This ladle refining unit removes unwanted particles, and maintains a constant temperature prior to casting.

◇ SOURCES OF ADDITIONAL INFORMATION

Minerals, Metals, and Materials Society
420 Commonwealth Drive
Warrendale, PA 15086

ASM International—American Society for Metals
Metals Park, OH 44073

Office of Minerals, Metals, and Commodities
US Department of Commerce
Washington, DC 20230

American Iron and Steel Institute
1133 15th Street
Washington, DC 20005

American Foundrymen's Society
Golf and Wolf Roads
Des Plaines, IL 60016

Forging Industry Educational and Research Foundation
25 Prospect Avenue, West, Number 300/LTV
Cleveland, OH 44115

Metals

American Cast Metals Association
455 State Street, Suite 201
Des Plaines, IL 60016

Materials Properties Council
345 East 47th Street
New York, NY 10017

Association of Iron and Steel Engineers
3 Gateway Center, Suite 2350
Plttsburgh, PA 15222

◇ **RELATED ARTICLES**

Volume 1: Machining and Machinery; Mining
Volume 3: Coremakers; Forge shop occupations; Heat treaters; Iron and steel industry workers; Job and die setters; Millwrights; Molders; Patternmakers; Pinsetter mechanics; Sheetmetal workers; Tool makers and die makers
Volume 4: Metallurgical technicians; Tap-and-die maker technicians

Military Service

General information

The American armed forces are responsible for the safety and protection of the United States. Five separate military services make up the armed forces: Army, Navy, Air Force, Marine Corps, and Coast Guard. These branches organize, train, and equip the nation's land, sea, and air services to support the national and international policies of the government. Those who choose to be members of the armed forces dedicate their lives to protect their fellow Americans.

America's first military force, the Continental Army, was established in 1775 to fight the British. So valued was the Army, that its commander and most revered general, George Washington, became the first President of the United States.

The Army remains the oldest branch of the military, followed by the Navy, which was officially established in 1798. The Marine Corps had been considered part of the Navy until 1834, when it established itself as both a land and sea defense force, thereby becoming its own military branch. Similarly, the Air Force was part of the Army until 1947, making it the youngest of the five military branches.

The Civil War was America's most tragic military incident, with Americans suffering more casualties than in any other war. America asserted itself as a military power in World War I, but social influences within the country led to a period of isolationism, where America reduced the size of its military and removed itself from foreign affairs. After the surprise attack at Pearl Harbor, America was forced into World War II, emerging as the strongest power of the Western world. Unlike the isolationist trend that occurred before World War II, the United States became involved in foreign affairs. Its presence was felt throughout the world, generating a new non-violent Cold War. Fear of the Communists led to propagandistic Pro-American sentiments and increased military spending.

This sense of American pride in its military extended through the Korean War. It was not until the Vietnam War in the mid-1960s that the American military policy was challenged by the younger generation. This challenge demanded a reevaluation of the American presence in foreign countries. For the first time in American history, the military was not a respected institution. Students burned their draft cards and others fled the country to avoid the draft.

Since Vietnam, the military has done much to improve its image, trying to make the military an appealing career option. The abolition of the draft has made it even more challenging for the military to recruit talented men and women.

Through the course of American military history, there have been a series of technological improvements that have changed the structure of the military. From the airplane to nuclear-powered submarines, chemical warfare to hydrogen bombs, the military has had to adapt and adjust its internal structure. These developments have changed the focus of the military, making many positions obsolete or less necessary and creating new ones.

While national safety was always a concern, the draft was not installed until the Civil War, when men were recruited for both the North and the South. At that time, military service was still not compulsory, rather the draft was established to inspire volunteers. After the war, conscription ended, reappearing years later for World War I. The draft ended a second time after World War I, being reinstated once again in 1940 for World War II. The government did not abolish the draft until 1973.

The Reserved Army Training Corps, otherwise known as ROTC, was established in 1916. It was designed to provide a basic college and military education to those who wished to become future officers. It gave these students the

A tank commander gives directions to other members of his group while practicing strategic maneuvers. Such military exercises prepare the army for combat in the event of war.

opportunity to qualify for commissions while in college. A similar program was installed for the Navy in 1926. In 1964, Congress strengthened the ROTC program by allowing it to award college scholarships and loans to students in exchange for military service.

The structure of the military services

Five separate services make up the armed forces. They are the Army, Navy, Air Force, Marine Corps, and Coast Guard. All are similar, but they are sufficiently different from the each other to warrant separate classifications.

The Army is the senior service. It is traditionally known as the branch that fights on land. Most of America's twenty-eight million living veterans have served in the Army, the largest of the services in total recruits.

The Navy, more than any of the other services, has a special way of life. Guided by traditions of the sea, it is in many ways more of a closed society than its sister services. Its officers and enlisted people work and live together at sea for long periods. Life at sea demands close attention to duties and teamwork. Ships and aircraft units visit many parts of the world. It is

a strange and wonderful life and strongly appealing to many who are looking for a different and exciting type of career.

The Air Force, newest of all the services, is highly technical and appeals to those interested in aviation and mechanical trades.

The Marine Corps, known as the "first to fight," operates on the land and sea. It is closely associated with the Navy, and like the Navy, it prides itself on meeting the highest possible standards in training, military bearing, and discipline.

The Coast Guard is a relatively small service and, as such, offers unique opportunities. It is oriented largely toward the enforcement of military law. In addition, it is involved with activities like searching and rescuing those in distress at sea and maritime law enforcement. Although opportunities exist for overseas assignments, many duties in the Coast Guard are related to the waters and shores of the United States. Unlike the other military branches, the Coast Guard is a service of the Department of Transportation except when operating as part of the Navy in time of war or when the president so directs.

Some decide to combine civilian life with part-time military service by becoming reservists or members of the National Guard. National Guard reservists agree to certain limited-duty assignments on weekends or during vacations. As service people, they serve their country and receive many special benefits (including retirement pay), but they work at civilian jobs in communities of their choice.

The actual structure of the miliary is pyramidal, with the President of the United States as the Commander-in-chief of the armed forces. The President's responsibilities include appointing top military officers and maintaining the nation's military strength.

The Secretary of Defense is an appointed position that is usually awarded to a civilian. He or she is a member of the President's Cabinet, presiding over the Department of Defense and directing the operations of all military branches. The Joint Chiefs of Staff, consisting of heads of four military branches, works with the Secretary of Defense to advise the President on military matters. The Department of Defense is located in the Pentagon, which also houses the Army, Navy, and Air Force.

There are two types of positions available in the military: enlisted personnel and officers. The enlisted members execute the daily operations of the military. The highest rank that an enlisted person may achieve in the Army is sergeant major (or related rank in the other branches). They are considered noncommissioned officers. Commissioned officers function as managers of the military, overseeing the work of the enlisted personnel.

Each service has nine enlisted grades and ten officer ranks. Promotion depends on a person's ability and on the time since the last promotion. On the average, a diligent enlisted person can expect to earn one of the middle noncommissioned or petty officer ratings (E-6 or E-7); most officers can expect to go to lieutenant colonel or commander (O-5). Outstanding individuals advance beyond those levels.

The names of ranks vary among the services. This is why the services have adopted a simple numbering system to denote rank. E-1 is at the bottom, with E standing for enlisted. An E-1 is a recruit. In the Army, the enlisted grades are private (E-1, E-2), private first class (E-3), corporal (E-4), sergeant (E-5), staff sergeant (E-6), sergeant first class (E-7), master sergeant (E-8), and sergeant major (E-9). Various technical specialists' designations are used among the three services for the enlisted grades. An E-9 is the most senior noncommissioned officer (in the Army) or petty officer (in the Navy).

An O-1 (O stands for officer) is a second lieutenant or ensign. An O-6 is a colonel or a Navy or a Coast Guard captain and an O-7 is a one-star general or rear admiral.

Military personnel are trained to operate many types of equipment and to perform in nearly all climates.

Women have become an integral part of the Army, Navy, Air Force, Marines, and Coast Guard. The five services accept women for officer and enlisted jobs. About 10 percent of the members of the services on active duty are women, and they are eligible for about nine out of ten military specialties. Federal law prohibits them from duty that may expose them to direct combat, such as service as a fighter pilot or tank crew member. Women are found increasingly, however, in many military occupations not traditionally filled by females, such as heavy equipment operations or helicopter maintenance.

Minimum terms of duty for young women wishing to enter the armed forces vary among the services. The requirements for women in some instances are different from those set out for the men. Service women must be high-school graduates and be eighteen years old. The Coast Guard will consider female candidates who are not high-school graduates but who have GEDs. The Coast Guard is the only service where women may enter all career fields. It should be noted that requirements change from time to time.

The pay for the equivalent grades in all services is the same. It starts comparatively low and rises to a more substantial salary for top officers and enlisted people. The services, how-

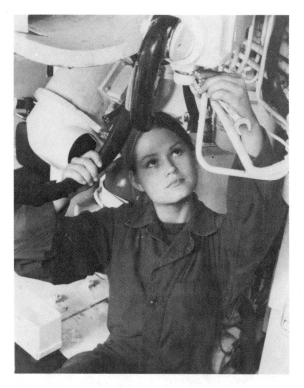

A mechanic repairs the hydraulic system in a tank turret.

Military people may apply for retirement after twenty years of service. At about age forty, a person is still in the prime of life for most work, and although the retirement pay is comparatively good, military retirees generally want to start new careers in civilian life and settle in one place. Thus retired service people often start new careers. The military training usually has prepared a person for a related trade or profession, and many military people look forward to the early retirement. They view it as an excellent opportunity to take a civilian job and keep the financial cushion of military retirement pay. Others, of course, prefer to stay in the service longer or for their entire working lives; generally speaking, only the more senior service members have that opportunity. Even in retirement, it should be noted, service people are subject to recall in times of national emergency.

Careers

The armed forces offer not just a single profession or trade but also a great variety of jobs wrapped up in a very distinctive way of life.

Members of the military services can be infantrymen, sailors, pilots, mechanics, physicians, radio repairers, engineers, gun crew members, lawyers, or deep-sea divers. Whatever the work, they are part of an ancient organization that has created its own society.

Each of the services offers a variety of trades and professions. Here is a small sampling of careers available:

Administrative support specialists: Administrative support specialists maintain files, record information, and type reports and correspondence. They usually work in office settings on land or aboard ship.

Air crew members: Air crew members operate in-flight refueling systems, defensive guns on bombers, or submarine detection systems. They work in all types of aircraft, from cargo planes and bombers to helicopters.

Airplane pilots: Airplane pilots plan flying missions and fly jet fighters, high-altitude reconnaissance planes, or cargo planes. They fly their airplanes to and from military bases in the United States and overseas.

Electronic weapons systems repairers: Electronic weapons systems repairers perform electrical, mechanical, and electronic repairs on one type of weapons system. Repairs are usually performed in specially equipped workshops.

Infantrymen: Infantrymen read military maps, fire weapons, and prepare for enemy at-

ever, also supply basic necessities—food, shelter, health care—that must be paid out of salaries in most civilian positions. Congress sets the pay scales after hearing the recommendations of the President.

In addition to the basic pay rates, hazardous duty pay may be earned by enlisted personnel who frequently and regularly participate in combat. Other special allowances include special duty assignment pay and foreign duty pay.

Generally, people retiring from the service receive at least one-half of their base pay at the end of twenty years and 75 percent of their basic pay at the end of thirty years. Retirement provisions are often changed, so all retirement provisions should be verified before enlistment.

Military men and women receive a number of additional benefits. They include recreational facilities, all medical and dental care, schools for dependents, and personal advice on matters of finance, legal assistance, and religious support.

The widow or widower of a service member who died on active duty or after a service-connected disability discharge will receive, for life or until remarriage, a monthly payment computed on the basis of the deceased spouse's rank. The surviving spouse also receives disability insurance.

tacks. They may also have responsibilities as drill instructors.

Intelligence officers: Intelligence officers collect and analyze information on the military forces, governments, and people of other countries. They often work with sophisticated intelligence-gathering equipment.

Military police: Military police (MPs) stand guard, conduct patrols, and enforce military rules and regulations. MPs are usually assigned to a security or law enforcement unit at a military base.

Radar and sonar operators: Radar and sonar operators identify, classify, and track objects. They work in operations centers or command and control facilities on land or aboard aircraft, ships, or submarines.

Special operations forces: Special operations forces carry out especially difficult and dangerous missions. They are trained to fight in all types of climates and environments. The Army Green Berets, the Navy SEALS, and the Air Force Pararescue Teams are special operations forces.

Members of each of the services often have responsibilities that are greater than those found at the same level of most other careers. A rifle-carrying private is responsible for the lives of the others in the squad; a sergeant leads and cares for a group of people; and an officer frequently will be responsible for thousands of men and women and millions of dollars worth of equipment.

Most military people expect to lead outdoor lives even in peacetime. Soldiers may train in tropical forests; sailors may cruise the Mediterranean and Far East; Marines may make mock landings on Caribbean islands; air crews may fly across the world; Coast Guard personnel sail along U.S. shores, but also explore Arctic ice fields and may go overseas.

Education

A person can enter military service at various ages and levels in education. Many recruits enter the military immediately after graduating high school. Educational opportunities, for those who wish them, are available after entering the service. The range of educational opportunities is diverse. A young person can be trained to operate the engineering equipment of an aircraft carrier or, with appropriate academic qualifications, proceed through medical training to become a military physician.

A broad general difference between the requirements for enlisted personnel and officers is academic preparation. There is no rigid rule,

A technician for the Navy tracks the position of a submarine.

but generally officers have college degrees, whereas enlisted people do not. Frequently, however, service members in both categories obtain degrees on their own initiative and with financial help while in the service.

The military services use every opportunity to advance the education of their recruits. More than 300,000 men and women are graduated from service schools each year, and many more thousands get financial help on outside education.

Leaders—the top enlisted personnel and the officers—must have special schooling as well as enthusiasm and drive. All service personnel get special training in military skills. Those who want to rise in the ranks will have the opportunity to attend school or undertake independent study and will be rewarded with advancement. Military education in many instances is related to civilian occupations, an added incentive for those who decide later not to make a career of military service.

Service schools for the most part, require more physical activity than their civilian counterparts. Servicemen and servicewomen almost always engage in some form of physical exercise. Some assignments require special athletic ability such as jumping from planes, swimming with underwater breathing apparatus, climbing cliffs, engaging in hand-to-hand combat, and hiking. Even service members with desk duty tend to exercise a great deal. They jog, play tennis and racquetball, swim, and participate generally in athletic activities.

Those who intend to serve as enlisted personnel should first finish high school and then

American military personnel are transported to stations all over the world. While abroad, they must operate under the rules and regulations of the military.

enlist. High-school graduates are more likely to be successful in the military than non-graduates, and the services accept very few non-high-school graduates. All applicants for each of the five services must take the Armed Services Vocational Aptitude Battery (ASVAB) as a requirement for enlistment. The ASVAB is offered at most high schools, in addition to being offered at approximately sixty-eight military entrance processing stations across the nation.

The different services' requirements for enlisted personnel are as follows:

Army: A man or woman between the ages of seventeen and thirty-five may enlist for two, three, four, five, or six years. High-school graduates may ask to take a special examination that will qualify them for schooling in one of scores of military specialties—many of which are directly related to civilian occupations.

Navy: Applicants between the ages of seventeen and thirty- four may enlist. Navy enlistment is usually for four years. However, three-, five-, or six-year enlistments are also available depending on the programs selected. Qualified high-school graduates can choose from special

fields and be guaranteed schooling in those fields.

Air Force: Applicants must be at least seventeen years old and enlist for a period of four years. Persons with enough education and a good score on the tests may choose training in one of four broad areas: electronics, mechanical, administrative, and general.

Marine Corps: The age for application is seventeen to twenty-nine, and the term of enlistment is three, four, or six years. Marines receive training and assignments in a wide variety of fields. Women are eligible to enlist in all occupational fields except combat arms (for example, infantry, artillery, and tank crews) and some combat support and aviation operations specialties.

Coast Guard: Persons aged seventeen to twenty-eight years old can enlist for four years. The Coast Guard prides itself on its ability to give personal consideration to the needs of its members in making training and duty assignments. After basic training, graduates will find challenges as diverse as serving on law enforcement vessels, search and rescue aircraft or ships, environmental task forces, or in the data-processing and telecommunication fields. Qualified persons can be guaranteed schooling in almost any field.

In addition to regular enlistments, all services offer reserve enlistments for persons who want a part-time military career or who want to try it out before regular enlistment. The requirements and opportunities are many and varied. Reserve and National Guard units, service recruiters, and the services whose addresses are listed at the end of this article can provide further information.

There are many routes to an officer's commission. A primary route for the nation's top high-school graduates is through the service academies—the Military Academy (West Point, N.Y.), the Naval Academy (Annapolis, Md.), the Air Force Academy (Colorado Springs, Colo.), and the Coast Guard Academy (New London, Conn.). Each academy furnishes college education and special military training. On graduation, each candidate receives an officer's commission and a bachelor of science degree. The Marine Corps draws some Annapolis graduates, but the primary source of Marine officers is the Platoon Leaders Class/Officers Candidate School program and college graduates enrolled as officer candidates at the Officer Candidate School in Quantico, Virginia.

To qualify for an academy, a candidate must have studied English and mathematics (plus science, social science, and the humanities) in high school, be seventeen to twenty-two years of age, and pass physical and mental examinations. Nominations to the Army, Navy, and Air Force academies are made by members of Congress and the President and by qualification under special laws for the sons and daughters of deceased veterans and of regular officers and enlisted personnel. Active-duty enlisted personnel can qualify too. The Coast Guard Academy is the only military service academy not subject to congressional appointments. Applicants to the Coast Guard Academy are accepted only by competitive examination. No matter what the route, academy appointments are highly competitive.

The most common route to a commission is through the Reserve Officer Training Corps (ROTC). There are some more than 500 units on about 400 college campuses all over the country. Students take regular college courses and add three to five hours of military science each week plus time spent at summer training camps or aboard ships. Each of the services offers scholarships that cover tuition costs and pay a monthly stipend.

All services also have special recruitment programs for college graduates or, in some in-

Logistics technicians control the command post area of the Strategic Air Command (SAC) Headquarters in Nebraska.

stances, for those who have partially completed college and who have other qualifications to become officers. College graduates in some specialties can be commissioned directly; some must attend officer candidate schools. The services encourage qualified enlisted personnel to try for promotion to officer rank.

Enlisted service people are almost always sent first to a basic training camp where they are tested, toughened, and trained. They learn the rudiments of marching, handling weapons, rules of conduct, first aid, and military customs. This can be the most demanding part of the recruit's early career. The work is hard with little time off.

Basic training varies from service to service as follows:

Army: Recruits are sent to one of a number of camps located across the country. Training takes eight weeks and includes mock battles, digging-in, rifle firing, and obstacle courses.

Navy: Recruits spend eight weeks and three days learning seamanship, gunnery, ship structure, survival, and Navy terminology.

Air Force: Recruits get six weeks of instruction in Air Force tradition, academic subjects, confidence courses, physical conditioning, and marksmanship.

Marine Corps: Recruits spend a little more than ten weeks becoming basic infantrymen. Training is rigorous, demanding, and challenging. It is followed by on-the-job training or specialist training in a formal school.

Coast Guard: Training of new enlistees lasts eight weeks. It includes guard duty, galley duty, and instruction in seamanship, communications, safety, and Coast Guard traditions.

Almost all officers receive special training, such as in aviation, ship handling, and weaponry. In some cases, officers are already qualified as historians, physicians, lawyers, veterinarians, or other professionals. All receive training in leadership and management.

Industry outlook

With rapid political changes occurring around the world, it is difficult to predict the outlook for careers in the military. In times of war or serious crisis, the services expand. The best judgment of responsible officials is that there will be no sudden shrinkage to the year 2000. Minor and gradual reductions or expansions in the size of the armed services could occur, but minor peacetime changes do not have great effect on careers.

There are many advantages to joining the military. In exchange for their service, the country offers important responsibilities and provides schooling, steady work, good pay, opportunities to develop new friendships, and travel. Also, military personnel are furnished care for their families, an excellent retirement plan, and a helping hand throughout their lifetimes.

All of the services offer special travel and recreation that add to the attraction of a military career. Since U.S. defense interests are worldwide, most service members can expect to travel abroad. Their assignments may give them an opportunity to know Europeans, Asians, and Africans, and during the annual thirty days of leave, many foreign countries can be explored.

Special social facilities are available to both officer and enlisted personnel—the Officers Open Mess or NCO (Noncommissioned Officers) Open Mess. The majority of the NCO Open Messes are open to all enlisted grades. These facilities usually charge dues to help offset expenses. The basic services offered by an Open Mess vary, but they often include a bar area, dining facility, entertainment area (dining/dancing/banquet) and offer family entertainment nights. The size of the facility and the variety of services offered vary according to the resources of the base or post on which they are located.

Military life, then, offers many extras, many benefits not found in most civilian occupations; but there are also some sacrifices and a high level of personal responsibility that a private civilian almost never faces. Navy people, for example, sometimes are at sea for weeks at a time, and during those periods cannot be home each night with their families. Air crews sometimes stand watches that require them to be on standby near their aircraft. Coast Guard crews may be away from home for weeks while coping with maritime disasters. Soldiers and marines frequently are required to conduct tough, exhausting field exercises. Many people in the service find excitement in these activities and a feeling of accomplishment. They represent experience different from the average civilian way of life, however.

A military life is regimented. Service members cannot always choose their assignments, their places of work, or their homes. Their whole purpose is to serve their country and their military unit, so the needs of their country and the service come first. The modern services try hard to give their members what they want—a good worker gets special consideration for the same reason a civilian employer rewards a top employee—but most service members at some time or other will probably work on the East Coast when they would rather be on the West Coast, go to sea when they would rather stay home, live in a house or barracks on the base when they would rather have an apartment in town, or serve a year in a lonely but important post abroad when they would rather be with their families.

The Army is the largest service, with about 785,000 men and women. The Air Force has more than 597,000 recruits, the Navy about 561,000, the Marine Corps more than 195,000, and the Coast Guard about 39,000.

◇ SOURCES OF ADDITIONAL INFORMATION

Interested candidates for military service in the Army, Navy, Air Force, Marine Corps, or Coast Guard should contact the recruitment centers listed blow. These centers will issue information concerning military duty, obligations, and recruitment procedures.

United States Army Recruiting Command
Office of Information
Fort Sheridan, IL 60037

Navy Recruiting Command
4015 Wilson Boulevard
Arlington, VA 22203

Commander, USAF Recruiting Service
Randolph AFB, TX 78148

Director of Personnel Procurement Division
HQ U.S. Marine Corps (MC-MR)
Washington, DC 20380

U.S. Coast Guard Information Center
1350 New York Avenue
Suite B-108
Washington, DC 20005

If a service career or tour of duty looks appealing, a young person should visit recruiting offices for up-to-date information about the requirements and benefits of each service. Young people should ask their high-school or college advisers for some of the information on service careers sent regularly to most American schools. Additionally, they may seek out and talk to active or retired military people in their own community.

◇ **RELATED ARTICLES**

Volume 1: Aviation and Aerospace; Civil Service; Engineering; Foreign Service; Health Care; Nuclear Sciences
Volume 2: Air traffic controllers; Astronauts; Cartographers; Engineers; Foreign Service officers; Pilots; Radio and telegraph operators
Volume 3: Aircraft mechanics and engine specialists; Airplane dispatchers; Automobile mechanics; Communications equipment mechanics; Electrical repairers; Flight engineers; General maintenance mechanics
Volume 4: Aeronautical and aerospace technicians; Avionics technicians; Biomedical equipment technicians; Electronics technicians; Mechanical technicians; Nuclear Instrumentation technicians; Surveying and mapping technicians; Weapons and ammunition technicians

Mining

General information

The mining industry finds valuable minerals beneath earth or water and removes them in the most economical and efficient way. Mined materials include energy minerals, such as coal, petroleum, uranium, and natural gas; nonmetallic minerals, such as limestone, salt, sandstone, and diamonds; and metallic minerals, such as iron ore, gold, and silver.

Mining is the discovery, valuation, development, exploitation, processing, and marketing of useful minerals. It conveys many different meanings to those outside the field. To emerging nations, mining is seen as a symbol of wealth, power, and a developing culture. To established nations, mining represents the ability to engage in trade, to provide for the welfare of their people, and to provide for self-defense. To those engaged in mining, the industry is seen as an adventurous, exciting, and engrossing occupation that contributes greatly to the welfare of humanity.

While early humans had used exposed minerals for ten of thousands of years, the earliest mine did not appear until around 8000 B.C. At that time humans extracted clay to make cooking utensils. During this period, humans also extracted hard volcanic rock for plowing, gold for ornamentation, and flint for basic weaponry. By as early as 3,000 B.C., man had entered the Bronze Age, mixing tin and copper to produce weapons and utensils that were stronger than flint. By 1200 B.C., or even earlier, humans had begun to use iron. During the Iron Age, humans mined valuable materials. Ceylon and India mined gems for trade, and the Greeks cut marble for their magnificent structures.

The usefulness of bronze and iron led to the development of more sophisticated mining techniques, which culminated during the Roman Empire. In addition to metals, the Romans mined volcanic ash, combining it with other materials to create very durable cement. For more than a thousand years after the end of the Roman Empire, mining techniques remained stagnate. It was not until the 1400s that the French, Germans, and Swedes began mining their territories with vigor.

Mining did not take hold in America until the 1700s, when French explorers discovered rich lead and zinc mines in the Mississippi River valley. In the mid-1800s, Pennsylvania residents developed numerous coal and coke mines, giving rise to the famous millionaires of the Gilded Age in American history: Andrew Carnegie, Henry Clay Frick, Andrew Mellon, and John Pierpont Morgan. Such cities as Pittsburgh, Gary, and Duluth grew rapidly, increasing the industrial and economic strength of America. At the same time, the discovery of rich oil fields in Texas introduced an entirely new industry in America.

After World War II, America entered the nuclear age, mining rare radioactive materials for nuclear energy and weaponry. More recently, the American mining industry has experienced its share of ups and downs. Facing intense competition from abroad, the industry has had to make many technological improvements to compete with other countries.

The mining industry is not populated solely by large integrated companies. Many organizations concentrate on just one or two facets of the industry; other concerns provide special services to mining companies. A mining concern may concentrate its efforts in the operational phases of the industry and rely on others to provide various services that it requires. For example, a company may perform just the drilling and sampling phase of prospecting and exploration. Similarly, there are concerns that only analyze samples for mineral content.

A number of small- and intermediate-size mining companies produce from 100 to 500 tons of ore per day and have a labor force of twenty-five or fewer. These smaller operations can pay a handsome profit on the investment of the individual entrepreneur. Whereas the general methods of development and exploitation remain the same, the small and intermediate companies usually do not have the extensive capital resources to purchase the many types of equipment needed for larger operations.

The structure of the mining industry

The basic elements found in the earth's crust are combined in many strange and beautiful ways to create many different types of minerals. The variety of raw materials is as diverse as the uses for them. At least 1,400 minerals of inorganic origin are known, approximately 300 of which have become useful to industry.

Basically, the output of the mining industry may be classified into three groups: energy minerals, nonmetallic minerals, and metallic minerals. Typical energy minerals are the fossil fuels, such as coal. Typical nonmetallic minerals include phosphate rock, used in fertilizers; limestone rock, used in cement, lime, and iron production; salt, used domestically and in industry for the production of basic chemicals; and sand and gravel, used extensively in construction. Typical metallic minerals are iron ores, copper ores, and bauxite, which is the raw material for the aluminum industry. The most heavily mined minerals are coal, iron, nonferrous metals, and construction materials, such as gravel.

In many ways, discovering the proper place to mine is an art. A trained and experienced professional is needed to discern an ore body—a mineralized mass technically, economically, socially, and politically minable at a profit. Geologists, geophysicists, and geochemists are engaged in the discovery activity. They need a fundamental understanding of the ways ore bodies developed on earth to discover more readily where ore bodies are likely to be found. Research into these basic issues is constant.

The easily discovered deposits that have provided minerals supply in the past are gone. Thus, the only available minerals are located deep in the earth. The development of special tools, techniques, instruments, and methods of interpretation help locate new mineral sources. Essentially, this side of the activity requires an understanding of the chemistry and physics of the earth. In addition, a person must develop some type of intuition about the earth and its ore deposits.

The discovery activity of mining requires a wide variety of talent. Scientists, engineers, and technicians are brought together into a team, usually with a specific kind of mineral target in mind. Initial efforts in locating likely mining areas may come from satellite photographs. This is followed by aerial photographs and geophysical sensing, which in turn is followed by more intense and detailed study of the geology, geochemistry, and geophysics of the targeted area. Sometimes the discovery is under water, such as the deep-sea nodules, or in the polar regions or even under existing towns.

Once the mineralized mass has been found, it is up to the valuation engineer to confirm the discovery and authorize the removal of the ore. The valuation function of mining ranges from understanding the geology of ore deposits to knowing the fundamentals of marketing the mineral products.

To answer practical matters such as cost and profitability, valuation engineers construct a three-dimensional sampling by geological, geophysical, and geochemical means. The valuation engineer must sift and analyze the accumulating data against a framework of profitable exploitation. To be profitable, the prospective ore body must be amenable to efficient extraction by present or foreseeable technology and equipment.

In mining the product, the valuation engineer must also consider social and political policy. Societal values change with time and the needs of people. Political parties and governments also change. A mining enterprise must respond to these changes and anticipate future trends and laws.

After the sample defines the limits of the ore body, the valuation engineers judge whether the area is worth mining. If so, their decision launches an ever-widening circle of design and construction activity.

The design sector of mining links the research and development phases with actual construction. Once management has stated its objectives in a given mineral project, the design engineers proceed to accomplish the objectives. Mining, industrial, and mineral engineers together must make a working system that will safely meet the output requirements with a minimum expenditure of staff and equipment.

For underground mining, the design engineers must plan detailed drilling and also determine the number and location of shafts, slopes (a diagonally dug shaft), and main extraction openings. The surface structure and roads are usually designed by civil engineers. In many cases, railroads are required. Engineers determine the size, number, kind, and layout of the various pieces of equipment. Electrical engineers and mechanical engineers are responsible for designing various controls and

This mine at Bingham Canyon, Utah is an example of a typical open pit mine, showing the funnel shape, the man-made terraces, and the transportation systems that carry the ore to processing centers.

the distribution of power and other services throughout the mine.

If the project is an extensive undertaking in a remote area, more often than not a town site with its services and facilities must be designed and constructed. This requires the further services of architects, water supply engineers, and sanitation engineers.

The design engineers hand over a set of plans and specifications to the construction engineers who are responsible for translating the plans into the reality of steel and concrete, head frames and mills, and shafts and tunnels. The actual construction may be handled by contractors or engineering concerns that specialize in heavy construction. Whether this is the case or not, the usual procedure is to determine a plan for construction, the quantities of material and other items needed, and the estimated cost of each construction operation.

Field work starts with a survey team sent to the site to lay out the mine and its facilities. The modern construction methods of the mining industry are characterized by the integrated use of many technicians, craft workers, and special-

ists, including carpenters, plumbers, electronic technicians, steelworkers, painters, and typists. Construction of access roads and auxiliary buildings begins immediately, and essential services such as electricity and water are established. The office workers continue the drafting, calculating, and accounting work begun earlier. Progress reports are submitted by the field workers and plans changed accordingly.

For underground mining, the construction phase entails sinking shafts and developing main extraction openings, underground workshops, and other openings important to mine operation. A choice must be made between conventional drill and blast methods versus shaft and tunnel boring with machines. The use of shaft and tunnel-boring machines is the newer method, but it must be carefully chosen to cope with the variety of geological conditions to be encountered.

Boring machines represent large capital investment items and hence must be operated, maintained, and used with skill. Teamwork among engineers, mechanics, and operating personnel is needed to bring the job to a successful conclusion. Essentially, these machines bore a twenty foot diameter or larger tunnel or shaft by thrusting an array of cutting bits against the rock face. The cutting head of the machine is then rotated and the bits chip and break off the rock in front of them. Large hydraulic jacks bear against the side of the bored opening and provide the restraint to the thrust of the machine.

Boring operations are continued on a twenty-four hour basis except for bit changes and repairs. Tunnel advances of 100 feet per day or greater can be accomplished in comparatively soft rock. Since the machine is boring blind, lasers are used to ensure that deviation from the underground target is minimal. When boring operations are completed, the shaft is equipped with the necessary supports and facilities.

Open pit mines are developed when the ore body is close to the surface of the ground. Typically, the pit is developed in a series of levels called benches. Haul roads are constructed between benches so that material can be moved from any location in the pit to various receiving points. Alternative haulage from the pit may be performed by conveyors or railroad trains. The receiving point may be the ore mill, the leaching dumps, the waste dump, or ore storage piles. Giant trucks move about on this network of roads, carefully scheduled so that no loading operation or receiving point is empty. Large drills, bulldozers, and power shovels work to ensure that the flow of ore out of the pit is a continuous operation. In this way, open pit mining can move more than 600,000 tons of ore and rock in a twenty-four hour period.

The nature of the mineral deposit makes for differences in how open pit mining methods are employed. Placer mining methods are used for the exploitation of platinum, tin, diamond, and gold deposits. In Florida, phosphates are mined by placer methods. Large quantities of material are mined and processed to find small quantities of these valuable substances.

The water treatment, handling, and safe disposal of mining wastes are large problems. Strip mining of coal may be done in mountainous regions as well as in the lowlands. Although the methods are fundamentally the same, the geometry of the resulting pit is different and gives rise to a host of different problems. One concern is land reclamation, which is more of a problem for coal producers than for hard rock mining companies.

Equipment and personnel are what makes open pit mining the cheapest and most economical method for producing low-grade or low-value material. Rock- and earth-moving equipment work on a scale hard to believe.

A geologist inspects core samples that reveal the depth and quality of the coal seam to be mined.

Power shovels and draglines capable of moving 100 tons at a time are common. High output rates mean that the scale of trucks, bulldozers, and other equipment must be large.

Operating personnel take over when construction is completed. The pace of work increases, for performance in meeting production goals is the criterion by which everything is measured. Teamwork and cooperation are essential. Drillers, blasters, loading machine operators, haulage operators, supply workers, and safety personnel work in a cycle of operations that meets production goals at the lowest possible costs.

The operation department also provides opportunities for mining engineers, metallurgists, mineral economists, industrial engineers, and chemical engineers. Process controls and performance standards must be established; jobs must be evaluated; employees trained; and cost control plans reviewed.

Maintenance of plant and equipment is sufficiently important to justify a separate department, since the dollar investment in both plant and equipment may be thousands of dollars per individual worker. The actual maintenance is in the hands of skilled craft workers and technicians such as mechanics, machinists, drafters, electricians, and instrument technicians, who are trained and equipped to overhaul all major plant facilities.

A mining engineer determines the number and location of mining shafts, plotting the measurements of the mine extraction openings.

All maintenance and operating work requires keeping complete and accurate records concerning equipment durability and efficiency. The analysis of these records also gives the information needed for inventory and stock requirements.

What resources to mine, when to start mining, how to finance, and where to market and at what price are questions confronting the mineral economist. Mineral economics is another vital part of the mining process. Since ore bodies are unevenly distributed throughout the world, a system has developed that distributes the output of ore bodies to those who want and need them. This system is motivated fundamentally by the law of supply and demand.

In addition, local townships, counties, states, nations, and international bodies desire to influence the workings of the fundamental law of supply and demand for minerals so that their own welfare can be maximized. The influences of these organizations on the policies of a mining firm must be thoroughly understood if the firm is to survive and prosper.

The sales force in the mining industry is responsible for cultivating buyers of their product and keeping in contact with them. Most mineral commodities are sold according to specifications. Industrial users need certain qualities in their raw materials and require suppliers to meet those specifications. The salespeople are vitally important since they person-

ally represent the company to the buyer. Knowing the wishes of buyers, they can apprise the company of the shifting demand for mineral products.

Salespeople in the mining industry must be familiar with the workings of the commodity markets and the flow of minerals in national and international commerce. Since they are required to compete in both price and specification, they must know their company's abilities and products intimately. They must know how various mineral commodities may interchange in the industry.

A key management role in the mining industry is played by the shift boss or mine captain. It is at this level that the desires of the upper levels of management are transformed into action. The responsibilities of the shift boss may be summarized as meeting the required daily output while considering the health and safety of the workers.

The shift boss must continually make personal inspections, regularly examining the fans and ventilation apparatus of an underground mine, looking at the condition of the shaft and main extraction openings, and examining the electrical system. In any type of mine, the shift boss must talk with the workers, formulate independent opinions of conditions, and report to the company managers. The shift boss may also meet with local representatives of labor and together negotiate solutions to any problems or concerns.

Mine managers keep informed by reports from the mine shift bosses, their assistants, and personal inspections and investigations. Mine managers and shift bosses differ in their responsibilities. The shift boss may have to decide: Should we replace float valve at pump station 1? Should we send people from production operations to the maintenance crew? The mine manager and the top management levels, on the other hand, might be thinking: Should we mine more actively in mine 2 than in 3? Is it possible to bring out a new mining venture without unduly disturbing the existing marketing structure? The choice among alternative plans that are broad in scope is management's responsibility.

Careers

There are many careers available in the mining industry. Below is a list of selected occupations.

Mining managers: Management of a mining industry deal with the grandiose issues. They set policy and make decisions concerning the financial welfare of the company.

Mining geologists: Mining geologists search for mineral deposits. In general, their work involves exploring areas for ore, taking samples, mapping prospective locations, and writing reports (see Volume 2: Geologists; Geophysicists).

Valuation engineers: In general, valuation engineers inspect a prospective mine location, determining its value. They sample the area, determine the amount of minerals present, analyze the profitability of a mine, and suggest whether or not the area should be mined. A fundamental knowledge of the capabilities of personnel, equipment, and methods and the interplay among them is needed to arrive at this decision.

The valuation engineer must also understand the nuances of capital investment and marketing of minerals. Some mining projects are so large today that a joint venture of several companies is formed or a combined government-private industry entity may be created to carry them out. These situations all have a bearing on the profitability of the venture.

Mining engineers: Mining engineers perform tasks similar to valuation engineers. In addition, they map the mining territory and devise methods of extraction.

Petrologists: Petrologists study rock formations to determine their mineral content (see Volume 2: Petrologists).

Design engineers: Design engineers execute a layout of the mine. They determine the location of shafts, openings, and roads to the mine opening. Such work relies heavily on the research preformed by the mining engineers, geologists, and valuation engineers. Designers must be able to think on paper.

Surveyors: Surveyors define the boundaries of the mine using specialized instruments (see Volume 2: Surveyors).

Mineral processing engineers: Mineral processing engineers design methods of refining the mined mineral into a marketable or useful product. Many mineral processing engineers work for those companies that purchase raw materials.

Shift bosses: Shift bosses supervise the day-to-day operations at the mine. The typical day of a shift boss is busy. He or she must first check the reports of the assistants that contain information on such mine conditions as ventilation, pumping, supplies, and output of ore. The reports describe the ground conditions in the working places, the state of the equipment and facilities used in ore production, and estimates of what must be done in the next twenty-four hours. On the basis of this information, the shift boss makes decisions as to what is to

In order to secure the overlying rock, miners drill into the mine roof and install steel rods, resin adhesive, and wooden planks.

be done and issues the necessary orders to accomplish the work (see Volume 3: Blue-collar worker supervisors).

Blasters: Blasters use explosives to create mine shafts, expose minerals at the surface, or loosen the minerals in a shaft.

Miners: Miners are the people who retrieve the minerals from the pit or shaft (see Volume 3: Coal mining operatives).

Construction equipment operators: Construction equipment operators run the bulldozers, trucks, and other forms of equipment used to haul the mined minerals from the shaft to the storage piles or onto cargo trains (see Volume 3: Operating engineers).

Operations personnel: Operations personnel includes electricians, plumbers, pipe fitters, instrument technicians, inspectors, and other craft workers and technicians involved in the operation of compressors, stationary diesel-powered generators, and electrical apparatus. They are usually responsible for mine and mill safety, including safeguards for individual workers and provision for fire protection and prevention.

Salespeople: In their daily work, the salespeople must know the answers to technical questions as well as know whether their companies can compete in price. They must study the products made available by their companies; travel among customers' plants, home offices, and factories; analyze customer complaints; represent their companies at technical meetings; report on field problems and innovations offered by competitors; and report on sales progress.

A blaster sets up explosives at a uranium strip mine in New Mexico.

Education

The activities of drilling and blasting, operating heavy construction equipment, and installing machinery all require experience and judgment that can be obtained only through actual practice. A beginner may join the construction team as a helper or laborer. He or she may then gain competency and experience and move to better-paying jobs and more advanced work. With a diligent application of talents, a beginner may someday become a supervisor or part of management personnel.

The training for engineering design must be broad since a major design encompasses many disciplines. Usually a four-year college education is required, with a strong background in engineering. More education may be required as technology advances. A knowledge of law will help in understanding contracts, building codes, and other legal procedures. A background in production and construction procedures is extremely helpful, for a good designer must keep in mind the difficulties in these areas.

Operating personnel must be skilled and trained on the job. The necessary training covers most of the basic fields of engineering as well as the skilled trades. The opportunity for an individual to rise to a position of authority is great, provided that the person has a feeling for the capabilities of workers and machines.

For the mineral economist, a thorough knowledge of economic decision making as it concerns the functions of valuation, design, production, and management of mining firms is essential. In addition, education and training in finance, national and international law, and political institutions are important.

Training for sales positions should include some business law, accounting, and mineral economics. A college education is helpful, though not necessary. A sales trainee may spend one to two years learning the company's products and their characteristics while working with a more experienced salesperson.

Shift bosses or mine captains usually come up through the ranks. Superintendents may come from the shift boss group or be promoted from other positions in the company. They frequently have backgrounds as engineers. As scientific management tools are more widely applied, people trained in mathematics, systems analysis, and operations research will find opportunities in this area.

Training for management is a mixture of technical know-how, business sense, economics, and sensitivity in human affairs. Persons with little formal education have risen to the top of management, but this will be increasingly difficult in the complex world of mining today. One can expect to start well down on the management ladder and progress as one's abilities, skills, and experience increase. A manager in the mining industry must have a basic understanding of human beings, as well as mineral economics, and the overall technical requirements of the industry.

Industry outlook

The mining industry is continually changing and improving. New mining techniques and methods, raw materials of different nature and kind, deeper and more difficult ore body situations, and changing supply-demand pictures will mold new patterns. With the changes in methods and machinery will come a change in career opportunities. Old jobs will take on added dimensions, and new jobs will be born to meet new needs.

Total employment in mining was about 171,500 in the late 1980s, of whom 132,000 were production workers. Jobs for mining engineers, however, are projected to grow gradually through the mid-1990s. Due to labor-saving equipment and economic trends, this number is expected to increase only modestly.

In 1989, the industry shipped $30.6 billion worth of ore. However, the prospective increases in jobs and shipments will most likely correspond to the rate of inflation, rendering the industry virtually unchanged. In particular, the coal mining industry is expected to remain stable. With few new nuclear plants or hydroelectric sites, coal-generated power will continue to be a useful commodity.

◇ **SOURCES OF ADDITIONAL INFORMATION**

American Mining Congress (AMC)
1920 N Street, NW, Suite 300
Washington, DC 20036

National Coal Association
1130 17th Street, NW
Washington, DC 20036

Society of Mining Engineers, Inc.
PO Box 625002
Littleton, CO 80162

International Union United Mine Workers of America
900 15th Street, NW
Washington, DC 20005

National Independent Coal Operators Association
PO Box 354
Richlands, VA 24641

◇ **RELATED ARTICLES**

Volume 1: Construction; Energy; Engineering; Metals; Physical Sciences
Volume 2: Construction inspectors, government; Cost estimators; Economists; Engineers; Geologists; Geophysicists; Groundwater professionals; Industrial designers; Industrial traffic managers; Management analysts and consultants; Oceanographers; Operations-research analysts; Personnel and labor relations specialists; Petrologists; Surveyors
Volume 3: Coal mining operatives; Construction workers; Electricians; Operating engineers (construction machinery operators); Petroleum drilling occupations; Petroleum refining workers; Soil scientists
Volume 4: Civil engineering technicians; Coal mining technicians; Drafting and design technicians; Electrical technicians; Geological technicians; Industrial engineering technicians; Mechanical technicians; Petroleum technicians; Surveying and mapping technicians

Motion Pictures

General information

The desire to go beyond static, nonmoving images started soon after the development of still photography. If one picture could capture a single moment, then a similar technique should be applicable to capturing a series of moments. Flip cards, the first version of moving pictures, worked on a simple principle. If one has a series of still pictures that capture the movements of someone running, showing the pictures in rapid succession would give the illusion of the movement of running. In 1877, Eadwaerd Muybridge successfully captured one single period of a horse in motion by using twenty-four cameras and trip wires that triggered the camera shutters as the horse ran along.

The famous inventor, Thomas Edison, produced a short movie called *The Sneeze* in 1894, using film for the first time instead of individual plates. Georges Melies introduced narrative films in 1899 in France, and in 1903 Edwin Porter filmed *The Great Train Robbery*, the first motion picture which told a story with modern filming techniques. Porter used editing to put together a story that he had filmed out of sequence.

Motion pictures became increasingly popular in the early 1900s, with the advent of the movie house and silent film stars such as Charlie Chaplin and Rudolph Valentino. It wasn't until 1927 that talking movies were made, when *The Jazz Singer* with Al Jolson was produced. Soon after that, color film reproduction allowed color films to be produced and distributed.

In the 1920s, the first animated films were released for theater distribution. The first Technicolor animated film, *Flowers and Trees*, produced by Walt Disney was released in 1932. Disney also produced the first full length feature cartoon in 1937, *Snow White and the Seven Dwarves*. Despite the advances in animation techniques, *Snow White* still remains a popular film today.

Throughout the past few decades, motion picture have become very sophisticated; advances in both the science and art of filmmaking have led to increasingly well-made films. Today the making of motion pictures has become a major industry in the United States.

The structure of the motion picture industry

Motion pictures are not only movies that you see at theaters. Television commercials, made-for-TV movies, documentaries, educational films, travelogues, industrial training films, and even music videos are all motion pictures of a type, requiring the skills of a motion picture industry worker.

The start of most motion picture productions is the selection of the story to be told. The movie may be based on a novel, a play, or an original script for a motion picture. With commercials or industrial films, the story line is the product or business that needs promotion, and with documentaries, it centers on the subject that is to be covered.

The second most important step after the development of the story line or subject is the funding. With commercial productions, it is almost always the company that is sponsoring the production that pays the production costs and approves the steps being taken. For political campaigns and public service announcements, it is normally an interested outside group that is covering the costs and making the production decisions.

Music videos and industrial films are normally sponsored at their inception by whomever is requesting the production. For motion pictures, though, it is normally started at the creative end, and a sponsor must be sought for financing the production.

In the days of the studio contracts, the conception, production, and financing of films was all done within one studio. For example, Twentieth Century Fox would have producers, staff writers, directors, and actors and actresses, from whom they would choose for any particular film.

Now the system has changed. Although there are people who will sign contracts to do several films for one studio for a prearranged salary, most people work on a project-by-project basis. Producers will bring a project to a studio, with an estimated cost of production, and perhaps the main actors and actresses selected, and a studio may agree to back the production. The studio will pay for the costs of producing the film, and will pick up the salaries of the crew and cast, in exchange for the profits realized off the film when it is released.

If the movie is successful, it will bring in more money from ticket sales than the film cost to produce. Movies have become a very expensive project, with some films costing several million dollars to produce. Those films require a huge turnout in the theaters to make any money for the company sponsoring the film. Small productions need not sell as many tickets, but frequently the actors and actresses are not well known, and selling tickets becomes more difficult.

With the increased cost of film production, the independent producer has to be a good salesperson to be able to sell a studio on the marketability of a film idea. If there are popular actors and actresses involved in the film, or a particular story line has done well before, the producer is more likely to find financing than if a new idea or unknown actors are involved. Some studios are more willing to take the risk of a lesser known cast and story, if the cost of production is not too high.

Occasionally, a producer will go to a studio with just the idea for a film. With studio backing, he or she may be able to attract bigger names to work on the film. Studios have developed a "step deal" for this and other arrangements. With a step deal, if the producer cannot get an adequate script or staff together, the studio cam withdraw funding from a project.

After funding has been arranged, the process of preparing the story for filming begins. For motion pictures, this will mean writing and rewriting the script to fit with the time limitations and the characters of the story.

Documentaries and educational films usually have more difficulties securing financing than a mass market motion picture. If the fund-

A camera operator runs a 35mm camera to film a movie. With the director's supervision, he controls the visual quality and cinematic atmosphere of the film.

ing is sought through endowments, government agencies, or broadcasting stations, then the producer and director should anticipate putting together a fairly lengthy proposal with extensive research on the selected topic. For example, the length of the documentary will need to planned out and explained. A time table for the research, filming, and editing will have to be calculated. The potential investors will also frequently want a biography of the more important staff members of the documentary to show the level of skill and the background of the people that they will be entrusting with their money. The producer may have to produce a shortened version of the idea (a pilot) to show what the full-length project would look like.

It can take six months to ten years to secure financing. For Public Broadcasting, there are stipulations on accepting a documentary based on who has supplied funding. If Public Broadcasting deems the sponsors to have a personal interest in the theme of the program, which may have influenced the objectivity of the writers, then the project may be rejected unless the project can be balanced with another funding source less directly connected with the subject.

With the expansion of cable stations that broadcast documentaries, the market for broad-

A technician operates the sound equipment during the filming of a movie. He creates the sound quality in accordance with the director's requests.

cast time is increasing, despite the cutback of documentary time on regular network television.

Once funding has been found for a project, a payment schedule is worked out with the producer of the documentary. Some funds will normally be supplied up front, with various amounts distributed along the way, and the final amount of money delivered after the completion of the project.

A film crew on a documentary or educational film can be as small as four people: a producer-director, a camera operator, a sound technician, and a lighting technician. For more large-scale documentaries, the staff can be quite large. As with other forms of film production, the more the cost is kept down, the easier it is to find funding.

The competition for funds is extremely keen, so the experience and reputation of the staff and a reasonable budget may help overcome the incredible competition for money.

Motion pictures, music videos, travelogues, and educational films all need scripting, even if there will be no spoken words. For all forms of motion picture, the action must be planned carefully. Timing, continuation of narrative, camera angle, and all the other many details that go into making a cohesive piece of work need to be worked out as well as possible before the filming begins. If the producer waits until the filming begins to decide on major aspects of the project, the costs will increase dramatically.

Decisions about where the filming is to be done, in a studio or on location, go into the cost analysis of the project. Casting of the actors, actresses, narrators, and other talent that will

be in the project will affect the budget. How long the filming will take, the special effects that are required, the overall size of the staff and production all determine the final budget for a film. The studio production department will need all this information before a final approval of contract can be made.

For animated features, the methods of funding can be either like that of the documentary or like a mass market motion picture. Animated features continue to have great appeal to the public and continue to be produced, despite the incredible time and detail that must go into the manufacturing of animated film. Each image that would be captured in a film of live action needs to be drawn onto a clear plastic sheet. Simple movement, like saying hello, would require at least eight different drawings, shown in sequence to recreate actions of the body and mouth. A full length feature takes at least two years to complete, and may use over one million different drawings.

Depending on the size of the project, filming can take several days to several months. The picture will normally be filmed out of sequence, which means that the director, technical crew, and acting staff will have to know how the pieces are to fit together to assure that details will match up when the film is finally assembled back in the studio.

The film can be shot in a studio on a sound stage, where everything is recreated to look like a real scene. The film can also be produced on location, in the actual setting where the story takes place.

Once the filming is done, the film is reassembled in a studio. Special effects, music tracks, and any conversation that may have been muffled by other noises during the filming, will be added at this point. This type of work is highly precise, and requires split-second timing to assure that the on-screen action matches the sound being heard.

Once the project is completed, the film is reviewed by the people in charge of the production. If the final product is acceptable, the film is released. This means that the film is distributed to the theaters.

Now it is up to the marketing and distributing staff to build an audience for the film. Their job is to encourage the public to watch the production, and make the public aware of the time and place that the film is shown. Without an audience, even the best motion picture will have little impact.

The advent of video cassette recorders has broadened and changed the movie market. While many people will not pay the full price to see a movie in a theater, they will gladly rent it later on.

Careers

A sampling of career opportunities follows below.

Producers: Producers are responsible for planning and coordinating the activities of all employees involved in a production. Motion picture producers coordinate the work of all employees engaged in writing, directing, filming, staging, and editing a show or movie. They determine the production schedule and overall budget for a particular show or film. They also discuss scripts with a variety of workers, including writers, directors, and editors. In general, producers make the final decisions on all matters related to a production and oversee the entire production.

Directors: Working closely with producers, directors read scripts, help select cast members, direct rehearsals, and oversee the activities of the writers and editors. Directors are responsible for getting the best possible performances from the actors. They also determine the camera angles and the way the picture will look on film.

Casting directors: Casting directors audition actors and actresses for productions. They observe the person's size, physical appearance, voice, expressiveness, and experience. They recommend players to producers and directors. Some casting directors may be involved with arranging contracts for performers.

Screenwriters: Screenwriters write scripts for movies, television shows, and educational films.

Film editors: Film editors work with producers and directors to create effective and accurate presentation of a script.

Art staff: Art directors, set designers, and set decorators are all involved with the selection, development, and design of props, scenery, costumes, makeup, and other artistic details.

Technical staff: Technical staff have a variety of production responsibilities. For example, recording mixers combine music and sound effects with a film's action. Grips are involved with a variety of behind-the-scenes duties, such as operating cranes, building mirrors and reflectors, and setting up backdrops and platforms. Production assistants help the technical or editorial crew in all types of work, from getting coffee to hauling production equipment.

Distribution and marketing staff: These staff members are responsible for finding theaters to show the film and arranging all advertising and promotional activities surrounding a film. How well a film does frequently can be influenced by the marketing. Bad projects may do somewhat better with good marketing, but good projects

Before a scene is filmed, technicians must carefully prepare the set. This includes placing the lights and microphones in the appropriate spots.

can certainly be hurt if the marketing and distribution are not as strong as possible.

Education

Many colleges and universities around the country offer classes in filmmaking, dramatic arts, and related subjects. In these classes, students are given hands-on experience on equipment and the basic steps of film production and direction. With an understanding of the history of filmmaking and a good technical background, a college student will develop some of the basic skills needed in the industry.

For the technical jobs, a technical school may be the best place to get experience with the equipment, although several universities include technical skills in their broadcasting majors. For production and direction jobs, a good liberal arts education is important. Good writing and research skills will allow a person to present funding proposals in an effective manner. Journalism backgrounds are helpful for producers because they will rely so heavily on the written word to convey the project they wish to show on film.

It is also desirable to get experience in high-school, college, or community stage productions. Broad experience on different types of projects helps develop the skills needed to work in film production.

321

A film laboratory technician inspects the quality of a recently developed segment of film.

Anyone interested in getting into motion picture work should be expected to start at menial tasks. Because of the competitiveness of the industry, the worker who does best is the one who is willing to work hardest at the entry-level jobs to develop a reputation as a solid crew member.

Industry outlook

The cable market, the video market, and a general heightened interest in non-fiction work (both in the print media and motion picture industry) has allowed for an expansion of the motion picture market at a time when most people has expected the market to fade. Years ago, television was expected to erode the motion picture industry, but other avenues have opened, and the industry remains strong. The video rental boom has made the greatest impact.

Although positions for film production are extremely competitive because of the vast number of people interested in working in film, the number of pictures being produced has qua-

drupled in the last ten years. The market for documentaries and independent film productions has increased with the number of cable stations now seeking projects, and the music video market is also expanding rapidly. With the rising cost of production, people investing in films will be more likely to invest with proven producers, so experience is essential in developing a good reputation.

◇ SOURCES OF ADDITIONAL INFORMATION

Association of Independent Video and Film Makers
625 Broadway, 9th floor
New York, NY 10012

American Film Institute
John F. Kennedy Center for Performing Arts
Washington, DC 20566

Society for Motion Picture and Television Art Directors
14724 Ventura Boulevard, Penthouse
Sherman Oaks, CA 91403

Screen Actors Guild
7065 Hollywood Blvd
Hollywood, CA 90028

◇ RELATED ARTICLES

Volume 1: Broadcasting; Marketing; Performing Arts; Recording
Volume 2: Actors and actresses; Advertising workers; Cartoonists and animators; Commercial artists; Dancers and choreographers; Fundraisers; Graphics programmers; Marketing, advertising, and public relations managers; Media specialists; Musical occupations; Photographers and camera operators; Recording industry workers; Reporters and correspondents; Writers and editors
Volume 3: Motion picture theater workers; Stage production workers

Newspaper Publishing

General information

The business of a newspaper is news. The newspaper provides information, explanation and interpretation, entertainment, and advice. The primary function, as it has been throughout the newspaper's 300-year history in America, is to inform, to bring the reader news and opinion of current events of interest. But its function also is to interpret and to explain, a responsibility that increased in importance as the world has grown smaller with instant communication. Other functions are to entertain and, through columns and features, to help the reader in his or her daily life. Advertising offers information about goods and services and supports editorial and production costs.

Newspapers, from big-city dailies to small-town and suburban weeklies, are a basic source of current and continuing international, national, and local events of interest to every conceivable sector of the public. More than sixty-three million daily papers are sold every day. "The paper," in its many forms, is a basic communications medium for practically everyone.

A newspaper serves its community. How well and in what way depends on the commitment of the owners, publisher, and editor. A newspaper is a business, and it can be a profitable one. But making money—the bottom line—is not the first concern when there is commitment to serving the community.

The print media, to which newspapers belong, are in a unique position: They are the only business protected by the Constitution. This gives them not only freedom and power, but it also places a heavy burden of responsibility.

This is why dedicated men and women are needed in newspaper publishing, from owners to editors and reporters. Newspaper journalism is an art, a craft, a skill. It can be regarded as a profession. It is certainly a calling.

Since their inception, newspapers have had a strong impact on public policy. Thomas Jefferson, though he disliked newspapers and suffered cruel abuse from the press, wrote in 1787: "Were it left to me to decide whether we should have a government without newspapers, or newspapers without a government, I should not hesitate a moment to prefer the latter." Napoleon, who answered press criticism with censorship and suppression, declared: "Four hostile newspapers are more to be feared than a thousand bayonets."

For more than two centuries, newspapers in the United States have exercised the freedom to print the truth and expose injustice and corruption. At times, they have abused their freedom. The first American newspaper, *Publick Occurences Both Foreign and Domestick*, appeared in Boston in 1690, but lasted only one issue due to censorship by the British government. The first continuously published paper in America was the Boston *News-Letter*, first published in 1704; the first daily newspaper, the *Pennsylvania Evening Post* began publication in 1783.

Producing these early newspapers was a painstaking process. Each letter had to be hand-selected and placed in a casing. When all of the words were set, individual sheets of paper were placed under a hand-operated press. Given the difficulty of obtaining news and the limited technology, these newspapers were small compared to today's newspapers.

As technology improved, so did the look of America's newspapers. The telegraph, the Atlantic cable, and the telephone greatly speeded the gathering and printing of news, and the typewriter quickened its writing.

The popularity of newspapers led to the establishment of modern journalism. As newspapers became larger and circulation increased, one person could no longer write, edit, and typeset a page, resulting in the emergence of full-time reporters and editors. By the mid to late nineteenth century, new types of presses

Once newspapers are printed, they are immediately transported via an assembly line to the circulation department where they are bundled and placed on trucks.

and suburban, standard size and tabloid format, small, medium, and large circulation, and general and special interest. Often cited as among the best newspapers are the *Boston Globe, Chicago Tribune*, Long Island *Newsday, Los Angeles Times, Miami Herald, New York Times, Wall Street Journal*, and *Washington Post*. These newspapers are also among the most financially successful. Others renown newspapers include the *Chicago Sun-Times, Christian Science Monitor, Louisville Courier-Journal*, and *Milwaukee Journal*.

The structure of the newspaper industry

The newspaper industry is made up of several departments that work simultaneously to produce a publication. Since most papers are published daily, the work is fast-paced and often exciting. From writing a story to soliciting an advertisement, producing a newspaper involves a great deal of coordination.

The editorial or news department of a daily newspaper generally is divided by subject area: City desk, National/foreign desk, News/copy desk (where stories are edited and decisions made as to what goes into the main news section), editorial page, opinion page, features, arts and entertainment, business/financial, real estate, sports, graphics (picture desk, photo department, art department), and Sunday magazine. Supervising these areas are the editor or editor-in-chief, the managing editor, and one or more assistant managing editors.

The largest departments within the editorial department most often are the city desk, features, and sports. On smaller daily newspapers, one person may be responsible for a function, such as the editorial page or business/financial. On a weekly newspaper, one person may be responsible for a number of subjects.

People interested in editorial work on a newspaper may aspire to a number of reporting, writing, and editing positions. In covering and interpreting the community, the nation, and the world for their readers, newspapers employ: general assignment reporters; beat reporters (covering the police department, city hall, the county building, the federal building, and various courts); rewrite men and women (who work in the office developing stories by telephone and writing them from reporters on the scene); copy editors (who edit copy for style and accuracy and who write headlines); specialists (including investigative reporters and consumer, education, labor, science, medical, ur-

were developed to increase production, and, more importantly, the linotype machine had been invented.

At this time, the great newspaper magnates appeared: William Randolph Hearst, Adolph S. Ochs of the *New York Times*, and Joseph Pulitzer. Each large city had several newspapers. With such intense competition for readership, sensationalism, otherwise know as "yellow journalism," flourished.

Since then, American newspapers have progressed from partisan journals and personal journalism through penny press, sensationalism, and muckraking to the Watergate era of the 1970s, which made investigative journalism the goal of almost every young reporter.

Perhaps the most dramatic technological change in the newspaper industry has been the advent of computers. Anthony Smith, in his book *Goodbye Gutenberg*, credits the computer with bringing about a third great transformation in human communication, comparable to the advent of writing and the invention of printing from movable type. In the 1980s and 1990s, reporters and editors on all of the larger papers now work at video display terminals and wire news comes by high-speed transmission. Computer-fed phototypesetters produce articles and headlines in "cold" (film) type at a rate of 2,000 lines a minute; whole pages are beamed by satellite in a matter of seconds to printing plants half a nation away. Gone are the noisy newsrooms with their competing typewriters, shouts of "Copy!" and never-ending clatter of teletype machines. Gone are the composing rooms with their clacking rows of linotype machines setting "hot" (metal) type.

Newspapers fall into various categories: daily and weekly, morning and evening, city ban affairs, political, and religion writers); and bureau reporters (assigned to nearby communities or the state capital). Larger newspapers have offices in several domestic and foreign cities. They also employ their own foreign correspondents, cartoonists, feature writers, columnists and critics, business and financial writers, news photographers, wire editors, photo editors, artists, news and layout editors, and editorial assistants.

While stories are being written and edited, the advertising department is busy soliciting ads and cultivating clients. Advertising is responsible for some 70 to 75 percent of the newspapers' revenue. Local advertising accounts for the largest portion of newspaper ad revenue.

Newspaper advertising is divided into display and classified departments. The display segment is further divided into national advertisements (usually placed through agencies) and local advertisements, which the newspaper sales force seek out. National advertisers and large local retail operations submit advertising copy to newspapers; however, in smaller communities, the advertising department often designs the local ads themselves. Larger newspapers maintain advertising sales offices in other cities.

The classified department includes small-print notices that clients purchase by the word. There is not a classified sales forces, rather people call in to place an ad. Many classified sections are divided into categories such as announcements, legal services, personals, help wanted, rentals, automotive sales, miscellaneous sales, and lost and found.

Once the stories have been written and the advertisement are set for the day, the production department pulls all of the text together and prints the paper. In other words, the production department is responsible for the finished product. It is divided basically into the composing room, where the pages are assembled and made up as specified by the editorial and advertising departments, and the pressroom, where the paper is printed. Such a process involves putting the words into type, laying out the pages, making photographic plates of the pages, and operating the press.

The electronic revolution has greatly changed newspaper production, making many pressroom jobs more technical. New publishing techniques are constantly being developed, making presses that were purchased only ten years ago nearly obsolete.

Once the paper is printed, it is up to the circulation department to get the newspaper to the reader. Circulation income from street sales, home delivery, and mail subscriptions

Given today's technological advances, the editorial aspects of newspaper publishing are almost entirely computerized.

provides 20 to 25 percent of the newspapers' total revenue. The department also develops sales and subscription contests and incentives.

Newspapers also have business offices; secretaries and clerical help are employed in all departments. In addition, many medium- and large-sized newspapers have separate departments for functions that require particular skills. For example the human resources department includes personnel, payroll, benefits, and training. Many newspapers employ labor relations specialists to handle union contracts with their editorial and other employees, circulation drivers, printers, and pressmen. In addition, many large newspapers have lawyers to assist them in libel suits. Some newspapers have market research departments that do their own market studies to find out about their audience and to assist in advertising sales.

Promotion and public relations departments furnish material such as ads, truck posters, contests, and giveaways to give the paper more exposure. Newspaper also sponsor special events like track meets, concerts, and children's programs. Such promotions help create a good image for the newspaper.

Careers

A sampling of newspaper careers follows below.

Publishers: The publisher is the person responsible for determining publishing policies

An account executive in the advertising department must cultivate good relations with his client. In this case, he is discussing the possibility of placing certain ads in the newspaper.

and for the overall direction of the company. He or she may be the owner or may be selected by the owner or owning group. In some cases, the publisher may assume some editorial responsibility, but for the most part, publishers are business-oriented.

General managers: Larger newspapers employ general managers, who like publishers are concerned with the money-making and the money-saving aspects of the business. They work closely with the publisher.

Editors-in-chief: The editor, who is the most autonomous of the persons reporting to the publisher, is responsible for determining editorial policy and exercises final authority over all editorial department decisions.

Managing editors: The managing editor is responsible for the smooth flow of all materials into production according to the priorities of the moment. This is especially tricky when there is more than one edition a day. In addition to responsibility for editorial content, the managing editor serves as the general manager of the news department.

Associate editors: An associate editor, when there is one, is in charge of the editorial page, reporting to the managing editor and, in a few instances, to the publisher.

Reporters: Reporters are responsible for finding newsworthy events and writing accurate accounts of what happened and why it happened. They may investigate certain happenings over a long period of time or be assigned to cover a local meeting and write an article for the next day's paper. Reporters may also write feature articles about important or interesting people.

Photographers: Staff photographers take pictures and develop them for publication. While some photographs are offered through wire services, photographers are needed to highlight local news. They often accompany reporters on assignment.

Advertising managers: Advertising managers oversee the entire advertising department. They assign accounts to the salespeople, keep track of those accounts, and, in smaller papers, solicit advertisements themselves.

Advertising salespersons: An advertising salesperson generally works on salary and commission. Sales ability is required as well as knowledge of the market, the product (the newspaper), and retailing. The advertising salesperson, especially on a smaller newspaper or weekly, may help the advertiser prepare an ad.

Classified salespeople: These people accept classified advertisements either over the phone or in the office.

Graphic artists: Graphic artists design special sections of newspapers and often work with the advertisers to create appealing ads.

Circulation managers: Circulation managers oversee the entire operation of the circulation department. It is their job to direct the drivers, supervise the carriers, and keep track of sales and subscribers. Circulation executives may also determine how many copies of each edition are printed, judging on the basis of such variables as the news and the weather.

Drivers: Drivers deliver newspapers to the newsstands, stores, and vending machines where they are sold.

Newspaper deliverers: Otherwise known as "paper boys" or "paper girls," these people bring the paper to home subscribers.

Camera operators: Camera operators develop special plates that represent finished pages of the newspaper. The plates are then placed on the press.

Press operators: Press operators run the presses. Such a task involves loading paper, adding ink, monitoring the reproduction quality, and repairing the press when it breaks down.

Education

James Gordon Bennett, Jr., publisher of the New York *Herald,* a century ago said a journalist should be "inquisitive, catty, human, eccentric, generous, and pernicious in turn, kindly and inexpressibly brutal from moment to moment, broad-minded, well-read, and suspicious." It is not necessary to be eccentric (though journalists can be), and catty, pernicious, and brutal are not recommended traits.

Yet Bennett's list indicates that a journalist may be many things in the search for truth.

A journalist needs to be inquisitive, inquiring, interested in people and their activities, their conflicts, and their tragedies. He or she must have a desire for facts and be concerned with all of Kipling's five Ws and the H—the who, what, when, where, how, and why—especially the why. Curiosity also is reflected in being well-read.

The second chief quality for journalism is demonstrated in Bennett's statement itself: A feel for and love of language and writing, for the meaning of words and the way they are used. Do not apply for a newspaper job and say, "I think I'd like to write"; if you don't know, you don't belong in journalism. If you like to write and want to write, read good writing. There are successful reporters on newspapers who are only average or even poor writers. But the men and women who hold the top positions and command the highest salaries are the best writers and editors.

The journalist also should be human and caring, sympathetic and understanding, fair and accurate, as well as questioning and suspicious. Other qualities that make a good journalist include enthusiasm, initiative, aggressiveness (but not obnoxiousness), and an outgoing personality. Most of all, a journalist must understand and reflect emotions; newspapers, like people, are more interesting when they are angry, enthusiastic, caring, or the like.

Many of the preceding qualities serve in other departments of the newspaper such as advertising and circulation. Enthusiasm, initiative, aggressiveness, and a positive personality are aids in selling as well as reporting. Writing ability is an advantage in any occupation, not only newspaper work.

Good preparation for a newspaper career is working on a school newspaper, in any capacity, both for the experience and to see what it is like. Another preparation, elementary as it seems, is to read a newspaper or newspapers regularly. Today a college degree is virtually a requirement for a writing or editing position on any newspaper. Business, marketing, and selling courses are helpful in other departments of the newspaper. Computer knowledge is also helpful.

Editors differ on whether they prefer a journalism degree or a liberal arts degree. But increasingly they welcome and hire the journalism graduate. Graduates who have served an internship improve their employment prospects. These graduates come prepared with both a knowledge of the field and some experience. Journalism students may work on newspapers as interns while still in school.

In the fast-paced environment of newspaper publishing, typesetters must work rapidly.

Industry outlook

Newspaper reporting and editing are not only interesting and challenging, but they offer opportunity for creative expression, satisfaction, and self-fulfillment as well. This is also true, in different ways, of other areas of newspaper employment.

The American Newspaper Publishers Association has listed these attractions of working for a newspaper: proximity to well-known public figures; access to inside information; satisfaction in recording the daily history of one's time (being there when news is happening); and the opportunity to write. The newspaper writer and editor also have the satisfaction of being able to influence events and public opinion through informing, interpreting, and providing comment. There is the excitement that reaches every department when a big story breaks, and the professionalism that operates to bring the story to the public quickly and accurately. There is the feeling of being the first or among the first to know.

Reporters, writers, and columnists sometimes become familiar figures to those they cover and to the public. The editor and publisher are important persons in the community. Newspaper experience also is a way to careers in other fields such as radio and television journalism; agency, corporate, and institutional public relations; advertising; and magazine journalism of various kinds. These fields look for and sometimes even require newspaper background. Newspaper writers go on to write books, novels, plays, and film scripts, drawing in various ways on their newspaper experience.

There were about 1,200 daily newspapers in the United States in 1990 with a total circulation (number of copies sold or distributed each day) at about sixty-two million. The majority of newspapers are distributed in the evening. Some papers publish morning and evening editions. In most communities, there is only one daily newspaper.

In addition to daily newspapers, there are approximately 7,500 weekly newspapers in the United States, including neighborhood and suburban papers as well as small town editions.

Individual newspaper circulations range from a few thousand or less to more than a million. There are special interest newspapers for banking, business, law, labor, medicine, real estate, home furnishings, oil, and other industries. Ethnic newspapers (including German, Greek, Japanese, Chinese, Polish, and Spanish) number in the hundreds.

The newspaper industry is expected to grow slightly through the 1990s. In the future it is expected that larger numbers of blacks, Hispanics, and other minorities will get involved in newspaper publishing.

◇ **SOURCES OF ADDITIONAL INFORMATION**

American Newspaper Publishers Association
The Newspaper Center
PO Box 17407
Dulles International Airport
Washington, DC 20041

National Newspaper Association
1627 K Street, NW, Suite 400
Washington, DC 20006

National Press Foundation
1282 National Press Building
Washington, DC 20045

Printing Industries of America
1730 North Lynn Street
Arlington, VA 22209

Newspaper Advertising Bureau
1180 Avenue of the Americas
New York, NY 10036

◇ **RELATED ARTICLES**

Volume 1: Advertising; Book Publishing; Broadcasting; Design; Magazine Publishing; Marketing; Printing; Pulp and Paper; Telecommunications
Volume 2: Advertising workers; Cartoonists and animators; Commercial artists; Designers; Marketing, advertising, and public relations managers; Media specialists; Photographers and camera operators; Public relations specialists; Reporters and correspondents; Writers and editors
Volume 3: Communications equipment mechanics; Electrotypers and stereotypers; General maintenance mechanics; Lithographic occupations; Printing press operators and assistants; Route drivers; Truck drivers, local and over-the-road; Typists and word processors
Volume 4: Darkroom technicians; Graphic arts technicians; Library technicians

Nuclear Sciences

General information

The nuclear sciences encompass a variety of industries ranging from medical treatment to weaponry. The most prominent application of nuclear sciences is in the field of energy. Nuclear energy is an important power source. From it has come new power plants, new forms of motive power, and new products. The nuclear energy field embraces parts of many different industries, from uranium ore mining to the packaging and distribution of radioactive compounds. Nuclear technology has applications in many areas of research and development.

Knowledge of radioactivity has existed for less than a century. While scientists have suspected the presence of radioactivity since the 1600s, it was not until 1896 that the French physicist Henri Bequerel discovered natural radioactivity in uranium. Two years later Marie and Pierre Curie worked with uranium ore and found two new radioactive elements: radium and polonium. Both Bequerel and the Curies discovered radioactivity through the use of photographic plates that, when exposed to uranium, detected the discharged rays.

The discovery of radiation led to further investigations of atomic structure. In the early 1900s, the British physicist Ernest Rutherford discovered high-energy radioactive alpha and beta particles and later located the nucleus of the atom. Meanwhile, the German scientist Max Planck proposed the quantum theory that described radiation as an emission of minuscule particles, not a continuous stream of energy as previously thought. Albert Einstein expounded upon the quantum theory, suggesting that the cause of particle emissions was due to the collision of photons with matter. Scientists later confirmed that radioactivity derives from both streams, or waves, and particles. In 1913, the Danish physicist Niels Bohr discovered the presence of electrons that orbit an atom's nucleus. He noted that, if the electrons are temporarily displaced from their orbit, they emit energy when returning to their position.

The reactions that were observed at this time occurred naturally and uncontrollably. When atoms are split due to the collision of a particle with an atom, the reaction is called fission. If volatile, radioactive materials are kept too close to one another, the particles that they emit strike nearby atoms and lead to more fission. This is called a chain reaction.

Physicists were aware of the dangers and potential benefits of fission. As they continued to unveil the structure of atoms in the 1930s, they tried to control the rate of radioactive emissions and harness the energy. In 1938, Lise Meitner and Otto Frisch of Austria created the first artificially-induced fission reaction. In 1942, Enrico Fermi and his team of scientists at the University of Chicago split the atom, thereby creating a chain reaction. This made possible the development of the atomic bomb and atomic energy.

During the 1940s and 1950s, American physicists dedicated much of their research to the development of nuclear weapons and nuclear-powered submarines. It was not until 1957 that Americans used their technical knowledge of nuclear sciences toward peaceful uses, establishing the first nuclear plant in Shippingport, Pennsylvania.

More than three decades have passed since the United States initiated its Atoms for Peace program to promote peaceful uses of nuclear energy as a national objective. During the 1970s, nuclear energy-related activity in the United States grew rapidly, with the number of firms involved in the manufacture and delivery of nuclear-related products and services more than doubling. Although much of this growth occurred in major areas of nuclear energy activity (the nuclear fuel cycle, power plants, reactor design and manufacture, and nuclear research), a large number of firms were engaged

329

A nuclear materials handling technician removes a dendritic deposit of uranium from an electrorefiner.

in many other related activities, such as nuclear facility maintenance, protective clothing, transportation and shipping, environmental monitoring equipment services, information services, and training of nuclear plant personnel.

In addition, other nuclear-related activities, such as radioisotope products and radiography services, continued to expand. The United States's nuclear energy industry has matured and shifted from emphasis on research and development to large-scale commercial activities.

The structure of the nuclear sciences industry

The nuclear sciences begin with natural radioactive sources that are carefully mined. Uranium mining is done mostly in New Mexico, Wyoming, Utah, Colorado, and Arizona. Workers in uranium mills extract uranium from uranium ore and apply metallurgical and chemical processes to prepare the uranium for further processing as feed materials. Uranium

mills are located in the same area as uranium mines.

At the beginning of the fission chain, uranium-bearing ores must be located and mined. After standard physical and chemical treatment, the heavy metal, uranium, is further refined to produce a concentrate that becomes feed material for further processing and purification. This material is the starting point for manufacturing nuclear fuels required for all types of reactors.

Uranium, being chemically active, is usually found in combination with other materials such as uranium silicate, sulfate, and phosphate. Actually, uranium is more abundant in the earth's crust than gold, silver, or platinum, although concentrations vary widely. Uranium metal occurs in more than a hundred different minerals. Few of these, however, contain large enough concentrations to make extraction economically viable.

Prospecting techniques have changed from relatively simple methods of recognizing radioactive outcroppings through the use of a Geiger counter to prospecting with aircraft equipped with sensitive radiation detection equipment. By study of topography and careful planning, large areas can be surveyed in a short time. Core drillings can then be made to determine how rich the deposit is and if exploitation is warranted. Obtaining these raw materials requires geologists, mining engineers, and chemists with a knowledge of uranium, its companion products, and their properties.

The feed materials processing represents an operation between mining/milling and reactor operation. By further purification, using solvent extraction techniques, the uranium is converted to the fluoride by hydrofluorination. At this point, some of the material may be reduced to the metal and used as a fuel in reactor operations. Reactors of this type use natural uranium, which has more than 99 percent uranium-238. U-238 is the principal naturally occurring isotope of uranium. The others are U-235 and U-234. Atoms of the same element have the same number of protons, but may have different numbers of neutrons in their nucleus. These variations are known as isotopes. Some are stable, whereas others may be radioactive. It was found that U-238 will absorb a neutron and shortly become the radioactive element of plutonium. Plutonium can be induced to undergo a fission reaction, or splitting, caused by internal neutrons as well as U-235.

Discoveries by early researchers showed that U-235 is the isotope that undergoes fission naturally. Since this isotope only occurs as one part in 140 of natural uranium, some effective means had to be devised to concentrate it. Of

Two nuclear reactor operator technicians monitor the controls at a nuclear power plant. They must be attentive at all times.

several different approaches, the gaseous diffusion process appeared to be the most effective.

Milled uranium is refined and enriched, and the uranium and thorium concentrates are converted into purified and enriched feed materials. This activity is centered in Ohio, Tennessee, and Kentucky. Many of the plants are highly automated and require highly skilled workers who are responsible for maintaining the plant and machinery.

While radioactive materials are being mined and processed, reactor manufacturers work on building and designing nuclear energy plants. This segment of the industry includes the manufacture of fuel elements for reactors; the design, manufacture, and assembly of reactors and reactor components; and the design and engineering of nuclear facilities, including nuclear reactor housings, nuclear energy laboratories, reactor fuel processing plants, and other facilities for nuclear energy applications.

A nuclear reactor consists of several components. One such component is the radioactive fuel, which comes in the form of bundles of long rods containing pellets. Then there are control rods, which contain elements such as boron that absorb neutrons and are used to control the power of a reactor by movement of the rods in and out of the core. The reactor core is the center of the reactor where nuclei split and energy is released. The core is surrounded by reflecting materials that bounce stray neutrons back to the fuel. The auxiliary equipment is composed of all the components necessary for the safe and efficient functioning of a reactor system, including pumps and valves which operate under extreme conditions of pressure and intense radiation level.

The nuclear reaction called fission, which is the splitting of any atom, but more commonly uranium, and radiation, which is the emission of alpha, beta, and gamma rays by nuclei, constitute the unique aspects of nuclear energy. The energy that is released comes from changes and adjustments in the nucleus of an atom. The energy we get from conventional fuel, such as coal, oil, wood, and the like, is called combustion. Combustion results from changes in the outer structure, or electron arrangement, of the atoms. A major difference lies in the much greater amount of energy available inside the nucleus.

Exploiting the use of nuclear energy for the benefits of humanity, while minimizing the harmful effects, is the job of scientists and engineers. Except for the unique problems caused by this energy and attendant radiation, work in the nuclear energy field does not differ significantly from work in many other fields.

As with a power plant that uses conventional fossil fuels such as coal, oil, or gas, the heart of the system is the furnace. In a nuclear

A nuclear scientist experiments with chemicals and drugs that may enhance the progress of nuclear medicine.

power plant, uranium or plutonium takes the place of fossil fuel. Heat is generated from the fission of the nuclear fuel. To convert this energy from heat to electricity, a conventional generator is used as the energy converter to produce electricity. In this oversimplified description, a few pounds of uranium, for example, are equivalent to tons of conventional fossil fuel. In addition to larger facilities, the reactor industry has developed small compact power plants for use on remote military and scientific bases.

An unfortunate by-product of nuclear energy is radioactive waste, which must be disposed in a matter that is not harmful to the environment. A segment of the industry is responsible for the packaging and disposal of radioactive waste materials, such as radioisotopes, protective clothing, and spent (used) reactor fuel.

Other than nuclear energy, there are many industries involved with the nuclear sciences. Nuclear instrument manufacturing is one of them. Engineers and technicians are employed by companies that make reactor control instruments and radiation detection and monitoring devices.

Perhaps the most versatile use of nuclear energy is the use of radioisotopes as tracers to follow what is happening in dynamic systems. Very few areas of scientific research have not benefitted from the judicious use of radioisotopes in one form or another. Radioisotopes also provide the medical profession with diagnostic and therapeutic techniques in the battle against disease. Medical technicians work closely with physicians in the application of these techniques.

One common medical use of radioisotopes is to determine how the thyroid gland of a patient is functioning. Under the physician's su-

pervision, a technician may be required to assay the radioisotope, in this case iodine-131, prepare the prescribed dose, and make the scan. Since the thyroid selectively takes up the element iodine, the radioactive atoms are also picked up. These signals are then measured with a sensitive counter, and a picture of the thyroid's function emerges. Similar tests using drugs and pharmaceuticals tagged with radioisotopes determine the function of other organs of the body, such as the kidneys and the liver. Other radioisotopes can be used to measure the total blood volume of a patient and survival time of red blood cells. There are numerous therapeutic uses that require skills in the handling and use of radioactive materials.

One of the most widespread applications arising from the development of the nuclear industry is radioisotope radiography. Radiography is the use of penetrating radiation, such as gamma or X rays, to examine voids in solid or welded specimens. These radiographic devices are often called cameras since they function in much the same way. The radiation, like light, exposes the film placed behind or around the object. Voids, cracks, or other weaknesses show up in the developed film without destroying the object. This application of nuclear sciences has resulted in an efficient and cost-saving way of meeting the higher quality and greater safety specifications required for many products today, both for civilian and military use.

Nuclear weapons and defense material production works extensively with nuclear materials. The production of nuclear weapons, weapons components, and other defense materials requires large numbers of physicists, chemists, and mechanical, electrical, and electronics engineers. These scientists and engineers are assisted by engineering and physical science technicians, drafters, and radiation monitors.

Other nuclear energy activities include processing and packaging isotopes; designing, constructing, and operating nuclear accelerators; and producing special materials such as beryllium, zirconium, and hafnium for use in reactors.

Over a thousand private companies are engaged in manufacturing and selling a variety of nuclear products and services, such as nuclear reactors, neutron howitzers, radiation detection equipment, and other items that are used in colleges, universities, and research and development facilities.

Some companies specialize in the manufacture of particle accelerators. Research in high-energy physics requires powerful machines that enable scientists to study the fundamental particles of nature. Other firms are engaged in the processing and packaging of radioisotope and specially labeled compounds for medical and research purposes. Still others produce smoke detectors, lightning rods, and radioluminescent lights, all using radioactive materials.

Much of the work in the nuclear sciences industry is overseen by the U.S. Nuclear Regulatory Commission.

Careers

Most of the people working in nuclear energy are engaged in designing and engineering nuclear facilities and in developing and manufacturing nuclear weapons, nuclear reactors, and reactor components. Many people are also involved in research and development. Most people working in the nuclear energy field are scientists, engineers, technicians, and craft workers. Other large groups of employees are service workers in production operations and office personnel in administrative and clerical jobs. A sampling of career opportunities follows.

Nuclear physicists: Physicists study the properties of materials or matter. They conduct research into the building blocks that make up matter—subatomic particles. The research may be about the physical characteristics of the matter or about the manner of motion of matter, either naturally occurring or induced. Quantum mechanics is the study of the structure and motion of atomic particles and the elements of radiation.

Nuclear engineers: On the experimentation side of nuclear physics, nuclear engineers conduct research to prove or disprove theories of nuclear structures and behaviors. They design and develop equipment in which to conduct nuclear tests, and they operate and direct the use of nuclear equipment, including reactors.

Physics technicians: Physics technicians usually assist scientists or engineers in the measurement of physical properties on a wide variety of materials. This type of work may include assisting in fundamental research or quality control testing to make sure materials meet specifications.

Metallurgy technicians: Metallurgy technicians often perform many of the same tasks as physics technicians, although they are more concerned with determining physical properties. Duties may include preparation of test samples, and determining tensile properties, compression strength, and hardness. This work is normally done in a laboratory associated with a research and development organization.

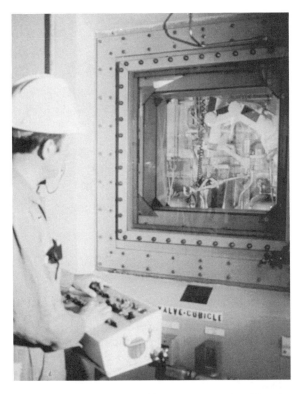

A nuclear materials handling technician removes contaminated items by operating a robot via remote control.

"Hot cell" technicians: These workers operate "slave manipulators" (mechanical devices that act as a pair of arms and hands) in an area enclosed with radiation-shielding materials, such as lead or concrete. By looking through thick lead-glass windows, these technicians operate remote-controlled equipment to test various materials and equipment. They may perform standard chemical and metallurgical tests using radioactive materials.

Power plant maintenance workers: As a part of a nuclear-fueled power plant's maintenance staff, such specialists as mechanics, millwrights, machinists, and welders must receive nuclear-specific training. Not only are they required to maintain and repair equipment unique to a nuclear plant but they also must be intimately aware of the precision tolerances, procedural requirements, and environmental conditions associated with the operation of a nuclear power plant.

Nuclear power plant operators: Nuclear power plant operators are responsible for the safe and efficient day-to-day generation of power in a nuclear power plant. These employees include licensed reactor operators, as well as auxiliary equipment and utility operators.

Miners and drillers: Miners and drillers collect radioactive materials.

333

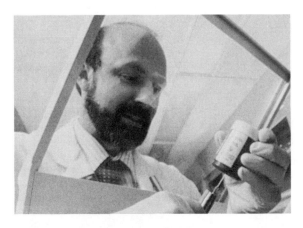

Many scientists dedicate their time to the advancement of nuclear medicine in the hopes of finding a cure for cancer.

Equipment operators: Equipment operators use machines that retrieve and transport materials from the mine to a processing plant. They work in both open pit and underground mines.

Geologists: Geologists use their knowledge of the earth's crust to help locate uranium deposits.

Mining engineers: Mining engineers are involved in the planning and design of mines. With the geologists, they must determine the location of the uranium. When the mines are in operation, they see that everything is running smoothly.

Chemists: Chemists are chief among the many scientists employed by research laboratories and other institutions. They conduct basic and applied research into nuclear energy.

Nuclear medicine technologists: Nuclear medicine technologists prepare and administer radioactive drugs that are used in the diagnosis and treatment of certain diseases. This is done under the supervision of a physician. Nuclear medicine technologists also perform laboratory tests of a patient's blood volume and fat absorption to determine the effect of the radioactive material.

Senior operators: Senior operators direct the activities of licensed and non-licensed operators. The licensed operator, who is responsible for manipulation of controls, mechanisms, and equipment operable from the control room, may be assisted in these tasks by non-licensed individuals.

Auxiliary equipment and utility operators: Auxiliary equipment and utility operators position valves, operate radiation waste systems, monitor local instrumentation, and perform other duties that are necessary for the safe and efficient operation of the facility.

Health physicists: Health physicists help protect individuals and property from radiation by detecting radiation and controlling exposures to it. They set up standards of inspection and establish procedures for protecting workers. They also supervise the inspection of work areas for radiation hazards and inspect radioactive waste and other materials to ensure compliance with government standards and regulations. A health physicist may also plan and supervise training programs concerned with radiation hazards and advise public authorities on methods of dealing with such hazards.

Health physics technicians: The health physics technician (or radiation monitor) usually works under the supervision of a health physicist. A technician in this field must be trained to monitor radiation-producing machines and radioactive sources used in research, industry, and hospitals. He or she should be able to analyze and compute the quantity of radioisotopes produced in a nuclear reactor, as well as monitor medical and dental X-ray installations. A radiological technician must be able to detect and measure the basic types of radiation, prepare and analyze environmental samples for radioactivity content, and perform decontamination procedures when necessary. This person should also be able to calibrate and help maintain radiation detection equipment.

Another important function of the technician is to analyze the monitoring equipment worn by workers, such as film badges and pocket detection devices that measure each individual's exposure. In certain types of operations, technicians have to calculate and prescribe the amount of time personnel may work in contaminated or high radiation-level areas.

Quality control technicians: The quality control technician tests, inspects, and audits materials, equipment, and processes to ensure that all are maintained within specified qualitative and quantitative limits. Such a technician may conduct nondestructive testing of materials and workmanship in compliance with regulations and specifications. It is the technician's job to ensure that the working environment is safe.

Chemical technicians: A chemical technician is usually a laboratory aide or assistant, depending on the amount of previous experience. He or she is normally part of a team working under the supervision of a professional chemist. The chemical technician performs a wide variety of analytical tests using standard chemical laboratory equipment, from microbalances to special nuclear equipment such as survey meters, radiation counters, and other nuclear instrumentation. High standards of precision and accuracy are required. In working on a research and development project, the technician may assist the chemist by setting up specialized apparatus and even conducting experiments.

Electricians: Electricians face unique technical problems as well as extreme environmental conditions (heat, stress, and radiation) while working in nuclear power plants. Electricians working in nuclear power plants require general nuclear training and orientation.

Education

The groundwork necessary for those who aspire to a professional career in science or engineering should begin in high school. An interest in mathematics and science is essential. The important sciences include physics, chemistry, and biology. Mathematics at this stage should be pursued through algebra, plane and solid geometry, and trigonometry. Subjects such as English, history, languages and other social sciences should not be overlooked. The art of communication is essential to any successful scientist or engineer.

During the first two years of college, training in mathematics and basic sciences should be continued. During the third and fourth year, the student should begin specialization in some field of science or engineering. Among the sciences, physics and chemistry have been essential in developing the basic ideas about the atom and the release of nuclear energy. However, other fields such as biology are also necessary for a more complete understanding of this energy and its use.

Graduate studies leading to a master's or doctorate degree provide academic specialization in a chosen field. To be adequately prepared for graduate study in nuclear engineering, competency in mathematics through differential equations is a prerequisite. A solid background in the engineering sciences and physics is also required. Familiarity with computer mathematics is desirable, as is an understanding of engineering design.

Qualified graduate students have opportunities for advanced study in virtually every field related to nuclear energy. College graduates wishing to pursue advanced studies in nuclear science and engineering or radiation science and protection may choose from a number of leading universities. For research work as a nuclear engineer or physicist, a doctorate is accepted as the minimum education for most jobs in private industry. For posts in research or teaching positions at universities, doctorates are also required.

The opportunities for specialized training in technical institutes and junior colleges is an option for students who are interested in positions where the work involves assisting some-

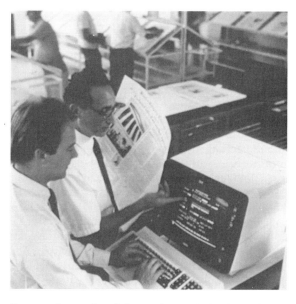

Two researchers monitor a fusion experiment at the Los Alamos Scientific Laboratory in New Mexico.

one with a graduate degree in nuclear physics. In general, the technical institute offers an educational program that specializes in one or more areas to prepare engineering or industrial technicians. These technicians function as assistants to professional scientists or engineers or frequently are operators of their own technical businesses.

A nuclear engineering program for technicians usually covers a two-year period with courses in subjects such as analytic geometry, calculus, physical chemistry, electronic circuitry, drafting, atomic and nuclear physics, principles of reactor operations, and nuclear instrumentation. Such positions as radiation safety technicians, chemistry laboratory technicians, and control instrumentation technicians can be filled by the graduates of such programs.

The term "technician" has been used over the years in many different ways, and has acquired widely different meanings, depending on the context in which it is used. This person is a semiprofessional. He or she may be expected to have a number of mechanical skills, but is usually not as intensively qualified as a specialized crafts person. Also, a technician must have some theoretical knowledge, but not as much as the scientist or engineer. A large number of employed technicians are persons who have advanced from the ranks of the blue-collar crafts person. The growing trend, however, is for two-year college or technical institute training as an employment requirement.

Industry outlook

Questions about public health and safety have continued to receive a great deal of public attention since the accident at Three Mile Island in Pennsylvania in 1979. In October 1985, the unharmed Unit One at Three Mile Island resumed operation after legal battles. Concern about the environmental effects of nuclear waste, actual and proposed state and federal moratoriums on new nuclear power plant construction and operations, rapidly increasing construction costs, changes in required power plant design and engineering, and a reduction in forecast growth in electricity requirements all contribute to present uncertainties that may reduce growth in the nuclear energy field.

Two major factors still contribute to the growth of nuclear power. One is competitiveness with conventional fuels. According to the American Nuclear Society, nuclear energy will be very competitive with coal despite high costs of nuclear units' electric power in the mid-1980s. The other factor is the knowledge that we have limited fossil fuel resources in a world of expanding requirements for power. Research and development on new reactor types have shown considerable promise in further lowering the cost of nuclear power and assuring an adequate source of fuel for the future. Breeder reactors, for instance, convert or breed more fissionable material than is burned in the operation of the plant.

Uranium metal oxidizes rapidly in air and under friction is highly combustible. For these and other reasons involving improvements in reactor design, the fabrication of uranium metal into fuel elements and other uranium-metal alloys is a continuing area of research and development.

Most of the employment in the nuclear energy field for scientists, engineers, and technicians is found in three segments—reactor design and manufacture, design of nuclear facilities, and nuclear-related research and development activities. The future of the design of nuclear facilities and reactor design and manufacture is obviously related to power plant development and redesign requirements. A reduction in nuclear power plant development for any extended length of time would probably cause a significant decrease in activity and employment in these two segments. Both of these segments employ a large number of scientists, engineers, and technicians with specialized skills.

Few new nuclear power plants are likely to be built before the mid-1990s, and employment of nuclear engineers is expected to increase more slowly than the average for all occupations. Safety standards and defense-related areas appeared to offer the best employment prospects for nuclear engineers.

Much of the nuclear-related research and development activities are government-funded, and most of the activity is located in government-owned, contractor-operated facilities. Obviously, the future of nuclear-related research and development depends primarily on future levels and directions of government funding. Several large-scale laboratories and accelerators are in operation in the United States, including Los Alamos National Laboratory (where nuclear weapons were developed), Fermi Nuclear Accelerator Laboratory, and the Stanford Linear Accelerator Center.

For the experimental research and theoretical study of nuclear physics, many in the profession will be employed by the universities. Many professors combine college research with private business research work. The use of nuclear energy and quantum mechanics helped develop lasers, transistors, and superconductors. With discoveries such as these, it is likely that private businesses will continue to invest in research into particle physics for some time to come.

◇ **SOURCES OF ADDITIONAL INFORMATION**

American Nuclear Society
555 North Kensington Avenue
La Grange Park, IL 60525

Society of Nuclear Medicine
136 Madison Avenue, 8th floor
New York, NY 10016

American Registry of Radiologic Technologists
2600 Wayzata Boulevard
Minneapolis, MN 55405

American Society for Engineering Education
11 Dupont Circle, Suite 200
Washington, DC 20036

◇ **RELATED ARTICLES**

Volume 1: Energy; Engineering; Metals; Mining; Physical Sciences; Waste Management
Volume 2: Biologists; Chemists; Drafters; Engineers; Industrial designers; Nuclear medicine technologists; Physicists
Volume 3 Electricians; Occupational safety and health workers; Operating engineers; Power plant occupations
Volume 4: Biomedical equipment technicians; Chemical technicians; Drafting and design technicians; Energy-conservation technicians; Industrial engineering technicians; Industrial radiological technicians; Industrial safety-and-health technicians; Instrumentation technicians; Mechanical technicians; Metallurgical technicians; Nuclear instrumentation technicians; Nuclear materials handling technicians; Nuclear power plant quality control technicians; Nuclear power plant radiation control technicians; Nuclear reactor operator technicians; Radiological (x-ray technologists

Packaging

General information

Packaging is wrapping, boxing, or bottling goods for consumer, industrial, and military markets. The packaging industry supplies almost every one of the hundreds of industries and thousands of manufacturing establishments that make up industry in the United States. Packaging is one of the largest employers. Increasing sophistication of technology has created a strong demand for packaging specialists.

Often, product innovations require dramatic new packaging forms. Such containers as aerosol cans and bottles, plastic squeeze bottles and trays, aluminum cans, tinplated steel rolled as thin as foil, and foamed synthetic materials have been invented and made into packages that protect products better and are easier for both individual and industrial consumers to use. Developments such as these require large teams of packaging engineers and technicians in user and supplier companies.

Packaging has pragmatic origins, allowing for processed products to be transported and stored with no damage. It was not until the Industrial Revolution in the late eighteenth century, however, that packaging became an important tool for marketing. At that time so many new products were being manufactured, that the consumer had a variety of choices. Often the package determined whether one product would be purchased over another.

While package design has played a vital role in the marketing of a product since the Industrial Revolution, the packaging industry has had to confront the development of new household products and changing American lifestyles. For example, the microwave oven has opened an entirely new packaging market. Many products are packaged in plastic so that they can be conveniently placed in a standard microwave. In addition, many single people want hassle-free meals, demanding individu-ally packaged meals that can be heated in a conventional or microwave oven.

Other household products that have changed the packaging industry include the refrigerator and the freezer. These appliances, in conjunction with new materials such as plastic, have broadened the industry.

Today it is possible to create an almost infinite number of new packaging forms possessing practically every characteristic desired by packaging people. Plastics with new cost-function relationships are being created almost faster than packaging people can learn about them.

The U.S. Food and Drug Administration in late 1982 issued new guidelines on the packaging of capsules and other products that are vulnerable to tampering. The new rules, drawn up in response to a wave of tampering cases, applied to many drugs or preparations that could be ingested, inhaled, injected, or otherwise used. The aim was to prevent deaths or injuries such as those that occurred in 1982 following ingestion of cyanide-laced Tylenol™ capsules. In general, the rules required the addition of tamper-proof seals.

Another recent concern involves the environment. Many packaging firms are developing biodegradable and recyclable products to protect the environment.

Packaging activity is generally spread throughout the United States, but there are, of course, concentrations of packaging plants for specific products. Canned and frozen foods are packaged to a large extent in the great fruit and vegetable growing areas of the Pacific Coast, Midwest, Florida, and the Middle Atlantic states. Specialty foods are packaged in or near large metropolitan areas, particularly New York, Chicago, and Los Angeles. These and other big cities are also centers for toiletry, pharmaceutical, and hardware packaging. In fact, packaging is part of the manufacturing process in just about every one of the manufacturing facilities in the United States.

The structure of the packaging industry

The creation of a package that will be successful in the marketplace involves virtually every department in a company. Thus, an array of talent in the packaging industry is necessary. Packaging is not a single science but a combination of such skills as mechanical and electrical engineering, physical and organic chemistry, food technology, sales, advertising, production, printing, and design.

When a marketable product has been developed, a manufacturing company hires a graphic designer to create an appealing package.

The graphic designer may be faced with either an existing product that needs to be repackaged or a new product. In the first case, the designer has to determine the suitability of new packaging materials to the product and establish a graphic image that is up-to-date and intensifies its competitive position. For a new product entering the marketplace, the designer has somewhat more freedom, but still has to consider the specific needs of the client, manufacturer, retailer, consumer, and economy.

A package is the last link in product communications, and, on the crowded shelves of a supermarket, must serve as a "silent salesman" that conveys the complete story of the product and of the company that produces it. The contribution that packaging adds to the product, however, goes considerably beyond this billboard function. A package is now expected to be functional too. It must adequately protect the product up to the point of sales and beyond and should provide consumers with easy opening and closing features and often assist in the use of the product. This is true, not only of consumer-type packages, but increasingly of containers for industrial and military items as well.

The American consumer is oriented toward self-service. The average U.S. supermarket carries from 8,000 to 10,000 items. While the customer wheels the shopping cart around, each product receives only a fraction of a second's attention. It is therefore extremely important that the shape, color, and graphic image is unique enough to warrant selection.

Within this overall concept, the graphic designer has to incorporate the various requirements specified under government regulations, such as net content statements. The package also has to protect the product against spoilage, breakage, and tampering. It has to contain the exact weight or measure as stated, and has to be convenient to the retailer to stack and to the

This machine bends pieces of cardboard to create creases. The creases then form the edges of a box.

consumer in its end use. Most important, the packaging has to be economical.

To this end, the designer has to investigate the adaptability of the new package to existing machinery as well as space availability on the supermarket shelf. Out of this investigation, the graphic packaging designer has often developed innovative use of methods and materials.

In addition to the package, the graphic designer is often involved in the development of shipping containers as well as point-of-purchase displays and other promotional material related to the presentation of the product to the consumer. Many graphic packaging design firms cover all these functions through in-house personnel; others hire outside consultant services. In either case, the graphic designer is a builder of bridges between manufacturer and consumer.

New package graphics are made possible by computer-generated design for type and other graphic elements, including logos. Many designers continue to favor three-dimensional, physical models, but the computer helps screen choices.

Once a package has been designed, it is up to the engineer to produce the package in mass quantities. It is no longer enough that the engineer be simply an expert in industrial, mechanical, or electrical engineering and apply classical principles to the solution of problems. The engineer who succeeds in packaging must create equipment that efficiently produces the packaging without changing the marketing objectives set forth by the company. Since engineering is a precise form of technology that does not normally encompass subjective considerations such as marketing, its application in the packaging field requires engineers with creativity and intuition.

Fresh loaves of bread are placed into plastic bags without being touched by human hands. Such packaging machines allow for a sterile baking environment.

The introduction of plastic packaging materials and the creation of new packaging forms such as plastic soft-drink containers and flexible food pouches have posed difficult problems in the manufacturing and handling of these packages on production lines. For this reason, the engineer has attained new importance in the packaging field.

As machine speeds increase, simple mechanical methods for controlling action give way to electronic controls. Thus mechanical engineers in packaging companies are being joined by electrical and electronic engineers. The leading professional group for these latter specialists, the Institute of Electrical and Electronic Engineers, has recognized this fact by establishing a packaging subcommittee to study the special problems existing in packaging equipment. The organization for machinery builders, the Packaging Machinery Manufacturers Institute, is also concerned with the recognition of packaging as a legitimate and separate branch of engineering.

Because the functions of machines and materials are interlocked in the creation of a packaging form, some machinery companies and even engineering groups in large packaging organizations now station chemical engineers in the same department with mechanical engineers to give them authoritative answers on materials properties. Chemical engineers are, of course, indispensable in the production of many packaging materials and containers, particularly those incorporating plastics, paper, and paperboard.

As packaging machines have become more automated and packaging operations more complex, there has been a need for closer study of the relationships between workers and machines and of the best methods to achieve efficiency in these production operations. This has led to increasing use of industrial engineers trained specifically in packaging operations.

To solve complex problems in packaging design many companies have turned to computers, making the computer specialist and data-processing staffs a vital part of the packaging function. It is difficult to overestimate the potential importance of these specialists. A majority of packaging professionals polled for a 1986 survey saw robotic packaging operations as an effective means of reducing direct labor costs on the production lines.

The person who often conducts the search for improved packaging technology is the packaging engineer or technologist, assisted by chemical engineers, structural designers, and specialists in quality controls and purchasing.

Increasingly, such research activities are carried forward by a centralized packaging group, directly responsible to top management. In biological or food product companies, these packaging groups (or the research departments with which they work most closely) contain bacteriologists, chemists, and food technologists who apply their backgrounds to the packaging process.

Some companies still use committees made up of representatives from all departments involved in the packaging function to work out packaging problems. In a packaging department, on the other hand, a relatively small group of workers devotes its whole time to working out what has become a continuing series of interconnected problems. Some companies have given the packaging function great status and head the packaging group with a vice president.

The executive in charge of packaging must know or have access to technical knowledge of the materials and methods for constructing packages and determine whether the desired constructions can be produced economically by outside suppliers or by in-plant facilities. There is increasing demand for packaging specialists to act as staff advisers on such technical matters and to coordinate packaging development.

As the American economy has expanded, sales has supplanted production as the key to business success. It is therefore not surprising that, in packaging, the marketing function is regarded as critically important.

To sell packaging materials or machines successfully in the competitive market that exists today, a salesperson must have knowledge of how the product will be used by packagers, and often must supply creative ideas on new package designs or production techniques. Many packaging supply firms employ specialists who can assist the salespeople, including experts in printing and the graphic arts, structural packaging design, and mechanical engineering. This is most true of those companies that convert basic raw materials into finished cartons, cans, and bottles. Basic manufacturers of such raw materials as plastic resins and metal sheet and foil also employ packaging technologists to assist their customers.

Careers

Packaging offers diverse opportunities to young people with imagination and training in engineering, science, and marketing, or in such technical areas as quality control, mechanics, and graphic arts. A sampling of packaging careers follows below.

Packaging engineers: Packaging engineers are involved in every aspect of packaging, from the design of the product to its manufacture. They are involved in such varied tasks as materials development, marketing and package design, and packaging testing. Packaging engineers also work on machinery design. Their expertise is utilized in every industry, from food and pharmaceuticals to industrial products.

Graphic Designers: The role of the graphic designer is a pivotal one in the packaging industry. The graphic designer has to produce a package that elicits a positive reaction from the consumer. The graphic designer also often coordinates the services of the structural designer, photographer, illustrator, typographer, and printer as well as market researcher.

CAD/CAM technicians: CAD/CAM technicians work with computers to design three-dimensional products.

Product managers: In most large packaging companies, overall guidance of packaging programs is frequently given by product managers whose primary training is in business administration, sales, promotion, or advertising.

In addition to those with specific tasks related to package development, the packaging industry also employs large numbers of computer specialists, chemical engineers, market research personnel, and other workers.

Education

Almost all those involved in packaging have a college degree. More than thirty universities and colleges, learning centers, and government agencies offer instruction in various aspects of packaging. Packaging programs in many large companies are often run by men and women

Many packaging designers use computer software programs that have the capacity to project three-dimensional graphics onto the computer screen. This feature allows designers to get a more complete view of the package.

originally trained in business administration, purchasing, or other fields.

Some of the schools that established degree programs include Arizona State University, Cornell University, California Polytechnic University, Indiana State University, Michigan State University, Pratt Institute, Rutgers University, and the universities of California, New Haven, and Wisconsin-Stout. Other universities, colleges, and institutes offer one or more courses in packaging in conjunction with one of their traditional schools of study.

Young people in schools without a packaging major must generally tailor their own program of studies, selecting a combination of science, engineering, and marketing courses. Students should also take courses in design, graphic arts, and technical subjects.

The reason for such breadth of training is that packaging development is rapidly moving toward the systems approach. In this approach, a complete packaging form is created to meet specific marketing objectives by the integration of mechanical principles and packaging materials. In other words, packaging development includes consideration of marketing, machines, and materials. Obviously, a specialist cannot work on a phase of such a systems problem without knowledge and appreciation of the work being done simultaneously by his or her counterparts. Therefore, although packaging people must specialize in a single subject area to attain the depth of knowledge necessary for

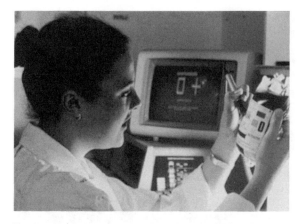

Many product packages contain bar codes that help institutions catalogue items purchased, supplied, or used. The codes are used in all types of goods, including medical supplies such as blood.

a professional career, they must also grasp the fundamentals of the other two facets of packaging so they can understand the objectives toward which they are striving.

Probably the best grounding for people interested in the marketing phase of packaging is business administration, sales, advertising, promotion, and graphic design. Young people interested in the mechanical phases should specialize in mechanical, electrical, electronic, industrial, or chemical engineering. Data processing and statistical control are also useful specialties. People wanting to follow package construction or materials development as careers should have chemistry, chemical engineering, or the technology of paper and paperboard, metals, or plastics in their background.

It cannot be emphasized too strongly that a packaging professional will benefit from knowledge in areas outside his or her specialization. It is impossible, even after a four-year program, for a person to graduate as a packaging expert; this can come only with experience in this complex field. Interested young people should concentrate on getting a broad variety of technical tools with which they can later work, according to the Packing Institute International and the Society of Packaging and Handling Engineers (professional organizations of the packaging field and good sources of information).

Graphics designers follow a different path, often obtaining degrees in the fine arts or other related fields. It is necessary, however, to have a technical background. The Advertising Design Department of the Fashion Institute of Technology in New York City offers a program in graphic packaging design.

Product managers may be trained in marketing, but are most effective when this training is supplemented by additional background

in the chemistry and technology of materials and in printing and mechanical engineering.

Industry outlook

Packaging is an important element in the total U.S. economy. In 1990, the value of selected packaging alone was about $20 billion.

The packaging industry is expected to grow slowly but steadily throughout the 1990s. There will be expanding employment for specialized engineers who can solve specific problems while understanding the total packaging concept.

The importance of packaging in regards to solid waste management will continue to grow. The materials used in the design and development of packages must be viewed as recyclable products. As packages become more and more recyclable, this will help relieve the large amount of packaging now being thrown away as waste matter.

Because the packaging field influences and is influenced by many corporate decisions, it is necessarily complex and dynamic. But for young people willing to grasp a challenge and grow with a job, the packaging field offers continued rewards.

◇ **SOURCES OF ADDITIONAL INFORMATION**

Packaging Institute International
20 Summer Street
Stamford, CT 06901

Society of Packaging Professionals
Reston International Center, Suite 212
11800 Sunrise Valley Drive
Reston, VA 22091

National Institute of Packaging, Handling, and Logistic Engineers
6902 Lyle Street
Lanham, MD 20706

Center for Packaging Education
32 Court Street
Brooklyn Heights, NY 11201

American Institute of Graphic Arts
1059 Third Avenue
New York, NY 10021

◇ **RELATED ARTICLES**

Volume 1: Advertising; Chemistry; Design; Engineering; Food Processing; Marketing; Plastics; Public Relations

Volume 2: Advertising workers; Commercial artists; Designers; Drafters; Engineers; Export-import specialists; Industrial designers; Marketing, advertising, and public relations managers; Marketing research personnel; Packaging engineers

Volume 3: Canning and preserving industry workers; Confectionery industry workers; Industrial chemical workers; Operating engineers; Plastics products manufacturing workers; Retail sales workers; Wholesale trade sales workers

Volume 4: CAD/CAM technicians; Drafting and design technicians; Graphic arts technicians; Packaging and paper products technicians; Plastics technicians; Robotics technicians

Performing Arts

General information

The performing arts are those performed before an audience. Acting, singing, dancing, and playing a musical instrument are all performing arts. The performing arts provide entertainment. They are a source of inspiration and ideas for the community at large, and they reflect social customs.

Ancient peoples often performed elaborate rituals as part of religious ceremonies. These ceremonies were often held to ask the gods for success in hunting or in battle. Often the high priest would put on a mask and colorful costumes. Religious ceremonies were also held to pray for the health of important individuals or to mourn the dead. These ceremonies combined music, dancing, and drama.

Prehistoric paintings found on cave walls in Africa and southern Europe show people dancing. The Egyptians used dance during parades, funerals, and religious ceremonies. The early Romans would dance around a Maypole on May 1, as part of a celebration to Flora, the goddess of spring. Other cultures also used dance as a way of communication with the gods. Many native Americans, for example, danced in an appeal for rain or a good harvest.

Ballet, a type of dance, begin in Italy in the fifteenth century. Ballet performances were held throughout Europe. During the mid-1600s, King Louis XIV of France was a great supporter of ballet. He also was known to participate in ballets.

Modern dance, developed in the early 1900s, began as a response against what was viewed as the formal, set techniques of ballet. Modern dance stressed a less-structured, more personal approach to dance.

In the United States, blacks developed tap-dancing in the 1800s by combining traditional African dances with English and Irish dance steps. People from around the world still use folk dances as an expression of cultural pride.

Drama was created by the early Greeks. These dramas explored a variety of moral dilemmas. Greek dramas were performed as early as 500 B.C. In these dramas, actors wore masks. Men played the parts of women. Usually, only two or three actors were on the stage at the same time. The Romans continued many of the traditions of tragedies and comedies initiated by the Greeks.

Theater spread throughout Europe, often being performed at royal courts and academies. The first public theater in England was built in the 1570s. Dramatic presentations were performed on large, open-air stages. Performances usually began in the afternoon and ended just before nightfall. William Shakespeare was and still is considered the greatest English playwright, but other notable dramatists included Ben Johnson, Thomas Middleton, and Richard Sheridan.

Early American drama (from the 1700s until the early part of this century) was largely patterned after European theater. Important American dramatists from this period include Eugene O'Neill and Thorton Wilder. More recently, Arthur Miller, Tennessee Williams, and David Mamet have contributed important plays.

The minstrel shows were the first authentically American form of show business. Minstrel shows began in the mid-1800s. Minstrel shows featured comedy routines, dances, and short skits. In most cases the performers were white entertainers who darkened their faces to appear black.

The origins of music go back thousands of years. Ancient people began to sing at about the same time they developed language. The Egyptians, Chinese, and other ancient people used music in religious ceremonies. Musical instruments are depicted in paintings from the Mesopotamians and the Egyptians from 3000 B.C. The Greeks had a type of lyre, the kithara, and reed instruments by 1000 B.C.

Dancers from the Hubbard Street Dance Company perform the piece "And Now This," choreographed by Margo Sappington. Dancers undergo rigorous training and many rehearsals before appearing on stage.

The Roman Catholic Church helped spread liturgical music throughout Europe. At first, chants were sung unaccompanied, but later these chants were embellished with melodies. Polyphony, two or more musical melodies being played at once, began in western music sometime between the seventh and tenth century A.D. Gregorian chants added words to musical chants, and began incorporating the singing of chords by different performers.

Not much is recorded of secular music, but it was present. Troubadours were poet-musicians who sang their poems in royal courts and while walking through the countryside. The poems often were words of love exalting a fair lady. Many troubadours were also jugglers and wandering musical entertainers. Troubadours began performing in the twelfth century and continued through the Middle Ages.

The 1600s brought about substantial changes to secular music. Baroque compositions in instrumental pieces developed two specific styles that continue to be performed today: the sonata and the concerto. This became the foundation for orchestral performances, where each instrument is treated as a different voice and the composer seeks to combine the voices in intricate and harmonious melody. Bach, Handel, and Vivaldi were Baroque composers.

The other major development was the opera. Stories were put to music to give them heightened dramatic effect. The Florentine Camerata, lead by the Italian composer Claudio Monteverdi, created the opera as a new art form. They felt that the combination of vocal bravado, music, and acting would form an all-encompassing medium for the performing arts. In the early 1600s, various elements were used with opera to achieve an entertaining performance. Dance, choruses, and spoken text were all used in operatic performances.

Classical music develop in Europe in the 1700s. Wolfgang Amadeus Mozart, Ludwig van Beethoven, and Joseph Haydn are among the composers who created pieces that still are performed throughout the world today.

In the United States, popular music, such as jazz, rock music, and country and western music have dominated the music scene for the last few generations. Rock music developed in the 1950s as a combination of different musical formats, particularly blues music and jazz. With the boom in rock music, the sales of records, cassettes, and eventually videos skyrocketed. Music performances by popular singers can attract thousands of people. It has become one of the most visible types of performing arts.

The structure of the performing arts

For any form of performance, the staff that is involved in executing the production extends far beyond the talent that is seen on the stage. There are workers ranging from directors to lighting technicians. The talent, however, is the most visible and the most well-known of the workers in performance arts.

Each type of performance has one performer or several. Plays have actors and actress. Dances have dancers; operas have singers, and occasionally dancers. Musicals have all three—actors, dancers, and singers. One person may be able to do all aspects of the performance as well. Instrumental music performances have musicians. Singers usually have musicians for accompaniment.

The setting of the performance may be on a stage, in a hall, or even outdoors. Where the piece is performed has a direct influence on the effect the piece has on the audience. The majesty, the intimacy, or the openness of the performance arena all enhance or detract from the performers. How that stage is set is one of the most fundamental elements of how well received a performance may be.

Designing a set is done by set painters, designers, light technicians, stage craftsmen, producers, directors, and other people involved in conceptualizing what will happen behind and around the performers. Scene designers may be hired that will oversee the entire production of scenery, lighting, and furnishings. They will decide what elements will be used and how to enhance the presentation. Scenery behind the performers sets the mood and the location. Lighting sets mood and highlights movements and performers at key points in the presentation. For musical presentations, such as rock concerts, lighting may be the single most important staging tool used to enhance the setting.

Properties, far more commonly known as props, are either set pieces or hand props. Set props are furniture, moving pieces, and other large elements of the stage design that extends from or is separate from the background scenery. Hand props are the things that the performers will carry, such as flowers or umbrellas, that help tell the story or embellish the mood.

Scene designers will draw up plans for each scene depicting how it is to be decorated. The lighting designer will also draw up plans for how each part of the show will be lit. The general lighting, specific illuminations (such as spot lights), and the special effects lighting are all charted, timed and choreographed to the performance.

Sound amplification, sound effects, and recordings are also well plotted before the performance actually begins. If microphones are to be used, the sound technicians will decide where they are placed, how much amplification will be needed, and when they are to be switched on and off. Body microphones, floor microphones, and boom (hanging) microphones all allow for different aspects of the sound to be emphasized. Sound effects are recorded in advance of the performance, if needed, or are recreated by sound effect technicians during a performance. Sound boards that control effects, amplification, and recording are controlled by the technicians during the performance.

Makeup and costuming are expressive elements of the appearance of the performers that augments and reinforces the mood and story. Makeup and costuming are regularly associated with plays, but they are a fundamental part of dance and opera as well. Even the most basic, simple costumes have been carefully chosen to help tell the story or present the spirit of the piece being presented.

All of these elements help establish the aura that will surround the performance. The actual performance is designed and developed by the workers who will direct the show. The directors work with actors, actresses, and singers; the choreographer works with dancers; and the conductor works with musicians. The role of the director, conductor, and choreographer is to plot out the movements, the voices, and the actions of the performers throughout the presentation (see Volume 2: Dancers and choreographers; Musical occupations).

Assisting the direction are stage managers, who may run auditions, attend rehearsals, and write down changes to direction during rehearsal so they can be incorporated into the master directing plan. Assistant directors may direct some elements of the performance and focus on particular performers for coaching and training.

Choreographers follow the same format for assembling a production that directors do. They must audition performers, rehearse the performers, block out the action that will take place on stage, then combine the elements of design, action, lighting, and sound into a cohesive piece. Such a task requires an understanding of music and storyline.

Conductors may be less concerned with the action of their performers in terms of visual presentation to the audience. An orchestra does not choreograph stage movement. The aspects of the performance that are primary to its success are the design, lighting, and sound. Sound is fundamental to the performance.

With orchestras, the staging is usually focused on combining many people into one group where no one attracts more attention than the rest of the group. This is why dress is usually simple black for orchestral musicians. For other performances, such as nightclub presentations, popular music concerts, and solo performances, staging is more important because the focus of the audience is on a small number of performers or on one individual. Staging increases the interest of the audience.

In almost all forms of performing arts, each of these elements—scenery, lighting, sound, costuming, staging, and direction—are considered and controlled to enhance the presentation.

Professionals in the performing arts have employment opportunities in a variety of places beyond the traditional theater and stage. For example, talent is used at and by summer resorts, on cruise ships, in gambling casinos, and at state fairs. A number of carnivals still travel and employ performers, though their main elements are rides and games of chance. Circuses are still extremely popular and have regular audition periods for performers. There is even a clown school for training for circus clowns.

Performing arts festivals of all kinds multiply here and in Europe, South America, Africa, and Asia. Often subsidized by national or local governments, such festivals present invited musical, dance, film, dramatic, jazz, or other talents, all of which helps promote cultural awareness and tourism.

Talent is also being employed as a form of diplomacy by governments. Cultural exchanges between the United States and other foreign governments provide performance opportunities for symphony orchestras, opera singers, jazz artists, ballet troupes, choirs, puppeteers, circuses, and others. Traveling is more than a possibility for successful performers and production workers; for most, it is essential to their career.

The performing arts primarily operate on a seasonal basis. Artistic performances of a given type rarely are produced year-round, but rather are performed during select times during the year. There are opera seasons, ballet seasons, summer concert series, and such. For example, many orchestras perform about twenty weeks each year. Very few of America's thirty to forty principal symphony orchestras and none of the over 100 metropolitan orchestras are able to assure their musicians year-round work. That means that concert musicians have another thirty-two weeks where they must either seek additional employment or live off the earnings from the concert season. Similar schedules are used for dramatic presentations, with plays

Two singers perform in Mozart's "The False Garden-Maid" at the Chicago Opera Theater.

running for a number of weeks and then closing.

Even if the worker in the performing arts is able to survive without seeking work outside of his or her community, there is still some chance that travel will be required. For many, a performance company's schedules demand travel. Ballet companies, theater companies, symphonies, and other groups often travel around the country or around the world for weeks or months at a time.

Many performances are at night. It is not unusual, for example, for musicians to perform late into the night. Dramatic presentations normally have several nighttime performances a week, with one or two matinee performances. Some performances may only be held once or twice. With singers, this is frequently true. Rehearsals are often during the day, so work can easily be twelve to fourteen hours daily.

Most producers and directors prefer to hire those who have experience. This sets up the age-old problem of how to get that first job. For many, the way to get an opportunity is through an audition. Casting directors for plays, operas, and dance performances tend to be reasonably polite, though courtesy is certainly not guaranteed.

Auditions may seem puzzling. Producers may be only mildly interested in talent, and far more in physical "type." An applicant may be effusively praised for a reading, a song, a dance, a bit of mimicking only to be eliminated from consideration as too tall, too short, too fat, or too thin.

When it is stated that an audition is "closed," it means that only performers already members of the union with jurisdiction may apply. Auditions are held all over town—in theaters, rented rehearsal halls, broadcast studios, corporation board rooms, and church basements. When the call is "open," anybody may appear, even amateurs. Should an outsider actually be hired, he or she may be required to join a union for performers. The Screen Actors Guild, the Directors Guild, and the American Federation of Radio and Television Actors are just a few of the unions to join.

In most cases, performing arts careers do not last a lifetime. For every Bob Hope or Elton John there are scores of once prominent entertainers who have become business people, managers, agents, or dropped out of the performing arts entirely. And for every one of the performers who has even briefly had a period of fame, there are thousands who never accomplish their goals in the arts. The same is true for the workers behind the scenes. The competition for positions in the arts is extremely keen. Most successful performing arts workers, from makeup artists to singers, will say that luck plays as much a role as talent.

One of the things that continues to attract the thousands of would-be artists is the fame and fortune associated with the occupations. Indeed, the financial rewards that flow to famous stars, virtuosi, producers, directors, and playwrights make them symbols of success alongside sports figures and industrialists. The great figures in the performing arts are admired and pointed out, not only because they are talented, but also because they are celebrities. Most artists, however, do not enjoy this fame.

The fame aspect can cut both ways, though. Once a person is recognizable to the general public, many aspects of his or her private life are opened to that public audience as well. The press, photographers, autograph seekers, and fans may become a daily element of every transaction of life. Eating out, banking, grocery shopping, and other mundane activities may become burdensome because of the attention. Private aspects of one's life may become stories in the press. Despite extraordinary efforts, some celebrities, such as Marlon Brando, have been unable to remove themselves from the public spotlight once they realized that they no longer cared to be in it.

The competition for positions, the fame, and the continual need to seek new employment opportunities are all aspects of a career in the performing arts that should be considered before deciding to pursue an arts vocation.

Careers

The performing arts provide a variety of career opportunities. People are needed not only to star in productions but also to help design, direct, and set up the performances. A sampling of career opportunities follows below.

Actors and *actresses:* Actors and actresses perform parts to entertain and inform audiences. They use facial expressions, body movements, voice modulation, and other devices in the performance of their roles.

Singers: Singers use their understanding of harmony and melody to perform in musicals, concerts, and other productions. They may sing character parts or perform in their own style.

Dancers: Dancers use their ability to move rhythmically to perform in ballets, modern dance ensembles, musical shows, folk shows, and other productions. They most often perform as part of a group, though some dancers may perform solo.

Musicians: Musicians play musical instruments as part of an orchestra, rock group, jazz group, or other entity. They may perform solo or as part of a group.

Talent agents: Talent agents represent actors, actresses, or other performers and try and find them appropriate parts. They often know a wide range of producers, directors, and other people capable of hiring talent, and thus may help performers find roles. Talent agents are usually paid by the performer.

Casting directors: Casting directors assist in selecting the appropriate talent for a performance. They work alongside the producer and director of a production.

Producers: Producers select plays or scripts that are to be performed. They coordinate the raising of funds to finance the performance and decide on the size of the production. Producers usually are responsible for hiring the director, the principle members of the cast, and writers.

Directors: Directors supervise the production of plays and other performances. They conduct rehearsals and select actors and actresses from auditions.

Choreographers: Choreographers create original dances and teach them to dancers and

Actors from Chicago's Steppenwolf Theatre Company perform "The Grapes of Wrath," an adaptation of John Steinbeck's novel. The troop then traveled to New York with the production.

other performers. They often direct the presentations of their work.

Script writers: Script writers develop copy for use in theater and other performance arts. They may do research to write historical material or they may create original works. Script writers may be hired on assignment or they may prepare a script and then present it to a producer or director.

Composers: Composers create original music for operas, jazz ensembles, symphonies, and others. They may assist in the interpretation of the performance of their work.

Makeup artists: Makeup artists apply makeup and other material to performers. They often create elaborate facial decorations.

Stage crew members: Stage crew members help construct the sets needed in operas, theatrical presentations, and other performances. They also operate lighting and sound equipment during a performance.

Lighting technicians: Lighting of the performance is designed, set up, and executed by lighting technicians. Manipulating the equipment, establishing the timing, and creating special effects are part of the lighting job.

Set designers: Background scenery, props, and stage decorations are all handled by set designers. To make a set interesting but not distractive, designers must be innovative and creative. Scenery painters, assemblers, and stage hands make and move the scenery as needed for a performance.

Costume directors: Costume directors select and help create the costumes for artistic performances. They often work with the director and producer of a show. Costume directors oversee the production of the costumes by designers and seamstresses. Such work often involves research. This is especially true for period pieces, where the performers must look as authentic as possible.

Sound technicians: Directing the amplification and recording of stage sounds is done by the sound technicians. Sound effect technicians record or create noises to enhance the performance. Their tasks may be focused on creating a recording of the noises or music needed before a performance or they may have to create some sound during the performance. They also tape record performances for recordings (see Volume 1: Recording).

This is a scene from the play "A Walk in the Woods." While some plays require a large troop, this one has only two actors.

Education

There is no magic formula to succeed in the performing arts. Therefore there is no educational path that can guarantee success. Often, luck and innate skill are as important as training. That having been said, it is still most likely that those who have practiced for a number of years and received the proper formal education will be most successful. Many elementary schools, high schools, colleges, and private studios offer classes in dance, music, acting, and art.

Those interested in the performing arts should become involved at an early age. For example, aspiring actors and actresses should participate in high school dramatic productions and also seek opportunities in local community productions. Similarly, those interested in dance or music should also get involved with local productions at an early age.

By participating in an actual production, students will gain experience and also develop a greater understanding of the pressures and challenges of live performances. This is as important for behind-the-scenes workers as it is for performers. The practice that comes with each performance increases the skills and talents of everyone involved in the execution of a presentation.

Those interested in a musical career should start lessons at an early age, with instruction in school and with a private teacher. Usually talent is recognized early, and, after high school, a student enrolls in a conservatory for more specialized training, or attends a college with a strong music program. Students must also study and practice on their own. Both musicians and singers should be able to read musical notations and have some basic understanding of musicology.

Many stagehands and other behind-the-scenes workers require only a short training period. Skills in the specific area of specialty may include construction, painting, sculpting, cosmetic makeup, and fashion design. For stage workers who will be required to recreate periods of history, some training in historical research is particularly helpful so that accurate knowledge can be applied to stage and costume design.

Stage managers, electricians, and other workers who help produce plays and other artistic performances must complete lengthy apprenticeship programs. These apprenticeships combine classroom instruction with on-the-job training.

In general a college education is seen as a plus in the performing arts industry. Courses in speech, drama, opera, broadcasting, and screen techniques will give aspiring performers a background in history and techniques. The attainment of fluency in at least one foreign language is also to be recommended since the performing arts are international by nature. A college education is especially appropriate for individuals interested in a serious vocal, orchestral, or other career that traditionally require an extended period of preparation.

Industry outlook

The number of dance performances, musical recitals, dramatic presentations, and other productions will continue to offer employment opportunities to skilled artists. While preparing for a career in the performing arts, however, it is important to remember that there are very few "stars." Virtuosi are rationed in any generation. In the legitimate theater, there are always three or four flops for every one hit. People who aspire to careers in the performing arts should recognize that although the possibilities of success exist and excite the imagination, the possibilities of disappointment are all too real.

The employment picture is clouded by fierce competition and too many applicants. Typically, performers make ends meet by branching out. They find a job here, a job there, in television or in an industrial revue. They may hope to connect in summertime with a stock company at some resort, or with one of the growing number of musical or dramatic road companies.

According to the acting unions, about 80 percent of registered actors make an insufficient income from acting to live on. At least 30 percent of the actors make no money from acting at all for the entire year.

Many people well trained in music, drama, or dance find work as teachers in arts schools or as private instructors. For those who do succeed, a career path often includes a variety of jobs. For example, a musician may give solo recitals, compose songs for other performers, and give private lessons. Some may compose jingles for advertisements.

The industry will grow in proportion to its ability to attract audiences. It is estimated that over thirty-five million adults visit an art gallery or museum each year, thirty million attend a musical play or operetta, over twenty million attend a classical music performance, and sixteen million attend a jazz performance.

◇ SOURCES OF ADDITIONAL INFORMATION

Theatre Communications Group
355 Lexington Avenue
New York, NY 10017

Directors Guild of America
7920 Sunset Boulevard
Hollywood, CA 90046

American Dance Guild
31 West 21st Street
3rd Floor
New York, NY 10010

American Symphony Orchestra League
777 14th Street, NW
Washington, DC 20005

National Endowment for the Arts
1100 Pennsylvania Avenue, NW
Washington, DC 20506

Contact the theater arts departments of universities and colleges for information concerning their programs.

◇ RELATED ARTICLES

Volume 1: Advertising; Broadcasting; Motion Pictures; Recording
Volume 2: Actors and actresses; Dancers and choreographers; Literary agents and artists' managers; Media specialists; Musical occupations; Painters and sculptors; Radio and television announcers and newscasters; Radio and television program directors; Recording industry workers; Writers and editors
Volume 3: Communications equipment mechanics; Cosmetologists; Motion picture theater workers
Volume 4 Audio control technicians; Audiovisual technicians; Drafting and design technicians; Graphic arts technicians; Light technicians; Sound technicians; Sound-effects technicians; Sound-recording technicians; Stage technicians; Studio technicians

Personal and Consulting Services

General information

Frank and Lillian Gilbreth developed time-and-motion studies that allowed them to evaluate the efficiency of industrial employees' work habits. They would be hired to survey the design of different companies and then prepare proposals for redesign of the methods used in the operations and tasks. Because of the demand for their specialized service, Frank Gilbreth started a consulting firm that would handle requests on a free-lance basis. This was one of the first consulting firms established in the United States.

In 1906, a reporter named Ivy Ledbetter Lee was named press representative for coal-mine operators. The operators had run into problems with the press and the hired miners. Lee convinced the mine operators to start responding to press questions and supply the press with information on the mine activities.

After a successful turnaround of the coal-mine operators' situation, Lee went on to work for the Pennsylvania Railroad and other clients. He developed a large group of clients for his services. He developed new policies for business: a practice of honesty and openness about the company's business and affairs, and a practice of sending out notices to the newspapers about noteworthy events in the company's development. After establishing himself as a public relations expert, Lee developed a consulting business in media relations.

Governments and corporations became regular users of consultants. During World War II, governmental agencies made a point of hiring publicity consultants, since public exposure aided funding and congressional awareness of the activities of the group. Later, the airlines hired public relations specialists to help with delivering information on airplane crashes, providing background and technical information to the press in a manner that would be readily understood.

It was inevitable to link consultants with politicians for two reasons. The first reason was the preponderance of media around candidates and the incredible importance of image in determining success in an election. The second reason was the need for experts for the short period of time preceding an election. To hire a full-time staff member with expertise on polling would be detrimental to a candidate on a limited budget. The flow of hiring in politics lends itself perfectly to a consultant's schedule.

In the 1950s, Dwight Eisenhower was the first president to use political television advertising on a national level. Hiring advertising specialists to design effective ad campaigns was a new and relatively radical method of running a campaign.

After Richard Nixon's unsuccessful bid for the presidency in 1960, Nixon hired public relations and press consultants to help him regain popularity in his bids for elected office. The experts redirected his method of dressing, speaking, and any other element of public presentation that might affect how he was seen by the voting public. He was able to reestablish a positive image among voters and was elected president in 1968.

As the arena of consultants expanded, hiring specialists as consultants became an established business practice. It was more cost effective to have a specialist on salary only for the time needed. If the company hired someone who had worked for many others previously, they were getting the benefit of someone who had worked in a variety of situations, making him or her more useful to the company requesting assistance.

The personal services industry began to move beyond consulting. Agencies were started that either handled a wide variety of services or specialized in one area. In the early 1970s, agencies began to open in larger cities, offering services like organizing a catered party, redesigning a wardrobe, developing a public image, and myriad other tasks for social and private life.

One of the biggest influences on the personal services industry has been the increased need for household help. In the majority of households in America, it has become increasingly difficult for families to find the time or energy to take care of many of the tasks that were handled by a housewife. Six million more families were headed by single women in 1980 than in 1960. By 1988, of the 64 million families in the United States, 41.5 million had only one parent in the home, or had both parents out of the house at full-time jobs.

In addition, more people found themselves working more than a forty-hour week. As the number of work hours increased, the ability to finish even the smallest of household chores became very difficult.

As the leisure time of the working class was eroding, the personal service industry was developing. It was geared to help people who could afford to pay someone to do household tasks. Service industries started in areas of household help, errand running, and such.

In larger cities, people were less likely to get to know their neighbors. Finding babysitters or someone to help out in an emergency became more difficult as the neighborhood environment broke down. It was increasingly important that someone be able to find a trustworthy person on a short notice to take care of such situations. Many of the agencies had interviewed and checked the references of the individuals doing the household tasks. This gave the clients a certain sense of trust.

More consulting services began springing up as well. By the end of the 1980s, services were developing in unusual areas. For example, someone could hire a consultant to come in and make sure the home was safe for a small child. The consultant would check for sharp objects, protruding corners, unguarded chemicals in cabinets, and other potential hazards. Then the consultant would either repair such problems, or itemize them on a list for the client to repair.

Some of the consultants started their businesses because they had trouble finding help in the area in which they now specialize. One woman who had problems adjusting to living abroad when her husband was transferred decided to start a consulting business that gave cross-cultural training and overseas information to families being relocated to foreign countries.

Many of the consulting companies spring from a real need in the community for the services offered. The personal consultants are able to handle problems that arise so that the client is free to do things that are more pressing or

This woman offers her services in plant care. For a given fee, she supplies, cares for, and waters plants in office spaces.

more enjoyable. The professional consultant is trained and has experience in the area of service offered, and can provide the best help for the least long term cost. Consulting has become a major industry, expanding beyond the original business and government clients, to a whole range of clients.

The structure of personal and consulting services

Because of the vast array of consulting and personal services offered, the structure of the industry varies considerably. There are, however, certain parallels that can be made across these broad areas.

Specialty services normally employ a staff that covers one particular job task. Consultants are specialists, with expertise in one field or another. Their services can range from business or political reorganization to giving grooming advice.

Consultant and advisory firms may have one or two people on staff, and they may hire other consultants and free-lancers when the work load requires it. Others may have a large full-time staff. Political consultants normally have an individual who sponsors the consulting firm, because he or she is well known in the political community. Staff members may be hired on a project-by-project basis. College students are frequently employed to help on projects. This provides training for the student, and inexpensive, educated staff for the consultant.

Specialized personal services may also have one or two individuals who run the organization and do most of the work, but who have

353

This woman prepares portable meals for the elderly. Once each meal is boxed, another person will deliver them to homes.

contact with others who are able to take on various chores.

General service firms may limit the range of their jobs to one area, such as catering, but the broadness of the category allows them to take on a wide variety of clients and tasks. Other general service firms may do an enormous variety of things, from clothes selection to organizing files at an office. These generalists tend to have a larger staff, where a large amount of the work can be done by unskilled labor. Moving, packing, cleaning, walking pets, and other tasks that mainly rely on physical labor can be done by a staff of students or others who are looking for part-time work. There is normally a core staff who run the organization and do the hiring of the part-time and temporary workers.

Specialists are trained to work with young children or older people. The services can range from all-day care in the home, to group care and individual needs fulfillment. Specialists can work on exercise, rehabilitation training, and general play activities. Service groups oriented to children have baby-sitters, nannies, health care workers, trained teachers, and assorted other skilled and unskilled workers. The skill level and training of the specialist will vary from business to business, and there is no method of employee certification.

For services to the elderly, the service providers come into the home to exercise with the elderly, take them shopping, or take care of health problems. Again, there is no set regulation on who is a specialist. Background training will vary considerably between firms.

Careers

A sampling of consulting career opportunities follows below.

Professional consultants: Consultants normally move into free-lance and temporary work after they have established a name for themselves in their field. They will have had several years of work related experience, be well known for their skills in their field, and have a good number of contacts for potential jobs. They may choose to work alone or with a few others.

Professional consultants normally do not require a large staff to run their consulting business; the services they supply are really their own knowledge.

General personal service directors: The organizers of the companies that provide a variety of services are in charge of hiring a staff that is capable of carrying out the demands of the customers. They are responsible for background checks into their employees' records to assure that the staff that is entering the home of a client is trustworthy and reliable. They need to provide training to staff members for all of the tasks that the company is assigned.

The director of the company may also be responsible for finding new clients, advertising the company, and maintaining client records and requests. For smaller operations, the director may be responsible for payroll, billing, accounting, and all of the day-to-day office tasks of running a business.

Personal service specialists: Like consultants, specialists are experts in their field, but they may not have the career background that a consultant has. For example, a health specialist may have finished training in geriatric care and start a personal service company for in-home care or meal preparation. The specialist need not have experience in a work environment as long as the educational training has been sufficient.

Business consultants: Business consultants provide information services for business on a variety of problems. Their expertise may be in marketing, public image development, time management, or any other area that may pose problems for a beginning or established business.

Political consultants: Political consultants have six basic areas of expertise: polling, media, fund raising, direct mail, phone banks, and general assistance. Two new political consulting areas that are beginning to catch on are negative research and computer software programming.

Political consultants start out by working on campaigns, frequently under the training of another political consultant. After a few successful campaigns, the consultant may establish his or her own client base.

Education

For most consulting work, a college degree in the area that is the target service is the most helpful first step in getting a consulting position. After education, though, experience is the single most important aspect to achieving success. The consulting and personal service industry is not an industry where most new graduates begin. It follows normally after a successful career in another industry that provides the training and expertise expected of a consultant.

Training under a consultant who has already established a firm is another way of learning the ropes, both in the skills needed for consulting and in the business management of a consulting firm.

Another method is to find a target market that does not have services currently covered by a consulting or personal services firm, and fill a need that is not currently met in the community.

Both of these routes are difficult, however, and the success rate is low for new firms. Consultant assistant positions are not common, and competition may be strong for the openings that do occur.

Internship positions are easier to find in political consulting. The demands of the work and the cyclical nature of the election schedule mean that consultants have periods of unemployment and are unlikely to hire permanent staff. Temporary assistants and interns are the best method of filling staff needs during campaigns.

Industry outlook

The industry as a whole is quite strong. There may be fluctuation in certain areas of consulting and personal services, but the overall need for professionals that can be hired on a temporary basis will be around for a long time.

Fluctuations in certain fields of specialty, such as political consulting, are based on the industry that hires the consultants. Because of the cyclical nature of the work, the longevity of most consultants is relatively short. They may opt to move on to more stable employment. For political consultants specializing in media or

Cleaning services have become increasingly popular for families where both the mother and father work full-time.

advertising, the advertising industry is a common field for retired political consultants.

◇ **SOURCES OF ADDITIONAL INFORMATION**

American Association of Professional Consultants
9140 Ward Parkway
Kansas City, MO 64114

American Consultants League
2030 Clarendon Boulevard, Suite 202
Arlington, VA 22201

Professional and Technical Consultants Association
1330 South Bascom Avenue, Suite D
San Jose, CA 95128

Association of Fashion and Image Consultants
7655 Old Springhouse Road
McLean, VA 22102

◇ **RELATED ARTICLES**

Volume 1: Advertising; Marketing; Politics and Public Service; Public Relations
Volume 2: Caterers; Economists; Fundraisers

355

Physical Sciences

General information

The physical sciences are concerned with the structure and properties of inorganic (nonliving) matter. Physical scientists study subjects ranging from the earth's interior to faraway galaxies, from tiny molecules to the composition of matter. The physical sciences include: physics, chemistry, astronomy, meteorology, and geology.

Even before the dawn of civilization, people contemplated the world around them. Although they were not able to understand the why and how of many of the things they observed, they were able to put into use much of what they learned through their perceptiveness and experience. They discovered such basic devices as the wheel and the inclined plane. They observed that some things that worked one time in a definite manner often worked again in the same way at another time and that certain things always worked in the same fashion. These preliterate people may, in the broadest sense, be called the world's first physical scientists.

The Great Pyramids in Egypt, some of which were built around 2600 B.C., are monuments to the theories developed in the physical sciences. Constructing these massive structures required a thorough understanding of what we now call mechanics, a branch of physics that deals with the force required to move solid objects.

Babylonian astronomy, developed about 1750 B.C., was one of the earliest scientific studies of the physical world. The Babylonians developed a system of arithmetic progressions that they were able to use to predict astronomical phenomena, such as the appearance of the new moon.

In the Western tradition, the ancient Greeks first recognized that there was order in the universe (things happen in nature consistently, according to definite rules). They realized that cause and effect relationships existed between occurrences in nature, and the Greek philosophers believed that these relationships could be discovered by means of observation and logic.

Greek science made great strides in an understanding of the universe for several centuries, reaching a high point around the time of the astronomer Ptolemy, about 200 A.D. After the Romans succeeded the Greeks, this emphasis on scientific understanding dwindled to almost nothing. In addition, pressure from leaders of the Roman Catholic Church further limited scientific discovery in the West.

With the rise of Islam in the seventh century, there was a revival in the study of the physical sciences. Many of the leading scientific books and papers were translated from Greek into Arabic.

The scientific revolution during the three hundred years spanning the fifteenth through the seventeenth centuries radically changed the way humans viewed the universe. In 1543, Nicolaus Copernicus published his theory that the earth revolved around the sun, rather than the other way around. In 1610, Galileo Galilei used a telescope to observe the moons of Jupiter and dispel the notion that the earth was the only planet to have a moon. He also defended Copernicus' assertions that the planets orbit the sun, and not the earth. In the late 1600s, Isaac Newton developed his three laws of motion, from which he was able to derive the law of universal gravitation.

In more recent years, scientists such as Max Planck, Niels Bohr, and Albert Einstein have developed quantum physics and other theories that have brought the physical sciences into the atomic age.

There is no "physical sciences' industry" as there are well-defined chemical and electronics industries. Yet physical scientists are widely employed throughout the entire U.S. economy, for physics and the other sciences are essential

Two technicians prepare a 25-foot centrifuge for experiments in geotechnical modeling at the Sandia National Laboratories in California.

to industry, education, and culture. The applications of the knowledge discovered in the fields of nuclear and solid-state physics, for example, as well as the areas of applied physics such as electronics, communications, and medical technology, have been shown to be of great commercial and military value. Both government and private industry spend hundreds of millions of dollars each year on basic research in the physical sciences.

The structure of the physical sciences

As the most basic of physical sciences, physics deals with the structure of matter and the development of comprehensive laws that describe natural phenomena. The scientific disciplines of astronomy, chemistry, meteorology, and geology developed as a result of the application of the general laws of physics to specific areas of study. Many of the early physicists, for example, studied astronomy. Although now, astronomy is considered a separate science, astronomers use instruments that have been designed by physicists and engineers. Astrophysics may be said to be a combination of astronomy and physics, just as geophysics may be called a combination of geology and physics.

Most big firms have well-established science laboratories, and the number of such companies and the sizes of these laboratories are constantly increasing. Although a number of companies are devoting some of their efforts to basic research, industrial scientists often must relate their investigations to the specific needs of their company. Nevertheless, the output of scientific papers from the laboratories of industrial firms is high, though most published papers in physics journals still come from universities.

Industrial research laboratories are almost always organized on a team basis with senior people, usually Ph.D.s, responsible for the work of perhaps thirty or forty scientists and technicians. Within this group, there may be several sections, each under the control of a leader who is responsible to the head of the group. This system has the advantage for the young graduate of providing a gradual introduction to the methods and responsibilities of organized research. Success in such a system must depend on an ability to work well with others and, as one gains senior status, to bring out the best in those for whom one may be responsible.

Today, most industrial jobs are primarily concerned with developing methods and processes to solve a wide variety of problems. Many physicists and other scientists, for example, conduct research to design lasers, electronic devices, and other equipment to increase or improve manufacturing methods. Certain positions do not involve research, but as a rule these posts are filled by scientists who have spent a number of years in the research or development departments. These positions include the administration of research, legal and patent work pertaining to developments in physics, as well as a variety of other areas.

The status of university appointments and the tradition of pure research in the universities combine to produce a strong attraction for the best scientists. The physical science departments of the major universities are highly esteemed and (coupling this with improvements in salaries) can often attract top people from industry and elsewhere to fill important positions.

Two men lower an apparatus into the ocean. The apparatus was designed by physicists at the Woods Hole Oceanographic Institution.

Various factors determine the amount of time a physical science professor spends in actual classroom teaching; however, a program of about nine hours a week of classroom teaching is common. A full professor at a large university may spend fewer than six hours a week in classroom teaching. On the other hand, classroom hours alone do not make up the professor's entire work load. The time spent actually teaching may be followed by hours of work on research, writing, and other professional activities, as well as preparation for teaching in the classroom, advising students, and participating in university or college affairs.

Often senior members of university staffs have supplementary sources of income derived from consulting work for industrial or governmental laboratories and royalties from books.

Federal scientific research and development has become a large scale, highly organized, and elaborate enterprise. Though considerations of national defense have been of overriding importance in this development, the heavy emphasis on defense research has not diminished government's interest in other kinds of investigations. The government offers a wide range

of positions to physical scientists, and the number of such posts is rapidly increasing. The Department of Defense, including the Army, Navy, and Air Force, employs a large number of the physical scientists working for the federal government. Other agencies employing a large number of physical scientists include the Department of Commerce, mainly its National Bureau of Standards, the Department of the Interior, and the Department of Energy.

Most of the jobs in the government are under Civil Service rules and salaries. Although the advantages of the scientific civil servant are substantial, government service does not appeal to all people. First, a civil servant can expect only the salary established for the grade and years of service. Second, government establishments must conform to general rules and regulations laid down to apply to a whole agency. Therefore, freedom of decision making for senior people in government agencies may, in many ways, be much less than that of persons of similar status in industry.

A major branch of the physical sciences is physical metallurgy. It concerns itself with individual metallic elements such as iron and copper; with mixtures of metals called alloys or inter-metallic compounds, such as steel and brass or iron carbide; and with combinations of metals and nonmetals called composite materials. The main task of physical metallurgy is to explain how the properties of metallic materials depend on their internal structure. The principal tools of physical metallurgy reveal internal structure; these tools are the optical microscope, the electron microscope, and the X-ray diffraction machine. Metallic structures are controlled by thermal, chemical, and mechanical treatment. Thus, by definition, physical metallurgy is the science of structure/property relationships in metal alloys.

Physical metallurgists become involved in every aspect of the work required to construct the machine, structure, or system. They serve as consultants to the designers and advise them about the types of metals and alloys to specify for specific parts. Since there are hundreds of thousands of actually or potentially useful alloys, physical metallurgists provide a very useful service. They also write the specifications for the metals and alloys that they and the designers have agreed on. This is an important and demanding task, and almost always requires negotiation and compromise between the physical metallurgist who buys the raw products for the company and the physical metallurgist in the metals-producing company that makes the raw product. It is the physical metallurgist who is held responsible for the quality of the metals and alloys bought by the

A physicist oversees the installation of a sonar device that he designed to chart the sea floor. Its purpose is to locate potential deposits of oil, gas, and precious metals.

company. He or she must be satisfied that the specifications have been properly met. This often requires considerable laboratory work, including the study of the internal structure of samples and the determination of their physical, chemical, and mechanical properties. To accomplish these tasks, physical metallurgists must operate complex equipment in the laboratory.

Physical metallurgists may also be required to design fabrication, heat treatment, and joining procedures that improve the properties of materials. They also assemble components into the finished structures in such a manner that the desired properties are not impaired. They have the responsibility of examining metallic components of the completed products after they have been in service to see if they are performing properly. If unexpected failures occur, the physical metallurgist must determine the causes of failure. Last, and not least, the physical metallurgist must constantly learn about new alloys, new specifications, new testing techniques, and new manufacturing procedures that will improve the product of the company and lessen its cost.

Careers

The physical sciences offer a wide range of career opportunities. Many careers demand very specialized education and training, but some career options are available to those with a more general education.

A sampling of career opportunities follows below.

Physicists: Physicists are concerned with the study of energy in all its forms, the structure of matter, and the relationship between energy and matter. The basic laws of nature are their source material, from which they attempt to draw mathematical relationships and conclusions. Physicists work in private industry, educational institutions, and in government service. Physicists are often referred to by their area of specialization.

Atomic and molecular physicists: Atomic and molecular physicists study the structure and properties of atoms and molecules.

Plasma physicists: Plasma physicists examine the behavior of ionized gas at extremely high temperatures.

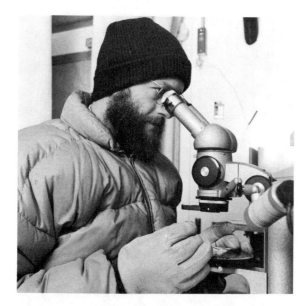

Dressed in cold-weather gear, a scientist examines the structure of ice crystals under a microscope.

Cryogenics physicists: Cryogenics physicists study the behavior of matter at extremely low temperatures.

Nuclear physicists: Nuclear physicists investigate the composition and behavior of the nuclei of atoms.

Geophysicists: Geophysicists study the chemical and physical properties of the earth's surface. They may, for example, study fossil remains of plant and animal life. Geophysicists also investigate the magnetic, electrical, and gravitational forces of the earth.

Geologists: Like geophysicists, geologists study the physical properties of the earth's surface. They conduct experiments to identify the chemical and physical properties of rock specimens. Geologists also apply their knowledge of the earth's structure to aid in oil exploration, the search for underground water, and the search for other resources.

Physical metallurgists: Physical metallurgists are responsible for providing tailor-made metallic materials that have just the right combinations of properties for specific applications. The microscopic and atomic structure of materials governs not only the mechanical properties but also their optical, thermal, and electrical behaviors. A tremendous variety of consumer and industrial products depend on the metallurgist's ability to manipulate these properties.

Meteorologists: Meteorologists study the physical and chemical characteristics of the atmosphere. They also study the way in which the atmosphere affects the rest of the natural environment. Many meteorologists forecast the weather.

Climatologists: Climatologists are meteorologists who study weather trends to help determine the overall weather pattern that makes up an area's climate.

Astronomers: Astronomers study celestial bodies such as the moon, sun, and stars. They examine scientific data relating to the composition of the universe and make observations using telescopes, radio telescopes, and other equipment.

Chemists: Chemists analyze natural and artificial substances to determine the structure, composition, and nature of these substances. They usually work in research and development, but many are also involved in teaching. Chemists often specialize in a subfield, such as organic or inorganic chemistry.

Semiconductor-development technicians: Semiconductor-development technicians test electronic semiconductor devices to compile data for evaluation of new designs. They usually work alongside engineers and other research personnel.

Education

All physical scientists require at least a bachelor's degree in their area of specialization and many have graduate degrees. A bachelor's degree with a major in chemistry or a related discipline, for example, is sufficient for many beginning jobs as a chemist. Graduate training is needed for most research positions, and most university professors require a doctorate degree. Beginning physical scientists should have a broad background in their area of specialization, with good laboratory skills. As a general rule, people in basic research possess Ph.D. degrees.

Physics is a fundamental science, and for this reason most other scientists need to study the subject. Chemists, astronomers, geologists, and meteorologists, as well as those in the medical professions, need a basic understanding of physics. This is partly the reason why many physicists often find themselves working in such related areas as astrophysics, geophysics, and biophysics, and they have to acquire specialized knowledge of such fields too.

In most colleges and universities, instructors are expected to have satisfied the requirements for a Ph.D. degree. In secondary schools and two-year colleges, however, where there are currently many opportunities for physical science teachers, Ph.D.s are not usually required. Often in colleges and universities, physical sciences' instructors are not promoted to a permanent staff position until they have published in the field or otherwise made important contributions to their area of specialization.

Industry outlook

The job outlook for physical scientists is fairly good, with the need for those with doctorate degrees especially strong. Some areas of the physical sciences may do better than others. The job prospects for physicists, for example, is expected to be stronger than the job prospects for chemists.

Looking toward the year 2000, the American Physical Society anticipates that the demand for college and university physics teachers, at all levels, will rise. The age distribution of current teachers is such that the need for replacement of retiring teachers is expected to increase. In varying degrees, this same trend seems to hold true for the other physical sciences.

The physical sciences offer more than teaching opportunities. Physical scientists have a choice of many different fields of endeavor; and in whichever field they elect to work they can be sure there will be a demand for their services and that they will be reasonably compensated for them. The desire for new and better products depends on an ever-increasing stream of scientific discoveries and on their application. The needs of national defense often demand increases in nuclear and electronics research and development.

◇ **SOURCES OF ADDITIONAL INFORMATION**

American Physical Society
335 East 45th Street
New York, NY 10017

American Meteorological Society
45 Beacon Street
Boston, MA 02108

ASM International (American Society for Metals)
Metals Park, OH 44073

American Geophysical Union
2000 Florida Avenue, NW
Washington, DC 20009

Society of Exploration Geophysicists
PO Box 702740
Tulsa, OK 74170

American Nuclear Society
555 North Kensington Avenue
La Grange Park, IL 60525

◇ **RELATED ARTICLES**

Volume 1: Biological Sciences; Chemistry; Energy; Electronics; Engineering; Metals; Nuclear Sciences
Volume 2: Astronomers; Biologists; Chemists; College and university faculty; Engineers; Geologists; Geophysicists; Groundwater professionals; Meteorologists; Physicists; Teachers, secondary school; Toxicologists
Volume 3: Industrial chemicals workers; Power plant occupations
Volume 4: Aeronautical and aerospace technicians; Chemical technicians; Geological technicians; Laboratory technicians; Laser technicians; Metallurgical technicians; Meteorological technicians; Nuclear instrumentation technicians; Nuclear power plant radiation control technicians; Radiological (X-ray) technicians

Plastics

General information

Since the first synthetic plastics were produced in 1909, plastics have become a part of everyday life. Plastics can be manufactured hard enough to use as dies for shaping metal or soft enough to weave nylon stockings. Surgeons can use plastic screws to join broken bones; architects use plastics that resemble marble, wood, or stone; space scientists use plastic nose cones, and others store certain chemicals in plastic containers. Plastics companies in the United States include material makers who make the resins, processors who shape the resins, and fabricators who make end products. Plastics are supplied to almost every type of manufacturer in the country.

Because of the diversity of plastics, many of their uses go unrecognized. Every consumer is aware of plastics used in housewares, toys, electrical fixtures, toothbrushes, packages, and household detergent bottles, but few are aware that the lifelines of all communications—television, radio, telephone, radar, sonar, and satellites—rely on plastics for insulation and other vital components.

Given the prominent role that plastics play in modern life, it is surprising that a little more than a century ago, no such thing as commercial plastic existed in the United States. The U.S. plastics industry officially dates its beginnings to 1868 when John Wesley Hyatt mixed pyroxylin, made from cotton and nitric acid, with camphor to create an entirely different and new product he called celluloid. Hyatt developed the plastic in response to a competition sponsored by a manufacturer of billiard balls. Faced with a shortage of ivory, from which billiard balls were made, the manufacturer was seeking a product to use in its place. This was the first commercial plastic in the United States. Other forms of plastic had been developed in England a few years earlier, but these proved to be of lesser quality.

As has been true of plastics materials ever since, celluloid quickly found new uses and moved into new markets. Such products as combs, curtains, and carriage windshields were made from celluloid. The photographic film used by George Eastman to produce the first motion picture film in 1882 was made of celluloid. As a highly flammable material, celluloid was not a perfect product, spurring further development of plastic product. The material, however, is still in use today (under its chemical name of cellulose nitrate) for making products such as eyeglass frames.

Forty-one years passed before the plastics industry took its next major step. In 1909, Dr. Leo Hendrik Baekeland introduced phenoformaldehyde plastics, more popularly known as phenolids, the first plastic to achieve worldwide acceptance. His new substance, called Bakelite, was intended as a resin. The versatility of Bakelite soon led to the production of many products such as cookware handles, telephones, and other parts for electrical equipment.

In the 1920s, scientists introduced polyvinyl chloride, which was eventually to become the second largest-selling plastic for such applications as flooring and wire and cable insulation. Another plastic, cellulose acetate, was commonly used as a waterproof varnish for the fabric of airplane wing coverings. Also during this period, the U.S. firm E.I. DuPont de Nemours & Company developed superpolyamide, otherwise known as nylon. This product is still widely used today.

During World War II, there was a shortage of natural materials, which encouraged chemists and chemical companies to develop even more types of plastic. The 1930s and 1940s saw the initial commercial development of many of today's major thermoplastics: low density polyethylene, polystyrene, and polymethyl methacrylate. These plastics were primarily used in packaging consumer goods.

The increasing demand for plastics in the 1950s and 1960s led to more and more types of plastics. Some of the more important inventions of the 1960s were heat-resistant plastics and ceramoplastics that have industrial uses.

In today's society, plastics are used in every aspect of American life. Plastics are used to manufacture countless objects including dishes, toys, signs, insulation, and appliance parts. The average car contains more than 300 pounds of plastics. Plastics are even used to replace defective heart valves, sockets, and joints, and other parts of the human body.

Some uses of plastics go unrecognized because they show up in combination with other materials. All paper cartons for milk, for example, have protective coatings of polyethylene, a plastic. Many metal cans have protective plastic linings. Many glass bottles have protective plastic coverings. Other plastics go unrecognized because their appearance is similar to other materials—such as plastic outerwear that looks like leather or plastic furniture with wood grain patterns.

Still other plastics go unrecognized because they are hidden in the finished product; for example, the myriad uses of plastics for electrical insulation in refrigerators. This use of plastics has resulted in more food-storage capacity without an increase in the outside dimensions of the refrigerator.

This opaque plastic bowl was formed through the molding process. Once it is cooled, it can be packaged and sent to a retailer.

The structure of the plastics industry

Plastics comprise a family of materials, not a single material. Each member of this family has its own distinct and special advantages. From different combinations of elements, it is possible to create different plastics with almost any quality desired in an end product. Some plastic products are similar to existing conventional materials but can be produced more economically. Some plastic products represent significant property improvements over existing materials. Finally, some plastic products can only be described as amazing materials unlike any previously known. This diversity has made plastics applicable to a broad range of end uses today.

One generally accepted definition of plastics classifies it as any one of a large and varied group of materials consisting wholly or in part of combinations of carbon with oxygen, hydrogen, nitrogen, and other organic and inorganic elements. At some stage in their manufacture, these materials are liquid, and are thus capable of being formed into various shapes, usually through the application of heat and pressure.

Thousands of companies in the United States produce basic plastics materials, fabricate plastics into products or parts, or finish these goods in some way, such as by decorating or other means. The companies that purchase these basic materials number well into the tens of thousands. Sometimes there is an overlapping of functions between industry and market. For example, customers such as automotive and packaging companies are themselves among the large processors of plastics into products and parts. There is also an overlapping of functions within the industry itself, as when materials manufacturers also do processing and finishing.

Materials manufacturers use chemical reactions to transform basic feedstocks into plastic materials. These materials are then sold in the form of granules, powder, pellets, flake, or liquids for eventual processing into finished products.

Between these manufactured materials and the finished compound that goes to the processor, there is often an intermediate step that involves the addition of modifiers, chemicals, and additives that impart special properties to the plastic or upgrade existing ones. For example, plastics can be colored with pigments or dyes or made more flexible by being treated with a modifier. The companies that supply these modifiers are often the materials manufacturers themselves. In other instances, they are separate companies specializing in the production of one or more specific types of modifiers for plastics.

A plastics mold drafter designs machines that mold new plastic products.

The compounding of the base resin into the finished plastic material that goes to the processor is usually performed by the materials manufacturer. However, a group in the plastics industry known as compounders will buy the base polymer from the materials manufacturer and then specially compound it by adding modifiers, additives, and so on for resale to the processor. It is also possible for processors to buy base polymers, modifiers, and additives directly and do their own compounding.

The processor is at the heart of the plastics industry. It is the function of the processor to turn plastics material into secondary products, component parts, or finished products.

The fabricator's role is to turn secondary products such as film, sheet, rod, tube, and special shapes into end products. There are several common ways in which this is done: molding, casting, laminating, extrusion, and calendering.

Molding a secondary product simply involves taking the heated liquid plastic, injecting it into a mold, and using intense pressure to shape the piece. For all items, the plastic is poured into a mold of the desired shape, whether it be a hollow bottle or a round object. Casting is very similar to molding; however, the plastic sets without the use of pressure.

In the lamination process, a piece of paper is placed between two transparent sheets of plastic. The three items are then heated to form a bond. Products such as tabletop and electrical insulation are laminated.

Extrusion is the process of making plastic tubes such as pipes and hoses. Basically, melted plastic is squeezed through an oblong object that excretes the finished product. Inside the tube is a screw-like part that pulls the plastic through it and squeeze the substance into the desired shape.

Calendering, like lamination, coats materials. In a process similar to printing, the substance to be coated is fed through a series of rollers. The rollers contain the plastic that coats the substance.

Finishing, decorating, and assembling the plastic products can either be done in-house by the plastics processor or fabricator, or by companies that may specialize in various finishing techniques.

Many workers operate machines that actually form plastic objects. For example, injection molders run machines that first liquify plastic powders or pellets. This liquid pellet is then injected into a mold and allowed to harden. The result is a molded plastic object.

Some plastics are cut into shapes rather than molded. Shaping-machine operators cut spheres, cones, and other shapes from blocks of plastic.

Technicians play an important role in the manufacturing of plastics. Some technicians install molds, watch over the molding process, maintain production schedules, and test both raw materials and finished products. Other technicians work in laminating.

The plastics industry also employs technicians as sales and service workers. Some sell plastics materials to manufacturers. Others work for manufacturers of the machinery used in plastics production.

Careers

The plastics industry offers a wide ranger of career opportunities. A number of the careers are discussed below.

Chemists: Organic, physical, analytical, and physical-organic chemists conduct research to form new plastics and to alter existing ones to achieve new, improved properties. Inorganic chemists often work with newer, more exotic plastics.

Plastics engineers: Plastics engineers are engaged in the manufacture, fabrication, and end use of existing materials, as well as with the development of new materials, processes, and equipment.

Chemical engineers: Chemical engineers are most likely to play a role in research and development. They devise economical ways to develop new plastics, and they may also get involved in the design of a chemical plant.

Mechanical engineers: The mechanical engineer, with a background in mechanics, pneumatics, hydraulics, and electronics, is likely to specialize in machine design, tool and die work, or product development. When a new plastic is developed, a mechanical engineer must design an economical method of production.

Material service and sales personnel: The material service and salesperson is responsible for selling raw plastics to fabricating companies. Sales personnel are required to be familiar with all plastic materials and their relationship with glass, wood, ceramics, and metals, plus their comparative costs.

Plastics mold drafters: Included under the category of technologist is the plastics mold drafter, who is adept at mechanical drafting and whose job it is to work out the detailed drawing from which the mold is made.

Product designers: The product designer is an artist who creates the plastic product. Such work entails full knowledge of many types of plastics.

Cost estimators: It is up to the cost estimator to determine the price of producing plastic items. Cost estimators must have the ability to read blueprints and understand engineering aspects of plastics technology. The cost estimator may have a background as an accountant or a statistician.

Plastics technicians: Plastics technicians perform jobs such as troubleshooting and operating machinery, for example, shaping machinery that transforms raw plastics into industrially usable products.

Plastic technicians also work as mold and tool makers. Technicians design these molds according to manufacturing guidelines.

Production color matchers: Production color matchers are responsible for color control. This requires a sound knowledge and understanding of elementary chemistry and testing techniques.

Plastics pattern makers: Plastics pattern makers create the mold and pattern that determine the final shape of finished plastic objects.

Grinding machine operators: Grinding machine operators run machines that grind particles of plastic into smaller pieces for processing.

Laboratory analysts: A laboratory analyst performs chemical and physical tests on plastic materials.

Plastic inspectors: Plastic inspectors test and inspect manufactured products for strength, size, and uniformity.

Blow-molding machine operators: Blow-molding machine operators run machines that

This plastics engineer uses a complex piece of equipment that creates new types of plastic for industrial uses.

mold such objects as bleach bottles by puffing air into plastic to expand the bottles.

Extruder operators: Extruder operators set up and operate machines that form plastics into tubes, rods, and film by drawing the liquid plastic through die.

Pad cutters: Pad cutters slice foam rubber into shapes for seat cushions and other foam rubber products.

In addition to these workers, the plastics industry requires sales personnel, office personnel, such as secretaries and telephone operators, as well as accountants, bookkeepers, truck drivers, and maintenance workers.

Education

Any type of technical work in the plastics industry requires at least a college education. Most scientists are graduates of the nation's leading engineering schools, and often have master's degrees or Ph.D.s. Plastics engineers generally graduate from four-year colleges with courses in engineering or polymer chemistry. As they gain experience, careers with administration management responsibilities become possible.

Technologists are often in contact with designers and engineers; therefore, a basic engineering background is helpful. Technologists generally graduate from two-year junior or community colleges with an associate degree, or they may possess equivalent knowledge

A plastics technician monitors the amount of plastic materials used in a machine that melts it and molds it into a particular shape.

through experience, training, and other means of education. The technologist can aim for promotion to general supervisor or plant manager.

Plastics technicians are usually graduates of technical high schools, vocational schools, or plastics industry seminars. They then take two-year courses at community colleges. A typical two-year curriculum for a plastics technician includes courses in introduction to plastics, compression molding procedures, fabrication of plastics, properties of thermoplastics, injection molding, and extrusion molding. A technician becomes fully proficient in his or her craft through on-the-job training. Plastics supervisors come from the ranks of technicians.

Plastic products manufacturing workers do not require college degrees. Often production workers learn their skill on the job. In high school, those desiring a job as a production worker should take classes in chemistry, physics, mathematics, drafting, and computer science.

Industry outlook

From its inception, the plastics industry has been phenomenally successful. It would be difficult to find a market in the United States today in which plastics, either by themselves or in combination with other materials, do not play a vital role. Plastics are diversified, and the end is not in sight. Hundreds of millions of dol-

lars continue to be spent by the industry each year in developing new plastics and improving existing ones.

Employing over 55,000 people, the plastics industry produces an estimated $3.8 billion in products annually. The U.S. government expects the industry to increase by at least 4 percent through the mid-1990s. While markets may open up in Eastern Europe, environmental legislation in the domestic front may curtail the production of certain plastics. This growing concern for the environment has led to the recycling of plastic products. In addition, scientists have recently developed biodegradable plastic bags that break down when exposed to sunlight for long periods of time.

In manufacturing plants, the demand for plastic machine operators and other plastics product manufacturing workers will be tied closely to general economic conditions and the ability of U.S. industry to increase productivity. Automated material handling and robot work stations may slow the rate of employment opportunities in this area.

The demand for qualified chemical engineers, Ph.D.s who know polymer science, and others with science qualifications is expected to be strong throughout the 1990s.

◇ SOURCES OF ADDITIONAL INFORMATION

Plastics Institute of America
Stevens Institute of Technology
Castle Point Station
Hoboken, NJ 07030

Society of the Plastics Engineers
PO Box 0403
14 Fairfield Drive
Brookfield Center, CT 06804

Society of the Plastics Industry
1275 K Street, NW
Suite 400
Washington, DC 20005

Plastic Metal Products Manufacturers Association
225 West 34th Street
New York, NY 10001

National Association of Plastics Distributors
6333 Long Street, Suite 250
Shawnee, KS 66216

◇ **RELATED ARTICLES**

Volume 1: Ceramics; Chemicals and Drugs; Chemistry; Design; Engineering; Machining and Machinery; Packaging; Rubber; Textiles
Volume 2: Biochemists; Chemists; Cost estimators; Designers; Engineers; Industrial designers; Industrial traffic managers; Management analysts and consultants; Packaging engineers; Wood science and technology careers
Volume 3: Industrial chemical workers; Iron and steel industry workers; Machine tool operators; Machinists; Manufacturers' sales workers; Molders; Operating engineers; Paint and coatings industry workers; Paper processing operations; Plastic products manufacturing workers; Printing press operators and assistants
Volume 4: Chemical technicians; Drafting and design technicians; Industrial engineering technicians; Mechanical technicians; Packaging and paper products technicians; Plastics technicians; Product test technicians; Testing technicians; Textile technicians

Politics and Public Service

General information

Politics can be traced back quite a long way in history. Early civilizations realized leaders were needed to run a community, and politics was born when more than one person wanted the same position.

In early Greek civilization, not only were there politics, but there were mud slinging political advertisements painted on the walls. The banding of the twelve tribes of Israel in Canaan was a political unification during an era when tribal cooperation was rare.

Organized politics in American history started right after the election of George Washington as president. Although Washington opposed the establishment of political parties, their existence in U.S. government was inevitable given the different philosophies of how the new government should be organized. The Federalists, led by Alexander Hamilton, were for a strong national government, and the Anti-Federalists (renamed the Democratic-Republican Party) opposed such centralized government, and wanted stronger state legislatures.

Although the party names and beliefs change over the years, the fundamental reasons for political parties and politics remains intact. Political structures allow for representation of the people in the government. The United States government is a representative democracy, which means representatives are elected to vote in the name of the public on laws and policies of local, state, and federal significance.

In other forms of government, the representation may be different. In single party structures, such as those in some Socialist countries, there is only one candidate running for office. The selection of the candidate is normally done by the party staff, so the public does not get a real voice in the selection process. The people in the party organization have the voices that determine the representatives in government.

Multi-party governments normally have several parties, none of which is strong enough to carry the entire parliament or federal governing body. In order to establish a majority voting block in the government, two or more parties must agree to work together, with either a formal or informal agreement. This type of arrangement is called a coalition government. Diplomacy and politics are the foundation for such negotiations.

More than a half million people held elected office in the late 1980s in the United States. Several million more worked on the election campaigns, political party staffs, or in the offices of candidates. Some worked as volunteers, others were paid for their services and expertise. Without people willing to run for office, or people willing to work for candidates who run for office, a democracy would not be able to function.

The structure of politics and public service

In the United States, public officials are elected or appointed to office. Their terms can run from two years, in the case of members of the House of Representatives, or for life, as in the case of Supreme Court Justices.

Appointments are given by a higher office, or another branch of the Federal government. Supreme Court Justices are nominated by the President, but the Congress votes to approve or reject the nominee. The appointment of judges is common, although they are elected in several states. However, judges are not allowed to be attached to any party during their campaign, since they are to remain neutral while deciding cases.

In state and local governing bodies, the status and duration of an appointment will vary according to the laws of each state. In some cities, for example, the position of chief of police may be an elected position. While in other communities, the police chief may be an appointed by the mayor's office and approved by a city council. The term of office for an official may also vary.

The method of removing appointed officers from their office varies as well. They may be removed by the desire of the appointing officer, by a recall vote, or perhaps by petition or impeachment. A Supreme Court Justice can only be removed by impeachment for corruption or abuse of the office. Each position has the means of removal of the officer stipulated in the same way the method of appointment is stipulated.

For elected officials, the entire process of obtaining office can be a long and hard struggle. The higher the office, the more time is spent by the candidate to campaign for the position. City council members, mayors, congressional representatives, governors, and the President are all elected officials. Most of them will be attached to a political party, normally the Democratic or Republican party. They will begin by announcing their candidacy for a position. In most circumstances, they will need to have petitions signed to show that there are several hundred or several thousand registered voters who would be interested in having that person as a candidate.

After announcing their desire to run for office, political candidates will proceed to advertise, speak in public and private gatherings, and meet with the public as frequently as possible in order to get their names in the minds of voters.

A candidate must meet all the requirements to be placed on the election ballot. This may mean having a certain number or percentage of voters vote for the candidate in a primary election, collecting enough signatures on a petition nominating the candidate, or submitting the candidate's name by a certain date before the election.

For each candidate running for office, there is a staff that works for his or her election. These people may either be employed by the candidate or by the political party. These workers may also be volunteers donating their time and energy to the campaign. Again, the higher the office, the more workers will be needed for the candidate to be successful.

Some people work for a candidate because they are particularly interested in seeing that particular person win the election. Others work because they support the party that the candidate represents. Still others make working for

An elected city representative speaks during a neighborhood festival. It is his duty to attend civic events that involve his constituents.

candidates their career. They become particularly well informed and skilled on how to run a successful campaign and are hired by different candidates.

Volunteers normally have the lower positions on the staff, and do a lot of the necessary clerical work for the office. This includes stuffing envelopes, handing out buttons and brochures, passing out pamphlets, going door-to-door or calling to talk to voters about their candidate.

The paid members of the staff will be mainly full-time employees. These people will be more specialized in areas of the campaign. Public relations and press representatives will be trained in presenting the candidate's views to the public and arranging as much press and media coverage as possible for every event. The head of the press office should have substantial background in handling the media and be able to deflect criticism from news stories that may not show the candidate in the best possible light. This position may be held by a consultant for candidates running for higher offices such as senator or president.

There will be media staff for commercials and televised events like debates. A logistics crew will handle hotels, airplane flights, ground transportation, and such. Aides will be hired to work on phone solicitation for finances and support. Financial specialists will cover major fund-raisers, government matching fund programs, legal matters for contribution, and other areas of concern for the candidate. General help, office staff, and other job requirements will be needed for a campaign, and the higher the office the larger the staff is going to be to handle large volumes of work.

During the Democratic convention in 1984, delegates and elected officials listened to speeches delivered by political leaders.

All of these people will work together to solicit as much support as possible from the public for the election of the candidate. They will work from early on in the campaign until the final weeks before the election, when the pressure and the time commitment become very demanding. The lower level staff will work on whatever area needs the help most. The higher levels will remain in their specialties, working to cover as much ground and contact as many people as possible in the time they have before the voting begins.

A congressional candidate will need to campaign mainly in his or her district. The presidential candidate must campaign across the entire United States. Presidential campaigns now start at least one full year before the date of the election and have campaign offices in all fifty states and the District of Columbia.

The candidate and staff will find out their future when they know the results of the election. For the winning candidate, a career is set for whatever the term of office is, and with the Senate and the House of Representatives, several terms may be set. More than 90 percent of the incumbent congresspeople win reelection.

Usually, several members of a candidate's campaign staff move into staff positions once the candidate is elected. Others will be able to move on to other election campaigns, or into positions in the party office. Depending on the level and the ambitions of the staff member, there are various opportunities for future political work.

Besides campaign workers and elected officials, there are plenty of other arenas for work in politics. In Washington D.C. the staff that assists Congress in all its tasks is quite large. Each representative has an administrative assistant to run the office in Washington. This person normally comes from the representative's own state, but that is not always necessary.

Legislative assistants and other assistants will work in the office, both in the home state and in Washington D.C. These staff members will vary in background and skill according to the representative's wishes and needs.

Subcommittees and Administrative Offices, such as the Senate Armed Services Subcommittee or the Health and Human Services Office, may employ a separate staff to run the day-to-day office work. This staff normally has considerable experience and knowledge in the area covered by the committee.

Lobbyists are also hired to sway congressional representatives to vote in the manner the lobby would like on certain pieces of legislation. The National Rifle Association, the National Wildlife Association, the Tobacco Industry, the American Medical Association, and the American Bar Association are all strong lobby groups, supporting the legislation that they feel will best help their industry and concerns, and opposing those which will not be helpful.

Lobbyists are frequently ex-government employee, because these people have the best contacts in the government and are familiar with the offices and the staff that they are contacting. There are restrictions on how long you must be out of office for certain positions before you are allowed to work for a lobbying group. Congressmen are not restricted, but administration employees above a certain authority level must wait a year before they may return as lobbyists.

The lobby group will also require a logistics staff to compile research and collect information on all other aspects of the business to make the group as effective as possible.

Consulting firms that work for political action committees and all sorts of government and government-related groups require a staff as well. Depending on the size of the firm and the specialization, the staff can vary in size considerably from firm to firm. The higher the position, the more likely it is that the staff will have extensive background in the field of interest for the firm. For example, military equipment consulting firms often hire ex-military personnel to enhance the quality of the services they offer to government agencies.

Consultants can be used to set up programs that will be executed by a permanent staff. Financial consultants will work for several campaigns a season, establishing the system of accounting that will be used by the candidate's campaign staff. The shorter term projects allow a consulting firm to move through several campaigns at a time, since their time will be needed only for a short period. It is, however, considered improper to move from one candidate to the opposing candidate during one election campaign.

General consultants working on structuring or establishing campaign strategies will have a strong background in politics and campaigning, but will not be interested in working on the day-to-day aspects of the campaign. This gives the consultant an opportunity to use his or her expertise, while not getting too involved with the more time-consuming tasks of campaigning.

Governor Thompson of Illinois addresses the state assembly in Springfield.

Careers

A sampling of career opportunities follows below.

Elected officers: For each community, the positions open through election may vary. It helps a candidate to have some experience in running for office or a history of working in a related field. This gives the candidate some exposure to the public. Although there are no restrictions on what the background experience should be, it is more likely that the candidate will be considered for senator, for example, if he or she has served in some capacity with the government before running for the senate office.

Some offices do have a restriction on the candidate's status as an American citizen and his or her age. For instance, a senator has to be thirty years old and the president has to be thirty-five years old at the time of the inauguration. In addition, the president must have been born an American citizen.

Appointed officials: Many of the same qualifications apply to appointed officials that apply to elected officials. It would be much more likely to be appointed chief of police, if one had served as a police officer. It will depend on the position and what the appointing official considers the strongest requirement for a candidate for the post. It is normally necessary that the candidate hold the same basic values toward the position as the appointing officer, so being a member of the same political party may make it much more likely for a person to be considered for a position when someone from his or her party is in the office doing the appointing.

In positions where the term of office is dependent on the appointing officer's continued approval, the appointee may find him or herself out of a job when new elections are held and a candidate from the opposing party is elected. Job stability may depend on the continued success of the party the appointee supports. For lifetime appointments, like the Supreme Court, this is of no concern to the appointees once they are in place.

Administrative assistants: These are the people who run the campaigns and offices of elected officials. They are like the general managers of a business, in charge of all aspects of the organization that they are running. They will need a good background in all elements of the campaign, with some understanding of all the needs, such as fund-raising, press relations, and brochure writing. They normally have moved up the ranks from a volunteer role in an earlier campaign, and have an established track record as a dedicated and competent worker.

Campaign staff: This comprises the organization that runs the campaign. Work areas will include a press relations officer; fund-raising officer; research staff for voter analysis, opposition analysis, and other topics; field workers, employed in regional offices to deal with all the elements of the campaign on a local level; drivers; telephone operators; canvassers; and assorted other staff members. Because of the long hours, relatively low pay for the paid staff, and the dedication to the candidate, political operatives are particularly open to newcomers. Hard working employees are difficult to find and are always needed, so the people on the staff are happy to help train beginners in a field of interest. Movement upward on a campaign

Staff members of party headquarters send out newsletters to people who are registered in their party.

staff can be fairly rapid if the worker is dedicated and remains on the campaign.

Congressional staff: Although the numbers and the variety of the staff positions are not as large as on the campaign staff, much of the work is the same. Campaign work can be fairly easily translated into congressional staff work. Frequently the administrative assistant for a campaign becomes the administrative assistant to the congressperson after election. The congressperson will need people to answer phone calls, letters, and questions from drop-in visitors to the office. It is important that the staff be good at fielding the requests in an efficient and courteous manner. Staff members may be required to be from the home state of the representative. Some background in political work may be required to be considered for a job. Congress has a placement office where resumes and applications will be kept on file for any requests that may come in from Congress.

The Democratic Study Committee and the Republican Study Committee both have job placement services as well.

Administration staff: The White House Administration requires a staff to organize its day-to-day activities. Responsibilities in this area are similar to that done in congressional offices.

Consulting personnel: Varying from highly specialized to very general in the information and services offered, consulting firms vary greatly in size. Entry-level positions for someone in the political field are very rare, with most of the staff consisting of experienced workers.

Education

Although no background is specifically required for many of the positions in this field, there are still some general guidelines to an academic background that helps the prospective worker. History, political science, and economy are all good courses of study. For fund-raising, finances, marketing, and economic courses are strong areas of study. For press and public relations, journalism courses, writing courses, and public relations courses are recommended. A bachelor's degree is recommended for most levels of employment, although there are staff employees who have moved up the ladder without a college degree.

Politicians frequently have law degrees, partly for the background, and partly because this will give them a solid job skill to fall back on when they are not in office. The period of unemployment between elections must be considered by the prospective candidate. A candidate cannot always count on being in office.

There are several suggested routes for developing a strong resume while in high school or college. Volunteering to work on a campaign is the single most effective method of gaining personal contacts, testing job skills, and finding out if the pace of life on a campaign is suitable to the prospective political person. For the dedicated volunteer, the prospect of earning money will come fairly quickly as skills are developed and contacts are made.

Internships exist for both high school and college level programs. They are fairly competitive and most are located in Washington D.C. The page program is probably the most well known.

The page program is structured so that each congressperson is allowed to nominate one student each semester. The student must be either entering or just out of his or her junior year in high school. There is a summer session, and two semester sessions, with about ninety pages selected each session. The competition for a page position is tight. A member of congress may get a candidate in once in four or five tries. The only way to get into the program is through nomination by the student's congressman. The pages live in a dormitory supplied by the congress, and are supervised by an in-house staff.

College internships are sponsored by either universities or by members of congress themselves. It is mainly for summer work in the offices of congress, but semester internships may also be available.

The Republican Party also sponsors the American Campaign Academy, a one semester program for people interested in further college level training on campaign skills and theory.

There are several skills that a strong political worker should possess. Having good writing and speaking skills, strong analytical skills, a solid, outgoing personality, and a real desire to work in politics and government all contribute to a good base for a political career.

Industry outlook

Although there is some discussion of cutting back staff on some local, regional, and even federal levels, the opportunities in politics still remain strong. The government will always require fairly extensive staffing to accomplish all the tasks assigned to it.

For the student looking at entry-level positions, starting as a volunteer and thereby getting to know people is the most effective and most recommended method of finding work. Because there is no pay in the beginning, it is best to get involved as early as possible so when an income is necessary, the prospective employee has the experience to get a paid position.

Any manner of making contacts with people currently in the political field is helpful. Internships and the page program are both important for that reason.

Advancement can be rapid for someone who is a fast learner and is independently motivated. Initiative is one key element to promotion. The movement from one area to another may be easier in politics than in other industries, because of the willingness of the staff to train newcomers.

One of the major drawbacks to be considered before venturing into politics is the job instability. Because of the continued dependence on election by both the candidates and the staff, the ability to determine long range job objectives is very difficult. There may be extended periods of unemployment, where living off of savings or other jobs may be necessary, and the prospective political worker should consider how adaptable he or she is to such situations.

Because of the frequent travel involved in campaigning and in holding office, someone with children may find the lifestyle increasingly demanding on the family. For this reason, politics tends to be populated with younger workers. It is certainly possible to continue working in politics for one's entire career, but the demands should be considered.

The other potential drawback to political life, mainly for the candidate for office but increasingly for the core staff on a campaign as

During elections, politicians strive to receive attention from the media. Such exposure increases their chances for election.

well, is that there is no real off-duty time. One is continually under observation by the press and public, and the personal life of a candidate and an office-holder is discussed frequently in the press. It is a form of celebrity, where a political figure is more closely watched than a person in the private sector.

◇ SOURCES OF ADDITIONAL INFORMATION

The Congressional Management Foundation publishes *The Congressional Intern Handbook* and *The Insider's Guide to Getting a Job on the Hill.*

The Congressional Management Foundation
513 Capitol Court, NE
Suite 100
Washington, DC 200002

Democratic National Committee
430 South Capitol Street, SE
Washington, DC 20003

The Democratic Congressional Campaign Committee and the Young Democrats of America, for youth between eighteen and thirty-five years old, are also housed with the Democratic National Committee.

Republican National Committee
310 First Street, SE
Washington, DC 20003

The Republican National Committee also has the Young Republican National Federation, for people between eighteen and forty years of age, and the

College Republican National Committee, for college students.

State capitol offices, regional offices of elections, and campaign headquarters are good sources of information and volunteer positions. Contact your congressperson for information on the page program and possible internships.

Also contact:

Public Service Research Council
8330 Old Courthouse Road, Suite 600
Vienna, VA 22180

◇ **RELATED ARTICLES**

Volume 1: Broadcasting; Civil Service; Foreign Service; Marketing; Military Service; Personal and Consulting Services; Public Relations
Volume 2: City managers; Economists; Foreign-Service officers; Fundraisers; Lawyers and judges; Legal assistants; Media specialists; Operations-research analysts; Political scientists; Public relations specialists; Statisticians
Volume 3: Court reporters; FBI agents; Occupational safety and health workers

Printing

General information

Printing is a diverse and highly technical industry. It involves the production of the millions of books annually, billions of newspapers and magazines, and untold numbers of paper money, wrappers, cartons, and even clothing.

Printing is among the most ancient and important means of communication. The history of modern printing is relatively short—about 500 years. However, the Chinese made substantial strides in printing hundreds of years before Western civilization had constructed its first press. In A.D. 105, Cai Lun of China invented paper, which proved to be an inexpensive medium for printed matter. In A.D 1045 Bi Sheng invented the first form of movable type with clay characters. Because the Chinese language has hundreds of characters, this method proved to be impractical. While the Chinese had progressed, inhabitants of the Western world were still writing text and drawing illustrations by hand on vellum, a costly and time-consuming task that was delegated to monks.

It was not until the late 1300s that Europeans used block printing to create illustrations for religious and artistic purposes. With the Renaissance fervor of the 15th and 16th centuries, the block printers could not keep up with the demand for reading material. With the invention of movable type in the 1440s by Johannes Gutenberg, printed matter could be produced quickly and inexpensively. Gutenberg used separate raised pieces of metal type, arranged them in a textual fashion, applied ink to the raised surface, and pressed the letters onto a piece of paper. This method is commonly known as relief printing. His first press could print 300 copies a day. In 1456, he completed the famous Gutenberg Bible.

The phenomenal success of Gutenberg's movable type press led to a flourishing of print shops all over Europe. By 1500, several million books had already been printed, but the technology had changed very little. Not until the early 1800s did the steam-powered cylinder press venture onto the markets. It could print up to 1,100 sheets of paper in one hour. Newer developments were continually introduced. In 1846, the American Richard Hoe created the rotary press, using revolving cylinders to make an inked impression on paper. This press could print up to 8,000 sheets per hour. The notion of revolving cylinders in printing presses still prevails in modern times with offset printing, where a series of cylinders are used to apply ink from a treated surface onto the paper. In this case, the plate never touches the paper. Such work is done on a web press.

Until the 1880s, platemaking was a laborious task where workers hand-selected individual letters and placed them piece by piece on a plate. In 1884, Ottmar Mergenthaler patented the Linotype machine which cast a full line of type into one piece of metal. Three years later, Tolbert Lanston invented the Monotype, which cast separate pieces of type.

Technological changes in the printing industry have proceeded at a rapid rate making it one of the most modern industries. The industry is constantly being altered by the development and widespread adoption of new technologies that increase productivity, accelerate output, and provide new tools to designers, editors, and others in graphic communications. Nearly everyone entering this field today, as well as those already in it, will be touched by these new technologies and will be faced with the challenge of using them effectively.

Printing is also one of the most diversified industries. Geographically, there is scarcely a town of any size without some provision for printing. Printing is used for many products, which range from books and periodicals to labels and cartons. Printing techniques are important to many other products such as electronic circuitry, textiles, sheet plastics, and metal decoration. The advent of affordable

This high-speed web offset press can comfortably print over 30,000 newspapers in one hour. It requires the attention of only four or five mechanics.

desktop publishing software and laser printers has made it possible for small businesses to be printing units, bypassing the use and expense of large printing companies.

The structure of the printing industry

Printing is one of the largest and most important of the service industries. Although it uses mass production techniques, every product of the printing press is tailor-made for a specific and unique purpose, usually performed against a rigid time schedule.

The process begins with the sales representative, who locates customers in need of some print work. He or she must convince them that the represented printing company is qualified to do the job. In smaller companies, independent sales representatives, or brokers, solicit clients. The broker will then call on specialized shops for services not available from the main supplier. Brokering can be highly remunerative, but, of course, such an operation is only possible in larger cities where a number of specialized shops are available.

Since every printing job is manufactured to fill a specific need, it follows that production time is extremely important. Periodicals must

be issued on regular dates, mailing pieces must be mailed within strict time limits, books must meet their publication dates, and financial reports must reach stockholders on specified dates. Production managers make things happen on time, and a good production person will have a number of such jobs under his or her control. Production management requires a high degree of accuracy, clear logical thinking, resourcefulness, and the ability to work with people.

When a project has been secured by a sales representative, the printing company prepares for the printing. Requests for estimates come from the salespeople and must usually be answered quickly, although the preparation of a single estimate may take several days before all the necessary information can be collected.

Estimates will be made for the purpose of giving established customers an indication of final production costs. Accurate estimates depend on accurate cost records in the particular plant; obviously, profits depend on accurate estimates of costs.

When a client has agreed to the estimated production costs, the text is then set into type. Composition is accomplished in a number of different ways, including setting metal type by hand, setting metal type by machine, and photographic composition. Additional variations are provided by applying various electronic aids (such as punched tape, magnetic tape, or computer disks) to machine and photographic methods. In addition, there are now composition systems based on modifications of the office typewriter and highly sophisticated optical scanners that "read" manuscripts and store the text without any of the traditional keyboard operations.

Hand compositors make up the oldest composing room occupation. Typesetting by hand, in the manner developed by Johannes Gutenberg in the fifteenth century, is limited to setting display type (large type used for advertisements), occasional short blocks of text, and other small jobs in which the setting of type by machine is impractical.

The traditional hand compositors read from the copy and set each line of type, letter by letter, in a small metal tray called a composing stick. This type is arranged upside down in lines, with spacing inserted as desired. As each line is filled, the type is transferred to a shallow metal tray called a galley. The galley tray, when filled, will hold all the type necessary to print a column of the text. This is a cumbersome process, requiring a great deal of patience.

All mechanical means of typesetting are organized around two basic steps. In the first step an operator, sitting at a keyboard, types out the copy that is to be printed. In the second step, metal type is cast and set according to the instructions entered at the keyboard. There are two methods for setting metal type by machine—the monotype method and the linotype method. In each method, hot metal is forced into molds and cast metal type is ejected into a galley tray. In Monotype, single letters or characters are cast and then ejected into the galley. In Linotype, entire lines of type are cast at once as single slugs and then ejected.

Monotype composition offers the additional feature that the keyboarding and the typesetting are done by two different machines and need not be done at the same time or in the same place. What the Monotype operator actually produces is a perforated tape that is then fed into the typesetting machine. This feature has led to Monotype's popularity because it allows for more flexibility and various kinds of electronic modifications to the system.

As with hand compositors, Monotype and Linotype operators must hyphenate and adjust small spacing to fit the width of columns. A thorough knowledge of spelling, grammar, punctuation, and word division is highly desirable for a compositor, as well as a high degree of finger dexterity. In addition, in small plants, operators may also be called on to maintain and repair typesetting equipment.

Although some highly specialized typesetting will continue to be done by hand or with Monotype and Linotype machines, more and more firms have switched to phototypesetting machines. In this method, a photographic process replaces the casting of type, and the final product is a film image of the type.

In phototypesetting, the output, a magnetic or paper tape or perhaps a disk generated by a computer word-processing program, may then be fed into a computer that is programmed to do hyphenation, enter typesetting codes, and arrange columns of text. A new tape or disk that contains both the text and these additional instructions about how to arrange it is generated. This new input directs a photocomposition machine that develops film for photographic type reproduction.

Once the text is fully typeset and edited, the text goes to press. Some printing is still done by letterpress (in which pieces of metal type are coated with ink and pressed against the paper), but offset printing (in which the printing plate does not actually touch the paper) has become the prominent method of printing.

Lithographers and photoengravers produce the printing plates that are used in the actual printing process. In photoengraving, ink is rolled over a printed surface that stands higher than the rest of the plate. When paper is pressed against the raised surface, the print or image is picked up.

The photoengraving process begins with making a photographic image of the material to be printed. An etcher makes the actual plate by dipping a piece of metal, with the image photographically printed on it, into a vat of acid that eats away at the areas that will not be covered with ink. Although many engravings are still made by hand, machines are now available that etch a large number of engravings in a few minutes.

In lithography, a plate is made from a photographic image of the material to be printed. In offset printing, however, the area to be printed is neither raised nor lowered. The image is printed on sheets of zinc or aluminum in such a way that the areas to be printed will pick up ink off of an inky roller while the rest of the plate will not. During the printing process, that ink is then transferred from the printing plate to a rubber roller, which in turn lays the ink down on the paper.

Closely allied with the printing process is the binding process, or the assembling of printed sheets by folding, gluing, and stitching into pamphlets or books. In binding, as in printing, the technological revolution is changing many of the traditional crafts, and automa-

Although typesetting is computerized, typesetters must still manipulate text carefully to make each page readable.

tion is eliminating many of the crafts that have existed for more than 500 years. Many high-speed printing presses now have automatic folders, stitchers, and trimmers attached, delivering a finished product.

Occupations in the printing industry tend to separate themselves into two categories—skilled craft workers and relatively unskilled laborers who tend, feed, and unload automatic machines.

Careers

The industry as a whole demands an extraordinary versatility and flexibility of its employees; even in routine crafts or highly specialized shops every order processed will differ in specifications, providing a continuing variety and challenge.

Although the craft occupations in the industry are rigidly specialized and specified by custom and union rules, jobs in administration tend to be more loosely defined, with a number of different functions often performed by the same person. The owner of a printing firm will frequently be its leading sales representative and will often participate in the day-to-day management of the shop. Servicing clients will often require the attention of the shop personnel.

A sampling of career opportunities in the printing industry follows below.

Sales representatives: Salespeople sell a printing service. They offer a tailor-made product that has not yet been manufactured. It is their job to convince a client that the company they represent can print the client's product. The high degree of confidence necessary for such a transaction tends to be dependent on the individual representative of the company. Once a project is completed, the sales representative must keep up good relations with the client.

Brokers: Brokers, who do not work for a specific firm, place the printing business they control with the shop that can give them the lowest prices or the greatest security in guaranteeing the quality of the product and schedule of deliveries. Brokers usually work for themselves, but they may have one or two assistants to supervise the jobs through the printing process. Often a broker will have an arrangement with a single shop that fills most of the orders and rents the broker office space.

Production managers: The production manager takes over the job from the sales representative or broker and guides it through the shop, coordinating the different operations to see that the components meet each other at the right time to fulfill the schedule requirements.

Plant managers: It is the plant manager's responsibility to maintain an organization of people and machines in efficient working order to achieve the schedule requirements requested by the customers. This requires an intimate knowledge of machines and processes, but, above all, a practical and effective working knowledge of how to deal with people, since the plant manager is senior in rank to most of the employees in a printing office. In all but the largest shops, plant managers act as personnel managers, recruiting not only the supervisors of the various departments but also the majority of plant employees.

Plant engineers: The plant engineer's job is to survey existing equipment and techniques and to recommend improvements in operations. Plant engineers in some firms will supervise separate departments of their own. Because of respect for tradition in this industry and the careful definitions of functions in all union contracts, a plant engineer will find that he or she needs to be a diplomat as well as a scientist to be effective in the job.

Estimators: It is the estimator's task to predict what it will cost to produce any given printing job. Estimators must therefore work out efficient plans of production in light of the techniques and equipment available in their particular printing plant, and then make precise calculations of the cost of each operation and of the materials required. Besides an ability to make accurate calculations, they must also have a theoretical knowledge of all printing processes and materials and a good measure of ingenuity.

A stripper prepares a multi-page signature by placing the negatives of each page in the proper sequence for printing.

Compositors: A compositor is anyone who participates in the arrangement of type for reproduction.

Phototypesetters: A phototypesetting system operator may type in the text without regard to column width or hyphenation.

Photoengravers: Photoengravers make the plates that are used in letterpress operations. They also make gravure cylinders on which the image is etched beneath the surface of the cylinder.

Lithographers: Lithographers make the plates used in offset printing.

Platemakers: Platemakers are responsible for operating and maintaining sophisticated machines and for ensuring that the plates meet quality standards. With increasing automation, the technical skills of a platemaker are becoming more important than his or her craft skills.

Camera operators: Camera operators photograph the material to be printed and develop the negatives.

Color separation photographers: Color separation photographers work exclusively with the process of reproducing materials in color.

Lithographic artists: Lithographic artists work with the negatives to enhance, sharpen, or reshape images.

Strippers: Strippers assemble the negative films, arrange them into sheets of the size required for the presses, and position them as required by sequence of pages, margins, fitting of multiple colors, and other elements.

Printing press operators: Printing press operators maintain, set up, and operate the printing presses that produce the finished products. In small shops, operators may run simple manual presses. In larger operations, operators may work in teams of several operators and assistants, feeding huge rolls of paper into giant machines that print the paper on both sides, cutting and assembling the pages, and counting the copies as they come off the press. In many modern plants, printing press operators control press operations through the use of computers and other sophisticated instrumentation.

Bindery workers: Bindery workers are involved with running the machines that put together the printed material. With books, this requires stitching, gluing, and attaching the cover. With other materials, such as magazines, only stapling may be involved.

Education

The occupations cited here are the traditional careers of the printing industry, most of which require an apprenticeship of from four to six years. But the entire industry is going through a technological revolution that will eliminate

A press operator and his supervisor examine recently-printed pages. If they notice any problems, they can correct them at this time.

some processes and create entirely new occupations. Some of these developments include new kinds of photomechanical typesetters, electronic page makeup devices, graphic creation stations and display terminals, and laser and ink-jet printing. Such developments call for engineers, chemists, mathematicians, and electronics experts. In addition, authors, editors, production managers, and many other people not originally trained in the use of high-technology equipment will need to learn what can and cannot be done. The advent of computers and especially desktop publishing has introduced these people to the mechanics of printing.

In the past, the printing industry recruited its trainees from those who were more interested in the practical arts and mechanical systems than in academic subjects. Students were taught principally through trade school courses and apprenticeships. Today, the conditions of the industry make this no longer practical, and the unions and management associations require prospective apprentices to bring a high level of aptitude and ability as well as a high-school diploma to the job. Apprenticeship programs for press operators last four years. Postsecondary education has become more important for job applicants.

Traditionally, the plant manager has come up from the ranks, having been promoted from supervisor of the composing room, the pressroom, or the bindery. Today, because of the

revolution in techniques and because of skills needed in the management of processes and personnel, the tendency is to select people who are trained as engineers.

Industry outlook

The printing industry is currently undergoing a technological revolution, as new and more advanced machinery is being developed. In many cases, these advancements have made some jobs obsolete. For example, photoengraving was traditionally the highest paid branch of the printing industry, and its union the strongest. The growth of offset and gravure, however, placed photoengraving at a competitive disadvantage.

Other occupations in the printing industry that did not expand because of newer competitive processes are electrotyping and stereotyping. On the other hand, the making of plastic printing plates, either by molding or photomechanical processes, has expanded in recent years.

Generalizations about the printing industry are difficult to make because of the extreme diversity in size and the many specialized smaller shops that limit themselves to a single function. Overall, however, the employment situation in the industry is dominated by the arrival of new, sophisticated laborsaving machinery. This will probably result in a scarcity of jobs for photoengravers, decreases in jobs for compositors, but some slow growth in opportunities for printing press operators (especially in firms outside the printing industry, like paper mills, which are now doing more of their own presswork), and a more rapid growth in employment opportunities for lithographers and other people involved in aspects of offset printing.

Although radio, television, motion pictures, and other media compete for the attention of the public, printing continues to grow in the United States. It is expected to produce almost $170 billion dollars worth of printed material annually in the early 1990s, increasing annually by over 7 percent.

Social factors such as the increase in the literacy rate and the increase in the population will boost circulation of printed matter such as newspapers, magazines, and books. Other large printing media such as direct mail packages and catalogues are expected to continue at full force. This will reflect postively on the printing industry. Since printed materials have a ease of access and simplicity in use that other media cannot always match, the printing industry has a bright future for the 1990s.

◇ **SOURCES OF ADDITIONAL INFORMATION**

Binding Industries of America
70 East Lake Street
Chicago, IL 60601

Graphic Communications International Union
1900 L Street, NW
Washington, DC 20036

In-Plant Management Association
1205 West College Avenue
Liberty, MO 64068

National Association of Printers and Lithographers
780 Palisade Avenue
Teaneck, NJ 07666

Printing Industries of America
1730 North Lynn Street
Arlington, VA 22209

◇ **RELATED ARTICLES**

Volume 1: Book Publishing; Magazine Publishing; Newspaper Publishing; Pulp and Paper; Wood
Volume 2: Cost estimators; General managers and top executives; Photographers and camera operators
Volume 3: Bindery workers; Blue-collar worker supervisors; Compositors and typesetters; Computer and peripheral equipment operators; Electroplating workers; Electrotypers and stereotypers; General maintenance mechanics; Industrial machinery mechanics; Lithographic occupations; Paper processing operations; Photoengravers; Photographic laboratory occupations; Printing press operators and assistants
Volume 4: Computer-service technicians; Darkroom technicians; Electronics technicians; Film laboratory technicians; Graphic arts technicians; Layout technicians; Photofinishing equipment technicians; Photographic equipment technicians; Quality control technicians; Telecommunications technicians

Public Relations

General information

Socrates, Plato, and Aristotle developed rules of rhetoric which involved ways of making arguments more effective. Emotional appeals, effective structures of logic, and methods of persuasion were explained for use in jury trials, teaching ethics, and other situations where reason guided the discussion. The development of persuasion for portraying a positive public image was used effectively in court defenses and other arenas where it was found that, by painting such an image of someone, opinion could be swayed to one's advantage. These are the origins of public relations.

In the late 19th century, newspapers decided to encourage advertisers by promising positive articles concerning businesses that chose to advertise in the paper. However, the free publicity in the form of news articles undermined the objectivity of the newspaper and eventually the practice was halted in the United States. In 1909, a newspaper committee was established to watch for abuses of free publicity to advertisers.

Despite the attempt to disengage public relations from newspapers, public relations continued to develop through journalists. The link between public relations and newspapers endured through reporters who were well skilled in the effects of language on public image and who were willing to use this to present a company in a positive light.

In 1906, a reporter named Ivy Ledbetter Lee was named press representative for coal-mine operators. The operators had run into problems because of their continual refusal to talk to the press and the hired miners. Labor disputes were becoming a large concern of the operators and they decided to bring in outside help to reform their standing in the public eye. Lee convinced the mine operators to start responding to press questions and supply the press with information on the mine activities.

After a successful turnaround of the coal-mine operators' situation, Lee went on to work for the Pennsylvania Railroad. They had been withholding information on railroad accidents and had developed a poor reputation with the press and the public. He revised their policy so that all information available on any accident would be given to the press.

He developed a large group of clients for his services. The term "public relations" had not yet been used, but it was certainly the service that Lee provided to those clients. He developed new policies for business: a practice of honesty and openness about the company's business and affairs, and a practice of sending out notices to the newspapers about noteworthy events in the company's development.

Governments became a regular user of public relations experts. England's Empire Marketing Board used publicity to promote trade in the late 1920s and early 1930s.

During World War II, governmental agencies in the United States made a point of hiring publicists, since public exposure aided funding and congressional awareness of the activities of the group. Groups looking for donations for rubber, scrap metal, and war bonds used press releases over the radio and in shops to promote their activity. Publicity was also used to recruit soldiers. The Office of Price Administration (OPA) under Chester Bowles used public relations tactics to promote rationing procedures, to persuade businessmen that prices had to be kept low, and to get legislation for the OPA passed through Congress.

By the end of World War II, almost every government agency had a public relations office. Public relations had become an accepted part of the operations of business and government. The airlines, for example, hired public relations specialists to help with delivering information on airplane crashes, providing background and technical information to the press in a manner that would be readily understood.

Politicians followed business's example. After Richard Nixon's unsuccessful bid for the presidency in 1960, Nixon hired public relations and press experts to help him regain popularity in his bids for elected office. The experts redirected his method of approaching interviews and press conferences, and any other element of public presentation that might affect how he was seen by the voting public. He was able to reestablish a positive image among voters and was elected President in 1968.

This relationship between politics and public relations was an inevitable occurrence given the preponderance of media around candidates and the incredible importance of image in determining success in an election.

Public relations specialists are now employed by all sorts of publicity-conscious people. Politicians, celebrities, artists, and even journalists now use specialists to help them receive positive coverage in the press. It has become a major industry, expanding beyond the original clients, business and government, to a whole range of clients who wish to put the best foot forward in their presentation to the public and get public exposure.

To gain as much public exposure as possible, companies hire public relations specialists to devise gimmicks such as hot air balloons.

The structure of the public relations industry

The first goal of a public relations worker is to present the best possible public image for a client. The public relations worker is responsible not only for providing positive information to the press about the activities of a client, but must also direct the client on the path to developing positive business practices.

The office of public relations for any company promotes good news and portrays bad news in a manner that would do the least damage to the company. In the case of an airline crash, legal necessity forces the airline company to be as straightforward as possible about the causes of the crash. In an accident which is the fault of the plane's design, for example, the public relations department must find out how the company plans to correct the problem, how long that will take, and what will be done in the interim to insure the safety of the passengers. The public relations staff assembles all the relevant information, assesses the situation, anticipates any questions from the press, and then presents the information to the news media. In a major disaster, the desire is to provide as much information as possible without guessing at any information that may be found to be untrue later.

In some situations, the company may wish to block the passage of information to the press. It then becomes the job of the public relations officer to redirect the focus of the media attention.

Interpretation of information for the media is the second major function of a public relations officer. This task is particularly important for a public relations staff of a scientific or technical firm. Public relations workers must be able to take technical information and explain it in such a way that non-specialists will be able to understand it. This interpretation of technical material must be done on press releases and any other information that comes from the technical side of the business and goes to the public.

In an organization such as the National Aeronautical and Space Administration (NASA), the need for a public relations specialist who has a good understanding of aeronautics is important. If a scientist is explaining a project to the public relations officer, the public relations officer must understand the explanation well enough to describe it to the media at a later time.

Research is the first step of public relations. It is important to get all the significant data and to analyze the attitudes revealed. Research personnel may be on the staff of a public relations

Public relations workers who specialize in the apparel industry organize fashion shows that feature both the sponsor, the retailer, and the designer in a single engagement.

department, or they may be employed by a separate research organization retained to do the job.

Research is important both for obtaining inside information on a topic that is to be presented to the public and for anticipating potential public response to the company.

A major goal of public relations is press publicity. Material provided for the media is called a press release. This may cover some aspect of the company that is deemed to be newsworthy by company staff. The press release will provide all relevant information to local or national press. It is one method of generating coverage of the company without buying advertising space. It may appear in various forms: newspaper spot news, magazine articles, or radio and television coverage.

Those who prepare news releases often have been trained as reporters and editors. They have learned to identify valuable news stories and how to write and illustrate a story so that it will be published. Such writers are part of every large public relations staff. Full-time photographic jobs exist only in the largest organizations; usually photographers are used on a part-time basis when photos are needed.

The use of advertising space for the presentation of an institutional message can be just as useful as the production of booklets, press releases, or similar public relations techniques. Such advertisements are sometimes written by

writers on the public relations staffs and sometimes by writers in the company's advertising agency. These advertisements can serve whatever need the company sees, but frequently they are used in response to a particular incident or crisis. After the 1989 major oil spill in Alaska, Exxon, owners of the tanker that was responsible for the spill, took out advertisements across the nation to explain the situation and the clean-up steps the company had decided to take.

Another use of the public relations advertisement is to announce mergers, enhance or fight takeovers by other companies, and inform the public on company policies and practices. It serves as the voice of the company, providing the information that they would like to send out, in a forum that is widely read or seen.

A further tool for informing people is the public relations periodical. This is a company magazine or house organ. It goes to the various groups served by the company or institution. Thousands of such periodicals are published in the United States. Some are equal in quality to the magazines sold on the newsstands. They often require a separate staff of editors and writers. They may maintain regular publication dates and often have large circulations. One of the most common is the airline magazine, provided on airplanes for the public to read.

Special events may involve displays, exhibits, meetings and conferences, awards, open houses, tours, contests, parades, or pageants. Activities that generate publicity, bring in a crowd that may not have been exposed to the company before, or produce a feeling of goodwill for the company are effective means of creating a positive image of the company. This is a method frequently used by groups that work on a non-profit or cultural basis. Zoos will sponsor activities centered around the animals, for example, to bring in families who may not regularly frequent the zoo.

Public relations practitioners also use oral communication. This primary method of human communication is usually organized through a speaker's bureau. Utility and other large corporations often offer speakers to community groups. Speakers with expertise on a subject serve two purposes in public speaking. The first is that they inform the public on a subject that is related to the work of the company who has sponsored the lecturer. The second is that they generate familiarity with the company name and projects that the company has undertaken.

Anniversaries are prime occasions for public relations specialist to engage in several promotions.

Careers

A sampling of careers in public relations follows below.

Account executives: Account executives are responsible for overseeing the public relations aspects of a company. Normally hired by a public relations firm that handles several corporate or private accounts, an account executive designs and controls the approach the company takes on all public relations matters.

Public relations managers: Hired by a business or individual for either permanent or temporary work, the public relations manager sets the agenda for public appearances, advertising campaigns, and other scheduled events that influence the public's image and awareness of the client. Public relations managers regularly work alone in small business and for individuals such as politicians. In a large corporation, a public relations manager may have a large staff with several researchers, administrators, designers, and other individuals who have specific skills in public relations and marketing.

Researchers: Working with an account executive or a public relations manager, the researcher collects information that reflects the public's attitudes toward a company. This may involve polling, interviewing, or reviewing others' data on a variety of subjects.

Media relations specialists: Possessing an extensive background in public relations work, the media relations specialist has a broad work-

ing knowledge of television and print journalism and has skills in establishing a controlled, positive image for the company or the person appearing before the press. Media relations specialists may also work in designing and presenting commercials, public statements, and interviews. Organizing such details as dress, make-up, background scenery, and audience are important to establish the image desired by the client.

Speech writers: Speech writers are hired to write all kinds of presentations given by politicians, company executives, and other people who need to speak before groups or the press. Since the way an idea or thought is presented is extremely important in getting the point across, specialists who write well are sought by people who have a speech to make.

For people who speak publicly on a regular or frequent basis, a full-time speech writer may be hired so that the writer understands the appropriate style of the speaker. This allows for speeches that reflect not only the beliefs of the speaker, but reflect the manner and natural rhythm of the speaker's own style as well. For someone who speaks infrequently before large groups, a free-lance speech writer may be hired to create one speech for a presentation.

In either case, the topic and information to be presented is selected by the speaker and given to the writer to research, write, and help in preparation of the presentation.

Speakers: For organizations that do not have enough staff or qualified individuals to give public presentations, a speaker may be hired whose skills involve public speaking, back-

Public relations workers issue press releases and photographs to media sources in the hopes that their company will get free publicity. In this case, a zoo released this photograph of Peter, the Aldabra tortoise, who is taking his seasonal stroll.

ground knowledge in the subject being covered, and, perhaps, name recognition by the public. For organizations looking for good press coverage, the familiarity of the speaker may draw enough coverage and audience to warrant paying a higher speaker's fee than would go to an expert who is less well known.

Depending on the organization and the goal of the public presentation, the qualifications of the speaker may range from having supported the organization financially to having a doctorate on the subject being covered.

For some organizations, speakers are hired on a permanent basis. Their job is to give public presentations, interviews, and press conferences on their company's business, and to keep up-to-date on the company and its concerns. For organizations that rely on public support and funding, public speakers are one of the most important facets of the business. For example, a conservation group may hire wildlife experts to tour the country speaking about conservation issues, increasing awareness of and membership in the organization.

Writers: Along with speech writers and public speakers, writers are responsible for generating coverage of the client in arenas that will give the client exposure to the public. Journals, newspapers, magazines, and newsletters are the fields of the writer. The coverage may be in internally produced documents or in outside publications. Creating articles and stories that will reflect the views and interests of the commissioning company or individual is the intent of the public relations writer.

Booking agents: Booking agents arrange for public speaking engagements for the representatives of a company or for an individual seeking public exposure. The agents arrange for engagements on talk shows, news shows, radio programs, lectures, panel discussions or any other forum that allows the speaker a place and an audience that will be receptive to the topic being covered. The booking agent is responsible for balancing the audience size to the potential audience response or participant response to the speaker. For example, the audience of a television show may be quite large, but the interviewer's questions may be difficult and unsympathetic to the speaker. The potential harms and benefits need to be weighed in selecting any speaking engagement.

Programmers: Programmers are responsible for scheduling coverage over a period of time. Determining the timing of advertisements, public engagements, and other presentations is all done by programmers. They evaluate the type of coverage the client wants, whether to run a long term program or a short term blitz, and they plan when and where the public exposure will come. Programmers may design public events and other sponsored events to generate coverage and media time for the client.

Information officers: Hired by companies and individuals to answer questions from the public and the press, an information officer may be responsible for handling problems, complaints, and concerns of customers of a manufacturer. He or she may handle questions on public events and any relevant information, such as directions, times, and schedules for sponsored events. The range of tasks of the information officer is determined by the goals of the office and the company employing the officer. A government information officer, for example, handles much different questions than a tourist bureau information officer.

Education

Colleges and universities have courses in public relations and some schools offer degrees in public relations. The specific skills needed by a public relations worker involve writing, planning, public speaking, and advertising. Course work that develops these skills will aid the candidate in a job search.

For specialists in an area of public relations, such as media relations, the course work should reflect the background knowledge needed for that specialty. The courses should be combined with the subjects already mentioned; those skills will also be beneficial to the specialist.

The majority of public relations offices look for candidates with at least a bachelor's degree, and some employers prefer master's degrees for certain positions. Writing skills are highly valued by both public relations firms and corporate offices looking for public relations workers. With smaller firms, the public relations worker is likely to be responsible for most of the work, so a person skilled in a variety of areas is the most valuable candidate to fill a position there.

Those wishing to enter the administrative phase of public relations should get an all-around business education. Some of the best training for such jobs is given by the graduate business schools of universities. Such courses cover business history, organization, financing, development, expansion, and personnel policies.

More than 3,880 firms offered public relations services in the early 1990s; employees on payrolls numbered more than 20,000. The total number of public relations workers is much higher because many corporations and institutions maintain public relations departments.

Industry outlook

Management, consulting, and public relations will remain among the fastest growing business services within the U.S. economy. Young people desiring to enter the public relations field should be knowledgeable in news-gathering and editing techniques and understand business methods. They should know business history and development, with emphasis on economics, social trends, politics, and labor relations.

◇ **SOURCES OF ADDITIONAL INFORMATION**

Public Relations Society of America
33 Irving Place, 3rd floor
15th and 16th Streets
New York, NY 10003

International Public Relations Association, U.S. Section
21 East 10th Street, #10A
New York, NY 10003

Society of Consumer Affairs Professionals in Business
4900 Leesburg Pike
Suite 400
Alexandria, VA 22302

International Association of Business Communicators
870 Market Street
Suite 940
San Francisco, CA 94102

◇ **RELATED ARTICLES**

Volume 1: Advertising; Broadcasting; Business Administration; Marketing; Newspaper Publishing; Personal and Consulting Services; Politics and Public Service; Travel and Tourism
Volume 2: Advertising workers; Marketing, advertising, and public relations managers; Marketing research personnel; Public relations specialists; Reporters and correspondents; Writers and editors
Volume 3: Public opinion researchers

Public Utilities

General information

The modern electric utility industry was born on September 4, 1882, at three o'clock in the afternoon. The birthplace was a modest red brick building on Pearl Street, near New York's business center. Thomas Edison signaled to an electrician, and the electrician threw a switch. Immediately, incandescent lamps began to glow in homes and offices in the surrounding neighborhood. People remarked that Edison's lamps gave a soft, even glow that was far more satisfactory than the hard, flickering light of gas jets.

The day's triumph was the result of several years' hard work for Edison and his assistants. Edison first became interested in the possibilities of electric lighting in 1878, when he was thirty years old. In the following year, he demonstrated the first practical incandescent lamp. Then he turned his attention to developing the machinery and equipment necessary to make electric service available to people. This equipment included generators, power-distribution systems, devices to regulate and measure the flow of electric current, sockets, fuses, and many other things.

Edison's experiments and the Edison Electric Illuminating Company (which was the official name of the Pearl Street station) were financed by investors, people who had faith in what Edison was trying to accomplish.

No special training was needed by workers in the early days of the electric power business. Workers needed only to be skilled with their hands, have a fair amount of "horse sense," and a large measure of faith. As one of Edison's assistants recalled many years later: "It should be remembered that at the time ... there were no manufacturing establishments either side of the Atlantic to produce the electrical machinery required. Scarcely any of the apparatus needed... was even invented, to say nothing of being designed."

Two big difficulties confronted the early electric companies. First, people had little use for electric service except for lighting streets and commercial establishments. This meant that most early electric companies operated only during the hours of darkness. Of course, this was an inefficient way of operating, and electric service for the limited hours of operation was very costly.

This obstacle was gradually overcome as people began making use of various other electrical appliances and devices, especially the electric motor. The electric motor made it possible, for the first time in history, for a tool to be relatively far removed from its power source. Electricity provided a clean, quiet form of power that could be sent directly by wire to the spot where it was needed.

A second problem was that the early power stations could transmit electric current only over short distances, so power stations had to be located near their customers. Also, two or more electric companies sometimes served the same community, so several expensive generating systems and costly transmission systems were operating where only one was needed. Since it cost much more to operate two companies than it would cost to operate one company, it was argued, customers wound up having to pay more for their electric service than they would have had to pay if one company acted as sole supplier for the area.

To make sure the electric companies provided good service and did not take advantage of the public by charging excessive rates, they were placed under government regulation. This was done because providing electric service was clearly a business "affected with a public interest." The idea of government regulation for businesses of this kind was not new; its roots extend to the heritage of English common law. In the United States, businesses that came under regulation included common carriers and investor-owned public utilities such as electric,

The Jardine Water Purification Plant in Chicago, Illinois, is built on landfill. In designing the plant, the architects sought to make its valuable lakefront grounds accessible to the public for fishing and swimming.

gas, water, and telephone companies. Today electric companies serve as sole suppliers within their franchise areas.

Early in the industry's history, electric companies began linking, or interconnecting their lines and generating equipment with those of electric companies serving neighboring areas. Those companies, in turn, interconnected their lines with still other electric power systems. Through interconnections, the companies could draw needed power from each other when generating equipment was being overhauled, at times of greatest local demand for electricity, or to meet emergencies. The efficiency and economy of interconnected operation proved advantageous, and vast networks of interconnected power systems today cover the United States.

Equally important, the ability to transmit electric energy over greater distances enabled electric companies to begin serving customers in thinly populated rural areas. As early as 1898, a farmer named John Onstott was persuaded that electric power would help him irrigate his twenty-five acre fruit ranch in California. He installed a five-horsepower motor, and an electric company built the power line to serve his farm. Today, virtually every farmstead in the nation receives electric utility service.

More than 200 electric home appliances are now available to enhance the comfort and convenience of everyday living. On the farm, electricity performs hundreds of tasks that formerly involved manual labor. And in the factory, a worker in the mid-1980s had the equivalent en-

ergy of more than 815 people working all year long.

By the late 1980s, the use of electricity had more than doubled over the previous twenty years and was expected to increase thereafter at about the same rate as real gross national product (GNP). Meeting the nation's electric energy requirements involves considerable long-range planning on the part of the electric utility industry. Electric companies have installed powerful new fossil fuel and nuclear generators to help meet future needs; these generators total millions of kilowatts of capacity.

Hand in hand with the planning and building of the electric utility industry have been the industry's continuing research and development efforts to enhance the economy and quality of electric service. In the early days of the industry, for example, more than eight pounds of coal were required to generate one kilowatt-hour of electric energy; today's highly efficient steam generators can do the same job with less than one pound of coal.

Important advances in the use of the atom as a source of power were made in a few short years. In 1954, Congress decided to permit American industry to proceed on its own initiative with the development of commercial nuclear power. Electric companies, equipment manufacturers, and other organizations began immediately to make plans to apply nuclear energy to the production of electric power. Some electric companies grouped together to share the extensive research, development, testing, and construction of plants to utilize this new

389

A utility worker performs a routine check up on some equipment in an electrical plant.

energy source. Others proceeded independently with projects for the construction of nuclear plants.

Electric companies were very enthusiastic about nuclear power in the 1970s, and dozens of plants were constructed. Serious questions were raised about the safety of nuclear power plants, however, after an accident occurred at the Three Mile Island nuclear power plant near Harrisburg, Pa., in 1979. Protests against nuclear power plants and concerns for community safety marked the early and mid-1980s.

Nuclear power plants in operation today function by a process called fission, popularly known as splitting the atom. But electric companies also have explored the possibilities of a process called fusion, in which the nuclei of certain atoms are compressed at high temperatures and pressures until the nuclei fuse together, with a resulting release of large amounts of energy. The extremely high temperatures involved in the process, however, thwarted efforts to sustain a fusion reaction for commercial applications, and fusion research moved ahead in the mid-1980s on a smaller scale than previously expected.

Nuclear power remains, for the foreseeable future, an irreplaceable component of the nation's electric generation system, according to the utility companies, and the electric utility industry remained committed to the continued development of nuclear power as an essential energy source. The use of nuclear power is seen as a potential source of cheap, efficient electricity. National average residential electric-ity prices were expected to increase at about the cost of living during the 1990s.

In the years ahead, heat or chemical energy may be converted directly into electricity by one of several possible direct conversion methods. One such method that seems to hold great promise is magnetohydrodynamics (MHD). In MHD, a jet of very hot and very fast moving electrically conductive gas passes through a magnetic field; this results in a flow of current in a surrounding coil. MHD was not a high priority for research in the mid-1980s, however. An area that electric companies continue to explore is that of advanced coal-burning technologies.

The industry's research arm is the Electric Power Research Institute (EPRI). It initiates research projects whose funding, including joint funding from other organizations, totals billions of dollars, with EPRI's share being the largest. From 1972 through 1986 EPRI funded almost 3,000 projects. EPRI's charter is to develop new and improved technology for the electric utility industry in transmission, distribution, generation, and utilization, with the idea of developing systems that are environmentally acceptable and cost-effective.

In 1983, the United States produced almost as much electricity as the next three leading countries combined—the Soviet Union, Japan, and Canada. U.S. production was 1.7 times Russian production and was almost double Russian production on a per capita basis.

The structure of the public utilities industry

The electric power industry is unique. It must produce its product the instant it is needed. Electricity cannot be packaged, wrapped, or stored. Therefore, power plants must be able to provide peak consumer needs at any hour of the day or night. They must be prepared for surges and debilitating storms. After electricity is generated, it passes to a switchyard where voltage is increased to carry it through transmission lines to the substations and ultimately to the consumer. The United States is the largest producer of all kinds of electric power. Power plants use various methods to produce electricity. These include steam, water, or gas turbine power plants; nuclear energy power plants; and windmills.

In the United States, about eight out of every ten people receive their electric service from electric utility companies, which are investor-owned and business-managed. The remaining

20 percent are supplied by various government-owned or government-financed power plants.

With an estimated total investment of billions of dollars in electric power plants and equipment in the early 1990s, electric utility companies comprise the largest single industry in the United States. From the early 1970s to the early 1980s, the generating capacity of the nation's electric utilities doubled.

The job of energy-management people is to help explore new and better ways of doing things with electric energy and to encourage customers to make use of these new ways. As a rule, electric companies employ a staff of specialists in each of four basic areas; industrial uses, commercial uses, farm uses, and residential uses.

Electric company industrial representatives help industries develop efficient methods of operation through the use of electric energy. Their work involves meeting regularly with their industrial customers, and also cooperating with manufacturers of electrical equipment, jobbers, dealers, contractors, architects, and consulting engineers.

The power company's commercial representative is concerned with every customer not covered by the words "home," "farm," or "factory." Hotels, motels, restaurants, schools, hospitals, retail stores, supermarkets, and many other places all have special electrical needs. The commercial representative seeks to identify these needs and to help develop the means for using electricity more efficiently and economically. While specific requirements vary from company to company, industrial and commercial representatives are usually technically trained, often with engineering backgrounds coupled with training or experience in energy management.

Through its farm adviser, the electric company encourages and participates in state or local programs that bring helpful information to the farm community about the use of electricity on the farm. Almost all of the farm adviser's time is spent in direct contact with farm customers or industrial agricultural customers. Major agricultural production equipment often costs more than $100,000. It is the farm advisor's responsibility to determine if the new application will benefit the farmer.

To perform this kind of service, the electric company's farm adviser generally has a degree in agricultural engineering or a similar agricultural specialization. In addition, many farm advisers have had firsthand experience in areas involving farm management.

Advertising and market research experts help to support industrial and commercial sales representatives, farm advisers, and the entire

Nuclear materials handling technicians operate robots via remote control.

company operation. Market researchers are concerned with analyzing the ways consumers use electricity, and when. They also seek out new areas for energy conservation. Through the use of newspapers, magazines, radio, and television, the advertising people seek to make consumers aware of the way electric energy can be used economically and efficiently.

While organizational structure varies from company to company, executives at the vice-presidential level generally oversee the smooth working of every major facet of the business including financial matters, legal matters, company operations, engineering, construction, conservation of electric energy, personnel, public relations, and purchasing.

The responsibility of company officers extends beyond purely corporate matters to the well-being of the community in which the electric company serves. This is because the electric company's progress depends upon the progress of its community.

Careers

A sampling of career opportunities in the public utilities industry follows below.

Engineers: The electric power industry is regarded basically as an engineering industry, and there will always be a strong need for top-notch engineers. Men and women who excel in applied engineering will become even more important to the industry as the economics of

391

Power line workers must wear rubber gloves and boots to protect themselves against electrical shock.

electric company service areas grow increasingly complex.

Engineers skilled to manage the planning of the increasingly sophisticated utility systems and computer-oriented people qualified to do economic analysis from a technical viewpoint will be of growing importance to the electric utility industry. These are predominantly graduates with degrees in electrical engineering, but mechanical engineers, nuclear engineers, civil engineers, chemical engineers, industrial engineers, and others are also well represented.

The design, development, and the production of equipment used to generate, transmit, and distribute electricity is done by electrical engineers. Power generators and transmission equipment are two of the most important elements that electrical engineers work with. They may handle the development phase, the installment, or the maintenance and improvement of old equipment.

Nuclear engineers plan, design, and develop nuclear power plants and equipment, including the instruments and controls that produce nuclear energy (see Volume 2: Engineers).

Electrical drafters: Designing the actual wiring diagrams, electrical drafters map out the wiring for power plants and hookups to homes, offices, and other areas requiring power lines or cables (see Volume 2: Drafters).

Electricians: Once the concept for a power plant has been developed and the blueprints drawn up, electricians come in and lay the wiring for the electrical lines and cables needed for electrical service. For high-powered electrical sources and plants, power plant specialists are normally used (see Volume 3: Electricians).

Inspectors: Because of the safety concerns of any electrical equipment, inspectors provide a vital role in the maintenance and installation of any power equipment. They must check to see that all wiring, transformers, and generators meet fire code and government regulations.

Quality control technicians: Quality control technicians are staff members for the power plant, assuring the continued safety of all elements of the generator and related power facilities throughout the life of a power plant. Technicians also conduct safety checks during the construction of a power plant (see Volume 4: Nuclear power plant quality control technicians).

Repairers: When the equipment of any electrical system is damaged or faulty, a repairer is called in to fix problems or replace defective elements. The work can be dangerous, depending on the type of repair being done. Downed power lines are one of the biggest concerns to a power company, both in terms of lost power to customers, but also for the element of danger imposed until the line is cut off from the power supply. Repairers frequently work in bad weather, because weather is the cause of many power problems (see Volume 3: Electrical repairers).

Power plant operators: Maintaining the facilities that supply energy to the customers, power plant operators regulate, check, and keep records on the generation of power at the plant. The operator is one of the most important elements in the safety of any power plant. Operators must be well trained to handle any emergency quickly and effectively (see Volume 3: Power plant occupations; Volume 4: Nuclear reactor operator technicians).

Transmission operators: Transmission operators, including line installers and station operators, determine the quality of the electrical power that is sent from the plant to the customer (see Volume 3: Transmission and distribution occupations).

Mathematicians: Because of the rapid technological advances and new data-handling systems being used, applied mathematics and other problem-solving disciplines are becoming increasingly important in the electric power business. Advanced applied mathematicians who can correlate the engineers' problems to computer science are needed for full utilization of engineering talent, especially in such areas as operations, research, and other areas of analysis and planning.

Finance officers: Electric company financial and tax work generally requires specialized knowledge. The timing of bond or stock issues and the determination of types of issues are important in the growth and development of electric companies, which are normally supported by bond sales. The ever-increasing complexities of federal, state, and local tax laws have a large bearing on business decisions.

Utilities business specialists Specialists work in areas such as financial programs and records, treasury, accounting and auditing, operating statistics, income and property taxes, property evaluation, rates and billing, insurance, credits and collections, budgets and reports, cash control, payroll, and purchasing.

Education

While company policies vary, many electric companies employ engineers with a B.S. degree and provide them with opportunities for advanced education and training while on the company payroll. Of particular value in this regard are postgraduate programs leading to a degree in law, business, accounting, or computer science. Individuals with these degrees become greater assets to their companies, and the additional education may aid them in advancing in a field other than engineering.

Engineers perform a wide variety of roles in electric companies, including system planning, design, and operation. A large percentage of top management personnel among electric companies have engineering backgrounds. Top executives also have degrees in law, business administration, accounting, liberal arts, and communications.

Many companies employ high-school graduates as technical assistants in such areas as electrical, mechanical, and civil engineering, and junior positions in customer relations, accounting, and sales. Companies hiring high-school graduates for such positions generally offer on-the-job training. These companies also encourage their high-school graduate employees to advance themselves through further training.

For graduates of colleges and universities, there are a multitude of career opportunities in the electric energy business. As a technically oriented business, this industry has a continuing demand for new engineering talent; but even in non-engineering areas, the career challenges of the electric companies can be as profitable as those offered by any U.S. business.

Industry outlook

All indications are that people's need for electric energy will continue to grow in the years ahead, and that the electric utility industry will grow to meet those needs. With that growth, the industry can be expected to require a great diversity of skills.

A power plant inspector looks over a newly manufactured transformer.

In the late 1980s, production of electricity in the United States equalled more than 10,000 kilowatt-hours for every American man, woman, and child. Today, generation of electricity accounts for approximately 36 percent of U.S. primary energy consumption.

In the future, people may be using electricity in many new ways. For example, more homes may be electrically heated and cooled, with individual climate controls in each room. In the mid-1980s, already millions of homes were electrically heated.

The walls and ceilings in homes of the future may be designed to radiate colored light. With this design, it may be possible to change the color scheme of each room at the twist of a knob.

Standard electrical appliances available for the home will be capable of performing more jobs, and doing them better. Many appliances of the future will be operated by fingertip control and many will be capable of operating automatically, with no manual controls at all. In the kitchen, an automatic electric console may perform the entire pantry-to-platter operation of preparing meals. Then it will wash the dishes. The house may be kept tidy with the aid of an automatic vacuum cleaner that steers itself about each room, seeking out specks of dust.

The family car may be driven by rechargeable electric batteries. Such electrically powered vehicles could help free community air of exhaust fumes. Through the Electric Power Research Institute, electric companies support research aimed at developing an improved battery system for electrically driven vehicular use.

Because the U.S. economy is expected to increase its electricity use at about the same growth rate as gross national product (GNP), the need for generating and transmission capacity will grow. Over the decade of the mid-1980s through the mid-1990s, part of the need can be met by using existing capacity more effectively, part can be met by extending the life of plants due for retirement, and part can be met by purchases from non-utility producers. Utilities estimated, however, that they would still need to build new capacity at about 2 percent a year over the decade.

Much of the new equipment will be far more advanced in design than any now in operation. This is because electric companies continually seek to develop better machines, better methods, and better materials to help provide their customers with the best of electric service.

◇ **SOURCES OF ADDITIONAL INFORMATION**

Institute of Public Utilities
113 Olds Hall
Michigan State University
East Lansing, MI 48824

Institute of Electrical and Electronic Engineers
345 East 47th Street
New York, NY 10017

Edison Electric Institute
Manager of Educational Services
1111 19th Street, NW
Washington, DC 20036

Electric Power Research Institute
3412 Hillview Avenue
Palo Alto, CA 94303

American Public Gas Association
PO Box 1426
Vienna, VA 22180

◇ **RELATED ARTICLES**

Volume 1: Engineering; Mathematics; Physical Sciences
Volume 2: Engineers
Volume 3: Electrical repairers; Electricians; Power plant occupations; Transmission and distribution occupations
Volume 4: Electrical technicians; Nuclear instrumentation technicians; Nuclear materials handling technicians; Nuclear power plant quality control technicians; Nuclear power plant radiation control technicians

Pulp and Paper

General information

The pulp and paper industry produces tens of thousands of paper products, including newsprint, facial tissue, paper bags, disposable diapers, paperboard shipping containers, wrapping paper, and writing paper. Paper is a versatile product, useful in itself in thousands of ways, but also adaptable for use in all industries. Thick or thin, light or heavy, flexible or stiff, tough or fragile—paper serves industry with applications limited only by human ingenuity and resourcefulness.

Before pulp-derived paper was manufactured, the ancient Egyptians wrote on papyrus, cutting the reeds into strips, arranging them in perpendicular crisscross patterns, and pressing them into sheets. The pressure released a glue-like sap that bound the papyrus strips. In 105 A.D., Cai Lun of China invented pulp-derived paper using fiber from mulberry trees. This proved to be much cheaper and easier to produce than the silk and wood used for the vast number of official documents during the Han dynasty. The Chinese later developed pulp with a combination of wood fiber, old fishing nets, rags, and hemp rope.

During the golden age of Islamic culture in the eighth century, the Arabs took great interest in paper, establishing a mill in 795. The use of paper travelled slowly to the Western world, taking well over 1,000 years. While the European traders and crusaders had been exposed to paper, the first mills did not appear until the fourteenth century. At that time, most Europeans were illiterate, with the exception of the clergy. Thus, most of the books produced were religious works. Monks produced beautifully hand-written and illustrated bibles on vellum—skin from an unborn calf. Such a painstaking process of book production dominated Europe throughout the Middle Ages.

It was not until the invention of the printing press by Johannes Gutenberg in the mid-

1400s that paper became an essential product for Europeans. Paper manufacturers at that time used a combination of rags and pulp to create durable paper. Paper was made one sheet at a time, by dipping a screen into a basin of pulp. The screen was then lifted, and as the water dripped through, the remaining pulp settled evenly on the screen. After sufficient drainage, the settled pulp was lifted from the screen and pressed. Thus, the size of the sheet was limited to the size of the screen.

There were very few improvements or changes until the early 1800s, when Nicolas-Louis Robert invented a moving screen belt that enabled paper manufacturers to produce paper in one continuous sheet. The Fourdrinier manufacturers in England perfected the technique only a decade later, and the process still bears their name. In addition, producers began experimenting with new sources of fiber such as groundwood and sulfite pulp.

While the technology for paper production has improved over the years, the basic process has not changed. Pulp is created by soaking pieces of wood; the pulp is filtered through a screen; the wet sheets are drained and pressed; and the paper is then treated with a protective coating.

The pulp and paper industry today manufactures a wide variety of paper products. The commercial printing industry consumes tons of paper daily for books—both hardbound and paperback—advertising promotion pieces, manuals, and catalogs. There is also a area of business requiring multiple forms with interleaved carbons, such as sales books, order forms, and records essential to the continuous daily conduct of business and industry.

One of the largest users of paper is the newspaper and magazine publishers. For the publisher, paper is the greatest item of expense, representing more than the total cost of the printing, ink, and binding. New, faster presses bring the demand for strong, smooth,

395

Reams of paper are being sent through a series of hot rollers that dry the sheets and press them into uniform thickness.

shipping, wrapping, marketing, delivery, and selling of products that make up every phase of the daily economy of the United States.

More than half of the production of U.S. pulp and paper is in the South. Many of the larger mills produce pulp as well as paper, and some also produce finished paper products.

The United States receives much of its newsprint from Canada. It is estimated that Canadian paper mills supply about 60 percent of the newsprint to U.S. newspaper publishers.

The structure of the pulp and paper industry

The production of paper depends on many factors, namely the materials used, the grade of pulp refinement, the type of machine used to make the paper, and the finishing treatment after the paper is formed.

The process of manufacturing paper begins in the woodlands where trees designated as pulpwood are cut into prescribed lengths, measured in cords, and hauled from the forests to the wood yards of the pulp company. Pulp is also taken from the waste products of woodworking. Paper manufacturers use all types of wood: oak, pine, aspen, beech, to name a few. The long fibers of soft wood gives paper strength. Hard woods produce short fibers that give paper a smooth and shiny surface.

Different paper products use different combinations of pulp. For instance, most newspapers are a blend of chemical pulp (one-quarter) and groundwood pulp (three-quarters). The glossy paper of magazines are coated with a solution of starch and clay. This type of surface is very good for printing. In high quality papers, such as stationary, money, and art products, linen and cotton are added to enhance the paper's strength and durability.

At the wood yards, the cords of lumber are placed on conveyor belts and fed into a giant, revolving drum barker, which strips away the bark and cleans the wood. Moving along on a conveyor belt, the chipper—a revolving disk with heavy, sharp knives set at an angle— quickly reduces the logs to millions of wood chips about an inch square and an eighth of an inch thick.

The wood, in chip form, travels on conveyors to the digesters, which are like a giant pressure cooker. Chemicals and steam are added and combine to break down the chips into soggy masses of cellulose and other elements of the tree. The chemicals are now removed, along with the lignin, resins, and natural chem-

lightweight, trouble-free papers that achieve the best reproduction of color printing, in illustrations ranging from museum art to food illustrations. Publication stock must have the strength for constant round-the-clock press runs to assure meeting news-breaking and news-making deadlines.

Paper and paperboard for packaging and for shipping containers comprise the largest tonnage sector of the paper industry. Shipping containers, also called fiber boxes, require millions of tons of paper and paperboard annually. Paperboard cartons of all types are used to package most of the prepared foods, soap products, cosmetics, and similar products that are used in daily life. In the United States, many thousands of different paper products are consumed at the rate of hundreds of pounds per person a year.

Paper and paperboard are used to package items as light as needles or as heavy as refrigerators, as fragile as eggs or as massive as motors. Infinitely thin or indestructibly strong, water repellant or water resistant, tissue soft or tough, disposable or permanent—paper and paperboard have an essential daily role in the icals found in the tree, leaving the cellulose fibers to be further processed.

The cellulose fibers—now called pulp—pass through many cleaners and screens to prepare them for the bleaching process, which will give whiteness and brightness needed for the grade of paper being manufactured. Once bleached, the wood pulp is ready to have dyes, pigments, or resin added to provide the paper or board with the appropriate finish.

For recycled paper, the pulping process is slightly different. A large machine called a pulper breaks down the paper into usable pulp. Chemicals are added to the mash that remove the dye and whiten the pulp. This kind of pulp is often called secondary fiber. Newsprint is the most common form of recycled paper.

The pulp, roughly 99 percent water and 1 percent fiber, is ready to be introduced into the paper machine through a headbox that stretches across the machine. Pumps spray a thin film of fibers onto the fast-moving, endless wire screen. As it travels along the wire, the water drops away and the fibers are matted into paper. Although still damp, the formed paper is picked up by and travels through a maze of hot rollers that press and dry the paper. From here, it is rolled and cut into various sizes.

In many paper mills where a fine grade of paper is produced for books, magazines, or for stationery and other writing purposes, a finishing department is maintained.

After the paper is finished, it is shipped to the appropriate manufacturer for further processing or sold to a wholesaler or retailer as a finished product.

Hundreds of rolls of paper, each weighing tons, are placed onto transportable bins where they will then be shipped to customers.

Careers

The versatility of the pulp and paper industry offers a great number of possibilities for employment. The work may include mill operations or manufacturing processes that involve converting paper and paperboard into any number of finished products. The work may be in the forest, in the research laboratories, or in the promotion, advertising, and selling of the many different end products.

Laws passed by the federal government in such fields as the environment, pensions, and equal opportunity have brought scientists, engineers, attorneys, and other professionals with training into the paper industry. In addition, the increase in the number of large companies in the industry—at least fifty are included among the thousand largest companies in the United States—has expanded the types of man-

agerial and marketing skills required. These huge companies operate in many different sectors of the industry, both nationally and internationally, and often work in many other industries as well. Today, the paper industry requires professionally trained people in the fields of management, marketing, accounting, and economics.

In addition to scientists and engineers who understand the papermaking process, the industry requires chemists and other scientists in the fields of toxicology, air pollution and water pollution, along with technicians and others who can operate in these fields. The mill management and the administrative field requires lawyers in corporate and patent law, tax law, real estate, and regulatory laws; experts on exports; and experts on labor, industrial, community, and employee relations.

Pulp and paper mill workers employed in plant jobs can generally be divided into three major occupational groups: production workers, who operate the various machines and equipment; maintenance workers, who maintain, install, and repair machinery, pipes, and equipment; and other workers, such as material handlers, stock clerks, and workers holding various administrative jobs.

A sampling of career opportunities in the pulp and paper industry follows below.

Industrial engineers: Industrial engineers are responsible for improving and maintaining operating performance, increasing efficiency and reducing waste, preventing delays, achieving cost reductions, and maintaining a high level of production efficiency.

To prepare wood pulp for paper manufacturing, chips of wood must be broken down into small bits of cellulose. The soggy material is then chemically treated so that the mass become uniformly smooth and white.

Power plant engineers: Power plant engineers are concerned with the design, supervision of construction, and operation of generating plants furnishing power.

Process engineers: Process engineers help establish schedules to ensure maximum use of available equipment, labor, tools, and capacity. They also coordinate production operations to meet delivery dates of finished paper products.

Quality control engineers: Quality control and production engineers are responsible for the installation of product inspecting and testing procedures that are used to establish quality standards.

Production time-and-motion employees: Production time-and-motion employees are responsible for maintaining efficient plant operation for maximum production with minimum loss of effort by machine operators.

Chemical researchers: Chemical researchers solve problems of production and manufacture and aim to extend product usefulness. They work closely with the chemist and engineer.

Timberland management researchers: These people conduct basic research in timberland management. They are concerned with the ac-

quisition, culture, harvesting, continued use of forest stands, and wood technology.

Barker operators: A barker operator is a semiskilled employee, who operates a machine that removes bark and dirt from the pulpwood.

Digester operators: The digester operator is a skilled worker who is in charge of the large kettle-like vessels, called digesters, that break down the wood chips through chemical action, heat, and pressure. The digester operator determines the amount of chemicals to be used, establishes cooking pressures and temperatures, and controls the cooking accuracy. In many mills, much of this work has been taken over by the computer, directed by process engineers, instrumentation engineers, and computer scientists.

Paper machine tenders: The paper machine operator, or machine tender, is a key worker who regulates and controls the flow of pulp onto the paper machine. The quality of the final product depends to a large degree on this person's skill and experience on the job. Computers have taken over the monitoring of the many functions of the papermaking machines, with machine tenders now working with computer scientists and technicians in the actual operation of the machine.

Supercalender operators: A supercalender operator, with several helpers, places huge rolls of paper on a machine that will give it a smooth and glossy finish.

Corrugating operators: The corrugating operator is responsible for tending the machine that makes corrugated packaging material (paperboard with alternate ridges and grooves) used largely in the manufacture of boxes.

Envelopment machine operators: The envelope machine operator feeds and tends an automatic machine that makes envelopes from die-cut blanks.

Education

Educational requirements for careers in the pulp and paper industry vary as to the specific nature of the job. For those in research and development or quality control, a college degree is almost always required. For those in a production capacity in a paper mill, a high-school diploma and some on-the-job experience may be the only necessary training.

Most quality control and production engineers have a B.S. degree in chemistry or chemical or industrial engineering, and from three to five years of experience in mill or plant production. Advancement may lead to the office of quality control executive. Those who pursue positions as engineers often have the opportunity to advance to managerial positions. Other advancements may lead to plant or mill executive positions.

Opportunities for those with a bachelor's degree or advanced degree in chemistry and/or paper engineering are extensive in the areas of basic chemical research or in developing solutions to technical problems. An advanced degree in organic chemistry, physical chemistry, and biochemistry is usually required to conduct independent investigations to develop new products or processes. There are also opportunities in basic physical research and product development for those with an advanced degree in physics.

Researchers involved with the study of forests and wood must have degrees from a college of forestry, with additional education in botany, chemistry, geology, zoology, and physics. Advancement may lead to the position of technical director or other executive posts.

Most members of the paper industry maintain their own established research facilities for use in improving their existing products and for developing new products as the need arises.

Fourteen rolls of paper are being mechanically transported from a dock to a ship.

These facilities require the employment of skilled engineers, chemists, physicists, and foresters. College graduates with degrees in forestry analysis find varied positions in timber management and forestry and genetic research, to name only a few.

Colleges, universities, and technical institutes that offer specialized programs and courses in paper technology include the universities of Alabama, Florida, Maine, and Washington; Miami University, Oxford, Ohio; Western Michigan University; Lowell Technological Institute, Lowell, Massachusetts; North Carolina State College; Oregon State College; State University of New York, College of Forestry, Syracuse; and the Institute of Paper Chemistry, Appleton, Wisconsin. All of these schools offer scholarships for students of merit preparing to enter the paper industry.

In addition to jobs that require some higher education as a necessary background, the industry offers many excellent opportunities for high-school and trade school graduates, as well as the semi-skilled worker. Entering the paper industry in a mill or woods assignment during school vacation may lead to opportunities with long-range potential for advancement.

Many top executives in the industry advanced from semi-skilled positions to more demanding positions, benefiting from familiarity with the various facets of the industry. Thus, a beginner with ambition, aptitude, and in-plant training may still reasonably aspire to increasingly responsible positions. However, many executives have college degrees and master's degrees in business administration.

Pulp and Paper

Industry outlook

The success of the pulp and paper industry has been an indication of the high standard of living of the people of the United States, as well as those in other parts of the world. In the United States, it is ranked as the tenth largest industry. The United States is the world's largest producer and supplier of paper. Nearly 625,000 people work in the pulp and paper industry, producing paper and allied products with a projected total value of about $130 billion annually in the early 1990s.

Economists predict a healthy decade for the pulp and paper industry, yet one of its greatest challenges for the 1990s will be addressing environmental issues. As waste disposal becomes an increasing problem and industrial waste becomes a key issue, the paper industry will have to make adjustments. Currently, the pulp and paper industry accounts for much of suspended solid material and other pollutants that make their way through the nation's waterways. The industry must anticipate stricter environmental standards. Certain changes will have to take place, such as developing nontoxic ways of producing paper and focusing on recycled products.

In the coming decade, the pulp and paper industry must anticipate huge investments in renewable forest reserves and in mills that must be updated for efficiency of plants and equipment. Vast consumption of electric power, water, chemicals, and other essential raw materials must also be part of the long-range planning.

Many pulp- and papermaking machines are partially or fully controlled by computers. This has opened up opportunities for process engineers, computer scientists, and technicians in these fields, taking over much of the work previously done manually.

◇ SOURCES OF ADDITIONAL INFORMATION

American Paper Institute
260 Madison Avenue
New York, NY 10016

Paper Industry Management Association
2400 East Oakton Street
Arlington Heights, IL 60005

American Pulpwood Association
1025 Vermont Avenue, NW, Suite 1020
Washington, DC 20005

Society of Wood Science and Technology
PO Box 5062
Madison, WI 53705

Society of American Foresters
5400 Grosvenor Lane
Bethesda, MD 20814

TAPPI (Technical Association of the Pulp and Paper Industry)
Technology Park/Atlanta
PO Box 105113
Atlanta, GA 30348

National Paper Trade Association
111 Great Neck Road
Great Neck, NY 11021

◇ RELATED ARTICLES

Volume 1: Biological Sciences; Book Publishing; Chemistry; Engineering; Magazine Publishing; Packaging; Printing; Wood; Waste Management

Volume 2: Chemists; Computer programmers; Engineers; Industrial designers; Wood science and technology careers

Volume 3: Bindery workers; Commercial and industrial electronic equipment repairers; Foresters; Furniture manufacturing occupations; Industrial machinery mechanics; Logging industry workers; Paper processing occupations; Printing press operators and assistants

Volume 4: Agribusiness technicians; Biological technicians; Chemical technicians; Civil engineering technicians; Forestry technicians; Industrial engineering technicians; Mechanical technicians; Pollution-control technicians; Quality-control technicians; Textile technicians

Real Estate

General information

The real estate business helps fulfill one of our most basic needs: shelter. For most families, buying a house is the most important single investment they will ever make. But real estate is more than just houses; it includes apartments, condominiums, cooperatives, farms, retail stores, office buildings, shopping centers, warehouses, industrial plants, medical centers, and many other types of property. Hundreds of thousands of licensed professionals work full-time in the selling of real estate. The industry also provides employment for many part-time salespeople and support personnel for the sales force.

The notion of property rights has existed since the beginning of civilization. Early nomadic societies distributed property rights among tribes, or families. For those nomadic societies where land was bountiful, tribes had no need to secure individual plots of land or establish permanent residences.

Historians and sociologists suggest that the early agrarian societies showed the first signs of individual property rights. Whether the lands were dominated by individuals, families, or clans, the agrarian societies practiced ownership of specific plots.

The urban orientation of ancient Greece caused the dissolution of communal properties. Individual and familial ownership of land was the norm. This notion of the absolute right of ownership continued until the end of the Roman Empire.

The Roman Empire extended throughout virtually all of Europe, protecting its dominion and upholding the law. With the decline of the Roman Empire and the subsequent barbarian invasions, families and landowners had little to guard their belongings and protect their land. This desire for security led to the feudal system of the Middle Ages. Feudalism entailed a lord who held vast lands in his dominion. Hence the word "landlord." Those who lived on his land and farmed it were called vassals. Vowing homage and fealty to their lords, vassals were guaranteed protection of their lives and their chattel. The lord, in turn, owned homage to his king, acting as the king's vassal.

So strong was the bond between vassal and lord, that vassals were considered unfree. However, they were not mere slaves, rather they were more like tenants, who paid their rent with the products they farmed. They were also expected to perform military services in times of war. While the lord presided over the land, vassals farmed individual plots of land and passed the property rights to their offspring.

With the dissolution of the feudal system in the 13th century, vassals were able to claim true ownership of the land that they farmed. In France, homage and fealty was not wholly abandoned until the Revolution in the late 1700s, when the aristocracy was abolished. At that time, the common man obtained unconditional freedom and with it the right to own land. Such rights had not been in existence since the Roman Empire nearly 1300 years before then.

The absolute freedom and rights of the common man during the late 18th century opened up the prospects for a better living. Thus, the purchase of land became a growing business that is known today as real estate.

While common people succeeded in asserting their rights to the ownership of land in Europe, ironically, European nations established vast empires overseas, claiming foreign lands as their own and subjecting the native inhabitants to their system of rule. Lured by the natural resources of these lands, the Europeans set up great trade routes that increased their wealth and power. Many Europeans considered it the "white man's burden" to civilize the inhabitants of these newly-claimed lands, while missionaries thought it was their duty to lead the natives toward salvation. The Spanish and

A real estate agent shows a house to a client. It is the agent's responsibility to represent to client during price negotiations.

the Portuguese took over Central and South America. The French dominated over other parts of North America, Southeast Asia, and northern and western Africa. The British annexed India, parts of North America, Hong Kong, Australia, and countless other areas. At Britain's peak, it was said that the sun never set on the British Empire.

It took centuries for natives of these conquered territories to claim independence. In North America, however, the native Indians never fully recovered their lost lands, rather the British colonists proclaimed their independence from England with little regard for the American Indian. Through various treaties and purchases, the United States acquired all of its land (with the exception of Alaska and Hawaii) by the 1850s.

As Americans moved westward in the nineteenth century, they claimed public lands with no title. By clearing the unclaimed land, farming it, and building a home there, settlers felt that they had earned the right to the land's title for free or for a nominal price. This established what is now known as squatter's rights. The Pre-emption Act of 1841 officially declared squatter's rights as legitimate. For another fifty years over 200 million acres of land changed from government to private ownership, until Congress abolished the act in 1891.

The real estate industry has grown dramatically over the last few years. With house values going up and people moving more frequently, many turn to real estate professionals to help in the stressful task of buying or selling property.

The word *Realtor* is a copyrighted and registered term belonging to the National Association of Realtors. Only agents and brokers who are members of this organization may use the term Realtor.

The structure of the real estate industry

The real estate business is essentially a service business. No product is manufactured, assembled, or sold. It is a business in which various functions are performed for the owner of a property or for a prospective owner. These functions are classified under the following general titles: real estate sales, management, land development, leasing, financing, appraisal, and consulting. The types of properties included in the activities of real estate people are houses, condominiums, apartments, farms, office buildings, stores, shopping centers, warehouses, factories, and other industrial properties including vacant land.

The income of a real estate business is from commissions paid to an individual or firm for the sale, management, financing, or other functions performed for the owner of a property.

Whenever the owner of a home, a store, or a factory desires to sell a property, that person almost always contacts one or more local real estate agents. In meetings with the agents, the owner discusses the price at which the property is to be offered, the plans for advertising and creating interest in the property, and the terms under which the owner will sell. The owner then commonly gives the selected real estate firm a contract authorizing it to be the agent for a certain period of time (several months) in trying to find a buyer for the property. Included in this contract is the amount of commission the real estate firm will receive for selling the property. If no buyer is found who will pay a price acceptable to the owner within the time specified in the contract, then no commission is paid.

Selling real estate requires the ability to price property accurately, to be imaginative in the use of sales and advertising methods, and to be particularly capable in dealing with prospective buyers. Good real estate agents, for instance, develop a keen knowledge of the neighborhoods they serve; they know the taxes, the schools, and the value of different locations. In selling homes, good agents know the houses extremely well, both their strengths and weaknesses. For instance, they know how much it costs to heat a given house per year, the

In areas where there is tremendous economic growth, real estate developers often purchase large tracts of land, design neighborhoods, and sell designated plots to new residents in the community.

amount of taxes paid monthly, and the age and condition of the structure.

Agricultural real estate agents deal with rural properties. Real estate people engaged in rural properties must know a great deal about agriculture: for example, the types of soil, the water supply and drainage, and the cost of labor in the area. Farming itself is changing rapidly, and the salesperson must keep abreast of these changes. In many places, yesterday's cornfield is now a shopping center.

Like agricultural properties, industrial real estate also demands special knowledge of real estate brokers and agents. A successful industrial broker must know a great deal about the needs of many different types of industries to suit the property to the potential buyer. He or she should know about transportation facilities; labor forces; local building, zoning, and tax laws; and such other factors as housing, parks, and school facilities for the potential employer's employees. A significant development in which brokers have played an important part is the growth and construction of industrial parks, large areas of land set aside for industrial use.

Industrial parks are one example of a larger trend, that of land development. Another form of land development is the housing development, sometimes just one block of houses, sometimes entire communities with shopping centers, schools, police and fire protection facilities, even country clubs. Unlike other phases of real estate, land development requires broad knowledge of all the phases of real estate: construction, appraisals, and leasing.

Land development is regarded as one of the most challenging forms of real estate endeavor. The developer's first step is selecting the site and buying the necessary tracts of land. Then, usually after borrowing money to finance the building, the developer will engage a contractor to put up the houses. Finally, the houses are put up for sale, either through a real estate broker hired by the developer or through the developer's own real estate organization.

Another important part of the management firm's responsibility is in the field of leasing—keeping a property fully rented. This requires a thorough knowledge of the rental market so as to obtain the highest rents and still keep the

Two real estate developers review the zoning of their community. They must ensure that the buildings they develop are located in the properly zoned areas.

apartments or offices completely rented. Office buildings are generally rented on leases varying from three to fifteen years, whereas most apartment leases may be for only one year. The managing agent must have sufficient knowledge of rental market conditions and possible rent control laws to advise owners of the desirability of increasing or decreasing rents to attain the highest degree of occupancy as well as the largest income for the property.

Leasing real estate is almost entirely concerned with apartments, shopping centers, office buildings, and retail stores. The owner employs an agent to rent the property and pays the agent on the basis of the total rent stipulated in the lease.

Leasing procedures differ somewhat according to whether the property is new and being leased for the first time or whether it is an existing property with leases made some time before. New properties require careful analysis by the real estate firm doing the leasing to ensure that the rent asked will represent an accurate estimate of the market. Owners want to obtain the highest possible rents, but it is also essential that the property rent quickly and without long exposure to the market. It is in this field of rental evaluation that the real estate firm makes a most significant contribution to the owner.

The real estate firm must use advertising, model units, personal calls to potential office tenants, and every possible sales device in the process of leasing a new property. The same type of sales ability is needed in leasing existing properties, but in these cases only one or two leases are up for renewal so the task is less difficult. The leasing of shopping centers is done on a national basis, whereas leasing apartments and office buildings takes place mostly at the local level. This phase of the real estate business is both challenging and demanding and requires considerable talent and knowledge.

Not all real estate is concerned with the purchase of property. A large branch of real estate involves the management of currently-owned buildings. Real estate management is primarily concerned with representing an owner in matters of leasing, collection of rents, payment of operating expenses, maintaining the property, and directing the work of the building employees. Owners of office buildings, apartments, shopping centers, and other types of income-producing real estate generally hire a real estate firm to manage their property. Those engaged in real estate management must account to the owner monthly concerning these activities.

Generally, management is done by a real estate firm, although sometimes the manager is an individual hired by the owner. The fee for managing real estate is usually based on the gross income of the property and is determined by negotiation between the owner and the agent. Property management requires both experience and business education.

Many income-producing properties are owned by investors living in other states or countries and they must employ a local real estate firm to manage their investments. They give a management contract to a real estate firm for periods from one to five years and pay fees based on the gross income of the property. These fees vary with the size of the property and the amount of work involved in the management.

Many real estate firms have mortgage banking departments, and these are an important part of the firm's activities. An important function of the mortgage department is to collect the monthly payments, the real estate tax, and monthly reserve and transmit these to the owner of the mortgage. The mortgage banking business performs a most important service in helping to finance the building of homes, apartments, or office buildings, as well as to finance the purchase and sale of existing real estate.

The responsibility in dealing with the mortgage investments of savings banks, insurance companies, or other companies is given to some real estate firms because of their ability to select valuable properties held by reliable borrowers. In other words, the real estate company, or the mortgage company as it is called, is paid to deal with the borrower. In cases of this type, the owner paying off a home loan sends the payments to the mortgage broker instead of the investor that actually holds the mortgage.

Appraising real estate is a specialized segment of the business and is engaged in by both firms and individuals. An appraisal might be made, for instance, to determine the value of a home that an individual wants to sell on the open market. The appraisal of real estate must take into account what similar pieces of property are selling for, and also include specific mention of any neighborhood characteristics that detract from or increase the property's value. The structural condition of a piece of property is also part of the appraisal report.

Because of the demanding nature of real estate sales and the fact the income depends on sales, many real estate agents work on a part-time basis, with money from other work supplementing their income.

Some real estate firms are dedicated solely to the leasing of office space. It is their responsibility to find tenants.

Careers

Real estate offers a variety of career opportunities. Some career options follows below.

Real estate brokers: In addition to selling real estate, brokers also rent and manage properties and make market appraisals. They often manage their own real estate offices and hire agents as independent sales workers.

Real estate agents: The three main activities of real estate agents are to obtain properties for sale, to develop lists of people interested in buying real estate, and to sell the specific properties they and their firms have to offer. In many cases, a real estate agent from another firm locates the buyer for the property. Two agents are then involved, and they typically share the commission. Most real estate agents are independent salespeople who contract their services to a licensed broker on a commission basis. Relatively few agents work as paid employees for real estate organizations.

Real estate managers: The manager of real estate must be concerned with problems of exterior repairs and maintenance, interior repairs and maintenance, heating, plumbing, decorating, employee direction and control, and equipment purchases and maintenance. Although the owner of the property will be consulted in important decisions, the day-to-day management of property is the responsibility of the real estate manager.

Leasing real estate agents: Leasing real estate agents rent out spaces in all types of buildings, such as office buildings, apartments, and warehouses. They represent the property owners who would like their space rented.

Appraisers: Appraisers set a dollar value on a piece of property. They may be hired by people wishing to sell their property or by estates wishing to sell the property of a deceased person. Appraisers are often used in business transactions, which may involve property worth millions of dollars. Appraisers also work for local governments, helping to determine tax rates.

Real estate developers: Real estate developers are people who purchase large tracts of land and build several structures. In some cases, they turn rundown commercial areas into bustling centers of commerce. Many developers have the ability to envision profitable ventures where others cannot.

Education

Every state requires that both real estate agents and brokers be licensed and pass a written examination on real estate fundamentals. In addition, brokers must have several years of experience in the business and pass an extensive examination. The length of time for a license renewal varies from state to state. Attendance at continuing education programs is increasingly required to qualify for license renewal.

Agents and brokers frequently take courses in real estate principles, law, financing, appraisal, and property management. These courses are offered by local real estate boards and by various schools and universities.

Anyone seeking to advance in the real estate field should acquire knowledge in finance, accounting, and appraisal. Most problems relating to income-producing real estate can only be solved with particular knowledge in these fields.

To become a leasing real estate agent, one must have experience and knowledge in the real estate field, particularly in the area of leasing office and retail properties.

For those interested in appraisals, most states offer licensing through state agencies. To be a qualified appraiser requires years of experience in the field of real estate and specialized training and knowledge in the techniques of appraising. This is true with property management as well.

Of particular significance to anyone considering the selection of the real estate business as a career is the possibility of entering the field with little capital, a very limited investment, and a small organization. As in any service business, the ingredients for success are education, sales ability, experience, and long hours of personal contact work. Many real estate organizations are made up of no more than three or four people, each of whose income depends on his or her own personal production.

Brokers expand their business by expanding sales staffs, and are often eager to introduce new salespeople to the business. With education and training, a hardworking and ambitious person could find both lucrative and interesting employment either with a firm or in self-employment.

Industry outlook

The real estate industry is subject to the fluctuations of the economy. If interest rates remain low, encouraging people to seek mortgages, then the future of the real estate industry looks bright. The real estate market can be very strong in some parts of the country and very weak in other parts of the country. Often, an area will be strong for a certain amount of time and then the number of real estate transactions will go down.

Employment in the real estate industry is expected to grow at a healthy rate throughout the 1990s. Due to the large turn-over of real estate agents, the opportunities are always open. Many of the approximately 400,000 real estate agents and brokers in the United States worked part-time.

It should be noted that experienced real estate agents and brokers often make considerably more money than those just starting out in the business. As in many other industries, those with training and good contacts are usually the most successful.

Recording

General information

Acoustical recordings were the earliest efforts in recording music. Thomas Edison invented a machine in 1877 that would record and play back sounds. Tin-wrapped cylinders were marked by the vibrations etched by a stylus, making an acoustical record. These machines posed a problem in recording lower strings, such as the bass and the cello, because the acoustical vibrations would not record accurately on the cylinders. Despite the technical difficulties with this type of recording, copies of classical performers and music became the standard type of record.

In 1887, Emile Berliner developed an alternate to the cylinder with his invention of the flat recording disk, to be played on his disc player "the Gramophone." The flat disks were easier to produce and store than the tubes, and soon gained in popularity.

The Gramophone Company established branches in several countries, and eventually expanded into the renamed Victor Talking Machine Company. Victor produced the Victrola, a record player that was unrivalled in popularity and sales for a great number of years after its introduction in 1901.

Columbia, a competitor to the Victrola, agreed to a cross-license arrangement with Victor in the manufacturing of records and phonographs. They combined patent assignments, allowing both to record on the newly developed wax disks. These records played for two minutes and held a recording on only one side of the disk. Most of the records were voice recordings since the reproduction quality was superior to that of instruments. Other early recordings were of vaudeville skits, readings, and popular music, such as ragtime piano pieces.

Cylinders continued to be made as well. In 1908, a new material called Amberol was developed, enabling the number of grooves on a cylinder to be increased. The higher number of grooves allowed for a longer recording, doubling the cylinder's playing time to four minutes.

By 1913, however, disks were matching the playing time of the cylinder. The increased number of grooves and the establishment of two-sided disks in 1908 enhanced the desirability and the utility of the disk. The development of the less expensive 78 rpm disks completely replaced the cylinders by 1915.

Spring motors powered the early phonographs. Hand cranks had powered the earliest versions but it was apparent the evenness of power was important to the sound quality and a regulated flow of power had to be developed. The Gramophone used a crank to wind a spring and then the spring released at a regulated speed to turn the phonograph.

In the 1930s, electrically powered motors were used to turn the phonograph. The turntable could now turn continuously and allowed for a more even speed on the turntable and longer playing time for the record. One of the reasons that phonographs were developed with an electric motor was the ability to combine the unit with a radio. The speaker system could be used for both, making the product more desirable for customers.

During the 1910s and 1920s, classical music recordings were by far the most popular type of recording offered. Popular music, jazz, and band performances began to catch on and record sales grew tremendously. However, the effect of the depression in the 1930s took its toll on record and phonograph sales. The ability of radio to fill the void by providing free music (once a radio was purchased) decreased the sales of phonographs.

With the decline came changes to the companies that had developed the industry. Victor was sold to the Radio Corporation of America (RCA). Columbia was purchased in 1938 by the Columbia Broadcasting System (CBS).

A sound-recording technician edits the sound track of a television program. He adds certain sound effects to appropriate moments in the program.

In 1948, RCA developed a vinyl disk that could play eight minutes of music. This allowed for an entire classical symphony movement to be recorded on one side on the record, avoiding the unusual breaks that had been a part of the 78 rpm recordings. The record played at 45 rpm and was seven inches in diameter.

Columbia developed a record that played at 33 1/3 rpm, and carried thirty minutes of music. With the development of these two speeds and lengths of records, both RCA and Columbia produced both types of disks by the end of the year.

Another major development for the record industry came in the method of recording. Magnetic tapes were used to produce the original recording. The quality of sound from the magnetic tape was the finest achieved to that date. Beyond the quality of the original recording, the tape allowed for patchwork correction to be done to a recording to replace sections where errors or poor quality sound occurred. It was no longer necessary to record the entire piece in one session.

Tape recordings also allowed for the music to be recorded on channels; a singer's voice may be one channel and the instrumental music another. This gave the producer an opportunity to mix the music with the desired emphasis. A flute, for example, could be enhanced beyond the original performance level, or the brass instruments could be quieted. Two track stereophonic recordings became commonplace in the 1950s, and phonographs were developed with two speakers to reproduce the stereo sound in the home.

Eventually the number of tracks recorded during a session increased to four, eight, and then sixteen tracks. This gave the recording engineers more leverage in the manipulation of sounds recorded.

The technology for recording boomed with the computer age. Synthesizers reproduced the sounds of orchestras electronically. Voices could be electronically enhanced, lowered, shifted in pitch, or adjusted to accommodate any change desired. The type of music recorded could be so stylized that it could not be reproduced in a live performance. The number of tracks recorded could be increased to meet the needs of an individual recording artist.

Along with the advancement in technology of sound recording, an advancement in the record disk began to chance the shape of the industry once again. Compact discs were invented in Japan in the late 1970s. Compact discs, or CDs for short, are digitally recorded discs that use a laser instead of a stylus to read the music. The benefits of CDs rest in the quality of the reproduction, the portability of the discs and players, and their ability to remain undamaged by wear or scratching.

The change by the record industry to CDs has been swift. Most popular music is now produced on CDs and the same is true for classical music. The more popular older albums are being re-released on CDs, and in some instances new or old albums may be available only on CDs and cassettes.

The record industry is striving to establish CDs that also produce a television image. This will combine the music video with the quality of a compact disc recording. The cost remains high for the stereo that runs the audiovisual compact disc, but as the cost of the CD players dropped dramatically, this will lower the cost of the new technology.

The structure of the recording industry

A recording artist, whether classical, popular, or some other music form, starts the process of getting a record made in the artist and repertoire (A and R) department. A and R executives are responsible for finding new talent and arranging the contract negotiations for a recording contract. They keep track of the new artists that are performing in clubs and concerts. They also keep in touch with the recording artists that are well known (see Volume 2: Recording industry workers).

The new artist is either approached by a representative of a record company, or the artist sends in a demonstration tape with around four songs to the artist and repertoire department of one or more companies. If the representative is interested in the artist's work, then arrangements are made between the company, the artist, or the artist's manager. The contract may be for a single recording, a series of recordings, or a flexible arrangement of number of recordings.

For a relatively unknown artist, an independent label is the most likely place to arrange a contract. The artist and repertoire staff are most active for independent labels in covering undiscovered artists or less mainstream types of music. Contracts for independent labels are commonly for several albums and if the artist becomes extremely popular, the contract may be bought out by a major record company. The independent label promotes albums to a lesser degree, and, for the smallest labels, the artist may be responsible for all album promotion.

For the established performer, contract negotiations may be carried on between several companies vying for the artist's work. Depending on the artist's desires and needs, he or she will choose the most favorable contract offered. Obviously, an established performer is in a much better negotiating position than a newcomer to the recording field (see Volume 2: Musical occupations).

More than half the recording artists in the popular music field were originally artists for independent labels. Once they developed a large national audience their contracts were purchased for a profit for the independent label. Elvis Presley is one of the best examples of an artist who was discovered by a small company, Sun Records, and eventually went national with another company.

Once the contract arrangements have been settled, then the process of recording an album is initiated. The songs that are to be recorded will be decided by the artist and the company representative assigned to the artist. A recording session is scheduled. Musicians, technicians, and support staff are hired by the record producer. For an artist that is regularly accompanied by certain musicians, arrangements may be made for those musicians to be hired.

During the session, several recordings will be made of the same song. The best sections of the song can be put together in order to provide the best version of the song. Each instrument and voice can be recorded separately and combined by recording engineers, who specialize in combining (mixing) different recorded sounds into a unified whole. Mixing the recording is one of the most important jobs performed

This recording engineer operates sound equipment during a music recording session. It is his responsibility to ensure that instruments and voices are blended in accordance with the producer's directions.

on the recording and can influence the sound as much as the performers can (see Volume 4: Sound-recording technicians).

For popular music, the tools of the recording engineer are used in a wide variety of ways to influence the sound produced or to create new sounds entirely. One of the criticisms of heavy technical mixing of a tape is that an untalented performer may be made to sound much better on a recording than is really the case. Similar criticism has been directed at classical music. Performers will not be able to reproduce the flawless performances given on a record because they only have one chance to play in a concert, and the record may be a compilation of several performances.

After the recording session, the producer, engineer, and artist combine the pieces of the recording into the finished product. This may involve re-recording parts, reproducing parts with a synthesizer, enhancing the sound of one or more voices, and otherwise combining the tapes into a whole. The finished performance is then added to the other performances to go on the album.

To record a live performance, the technical end is just as necessary, but the performer only has one shot at the recording. After the performance, the engineer can work with the dif-

A performer reads text during the recording of an advertisement that will be broadcast on radio.

ferent tracks of tape to erase flaws, outside noises, and juggle with the volume and intensity to smooth over rough patches in the performance.

One of the most important aspects to the recording of a live performance is the position of the microphones. Setting microphones for a symphony determines the strength of the different sections of the orchestra. If solo performers are to be heard, a single microphone may be assigned to their position on the stage to capture their performance separately. To maintain a balanced sound in the reproduction of a large performance such as a symphony, the recording much match the balance that is achieved for the audience sitting in an orchestral hall.

Once the recording is finished, and the album put together, the production department takes over. They are responsible for the actual recording onto discs, records, and cassettes. The press run (the number of albums produced) is determined by previous sales of the artist, and the anticipated increase or decrease in sales for this release. The artist and repertoire department and promotion departments are responsible for knowing the market and the estimated value of a recording. Re-pressing a recording that is selling well is an easy process once the master tape is made.

While the record is in production, the art department is producing cover art and inside art if there is any. Type design is chosen for all written matter. Various designs are presented to the company representative, the artist, and the record producer. For smaller companies, the artist may make all the final decisions on art and packaging. A final design is selected, then

completed by the artists. For re-issue albums, the art department may decide on their own what design to use on the cover (see Volume 1: Design).

The editorial department is also at work on the liner notes, the information that is written on the cover and interior of the album casing. The lyrics for songs may be included in the packaging. The words must be checked, verified, and proofread for typographical errors.

The advertising department of the record company creates the ads that will run in newspapers, magazines, on television, and in stores for each album produced. Posters, show cards, displays, and any other promotional material are designed and developed in the advertising department as well. Advertising can greatly enhance sales of an album by generating an interest in the record either before its release or after it has been moved into the stores (see Volume 1: Advertising).

One of the chief methods of generating interest in an album, particularly in the popular music category, is air play on the radio. The promotion staff is expected to keep up-to-date on the staff and audience of radio stations. They should be aware of what audiences are covered in each region of the country, and how to best promote the new product to the audience that is interested in that type of music.

The promotion and publicity department is responsible for sending out copies of the recording to reviewers, along with press kits providing information and photos of the artist. This press package is mainly geared toward the air play time that can be generated by favorable reviews and frequent audience requests to the radio station (see Volume 1: Marketing).

Other forms of publicity used to create an interest in the recording include concert performances, interviews on television and the radio, press coverage in the printed media, public appearances, and any other promotion that brings the artist into the public eye (see Volume 1: Public Relations).

Once album sales are underway, determining the success or failure of a recording is directly linked to the number of recordings sold. For a successful classical album, the number sold may be 5000 to 10,000 copies. For a popular music album, the numbers are more likely to approach or exceed a million copies. Well known performers regularly have record sales that exceed a million copies.

After the record is sold, the recording may be re-released or may go out of print. Sales of most albums decline quickly after release and may not need a second pressing. Some albums, however, may be marketed successfully for years.

Careers

A sampling of careers in the recording industry follows below.

Artist and repertoire executives: Artist and repertoire executives are responsible for following the trends in their area of recording. They review prospective new artists, maintain ties with contracted artists, and decide on contracts and recordings. They negotiate all contract and recording arrangements. They are frequently employed by independent labels.

Artist and repertoire staff: The artist and repertoire staff scout for new talent, attending performances, concerts, and other events where talent may be discovered. They listen to recordings sent to the department, plan production of a recording, and assist in recording sessions. They need to know what the newest names and trends are in their category of music.

Executive producers: Executive producers direct the recording session. They work directly with the artist on the recording session, selecting studio musicians, technicians, engineers, and other staff needed for a recording session. They also work on the final mixing and editing of the tape.

Recording producers: In charge of all aspects of taping a recording session, the recording producer supervises the technical staff in their tasks. Producers monitor and control the technical elements such as microphone placement, tracks used, and anything else that influences the quality of sound.

Mastering order editors: Mastering order editors book time for the tape editing after the recording is completed.

Recording engineers: Operating the controls of the recording equipment, recording engineers monitor each individual machine in operation. They oversee the technical end of the recording.

Production managers: After a recording is edited and ready for copying, the production manager supervises the reproduction of the tape into a record or compact disc. Managers also supervise the design of the packaging, the writing of the liner notes, and the records release to the manufacturing department.

Art department staff: Art staff design rough drafts of record or CD covers. The record company executive and the artist select the cover desired. Artists in the department then draw or photograph the final art that will run on the album cover. For re-releases that are repackaged, the art department may work independently, making their own decisions about art to be used (see Volume 1: Design; and Volume 2: Commercial artists; Photographers and camera operators).

A recording engineer must know how to operate all of the equipment on the control room.

Editorial department staff: Editorial department staff write all the information found on the liner notes and cover. Any information to be presented as fact is verified, all lyrics are proofread, and all information is presented to the company executive and artist (see Volume 2: Writers and editors).

Advertising department staff: Once the recording package is ready, the advertising department creates point-of-purchase materials that will draw attention to the recording. This may include posters, show cards, brochures, standing displays, and such. Advertisements for the newspapers and magazines are designed and selected. Commercials, videos, and other promotional ads are created to enhance sales. Selected audiences are targeted through the placement of all promotional materials (see Volume 1: Advertising).

Promotion and publicity staff: All the information that is provided to reporters is written and developed by the promotion staff. Press kits with biographical information, promotional information, and photos are presented to the members of the press that review albums. The promotion staff arranges interviews, autograph sessions, and concerts. They maintain contact with radio executives and disc jockeys to promote air play of the albums they handle. For most small labels, the artist's business manager and the artist handle record promotion (see Volume 1: Broadcasting; Public Relations).

A singer discusses vocal techniques with the producer before recording his music.

Composers: Composers write music to be recorded. They may write orchestrations or arrangements (music to accompany the original composition) or they may create new pieces (see Volume 2: Musical occupations).

Singers: The singers may be the main performer on a recording, or they may be part of a chorus or back-up group that enhances the performance of the main singer. Choral arrangements, where no performer stands out, are also a regular part of the recording industry.

Music publishers: Once the song is composed and recorded, sheet music will be produced that allows others to play the song. Songs recorded by another artist earn royalties for the company and the composer.

Artist managers: Handling the business end of a performer's career is either the artist him or herself or a manager. The manager arranges contracts, performance schedules, commercial endorsements, promotional presentations, and the image building of the artist. A manager's fees are paid by the artist and are normally 15 to 20 percent of the cash intake.

Artist agents: Different than a manager, an artist agent books performance and interview assignments for the artist. The groundwork for scheduling, exposure, and coverage are handled by the agent. The agent is also hired by the artist and is paid on a percentage basis of ticket intake or income as well (see Volume 2: Literary agents and artists' managers).

Publicists: The need for a publicist presents itself once the artist has achieved some level of prosperity but needs publicity to become a more familiar name. The publicist is usually hired by the artist (see Volume 1: Public Relations; and Volume 2: Marketing, advertising, and public relations managers).

Education

The education requirements in the recording industry vary widely from task to task and from company to company. The largest companies for the recording industry require the highest level of education. The competition for the job openings allow for those with more experience and/or better education to have a better chance.

In classical music, a degree in musicology, music history, or some other education in music theory or history is most helpful. For students looking to find employment in the editorial department, writing classes or experience also helps.

Art department employees either have experience or education in commercial arts, graphic arts, computer arts, or fine arts.

For other areas of specialty, the best education is the one that follows most directly with the position of interest. For example, publicity department staff should have some working knowledge of promotions, marketing, and demographics. College graduates in business administration majors will usually handle the business and financial positions in the recording industry.

Since the smaller recording companies have fewer staff members, flexibility and the ability to handle many different tasks are important skills for the successful candidate. Once the employee is hired for a certain position, chances are that he or she will be trained to handle other jobs as well.

The salary levels vary widely, depending on the size of the company. For both the large and the small companies, though, the hours can be extremely long. Frequent travel and irregular working schedules may be necessary to scout new talent or produce a record on time. Many employees work twelve hours a day, and low pay is the reward.

The point most often emphasized by the staff hiring new employees is that candidates must have a real love for the music with which they will be involved. A broad background in all types of music helps, but a strong education and knowledge in the area of specialty is essential.

Industry outlook

With the transition to compact discs, the jobs that were specific to vinyl recording reproduction are almost completely obsolete. The number of people that will be hired to replace the staff that leaves will diminish until the conversion to compact discs is complete.

Sales of long-playing albums are down to less than one third of what they were ten years ago. In 1980 the record industry in the United States sold 322 million long-playing albums. But by 1988, this figure had dropped to 107 million albums sold.

Over the same ten-year period, audio cassettes have risen in sales. Cassette sales are almost four times as high as they were in 1980. The market for cassettes has expanded enough for the industry to begin experimenting with cassette singles as a possible new market.

The biggest boom has been in the compact disc (CD) market. Since the first sales statistics were gathered in the United States in 1983, the market has expanded to 100 times its first year sales figures. With the increased efficiency in production, the cost has come down, and the popularity of CDs has skyrocketed. Only with the increased sales of CDs has the recording industry been able to match its earlier sales records of the late 1970s.

Overall the industry is maintaining a solid sales level. The staff for smaller companies continues to be tight, and the competition for jobs in the large companies is keen. But once a person has established a base in the industry, the stability of the industry should maintain employment possibilities for that person.

◇ SOURCES OF ADDITIONAL INFORMATION

Recording Industry Association of America
1020 19th Street, NW, Suite 200
Washington, DC 20036

Society of Professional Audio Recording Services
4300 Tenth Avenue North
Lake Worth, FL 33461

American Federation of Musicians of the United States and Canada
Paramount Building
1501 Broadway
Suite 600
New York, NY 10036

National Association of Schools of Music
11250 Roger Bacon Drive
Number 21
Reston, VA 22090

American Guild of Musical Artists
1727 Broadway
New York, NY 10019

◇ RELATED ARTICLES

Volume 1: Advertising; Broadcasting; Design; Marketing; Motion Pictures; Performing Arts
Volume 2: Recording industry workers; Writers and editors
Volume 4: Audio control technicians; Audiovisual technicians; Electronic organ technicians; Sound technicians; Sound-effects technicians; Sound-recording technicians; Studio technicians; Video technicians

Recreation and Park Services

General information

Devotion to recreation developed early in civilization. Recreation became important when people were able to gather enough food and protect themselves from harm by others or by nature. Only when these necessities were taken care of were they able concentrate on other activities. Ancient people developed many forms of amusement and distraction which we continue to use today.

Sporting events have a long history. The Olympics were held regularly in ancient Greece, starting in 776 B.C. Before that, regular festivals were held every four years around Greece which were a combination of athletics and festivities. These have been traced back as far as 1400 B.C.

The Greeks in ancient times ranked the four most important areas of study; athletics, music, fine arts, and scholarship. It was believed that a well-rounded individual would possess abilities in all areas.

The European Renaissance also developed the same idea. The ideal Renaissance Man, the courtier, would be educated in art, athletics, swordsmanship, music, writing, speaking, and many academic topics. With this balance of talents, one would have some understanding of any endeavor.

Developing skills for hunting and other outdoor activities became noble. As the upper class developed a liking for certain activities, the negative association of hunting and other activities was lost. This was true for both what people did and where they lived.

The need for recreational areas as well as the growing urban population combined to popularize the notion that large areas of countryside should be left undisturbed for people to enjoy. The countryside was seen less as farming area and more as a retreat to natural beauty and leisure. With overcrowding and pollution in urban areas increasing, the need to protect the natural environment became more apparent.

The concept of national parks and sanctuaries can be traced back to 1872 in the United States. Yellowstone National Park was the first protected wildlife area. Cornelius Hedges, a Montana judge, asked Congress to consider preserving the Yellowstone area, with all its natural wonders, so that future generations would be able to enjoy it. Congress agreed, and by 1900 Congress added Yosemite, Sequoia, Kings Canyon, and Mount Rainier to the National Park system. The National Park Service, in the Department of the Interior, was established in 1916 to maintain the parks and establish new sites for preservation.

Since its founding, the National Park Service has added to its list of goals. Education of the public through walks, tours, and presentations has helped increase awareness of ecological concerns. The Parks have also become a shelter for endangered and threatened species. Conservation of animals and nature is the task of several programs that are held under the National Park Service. The Land and Water Conservation Fund, and the National Wild and Scenic River System are two of the programs sponsored through the Parks Service.

Development for recreation and beautification of urban areas is also the task of the National Park Service and the Department of the Interior. The Urban Park and Recreation Recovery Program and the National Register of Historic Places work to upgrade and maintain the parks and buildings of urban areas, as well as historic locations outside of the large cities.

Recreation now is a regular part of the average person's life. Vacations are planned around what type of recreational facilities are available. Cities are designing facilities for outdoor activities and nature preserves. Recreation for the elderly, the handicapped, and anyone else who may not have been considered in the past is now being addressed by the people who work in recreation. The business of recreation is booming and it is covering a vast number of areas of concern.

The structure of the recreation and park services industry

Professional people working in the field of recreation are concerned with meeting the needs of people of all age groups. Most municipalities in the United States have recreation programs for children and adults, and many companies have programs for their employees. Planned recreation programs cover many areas of activity: camping, hobbies, crafts, art, music, dramatics, aquatics, games, and sports.

People are starting to take seriously the words of Henry David Thoreau: "We have lived not in proportion to the number of years we have spent on this earth, but in proportion to the number we have enjoyed."

No longer does youth dominate the services of the recreational system. Seniors, young adults, and special population groups now demand equal recreation opportunities. Many of these people have poor leisure skills or attitudes, and the profession is working to provide opportunities for people to learn to participate in activities that may have been unavailable to them in the past.

Another challenge is to furnish a balance of cultural, social, and educational opportunities to go along with the traditional recreational activities of sports and fitness pursuits. Also, activities for the different skill levels must be provided. The essence of recreation today is the participation of a diverse population with a variety of interests and needs.

Thousands of organizations and groups provide various types of recreational facilities and resources. The YMCA and the YWCA are probably the most familiar urban facilities. This type of organization provides facilities for all sorts of exercise and outdoor activities. They may sponsor camps for youths, classes in swimming and other sports, art centers, gyms, and exercise facilities to members of the community for a fee. Schools, universities, churches, civic groups, and a variety of other groups may sponsor facilities to provide recreational services to their members or the community at large.

Staffing may vary from a completely volunteer staff to a full-time trained staff. There are certain restrictions by the local and state governments on who may teach or oversee certain activities. Swimming pools have the most fa-

A conservationist takes a group of students on a nature walk. He is teaching them the structure of tree trunks.

miliar rules. It is unusual to find a pool with a lifeguard who has not taken a lifesaving test. Swimming instructors normally have lifesaving and CPR certificates as well.

Summer is the season when most of the staff is needed at outdoor facilities. Camps, beaches, playgrounds and such require staffs as students get out for summer vacation and the weather warms up enough to spend the day outdoors. Seasonal work is very common, and frequently recreational staffs are made up of students and other people looking to get into recreation as a career.

The Park Service will hire both senior citizens and students for a variety of positions. The work may require living in dormitories if the assignment location is far from an urban center. Certain skills and knowledge will be required for different types of services. Taking people on tours of the Grand Canyon, for example, would require more historical knowledge than supervising a group of swimmers. Evening tours might require some knowledge of the constellations. There are a variety of subjects and skills for each job.

All recreational activities need space. People's interests are increasingly diverse, and the demand for places to play has increased proportionately. Neighborhood parks, recreation centers, playing fields, art centers, trails, campsites, and other facilities need to be provided. Efficient use of existing space in unused schools, churches, and other community build-

Dressed as a pioneer, a park volunteer demonstrates food preparation at the Lincoln Park Village.

ings has assisted in meeting increased demand. The development of new parks and open spaces and the renovation of old parks to new uses have presented interesting challenges to planners. The field of park resources concerns itself with just such problems.

The planning, maintenance, and administration of cultural, historical, and environmental sites requires certain skills. The resource staff should have good administrative skills, with the ability to present proposals, write site-development plans, determine planning and maintenance costs and schedules, and do a variety of other tasks.

The interest of many localities in developing recreation facilities can be traced to the new public awareness of the need for recreational pursuits. Many parks and other recreational facilities have been created in both urban and wilderness areas. Federal government grant-in-aid programs for the acquisition and development of parks and open spaces has greatly influenced the expansion of local, state, and federal park systems. Likewise, some states have greatly expanded capital budgets for statewide facilities, and some have instituted grant-in-aid programs

for local governments to aid in building new facilities.

Careers

A sampling of recreation and park services careers follows below.

Park and recreation staff: These are the employees of the municipal, county, state, and national park systems. Conservation and natural resources are the two main areas of work for the park staff. This would include wildlife management, fire control, and gathering data on the environment. Staff members also work on law enforcement, violation investigation, accidents, and search and rescue operations. Campground operators, tour guides, and information center staff would also work in the park and recreation category.

The training and background for staff jobs differs with the needs of the site. Those who work in forest areas, for example, require a background knowledge of forest wildlife, fire management, rugged terrain rescue, and other sorts of skills required for that environment. Those who work in a National Park without a lot of trees, on the other hand, would need a different educational background, with different wildlife management skills.

Some positions can be filled by volunteers while others, such as the position of park ranger, require highly-trained workers. Some skills may be learned on the job, while others require a college degree (see Volume 3: Park rangers, Ranger managers, Tour guides; and Volume 4: Park technicians).

Armed Forces recreation staff: These employees supervise the recreational events for the military, both at U.S. bases and the bases abroad. They also maintain the recreational facilities at military bases.

Aquatic recreation staff: The staff that runs the swimming pools, marinas, beaches, and water sport facilities fall into the same range of skills and titles as the park and recreation staff. Summer staff would include lifeguards, swimming instructors, and maintenance staff. Full-time positions are held in management, education, conservation, and other day-to-day operational elements (see Volume 2: Sports instructors; Volume 3: Swimming-pool servicers; and Volume 4: Marine services technicians).

Park resources and design: The Park Service has an interpretive design center in Harpers Ferry, West Virginia, and a planning and design facility in Denver, Colorado. This staff consists of the engineers, architects, recreational planners, and other design-oriented workers responsible for the production and development of facilities, both new and under renovation. The resources staff includes the local staff that work on enhancing the educational and cultural elements of the park (see Volume 2: Architects; City managers; Landscape architects; Urban and regional planners; and Volume 4: Surveying and mapping technicians).

Therapeutic recreation staff: This is the most rapidly expanding field in recreation. The development of classes, sites, and opportunities in recreation for the mentally and physically disabled is a relatively new area in research and development. Recreation for the aging is also expanding, with the increase in the number of senior citizens and the interest in continuing activities that involve the recreation facilities around them. The vast array of areas being explored include skiing for the physically impaired, hiking trips for older groups, and swimming classes for the blind. This field requires certification in therapeutic recreation, with an emphasis on medicine for some positions (see Volume 1: Health Care; and Volume 2: Recreational therapists).

Resort and commercial recreation: This is mainly a private industry field, including golf courses, amusement parks, resorts, and health spas. The type of facility will normally indicate the type of background required. Golf course maintenance requires a knowledge of grounds keeping, for example, while the amusement park area requires skills in crowd control and the ability to supervise a large number of employees for public assistance and service.

Spas and resort facilities need educational instructors for various sport and art courses and a staff for entertainment and recreation coordination. The tourist industries are a profit making venture, and there are several courses offered by different universities that may help the prospective employee get background skills for such work (see Volume 3: Hotel and motel industry workers; Landscapers and grounds managers; Ski lift operators).

Park police: The staff of the park district police is employed by the Park Services. The guards for park facilities are also Park Services employees. These jobs are mainly located in large urban areas (a significant number are in Washington, D.C., around the large collection of monuments in the Mall). Most start working in Washington, D.C. and then, after training, may be assigned to any of the park services area. The staff includes the mounted police, the motorcycle, helicopter, canine, special equipment and tactics teams, and the investigations units.

Museum staff: The federally employed museum staff is small in numbers; most museums

A recreational planner at Harpers Ferry in West Virginia helps renovate old park facilities.

hire on an individual basis with each staff determining the qualifications for the positions available. Positions range from volunteer tour guides to curators. Museums employ people to create and set up exhibitions, prepare exhibition catalogues, care for art pieces, and keep records on the history of the pieces and their condition. Curators will normally possess a specialized degree with at least a master's, and probably a doctorate in the area of study required by the museum. For an art museum such a degree would most probably be in art history or museum studies (see Volume 2: Archivists and curators; Museum occupations; and Volume 4: Exhibit technicians; Museum technicians).

Zoo and aquarium staff: Biology and wildlife studies are the most important elements for most of the staff at a zoo or aquarium. The people who work directly with the animals will need to have a strong understanding and education for all of the facets of animal management. The support staff would include public relations, publications, education, graphics design, and various other positions needed for the operations of a public facility (see Volume 1: Biological Sciences; Volume 2: Veterinarians; and Volume 4: Animal health technicians; Animal production technicians).

In most parks, campers must register before entering the grounds.

Education

Individuals interested in professional-level employment in recreation should plan to complete a college degree in the field of interest. Nearly 500 colleges and universities offer professional and paraprofessional curricula in recreation, parks, and leisure services. Students majoring at the bachelor's level should investigate programs accredited by the National Recreation and Park Association/American Association for Leisure and Recreation (addresses are listed at the end of this article).

For those interested in the technical aspects of recreation, technical institutes, universities and some community colleges offer educational and vocational training in a variety of specialties. Check the catalogues of these institutions for related courses. Zoo, aquarium, and some park district work will require a background in wildlife management, zoology, marine wildlife management, or veterinary medicine. The other technical jobs vary with the tasks. The best method for finding the specific requirements, if there are any, for a technical position is to contact the facility hiring for that post.

Preparation for a career in recreation should begin in high school. Courses in English and communications, social sciences, art, music, drama, and vocational arts are particularly useful. Participation in extracurricular activities and part-time or volunteer work are excellent training for this field. An interest in people and their welfare, a desire to serve, an interest in organizing, a tolerance for all abilities, and a sympathy for disadvantaged people are personal qualities necessary for a successful career in this field.

Industry outlook

In many sections of the country, an oversupply of professionally prepared individuals has developed. This has been caused by a slowdown in the expansion of services by many of the traditional agencies: public recreation and park departments. Also, individuals with professional preparation in related fields (social work, education, and so on) have sought positions as opportunities in their own fields have diminished. The need for certain specialists and paraprofessionals and technical workers such as park maintenance personnel and activity leaders is affected by the often seasonal nature of the field. Nevertheless, career opportunities in both the public and private sector continue to be created and developed. The areas of fastest development are therapeutic recreation and private recreation facility staffing.

The most competitive positions are for the park rangers and the wildlife management positions in all the areas of employment. Some potential zoo staff members have waited several years before an opening became available in a zoo. The wages are usually low for the most competitive jobs, with prime positions taken by veterans who have extensive background in the field.

Compensation for recreation work varies greatly. Generally, professional salaries are comparable to teacher and education administrator salaries. Paraprofessional and technical personnel are paid comparably with allied personnel in related fields. The field of recreation offers a variety of duties involving people and places. Opportunities for creativity and innovation abound.

The hours of work are often long, but usually not dull. Since recreation workers work while others play, the hours are irregular with weekend and evening work quite normal. Fringe benefits are comparable to those for most workers, and working conditions are often very pleasant.

◇ SOURCES OF ADDITIONAL INFORMATION

United States Department of the Interior
National Park Service
PO Box 37126
Washington, DC 20013

National Recreation and Park Association
3101 Park Center Dr, 12th Floor
Alexandria, VA 22302

American Association for Leisure and Recreation
1900 Association Drive
Reston, VA 22091

Society of American Foresters
5400 Grosvenor Lane
Bethesda, MD 20814

◇ RELATED ARTICLES

Volume 1: Biological Sciences; Health Care; Hospitality; Sports; Travel and Tourism
Volume 2: Architects; Archivists and curators; Hotel and motel managers; Museum occupations; Occupational therapists; Recreational therapists; Recreation workers; Sports instructors
Volume 3: Fire fighters; Landscapers and grounds managers; Park rangers; Ranger managers; Ski lift operators; Tour guides
Volume 4: Animal health technicians; Animal production technicians; Fire safety technicians; Fish production technicians; Forestry technicians; Marine services technicians; Museum technicians; Park technicians; Planetarium technicians; Soil conservation technicians; Surveying and mapping technicians

Religious Ministries

General information

Many people consider religion a hard word to define, but, generally speaking, most see it as a system of beliefs and practices having reference to our relation with the divine. Religions, as spoken of in this article, are the principal organized religions, specifically the largest in the United States: Protestantism, Roman Catholicism, and Judaism. Though beliefs differ, the common link of those involved with religious work is each individual's dedication to religious pursuits.

Of the three most practiced religions in the Western world—Protestantism, Roman Catholicism, and Judaism—Judaism is the oldest. Its 4,000 year history spans countless civilizations.

Much of the first two thousand years of Jewish history is recorded in the Torah, often referred to as the Old Testament. During this Biblical era, Jews evolved from twelve loosely-related tribes to a small nation that was situated in modern-day Israel. Thus, Judaism was more than a religion; it was a way of life, an identity, and a social structure. Such laws and codes of ethics were handed down by their God, known as Yahweh.

As a nation, Israel was subject to political disputes, tenuous coalitions, civil disturbances, and wars. This brought about a weakening of the state, and led to the movement of Jews to other regions. Such places were known as the Diaspora. Many Jews followed the trade routes, but in general, they traveled to places where they were welcome. Restrictions on living in certain areas varied, depending on those in power at the time. The ancient Romans, for instance, let Jews practice their religion and their trade with few restrictions, allowing them to settle in Syria, Asia Minor, Babylonia, and Egypt. However, their benevolence was limited to mere toleration; they eventually dissolved Israel in about 70 A.D. and incorporated it into the Empire.

With the Jewish nation shattered and it citizens spread throughout the Roman Empire, the Jews needed some cohesive element that would help maintain a uniform identity. The rabbis provided the necessary leadership. They developed the Mishna (oral law) over a 400 year period, roughly between 200 B.C. and 200 A.D. The Mishna essentially regulated every aspect of Jewish life. This was a code of conduct that all Jews in the Diaspora followed. The rabbi, known as the teacher, became the authority on the Mishna and thus a scholar and community leader. The codes set forth in the Mishna were constantly debated among rabbis, inviting interpretation and reevaluation as times changed.

Along with the Mishna, rabbis compiled the Talmud (the combined text of the Mishna and the later oral law called the Gemara) over approximately a 600 hundred year period, from about 500 to 1100 A.D. The Talmud was the rabbis' interpretation of the Torah, and as such outlined the laws and ethical and moral guidelines that were to shape Jewish life.

Rabbinical scholarship continued through the Middle Ages. By then, Jews had settled throughout Europe and Russia, often living insular and secluded lives. Nonetheless, those Jews involved with trade mingled among the non-Jews and often longed for assimilation. By the end of the 1700s, many Jews began to change their focus from isolated religious lives toward more secular lives that concentrated on personal and national fulfillment. This ideology led to the Reform movement, which began in Germany in the mid-1700s, and later moved to America in the mid-1800s. At the same time, the Conservative movement gained acceptance among non-Reform Jews in America. Conservative Jews had a more traditional approach to the practice of Judaism without the strict observance practiced by Orthodox Jews.

Judaism was already 2,000 years old when Christianity was founded. It began as a movement within Judaism, but due to issues concerning the messianic role of Jesus and the validity of Mosaic Law, it never attracted many Jews. In addition, the Jews of the Diaspora were struggling to maintain their identity through traditional customs and strict rules of conduct. Thus, the universality of Christianity was not appealing to most Jews.

The Romans considered Christianity a threat to their empire and proclaimed the practice of Christianity illegal. For the first three hundred years, Christians were brutally persecuted and killed. In A.D. 312, the Roman emperor Constantine saw a vision of the Greek letters *chi* and *rho*, the first letters of Christ's name, before engaging in battle against his rival Maxentius. Upon winning the battle, he became a strong supporter of Christianity, and in A.D. 313, he issued the Edict of Milan, legally recognizing the Christian faith.

The structure of Christianity evolved over hundreds of years. Bishops, particularly in the Western provinces of the Roman Empire, presided over large areas known as dioceses. The Bishops of Rome, Alexandria, Antioch, Jerusalem, and Constantinople were the most powerful authorities of the church. In 461, the Bishop of Rome, Leo I, asserted his position of pope, the primary leader of the church. The first clergymen were responsible for preaching, distributing alms to the poor, administering baptism and the Eucharist, and representing their communities during religious conferences.

During the early Middle Ages, Christianity spread throughout Europe, providing a powerful network that ensured political and social stability. Numerous monasteries were established as centers of scholarship and bastions of culture. The ethics and teachings of Christianity became the overriding preoccupation of all Europeans. Popes and bishops were as powerful as emperors, and many of the political ceremonies centered around Christian rituals.

While the structure of the church remained a dynamic and ever-changing force in Europe, a major schism occurred in 1517 when a dissatisfied young monk named Martin Luther posted a list of ninety-five theses on the door of a church in Wittenberg, Germany. The theses enumerated several theological problems with the church that Luther found antithetical to religious salvation. Although Luther had not intended to break away from the Catholic Church, he was excommunicated by Pope Leo X in 1521.

The movement by Luther and others such as John Calvin, known as the Reformation, initiated many more revolts against the church, establishing such Protestant sects as Lutheranism (named after Luther), Anglicanism, Pres-

An episcopal priest in Vale, Oregon, conducts services. As a community leader, it is her responsibility to offer any assistance to members of her congregation.

byterianism, Methodism, Unitarianism, and several more.

Both Protestants and Catholics had extensive missionary ventures all over the world. Many Protestant sects are still active in missionary services.

In the United States today, approximately 55.1 percent of the people identify as Protestant, 29.7 percent identify as Roman Catholic, and 3.2 percent identify as Jewish.

The structure of religious ministries

Those involved with in religious ministry work often have similar duties. For example, all religious leaders tend to the needs of their congregants. Religious leaders also often have similar administrative tasks, overseeing the functioning of an office. Despite the similarities in duties, however, the clergy representing each religion do have differing religious responsibilities.

While lighting the candles for the Sabbath service, a rabbi recites prayers in the memory of Holocaust victims.

The particular activity into which any Protestant minister is channeled depends on the number of suitable openings in that area, or the area the minister prefers, and also on favorable action by a directing authority, such as a bishop, conference, synod, district superintendent, or denominational board. In churches with congregational authority, the minister is retained directly by vote of the congregation, acting on recommendations of a search committee who chooses from a list of eligible candidates supplied by the denomination.

In most churches today, the pulpit is only one of the minister's responsibilities. In smaller congregations, the minister looks after all functions. In larger churches, however, associates and assistants are retained not only to preach and officiate at the growing number of second services on the Sabbath and on other special days but also to administer christenings, conduct marriages, preside at funerals, supervise religious instruction, spearhead various programs of lay activities, and direct the music program.

Moreover, in some denominations, the ministry goes far beyond the local church. There are home missionaries carrying on religious, educational, and welfare functions, as well as directing medical programs, among the underprivileged. Foreign missionaries carry on the same work and direction abroad, in Asia, Africa, the Middle East, and Latin America. Then there are chaplains in the armed forces, on university and college campuses, and in institutions (hospitals, mental health facilities, orphanages, and penitentiaries, for example).

Further afield, ministers are responsible for administration and teaching in private schools, colleges and universities, and seminaries. They are also found on the editorial staffs of religious newspapers, church magazines, and religious book publishing firms. At denominational headquarters, ministers direct church-wide educational programs, finances, personnel, radio and TV programming, men's work, women's programs, and youth activities. Similar responsibilities are exercised by ministers assigned to interdenominational organizations.

A minister's work is not restricted to the altar and the pulpit; it embraces all forms of counseling and teaching of human relations, as well as such areas as the teaching rostrum, physical and mental healing, the printing press, and electronic communication.

It should be emphasized that personal counseling, sometimes the principal assignment of an assistant minister in a larger congregation, remains one of the important responsibilities of members of the clergy in whatever work or in whatever area they may be engaged.

Although the ministry is hardly a calling to financial affluence, members of the clergy do receive basic living expenses.

In larger congregations with more than one minister, the senior minister will need experience and administrative ability. He or she will be called on to provide direction in areas of finance, personnel, human relations, and public relations.

Assistant ministers engaged by local churches to head up activities in religious education and to direct music programs will need the firm foundation of special seminary studies and music courses. Continued professional education can be obtained in summer school courses and from reading the current literature.

Ministers working with the underprivileged, migratory, minority, and foreign groups, as well as on Indian reservations, must be able to live under adverse conditions, to improvise and make do with limited resources, to adjust to different outlooks, and, with foreign groups, to have a working knowledge of the language and culture of the people. Tact and persuasiveness also are helpful qualities when the home missionary is called on to deal with the representatives of government and private agencies and with employers.

Denominational home mission boards are financially responsible for the men and women they assign to the field, as they are for retirement and other benefit provisions.

Ministers engaged in the administration of schools, colleges, universities, and seminaries need to have training and experience in general administration involving fund-raising, personnel work, and industrial relations, as well as a good grounding in education and educational methods. Those who teach in such institutions must reinforce their ministerial training with specialization in education and continue advanced study in their subject of instruction to earn the necessary degrees.

The religious field offers two highly specialized opportunities specifically for lay people: the deacon or deaconess and the church business administrator. Although in many denominations deacons and deaconesses are appointed in local churches only for the volunteer performance of simple tasks, they are formally engaged in full-time service mainly by the various Lutheran bodies, the Methodist church, and the Protestant Episcopal church.

A priest gives his blessing over baskets of food during Holy Saturday.

Denominations engaging deacons and deaconesses for full-time service are financially responsible for them. Domestically, this service may be in local churches, in settlements and community centers, in educational institutions and hospitals, and in social agencies. Abroad, there are numerous positions in foreign missions.

The area of church business administrator is relatively new in the religious field. Openings are very limited, but the financial compensation (paid by the retaining congregation) is greater than that received by most ministers. Only very large or wealthy congregations can afford such specialized service.

In the Roman Catholic Church only men are ordained and marriage is forbidden to the clergy. The opportunities of religious life are extended to men as brothers and to communities of sisters, and for both, the vows of obedience, poverty, and celibacy can be lifted only with special reasons and permission, usually from the pope.

The Roman Catholic Church has two types of priesthood: diocesan (secular) and religious. The religious clergy belong to a religious society and are immediately responsible to a superior. The members of the secular clergy are immediately subject to the bishop of a diocese, and are usually devoted to parochial work, administrative work, and other various duties. Members

423

In addition to their regular duties, religious leaders offer their services to the general community as well. This priest prepares meals in a local soup kitchen.

of both the secular and religious priesthood receive their assignments from their superiors; however, assignments today are always made with the interests and abilities of the individual in mind. Every effort is made to place a priest in the type of ministry he feels called to offer the community.

The religious priest belongs to a given order, each of which has its own specialty: members of the Society of Jesus (Jesuits), for example, are known as educators; members of the Order of Preachers (Dominicans) are known as philosophers and preachers; the Paulists specialize in home mission work; and the Maryknoll fathers work primarily in the foreign mission field.

Religious priests are often involved in the operation of schools, from high schools through colleges and universities, and also many special schools for boys, such as orphanages or training schools. Members of the order, whether priests or brothers, do everything from being president to driving a tractor. In most religious institutions today, an order would serve in collaboration with lay people. For example, at the University of Notre Dame, founded by the Congregation of Holy Cross in 1842, the majority of the faculty members are lay people.

Having taken the vow of poverty, the religious priest and monk may keep no money given to him or willed to him. It must go to his order. On the other hand, the order takes care of all his needs: food, clothing, shelter, medical and dental care, and some leisure opportunities, as well as a limited amount of money for

necessary travel, local transportation, and sundries.

Christian monks, nuns, and priests also take vows of chastity, requiring them to foreswear sexual relations and marriage. They also take vows of obedience, stating they will follow the decisions of the church leaders.

There are two kinds of brothers in the Roman Catholic Church. In both cases, they are religious men who are not ordained, which means they cannot celebrate Mass, hear confessions, or perform other ecclesiastical functions.

The largest groups of brothers are orders of brothers, such as the Brothers of the Christian Schools (Christian Brothers), Marist Brothers, and the Christian Brothers of Ireland. Most orders of brothers are engaged in educational or hospital work.

The other kind of brother belongs to a priestly order and, although not a priest, follows the rule of the order.

Religious congregations of nuns are differentiated according to the nature of their life. Some are contemplative; their purpose is the objective worship of God and they exclude the external works of an active life. Other religious women are noncloistered, and are active in community work and education at all levels, from preschool through college. They minister to the aged and the infirm and engage in child care and other social work.

Nuns are responsible to the superior of their order, and conversely the order is responsible for the care of all its sisters.

In the United States, there are more than 300 religious orders with thousands of religious women. They too take vows of poverty, celibacy, and obedience.

More church officials are giving responsibility to lay people as church needs have multiplied. Diocesan and archdiocesan headquarters need trained office personnel, as do the many church-affiliated organizations. And this goes beyond clerical and stenographic help— lay executives are engaged in administration, public relations, finances and fund-raising, accounting and promotion. The charitable arms of the church need experienced social welfare workers; church hospitals, orphanages, and senior citizen homes need nurses, administrators, laboratory technicians, and dietitians. But perhaps the greatest need today is for teachers in parochial schools and in the church's institutions of higher learning.

Traditionally, Roman Catholic foreign missions have been spearheaded by religious priests with the assistance of brothers and sisters. But now, in line with the greater emphasis being given the laity in church activities, specialists in teaching, sanitation, nursing, medicine, and dentistry are being sought on a volunteer basis for limited tours of duty in foreign missions. Lay people assist the priest in preaching, baptizing, witnessing marriages, and giving communion. They do not say Mass or hear confessions, but they are trained in many areas formerly reserved for priests.

The laity has also been invited into the activities of the church by the establishment of diocesan pastoral councils and parish councils.

Jewish religious life offers a wide variety of opportunities to its rabbis. They serve congregations affiliated with four different divisions of American Judaism: the Orthodox (traditional), Conservative, Reconstructionist, and Reform (liberal).

All rabbis, regardless of which type of congregation they have, perform similar duties. They are available to counsel members of their congregation, deliver sermons, visit the sick, perform funeral services, help the poor, officiate at weddings, conduct religious services, supervise religious educational programs, frequently teach confirmation and adult education classes, and often assume community responsibilities.

Many institutions of higher learning have sizable numbers of Jewish students requiring campus chaplains (placed through the B'nai B'rith Hillel Foundation). The Armed Forces and the larger public institutions also have a need for chaplains. Finally, the Jewish seminaries and day schools require religious leaders for their staffs.

A role of increasing importance for lay people in the Jewish religious field is that of synagogue administrator. Training, duties, and compensation for the synagogue administrator are similar to church administrators.

An important social force in areas with a growing Jewish population is the Jewish community center. The responsibilities of its director are among the most important that can be assumed by a lay person. It calls for an interest in and a liking for people, as well as both tact and diplomacy.

The Jewish day school offers both Jewish and secular curricula. The teachers in such schools are often ordained rabbis and they work closely with the members of the Jewish community. Jewish schools and other institutions also have regular need for principals, directors, teachers, office personnel, and administrative executives.

The military chaplaincy is open to clergy of all faith groups. Military chaplains serve as commissioned officers in one of the branches of the Armed Forces either full-time on active duty or in one of the Reserve components. In

Many religious communities run programs that aid the less fortunate.

addition to meeting the ordination, educational and physical requirements, the applicant must receive ecclesiastical endorsement from a denomination recognized by the Armed Forces Chaplains Board. A favorable National Agency check is required, and in most cases, pastoral experience after graduation from a religious institution. Duties of miliary chaplains are analogous to those of civilian clergy, but they are performed in a military environment. They work cooperatively with chaplains of other faith groups to insure the free exercise of religion for all military personnel (see Volume 1: Military Services.)

Campus chaplains fall into two categories. In the first category, chaplains are retained by the institution to minister to the student body as a whole; chaplains in the second category are assigned by their denominational board of education to serve member students. In addition to the requirements for the ministry in the local church or synagogue, campus chaplains must be able to deal effectively with young people who have inquiring minds and are impatient with traditions. Campus chaplains are responsible for many functions, such as promoting social gatherings, organizing seminars to deal with current issues, and celebrating religious holidays with students. All these activities are done in addition to conducting worship services.

Full-time institutional chaplains of Protestant, Roman Catholic, and Jewish denominations are retained by hospitals, reformatories, orphanages, penitentiaries, and other institutions. These institutions may be operated by federal, state, county, or municipal governments. Part-time chaplains may be engaged by city councils of churches to minister to the inmates of local institutions.

Religious Ministries

Careers

Although there are a wide range of careers in religious ministries, usually a person has a certain set of beliefs and opinions that limits somewhat the specific area of interest.

Protestant ministers: Protestant ministers lead their congregations in worship services and administer baptism, confirmation, and other rites. They also perform marriages and other religious ceremonies and provide moral and spiritual guidance to their congregants (see Volume 2: Protestant ministers).

Catholic priests: Catholic priests provide for the spiritual, educational, and social needs of Roman Catholic congregations. They offer Mass, administer the sacraments, perform wedding and funeral services, hear confession, and perform other religious duties (see Volume 2: Roman catholic priests).

Rabbis: Rabbis are the spiritual leaders of Jewish religious congregations. They interpret Jew law and tradition and conduct religious services. They also perform wedding and funeral services, counsel congregants, and perform other religious duties. In all but the Orthodox community, women can become rabbis (see Volume 2: Rabbis).

Cantors: The cantor leads the choir or congregation in singing and is the soloist in a synagogue. Cantors often teach Jewish boys and girls who are to become bar and bas mitzvah at the age of thirteen.

Military chaplains: Military chaplains have the same responsibilities as civilian clergy, but perform those duties in a military setting (see Volume 1: Military Service).

Monks or brothers: Taking vows of poverty, chastity, and obedience, monks and brothers of the church work, pray, and meditate, according to the rule of their religious order. Brothers have not taken the rites of ordination, or the holy orders, to become a monk or priest.

Friars: Members of one of the ten mendicant religious orders of the Catholic Church, friars combine monastic life with outside activity. Mendicants were originally brothers who had taken a vow of poverty and lived by begging. Mendicant orders include the Dominicans and Franciscans.

Nuns or sisters: With the same types of vows as monks, nuns work, pray, and meditate according to the rule of the religious order of which they are members. The initial period of training is known as the novitiate, lasting between five and ten years. Then simple vows are taken to become a sister, and solemn vows are taken to become a nun. Solemn vows are irrevocable and personal ownership of property and such are prohibited under canon law.

Education

Protestant ministers should have completed a college or university course plus a three-year graduate program in a recognized religious seminary. For the rural calling, supervised field work in rural communities (provided by some seminaries) or summer courses at an agricultural college or a rural internship (provided through some seminaries or denominational boards of home missions) is valuable.

As previously emphasized, personal counseling remains one of the prime responsibilities of the minister, whether in a local church, in mission work, engaged as a chaplain, or heading up a program at church headquarters. Seminary study of counseling and college and university work in the social sciences are useful. Following completion of seminary study, the effective counselor must continue to be conversant with the latest authoritative literature on the subject and will benefit by taking advantage of such related courses as may be available to the clergy, often at nearby hospitals and medical schools.

The institutional chaplain should have the same education qualifications as the minister in the local church, plus pastoral experience. In addition, a year of clinical pastoral training, obtained by assisting an accredited full-time chaplain, is desirable.

Aspiring deacons and deaconesses should be imbued with the desire to share their faith and to minister to the needs of others. Good health, love of people, emotional stability, and adaptability are important attributes. A bachelor's degree from an accredited college plus specialized training in religious education are basic educational requirements. For teaching, a certificate from a state department of education is also required. For nursing, certification as a registered nurse is the second requirement. Those engaged by a Lutheran body or by the Protestant Episcopal church must expect to wear special garb.

Those interested in church business administration must be endowed with tact and persuasiveness; they must be prepared for much extra duty as so many church activities are in the evening and over weekends. Training may include a bachelor's degree or equivalent experience in business administration and a knowledge of church customs, practices, and activities.

Priests may serve in a wide variety of ministries ranging from counseling full-time and working in social services to being chaplains in the armed forces, prisons, or hospitals.

The religious priest is a college graduate who has completed a three-year program in theology beyond the undergraduate degree. After serving a year or two in a deacon internship program, he may be assigned to a parish or to work as a chaplain in an institution or on a campus, as a teacher in a school, college, or seminary, on the editorial staff of a church periodical, or in any of a number of jobs.

The secular priest today is a college graduate who has successfully completed a course in a Roman Catholic diocesan or archdiocesan seminary and has been ordained. He normally can expect to become the pastor of a parish. Although he may later be transferred to the chancery, appointed to teach in a seminary, assigned to a church publication, or even possibly made superintendent of parochial schools, the secular priest usually will stay with the same diocese or archdiocese.

Monks, nuns, sisters, and friars are trained within the community where they wish to take their vows. Training is several years in length and the structure and length of training vary between the orders.

Rabbis are college and university graduates who have completed the prescribed course of study in a Jewish seminary. Training at the graduate level is now available at various colleges throughout the United States for those wishing a career in Jewish communal service.

To work in a Jewish community center, an undergraduate degree, a master's degree in social work, and experience in administration and group work or their equivalents are usually required. Work in such organizations as the Young Men's Hebrew Association should provide excellent experience and training.

Industry outlook

The prospects for employment as a religious community leader remain stable. For the most part, the greatest opportunities are in small communities. Given the ever-changing ethnic affiliation of neighborhoods in metropolitan areas, many churches and some synagogues in large cities have not been able to maintain sufficiently large congregations to operate. However, new communities continually develop, and churches and synagogues are often built to accommodate the new populations. In addition, religious leaders are needed to manage social service organizations such as youth programs, charitable foundations, and homeless facilities.

Opportunities for Protestant ministers are relatively favorable. Graduates of theological seminaries will face less competition for positions as ministers than in the past; however,

the situation varies among Protestant sects and regions within the United States. Most of the positions available will simply be replacements for retirees.

Both the increase in the number of Catholics and the decrease in seminary enrollment has lead to many employment opportunities for Roman Catholic priests. Due to the current shortage of priests, many of the priests' nonreligious functions have been taken over by the Catholic laity.

As with Roman Catholic priests, there is also a shortage of rabbis in America. The decrease in enrollment in Jewish theological seminaries allows for many employment opportunities. While it is still difficult to get positions in large metropolitan communities, rabbis may find employment in small cities, especially in the South, Midwest, and Northwest.

◇ **SOURCES OF ADDITIONAL INFORMATION**

Interested candidates should consult with religious leaders of their faith for evaluation of qualifications and guidance on formal educational preparation and opportunities.

For information concerning the work of military chaplains, contact:

National Conference on Ministry to the Armed Forces
4141 North Henderson Road, Suite 13
Arlington, VA 22203

Information on the Protestant ministry is available from:

National Council of Churches of Christ in the U.S.A.
475 Riverside Drive
New York, NY 10115

Information about the Roman Catholic priesthood and monastic orders is available from:

American Catholic Union
PO Box 1152
San Rafael, CA 94915

Practicing rabbis can advise on vocational preparation in one of the accredited seminaries and theological schools. Information is also available from:

Rabbinical Council of America
275 Seventh Avenue
New York, NY 10001

Religious Ministries

◇ **RELATED ARTICLES**

Volume 1: Business Administration; Education; Social Services
Volume 2: College and university faculty; Guidance counselors; Protestant ministers; Psychologists; Rabbis; Rehabilitation counselors; Roman Catholic priests; School administrators; Social workers; Teachers, kindergarten and elementary school; Teachers, secondary school

Retailing

General information

Retailing is the last link between the manufacturer and the consumer. The retailing field consists of supermarkets, department stores, chain stores, specialty stores, variety stores, franchise stores, mail order houses, leased departments, sidewalk vending, and door-to-door selling. Retailers buy their goods wholesale, stock them, and resell them to individual consumers in small lots. Retailers must know their customers' needs and wants, and they must also advertise and attractively display the goods that they sell.

Small stores specializing in one type of merchandise and general stores featuring many lines were the familiar methods of retailing in the days of the colonies. In addition, the itinerant peddler served customers in outlying areas by selling goods from house to house.

In the 1850s and 1860s, United States retailing grew and expanded extensively. Chain organizations such as the Great Atlantic & Pacific Tea Company were established. Firms such as Macy's and Marshall Field's grew into sizable department stores. The introduction of low postal rates gave rise to large mail order firms such as Montgomery Ward and Sears and Roebuck. F. W. Woolworth organized another familiar type of retailing, the five-and-ten-cent store, better known today as the variety store.

Following World War I, self-service was introduced in the clothing and accessories fields and in the grocery business. These self-service stores were planned so that the merchandise and the displays rather than salespeople were used to induce customers to buy. Horse-drawn streetcars and later electrified streetcars brought people to central locations in cities to do their shopping.

The movement of people to the suburbs in the 1950s and 1960s stimulated the creation of a new type of merchandising, the one-stop shopping center where all merchandise would be located in an easily accessible area with ample parking space available. Here all types of retailers joined to provide the many kinds of goods and services sought by the families who lived in surrounding communities. At the same time, some large department and specialty stores and mass merchandisers, aware that suburban customers no longer made frequent shopping trips to the city, established branch stores in the suburbs.

The first "discounters" based their appeal on low prices, and often provided limited lines of merchandise in out-of-the-way places such as abandoned textile mills or old warehouses. These firms later developed into famous mass merchandisers such as the K Marts, Korvettes, Woolco stores, and Two Guys shopping emporiums.

Another familiar form of retailing, the vending machine, initially was used to sell gum and candy. Today, it also offers coffee, hosiery, greeting cards, books, sandwiches, and a host of other products.

Door-to-door retailing, sidewalk vending, and mail and telephone order networks have increased in popularity as people's lives have become more rushed and time for shopping has become more limited.

The widespread nature of the retailing industry makes it unique among career fields. Retailing exists in every hamlet, town, and city—in downtown areas, in suburbs, and in shopping centers. No matter where you live or where you move, a retailer is nearby.

The first high-school courses in retailing were instituted in Providence, Rhode Island, in 1910. The real incentive for the expansion of retail training was provided through the passage of the George-Deen National Vocational Education Act in 1936 and by subsequent acts in 1960s and 1970s. These acts made funds available for the cooperative (work-study) education of full-time high-school students and for part-time adult students in evening classes in

Indoor shopping malls provide convenient retail outlets for both rural and urban communities. They maintain pleasant shopping environments during all seasons.

distributive education programs. Hundreds of thousands of young people and adults in the years since 1936 have been introduced to retailing occupations through these high-school and post–high-school distributive education programs. DECA, the national Distributive Education Clubs of America, is the foremost organization that supports and encourages education for distributive occupations throughout the country. Both high-school and two-year college students are eligible to belong to this organization.

Collegiate education for retailing was organized initially to train teachers of retailing. By 1915, the Prince School of Salesmanship, which was affiliated with Simmons College in Boston, was established. Retailing was then incorporated into the curricula of the Carnegie Institute of Technology in 1918 and of New York University in 1919. Today, hundreds of junior and community colleges, as well as four-year colleges include retailing as part of their business and/or home economics curricula. The American Collegiate Retailing Association lists many of the four-year colleges that offer several retailing programs.

The structure of the retailing industry

Although shopping in a retail store, from a catalog, or from a door-to-door vendor is a familiar activity for everybody, actual work in a retail organization is a mystery to most people. Without prior study, you would be unlikely to know about the different kinds of retail firms or the variety of work done by retailers. The average person's contacts with retailing have been with those staff members who handle the merchandise or the money.

The retailing field is challenging because it is a business of constant change due to innumerable trends. Change exists in the kinds and styles of goods carried, in the living habits of consumers, and in the resulting demands made by those customers. In addition, competitors who sell similar goods and services are constantly seeking new and different products, modifying prices, and improving the layout and arrangement of their stores. This competition makes each retailer race to get the merchandise first, to offer the best service, and to provide the most attractive setting so that customers will be lured into that particular establishment.

Retailing is a fast-paced business that requires the retailer to anticipate the customer's wishes days, weeks, and sometimes even months before the customer is aware that goods will be needed or wanted. Alert retailers make sure that they have those goods in stock when the customers do make their decision to buy.

To serve American consumers with the most efficient and effective distribution system in the world, a variety of retailing organizations exist. These may be classified as store and other establishments. Stores, in turn, are subdivided into two major groupings: specialty stores and general merchandise stores. Retailing in settings other than stores is divided into mail order houses, sidewalk selling, door-to-door selling, and vending machine retailing.

Specialty stores carry just one category of merchandise or several types of closely related merchandise. Specialty stores include apparel shops, building supply stores, automobile dealers, gasoline service stations, household appliance and radio and TV stores, tobacco shops, florists, optical goods stores, news dealers, drugstores, shoe stores, bicycle shops, and videocassette rental and small computer and software sales outlets. Supermarkets are expanded food stores. They specialize in offering, through self-service, foods and household products for the convenience of their customers.

General merchandise stores include variety stores, junior department stores, and department stores. General merchandise stores stock a multitude of different items under one roof. Variety stores carry these broad assortments of goods at limited prices. Junior department stores carry various categories of merchandise in somewhat broader price ranges. Department stores carry large assortments of apparel, home goods, and staple items in fairly extensive price ranges.

When specialty stores or general merchandise stores feature self-service and bargain prices, they are usually called mass merchandisers.

Any of these stores may be single unit or multi-unit, with the latter having as few as two stores in the group or as many as several thousand. Chain organizations are multi-unit operations, as are parent stores with branches. Franchisers are firms that may operate or sell their merchandise to special owners within large stores, or they may franchise entire inventories of merchandise or food to persons who invest in their lines.

Although the main business of retailing is to buy and to sell goods and services, the many types and sizes of firms and their diversified

A purchaser in the linens department of a store orders more towels. It is his responsibility to maintain ample stock of each item.

activities require people with varied abilities, backgrounds, and education.

To attain the needed volume of business to serve millions of shoppers, the people engaged in retailing must anticipate the wants and needs of their customers. To do this, retailers search the marketplace for the goods that will meet those requirements. They bring the goods to their firms in the desired quantities at the times the customers will be seeking them. Retailers then price the goods to cover the costs of the products as well as the costs of transporting, housing, and distributing them. Retailers display and advertise the products so customers are aware of them. Retailers sell products in person or by phone or mail, provide for payment by cash or charge, and offer wrapping and delivery service if needed. To accomplish these various tasks requires a veritable army of retailing workers. Millions of sales clerks work in American retailing, along with great numbers of stock clerks, clerical and accounting personnel, and route delivery drivers. With sales figures in the hundreds of billions each year, retailing is a crucial segment of the American economy.

Even though retailing is a diversified field, all retailers must perform certain functions. The main differences between the activities of large and small organizations depend on the numbers of people available to perform each task and the resulting degree of specialization each person can bring to the job.

The major functions of retailing may be divided into five categories: merchandising and

Some urban malls have been designed as restoration projects to revitalize run-down areas. Such projects have been successful in Milwaukee and Boston.

these records are examined and the amount of such merchandise already in the store is determined, the executive decides on the amount of new merchandise to be purchased. The person who does this kind of planning and supervising in a large organization is called a merchandiser.

After the general buying plan has been established, the buyer must go to the manufacturer's showrooms or to the factories in the United States or abroad to look at the merchandise and select from the available items that will be in demand for the coming season. Contracts are then signed for the delivery of the goods. Buying may be completed as much as six months before the buyer anticipates selling the goods in the store.

Store managers of chain stores and department managers in branch stores have a job that combines responsibility for merchandise and for department or store operation. The department manager acts as a departmental supervisor for the buyer in the branch store, but does not have the responsibility for actual selection and purchase of merchandise.

In a small store, usually one store manager has the final responsibility for all operational activities. In a larger organization, each function may be supervised by a separate manager. Managers may be in charge of receiving goods, marking them, placing them in the stockrooms or warehouse, and subsequently moving the goods to the selling floor. After the merchandise is sold, other managers may be in charge of wrapping stations and of delivery services. Supervision of the selling floor and handling of customer returns and complaints are also activities carried on by operating personnel. Elevator service, housekeeping service, and the relocation of goods for special selling seasons are further responsibilities of operating personnel.

Many large retailing organizations maintain sales promotion, advertising, and display staffs. The people who work in these fields are responsible for the overall impression that the store creates in the community it serves. A favorable image generates more business for the retailer. Those who produce the advertising include the advertising manager, copywriters, artists, photographers, and typographers.

Creative talents are needed for most of the positions in marketing. Therefore, those who apply for these jobs usually have excelled in writing or in artwork, or they have had experience in staging shows or running school publicity events.

In small stores, most owners or managers employ part-time accountants to take care of the financial records of the firm. The finances of a large store or chain of stores are usually administered by a controller who has an account-

buying; store operations; sales promotion; bookkeeping/accounting; and personnel. Merchandising and buying determines the assortment and amount of merchandise to be sold. Store operations maintains the retailer's building and provides for the movement of goods and people within the building. Sales promotion and advertising inform customers and potential customers about the goods and services that are available. Bookkeeping and accounting workers are charged with the task of keeping records of money spent and received, and records of payrolls, taxes, and money due from customers. Personnel staffs the store with people who are qualified and trained to handle the work that needs to done.

Many people are involved in buying merchandise in large organizations, whereas in small stores one or two persons may do all the buying. Before merchandise can be purchased, however, store executives must plan for the kinds and amounts of merchandise to be bought. Analyses of previous sales reveal how successful the store was in selling similar merchandise during a comparable period. After ing background and knowledge of computer systems.

Large numbers of mass merchandisers and supermarkets need cashier-wrappers. Young men and women find employment opportunities as cashier-wrappers in stores that may or may not also employ salespeople.

Careers

Retailing abounds around all of us, but young people who are planning their future occupations often overlook it as a career choice unless they have had some experience in the field. Once they become acquainted with retailing, they may come to recognize it as a career choice that combines fascination, variety, and change.

Retailing merits serious consideration as a career field for both men and women. Both have opportunities at every level of retailing, from stockwork to supervision. Retailing has a place for men and women in managing, planning, buying, selling, promoting, computerized record keeping, employing, and training. A sampling of career opportunities follows below.

Store managers: The store manager has responsibility for seeing that merchandise in the correct amounts is available at all times for the customers of the store. Store managers also supervise salespeople and other workers as they do their work.

Department managers: The department manager is responsible for having the goods on the selling floor, for counting the merchandise on hand, and for reordering merchandise from the main store.

Distributors: Distributors gather information from company stores regarding merchandise needs. They then allocate the merchandise to the individual stores. Thus, the job of the distributor combines record keeping, stock keeping, and decision making. Distributors work in the main store, the central buying office, or the warehouse of the firm.

Home furnishing coordinators: Home furnishings coordinators assist buyers of furniture and accessories to stock merchandise that will be harmonious when assembled in the home of the customer.

Advertising managers: Advertising managers oversee the production of promotional material designed to bring customers into the store.

Special-feature publicists: Special-feature publicists plan special events such as fashion shows, parades, special exhibits, and television and radio shows sponsored by a retail outlet.

Window display managers: Window display managers develop merchandise displays to attract people into a store.

Education

Although education beyond high school is not required for some of the beginning jobs in retailing, those people who progress through the ranks into managerial or executive positions find that a college background is important. Increasing numbers of retailing executives hold college degrees. Because of the diversity of work available in retailing organizations, graduates of all types of programs may find positions. Backgrounds in liberal arts, business administration, engineering, law, education, and other fields are useful in the retailing business.

For young men and women who have had education beyond high school and who are interested in being employed full-time by a retailing organization, an avenue for beginning a retailing career is the training squad. Training squads provide on-the-job training in all aspects of retail operations. Larger department and specialty stores, chain stores, mass merchandisers, and supermarkets provide this type of learning opportunity for those who have graduated from two-year and four-year colleges.

People selected to be on training squads are carefully chosen because they will be given opportunities to become junior executives following their training period. The length of training varies, and on-the-job experience is usually accompanied by classroom lectures and assignments. Constant evaluation of the trainees enable the executives to decide where the aspirants would be most valuable after completing the training course.

In addition to those selected from graduating classes, occasionally outstanding people from the firm's own sales force or the stockroom staff are invited to join the training squad.

To become a merchandiser or buyer usually requires several years of apprenticeship training. A buyer should have an appreciation for merchandise, be a skilled observer, and have good taste. He or she should acquire technical information about the products to be purchased and should have good mathematical skills. Although a college education is not required for such a position, many buyers have graduated from college or have completed some college studies in addition to gaining several years of experience in various positions in retail stores.

The young people who are sincerely interested in opening their own retail business are

Fashion models work on demanding and often sporadic schedules. Much of their work depends on the season.

Knowledgeable management is a requirement for success today.

With a maturing population, the influx of persons from other cultures, the mobility of the populace, the increased standard of living of the American people, and the growth in the number of media outlets, retailers face a constant challenge to serve the public more efficiently and more effectively.

Because retailing is still primarily a business of people working with and serving other people, the application of computerized systems for record keeping, mechanization for handling merchandise, and automatic vending machines has displaced comparatively few persons.

◇ **SOURCES OF ADDITIONAL INFORMATION**

National Retail Merchants Association
100 West 31st Street
New York, NY 10001

International Mass Retailing Association
570 7th Avenue, Suite 900
New York, NY 10018

Institute of Store Planners
25 North Broadway
Tarrytown, NY 10591

American Collegiate Retailing Association
Marketing Department
Miami University of Ohio
Oxford, OH 45056

American Management Association
135 West 50th Street
New York, NY 10020

best prepared if, in addition to their background education, they obtain a position in a retail business and learn the rudiments from someone who has been successful. Hard work, study, constant analysis and evaluation, and sufficient capital may then assure the success of the new business venture.

Industry outlook

Retailing throughout the years of America's growth has been a field in which young entrepreneurs with courage, hard work, and a small amount of money could open a business that would grow as the population of any given area expanded. Although opportunities are still present, retailing in today's economy demands both knowledge and management ability if the owners are to achieve success. More competition, better educated customers, and more diversified types of retailing allow for fewer errors on the part of small firm owners.

◇ **RELATED ARTICLES**

Volume 1: Advertising; Apparel; Foreign Trade; Franchising; Wholesaling
Volume 2: Buyers, wholesale and retail; Management trainees; Retail business owners; Retail managers
Volume 3: Bookkeeping and accounting clerks; Cashiers; Counter and retail clerks; Display workers; Door-to-door sales workers; Models; Retail sales workers; Stock clerks

Rubber

General information

Natural rubber is a pliable, stretchy material made from the milky juice of various tropical plants. Synthetic rubber, made of chemicals, was developed as a substitute for natural rubber. The material is called "rubber" because one of the most practical uses of the gum, it appeared, would be to rub out, or erase, pencil marks. Hence, the name rubber.

Rubber, whether natural or synthetic, is an essential raw material. No other material is as good for holding air, keeping out moisture, resisting electricity, and stretching. Much synthetic rubber is used today, owing to the greater variety of uses to which it can be applied and the different ways it can be altered for use. More than half of all the rubber produced is used for tires and tubes for automobiles, trucks, and other vehicles; it is also used in making rainwear, shoes, rubber gloves or syringes for medical use, large storage containers, floor coverings, balls for sports, insulating materials, and many other products.

Christopher Columbus, while on one of his voyages to the New World in the 1490s, observed natives in Haiti playing with a ball that bounced. It was made from a sticky substance drained from a certain tree through a cut in the bark. Later explorers observed American Indians using the substance to make footwear by applying the substance to earthen molds and allowing the molds to dry.

For a long period of time, people tried to use the milky substance to waterproof their clothing. It worked in the rain but melted in the sun. This problem plagued the would-be users of this promising material for centuries.

In 1839, however, Charles Goodyear, an American who had become obsessed with finding a way to make rubber useful in all seasons, discovered the process known as vulcanization. He dropped a glob of rubber mixed with sulfur on a hot stove. When the mixture cooled, it remained pliable in the cold and did not become sticky when exposed to heat.

Goodyear's discovery was the beginning of the rubber industry because it made rubber practical for countless uses. Rubber manufacturing plants were established in New England and later in other parts of the country.

Rubber moved to the Midwest in the 1870s. This was the hub of the carriage-making industry to which the rubber industry supplied solid, and eventually pneumatic (air-filled), tires. Many of the carriage makers went into automobile manufacturing in the early part of the twentieth century, establishing the Midwest as the country's most important rubber manufacturing area, with Akron, Ohio, as its capital.

As the industry grew, manufacturing tended to become centralized in large plants at one location. During the 1930s, however, the trend toward decentralization began. Los Angeles was established as a center on the West Coast, and later, many factories were opened in southern and other midwestern states.

Meanwhile, export trade expanded. But tariff barriers and import quotas imposed by foreign countries, as well as monetary exchange problems led to the development of U.S.–owned rubber factories in foreign countries. The result has been wide U.S. ownership, either wholly or partially, or rubber factories throughout the world.

The larger companies in the rubber industry are multinational organizations that manufacture and sell their products around the world.

The structure of the rubber industry

Natural rubber usually is grown on plantations in hot, moist climates. Most of the world's natural rubber is grown in the Far East, primarily Indonesia and Malaysia. Although natural rub-

A worker in a tire plant prepares an airplane tire for inspection prior to vulcanization. Due to their multiple plies, airplane tires are considerably heavier than automobile tires.

Synthetic rubber can be produced in a variety of ways, depending on its final use. For example, styrene-butadiene synthetic rubber is made from mixing a gas (butadiene) and a liquid (styrene). These chemicals are combined in specific proportions in a big tank containing soap and water. The ingredients are heated or cooled and then mixed until the chemicals form a milky-white fluid called latex. The latex is thickened to form rubber.

Rubber manufacturers obtain dry rubber from plantations or from synthetic-rubber manufacturers. Rubber goods are formed from the dry rubber or sometimes from latex, which is shipped to the manufacturing plant in tank cars. Different rubber products are produced through different manufacturing processes, but generally all rubber is heated, shaped, and finished. Most of this work is done by machine.

The first step in rubber goods production is breaking up and mixing the crude rubber. Rubber cutters cut bales of crude rubber into pieces, moving levers on a large hydraulic cutter. Rubber-mill tenders then mix, blend, knead, or refine the crude rubber by running it through a mill with corrugated rolls that break it apart and soften it. Plasticator machines also grind and soften rubber, making it easier to mold. The rubber is then mixed with chemicals to keep it from spoiling in light, heat, or air.

The rubber then goes through a series of steps designed to blend and shape it into its final form. These steps include: compounding, shaping, and vulcanization.

Once the rubber is produced, manufacturers must find markets for the finished product. Career opportunities in sales and marketing throughout the rubber industry are among the most diversified anywhere. The industry offers careers in retailing, industrial products, chemicals, packaging and sheeting films, and foam products materials.

For the various companies within the industry to maintain a strong market position, each must obtain its share of the available business in all markets. Since markets are constantly changing, a company's distribution network must adapt to keep pace. To improve position, it must expand faster than the market. This means constant expansion of the various retail outlets that sell rubber products to the consumer.

For the replacement tire market, the industry distributes its product mainly through independently owned dealerships and company-owned retail stores. These retail organizations provide training for many people in the industry, including those who ultimately may sell to manufacturers of original equipment, such as Detroit's major automobile makers.

ber still accounts for some of the rubber used today, synthetic rubber is used more widely. Synthetic rubber can be produced at a cost that makes it competitive with natural rubber and it has more applications. For example, synthetic rubber has superior air retention, an important consideration in the manufacturing of tires and many other rubber products. The United States is one of the leading producers of synthetic rubber.

Natural rubber comes from latex, the milky white substance of a number of plants, including the rubber tree. Workers collect the latex by cutting a narrow groove in the bark of the tree and catching the latex in a cup as it flows out of the tree. Trees of rubber plantations may be tapped every day for about two weeks and then allowed to rest, or the trees may be tapped every other day. Since natural latex is only about one-third rubber (the other two-thirds being mostly water, with some resin and protein as well), plantations make crude rubber through a coagulation process that separates the rubber from the other components of latex.

The sale of tires accounts for roughly two-thirds of the industry's sales volume. The other one-third of sales is derived from the general product areas, such as industrial products, chemicals, flooring, and metal products.

Manufacturers' sales representatives are concerned with the sale of raw materials and finished products to business and industrial firms in the United States and foreign countries. Typical examples are the sale of tires to car manufacturers, chemicals to paint companies, and rubber piping to the oil industry.

Careers

Because of its size and diversification, the rubber industry offers a wide range of employment opportunities for a variety of skills, talents, and interests. Careers are available in manufacturing, finance, administration, research and development, sales, and various other support functions. A sampling of career options follows below.

Rubber goods production workers: Rubber goods production workers use machines to heat rubber and form it into thousands of different products, such as balloons and rubber gloves.

Tire development engineers: Tire development engineers design tire structures, molds, test fixtures, and equipment. They engineer fabric-rubber components that must handle stresses ranging from lightly loaded motorcycle tires to giant earthmover tires.

Calendar operators: Calendar operators run machines that rolls rubber into sheets of specific lengths. The calendar machine cuts the rubber sheets into various sizes and patterns, or stocks the sheets in layers to make products such as flooring and bed sheets.

Calendar-let-off operators: Calendar-let-off operators run machines to cure and dry coated rubber fabrics.

Rubber-cutting-machine tenders: Rubber-cutting-machine tenders use a guillotine or other sharp object to cut rubber slabs.

Sponge-press operators: Sponge-press operators run machines that roll and cure sponge rubber into sheeting for automobile gaskets, insulation, and carpet padding.

Injection-molding machine tenders: Injection-molding machine tenders operate a machine that injects hot rubber into a mold and ejects a molded product.

Machine cutters: Machine cutters operate machines that cut rubber. They then verify the size of the rubber goods, using rulers, calipers, and other measuring instruments.

An inspector tests a newly manufactured rubber belt. The belt will be used in large photocopying machines.

Tuber-machine operators: Tuber-machine operators set up and run tube machines, which shape rubber products. Tube machines squeeze soft rubber through a hole. The shape of the rubber depends on the shape of the hole.

Chemists: Chemists work in the area of compounding, which includes the formulation of rubber and plastic compounds tailored for specific performance properties, such as wear, flexibility, and traction (see Volume 1: Chemistry; and Volume 2: Chemists).

Chemical engineers: Chemical engineers design new product applications, such as developing new adhesives and fiber combinations to strengthen rubber tires (see Volume 1: Engineering; and Volume 2: Engineers).

Pipe fitters: Pipe fitters construct and maintain systems that supply steam, air, gas, water, and other liquids to the rubber manufacturing plant (see Volume 3: Pipe fitters and steam fitters).

Manufacturers' sales representatives: Manufacturers' sales representatives are responsible for selling the rubber products to customers. It is their job to maintain good relations with old customers and generate new customers.

Many railroad crossing pads are made of rubber. This experimental pattern is designed for better impact resistance, shock absorption, and smooth riding.

Education

A person enters the rubber industry in essentially the same manner as in any other business. The applicant is selected on the basis of academic qualifications, work experience, and other job-related criteria. Many college-trained applicants have the opportunity to enter special training programs for exposure to the many operations of the rubber manufacturer. Through a series of job assignments, new employees can find their proper area of specialization in the organization.

The traditional on-the-job training methods, in which new employees assist other workers to learn the ropes, are becoming as obsolete as the one-room schoolhouse. Modern plants now have training centers where new employees are assessed, evaluated, and effectively trained for a given position before they ever set foot inside the plant. Today's training centers have both the facilities and skilled instructors necessary for skillfully and quickly teaching trainees in the correct step-by-step methods for carrying out each job.

The rubber industry has traditionally promoted from within, and therefore the opportunity for advancement is available to those employees with the training and experience needed.

Most positions in administration, the technical fields, and sales are open to college graduates with degrees in business administration or more generalized liberal arts subjects. In some certain administrative and sales jobs, a high-school education is sufficient if combined with a number of years of appropriate work experience.

Candidates can find a wide variety of jobs in factory employment even though they have no previous experience. Once on the job, beginners are trained to perform specific jobs. As a practical matter, not all production jobs are available to new employees because of various seniority rules.

Jobs will have learning times that vary according to the degree of skill and responsibility involved. Relatively unskilled jobs, such as a position as a rubber cutter, will usually require three weeks or less to learn, whereas more skilled jobs, such as a position operating a tuber machine, range from three weeks to a year or more.

Most craft training is available through apprentice programs, combining selective work assignments with related formal instruction. Training is provided internally by the sponsoring manufacturing plant, often in conjunction with vocational schools and other learning institutions. The current trend is to advance trainees through the program as they demonstrate a standard of job competency rather than by a predetermined time schedule.

Opportunities also exist for graduates with associate degrees in technical areas. For example, a person with an associate degree in chemical technology could work as a chemical technician under the supervision of a Ph.D. chemist in the research division. An associate degree in an engineering discipline could lead to a position working with engineers in plant design.

Educational assistance, offered by many of the rubber companies, makes it possible to continue college and obtain a four-year degree while working and learning on the job.

Non-college graduates can find positions as drafters, lab assistants, technicians, test-car drivers, and tire test operators. Tire test operators gather reliable test data so that the new tire designs can be evaluated.

A basic knowledge of retailing is required at each level of management because a substantial portion of the industry's total income comes from retail sales. Many managers acquire graduate business degrees.

Normally, after a brief training program, the sales employee will receive on-the-job experience in specific retail positions. These entry-level positions are followed by assignments in retail store management. The career path from this point through the various areas of distribution—retail, wholesale, and technical areas—depends on the individual's performance and interests.

Manufacturers' sales is a highly specialized field and considerable experience is necessary. In many instances, a technical education is an essential qualification for a job.

The growing complexity of business operations is putting a constantly growing burden on management personnel in the rubber industry. Management training is designed to keep managers abreast of constant changes in the business world while keeping them updated on more effective management techniques and principles.

Throughout the industry, most of the larger organizations have training divisions that offer complete training in each area of their business. These programs consist mainly of classroom and on-the-job training. One company developed regional centers throughout the country to implement various phases of its training programs.

Industry outlook

The rubber industry is expected to grow somewhat slowly in the coming years. It is estimated that sales of synthetic rubber, already accounting for over one billion dollars in annual sales in the United States, should grow by 1 or 2 percent a year through the mid-1990s. Demand for synthetic rubber will primarily depend on the economic success of the tire industry, because the majority of synthetic rubber in the United States is used to produce tires.

The advent of the long-wearing radial tire, combined with the increasingly expensive capital expenditures needed to stay competitive, will cause some long-established tire and rubber companies to diversify into other areas, leaving the bulk of the U.S. and world tire market to the healthiest of the American companies and to some foreign competitors. Overseas rubber manufacturers may receive a boost because the United States is increasing its use of foreign-made rubber parts.

The economic shakeout and repositioning of the rubber industry will result in product design challenges and innovative production techniques. It may include the financial restructuring of companies through mergers, divestitures, and even re-deployment of assets that will place greater emphasis on product lines other than tires.

In addition to establishing a sound financial and production base, the industry must meet the challenge of innovative development in the creation of new products for the years ahead.

The rubber industry is undergoing a wave of modernization, owing to the introduction of

A tire manufacturing inspector sorts through radial truck tires. He is searching for tires that do not meet the company's standards.

product innovations, new computer systems, and the development of new and better materials. These breakthroughs have stimulated further research and development.

◇ **SOURCES OF ADDITIONAL INFORMATION**

Rubber Manufacturers Association
1400 K Street, NW
Washington, DC 20005

International Institute of Synthetic Rubber
2077 South Gessner Road
Suite 133
Houston, TX 77063

Malaysian Rubber Bureau
1925 K Street, NW
Suite 204
Washington, DC 20006

International Tire Association
PO Box 1067
Farmington, CT 06034

National Tire Dealers and Retreaders Association
1250 I Street, NW, Suite 400
Washington, DC 20005

United Rubber, Cork, Linoleum and Plastic Workers of America
87 South High Street
Akron, OH 44308

◇ **RELATED ARTICLES**

Volume 1: Automotives; Chemicals and Drugs; Engineering; Plastics
Volume 2: Chemists; Engineers; Industrial designers
Volume 3: Machinists; Manufacturers' sales workers; Molders; Retail sales workers; Rubber goods production workers; Wholesale trade sales workers
Volume 4: Chemical technicians; Engineering technicians

Social Science

General information

The social sciences are concerned with the transmission and communication of knowledge and information about human social behavior. Many social scientists are involved in teaching and with research and investigation. Among the occupations included in the social sciences are those of anthropologists, economists, historians, political scientists, social psychologists, sociologists, social statisticians, social geographers, and social workers.

In one way or another, social scientists find themselves making observations about the behavior associated with personality, society, and culture.

Social scientists are not only concerned with the communication of existing knowledge. Like other scholars, they are forever exploring new cultures and civilizations, digging up new information about past civilizations, experimenting with novel techniques for measuring human responses, or gathering up-to-the-minute data on human opinions, attitudes, and motivations.

Although the social sciences as scientific disciplines are relatively new, the origins can be traced back to the ancient Greeks and their rationalistic investigations into the nature of human interactions and the principles of government.

Under the influence of philosophers such as Rene Descartes in the seventeenth century and John Stuart Mill, society at large began to accept the notion that the world could be understood through several fundamental principles of reality. These principles, be they economic, social, or political, could be applied to develop theories that would explain human behavior.

The development of the social sciences and their increasingly important role in society resulted from the industrial, urban, and scientific revolutions. Industrialization, urbanization, and rapid technological innovations heightened the rates of social change, transformed the nature of human communities, and accelerated the number and kinds of adjustments individuals have had to make to the world about them.

The structure of the social sciences professions

Social scientists are dedicated to a better understanding of the nature of individuals and society. But they also want to put that knowledge and understanding to work for the benefit of humanity. Thus they not only acquire and transmit knowledge but they also attempt to put it to practical use. They seek to solve complex personal and social problems by applying social science knowledge to concrete situations.

The social sciences are usually divided into several broad disciplines, each of which views human social behavior from a different angle. The commonly recognized fields are anthropology, the science of humankind and its many cultures; economics, which studies human behavior in obtaining goods and services; history, the study of people and society through time; political science, the study of government; social psychology, the study of human individuals in all their social relationships; sociology, the science of society and social institutions and groups; and social statistics, the science of quantitative method applied to social phenomena.

Perhaps the largest number of social scientists teach in schools and colleges and universities. However, government organizations, museums and other cultural organizations, international organizations, hospitals, clinics and other health units, and research and statistical institutes also employ considerable numbers of

Three sociologists discuss the disparity between American and Japanese cultures. Through understanding and respect for foreign cultures, many international problems can be avoided.

social scientists. A small but increasingly significant group of social scientists are self-employed, for example, clinical psychologists and sociologists.

The interdisciplinary sciences, or the borderline sciences that are considered integral parts of biological and physical sciences, but have significant social science orientations, include demography, the science of population; physical anthropology, the science of the races of humans and their physical characteristics; and social geography, the science of humankind's relation to the environment.

Many subdivisions and specialties exist within the main branches of the social sciences. A sociologist may be a criminologist or a family specialist, for example, and an economist may be a banking and finance expert or a specialist in consumer behavior. There is also considerable overlapping among the social sciences disciplines, as, for example, in the field of economic history or economic geography, as well as important overlapping between the social sciences and natural sciences.

The activities of social scientists can be classified under four main headings: teaching and training; research and investigation; social service and assistance; and administration and management.

The social sciences, as scientific disciplines, are concerned with the transmission and communication of knowledge and information about human behavior. Therefore, a very large number, if not a majority, of social scientists are

engaged in teaching and training occupations. They teach in all levels of educational institutions and in governmental and business organizations. Some become social studies teachers in elementary schools, teaching the basic facts about the social world in which we live. Others teach more specialized disciplines at the high-school level, such as economics, history, anthropology, psychology, government, and sociology. A third group become teaching specialists in institutions of higher learning and assume positions as professors and instructors in community and junior colleges and colleges and universities.

But social scientists do not confine their teaching to schools and colleges. Many teach in governmental organizations, such as the various schools and institutes of the military establishment and the foreign training institutes of the Department of State. Many work as consultants for state and local governments. Others work in museums and other cultural institutions. Anthropologists, for example, train foreign service officers in the culture and language of the areas to which they may be assigned. Management specialists give in-service training to young administrators in public, private, and nonprofit sectors.

In addition to teaching, social scientists also conduct both basic and applied research. Basic research involves the pursuit of knowledge to satisfy the fundamental desire to know and understand the world around us. Applied research addresses itself to the solution of a practical problem. Professors at the college and university level frequently combine their teaching duties with an active program of research. A professor of history may teach courses in American history, for example, and, at the same time, collect manuscripts and other materials that may shed new light on the causes and consequences of the Civil War.

The results of an individual's research efforts are often reported in books and scholarly journals. They frequently give the social scientist not only the satisfaction derived from contributing new knowledge but extra income as well.

Social science research provides a fascinating variety of opportunities for investigation. Some researchers use historical methods, such as the collection and analysis of letters, manuscripts, and autobiographies. Others, especially psychologists, may conduct experiments in a laboratory. Political scientists work in scholarly institutions such as university libraries to conduct research, while others travel extensively, studying current political and social events. Anthropologists and sociologists do field work. This takes them to communities and cultures all over the globe and permits them to observe and study behavior patterns very different from their own. Anthropologists and sociologists examine cultures and peoples in Latin America, Asia, Africa, Australia, Europe, and in such out-of-the-way places as New Guinea and Samoa. They also study both traditional cultures and modern peoples closer to home. American Indians, Eskimos, and various immigrant and ethnic groups have been carefully investigated.

Statistical research is also important, especially in population and economic studies. Clinical research—research with individuals outside the laboratory—is conducted in a large number of instances, especially by psychologists and sociologists interested in physical and mental health problems, both in the community and in hospitals and clinics.

Social scientists are involved in a number of disciplines, including social work, criminology, psychology, and economics. A major area of emphasis is social work. Social work agencies deal not only with individuals and families but frequently with whole communities as well. Individual case workers, community organization specialists, psychiatric social workers, social workers in hospitals and clinics, and group workers assist people through the use of discussion groups, recreational activities, and other joint actions.

Social scientists have specialized understanding of how people behave in groups and how organizations and institutions are created to achieve collective goals. It is not surprising, therefore, that social scientists are frequently found in administrative and managerial positions. College and university presidents and deans are often trained social scientists. Psychologists are executive officers in hospitals, clinics, research laboratories, and business organizations. The administrative heads of welfare agencies and social security organizations are frequently individuals with training and experience in these fields. Many of the chief administrative officers of major foundations are social scientists. Administrative and managerial skills are often developed as a direct result of study and experience in the social sciences.

Careers

The social sciences offer a wide range of career choices. A sampling of career opportunities follows below.

Social workers: Social workers attempt to help people overcome personal and social difficulties. They are particularly concerned with

Many sociologists are employed by universities, where they are required to teach classes and conduct extensive research in the area of their expertise.

the poor and incapacitated. Other areas of concern involve delinquents and criminals.

Political scientists: Political scientists study the ways that the political process impacts on individuals and society. They serve as managers, organization specialists, budget analysts, fiscal officers, planners of urban, regional, and state affairs, civil service directors, management experts, researchers, policy specialists, advocates in government institutions, community organizers, and in many related important capacities.

At all levels of government, from the unincorporated village to the most complex international organization, the skills and knowledge of political scientists are in demand. Growing international communications requires specialists who can advise governments, attend to the public's business, organize a civil service, maintain a well-trained foreign service corps, and contribute constructively toward the universal aims of peace, goodwill, and cooperation.

Psychologists: Psychologists study human behavior. They are in great demand to make proper assessments of an individual's capacities, aspirations, motivations, aptitudes, and attitudes. Psychologists are frequently called on to make personality evaluations and to give guidance and counseling to individuals and families. They use a battery of technical instruments such as tests, interviews, rating scales, inventories, personal histories, and direct observation. Many psychologists find employment in school systems. Others serve in the

A psychologist examines the social patterns of handicapped children and the tendency for these children to cling to adults.

personnel departments of industrial and commercial establishments.

Economists: Economists investigate the way society distributes its finite resources. They are employed by business and industry and by governmental agencies to determine what is sound fiscal policy, how the economy can be developed and strengthened, and how unemployment and poverty can be reduced. In a variety of capacities, economists may be called on to apply expert knowledge about economic institutions and behavior, national income, and business trends. They also serve as statistical specialists, gathering and analyzing huge volumes of data. Some are particularly concerned with the problems of housing, transportation, taxation, and marketing; others may concentrate on the problems of agriculture.

Criminologists: Criminologists study the nature of various types of deviant behavior.

Probation and parole officers: Probation and parole officers help courts and judges to determine the best courses of action for the proper rehabilitation of prisoners.

Penologists: Penologists examine prisons and try to work out the most humane and beneficial methods of incarceration.

Anthropologists: Anthropologists study the language, way of life, and physical characteristics of different peoples. They provide practical assistance, especially in matters relating to the impact of new technologies on existing cultural practices and to the problem of how new ideas and other innovations can be effectively intro-

duced without destroying the basic values of a people.

Historians: Historians research and analyze the past. Many industrial and commercial organizations call on historians to provide insights into the past practices of their industry as a means of understanding the present and assessing the future. Historians also examine the history of modern countries to determine what guidelines might be furnished for the new developing nations.

Education

Many social science teachers at the elementary school level can obtain positions with a bachelor's degree from a four-year college. A master's degree is very helpful, although not essential, at the high-school or junior college level. A doctor's degree is normally expected of those preparing to teach in a college or university.

As you plan a career in the social science field, you should think of earning at least a bachelor's degree from an accredited college or university. You should aim for a good academic record and be prepared for graduate study if you are thinking of a professional career as a scholar in any of the social science disciplines. A liberal arts degree with an undergraduate major in one of the social sciences will give adequate background for some careers in business, social work, government service, journalism, and other areas in which human relations are especially significant. Advanced graduate study is necessary for research and higher levels of teaching. A Ph.D. degree is a minimum requirement for most positions in colleges and universities and is important for many top-level nonacademic posts. In some nonacademic areas, practical experience may be deemed to be the equivalent of additional formal education.

Those in research should also have at least a undergraduate degree in their area of specialization. Many researchers have master's or doctorate degrees.

Industry outlook

As long as we live in a changing world—and change is the key phenomenon of the modern age—there will be social problems requiring solutions. Applied social scientists are fortunately available to offer their knowledge, professional skills, and technical assistance in helping solve complex problems. In the decades ahead, there will be demands for their services in such areas as welfare, security, health, economic well-being, political organization, international relations, mass communications, urban planning, intergroup relations, and related fields.

Our survival as a species is now dependent on our ability to solve the numerous problems of peace, economic well-being, diminishing natural resources, and intergroup relations that developments over the past several decades have created for us. The social sciences are an expression of the fundamental idea that rational knowledge about human social behavior and a fuller understanding of humans and their society can contribute significantly to the solution of these problems.

Employment of social scientists is expected to grow about as fast as all other occupations through 1995. In anthropology, history, political science, and sociology, graduates may face strong competition for teaching openings that do occur. Openings would arise chiefly because social scientists retire or leave the profession for other reasons, though there is evidence suggesting that the field of teaching is expanding.

The number of social scientists in some disciplines, such as anthropology, is relatively small. In such disciplines as anthropology and sociology, little if any growth is predicted in the academic sector during the 1990s. Efforts are under way to acquaint new graduates with career opportunities in applied areas such as program administration and evaluation research. Such positions are available in federal, state, and local government agencies, research organizations and consulting firms, hospitals and other health agencies, labor organizations, trade associations, nonprofit organizations, and business firms.

A social science career will not necessarily make you rich, but you can depend on earning a comfortable living. Numerous benefits include long vacations and sabbatical leaves for those in schools and colleges and universities. There is also the personal satisfaction of knowing that you are contributing to a better understanding of human social behavior and helping find a solution to the vexing problems of social life.

A psychologist conducts a group therapy session where people are invited to discuss their problems and offer advice.

◇ SOURCES OF ADDITIONAL INFORMATION

Consortium of Social Science Associations
1625 I Street, NW, Suite 911
Washington, DC 20006

American Anthropological Association
1703 New Hampshire Avenue NW
Washington, DC 20009

Society for American Archaeology
808 17th Street, NW
Suite 2000
Washington, DC 20006

American Psychological Association
Educational Affairs Office
1200 17th Street, NW
Washington, DC 20036

American Sociological Association
1722 N Street, NW
Washington, DC 20036

American Society of Criminology
1314 Kinnear Road
Suite 212
Columbus, OH 43212

American Historical Association
400 A Street, SE
Washington, DC 20003

American Political Science Association
1527 New Hampshire Avenue, NW
Washington, DC 20036

American Economic Association
1313 21st Avenue, South
Nashville, TN 37212

National Council for the Social Studies
3501 Newark Street, NW
Washington, DC 20016

Social Science

Social Services

General information

Social welfare, taking care of the less fortunate or the less capable in society, has been part of the general structure of society since the beginning. The methods, however, of handling these people have changed dramatically in the last century.

The ancient civilizations believed that people with mental disorders were being punished by the gods. The mentally ill were banished from society or punished. Class structures that included slavery incorporated paupers into slave or indentured servant status. Other problems of support fell upon the family to fulfill or solve.

Hippocrates is credited with recognizing natural causes for illness, including mental illness, and attempting to treat the illness with medication and rest. The Greeks and Romans treated the mentally ill as they did the physically ill, by diagnosis and curative treatment.

The rise in the belief in witchcraft during the twelfth to eighteenth centuries put the general population back in the position of regarding mental illness as punishment from the gods or possession by demons. Physical deformities and handicaps and mental handicaps brought upon the sufferer a life of begging and vagrancy. Hospitals for the socially outcast were crude and treatment was often cruel. Although there were hospitals and facilities through the centuries where treatment was humane, the majority were inhumane in their handling of patients and prisoners.

For the poor or financially unstable people whose families were not available or capable of providing assistance, there was little in the way of public aid. The monasteries and churches provided alms. Almoners, distributors of alms to the poor, were common by the thirteenth century. Sponsored by the churches and the royal courts, alms were charitable donations of money, food, and clothing to the needy.

Poor laws were established in England to handle the needs of the poor, aged, and ill. Established in 1597, the poor laws developed parish workhouses for paupers, and care services for the ill. Foundling homes are believed to have existed for the housing of orphans by 1552. Run by families or private institutions, they served to house orphaned and abandoned children. Children were apprenticed to jobs when they were old enough to work—seven, eight, or nine years old. They were also given to the lowest bidder for service in the home, and the bidder was paid by the local government for housing the child.

Conditions for the poor were extremely difficult. Some early efforts to remedy this and assist the poor included the Speenhamland system of financial assistance. Enacted in 1795 in England, the system provided wage enhancement to workers whose wages were determined to be below minimum living standards. Although intended to bolster every worker to a minimum income level, the Speenhamland system was abused. Employers, knowing that the government would provide the extra wages, would lower wages of their employees. They could also charge more for rents because the government would provide the money for the increases. Such deception made life harder for the underprivileged.

The public support for government relief programs was rapidly turning against the poor in England. In 1834, sweeping reforms to the poor laws were made. The reforms used the Victorian work ethic to decrease tolerance of and assistance to the poor. Armed with the belief that poverty was a moral failing, the laws decreed that no aid would be provided to those living in their own homes. The only assistance was to be issued through the workhouses. This system was meant to make the receiving of public aid as punitive and degrading as possible, in order to combat laziness, according to the philosophy of the day.

A social worker advises an underprivileged woman on potential career paths and places of employment.

Toward the end of the 1800s, the initial changes in social welfare philosophy began to take hold. The Charity Organization Society in the United States, and similar charitable organizations in Europe, took up donations to assist the needy that were determined by the societies to be deserving. By labeling categories of people as "deserving needy," and "undeserving," the charities were able to circumvent the stigma attached to public assistance. Help for the aged, the physically ill, and the mentally ill was the first to be established.

Two basic elements of social services were developing in the 1880s. The first, welfare services, provided assistance to the poor, ill, and emotionally disturbed. Social services, the second element, provided training, education, health care assistance, and other counseling services. Social services were to assist neighborhoods and the general population. Welfare groups were to help vulnerable groups.

One form of social service that developed before the turn of the century was the neighborhood education and training center. Settlement houses began with Toynbee Hall, in London. Founded by Samuel A. Barnett in 1884, the Hall served as the residence to several college trained workers who developed adult education classes, counseling, and general assistance programs for the families in the deprived neighborhood.

In 1887 or 1888, Jane Addams visited Toynbee Hall. Impressed with what she saw, Addams returned to her native Chicago and established Hull House, a settlement home in an immigrant neighborhood. With Ellen Starr, Addams designed Hull House in 1889 to assist neighborhood residents to improve their status in life. Initially run as a kindergarten, Hull House expanded into day care. With a large immigrant population in Chicago, Addams eventually included English language training, civics courses, and practical manual skills such as sewing and carpentry to provide the population with the skills needed for the workplace.

Social agencies began to spring up to serve the needs of the population. Relief agencies were abundant after World War I and II. Mental hospitals, orphanages (and eventually foster parent programs and adoption offices), and public aid offices were improved. By the end of World War II public aid was incorporated into many western government programs. Social security was established in the United States in 1935.

In 1990, federal, state, and local governments spent more than $800 billion on social welfare programs in areas such as public aid, food stamps, medical insurance and assistance, and housing. Housing assistance, through such programs as low income housing rent and housing costs subsidies, makes up less than 2 percent of the welfare budget. Social security, employee disability, workers compensation, and other social insurance programs receive more than half of the welfare budget.

Most people involved in social services are employed by state and local governments, or by private and volunteer organizations designed to assist the underprivileged and needy.

The structure of the social services professions

Social services can be categorized into four areas: preventive services; supportive services; remedial services; and emergency services. Many of the careers are present in each of the service branches; it is the objective of the branches that differs. Many of the programs overlap to work on and solve the same problems.

Preventive services is one of the newest concepts in social work. Social programs usually originated to alleviate a problem once it was determined to exist. Preventive services is designed to foresee problems, their causes and roots, and take action before the problem reaches crisis level. Well-baby programs are an example of preventive service. After studying the health of expectant mothers in poverty ridden areas, the social services specialists realized that inadequate health care was leading to lower birth weights and survival rates among the infants. It was determined that ignorance of prenatal care may lead mothers-to-be to engage in behavior that is harmful to their infants. Counselors were then provided to give information, assist in physical examinations, provide nutritional information and, in some cases, give baby formula and food.

Preventive programs are designed to combat drug use, alcohol abuse, child abuse, and other problems that can be prevented through education, counseling, and assistance.

Some of the newer programs center around prevention of homelessness for families on public aid. One of the programs established on a municipal level provides budget training, financial planning for previous debts, and rent repayment plans for families at risk of eviction.

Supportive programs are designed to help those currently in need. The obstacles may be financial, medical, or personal. Some types of support programs are familiar to everyone. Hotlines to assist abused children, runaways, battered wives, alcohol and drug abusers, and others exist in almost every community. The programs may be funded through government programs, either local or state, or they may be privately funded by churches, synagogues, or other community groups.

Financial programs to assist in rent, food purchase, and medical care have been established to aid families with dependent children and individuals with disabilities. Caseworkers assigned to individuals and families are responsible for providing information and services to those in need with the facilities and resources that are available to them. Federal programs include food stamps (where stamps issued by the government purchase certain food), medicaid for medical insurance, and subsidized low income housing.

Remedial care functions to remedy situations that are critical or pose acute problems for the individual. Foster care for children who have been abused or abandoned by their caretakers is one primary example of remedial care. Foster programs are designed to remove the child from harm, provide security and shelter for the child, and to establish a long range plan for the child's welfare. Support programs in the form of counseling and financial assistance may also be available, but the goal of the remedial program is to ameliorate the child's situation as quickly as possible.

Another remedial program is nursing care for the elderly and acutely ill. Nursing homes provide service to those who require considerable assistance but who may not require the continual medical care provided by hospitals.

The fourth category of social service, emergency care, is most readily associated with crises and catastrophes. The Red Cross and other

Volunteers dish out a traditional Thanksgiving meal to several hundred people in Washington, D.C.

agencies provide emergency assistance and relief to flood, hurricane, and earthquake stricken areas. Relief may be through provision of food and shelter. Once initial arrangements are made for the subsistence of the population, then redress for the losses begins. There are numerous programs nationwide that handle rebuilding of homes, shipping of medical supplies, and financing for the many things that may need to be replaced for each individual affected by the disaster.

Other emergency programs exist for war-torn areas. Famines, droughts, and other natural disasters are regularly handled by emergency relief organizations. Other types of emergency services are temporary counseling and support programs, such as group counseling for students who have sustained a tragedy like a student suicide. Medical emergency teams are employed to vaccinate against epidemics, treat wide-sweeping diseases to prevent further contamination and infection, and test for sources of illness and disease. Emergency social service is normally used to manage, on a temporary basis, the needs of a population in distress.

With that general breakdown of the types of services offered, the structure of the social services can be covered as a whole. Depending on the organization, the level of service provided and the number of people being handled by the service, each of the following elements may be operated internally by one social service or may be covered by different organizations.

To set up a program and implement it effectively usually requires a staff of policy makers. The director of any social service program can normally be assumed to be the head policy maker, unless he or she operates under a par-

A home health technician takes care of two elderly women who need assistance in daily chores.

ent program. Policy-making involves the decisions on the setup, operation, and financing of any program. In order to determine the goals and intended recipients of the program, the policy makers set forth the directives and organizational plans. The people in charge of this are normally specialists in their field, with an extensive background in program direction and implementation. They usually have considerable administrative training, and they may have done field work, although this is not necessarily required.

Once the program goals and methods are established, the next goal for almost any social service program is to obtain funding. As the federal government moves more and more into an administrative role, social services subcontractors are normally the implementors of government programs. Those subcontractors (a type of independent social work business) may be developed specifically to fit the need of the governmental program, as was in the case of early homeless programs, or the funding may go to already established organizations. Fundraisers, grant proposal writers, and grant reviewers are responsible for finding out about financial resources available in the field they work. Grant applications are used for both government and private foundations that sponsor social programs. Some grants are quite program specific, such as those only for child care, and some are broad in potential application. Most organizations will apply for many different grants and may be awarded more than one in each fiscal year.

Fundraising is also a key element to the financing of many social services programs.

Fundraising can be done through individual donations, corporate sponsorship, or fundraising events. Telethons are a familiar example of event fundraising.

Once funding is awarded and operating expenses can be met, the fund monitoring and fund implementation staff keeps track of where the money goes. In small organizations, this may be done through the fundraising departments. In large organizations, the departments may be quite separate. The government oversees much of the actual dispersal of funds, so monitoring is a key aspect to the continual survival of an organization. Because of the large quantity of money being contributed by the private sector, assuring no abuse of the finances allows confidence in the programs.

For many social services, proving the effectiveness of the program is a continual objective. Statisticians, in-house reviewers, and outside reviewers evaluate programs and methods of operations to assure the quality of the program.

The individuals who work with the recipients of the programs are the field workers. Social workers with clinical training are the most familiar of the field workers. Case workers, caretakers, psychologists, and other specialists manage different aspects of program implementation. The type of field worker is determined by the needs of the programs. These individuals are responsible for delivering the services that the program is designed to cover.

Careers

Field work positions are specifically social work oriented. Many of the other careers are not necessarily social work specific. A brief description of both types of work follows.

Social workers: Social workers can denote everyone who works with clients, but social workers here means those who have the bachelor's in social work (BSW) or the master's in social work (MSW). Social workers can specialize in clinical service, direct service, administrative service, or policy-making. Inside each of those divisions are more specialties: child welfare, chronically mentally ill patients, and adult protective services to name just a few (see Volume 2: Social workers).

Psychologists: As doctoral and master's degree graduates in psychology programs, psychologists assist mentally and emotionally disturbed patients, distressed clients, and others in need of psychological support and evaluation. Clinical psychologists work with patients (see Volume 2: Psychologists).

Human services workers and caseworkers: This group of employees covers a number of different jobs. They handle day-to-day client transactions, including assisting in paperwork, filling in applications for assistance, directing a client to counseling centers, and transporting clients to sites.

Rehabilitation counselors: Providing guidance to the physically and emotionally impaired, rehabilitation counselors train the impaired to gain or regain skills needed for self-help and vocational training.

Therapists: Various forms of therapy are used to aid clients with a variety of problems. Physical and emotional problems are worked on in a variety of programs with different methodologies. Dance therapy, art therapy, and physical therapy are a few of the varieties offered (see Volume 2: Therapists, miscellaneous).

Medical staff: Depending on the needs of the organization and the program, medical staffs may require physicians, nutritionists, practical nurses, or a number of other medically trained individuals.

Homemakers-home health aides: Assistance for the elderly, the disabled, and the ill is provided in the client's residence by homemaker-home health aides. The level of assistance is determined by the needs of the clients and the training of the aide, but can include cooking, cleaning, exercising the patient, assisting in bathing and other day-to-day needs, and all other aspects of daily care that would allow a client to remain in his or her home instead of an institution.

Child care workers: Specifically trained to work with small children, child care workers may handle infants to elementary school children who must be taken care of while a parent works.

Fundraisers: Applying for grants, soliciting contributions, and seeking other sources of revenues are the roles of the fundraisers. Essential to most social work organizations, the fundraiser combines skills as writer, researcher, and investigator to develop as large a revenue base as possible.

Services administrators: Overseeing the staff of social workers and human services workers, the services administrator will assign tasks, schedules, hire and fire personnel, and handle clerical and administrative tasks that are essential to the management of the office. This role will vary from organization to organization, with the tasks determined by the needs of the group.

Statisticians: Analyzing the effectiveness of the system, the statistician gathers the data on operations to determine if the systems being

Volunteers form a substantial portion of the work force in social service agencies. This woman offers her time to work for an emergency hot line.

used are effective and efficient. For further funding, many organizations require statistics to provide evidence to contributors that the program is effective and essential.

Education

Social workers, psychologists, and counselors have the possibility of fulfilling different degree requirements. Bachelors degrees are available in psychology and social work. This is the minimum requirement for social workers. The bachelor's degree may be sufficient for field work, but the master's is almost always the minimum requirement for supervisory and administrative positions. For psychologists, a master's or doctorate is usually required for clinical work. Clinical work education requires a supervised internship.

For social workers, the decision should be made before applying to a graduate program what the field of specialty will be. Different graduate schools specialize in different aspects of social work. Direct service and clinical work, administrative work, and policy making are distinct areas of study. One way of determining one's area of interest is to gain practical experience during college. Volunteer work, summer employment, and internships are readily available in almost all sectors of social work. Social work depends heavily on volunteer spirit, and it provides up-front opportunities to handle some of the tasks that social workers confront every day. This also allows the student to work in different subsections of social work, like child welfare and geriatric assistance.

Fundraising has no specific educational requirements. Training is usually done on the job. Experience in fundraising is available, again, through volunteer experience. Fundraising is a job that extends well beyond the field of social work. Grant writing, however, has some quite specific skills and requirements. A college degree with an emphasis on research and writing skills is a minimum obligation of students looking to work in social services fundraising.

With most of the posts in social services, the higher level of education provides more advancement opportunities. Bachelor's degrees are a minimum requirement for all but a few positions. Licensing, certification, and other 2 testing varies from program to program and state to state. By contacting local agencies, more information can be obtained about specific requirements in the field. For most administrative and policy-making positions, though, the student can assume that graduate work will be expected of any candidate.

Industry outlook

There are two factors that will directly affect employment opportunities in social services. The first is that the population is, on average, getting older. The number of people surviving into old age is increasing with improved medical care, and the baby boom generation—the largest segment of the population—is getting older. This means that services for the elderly will have to increase to meet the rising demand.

The second factor that influences hiring is the availability of funds for social services. Funds have regularly been cut by municipal, state, and federal programming. The overall spending fluctuates and may rise in actual dollars, but real spending is believed to be decreasing. The private sector is picking up some of the costs, but the direction of future contributions cannot easily be predicted.

The number of new hirings in social services is expected to increase over the 1990s, partly due to an increase in programming and partly due to retiring and resigning social workers. Social work does not pay at the high end of the wage scale. Competition for the best paying jobs will be quite competitive, but the lower wage earning jobs will revolve more frequently, as staff is promoted or leaves the field.

Although most careers require interest and dedication to the work, social work, like medical work, requires an enormous commitment of time and energy and the people who do best in the field are those who cannot imagine doing anything else.

◇ SOURCES OF ADDITIONAL INFORMATION

For information on educational programs, job opportunities, and job placement, please contact:

American Public Welfare Association
810 First Street, NE
Suite 500
Washington, DC 20002

Council on Social Work Education
1744 R Street, NW
Washington, DC 20009

National Association of Social Workers
7981 Eastern Avenue
Silver Spring, MD 20910

National Mental Health Association
1021 Prince Street
Alexandria, VA 22314

National Urban League
500 East 62nd Street
New York, NY 10021

U.S. Department of Health and Human Services
Bureau of Health Professions
Rockville, MD 20857

For information on certification for professionals and on accreditation of schools and universities, write to:

Council on Social Work Education
1744 R Street, NW
Washington, DC 20009

For other information, contact:

American Psychological Association
Educational Affairs Office
1200 17th Street, NW
Washington, DC 20036

Welfare Research, Inc.
112 State Street
Albany, NY 12207

◇ **RELATED ARTICLES**

Volume 1:   Health Care; Personal and Consulting Services; Social Science
Volume 2:   Career counselors; Employment counselors; Fundraisers; Health services administrators; Human services workers; Psychologists; Rehabilitation counselors; Social workers; Statisticians; Therapists, miscellaneous
Volume 3:   Child care workers; Homemakers-home health aides; Nannies; Nursing and psychiatric aides
Volume 4:   Home health technicians; Physical therapist assistants; Psychiatric technicians

Sports

General information

When people think of sports, they often immediately think of highly-paid athletes performing in front of huge crowds. But the sports industry is a highly diversified field, made up of a variety of professionals, from athletes and coaches to executives and grounds keepers. The sports industry also includes managers and scouts, and those who produce the uniforms and equipment needed in the various sports.

The first organized athletic events took place in Greece around 776 B.C., with the advent of the ancient Olympic games. The Olympics featured running races and other competitive events, with the greatest athletes from the Greek empire competing in the contests. The Olympics were very colorful events and people from around the world gathered to watch the events. The ancient Romans, although initially scornful of sports, also participated in events of their own, such as chariot races and gladiator battles.

Different cultures and societies developed different sporting pastimes. Bowling, for example, has been around for centuries; a stone ball and nine stone pins were found in the tomb of an ancient Egyptian child. Native American tribes played lacrosse with webbed sticks and hard wooden balls centuries ago. Soccer, perhaps the most widely played sport, is believed to have been first played in England about 200 A.D.

In the United States, the interest in sports grew during the 1800s. The English sport of rugby lead to the development of American football, and, in 1869, Rutgers and Princeton played the first intercollegiate football game. Many other sports soon followed. Baseball was first played in 1845 and basketball was invented by Dr. James Naismith in 1891. Golf and tennis were organized into competitive events soon after, and the first championship boxing match was held in New Orleans in 1892.

As the popularity of sports grew, so too did employment opportunities in sports-related occupations. The increasing number and variety of professional sports teams not only created a need for professional athletes, but also brought a need for coaches, managers, trainers, and scouts. High school and college athlete programs became highly organized, and many additional jobs were created.

The 1980s have seen a rapid growth in sports in the United States, whether the professional variety, with its emphasis on the business of public entertainment, or amateur sports, which underscore participation. Professional sports, with their strong spectator appeal, monopolize the sports pages and a large portion of the TV programming, especially on weekends. Organized competitive school sports also draw vast audiences of spectators. The general population, moreover, is participating in sports of all kinds in unprecedented numbers.

The structure of the sports industry

In the United States, the five major team sports are baseball, basketball, football, hockey, and soccer. All are structured along much the same general lines—a good thing to know when planning a job search.

There are also a wide number of sports which require fewer participants. These sports include tennis, golf, boxing, wrestling, horse racing, running, and race car driving.

Most sports teams are owned by one person or a number of people. These owners not only pay the salaries of the athletes and other personnel, but they also often exert a strong influence on the personality of a team. Owners often select athletes that appeal to them and set rules and regulations that create a particular atmosphere in the clubhouse. Owners often view their team as a business, and teams may be bought and sold at the discretion of the owner.

General managers and business managers are often brought in to run the day-to-day operations of a team. They deal directly with the coaches and athletes, and may consult with owners when making personnel changes or other decisions.

All professional sports depend on full-time scouting to find talented athletes. Clubs support individual scouting staffs and also participate in pool scouting, in which one report from a highly skilled team of observers is furnished to four or five teams.

Professional sports are divided into seasons, and the athletes usually train the rest of the year to stay in shape. Baseball, for example, is primarily a summer sport, but athletes begin training early in spring and the season does not end until early autumn. Hockey is played primarily in the winter, but training and post-season activities keep hockey players busy almost the entire year.

An actual sporting event may take only a few hours, but athletes must arrive several hours early to prepare for a game and often must stay well after a contest is over in order to discuss the outcome of the game. Schedules for athletes depend on the sport in which they are participating. Many of the games are played at night or on weekends, when the majority of people can watch a contest. There may be a number of games of week or only one or two. Baseball players, for example, may play five or six days in a row. Football players, on the other hand, usually only play one game a week. Of course, practice and travel make sports a full-time profession, especially during the season.

Umpires and sports officials play a vital role in the sports industry. They ensure that the rules and regulations of a particular sport are observed and make other decisions during the course of a game. Often, a number of umpires or referees work at each sporting contest.

For those who do not play professionally, many avenues are open in sports work. Teaching and coaching, full time or as a part of other duties in the academic field, are two of these. Some athletes will inevitably realize that, although they can outthink the opposition, they are not themselves fast enough, strong enough, or big enough to be truly outstanding players. These people may become top candidates for jobs in coaching, teaching, or officiating.

In the past, a sick or injured player may have been sent to a regular doctor or, if necessary, to a specialist. The care of the player, in these days of million-dollar, no-cut contracts, has become a matter of top priority to both player and the club's top administrators. Many

Professional athletes must continue rigorous training throughout the year.

precautions are taken to ensure good health and fitness, and contracts often spell out the team's and player's responsibilities in this regard. Sport physicians and physical therapists accompany players to the games, and any injury is immediately treated.

The media have always been an important part of the sports industry. Newspapers and magazines did much to publicize the exploits of the athletes and radio brought the games to large audiences listening at home.

Today, television has become the dominant financial factor in professional sports. TV sports require a large variety of people. There are writers, researchers, publicists, producers, directors, and announcers.

Work in radio and television is accompanied by tremendous pressure generated by the need to make decisions or perform on a split-second schedule, and by the awareness that the audience may be in the hundreds of thousands or the millions. It calls for a cool head and an ability to work with other people. For television, many kinds of replay refinements, split-

Coaches work with athletes of all ages. This coach helps young gymnasts in a program sponsored by the YMCA.

camera work, and other special effects have been developed.

Sports publicity offers the opportunity to provide others with information, arrange interviews, and offer a number of other services to the press and the public. The club's publicity person in football, for example, runs the press box and is charged with a great many supervisory tasks, such as operating the public address system, maintaining statistics, and following up with information to the public on events, such as if a player has to be taken to the hospital during a competition.

Sports statisticians customarily work under the publicity director, although there are bureaus that provide the statistics for the various leagues and talent-scouting organizations. The statistician prepares figures for the press book issued before the start of the season and also helps put the book together. These publications must come out a month or two before formal competition begins.

Television networks also use statisticians to work alongside the announcers, providing up-to-date figures to be flashed on the screen as the contest progresses.

Sporting goods manufacturing are involved in producing the equipment needed in the various sports. They produce equipment such as golf clubs, basketballs, baseball equipment, tennis racquets, and skis.

Careers

Careers in professional sports are numerous and varied. Few other industries can match sports in the opportunities it affords for something new every day. The performer or athlete is the most glamorous position, but managers and other administrative people also play key roles. Radio and television sportscasters, newspaper sportswriters, publicity people, statisticians, officials and umpires, teachers and coaches, and talent scouts—all play major roles in presenting players and sports activities to the public. A sampling of career opportunities follows below.

General managers: The general manager is the executive who runs the day-to-day operations of a team. The general manager negotiates player contracts, makes trades with other clubs, and develops long-range strategy. In these capacities, the general manager works closely with the team's coach or field manager and with the club's personnel director. The general manager also negotiates contracts for TV and radio rights to broadcast games and consults with the stadium manager, who is responsible for ticket sales, concessions, and security. The general manager will also want to know about injuries, and calls on the trainer and the team physician for expert guidance.

Business managers: Business managers are concerned with purchasing the necessary equipment and other supplies to keep a team functioning smoothly. They are also responsible for arranging the transportation to move the players to other scenes of competition. On the road, the business manager (sometimes referred to as the road secretary) also arranges transportation for the media people attached to the club, including newspaper writers and TV reporters.

Professional athletes: Professional athletes compete in athletic events, such as baseball, football, hockey, and basketball for pay. Only a very small number of talented athletes ever become professionals.

Teachers, trainers, and *coaches:* The teaching and coaching aspect of sports is a broad one and ranges from coaching a school football team to individual tutoring in sports like tennis and golf. There is no limit to how long someone can coach. The idea, however, is to get a coaching start early in one's career because it is a long road up to the premium jobs, and experience counts heavily. Some coaches are able to communicate best with young people and are completely happy at the school or college level. Others respond to the challenges and the pressure of the pros, where intricate strategies go hand in hand with high stakes.

Sports officials and *umpires:* Sports officials and umpires ensure that the rules and regulations of a particular sport are maintained during the course of a contest. They have different responsibilities depending on the type of sport they oversee. Referees in tennis, for example, decide when a ball is in or out of play. Umpires in baseball determine when a pitched ball is in or out of the strike zone. Boxing referees watch for illegal moves and signs of fatigue in boxers.

Television announcers: Television announcers describe a contest for viewers watching on TV. Announcers come from various backgrounds. Some are ex-athletes, like Pat Summerall and Tom Brookshier. In basketball, former stars like Keith Erickson and Hot Rod Hundley became successful announcers. Some announcers learned the game as college players. Curt Gowdy was a top basketball player at Wyoming; Vin Scully patrolled the outfield for Fordham University's baseball team. Some were professionals in other fields; Howard Cosell decided sports was more attractive than practicing law (see Volume 1: Broadcasting).

Sports journalists: Sports journalists may travel with a particular team and report on the successes and failures of the team. They may write articles or broadcast reports about the results of a particular game or about interesting personalities associated with the team. Sports journalists with national sports publications cover one or two sports, reviewing the events of competitions across the country and sometimes around the world.

Publicists: Publicists arrange interviews with athletes and provide a number of other promotional services to teams. They may run the press box and have other media-related responsibilities (see Volume 1: Public Relations.)

Statisticians: Statisticians maintain records of the performance of individual athletes. Since these records often change frequently during a contest, speed and accuracy are at a premium. Since the figures have become more and more sophisticated, statisticians today rely heavily on computers. The club's up-to-the-minute statistics may be recalled at a moment's notice, ready to be photocopied for quick distribution in the press box and to all other interested parties.

Sports photographers: Most major papers have at least one photographer who specializes in sports, and the major wire services operate extensive photographic services with bureaus worldwide. National sports publications normally staff all major events with their own photographers as well. Stringers, or photographers who work on a free-lance basis for the publication, cover other events.

Sporting goods production workers: Sporting goods production workers are involved in all

Many college athletics programs provide the proper training needed for promising athletes to enter professional sports.

aspects of manufacturing, assembling, and finishing sporting good equipment. They produce the equipment needed in such sports as baseball, football, tennis, hockey, and badminton.

Indoor and outdoor grounds keepers: Indoor and outdoor grounds keepers maintain playing fields so that the fields are in good condition. For example, grounds keepers make sure grass or artificial turf is in the best condition possible at game time.

As in other industries, there is also a need for administrative workers, such as bookkeepers, secretaries, and computer programmers.

Education

People in sports will usually tell you that their interest started early, some when they were only toddlers. They may recall that they read the sports pages along with their grade-school books, but others recall being attracted by some particular phase of sports only after they were well into their teens. And some reached maturity before they made their crucial decision to make sports a life's work.

There is no best way to become a professional athlete. Most athletes train for many years before becoming professionals. It takes a combination of dedication, physical fitness, talent, plenty of experience, and a little luck to make it to the pros. It is very important for a talented athlete to receive proper coaching early in life so as to develop in the best possible

Many sports broadcasters are able to analyze and comment on a variety of sports.

rules and regulations before being certified to become an umpire at the professional level. Umpires and other officials below the professional level also receive some training, but do not have to undergo as lengthy a training period.

All publicity jobs require an ability to remain calm under a barrage of requests for information. Fortunately, once a season gets under way, things fall into a pattern, with different tasks allotted to different days. Often publicity workers have a background in communications as well as plenty of knowledge concerning a particular sport. Public relations, marketing, and advertising degrees are often recommended for applicants looking for publicity work.

Those interested in television announcing should be armed with an interest in sports and a dedication to the spoken word and how it affects others. Radio and television are for people who can say something well and in a manner that holds the attention of listener. In addition, a candidate should be comfortable in front of a camera. There are several on-air sportscasters who have journalism training; however, there are several well known sportscasters who have had no formal education but have developed a talent for on-air coverage.

Newspaper sportswriters and news sportscasters are usually college educated with a major in journalism, English, creative writing, communications, or some other program that trains the student in communication skills. Knowledge of sports, particularly if the journalist is interested in specializing in one sports coverage, is essential. Working on college newspapers, stringing (working on a free-lance basis) for newspapers, and any writing opportunities in sports coverage while in school is recommended. Portfolios are usually requested by employers to demonstrate competency in sports coverage.

Those who seek an opportunity in the technical end of radio or television should be interested in the operation and mechanics of electronic equipment. Special courses in electronics are available. Some colleges have technical training on broadcasting equipment in their communications programs. There are two year technical schools that have technician training programs specifically for broadcasting. High school guidance counselors can offer assistance in finding college and university programs that provide effective training. Whether operating a camera, mixing sound in the control truck parked outside the stadium, or giving directions on which part of the action to pick up, the technical staff must know what the equipment can and cannot do.

manner. College athletics often provide the training ground for athletes who make the transition to professional sports. Some athletes are able to make the transition directly from high school. However, the choice to move directly into professional athletics should not be made lightly. If the athletic career is short lived, then the athlete has little training for another career and may have to return to school for more education.

There is no particular educational requirement for sports managers, although a good deal of experience in a particular sport is absolutely necessary. A baseball manager, for example, should have played the sport at least on the college level and have many years of working with a ball club in other capacities.

Scouting relies heavily on former players, but it is not an absolute necessity to have playing experience. A knowledge of the game and interest in personnel are of primary importance.

Umpires and other sports officials often go to special schools to receive training. They must have a comprehensive understanding of all

Industry outlook

The greatest number of job opportunities exists with professional teams. There are more than 100 professional football, baseball, hockey, soccer, and basketball teams on the major-league level.

The number of professional teams, in all sports, is relatively stable. This means, however, that the number of jobs is also relatively stable. For jobs that are specifically sports related, such as managers, coaches, umpires and referees, job openings will occur as people retire or otherwise leave the profession. For other occupations that are also open in other fields, such as journalists, publicists, and business managers, there is some movement of trained individuals into and out of the sports sector. The competition for all these jobs is fairly keen. The number of people interested in working in sports far exceeds the number of openings.

As tough as positions are to get for non-athletic positions, the competition for a professional job as an athlete is much tougher. In football, for example, there are almost 200 Division 1 College football teams. There are countless other teams for other divisions. There are only 28 American professional football teams in the National Football League. For all of the athletes who wish to make the pros who play in college, there will be few chosen. Of those chosen, many will not last the season; others will not play for more than a few years. The number of professional football players who make a career of the sport is minuscule. The same is true for other sports as well.

Golf, tennis, and other individual sports enable professionals to play at the international level. But the financial incentive for players who do not win tournaments is limited. It is only a few players who will make the large salaries of an athlete on the level of Jack Nicklaus or Chris Evert.

◇ SOURCES OF ADDITIONAL INFORMATION

Federation of Professional Athletes
2021 L Street, NW
Washington, DC 20036

American Alliance for Health, Physical Education, Recreation, and Dance
1900 Association Drive
Reston, VA 22091

National Sporting Goods Association
Lake Center Plaza Building
1699 Wall Street
Mount Prospect, IL 60056

National Sportscasters and Sportswriters Association
Box 559
Salisbury, NC 28144

American Sports Education Institute
200 Castlewood Drive
North Palm Beach, FL 33408

Sports Foundation
Lake Center Plaza Building
1699 Wall Street
Mt. Prospect, IL 60056

◇ RELATED ARTICLES

Volume 1: Broadcasting; Business Administration; Health Care; Magazine Publishing; Newspaper Publishing; Performing Arts; Public Relations
Volume 2: Literary agents and artists' managers; Marketing, advertising, and public relations managers; Media specialists; Photographers and camera operators; Physical therapists; Physicians; Podiatrists; Professional athletes; Public relations specialists; Radio and television announcers and newscasters; Radio and television program directors; Recreational therapists; Reporters and correspondents; Sports instructors; Sports occupations; Statisticians; Teachers, secondary schools; Writers and editors
Volume 3: Landscapers and grounds managers; Sporting goods production workers
Volume 4: Audio control technicians; Audiovisual technicians; Cable television technicians; Field technicians; Physical therapist assistants; Sound technicians; Transmitter technicians; Video technicians

Telecommunications

General information

The telephone industry is the nerve system of the United States, consisting of millions of telephones and a vast network of switching and transmission systems. To provide the kind of service required for constantly increasing communications needs, this industry employs many people in many kinds of jobs. Competition and technological innovation characterize the changing telecommunications industry.

Although the telephone industry is big business, it is also a retail and service organization in each community. Its business is to send individual calls, install and service individual phones, and serve the needs of the smallest community.

Alexander Graham Bell invented the telephone in 1875. Bell, a speech teacher who studied electricity as a hobby, wanted to develop an harmonic telegraph so that two or more telegraphic messages could be sent over a single wire at the same time. By chance, the essential principles of the telephone were discovered.

The telephone earned praise when it was demonstrated at the Centennial Exposition in Philadelphia in June of 1876, but it did not gain widespread support until 1877, when Bell gave a number of public demonstrations of his invention. By 1892, Chicago and New York were linked by long-distance telephone lines, and by 1915 it was possible to make a telephone call between New York and San Francisco.

The last several decades have seen a number of improvements in the telephone communication systems. The use of TASI (Time Assignment Speech Interpolation) makes it possible to shift conversations along a transmission line automatically. Satellites make it possible to complete overseas calls in a matter of seconds.

Recently, technological advances such as fiber-optics systems, which use bundles of extremely fine glass fibers to carry calls on laser beams, and cellular telephone systems, in which phone calls are transferred from one transmitter to another allowing for an uninterrupted mobile conversations, have revolutionized the industry. An outstanding recent development has been the ability to transmit visual images over the telephone line through the use of facsimile (fax) machines.

The Bell System, which operates most of the nation's phones, was once one giant corporation supervising the work of local operating companies. American Telephone and Telegraph Company (AT&T), the parent corporation, was the subject of a successful antitrust suit by the U.S. Department of Justice. Effective January 1, 1984, the local companies—organized into seven regions—were divested (separated from the control of AT&T) and made autonomous over local phone service. Independent companies were meanwhile offering competitive long-distance call packages, taking some business away from AT&T. The two systems—the independent and Bell—offer many of the same services.

The partial deregulation of the industry, dating from the late 1960s, and the AT&T divestiture of January 1984 led to major changes in the telecommunications industry. Other common carriers, among them MCI and GTE/Sprint, built long-distance networks to serve public and private users. By the mid-1980s, more than fifty firms were providing some form of long-distance service, and many launched advertising campaigns that were designed to attract new system subscribers. The seven regional Bell operating companies formed under the AT&T divestiture agreement were principally engaged in providing local telephone service, but they too began to seek new markets and protect the ones they had.

The large number of long-distance companies led to various marketing techniques to differentiate one company from another. One company might claim that it provided the most reliable service, for example, while another company might claim it had the lowest rates.

The structure of the telecommunications industry

All telephone companies are privately owned and operated; but all come under regulation by the Federal Communications Commission for interstate rates and services and have been required to follow a uniform system of accounting. State commissions have jurisdiction over intrastate services and rates; and in some instances, local governments have certain regulatory powers. No two companies operate within the same jurisdiction, but the phones of all companies interconnect. Telephone service is provided by companies in one of two groups or systems: the independent companies or the Bell companies.

The independent companies supply service for a relatively small percentage of the nation's total phones. Though some of the companies are relatively small, others have thousands of stockholders and operate in areas of growing populations.

The growth of the telecommunications industry has been fueled by the use of business-oriented services, such as computer communications over telephone lines and the use of toll free 800 numbers (also known as inbound WATS service). Other services provided by the telecommunications industry include directory assistance, emergency numbers, and the publishing of telephone books.

When a person makes a telephone call, the sound waves of the caller are converted by a transmitter into a pattern of electric waves that travel over a series of wires. The phone receiver getting the call converts the electric waves back into sound.

A local telephone call travels over wires or by radio to a central office. Switching equipment is then used to connect the telephone call to the appropriate phone line. If the local call is to a person served by the same central office as the caller, the call is connected by the central office that serves both parties. However, if the call is to someone served by another central office, the call must travel along a trunk cable that connects numerous central offices. Over 99 percent of all telephone calls are connected automatically through electrical switches. A small number of calls are still connected manually by telephone operators.

Long distance telephone calls can use the same types of wires and cables as local calls.

When new housing developments are built, telephone line installers must connect all of the new houses to the local telephone service.

However, the electrical signals used to transmit the sound waves are often not strong enough to carry over tremendous distances. Therefore, long distance telephone lines are equipped with amplifiers that strengthen the signals as they pass along the wires.

With local telephone calls, the wires and cables needed to transmit a call are placed underground or strung along telephone poles. Long distance calls often use radio relay systems to transmit calls via radio waves.

The job most frequently associated with the telephone industry is that of the telephone operator. There are two basic operator jobs—long distance and directory assistance. They help provide a vital service. They must be alert, particularly in emergency situations, and be able to adapt to different types of customers and varied work situations.

Research involves developing new methods and procedures, as well as evaluating costs and effectiveness. Such tasks are the responsibility of the engineers throughout the industry. Electronics engineers, for example, will often design, plan, and test new cable systems or other equipment that will improve the lines used in transmitting telephone calls.

Today's telecommunications marketplace is increasingly complex in terms of products and services and ever-changing in response to competition under partial deregulation and to customer needs. The challenges are great and the rewards commensurate for recent technical and business graduates and seasoned marketing specialists with the abilities to sell and deliver the integrated, multi-functional, data-oriented systems that will support communications now and in the years ahead.

461

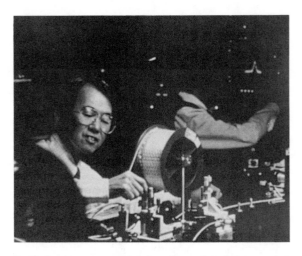

Electrical engineers are experimenting with new fibers that can conduct communications transmissions efficiently.

Due to the increased competition created by the breakup of AT&T, marketing is becoming extremely important as telecommunications companies scramble to develop strategies to keep current customers and attract new ones. Each company tries to sell itself by making its services known and differentiating its product from the competition. Some companies might try to advertise reduced costs, while other companies might try to use new technology, such as fiber optics, to attract customers.

The technical aspects of the telecommunications industry are subdivided into two groups, depending on where the work is performed: inside technical jobs and outside technical jobs.

Inside technical jobs are repairing, rearranging, and maintaining central office switching equipment or locating trouble in the lines. This may include inspecting and testing equipment and analyzing test data and maintenance reports.

Outside technical jobs are quite varied. People performing outside technical jobs may install or repair telephone equipment ranging from single telephones to complex switching systems in customers' homes and businesses. Employees in some outside technical jobs connect individual telephone wires to underground cables, along pole lines, and in cable vaults in buildings. Still others set telephone poles, lay telephone cable, and do the wiring work needed to interconnect central office equipment and cables. All of these jobs require working outdoors in all kinds of weather, climbing telephone poles, and driving company motor vehicles. Some require the operation of heavy equipment.

Careers

The telecommunications industry offers a wide range of career opportunities. Not everyone in this industry requires a college education, but increasingly a college degree is becoming vital to those who want to advance into management, engineering, marketing, and other specialist fields. A sampling of career opportunities follows below.

Electrical engineers: Electrical engineers who work in the telecommunications industry are responsible for the design, development, and production of electrical equipment used in the transmission and distribution of telephone calls. They may work with overhead or underground telephone lines or other types of equipment.

Telephone line installers: Telephone line installers place lines and poles, and install wires and cables that run from the customer's phone line to a central office.

Telecommunications technicians: Telecommunications technicians install, maintain, and repair a wide variety of telecommunications equipment. Switching equipment technicians, for example, are telecommunications technicians who install, test, and maintain the equipment that automatically connects telephone calls. Submarine cable equipment technicians work with machines and equipment used to send messages through underwater cables.

Marketing personnel: Marketing personnel help promote a particular telecommunications company to potential customers and thereby convince those customers that a particular company is best equipped to meet the customers' telecommunications needs. Marketing personnel may use various methods, such as television advertising or a direct mail approach.

Account managers: Account managers usually work with business clients to ensure that the business client remains please with the level of service from the company. An account manager will keep up-to-date on the latest technology to make sure clients have the best possible telecommunications service.

Programmers: A programmer will write computer program codes, test program modules, develop test data, and document and maintain computer programs used in telecommunication systems.

Field engineers: Field engineers set up and operate portable radio and television transmitting equipment. They obtain a link with the station by location telephone wires that can carry transmissions, then they connect microphones, amplifiers, and a power supply to the lines. Field engineers are sometimes referred to as field technicians.

Frameworkers: Frameworkers install, change, or disconnect customer telephone lines that are connected in central office equipment rooms. Frameworkers work with hand tools, test equipment, and maintain administrative records.

Telephone and PBX installers and repairers: Telephone and PBX installers and repairers install, service, and repair telephone lines, telephone switchboards, and other specialized telecommunications equipment. They work in private homes and in places of business.

Long-distance operators: The long-distance operator is the service specialist who assists customers in completing person-to-person, collect, credit card, emergency, and other special kinds of long distance calls.

Directory assistance operators: The directory assistance operator assists customers and other operators in locating telephone numbers that they cannot find or that are not printed in the directory.

Customer service and sales workers: Customer service representatives discuss and sell telephone service; answer customer inquiries regarding costs, billing charges, and company policies; make credit decisions; and maintain customer records. Some of these individuals work in telephone company business offices, while others work in phone centers or stores. Sales representatives have direct contact with business customers regarding their communication arrangements or their yellow page directory advertising programs. They analyze the business customer's present communications arrangements and develop and make presentations on the types of services that customers should consider to meet their business needs.

Coin collectors: The coin collection job consists of collecting money deposited in coin telephones, inspecting coin telephone booths and equipment, keeping records, and preparing reports.

Education

A variety of jobs are available in the telephone industry for the student entering the job market from high school. The majority of these jobs do not require any previous training or experience. Such positions include frameworkers, general maintenance workers, installers and repairers, operators, customer service workers, and coin collectors.

Training for most jobs begins when the employee starts work. For some jobs, however, an applicant may be required to have a particular

A telecommunications technician tests fiber optics materials with advanced laser technology.

skill to be employed, for example, typing or stenography.

The training may be given on the job by a person who has previously held the job or through individual or group instruction. Slides, films, videotapes, and other audio and visual aids may be used to make the learning process an interesting one.

Training is a continuous process. As new developments or procedures come along, additional training or special courses are provided to keep the employee abreast of new technology. In addition, employees are encouraged to present their own ideas on how the companies can improve the services which are provided.

The changing environment within the telecommunications industry has created new challenges for the talented administrative specialists who provide the broad spectrum of support services. Some of these services such as completing rate and tariff studies, require strong analytical capabilities and technical knowledge in such areas as mathematics and statistics.

To become involved in programming in the telecommunications industry, college graduates will usually need a strong academic record in

Telecommunications satellites have strengthened communications throughout the world. This particular dish is located in Moffett Field near San Francisco.

computer science, mathematics, engineering, or physics.

Challenging career opportunities exist for outstanding engineering graduates—particularly those with electrical, mechanical, and industrial degrees—as well as mathematicians and economists with an interest in technical applications.

There are a number of opportunities for advanced training and study. Depending on an individual's background, interests, and entry position, development may include on-the-job training, regular or periodic classroom training, seminars or workshops conducted by specialists, or enrollment in an advanced degree program, with full or partial tuition reimbursement for career-related study.

Industry outlook

The telecommunications industry promises strong growth in the years ahead. As technological advances such as fiber optics, satellite transmissions, and facsimile machines revolutionize the industry, there will be a continual need for trained engineers and other technical specialists to develop new applications for these products. In addition, society's need to quicken the pace of communications will lead to job opportunities in research and development.

As telecommunications companies grow, there will be a corresponding need for service personnel to work with customers. The intense competition in the telecommunications industry may lead to a reduction in the number of companies providing service, but overall employment opportunities should remain strong. Currently, more than 2,000 companies provide telecommunications services in the United States.

The complex field of telecommunications and information handling is a national resource. There is a need for exceptional people to share in the determination and commitment necessary to develop that resource.

◇ SOURCES OF ADDITIONAL INFORMATION

Those seeking information about jobs within the telephone industry should visit the employment office of the local telecommunications company. Information is also available from:

United States Telephone Association
900 19th Street, NW, Suite 800
Washington DC 20006

North American Telecommunications Association
2000 M Street, NW, Suite 550
Washington, DC 20036

Telecommunications Industry Association
1722 I Street, NW, Suite 300
Washington, DC 20006

Tele-communications Association
858 South Oak Park Road, Suite 102
Covina, CA 91724

◇ RELATED ARTICLES

Volume 1: Electronics; Engineering
Volume 2: Engineers; Radio and telegraph operators
Volume 3: Communications equipment mechanics; Computer and peripheral equipment operators; Line installers and cable splicers; Office-machine servicers; Switchboard operators; Telephone and PBX installers and repairers; Telephone operators
Volume 4: Computer-service technicians; Electrical technicians; Electromechanical technicians; Electronics sales and service technicians; Telecommunications technicians

Textiles

General information

Although the term textile originally referred only to woven fabrics (those made by weaving yarn on a loom), today the textile industry includes knitted goods, braids, and other fabrics that are made from fibers, yarns, and other materials. Textiles may be made from natural products or from synthetic materials. The textile industry produces fabrics for clothing, as well as fabrics for home furnishings, carpeting, towels, and sheets.

People began weaving the four basic natural fibers (cotton, linen, wool, and silk) into cloth as early as the Stone Age. Pieces of woven cloth dating from about 4,000 B.C. have been discovered in Europe, Asia, South America, and the Middle East.

The making of cloth had always been a time-consuming task, because everything had to be done by hand. When the Industrial Revolution began in the eighteenth century, textile manufacturing was one of the first industries to be affected by the development of the new machines. The machines used to produce textiles saved time and dramatically cut the cost of producing clothing.

Until two hundred years ago, almost no cloth was manufactured in the United States; most was imported from England. The textile industry was so important to England that English officials refused to allow either the drawings of textile machines or the mechanics who operated the machines to leave the country. In 1789, however, an English textile mechanic named Samuel Slater disguised himself as a farmer and sailed to the United States. He carried the details of the machinery in his head. A few years later, he opened a spinning mill in Rhode Island.

The first synthetic fibers were developed near the beginning of this century. Since then, synthetics have improved the function and versatility of textiles. For example, new fibers and finishes have made clothes less costly. Durable, soil-resistant synthetic carpets cover the floors of homes, schools, offices, and hospitals. The car industry uses synthetic fibers in seat belts, upholstery, and the reinforcement of tires, belts, and hoses.

Although textile plants are located throughout the United States, the majority are in the Southeast. Some are in the cities, whereas others are surrounded by farms and forests. Frequently, manufacturing plants are found in small towns within a few miles of larger cities. Most companies also have regional or district sales offices in major cities throughout the country. With few exceptions, textile research and development centers are located in industrial areas of the Southeast. These facilities usually are equipped with the latest in scientific equipment.

The structure of the textile industry

The process of manufacturing textiles involves basically the same steps as weaving cloth by hand. The main difference is that now large machines are used to twist the fibers into yarns and then knit or weave the yarns into fabric. In almost all cases, the process is completely automated, with textile manufacturing workers operating the machines and making sure that the machines run smoothly.

The large majority of fabrics are produced by weaving or knitting. Woven materials are made from two sets of yarns. One set of yarn (called the warp) is threaded crosswise through a series of frames. During the manufacturing process, some of the warp yarn is raised and some is lowered. This creates a space through which the other set of yarn (called the filling or weft) is pulled to form the crosswise pattern. Various patterns are formed depending on the

465

A fashion designer looks at many types of textiles to determine which ones will suit her latest fashion design.

amount and type of spacing between the warp and filling.

Knitted materials can be made either from a single yarn or a set of yarns. A knitting machine with automatic needles is used to make loops in the yarn and join the loops together, thereby producing cloth.

Cotton is the most widely used natural fiber in textile production. Another widely used natural fiber is wool. Synthetic fibers are made from nylon, polyester, acrylic, and olefin.

Research and development is an important function of many textile firms. Research is continually being conducted to find new synthetic materials, experiment with dyes and weaves, test fiber strength, and develop computerized equipment.

Another important area of concern for some researchers is improving the plant environment, especially methods of reducing noise and exposure to hazardous materials. Textile research and development people are innovators. They are professional scientists who put their knowledge to work to develop new ideas in textile making.

Textile science facilities often include laboratories in which textile products are tested for such qualities as strength, durability, soil resistance, and other characteristics. Although the actual testing is usually done by technicians, a scientist oversees the operation.

While the research and development departments refine the process of textile production, the stylists and designers generate fabric designs. The textile industry offers careers in styling and design for creative people with a love of color and artistic talent. An increasing amount of designing is being done by computer. For example, CAD/CAM technicians use computer-controlled systems to create the diagrams and drawings required for textile manufacturing (see Volume 4: CAD/CAM technicians).

Once a design is approved, it is ready to be manufactured. The first step is to purchase the material needed to produce the fabric. Textile firms divide purchasing into two categories: raw fiber and general purchasing. Raw fiber procurement is a highly specialized field and requires knowledge of fabrics, market prices, market demand for various textiles, and other topics. General purchasing includes everything from office supplies to large machinery.

With the materials available, the production of the fabric may begin. Textile plant operations include many processes: opening of bales of fibers; cleaning the fibers; carding them so that the strands will lie parallel; twisting and roving the fibers; spinning the fibers into yarn; weaving or knitting the yarn into fabric; and chemically finishing the fabric. Each of these steps requires special machinery.

Textile plants have many kinds of machines doing different kinds of jobs. There is a constant flow of materials between departments. The machines that do most jobs are complicated and must be handled with skill. The people who control them have a great deal of responsibility. They operate many kinds of machines and must be able to do so without supervision.

Color and pattern are important features of many textile products. Computers are often used in the formulation of dyes and matching of colors to assure uniform quality, but expert dyers supervise the adding of color to yarn or fabric. Die-range operators control the dyeing machines, in which widths of cloth are spread on a dye pad and then dried.

After textile products are woven or knitted, they are treated to give them special properties. This operation is known as finishing. Finishing processes that enable fabric to resist shrinkage, repel soil, resist burning, or hold its shape are chemically based.

To satisfy the ever-changing needs, tastes, and values of consumers, the textile industry has employees who are involved in the challenging and extremely competitive world of merchandising—the business of selling fabric and consumer products. Those involved with marketing design products to meet consumers' needs and work with store managers, garment makers, and designers to produce and distribute high-quality products.

Advertising and sales promotion personnel must create demand for textile products with a variety of communications tools. Methods used might include television advertisements or ads in consumer and trade magazines. Other promotional activities might include point-of-sale displays, attractive packaging, exhibits at fashion shows, or promotions within department stores.

Another textile-related field involves textile conservation. Textile conservationists restore and repair damaged textiles using highly-technical methods. The most common problems are due to the normal wear and tear of fabrics. Some of the textiles are found buried, which leads to even further disintegration. Some of the basic tasks of conservationists include analyzing dyes, identifying fibers through microscopy, documenting fabric construction, assessing the proper construction of exhibition mounts, determining methods of storage, and repairing damaged textiles.

Roughly half of the conservationists are employed by museums, while the remaining conservationists have private practices, where they assist the general public and smaller museums that have no conservation labs. The conservationists use such high-tech equipment as x-ray machines, scanning electron microprobes, and microscopes to locate problems and analyze the fibers.

This loom operator loosens a thread that is caught in the loom. In order to weave a perfect sheet of fabric, she must pay attention at all times.

Careers

The textile industry offers a wide range of careers, including salespeople, engineers, printers, textile chemists, dyers, computer specialists, fashion designers, knitters, environmental scientists, weavers, researchers, secretaries, manufacturing specialists, truck drivers, health specialists, and many others. A sampling of career opportunities follows below.

Textile researchers: Textile researchers develop new products and look for ways to improve manufacturing processes and machinery to reduce costs of production while keeping quality high. Textile researchers are involved in the design or improvement of textile machinery, the development of new dyeing or finishing techniques, or the invention of completely new fabrics. Knitted replacement arteries, space suits for the astronauts, fake fur, and inflatable buildings are all results of textile research.

Textile technicians: Textile technicians assist in producing textiles and making apparel and other products. They may work in textile research, design, development, or production.

Dye-lab technicians: Dye-lab technicians use sample dyeing equipment to color cloth according to dye formulas. They verify that products and colors meet company specifications. They calculate the amount of dye required for machines of different capacities, and they weigh and mix dyes and other chemicals.

Stylists: Dealing primarily with fabric colors, weights, and textures, the stylist is responsible for most long-range fashion planning. From the time an idea for a fabric is born until it is produced, the stylist and designer work together to produce the desired material. The successful stylist should understand what consumers want, sometimes in advance of a noticeable trend. And the stylist can even stimulate consumer desires.

Designers: The stylist's idea for a fabric design may be executed by the designer. Many designers create their own original designs in addition to executing a stylist's idea. The design might be for fabrics that are knitted, woven, or printed. And the fabrics can be made from wool, cotton, silk, synthetic fibers, or a fiber blend. A designer must know textile man-

467

A textile conservationist instructs a group of students on the weave of fine cotton and the structure of individual threads. A sample piece of cloth has been placed under a microscope and the image is projected onto a television screen.

ufacturing processes in addition to having artistic skills.

CAD/CAM technicians: In the textile industry, CAD/CAM technicians use computer-controlled systems to assist industrial designers in designing textile products and carrying out automated industrial processes. CAD is an abbreviation for "computer-aided design." CAM is an abbreviation for "computer-aided manufacturing."

Industrial engineers: Industrial engineers set standards for each kind of textile machine, determine the most efficient methods of materials handling, measure cost of production, and make sure that all of the production operations are being carried out at optimum efficiency. When they determine that changes are necessary, industrial engineers work with management and the plant engineer to develop the best way of putting the new procedure into operation.

Plant engineers: Plant engineers are responsible for the smooth functioning of a manufacturing plant's heating, air-conditioning, and other internal systems. Plant engineers and their staffs make sure all these systems are op-

erating properly and oversee any changes or modifications in the systems.

Manufacturing supervisors: Manufacturing supervisors have responsibility for yarn preparation, weaving, knitting, finishing, or printing in the plants. Working in the production area, they may direct the activities of hundreds of people and the operations of hundreds of machines. They may schedule employees for different shifts and overtime work.

Machine operators: Machine operators run and service several kinds of machines, such as weaving machines and dyeing machines. The nature of each job varies with the kind of machine used. Some require operators to use their hands extensively, whereas others may call for operating electronic controls. Jobs require the use of the mind as well as the hands. The ability to solve problems and organize time is often as important as knowing how to operate machines.

Machine technicians: Complex textile manufacturing equipment requires expert technicians to keep the equipment in good working order. Machine technicians are often former operators with especially good mechanical skills.

Frame operators: Frame operators tend machines that draw and twist strands of fiber into yarn. Frame operators are often referred to as frame spinners.

Beam-wrapper tenders: Beam-wrapper tenders work at high-speed machines that wind yarn onto beams before the weaving process begins.

Loom operators: Loom operators run a battery of automatic looms that weave the yarn into cloth. They observe the weaving process carefully to detect flaws in the cloth, breaks in the threads, or mechanical defects. Loom operators are often referred to as weavers.

Dyers: Dyers control the machines that dye and dry cloth.

Finishers: Finishers treat fabrics with a variety of chemicals to make the fabrics more durable or water-resistant.

Textile marketing managers: The textile marketing manager is responsible for planning and directing the smooth flow of the finished product, from the textile plant to the customer. A marketing manager must know and understand each link in the complex merchandising chain. Some of those links include styling and design, manufacturing, market research, advertising, and, of course, sales.

Salespeople: The salesperson is the key figure on the marketing team. Whether selling cloth to an apparel manufacturer, sheets to a retail chain, or industrial fabric to an automobile manufacturer, the salesperson is the one who has direct contact with the company's sources of income. By developing a continuing relationship with a customer, the salesperson learns to understand and anticipate the customer's needs. As the supplier-customer liaison, the salesperson also serves as a consultant and adviser on new product developments.

Textile conservationists: Textile conservationists restore damaged textiles. The textiles range from rare museum pieces to items from private collections. Conservationists use a variety of scientific techniques to isolate the damage and repair the textiles.

Education

Career opportunities in the textile industry are open to college graduates in a variety of majors, including liberal arts, business, and the sciences. There are also textile colleges that provide complete educations concerning the textile industry. In many cases, the potential for promotions and increased earnings are better for a graduate from a college with a program in tex-

A textile worker positions yarn to be fed directly into a knitting machine. The fabric will be used in blouses and dresses.

tiles. An advanced degree may be required for some jobs.

There is no standard formula for getting started in textile research, and requirements vary from company to company. Some firms require their researchers to have one or two years of experience in at least one area of textile manufacturing. These companies rarely hire people straight out of school for research jobs, although there are exceptions. Employees without advanced degrees are often encouraged to further their training, and may be reimbursed for tuition and other educational costs.

High-school graduates are hired as technicians and are often given substantial responsibility. In some cases, their work schedules are arranged to allow them to go to college while employed.

Persons majoring in fabric design or textile design take courses in dyeing, loom operation, and screen painting. They often do research at museums and galleries, and will usually take

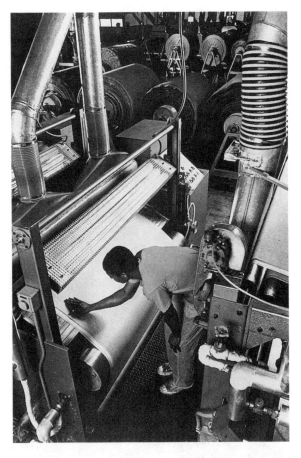

A manufacturing supervisor inspects the uniformity of the weaving and the quality of newly manufactured upholstery fabric. The fabric is woven on an fully-automated loom.

tem. Regular travel is not a part of most administrative positions. Most firms, however, encourage their management personnel to attend seminars, workshops, classes, and other functions that help to keep them abreast of current developments in the industry.

Many companies conduct management-training programs that prepare college graduates for supervisory positions. The ability to organize work and to solve problems is important. There are specialized textile degree programs that help the graduate apply his or her college education in the sciences, mathematics, or humanities to textile industry operations.

Manufacturing supervision is often the most direct route to higher levels of management responsibility. Because they become totally familiar with the manufacturing process, supervisors rapidly gain the experience and knowledge that will make them valuable in sales, administration, research and development, as well as in manufacturing.

People who operate machines are generally trained on the job. A high-school education is adequate background for most jobs. For machine technicians, those who have the interest and the ability may be promoted to supervisory or management positions. Others may become full-time instructors, teaching new employees job techniques. Some may go into research, testing, or other fields related to manufacturing.

The finishers should have a knowledge of chemistry. Finishers are also trained by the company in most cases, but college training in chemistry or textile chemistry is important.

Sales is also one of the most direct paths to management. Most textile marketing and merchandising managers and many company presidents have had strong sales experience. A sales career also offers the opportunity of being on one's own, meeting a great variety of people, and eventually setting one's own hours.

Most companies now require that a salesperson have a college degree, preferably in business administration or marketing. Textile college graduates are also in demand, but many graduates with liberal arts degrees are successful in textile sales. The person who is technically oriented or who has training in the social sciences or engineering might choose a career selling industrial textiles.

To be a textile conservationist, one must have an undergraduate degree in a related field of specialization. This may include textile science, home economics, art history, and anthropology. Graduate work is often necessary, though apprenticeships are widely accepted as legitimate forms of educations and training.

seminars with industry people. The student's course load also includes liberal arts courses.

In addition to creative talent, those seeking styling and design careers need training in the fine arts, textile sciences, and computers. They should understand the textile marketplace and should know what machinery used to make fabrics can do. Stylists and designers can advance into broader areas of merchandising, management, and fashion promotion.

Industrial engineers are generally taught their jobs in special management training programs conducted by the company. Most college degree programs provide useful backgrounds for careers in industrial engineering. Many companies prefer graduates with industrial engineering or textile manufacturing degrees.

Plant engineers often begin their careers as electrical, mechanical, or air-conditioning engineers within the plant. A degree in engineering is required.

A career in textile administration is best aided by a knowledge of general business principles and an understanding of the market sys-

One needs a chemistry background to qualify for graduate school in textile conservation. There are several schools of conservation in the United States, notably New York University, the University of Delaware at Winterthur, and the Courtauld Institute at Hampton Court in England.

Textile conservationist must have a variety of knowledge concerning exhibitions, storage methods, textile manufacture, and textile history. They attend annual conventions that keep them abreast on the newest conservation methods. In addition, they read and contribute to conservation journals that publish the latest findings.

Industry outlook

In 1989, the textile industry was worth nearly $69 billion in total shipments, increasing by 5.2 percent from the previous year. Due to the continual need for clothing and other products, the industry shows promise in the 1990s of steadily increasing growth. Currently, an estimated two million people are employed in the U.S. textiles industry.

The textile industry is constantly creating new products and expanding its client base by supplementing other industries. Recent developments include producing materials for highway construction, erosion control, and space exploration.

New methods of spinning, new weaving machines, better printing processes, and increased adaptation of computers to manufacturing operations have made the textile industry one of the most efficient and productive in the world. As new machines and methods are developed and put into place, new technical jobs will follow. Consequently, machine operating jobs are diminishing with the advent of computerization.

Computers have also improved the marketing aspects of the textile industry. Computer programs have created efficient electronic linkages among the manufacturers, wholesalers, and retailers. These programs shorten the response time between the demand for products and the supply of them, saving time and money.

Recent concerns for the environment have led to efforts to reduce the amount of pollution generated by manufacturing plants. For the textile industry, environmental awareness can mean such steps as changing ingredients in a chemical used for dyeing, building a water purification system, making a financial contribution for the construction of a municipal waste-treatment facility, or studying the recycling of liquids. In the years ahead, there will be an increasing demand for people who are trained to protect the natural environment. Such positions may be open to chemists, chemical laboratory technicians, environmental law specialists, environmental scientists, or other specialists.

◇ **SOURCES OF ADDITIONAL INFORMATION**

American Textile Manufacturers Institute
1801 K Street, NW, Suite 900
Washington, DC 20006

American Association for Textile Technology
295 Fifth Avenue, Room 621
New York, NY 10016

National Council for Textile Education
PO Box 391
Charlottesville, VA 22902

Textile Designers Guild
11 West 20th Street, 8th Floor
New York, NY 10011

American Institute for Conservation of Historic and Artistic Works
1400 16th Street, NW, Suite 340
Washington, DC 20036

American Apparel Manufacturers Association
2500 Wilson Boulevard, Suite 301
Arlington, VA 22201

◇ **RELATED ARTICLES**

Volume 1: Apparel; Design; Engineering
Volume 2: Chemists; Designers; Engineers; Industrial designers; Industrial traffic managers; Museum occupations; Purchasing agents
Volume 3: Industrial machinery mechanics; Manufacturers' sales workers; Textile manufacturing occupations; Wholesale trade sales workers
Volume 4: CAD/CAM technicians; Chemical technicians; Drafting and design technicians; Graphic arts technicians; Industrial engineering technicians; Industrial safety-and-health technicians; Textile technicians

Toys and Games

General information

Toys and games are centuries old. In 1600 B.C. swings were used by children on the island of Crete. Dice have been found in Egyptian tombs over 2000 years old. Indian, Eskimo, Chinese, and African dice and other playing pieces have also been found from archeological digs. Dice are the oldest game pieces, with a variety of games using cubes designed by different cultures.

Both physical games (such as tag, capture-the-flag, and hopscotch) and intellectual games (such as chess, guessing games, and riddles) have been traced back through many generations in many civilizations. Games provide a training ground for skills for children and serve as entertainment and exercise. The games normally use simple rules and activities and involve two or more people.

Toys such as dolls and wooden soldiers were originally made by parents or craftsmen. Toys were developed in civilizations that had some leisure time to dedicate to carving and sewing non-essential items. Balls, hoops, pull toys, dolls and animal shapes were the oldest types of toys made. They were simple designs to make and provided entertainment to different age groups.

Toys produced in the early periods were made from clay, wood, ivory, or stone. The earliest dolls found by archaeologists in Egypt were not for play; they were used to symbolize aspects of religious beliefs. However, Greek historians explain that toy dolls were used as playthings in their culture.

Dolls became less prominent during the Middle Ages. Society's attitudes toward children shifted from some acceptance of childlike behavior to tolerance of only what was deemed to be adult behavior. Toys and games were meant to be training material for skills needed as an adult, and playthings used merely for entertainment were less common.

Manufactured games were developed in the 1600s for instruction in schooling. For example, geographical games were made where each country was cut out to enable the child to fit the countries back together correctly. This was the earliest type of jigsaw puzzle.

By the 19th century, the awareness of a child's need for playthings emerged. Toy manufacturing developed into a fledgling industry. Germany had been the forerunner of the toy making industry, starting in the 1600s, and with the new international interest in toys, Germany found itself in the best position to make use of its experience in toy development. The country had hosted toy fairs during the Renaissance, with one of the largest annual fairs held in Nuremberg. It continued to build off of its reputation of training master toy craftsmen, as the expansion of toy sales began.

The development and relative cheapness of certain materials allowed for production of new types of toys. Rubber was discovered and became an ideal material to make bouncing balls. Paper became cheaper to manufacture and China began to export kites.

Germany developed several of the most popular types of dolls, starting with wooden dolls in the 1800s. Papier-mache dolls were developed in Germany in the 1800s as well; these were easily molded when wet and became strong and hard when dry. Papier-mache doll heads were sold separately so cloth bodies could be made at home. Full dolls were also produced. Wax dolls were developed later, where papier-mache was dipped in wax to give a nicer quality to the skin of the doll.

France followed as a large manufacturer of toys, particularly in doll-making. Porcelain dolls, started in Germany, were developed as luxury dolls in France. The dolls were dressed in elegant, formal outfits and were not really intended for play. The outfits could be changed and wardrobes could be purchased for the dolls.

Baby dolls were not manufactured widely until Augusta Montanari and her son Richard produced wax baby dolls in England in 1850. Eventually baby dolls became the most popular type of doll with *Kewpie, Bye-Lo, Raggedy Ann*, and other popular mass-produced dolls beginning to sell by the hundreds of thousands.

As the industry grew, the mass production of games and toys became a more profitable enterprise. Board games, inexpensive to produce, increased in popularity with both adults and children. *Snakes and Ladders* was first made in the 19th century and is still produced in various forms today. *Monopoly* was developed in 1933 and has expanded with many international versions to become the best selling board game ever. Puzzles, originally hand cut, became inexpensive when mass production was possible.

Barbie dolls and G.I. Joe were popular worldwide. They combined the wardrobe variety of the early French luxury dolls and the durability of a play toy. G.I. Joe was the first internationally popular doll for boys.

Toys and games became more mechanized. Dolls could move head, arms, and legs. Some could talk, walk, and move with a remote control. Electronic games were built so a partner was no longer required for board games. One could play against a computer or other machine.

With the advent of the home computer, computer games were built that included such programs as ping-pong and eventually moved into three dimensional graphics in maze games. As the graphics and movement capability of the games improved, the skill levels for players became broader. However, advancement in electronic technology for computer graphics is moving so rapidly that games that seemed advanced two years earlier appear simplistic and outdated against the competition of the day. Because of the continual updating of the technology, lulls in computer game sales have created major dips in the market. Companies that were based on great sales on one or two games have gone out of business. Although the popularity of the games has boosted the market overall, the lack of one specific best seller has kept the sales of toys and games at a lower level than in the past.

The complexity of the electronic toy is being offset by the renewed popularity of the simple toy. Hoops, balls, jacks, and cloth dolls are regaining popularity with children. Partly because of the quick rise and fall of the more complex, expensive video and computer games, simpler toys are touted as the better investment for a child's entertainment and education. Both types of toys, however, maintain strong sales in the marketplace.

Computers are helpful in designing machines. This industrial designer is creating a machine that will produce toy vacuum cleaners.

The structure of the toy and game industry

The beginning of all games and toys are in the design department. They start with a concept for a new game or toy and evaluate its prospective use. They determine what age group would use the toy, what would be the competition for the toy on the market, and how the toy would be made. New designs are submitted constantly to toy manufacturers by the in-house design staff and outside designers interested in selling a new product. For some of the larger companies, at least one third of the designs that are produced come from non-company employees.

The designer creates several sketches of what the new toy will look like, from different angles if necessary. The materials to be used may be listed and the potential cost of production of the toy using these materials would be figured out.

The sketches move on to the research and development department. There, they research the potential sales of the new toy. Determining how appealing the toy is, what age group would use the toy, and how well similar toys have done in sales, are all areas that the research and product development departments will investigate before beginning to produce the new item.

If enough potential is seen in the new design, then models are made of the toy. The design department engineers, artists, and model makers construct prototypes of the new toy so development and testing can see and use these toys to judge the quality and interest in the toy. Testing a toy means giving it to children to play

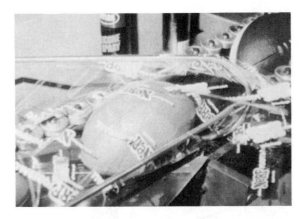

Toy packaging is designed to appeal both to children and their parents. In this case, the packaging simply reveals the product, which is colorful and attractive.

with while trained observers take notes on the use of the toy. Suggestions for improvement in design, size, color, and other areas that the observer notes will be passed back to the design department for potential incorporation into the next stage of the toy's design. If the toy is changed then the toy will go through another period of trial and observations.

Child testers, the children who use the toys during the testing period, are normally participants in a company-sponsored or university sponsored play-group. Child care centers and school groups may also be participants. Observers are often specialists in child development, child psychology, or pediatrics.

With the help of one-way mirrors and unobtrusive viewing positions, trained staff note which toys are used frequently and creatively and which toys are ignored or used only briefly. The collection of toys on the floor may include several of the company's toys, some of the competition's, and the experimental toys.

While the observation end of the research team is at work, the marketing research team is out collecting information. Consumer research involves asking parents questions about the toys they have purchased and their experience with the toys. This may mean standing in a shopping mall questioning parents coming out of a toy store, sending questionnaires to customers, or conducting in-depth phone interviews with parents. The information they gather will be used to determine the quality and desirability of the products they have already produced, and they can find out the types or styles of toys the parents are looking for but have not found. For example, it was through consumer requests that the toy industry began producing black, ethnic, and boy dolls.

The engineering and safety experts continue with the investigation into the new toy's viability. They conduct stress tests on the new toy to make sure it is safe, reliable, and relatively indestructible in the hands of the child. The mechanical and functional parts are tested for wear and strain. If the toy is for small children, the size of the pieces that make up the toy have to be checked to be sure they cannot be swallowed. Each age group has certain limitations for what is safe in a toy design.

The U.S. government has established a voluntary age grading guideline to assist parents in selecting appropriate toys for their children. The guidelines are based on four areas: physical ability, mental ability, play needs and interests, and the safety aspect of the toy. For a child under a few years old, small objects can be swallowed and should be avoided. Even for a child that is above average in mental skills, the physical coordination required for toys in the age group above may be beyond the capacity of the child. All four aspects of the toy's use have to be considered by the toy maker and in cases where the toy may be dangerous to younger children, additional warnings are included on the package. For example, electrical toys are not considered safe for children under the age of eight, and most electrical toys will include a warning to parents about allowing younger children to use this toy.

The government has the U.S. Consumer Product Safety Commission test and judge the safety levels of toys and games. If a toy has a repeated history of accidents then the toy can be recalled from the market, making it unavailable for sales. If the design of a toy is found to be inherently dangerous, the toy can be banned permanently from sales, as was the case with lawn darts. The Commission samples several thousand toys each year for safety inspection, but not all toys are investigated before being placed on the market.

Both art designers and industrial designers working on the manufacturing of a new product pay attention to the safety aspects of the design. They consider all of the elements that go into a design and adjust accordingly during the testing period for a new product.

Toys that are being sold abroad have to meet safety standards of the country they are sold in. Toys that are being sold from other countries in the United States have to meet U.S. standards. However, the sheer quantity of toys brought in exceeds the number of toys that can be tested by the Consumer Product Safety Commission, so parents are also responsible for checking toys to make sure they are safe.

Before the toy has been approved for production, the feasibility studies on sales are completed. This gives the company some idea about the sales potential of a toy. The cost of producing reasonably priced, safe, durable toy depends on the sales figures. A toy that sells millions of copies costs less per item in production than a toy that only sells several thousand copies. For both toys, the company must pay for production labor and equipment, the molds used to make the toy, the packaging designers, and all sorts of other costs. The larger the sales, the smaller the distribution of the costs are for each individual sale.

Colors of the toy, the package, and other design characteristics are discussed and decided upon. Advertising campaigns are discussed as well. Marketing strategies, including placement on the store shelves, are presented. From all this information, and the information from the research and design staff, the decision is made to go ahead with or cancel the production of a toy.

Once the toy has been approved for production, the manufacturing and purchasing departments begin their part of the work on the new design. Manufacturing of the toy, frequently done abroad in foreign plants, is initiated by the manufacturing staff inside the company. Orders are placed to either produce the material directly or have someone else produce some aspect of the product. For doll clothing, for example, it is frequently easier and more cost effective to buy the products wholesale from an independent manufacturer than to order a new production of the item needed.

Items that are purchased wholesale are tested for durability and safety as well as the products that are ordered directly for the company. Colors are matched and quantities ordered and shipped to the factory for assembly. Inspectors are on site at the factory to randomly check the production run. Inspectors also check random samples of the shipped products during quality-control inspections.

The toy that is being produced will have the production orders established before the actual production begins. Woodworkers will be hired for the wooden toys, plastics manufacturers for the plastic pieces, and metal workers for the pieces being ordered in metal. Assemblers and finishers work on putting the pieces together and polishing up the rough edges of the product after the pieces of the toy are made. This is a large enough industry that specialists in certain areas have been developed; for example, doll wig makers work only on doll hair, setting the synthetic hair into the holes in the dolls' heads and combing and shaping the hair.

Once the toy is produced, whether it is assembled abroad or in the United States, customs specialists are responsible for the move-

A researcher observes a child while she plays with a newly-designed toy. If the child plays with the toy as expected, the toy will be marketed to the general public.

ment of all goods needed by the toy industry into the United States. They are responsible for knowing all the regulations that the toy industry is affected by, and they insure that the regulations are followed. They research the tariffs and duties required of incoming goods to arrange the best financial situations for the manufacturer. The customs department is also responsible for arranging the shipment of produced toys to foreign markets.

Once the toy is made, boxed and ready for sales, it is sent in quantity to the stores that will be selling the toy to the consumer. Toy sales reach a peak just before the Christmas and Hanukkah holidays, so manufacturers try to get new toys on the market during the three month period before the holidays. Competition for shelf space in the store is strong, and the manufacturers will try to arrange for the best location and sales point for their products in the store. One standard way to encourage purchase of their toys by store owners is to allow stores to order toys in the third quarter of the year and not make payments on the shipment until the fourth quarter.

Once the toys are on the shelf and the advertising campaign has begun, the consumer decides which products will be big sellers. Having a single large selling product can maintain a toy company for a few years, but if sales slide off on the product, the company may not remain profitable. However, one continually well selling toy, such as a G.I. Joe, can be a large part of the continued success of the company.

With most of the largest manufacturers of toys, there is one toy or game that continues to be a best seller for the company. This estab-

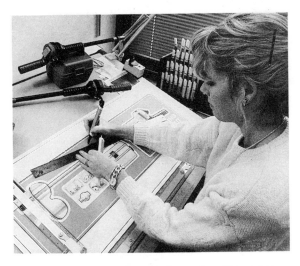

An designer sketches a possible advertisement for a children's fishing rod. She must emphasis the safety features of the toy.

lishes the company's place in the market in two ways: it allows the company a guaranteed money making product, and it encourages satisfied consumers to try new products from a company the consumer has familiarity with. For toy manufacturers, the company's public image is a large part of its success in sales.

Careers

A sampling of career opportunities follows below.

Art designers: Art designers are responsible for creating the image of a new toy. Dolls, board games, and such start with a concept for the product. Art designers must produce a visual image to accompany the information that will be presented to decide which toys to produce and which ones to let lay. The design is a key element in the success of a toy or game and the designer must create a competitive, attractive, marketable product.

Industrial designers: Industrial designers concentrate on both the technical and the artistic elements of a toy design. They must consider the qualities of the materials as well as the aesthetic goal of the object under consideration. The industrial designer is responsible for developing the least costly design acceptable for the market and target customer. They work with the artistic designer in developing prototypes of toys for the test markets.

Engineers: Depending on the materials used in production, engineers are used to develop the molds, materials, and pieces that will be part of the new toy design. Electrical toys re-quire an electrical engineer to design the elements that make the toy work. Ceramics engineers will design toys that use clay, glass or other ceramic products. For other types of toys, other specialists can be hired to handle the development and production of the new product.

Graphic artists: When graphics are included on a board game, toy, or on the packaging and advertising, graphic artists are responsible for the designs that are used. On a board game, the pictures, paths, images and other art work are all the product of the graphic artist's pen.

Model makers: Model makers develop the prototype examples of toys. They create the first working models of a new design so any changes requested will not require extensive additional costs. Since the models can be created one at a time, initial molds may not be needed, and this keeps the cost of the model down.

Researchers: Involved in several different areas of toy and game production, researchers are trained to study one area or more of the many that are used. Areas such as the educational needs of children, advertising effectiveness, and consumer expectations are topics that the researcher investigates before, during, and after production of a new product.

Safety engineers: Safety is one of the most important factors in toy and game design. There are strict government regulations on what materials can be used, and there are voluntary government guidelines for age factors in product recommendations. Safety engineers evaluate designs for potential safety problems. They investigate the wear and tear on the toys, the weaknesses and strengths of the design, and the potential for bodily harm in misusing the toy.

Packaging designers: Once a product is developed, a package that enhances sales is designed. The packaging of a toy has several areas of consideration: protection of the product so it is not broken or damaged in shipping and handling; accessibility in viewing or depicting the product in the package; and easy removal from the packaging without damage to the product. Packaging designers need to consider who will be selecting the toy and what the likely element of interest is, so that point can be emphasized in the packaging design.

Production supervisors: When the product is designed, the production of the toy or game on a mass scale is started. A production supervisor will oversee the making of one part, several parts, or the entire toy, depending on the design. Production supervisors can specialize in one type of production (for example, mold casting plastic pieces), or they may have a general background for different types of production.

They are responsible for covering the various elements that go into production, such as accounting, ordering materials, and labor negotiations.

Production inspectors: In order to ensure the quality of products that are produced, a production inspector evaluates random samples of the item being produced. Pulling samples from the production line, checking samples of already produced shipped items, or checking the quality of items already assembled, are all part of the inspector's job.

Sales representatives: Sales representatives talk to store owners about the new products that their company has produced. They take orders for new toys, solicit reorders on the older toys, and handle questions and complaints.

Consumer affairs officers: The consumer affairs officer handles questions, complaints, and concerns of the people purchasing the product. The officer may also be responsible for handling press interviews and questions, although most large companies will also have a press office (see volume 1: Public Relations).

Education

For skilled labor in design, development, and manufacturing of toys, apprenticeships and trade schools offer an opportunity to gain the skills needed in whatever trade work the student selects.

Line production workers are trained on the job. The skills required for such positions as assembler, hand finisher, or toy stuffer are all learned while working. Promotion is earned through skill and reliability.

Managerial and creative positions require a college degree for most companies. For creative positions, a degree in fine arts, commercial art, or graphics arts would be a common route to employment. For researchers and developers there are a variety of possible programs to follow. Child development, elementary education, psychology, sociology, marketing, or business administration are all potential avenues to a career in toy and game production. It depends on the interests of the student and the area of employment that the student targets.

Industry outlook

One factor in the growth of the toy industry is the increase in the number of children between the ages of one and fourteen. In 1988, the toy industry had an estimated $10.4 billion in total

Many advertisements are geared towards parents who want to ensure that the toys they purchase have educational value for their children.

worldwide sales. Each year's sales have been larger than the year before. This suggests a continued growth in the toy industry, although much of this growth will take place overseas, especially in Asia. Video games continue to be a big attraction, and doll sales have also been strong.

Although the toy industry should continue to expand, individual companies may or may not succeed. A toy company is often only as strong as the sales on its most recent product. There are hundreds of small American toy companies. Some will grow rapidly, others may go out of business.

◇ **SOURCES OF ADDITIONAL INFORMATION**

Toy Manufacturers of America
200 5th Avenue
New York, NY 10010

Toy Wholesalers Association of America
66 East Main Street
Moorestown, NY 08057

National Association of Doll and Stuffed Toy Manufacturers
200 East Post Road
White Plains, NY 10601

For a list of accredited schools in design, contact:

National Association of Schools of Art and Design
11250 Roger Bacon Drive, Suite 21
Reston, VA 22090

◇ **RELATED ARTICLES**

Volume 1: Advertising; Design; Foreign Trade; Marketing; Packaging; Plastics
Volume 2: Commercial artists; Designers; Industrial designers; Marketing, advertising, and public relations managers; Marketing research personnel; Packaging engineers
Volume 3: Molders; Plastics products manufacturing workers; Toy industry workers

Trade Unions

General information

The idea of workers or craftsmen banding together for their mutual benefit has existed in Europe since the 11th century. In the Middle Ages, groups of craftsmen, such as blacksmiths, carpenters, and weavers, organized themselves into guilds. The guilds established product quality standards and wage standards. They also set forth the requirements for entering their trade or craft, and erected barriers against outside competition.

Craft guilds were important to the economic life in Europe from the 12th to the 15th century because they affected the economic welfare of both the guild member and the consumer. The guild members were highly regulated and governed, while the consumer benefitted from the high quality of goods produced. By the 14th century, guilds had begun to compete with the rich merchant class for the right to govern. In some municipalities, they succeeded in taking control.

In the 15th century, guilds began to lose their power as municipalities deprived them of privileges and placed restrictions on them. During the French Revolution, all guilds in France were abolished and in England guilds were abolished by acts of Parliament in 1814 and 1835.

In the United States the first guilds were shoemakers, carpenters, and printers, and they were organized as early as 1791. These early unions were not strong because they were not able to include all the workers in their crafts. But they still did their best to seek higher wages, shorter work hours, and the enforcement of apprenticeship regulations. Unions also established the principle of the "closed shop," which eliminated non-union hiring. The first recorded meeting between worker and employer representatives occurred in 1799 between the Philadelphia shoemakers and their employers.

The forerunner of today's business agent grew out of an early need for unions to enforce the union wage scales. "Tramping committees" were formed, made up of unpaid representatives of the union that would visit the different shops. As the unions grew, these representatives became specialized, paid "walking delegates."

The wage question increased in importance as unions became stronger, and employers tried to organize to resist the union wage demands. From 1806 to 1814, legal battles were fought in the courts in Philadelphia, Pittsburgh, and New York, over the controversy concerning unions as a conspiracy to restrain trade. This controversy lasted through the 19th century, with its emphasis shifting toward the means in which a union restrained trade. As a result, unions became lawful but their means to bargain (strikes, boycotts, and other methods) became unlawful. This was the focus of much court action.

In the larger cities around 1820, organizations for the tailors, hatters, weavers, nailers, and cabinetmakers arose, and for the first time there were organizations for factory workers.

By 1836, unions were organizing on a city-wide basis and were moving toward organizing on a countrywide basis until the period of depression and unemployment hit that lasted through most of the 1840s. By the late 1840s, industry had revived and the unions became more active. Most of the important trades had some degree of union organization by 1854.

In 1869, the Knights of Labor was founded. Initially developed as a secret organization out of fear of employer retribution, the union was the first to organize a broad spectrum of workers into one union. With the election of Terence Powderly to the position of Grand Master Workman in 1879, the union shed the cloak of secrecy and membership grew with the power of the union. One of the most significant events for the union was the successful campaign in

Mining was one of the first industries to become unionized. The union lobbied for reasonable work hours and more extensive health and safety regulations.

1885 against railroads held by Jay Gould, in which workers struck for improved working conditions. The membership peaked in 1886 with 702,000 people, but declined soon after from the combination of anti-union sentiment and the resulting fear from the Haymarket Riot.

The Haymarket Riot was centered around the violent confrontation between labor protestors and the police in Chicago, on May 3, 1886. One person was killed during the clash between strikers, strikebreakers, and police in front of the McCormick Harvesting Machine Company. The strikers had been pressing for an eight-hour workday, a reduction in the number of hours the workers were required to work.

A meeting was called for May 4, 1886 to protest police brutality in the handling of the situation the day before. The site was the Haymarket Square where the anarchist leaders that had called for a demonstration would hold their rally. Several thousand workers and onlookers gathered in a peaceful congregation until a group of policemen attempted to drive the crowd off. An unknown person tossed a dynamite bomb into the crowd, killing several policemen and injuring dozens in the crowd. Police then opened fire on the crowd, with some workers firing guns as well. Seven alleged members of the anarchist group in the labor union were sentenced to death for the incident, with four actually executed, including the purported leader August Spies. One other killed himself, and the remaining three were par-

doned by the governor in 1893 on grounds of insufficient evidence for conviction.

The overall effect of the Haymarket Riot was to increase dissatisfaction and distrust of union workers and leaders. It brought about a decrease in the number of union members and the authority of the unions in negotiation.

Despite the sentiment that adversely affected the Knights of Labor, another union was forming that would eventually supersede it. In 1886, The American Federation of Labor (AFL) became one of the first national unions. The AFL joined the Federation of Organized Trades and Labor Unions of the United States and Canada. Its main power was developed in collective bargaining—the use of representatives to voice the needs and wants of the workers, with its strength in numbers of workers who are union members. Through its intensive lobbying, the AFL was able to get child labor laws passed and was also able to get higher wages, shorter hours, and workmen's compensation for its members. Samuel Gompers was elected president and led the AFL until his death in 1924.

The fluctuation in the U.S. economy throughout the 19th century was, at times, damaging to union growth, but collective bargaining grew stronger as a negotiating tool. The first Labor Day parade was held on September 5, 1882, in New York City.

The beginning of this century saw huge growth in union membership, which jumped from less than 800,000 in 1900 to more than five million by 1920. During this time, unions lobbied for better working conditions, eight-hour workdays, and wage increases. In 1914, through the insistence of the AFL, clauses were inserted into the Clayton Anti-trust Act, exempting unions from being prosecuted on the grounds of the restraint of trade. But this victory was short-lived, as court interpretations almost nullified the Clayton Act.

Labor shortages during World War I brought about union expansion and, for the first time in history, a federal labor agency set forth the right of workers to organize into trade unions and to collectively bargain with employers. This was accomplished by the Department of Labor, established in 1913.

Unions received a further boost from the New Deal legislation with the Wagner Act in 1935, giving unions more ability to organize in the face of strong employer opposition. The Wagner Act established the National Labor Relations Board to handle labor disputes.

It was also in 1935 that an internal rift occurred in the AFL between the craft and the industrial unions. There were essentially two types of unions within the AFL: the craft union, whose members were all skilled in a certain craft such as carpentry or electrical work; and the industrial union, whose members all worked at various jobs within a certain industry, such as automobile or steel manufacturing.

The Committee of Industrial Organizations, later renamed the Congress of Industrial Organizations (CIO), came into being, and split with the AFL. The CIO represented the industrial unions' interests, such as the United Mine Workers, rather than the craft unions' interests. This actually proved beneficial to union membership as a whole because of the competition that developed between the AFL and CIO.

In 1955, the American Federation of Labor and the Congress of Industrial Organizations merged, and the AFL-CIO was founded. The alliance proved successful in serving the needs of both types of unions.

In the early 1990s, there were more than forty unions with 100,000 members or more. The National Education Association had almost two million members, making it the largest in the United States. The AFL-CIO affiliated unions have more than twelve million members nationwide. The total number of union members is estimated at seventeen million, with another three million workers represented by unions but not holding union membership.

The number of strikes have dropped from 222 in 1960 to 46 in 1987. Almost 900,000 workers were involved in the strikes of 1960; only 174,000 were in striking groups in 1987. There were 425 collective bargaining settlements for companies with 1000 or more employees, which meant that contracts were negotiated to the satisfaction of both sides without the use of a strike.

The structure of the trade unions

Organizers begin the process of establishing a union for a group of workers. The organizers may be independent, but frequently they are affiliated with an established union and have been trained in organizational skills specifically oriented toward unions. They initiate interest in a local chapter of the union for a group of employees. The group normally holds a vote to determine if the majority want to pay the annual dues and agree to the rules of the union for wage negotiation and honoring strikes. The organizers from the union should be familiar with labor laws, strategies in planning publicity and other elements of the union building, and should be able to handle the disputes and controversies that may arise between the business

A union representative meets with management to discuss the issues that will be raised during the next union negotiations.

management and the workers interested in unionizing the establishment's workers.

Once a union is established, the union members select someone to be the officer in charge of day-to-day functions of the union. The position is usually a paid, full-time job, with a person chosen from the ranks of union members and workers in the trade represented. Therefore, an auto worker would be elected to the position (called president) of the local automobile union.

In industrial unions, the locals are directed by a central union, which is led by a regional director and is part of a large national or international union. Craft unions are organized somewhat differently. Each craft is represented by a different business manager, and several of these managers work on the staff of a district council. These district councils are like an organization of unions. Each is governed independently of the others, but band together for bargaining strength.

One of the most important aspects of the job of union business manager is the role of liaison between workers and employers. This role becomes most important when the union and its contributing employers need to negotiate a new contract for the employees. The business manager needs to know what the union members want when talking with the management about wages, benefits, pensions, working conditions, layoffs, workmen's compensation, and other issues.

The president or manager will explain the union's position to the management during pre-bargaining talks. During negotiations, the union staff will keep the union members in-

The automobile industry is heavily unionized. Such an organization provides its members with an effective means of improving work conditions and increasing benefits.

formed of the progress of the contract talks, advising them of the management's position. The union representatives need to be able to drive a firm bargain with the employers, yet be aware of the realities of the employer's position, so that a contract can be written that is agreeable to everyone. If a contract agreement cannot be reached, the union may have to organize a general strike, which can be difficult for both labor and management.

The union has the responsibility of making certain that it is serving its members properly. The president often handles grievances expressed by union members and, if necessary, will work with people in the company to solve them. It is also the president's job to insure that the terms of the union's contract are being carried out by the employers. The union staff is in constant contact with the union members through the shop steward, who can be elected by the membership or appointed by the business agent.

The public image of the union is also an important concern for the union press agent. This involves everything from contacting newspaper reporters and other members of the media to organizing charity drives.

The national and international (the United States and Canada) unions are formed by groups of local unions who band together for stronger sway in negotiations of contracts with employers. Representatives from each of the locals are voted on by the local membership. Those representatives are responsible for electing the board that runs the national or international union. The union president will be elected from the delegates and the executive council members will also be elected. Frequently the union president is a previous office

holder from the executive council. Somewhat like governmental elections, the conventions are held regularly at least once every five years, as designated by federal labor laws. They are usually held every two or three years. Delegates may be one from every local or one for every thousand or so union members.

The national and international level unions hire permanent staff to cover different areas of running the organization, such as press agents, publications staff, research staff, and lobbyists.

Careers

A sampling of career opportunities follows.

Union business agents: Also known as administrative officers, executive secretaries, and other titles, agents are representatives of the working members of a union. Agents are usually elected by those members in a democratic fashion, although sometimes they are appointed by the union's elected executive board.

In an industrial union, a business agent would speak for workers in several small plants or a single large plant. In a craft union, the agent would represent a single trade or group of crafts people.

Local representatives: Local representatives take care of a large number of duties that are required in the running of a union. Duties will usually include organizing, contract enforcement, handling grievances, and bargaining. Local representatives do many of the same things that business agents do, and the role varies from union to union.

Organizers: Specifically brought in by the national union that has been approached for possible representation for a group of workers, the organizers are responsible for orchestrating all the moves that will be made on the part of the union to establish a local for that group. There are strict guidelines to be followed which have been set up by the government for both the union representatives and the employer. It is the chief responsibility of the organizer to follow those guidelines while presenting the union in the most favorable light for acceptance among the voting employees. Organizers have a heavy travel schedule.

International representatives: With background in running local unions, international representatives are provided to the local unions to help them organize, bargain, and run the local union. They frequently work with the smaller unions that do not have a paid staff. They conduct training and education programs for members of the local union who are or plan on becoming involved in union operations. International representatives frequently have more than one local union that they are responsible for handling, so travel is a major part of the job.

Research analysts and researchers: Collecting information that will help a union in bargaining and organizing is the role of the research staff of the national or international union. Research analysts decide what information should be collected, how it should be interpreted, and how to present it to union officials, management, and the union members.

Division directors: For different areas requiring supervision by the union, the union may employ a director to oversee the quality of care and consideration the management has for a specific area of concern. For example, a human rights director polices the affirmative action programs in the work place while the health and safety director checks on potential health code violations and distributes education information to workers on industry safety problems.

Legal staff: Lawyers, legal assistants, and councils, are hired on a retainer or as permanent staff, depending on the size and needs of the union. For an organization as large as the AFL-CIO, there is a staff of lawyers who specialize in labor law and contracts.

Press staff: Disseminating information to the press and public on the activities of the union, the press staff of the national and international union prepares press releases and information packages (see Volume 1: Public Relations).

Union presidents: Normally elected from the staff of the executive council, and usually a past member of the executive council, the president is the director of the union's activities on a long term and short term level.

Executive council: The second highest authority in a national or international union, the executive council are the union members in governing positions. The executive council members are normally given titles such as vice president.

Education

To succeed as a union representative, a person needs to have leadership qualities. Union business agents must be committed to the cause of the union and to the rights of the workers. Their role in negotiations requires intelligence, persuasiveness, patience, and self-discipline. They must be able to command respect from both the employer and the union members.

Union staff should have first-hand experience in the trade, industry, or profession whose union they wish to represent so that

Union members attend a meeting at their local chapter to review current union policies.

they can appreciate the problems and concerns facing the workers. Most union staff members join a profession or apprentice a trade, after which they get involved with the union as members and work their way up through the ranks of leadership. If no union exists at their company, they can organize one.

Communications skills are essential if an agent is to vocalize the concerns of the workers, understand the terms of union contracts, and convince representatives of a company to accept an agreement. If the union leadership has reached a decision that may be unpopular, the agent will have to be persuasive in explaining the reasoning behind the decision to the rank and file.

A high-school diploma is important to a union business agent. Course work should include English, mathematics, and public speaking. History, political science, and economics are also useful, as are technical courses in the skills required in the industry or craft chosen. To gain experience in policy-making and to nurture leadership qualities, students should get involved with the student council, the debate society, and other high-school clubs.

A college degree can also be very valuable for union business agents. Many colleges now offer curricula in labor and industrial relations. Additional courses that agents would find useful include psychology, collective bargaining, labor law, occupational safety and health, and economics. Some unions may offer to reimburse the costs of seminars and college courses for those people interested in rising in union leadership. Some unions have programs to prepare for leadership within the union local. In those cases, business agents will receive less formal training, and more on-the-job training with experienced union leaders.

An agent's dedication to the union often dictates the amount of hours worked every week. Most agents work a forty hour week, but they may work much longer during contract bargaining talks and membership organizing drives. They are also expected to be available twenty-four hours a day to handle emergencies.

Agents generally split their time between field work and office work at council or local headquarters. They spend many hours visiting factories and construction sites, meeting with stewards and listening to the opinions of the rank and file. In these visits, they have to deal with the working conditions of their industry. Agents also travel a great deal, and can be on the road for long periods of time.

Because of their role as liaison between the workers and the management, and between the workers and the union hierarchy, agents can experience a great deal of emotional stress as they listen to the concerns and demands of each side. Negotiation requires a great deal of judgment, persuasive ability, and mental and emotional strength. To reach an agreement, business agents may have to give up some demands and agree to others. If an agreement cannot be reached, the agent may have to help arrange a strike. This is a drastic step that may or may not be successful. The job of a union business agent is not an easy one, but it can be personally rewarding to improve the lives of the union membership, while promoting the interests of the union.

Industry outlook

The success of union business agents depends to a great extent on the strength and growth prospects of their particular union, and their industry in general. Union membership continues to grow, but not at as fast a rate as the labor force as a whole is growing. The best opportunities, then, for employment and advancement, exist in those industries expected to grow in the years to come.

Recent years have seen a shift in the U.S. economy away from manufacturing toward service industries. The U.S. Bureau of Labor Statistics predicts that, by the year 2000, nearly four out of five jobs will be in the industries that produce or render services. These industries include insurance, banking, legal services,

health care, accounting, retailing, data processing, and education. The growth of these industries and the industries that support them will provide the greatest growth in jobs in the upcoming decades, and so may provide the greatest opportunities for unionization and union workers. The teachers' union, the National Education Association, is an example of one of the largest single group unions in the United States.

Opportunities for union employees will arise around the fields of health care, computer sciences, and secretarial work. Workers, such as nurses, nursing and medical assistants, technicians, custodians, sales workers, and data processors are likely to form unions as the demand for their services grow.

The manufacturing sector of the economy, which traditionally has been very unionized, is expected to lose jobs to increasingly efficient technologies and competition from overseas. However, certain areas of opportunity will still exist. Increases are expected in certain durable goods industries such as electronic computing equipment, medical supplies, plastics, glass, and commercial printing.

The earnings of business agents vary from union to union. Their pay is usually prescribed in the union's bylaws or constitution. Normally agents' wages conform closely to the wages of the other members of the union. In addition, agents get the same benefits as other union members, such as paid holidays, health insurance, and pension plans. Some agents may drive a car owned by the union and have their expenses paid for while they travel on union business.

◇ **SOURCES OF ADDITIONAL INFORMATION**

American Federation of Labor and Congress of Industrial Organizations (AFL-CIO)
815 Sixteenth Street, NW
Washington, DC 20006

International Brotherhood of Teamsters, Chauffeurs, Warehousemen and Helpers of America
25 Louisiana Avenue, NW
Washington, DC 20001

International United Automobile, Aerospace and Agricultural Implement Workers of America (UAW)
8000 East Jefferson Avenue
Detroit, MI 48214

United Steel Workers of America
5 Gateway Center
Pittsburgh, PA 15222

US Department of Labor
Employment and Training Programs
200 Constitution Avenue, NW
Washington, DC 20210

◇ **RELATED ARTICLES**

Volume 1: Business Administration; Politics and Public Service
Volume 2: General managers and top executives; Labor union business agents; Personnel and labor relations specialists

Transportation

General information

Transportation is a service-producing rather than a goods-producing industry. It provides the ability to move passengers and packages from one point to another, a service so vital to all industries that transportation is sometimes called a utility, as essential as electricity, phone service, and running water. Almost everything Americans eat, wear, or use at home or in business is made accessible thanks to the transportation industry.

The transportation industry comprises four major modes: water, rail, motor, and air. The industry's two main functions are moving passengers and cargo. Each mode contributes to a complete transportation system. For example, a truck can transport a product from San Francisco to New York. This material can then be loaded on a ship to take it across the Atlantic Ocean to Europe. The combined use of different modes of transportation extends the reach of freight far beyond the cities served directly by airlines, trucks, trains, or ships.

Even before the invention of the wheel over five thousand years ago, transportation played an important role in bringing people and products together. Ancient civilizations, such as the Phoenicians, used boats and other methods to establish trade routes. Transportation networks were also used for military purposes. The Roman Empire established a network of roads that enabled it to conquer the world. Roads were originally needed for movement of armies, but the roads also provided routes for trade. The trade established Rome as the financial center of the western world for several hundred years. Early explorers relied on ships and navigation techniques to sail around the world.

Today, transportation continues to play a crucial role in the world economy. Trucks, trains, airplanes, and ships carry goods to warehouses, stores and manufacturing plants. These same transportation systems carry millions of passengers on business and pleasure trips.

The history of transportation has depended not only on technological progress, but on structural changes as well. For example, the steam locomotive was invented in 1830, but it was another forty years before railroad tracks were laid all the way to the Pacific coast. Therefore, while rail transportation was booming east of the Mississippi River by the middle of the 19th century, travelers had to make do with wagons and stagecoaches as they moved west. Today, air travel dominates the transportation industry, but its growth is limited by the number of airports available, and the need for radio control towers to regulate air traffic for safe travel.

Modern technology has revolutionized the transportation industry. With airplanes, people and products can fly across the country in a matter of hours. Spacecraft now transport satellites and other materials thousands of miles into space. Here on earth, computers are helping to automate many of the tasks involved in establishing an effective transportation system.

In the United States, trucking employs just over 50 percent of the estimated three million people who work in the transportation industry. Air transportation employs another 24 percent, railroads employ 10 percent, local transportation employs about 10 per cent, and water transportation employs about 6 percent of the work force.

Land transportation carries most of the freight in the United States. Railroads carry about 33 percent of the freight and trucks carry about 25 percent of the freight. Trucks are getting more of the high-value, lighter-weight, short-distance shipments. Rail traffic has shifted gradually to longer hauls of bulk commodities.

Because of the greater cost, airlines do not carry a lot of freight, but airlines carry the majority of passengers, both nationally and internationally.

Freight trains are an efficient means of transporting livestock, coal, and other bulky materials. This train is carrying automobiles from a General Motors plant in Oklahoma City, Oklahoma.

Over the last several decades, water transportation has declined as a way of moving people and cargo. Ships are still used to carry heavy materials, such as grain and oil, around the world.

Amtrak is a quasi-government agency, created by Congress in 1970 to relieve freight railroads of the financial burden of operating passenger trains. Amtrak provides passenger and commuter service, primarily between major cities. On the local level, government has continued to provide most of the public transportation (mainly buses and trains) that carries commuters and other travelers on local trips.

"Piggybacking" (carrying truck trailers and containers on railroad flat cars) has been the fastest growing segment of today's railroad industry. Truck trailers with two separate sets of wheels (one set for highways and one set for rails) have added a new dimension to the piggybacking concept.

Rail bridges are an extension of the piggyback concept. They are services that move overseas cargo in containers by rail between U.S. seaports on opposite coasts or between a seaport and an inland city. To generate the high traffic volumes necessary to make these systems profitable, effective coordination of operations and marketing is required. As one means of doing this, ocean liner companies have acquired or become partners with freight-forwarding companies and other third parties.

The deregulation of the transportation industry, which occurred in the late 1970s and early 1980s, increased flexibility and allowed carriers to respond more quickly to the pressures of the market. Government regulation had set shipping and passenger rates and established other requirements that limited competition. Deregulation legislation allowed transportation companies to set their own rates and develop alternative transportation methods.

A truck dispatcher for a bakery gives a truck driver his schedule and list of destinations for the day.

The structure of the transportation industry

Most of the employees in the transportation industry work for common carrier establishments. Common carriers are companies whose business is moving goods or people from one place to another, usually over certain routes and according to fixed schedules. Bus systems, truck lines, steamboat companies, airlines, railroads, and pipelines are all common carriers. Job opportunities are also available at transportation terminals, and with freight forwarding, packing, warehousing, and storage companies.

Motor carriers include commuter bus companies, taxi cab companies, intercity bus lines such as Greyhound, tour-bus and school-bus services, furniture moving companies, small local package-delivery companies, and long-distance trucking companies.

Air carriers include cargo and passenger plane companies, as well as air-ambulance, helicopter, and private charter services. In the early 1990s there were approximately 200 commercial air carriers employing more than 400,000 people. The industry is highly concentrated, with approximately ten passenger carriers accounting for about 90 percent of all revenue passenger miles. (A revenue passenger mile equals one paying passenger flying one mile).

Rail carriers include freight trains, intercity passenger railways, and commuter systems such as subways and elevated trains. In the early 1990s, there were about twenty major car-

riers and 500 smaller carriers employing nearly 200,000 people.

American water transportation includes foreign and domestic transportation, Great Lakes-St.Lawrence Seaway carriage, inland waterway movements, as on the Mississippi and Ohio Rivers, and local cargo shipments. Water carriers, also known as the merchant marine, comprise tankers, ocean liners, tugboats, canal barges, and ferries. The water transportation industry employs approximately 150,000 people.

No matter what mode of transportation is used to move cargo, the shipping process is basically the same. Traffic clerks record information about incoming and outgoing merchandise, such as its weight, value, and destination. To correctly establish rates, clerks must consult rate sheets. The value of merchandise is often entered on a computer, so that the accounting department and other managerial personnel have quick access to it.

Before goods are sent to a customer, shipping clerks make sure that the order has been filled correctly. They then wrap the merchandise in appropriate material and place it in a container. Different types of containers may be used, depending if the package is going via land, sea, or air. Clerks also address the containers and record the weight and cost of each shipment. The shipping clerk then takes the container to the shipping dock to be loaded on a truck or other vehicle.

Receiving clerks have many of the same responsibilities as shipping clerks only in reverse. They make sure that the delivered containers have the ordered material. They verify that none of the material has been damaged in transit. Often, clerks record this information on computer. The containers are then unloaded and routed to the correct location.

In small companies, one clerk may do all the above duties. In larger companies, a number of clerks take care of these record-keeping responsibilities.

Careers

Many of the jobs in this field are specific to the transportation industry, such as air traffic controllers and traffic engineers. Other occupations, such as computer specialist, can be found in other industries.

Most jobs fall within one of three broad categories: jobs that require no specialized training; jobs that require some specialized training and experience; and jobs that require advanced training and experience. The occupations listed below, highlighting the variety of jobs available in the industry, contain jobs in these three categories.

Airline baggage and freight handlers: These workers take care of freight and luggage in airports. They load and unload planes and place luggage on trailers. The luggage is then transferred to the terminal or to another plane.

Railroad brakers: Railroad brakers display warning lights and signals to notify train engineers of unexpected stops. Brakers may work with engineers or conductors.

Intercity bus drivers: These employees drive the vehicles that carry passengers on city-to-city or interstate routes. They inspect buses before trips to make sure they are safe.

Aircraft mechanics: Mechanics examine, service, repair, and overhaul aircraft and aircraft engines. They also repair, replace, and assemble parts of the airframe (all parts of the plane other than the engine.) Aircraft mechanics work for commercial airlines, private companies, and the military.

Diesel mechanics: Diesel mechanics repair and maintain diesel engines that power such machines as buses, ships, trucks, and railroad trains.

Parking analysts: Parking analysts develop plans for the construction of parking facilities. They help determine the best location for a parking lot and then estimate how much it will cost to build. Analysts prepare maps and graphs to explain their findings.

Truck and bus dispatchers: Dispatchers assign trucks and buses to drivers and otherwise coordinate the movement of vehicles in and out of a terminal. They ensure that schedules are kept and the correct freight is loaded on each vehicle.

Air traffic controllers: Air traffic controllers give instructions, advice, and information to pilots as planes fly between or in the vicinity of airports. They work in control towers and give pilots permission to take off or land. Controllers use radar screens to track planes and must always be aware of weather conditions.

Traffic engineers: Traffic engineers design and plan roads and highways. They must examine traffic flow and other factors when planning safe and economical roads.

Merchant marine pursers: Merchant marine pursers keep a ship's accounts and other paperwork necessary when a ship enters or leaves a port.

Directors of operations: These workers keep vehicles, passengers, and shipments moving to their destinations, safely and on schedule. The director of operations coordinates the movement of vehicles and shipments between company terminals. Workers under the director's

A truck driver checks all of the wiring between her truck and the load. Such safety precautions are necessary when traveling long distances.

supervision are terminal managers, freight supervisors and handlers, checkers, dispatchers, and the people who operate the vehicles.

Freight handlers: Freight handlers load and unload cargo and keep records of their actions. They are employed by both carriers and terminal companies throughout the transportation industry. Usually, special personnel are hired as freight handlers, but in the trucking industry, drivers often unload their own cargo. In air transportation, these workers belong to the ground crew. In the merchant marine industry, they are known as stevedores.

Freight handlers are supervised by terminal managers, who, in turn, report to district managers, who coordinate the freight operations at various terminals throughout a region.

Ticket agents: Ticket agents make and confirm reservations for passengers. They use time-tables, manuals, reference guides, and tariff books to plan routes and compute ticket costs, and they may also maintain an inventory of passenger space available. Some agents check baggage and assist passengers in boarding.

Flight attendants: Flight attendants provide personal services to passengers of airlines to make their traveling as comfortable and enjoyable as possible.

A towboat pilot moves coal barges at a preparation plant in southwestern Pennsylvania. Once he has gathered several barges and tied them together, the barges are then transported to an electrical utility.

Maintenance workers: These employees make certain that vehicles are serviced and ready to go on time. Their primary concern is not with repairs but with preventive maintenance—keeping the equipment in shape so it will not break down and cause the delays that hurt customer relations and reduce company profits.

Among the most important and highly specialized jobs in maintenance departments are those of inspectors, engineers, mechanics, and machinists. Other maintenance personnel include sheet metal workers, carpenters, electricians, painters, drill press operators, and upholsterers.

Maintenance personnel may be employed on actual vehicles or in terminals such as airports, harbors, and bus, truck, and bus terminals. Transportation companies often have one main overhaul base, where the greatest percentage of its mechanics are employed.

Flight engineers: Flight engineers monitor the operation of various mechanical and electrical devices aboard airplanes to make sure they stay in good condition.

Avionics technicians: These technicians inspect, test, adjust, and repair the electronic devices that are the components of aircraft communication, navigation, and flight control systems.

Traffic, shipping, and receiving clerks: Clerks keep track of good transferred between businesses and their suppliers and customers. Traffic clerks record information about incoming and outgoing cargo, such as its destination, weight, and charges.

The traffic department is responsible for maintaining close contact, not only with shippers, but also with the company's sales, accounting, and operating departments to coordinate information about proposed changes in routes and rates. Traffic officials may appear before government regulatory bodies to request permission to change routes and schedules.

Marketing agents: Marketing agents try to determine customer needs and then confer with upper management to develop programs to fill those needs. Marketing agents determine needs both by conducting surveys and by conferring with sales representatives.

Sales representatives: Sales representatives show prospective customers why their transportation company can outperform competitive carriers. Their job is not just to sell a service but to help customers solve their physical distribution problems.

Salespeople often specialize in the transportation of one particular commodity, such as chemicals or textiles, and they become experts on the distribution patterns and problems of a single industry. Sales representatives prepare for their specialty by acquiring a thorough knowledge of their company's freight rates, routes, minimum transportation time between major points, and special loads.

Safety managers: Safety managers identify hazards and appraise conditions that could produce accidents. They also coordinate programs to minimize potential problems.

Education

The educational requirements obviously differ according to the type of job desired. For those who want a job that requires no training or experience, a high-school diploma should be sufficient to get an entry-level job. Jobs in this category include airline baggage and freight handlers, traffic, shipping, and receiving clerks, railroad brakers, intercity bus drivers, and dock workers. Workers in this category usually receive on-the-job training in the appropriate area.

Those interested in a job that requires some training and experience will need at least two years of vocational training, junior college, or college. Jobs in this category include aircraft mechanic, automotive mechanic, parking analyst, and truck and bus dispatcher. Workers in this area receive in-depth on-the-job training in the appropriate area.

For jobs requiring advance training, an undergraduate or graduate degree is usually required. Some colleges offer degree programs in transportation. Jobs in this category include air traffic controller, traffic engineer, and operations manager. Many transportation companies also offer management trainee programs for college graduates in this area.

As the transportation industry becomes more complex, proper education and frequent upgrading of skills are essential to a successful career. For example, those interested in a career in water transportation should keep up with changes in true motion radar, facsimile receivers, loran, radio teletype, very-high-frequency radio telephones, and other telecommunications equipment.

Some jobs in the transportation industry, such as pilots, dispatchers, and aircraft inspectors, require a license from the federal government. There are a number of privately owned and operated schools where one may obtain the training needed to qualify for federal certificates.

Industry outlook

The health of various transportation modes is affected by both external and internal factors. The external factors are linked directly to the country's overall economy and to the health of other industries. For example, when the dollar is weak, foreign countries may find it cheaper to hire American carriers for their exports rather than those owned by non-Americans.

Energy costs have a great impact on transportation companies. Coal tends to be transported by railroad, while oil tends to be transported by tank trucks or ships. Therefore, when foreign oil is expensive and electric utilities turn to coal, the railroads benefit and vice-versa. When foreign oil is cheap, however, there is less offshore drilling in the United States, adversely affecting the service boat industry, which transports workers and supplies to rigs.

Across the transportation industry, pressure is on to increase productivity through automation, which translates into fewer employment opportunities. This is especially true for many of the clerical positions, as computers are used to store and retrieve information. There is also movement to incorporate advances in such areas as computerized tracking of freight and scheduling of vehicles.

The outlook for trucking over the long term appears favorable. Since federal deregulation of trucking wages and shipping rules, the number of drivers has decreased enough to affect the industry. Wages dropped for all drivers but non-union long-distance drivers had the biggest decrease. As competition for qualified, safe drivers increases, wages are expected to rise. Job opportunities in the trucking field currently account for over 50 percent of all jobs in the industry and this trend should continue throughout the 1990s.

Passenger service and available flights have increased significantly, and cargo service, while still small, is becoming more important to the airline industry, though not necessarily for major carriers. Instead, package-delivery air fleets are expanding, and aircraft-truck companies are starting up to meet growing demand for door-to-door package delivery. The increase in air cargo shipments from 1975 to 1987 was 425 percent. Private companies specializing in overnight and two-day cargo delivery are expanding rapidly.

Air travel can continue to increase if airport facilities and the air-traffic management system are expanded. Air cargo carriers are less limited by these variables because they often provide their own ground facilities and use off-peak hours.

Because of the expansion in service, there may be a need for more experienced workers. On the other hand, stricter safety regulations may reduce airport congestion and improve service performance, but will require reduced flight schedules, which translates into fewer jobs.

In addition to piggybacking, railroads are increasing their freight volumes with double-stack container cars. This technology is especially efficient for transcontinental shipments, and makes trains more competitive with trucks. Railroad employment is decreasing, but people are not getting laid off so much as retiring early with special retirement packages. The railroad industry in the United States is being restructured slowly to encourage more shipping by trains.

The health of the American water transportation industry depends heavily on the strength of exports. The U.S. shipping industry carries goods between the United States and foreign ports in direct competition with international operators. The U.S. liner industry operates in a highly competitive international market, resulting in a decline of freight rates.

The annual average number of U.S. seafaring jobs has dropped steadily, but skilled personnel who bring appropriate training and a willingness to serve at sea remain much in demand. Job opportunities are expected to remain more favorable for officers who are graduates of training schools than for merchant marine sailors.

Transportation

◇ SOURCES OF ADDITIONAL INFORMATION

American Public Transit Association
1225 Connecticut Avenue, NW
Washington, DC 20001

American Trucking Associations
2200 Mill Road
Alexandria, VA 22314

Intermodal Transportation Association
6410 Kenilworth Avenue, Suite 108
Riverdale, MD 20737

Transportation Clubs International
203 East 3rd Street
Sanford, FL 32771

Transport Workers Union of America
1980 Broadway
New York, NY 10023

◇ RELATED ARTICLES

Volume 1: Automotives; Aviation and Aerospace
Volume 2: Air traffic controllers; Conductors, railroad; Merchant marine occupations; Pilots
Volume 3: Aircraft mechanics and engine specialists; Airplane dispatchers; Automobile-body repairers; Brake operators, brakers; Bus drivers, intercity and local transit; Diesel mechanics; Flight attendants; Flight engineers; Industrial-truck operators; Locomotive engineers; Motorcycle and small-engine mechanics; Railroad clerks; Reservation and transportation ticket agents; Route drivers; Shipping and receiving clerks; Signal mechanics; Stevedoring occupations; Traffic agents and clerks; Truck drivers, local and over-the-road
Volume 4: Aeronautical and aerospace technicians; Avionics technicians; Marine services technicians; Traffic technicians

Travel and Tourism

General information

The travel and tourism industry is concerned with accommodating the growing number of people with leisure time. It is a huge industry, encompassing hotels and motels, resorts, travel agents, airplanes and other forms of transportation, and other sectors of the economy.

When Rome was at the peak of its power in A.D. 100, it had built cobblestone roads to all of the major cities in Europe. The roads were the most extensive, best constructed roads ever seen, and covered more than 50,000 miles. The road system was constructed by and for the Roman troops but was used mainly for people in commerce and trade. Because of the long voyages taken by travelers, inns and restaurants developed along the roads.

As transportation improved, the numbers of people traveling increased. Pilgrimages to the holy lands, sacred places, and the sites of miracles became more common undertakings for the population. Long voyages of several hundred or thousand miles were traveled by people in search of adventure or commerce.

Eventually travel began to be accepted for the sake of entertainment and enjoyment. Travel provided a diversion for those with sufficient time and money. Coach travel and ship travel designed for the wealthy voyagers was a developing business. These trips were not short jaunts; they commonly lasted for months.

As technology improved the modes of transportation, the numbers of tourists increased. Trains, air balloons, cruise ships, and eventually airplanes and automobiles all added to the methods and means of travel. Tourism was not limited to the idle rich. The working class could afford train fare to the countryside or the big cities. For Americans, a trip to Europe became an achievable goal. Although the cost was still quite high, it was within the grasp of enough people to save for and plan the trip. In the late nineteenth and early twentieth century, a trip abroad was a regular gift to the graduating student. Referred to commonly as a "grand tour," it was seen as a reward as well as a learning experience for the college graduate.

With the advent of regular travel came the necessity of planners for trips. Travel agents who knew which hotels were good, how to get reservations, and how to make travel plans found themselves in business. Thomas Cook, in England, began his business with the guided tour in 1841. He specialized in excursions that serviced hundreds of thousands of people a year. Exotic places like Egypt and the Orient were open to travelers on the Cook tours.

Travel agencies developed everywhere in the West. Travel specialists who could arrange tours and travel guides who knew the ins and outs of faraway places became cherished business people to know. The booming travel industry relied on experts to steer tourists to their establishments.

Luxury cruise ships to carry passengers to Europe were built with the best accommodations and features that could be put on a ship. Orchestras, ballrooms, fine dining halls, and such were the features of these vessels. The Queen Elizabeth was probably one of the best known, most traveled of the luxury liners. Ship travel was intended to be leisurely. Crossing the Atlantic by ship took weeks.

As the airline industry developed, advancements in plane design allowed for a greater number of passengers on a greater number of routes. Small cities were able to establish airports for smaller vehicles, and large cities found themselves with several runways and substantial air traffic.

In the past several years, the airline industry has seen an increase in travelers to the point where air travel is an everyday experience for some business travelers. Cruise ships are rising in popularity, and travel agencies and tour agencies are providing services for a greater number of tourists than ever before.

A group of skiers in the Rocky Mountains are taking lessons in the mornings. This is a good way to meet other vacationers and hone skills for the afternoon runs.

The structure of the travel and tourism industry

The elements of the travel and tourism industry focus on the provision of transportation, lodging, dining, and entertainment. The tourist may choose to combine one or more elements in a package arrangement where someone else has handled the logistics, or the tourist may choose to create a vacation where each of the four elements are selected personally. In all these instances, several travel specialists will be involved in assistance—providing guidance, information, and services to the traveler.

A person who decides to take a trip will normally start out by consulting a travel agent, a guide book, or an information office that provides information on the location to be visited. The information gathering stage of traveling involves pricing the cost of transportation, lodging, and food. The entertainment aspects of the destination are considered as well. Some locations are interesting for their historical relevance, others may provide pleasant natural surroundings.

The goal of the travel agent is to assess the desires of the customer and the requirements of

the vacation in terms of interest and potential cost. The travel agent is responsible for making transportation reservations, hotel reservations, providing relevant information such as visa requirements for travel abroad, and providing any other available information the traveler may desire.

If the traveler is planning the trip without the aid of a travel agent, the resources available are varied, depending on the destination. Embassies and consulates can provide information on immunizations and visa requirements for their country. Information bureaus are available that handle tourist information for countries, states, and cities. These offices may provide brochures, travel planning packages and such. Some make reservations, check hotel availability, and can offer guidance for travel destinations if the visitor so desires.

Travel and tourism is a vital industry in many areas. For example, Hawaii's primary industry in 1989 was travel, with approximately $6.6 billion spent by out-of-state visitors. The Virgin Islands are also supported primarily by more than one million visitors each year. To be competitive against the many other possible places to travel, both Hawaii and the Virgin Islands have advertised heavily on television and in newspapers and magazines. Travel packages to these destinations are readily available and information is easily obtained through any travel agent or from information services.

Tourist information offices are found in every state in the United States. Chambers of Commerce also provide information for towns, counties and regions in the U.S. Cities such as Chicago and New York have active tourist information offices that provide information to out-of-state visitors as well as people who drop by their offices. They may publish books, catalogues, or brochures that list upcoming events so travel plans can be geared around a special activity. They also carry hotel guides, maps of the city and surrounding areas, and calendars of events.

Stratford, in Canada, has built an entire tourist industry around the Shakespeare festival it holds each year. New Orleans has the Mardi Gras parade and its jazz festival, which attract millions of visitors to the city each year. Sports events, such as the Olympics, can be a huge draw for tourists, and the increase in tourism may continue for a long time after the event because of the increased awareness of the location and because of the increased availability of accommodations and activities for visitors.

Packaged tours are available for those who wish to have many aspects of a trip planned in advance. Package tours can range from several days to several weeks. They may cover a number of countries or they may stay in one city the entire time. Tourists have a wide variety of tours to choose from to meet their specific needs and interests. Travel agencies, private groups, museums and other institutions are just some of the organizations that provide package tours.

Beyond the package trip, the tourist may be able to schedule his or her itinerary through a travel agent or the tourist information services. Assistance in checking for museum schedules, holiday schedules, special events and any other dates and times that may affect the trip are all available through agencies or by contacting the place directly.

Written travel guides are available for almost every major city and travel guides for entire regions and countries are also abundant. The guides vary in their design, focusing the information on cost, interest, and time to be spent traveling. For budget minded travelers, several guides for the United States and Europe exist that list inexpensive restaurants, hotels, and travel services.

Many travel guides have lists of reference information for restaurants, including the types

Travel agents can perform a variety of tasks from issuing plane tickets to planning group trips.

of food to order, what the local specialties are, and the average cost of the meal. For more extensive information, there are guides that only cover restaurants, bars, and such.

Language books for travel abroad give translations and pronunciation guides for commonly needed phrases. Cassette tapes are also available for travelers who wish to learn a little of the local language before heading abroad. This sub-industry of travel and tourism has become a booming business. Classes, television shows, and an endless variety of records, cassettes, and books are available for foreign language instruction specifically geared to the traveler. All the commonly studied languages are widely available and many of the more unfamiliar languages, such as African tribal languages, and languages of the slavic regions, are also available.

For tourists interested in spending much of the time actually moving from one point to another, cruise ships provide a slower, more leisurely type of travel. Cruise ships were the only form of travel across the oceans for hundreds of years. With the onset of air travel, cruise ships fell out of favor. It has only been in the past few years that cruise travel has once again gained in popularity.

Cruise ships provide enough entertainment so that some passengers regard them as floating vacation spas. The locations visited by the ship may not be that important to the cruise passengers who choose whether or not to disembark at ports. Cruises can run from three days to several months and may dock in two or three cities or may voyage around the world. Some of the most popular cruises in the early 1990s were to the Arctic, the Antarctic, and

Cruises offer continuous activities for their patrons. This gives people the option of relaxing on the ship or participating in the activities with other vacationers.

Alaska. The rugged terrain and remote wilderness provide an ideal view from the water.

Health and recreation spas serve some of the same functions as the cruise does. Everything required for the vacation is present in one location. If the guest decides he or she does not want to leave the grounds until the end of the vacation, the facilities provide everything from food to entertainment to keep the guests happy. The spas may choose to have an operating theme, such as physical health care, and many of the day's activities will focus on that. A health spa will include health conscious menus, exercise classes, massages, relaxation therapy, and other aspects of health training and support.

Careers

There are a variety of careers and work settings available in the travel and tourism industry. Reservation agents, for example, may work for hotels, airlines, health spas, cruise ships or a number of other facilities directly related to one form of vacation or another. The goals of service to the customer are the same for everyone in the industry. A sampling of career opportunities follows below.

Reservation agents: When someone requires a space on a plane, hotel, train, or ship, a reservation agent will be responsible for checking the availability of accommodations, and reserving a place for the customer. Agents will confirm schedules, arrival times, departure times, and all the necessary information for the customer to ensure smooth travel arrangements.

Ticket agents: Like a reservation agent, the ticket agent is responsible for finding an open place for a customer and verifying the schedule of arrival, departure, and other necessary information.

Car-rental agents: Providing a car to tourists and travelers, car-rental agents fill requests for all types of cars for travelers who require a car while in that city.

Travel consultants: For clients seeking specific assistance and information on certain types of travel, a travel consultant is available to help customize a vacation or travel plan. This assistance may include obtaining a visa for foreign travel, arranging special accommodations for the client, or adapting a schedule to fit the client's needs.

Travel agents: Serving some of the same functions as the travel consultant, the agent issues tickets and reservations as well, and may be able to design group packages and tours for a number of clients traveling together. Travel agents may specialize in one region or one form of transportation.

Vacation tour guides: Accompanying the travelers on their trip, a tour guide provides assistance with accommodations, foreign languages, logistics of travel, and provides information about the places that will be visited while traveling. The tour guide is often responsible for the arrangements required for everything from transportation to and from airports, to the menu to be served in the restaurants where the tour members will eat.

Location tour guides: In many locations such as castles, museums, and historical sites, tour guides are available to present the place in an orderly manner with information that the tourist may not know. Frequently designed to last an hour to several hours, a tour guide gives the tourists an entertaining and informative portrayal of the place they have come to visit.

Food service staff: In locations such as spas, cruise ships, and cross-country trains, food is provided to the tourists while they are in residence. The food staff have different titles in different locations but function as cooks, bakers, waiters and waitress, and hosts and hostesses.

Entertainment directors: Entertainment directors plan parties and other events. They also often act as hosts or hostesses. People who are naturally outgoing are more comfortable with the ceremonial aspects of the job.

Cruise directors: Functioning as the entertainment director on a ship, the cruise director administers the staff that provides all entertainment on the ship. The entertainment staff includes performers, movie theater workers, fitness instructors, and any other staff that provides entertainment service to the passengers.

Hotel directors: In all lodging facilities, the hotel director oversees the staff that provides lodging service to the guests.

Cruise hosts and hostesses: On large cruise ships, hosts and hostesses handle many of the day-to-day aspects of moving the passengers to and from their entertainment activities.

Spa directors: Designing the theme and activities, and hiring staff for spas, directors administer the functions of the spa that give it its unique characteristics and image. They may be the owners of the facilities as well.

Education

For many of the management positions in travel, a college education is the minimum requirement for obtaining work. For cruise directors, travel agents, tour guides, and others, the liberal arts degree is sufficient for entry level positions that are on a career path that leads to these positions. It may be, however, that some companies require more specific educational backgrounds. If one is a tour guide for an agency that specializes in Asian tours, for example, a degree in Asian studies or languages may be needed.

For many of the international travel positions, fluency in at least one foreign language is a necessity. For Norwegian Cruise lines, one of the major cruise ship companies, the host and hostess position requires fluency in three foreign languages and English. For tour guides who handle arrangements and tours in foreign countries, it is usually essential that they speak the language of the country where the tour takes place. For anyone looking to find positions that provide travel abroad, four years of language study at the college level is often a minimum requirement.

While in college, working in service occupations is also quite helpful for developing the skills needed for travel and tourism. Teaching, volunteer work, or work in the public sector all provide opportunities to develop interpersonal skills that are required in almost every travel-related job. Except for some behind-the-scenes staff in food preparation, lodging, and maintenance, almost every other worker will come in contact regularly with customers and travelers. The skills include communication and patience. The ability to help others is basically the goal of the profession.

For specific fields, such as lecturer on educational tours, the educational requirements are

There are many resorts that specialize in particular sports activities. This resort in Colorado features golf in the summer and skiing in the winter.

quite rigorous. Normally these positions are filled by people who are not primarily in the travel industry. They are professionals from another field who are hired on a temporary or free-lance basis to handle specific needs of the travel group. They may be archaeologists, linguists, historians, or another specialist covering the area of interest on a tour.

It is difficult to learn the skills needed for positions in travel without working from the entry level up. It is with the experience of working with travelers that the most important skills are learned.

It is recommended that anyone interested in working in tourism gain experience in working with the public, and gain skills in at least one foreign language. The competition for many jobs in travel is extremely vigorous because it is seen as a glamour industry. Only those candidates with the best resumes and qualifications are likely to find employment. Competition for international jobs is the most intense.

Travel industry jobs, except for positions such as ticket agent, some travel agents, and reservation clerks, require extensive travel. Employees may travel up to ten months a year. The work can be difficult. Employees who are traveling with a group of tourists do not really have time off. When they are with their clients they must behave politely and courteously. They are responsible for the happiness of the travelers and are seen as the travelers' assistant and leader.

497

Travel and Tourism

Industry outlook

As the third largest retail service industry in the United States, travel and tourism is a booming business. It is estimated that there are currently 1.5 million workers in the industry and this number grows by about 100,000 each year.

Changes are affecting the way the industry is structured, though. More people are taking shorter vacation. Three and four day weekends are replacing the two-week vacations that were common in the 1960s and 1970s. As the working population in the United States finds it more difficult to take extended vacations, many travel organizations have had to gear their programs around shorter trips.

The abundance of travelers from abroad to the United States has also increased the need for multi-lingual staffing in areas where foreign tourists are common.

Trying to target specific needs of a specific clientele has proven to be more successful for many travel companies. This may be in terms of economic specialization, with such developments as budget or luxury hotels. It may also be for educational purposes. Cruises to Alaska, for example, have hired wildlife specialists that can give in-depth information about the wildlife seen from the ship.

When the U.S. dollar rises, more Americans travel abroad since they are able to buy more of the foreign currency for each dollar. Foreigners are less likely to travel to the United States when the dollar is strong because they are forced to spend more of their currency. These market fluctuations change regularly and it is difficult to forecast far into the future about the strength of the dollar and its influence on travel.

Despite strong fluctuations in the market, though, it is extremely likely that travel will remain a strong industry for many years to come. It remains the single most important industry in many cities and regions and the tourist trade is readily shifted to meet new demands of the market.

◇ SOURCES OF ADDITIONAL INFORMATION

American Guides Association
8909 Dorrington Avenue
West Hollywood, CA 90048

American Sightseeing International
309 Fifth Avenue
New York, NY 10016

American Society of Travel Agents
1101 King Street
Alexandria, VA 22314

Travel Industry Association of America
2 Lafayette Center
1133 21st Street, NW
Washington, DC 20036

◇ RELATED ARTICLES

Volume 1: Aviation and Aerospace; Food Service; Hospitality; Personal and Consulting Services; Recreation and Park Services; Transportation
Volume 2: Hotel and motel managers; Interpreters; Merchant marine occupations; Pilots; Recreation workers; Sports instructors
Volume 3: Car-rental agents; Hotel and motel industry workers; Railroad clerks; Reservation and transportation ticket agents; Tour guides; Travel agents

Waste Management

General information

The waste management industry is responsible for the collection, storage, and processing of solid waste, liquid waste, and gaseous waste. Waste management promises to be one of the main issues of the 1990s. One reason is that America is a throwaway society. The United States generates about ten billion metric tons of solid waste per year. Another reason is the growing awareness of the environmental and economic problems caused by this huge volume of waste. Politicians from the President on down identify themselves as environmentalists and citizens of all ages and backgrounds are taking an active interest in resource-recycling, resource-conservation, and other waste management issues.

People have always been troubled by waste management concerns. Centuries ago, when much of the waste was agricultural material, individuals disposed of waste in abandoned pits or they burned it on their own property. Because there were not many people in any one area, there were not many major pollution problems.

When people first began to live in cities, however, the sheer quantity and concentration of garbage, sewage, and other substances became so great that the material could not be readily and harmlessly dispersed in the environment. Local buildups of pollution prompted a variety of attempted solutions. The ancient Romans, for example, had trenches outside of cities where they put their trash, a disposal method that ensured periodic epidemic diseases.

With the beginning of the Industrial Revolution in the late eighteenth century, health problems created by smoke and other by-products of manufacturing became significant. Areas with large numbers of factories experienced markedly higher death and disease rates than areas with little industrial development.

Some bodies of water became reservoirs of chemical wastes from untreated sewage, thus posing a major health hazard. In some cases, the air was heavily contaminated with smoke particles and with a variety of harmful gases, both of which contributed greatly to respiratory ailments.

The technological advances of the twentieth century added new and different pollutants to the environment. As automobiles began to play a central role in American society, automobile exhaust increasingly polluted the air. More products were manufactured and consumed, generating more waste material.

The proper disposal of waste did not become an important public issue until the last several decades. Until then, sanitary landfills took most of the refuse and the rest was burned through various incineration methods. Most people did not recognize the dangers of improper waste management. Not until after World War II did the public begin to see the air, water, and land as deteriorating because of pollutants and decide that responsible action was needed to minimize the damage. New pollution-control laws and programs began to be instituted in the 1950s.

In the early 1970s, people began to recognize the dangers posed by hazardous waste and toxic chemicals. Until that time, most hazardous wastes had been simply dumped in landfills across the country. As awareness began to be raised that these landfills were polluting underground water supplies, harming farmland, and causing other ecological damage, a movement began to safeguard against hazardous waste contamination. In 1976, Congress passed the Resource Conservation and Recovery Act, which stated that toxic wastes must be disposed of in specially permitted locations. In 1980, Congress created "Superfund," a five-year, $1.6 billion bill that financed hazardous waste cleanup. The Environmental Protection Agency (EPA) was responsible for administer-

499

A pollution-control technician analyzes a water sample that was taken from a stream near an underground coal mine. She is testing the water to ensure that the mining activities have a minimal environmental impact on the fresh water supply.

ing the cleanup. In 1986, Congress extended the Superfund legislation, increasing its budget to over $8 billion.

The EPA estimates that over 2,000 sites may eventually qualify to be cleaned up under Superfund legislation. Other experts, both in and out of the U.S. government, estimate that over 10,000 sites nationwide may eventually have to be cleaned up.

The EPA also is responsible for setting regulations for air and water pollution. Other governmental agencies are also involved in waste management issues. For example, the Department of Defense will spend an estimated $10 billion over the next ten or twenty years to clean up contamination on military bases.

The proper disposal of waste products is very important. For example, toxic wastes include chemical and other substances linked to cancer, heart attacks, hypertension, and other disorders. It is estimated that eight out of ten Americans, approximately 200 million people, live near a source of toxic waste or a toxic waste site. New landfill technologies are being used to protect surrounding communities. For example, new landfills have layers of low-permeability clay and synthetic material line the landfill, minimizing leakage. This technology is expensive, and many communities have experienced dramatically higher waste disposal fees. The cost of waste disposal will continue to be an issue of public debate in the future.

Although the federal government is involved in waste management issues, state and local political bodies will continue to make vital decisions that impact how much waste is created and how it is disposed. For example, supporters of Bottle Bill legislation, which requires a five or ten cent deposit on bottles, maintain that a deposit on bottles more would encourage more people to return the bottles, thus reducing waste. Critics maintain that the Bottle Bill would not help the environment that greatly. Several states, including Michigan, have adopted Bottle Bill legislation. Cities, like New York City, passed local bottle laws.

There is also a move on the part of many municipalities to limit the disposal of certain materials. Many cities, for example, are not allowing people to dispose of grass in their regular garbage. City leaders are encouraging people to leave the grass cuttings on the lawn. If people do dispose of the grass with the rest of their trash, they usually have to pay additional fees to have it hauled away.

Many cities have drafted legislation that prohibits the establishment of new landfills. With current landfills quickly overflowing with waste, new policies are needed to cope with it. One technique is recycling. Many towns and cities have now established a system whereby residents put papers, glass, and aluminum cans in colored containers. This material is then picked up by special crews and brought to recycling stations rather than the landfills.

With the increased environmental awareness on the part of politicians and the public at large, there has been a move to improve the waste management industry. The private section cleanup industry is quickly becoming a billion dollar annual industry. Obviously, waste problems that took years to accumulate will take years to resolve. But some critics argue that not enough money is being put into cleanup. A congressional study forecasts that cleanup will cost at least $300 billion over the next fifty years. Critics say this is not enough money to invest to safeguard the nation's health.

At this point, most of the emphasis is on limiting the negative impact of waste disposal on humans and the natural environment. But environmentalists such as Barry Commoner argue that the ultimate solution is not in regulating how much of a contaminant is allowed in the environment, but in not allowing contaminants into the production process in the first place. Commoner argues, for example, that the U.S. government was most effective in getting lead out of the air by mandating that lead-free gas be used. Commoner argues that designing expensive technology to extract lead from the air is not effective; better, he says, not to allow lead into the air in the first place.

Many people are now moving toward an understanding that an effective way to reduce waste is to not produce it in the first place. This is known as resource-conservation. For example, there has been a move to reduce the amount of packaging on products. It is estimated that almost 50 percent of residential solid waste is paper of some type. Almost one-third of this trash is estimated to be consumer product packaging and containers. People are most concerned with plastic goods because they take up nearly one-quarter of landfill space. The use of polystyrene, a type of plastic used in fast-food containers, was restricted by some states in 1989. Now, several U.S. chemical companies are opening recycling centers for the plastic in the hopes of recycling 25 percent of the polystyrene by the mid-1990s. There is also a move to reduce the amount of paper and other substances used in packaging.

The structure of the waste management industry

The waste management industry is a highly diversified industry with separate processes designed to handle solid wastes, waste water (sewage), air contaminants, and hazardous wastes.

At present almost three-fourths of all municipal solid waste is deposited in the approximately 6,000 landfills across the country. Another 10 percent is disposed of in open dumps, and about 10 percent is incinerated.

As greater numbers of people become concerned about the negative impact of landfills on health, property values, and the natural environment, the reliance on landfill disposal is being challenged. Legislation is limiting the amount of landfill space available and regulations are greatly increasing the standards of landfill design. Over 1,000 landfills are scheduled to close by 1995 and many more will have to be redesigned to be made safer from leakage.

As a result of the decrease in landfill space and the increase in the cost of pollution-control features, municipalities are looking for ways to reduce their dependence on landfills. This has led to the development of integrated solid-waste management systems, which include conservation programs to reduce the creation of waste, recycling programs to reuse waste into usable goods, new landfill technologies to dispose of waste, and improve incineration technologies to reduce the volume of waste.

Two pollution-control technicians test the level of toxicity in barrels that contain harmful chemicals.

One reason that conservation and recycling techniques can be so effective on the solid waste is that so much of it is paper and other easily reusable material. According to the EPA, about 50 percent by weight of solid waste is paper, paperboard, and yard wastes (grass clippings, etc). Nearly 40 percent of the solid waste is composed of metals, glass, food wastes, and plastics, and 10 percent is made up of rubber, leather, and other inorganic material. More than 75 percent of this solid waste is recyclable material, but this percent of recycling has not been reached due to lack of public cooperation, insufficient markets, and deficiencies in technology. Successful recycling programs today can recycle 30 to 50 percent of the solid waste.

The landfill process usually involves trucks hauling waste to a central site where the waste is spread into layers of uniform thickness. At the end of each day, the layer is covered by a layer of compacted soil to seal the waste from animals and to prevent the release of organic material into the air. When a landfill is full (a process that takes a number of years, depending on the size of the landfill and the amount of waste placed there), it is covered with clay, sand, gravel, and vegetation to minimize erosion. These areas are then often used as recreational sites.

A disadvantage of the use of landfills is that as the need for waste disposal sites grows, less and less suitable land is available. This is compounded by the fact that few people want sanitary landfills located in their communities. At times, trains have been used to haul compacted refuse from transfer station in large metropolitan areas to landfill sites in unused quarries and other rural sites. But more and more fre-

Many waste management businesses collect glass, aluminum, newsprint, and plastic for recycling.

quently, rural communities are refusing to become the dumping ground for waste from neighboring communities.

Another major disadvantage to landfills is that pollutants can leach into the ground and contaminate surrounding land and ground and underground water supplies. As noted, synthetic and clay liners are helping reduce these problems, but during the operation of a landfill the ground water must be continually monitored.

Although landfills are problematic, even after municipal waste has been recycled and incinerated, at least 20 percent remains to be disposed of. Therefore, landfills are a necessary component of any waste-management system.

Incinerators have always been used to burn solid waste to reduce volume. Incineration reduces solid waste approximately 90 percent by volume and 75 per cent by weight. The incombustible solid residue is usually disposed of in landfills. The rest of the material is discharged into the atmosphere as carbon dioxide and water vapor.

A major problem with incineration is that many incinerators cause air pollution by spewing carbon monoxide, hydrocarbons, and particulate matter into the air. When air-pollution laws were enacted in the 1970s, incinerators had to be equipped with pollution-control equipment, such as afterburners that burn most of the polluting gases and special dust collectors to clean the exhaust gases. Due to the cost of this technology, many of the smaller incinerators were forced to shut down.

Increasingly, incinerators are being used for energy recovery. The furnaces that burn the waste heats a boiler that is used to produce steam for generating electricity, heating building, and other industrial processes.

Treatment of sewage is regulated by the Clean Water Act of 1977 and related laws. About 80 percent of the sewage in the United States comes from industrial sources (most of the remaining sewage comes from homes and small businesses). Although some industries operate their own waste water treatment facilities, most sewage is treated in public sewage systems. In most cases, water goes through primary and secondary treatment before being reused or released into a natural waterway.

Primary and secondary treatment remove about 95 percent of the waste material in sewage. In primary treatment, screens trap the largest pieces of solid matter. Other solids settle in a clarifier and are then removed. In secondary treatment, bacteria are used to further purify the sewage and many of the smallest solids sink to the bottom of secondary clarifiers and form sludge. This sludge is removed and is often buried in a landfill. Sometimes chlorine is added to the water to kill most of the remaining bacteria.

Tertiary treatment is sometimes used to remove even more of the contaminants from the waste water. Tertiary treatment involves various methods, including chemical treatment, microscopic screening, and discharging the waste water into lagoons to enhance the settling of solids.

The treatment of waste water has become much more efficient over the last several years, and many lakes and streams are significantly cleaner than they were just a short time ago. Lake Erie, once severely polluted, now has fish.

There are two approaches to responding to hazardous waste problems—removal actions and remedial actions. Removal actions are the immediate responses to accidents involving hazardous wastes. An example would be a truck spilling a load of highly toxic chemicals.

Remedial actions are designed to remove the cause of the contamination, such as leaking chemical drums, and also help reverse the contamination of the soil, surface water, and ground water. Superfund and other clean-up programs are remedial projects.

Because hazardous waste sites differ in the kinds of waste they contain and their geological composition (the composition of the soils and the presence of hills and other features, for example), a separate plan must be established for every cleanup operation. There are basically four steps in every hazardous waste cleanup operation—remedial investigation, feasibility studies, remedial design, and remedial construction.

Remedial investigation entails a comprehensive site investigation to define the extent of the problem. Analysis is often a long, complicated process. Hundreds of samples must be taken.

Using the findings of the remedial investigation, the project manager and other professionals put together a feasibility study discussing the various cleanup alternatives. These studies must discuss possible solutions in light of how effective they would protect the public, if the technology presently exists to implement the solution, and how much it would cost.

When a remediation plan has been approved, design plans are finalized and construction begins. Special care must be taken to ensure that workers are protected against contamination and that safeguards are in place to protect the public from any release of toxic material. To date, relatively few hazardous waste sites have been cleaned up. As of the late 1980s, work had been completed at about fifteen sites.

A technician tests the contamination level of soil by taking samples from various depths.

Careers

A wide range of careers are available in the waste management industry. Some required many years of professional preparation; others required training in a specific area. A sample of careers follows below:

Environmental health inspectors: Environmental health inspectors examine places where pollution is a danger, test for pollutants, and collect air or water samples for analysis. They determine the cause of pollution and initiate action to stop or control it.

Hydrologists: Hydrologists study the circulation, distribution, and physical properties of surface and underground water. They often take water samples to determine if and how a body of water has been polluted.

Nuclear engineers: Nuclear engineers design, develop, monitor, and operate nuclear power plants. They may also work on the safe disposal of the waste produced by nuclear energy.

Analytical chemists: Analytical chemists identify the presence of chemical pollutants in air, water, and soil. They also may help develop techniques which save energy and reduce pollution, such as improved oil refining techniques.

Industrial hygienists: Industrial hygienists check for health hazards in the work place. These hazards may include dust, fumes, and gases. In many cases, industrial hygienists must wear protective gear to monitor pollution

levels. They often suggest ways to reduce pollution-related problems.

Hazardous waste management technicians: Hazardous waste management technicians dispose of chemical and nuclear wastes in a manner that will not harm human health or the environment. They may, for example, remove toxic chemicals from a regular landfill and transfer them to processing centers or to safe disposal areas.

Refuse collectors: Refuse collectors pick up garbage and other waste materials from homes, businesses, and industries and transport the material to landfills or incinerators for disposal or burning.

Incinerator operators: Incinerator operators run private and municipal incinerators. They make sure that the burning of waste products does not exceed legal limits.

Sanitary landfill workers: Sanitary landfill workers operate bulldozers, tractors, and other equipment to cover garbage with layers of earth.

Water and waste water treatment plant operators: Water and waste water treatment plant operators control processes and equipment that remove solid materials, chemicals, and other substances from the water. Operators read and interpret meters to make sure equipment is operating properly and adjust controls as needed.

Pollution-control technicians: Pollution-control technicians, or environmental technicians, test water, air, and soil for contamination. They work in laboratories and outdoors to find ways to identify and control pollution.

Pollution-control engineers: Pollution-control engineers design systems for air and water quality control and solid waste disposal. They study the problem, devise methods of identifying and measuring pollution, and design and build systems to reduce the pollution.

Education

Opportunities in the waste management industry are divided between positions that required at least a college degree and those that do not. Even the positions that do not require a college degree, however, require specific technical skills that demand training and the ability to pay attention to detail. In some cases where an undergraduate degree is desired, experience may substitute for the educational requirements.

An environmental engineer must possess at least a bachelor of science degree in engineering. A bachelor's degree in geology or earth science is a prerequisite for employment as a hydrologist. Environmental geologists and environmental chemists must also have at least a bachelor's degree in their area of specialization. Many professionals do graduate work in their area of expertise. It is extremely important to keep up with the rapid technological changes in the field.

Students interested in pursuing a career in environmental chemistry are usually curious individuals with an ability to concentrate on details. They must also enjoy working with groups and on their own. On the college level, it is wise to concentrate in the sciences with continual exposure to laboratory procedures.

Pollution-control technicians and others with similar job responsibilities do not generally need a four-year college degree. However, a two-year program in pollution technology is usually required. Courses would include introduction to atmospheric pollution, air and soil quality management, technical mathematics, chemistry, environmental science, and statistics. New employees are given extensive on-the-job training.

Water and waste water treatment plant operators also receive extensive on-the-job training. Operators need mechanical aptitude and should have a strong background in mathematics. Some two-year programs leading to an associate degree in water and waste water technology are available.

Refuse collectors may not always need to graduate high school, but as the industry becomes increasingly automated more and more cities are requiring at least a high-school diploma.

Industry outlook

Spending on waste management has skyrocketed in the last several years. Waste management is now a multi-billion dollar industry. It is estimated that the public and private sectors will spend hundreds of billions of dollars on waste management during the 1990s. The rapid rise in cleanup operations has created a strong market for those with an expertise in waste management. Opportunities are especially strong in the hazardous waste field, but skilled scientists and technicians should find a strong job market in all sectors of the waste management industry for the foreseeable future. For example, it is estimated that jobs related to Superfund legislation will grow from about 3,500 in 1984 to an estimated 23,000 by 1995. Many of the openings will be for hydrologists, toxicologists, environmental engineers, and other highly-skilled professionals.

Many of the jobs in waste management are tied to government funding and regulation. If the government is strict about enforcing environmental legislation, private businesses will hire more people to ensure compliance. Private companies will also invest in developing alternative disposal techniques and waste reduction plans.

Private companies specializing in providing technical assistance in cleanup operations will also flourish.

◇ SOURCES OF ADDITIONAL INFORMATION

Environmental Protection Agency
401 M Street, NW
Washington, DC 20460

Water Pollution Control Federation
601 Wythe Street
Alexandria, VA 22314

The National Solid Wastes Management Association publishes a monthly magazine *Waste Age: The Authoritative Voice of Waste Systems and Technology.* Information is available from:

National Solid Wastes Management Association
1730 Rhode Island Avenue, NW, Suite 1000
Washington, DC 20036

Hazardous Waste Treatment Council
1440 New York Avenue, NW, Suite 310
Washington, DC 20005

Plastics Recycling Foundation
1275 K Street, NW
Suite 400
Washington, DC 20005

**Portable Sanitation Association
International**
7800 Metro Parkway
Suite 104
Bloomington, MN 55425

Air And Waste Management Association
PO Box 2861
Pittsburgh, PA 15230

**National Environmental Training
Association**
8687 Via de Ventura
Suite 214
Scottsdale, AZ 85258

American Water Works Association
6666 West Quincy
Denver, CO 80235

Institute of Scrap Recycling Industries
1627 K Street, NW
Suite 700
Washington, DC 20006

◇ **RELATED ARTICLES**

Volume 1: Agriculture; Chemistry; Energy; Engineering; Nuclear Sciences; Packaging; Physical Sciences; Plastics; Pulp and Paper
Volume 2: Biochemists; Biologists; Biomedical engineers; Chemists; Cost estimators; Engineers; Geographers; Geologists; Geophysicists; Groundwater professionals; Health and regulatory inspectors; Industrial designers; Management analysts and consultants; Medical technologists; Operations-research analysts; Packaging engineers; Petrologists; Toxicologists
Volume 3: Agricultural scientists; Foresters; Industrial chemical workers; Occupational safety and health workers; Paper processing operations; Refuse collectors; Soil scientists; Wastewater treatment plant operators
Volume 4: Agribusiness technicians; Chemical technicians; Energy-conservation technicians; Hydrological technicians; Industrial engineering technicians; Industrial safety-and-health technicians; Medical laboratory technicians; Nuclear materials handling technicians; Packaging and paper products technicians; Plastics technicians; Pollution-control technicians; Soil conservation technicians; Water and wastewater treatment technicians

Wholesaling

General information

The wholesaler is the middle person in the distribution chain between the producer of merchandise and the retail store in which the merchandise is sold. Wholesalers deal in such products as automobile parts, pharmaceuticals, clothing, health care products, books, and food. The wholesaler buys good in large quantities directly from producers and sells primarily to retail store owners. The store keeper then sells individual items to customers. By providing the retailer easier access to a variety of products, the wholesaler makes buying easier for the retailer and acts as a vital part in the smooth and effective flow of commerce.

Up until a little over 100 years ago, the buying and selling of merchandise was relatively uncomplicated. Retail store owners would travel to major seaports and manufacturing centers once or twice a year to purchase new products for later resale. Industrial concerns usually manufactured or purchased locally components for the goods that they produced.

The earliest wholesalers in the United States were probably the ship chandlers in New England who assembled goods required by merchant and military ships. Shipowners found that a specialized and centralized supply source enabled them to equip vessels quickly and send them back out to sea.

With the introduction of mass production and mass marketing techniques in the nineteenth century, wholesaling became a vital component of the buying and selling process. Without wholesalers, manufacturers would have had to deal with large numbers of retail store owners or individual buyers, and retail store owners and individual buyers would have likewise have had to deal with large numbers of manufacturers.

The need for wholesalers grew as industrialization changed U.S. manufacturing capacities and consumer tastes, and more complex retail establishments replaced general stores. Individual manufacturers found they could sell more reasonable through the use of a wholesaler. Purchasers of goods found it more convenient to deal with a few sources of supply rather than hundreds of organizations.

The wholesaling industry has continued to grow and expand. By 1990, the U.S. wholesaling industry handled approximately $1.6 trillion worth of merchandise annually. A major development in wholesaling has been the merging of a large number of wholesalers. It is estimated that about 10 percent of the nation's 300,000 independent wholesalers merged with other wholesalers between 1985 and 1990. This concentration of merchandise into fewer and fewer hands is forcing wholesalers to specialize. Wholesalers are now more likely to carry only a limited number of products, rather than a variety of merchandise.

As an integral part of the system of production, distribution, and merchandising of goods, wholesalers play an important role in the economic system that allows consumers to purchase what they want or need. Moving the product from the supplier to the customer destination is the lifeblood of the wholesaling business. This includes warehousing, purchasing transportation, and order processing.

The structure of the wholesaling industry

There are three main types of wholesalers—merchant wholesalers, manufacturers' sales branches, and merchandise agents and brokers. Merchant wholesalers buy large quantities of merchandise from manufacturers, process and store that merchandise until needed, and then redistribute it to retail shop owners and others. Merchant wholesalers operate as independent businesses; they make their profit from the markup in price they add to goods as they sell them. Merchant wholesalers comprise the largest number of wholesalers and are responsible for a great percentage of the total sales in the industry. Of the approximately 210,000 wholesalers in the United States, over 80 percent are merchant wholesalers. Merchant wholesalers usually hire sales workers to call on retail customers.

Manufacturers' sales branches are another important component of the wholesaling industry. Manufacturers' sales branches are businesses established by manufacturers to sell directly to retail shop owners. These branches allow the manufacturer to deal directly with retailers. Manufacturers' sales branches tend to be set up by large manufacturers.

A third type of wholesaler, merchandise agents and brokers, represent either the buyer or the seller in a transaction. Unlike the manufacturers' sales branches or the merchant wholesalers, the agents and brokers do not buy or take direct control of the goods being sold. Rather, they act as intermediaries for either the buyer or seller. As representatives of businesses that buy or sell products, agents and brokers receive commissions for their services. Agents often contract with a manufacturer to sell a product or group of products to retail stores, industrial plants, and local distributors in a specific geographic region. They often represent more than one manufacturer.

Wholesalers may provide full-service or limited service. Full-service wholesalers operate warehouses, supply credit, employ sales workers, and make deliveries. They also might be involved with advertising, packaging, and providing other services to customers.

Limited-service wholesalers, on the other hand, may only ship merchandise from the manufacturer to the retailer or sell and deliver merchandise directly from their truck. Limited-service wholesalers are smaller operations but can often deliver products at a lower cost.

Wholesalers are experts in their particular line of work. They must know everything there is to know about their product and also keep up to date on what competing wholesalers are doing.

Numerous workers in the wholesale industry are salespeople. There are two types of sales workers—those who work in an office and those who do most of their work while on the road. "Inside" sales workers usually work by phone, taking and soliciting orders. They also monitor inventory levels for their customers and process orders.

Sales workers who travel call on retail store owners and try and persuade them to buy their

A wholesaler specializing in fresh produce loads his truck with his products. He intends to sell them to restaurants at an open market.

products. They must make periodic calls on regular customers; inform customers of new and old products, availability of supply, and prices; help with inventory control; arrange for delivery or installation; handle customer complaints; check on the activity and products of competitors; attempt to lure customers away from other companies; and in general do all that they can to most effectively represent their company.

Sales workers must be able to ascertain directly such product elements as purpose, construction, durability, quality, and style. Additionally, sales workers must be well acquainted with the best sources of supply for each type of good they purchase. A wholesaler who handles sporting good equipment, for example, must keep up-to-date on the latest athletic products and keep in constant contact with coaches, athletic directors, and other experts in the field. A wholesaler who sells food products will similarly read the latest literature and speak to experts in the food industry.

Sales workers who sell highly technical machinery, such as those who sell machines to steel producers, frequently must begin by analyzing the customer's specific needs, and then

Many wholesalers store their goods in large warehouses near shipping docks. This gives them the opportunity to transport the goods to their customers as quickly as possible.

adapting products to a customer's specialized needs. They usually prepare an extensive sales presentation that includes precise information on the equipment recommended for purchase, the cost of the equipment, and the total effect upon the customer's profits or quality of service.

Modern technology is beginning to play an increasingly important role in wholesaling. For example, computer systems can now expedite the ordering of materials, allowing the sales representative to know at the touch of a bottom when a customer may need to reorder merchandise. Computers are also being used to improve the delivery and handling of inventories.

Because of its favorable location, excellent port facilities, and large population, New York City is considered the leading wholesale trade center in the United States. Other important wholesale trade centers include cities such as Chicago, Kansas City, St. Louis, New Orleans, and Los Angles.

Careers

There are a large number of career options for those interested in the wholesaling field. Because sales are such a vital part of the wholesaling industry, many of the job opportunities

entail some sales work. Other important jobs in wholesaling involve ordering and processing the merchandise. A sample of career opportunities follows below:

Specialty wholesalers: Specialty wholesalers are full-service wholesalers who usually handle only one product, such as chocolate or coffee.

General-line wholesalers: General-line wholesalers are full-service wholesalers who carry a broad assortment of merchandise, such as groceries.

Commission merchants: Commission merchants usually trade in fresh fruits and other perishable goods. They often have their own warehouses.

Merchandise brokers: Merchandise brokers are hired by individuals or companies to buy or sell products for them. Unlike merchant wholesalers, brokers do not own the products they buy and sell, but are rather paid a commission on all transactions. Brokers work mainly in select fields, such as foods, grains, and gas and other petroleum products.

Manufacturer's representatives: Manufacturer's representatives sell the products of one or more factories in a specific territory. They usually call on customers (retail merchants, business concerns, and institutions) at their places of business.

A growing number of manufacturers use this sales method to sell directly to retailers or individual customers. The food products industry is the largest employer of manufacturer's representatives. Other fields with large numbers of representatives include printing, publishing, fabricated metal products, chemicals and dyes, electrical and other machinery, and transportation equipment.

Drop shippers: Drop shippers are limited service wholesalers who buy and sell goods but do not take possession of them. They arrange for the goods to go directly from the manufacturer to the buyer.

Wholesale sales workers: Wholesale sales workers sell products to buyers in retail stores and in commercial or industrial companies. They usually represent a wholesaler that does not manufacture products but purchases them for resale. Most sales workers specialize in a certain type of product and work in one region or district. Wholesale sales workers may work in an office or travel extensively.

Industrial distributors: Industrial distributors are manufacturer's agents who handle one or more products for only one manufacturer. Usually manufacturer's agents represent more than one manufacturer.

Purchasing agents: Purchasing agents determine the quantity and quality of the items to be purchased, and negotiate costs, delivery dates, and sources of supply. They keep records pertaining to items purchased, delivery costs, product performance, and inventories. Purchasing agents may work under managers of procurement services, who coordinate all the activities of personnel involved in purchasing and distributing materials. They may also handle dispersal of surplus goods. Procurement services managers also analyze market conditions to determine present and future availability of desired materials.

Contract administrators: Contract administrators examine estimates of production costs, performance requirements, and delivery schedules to ensure completeness and accuracy. They prepare bids and other exhibits that may be required.

Contract specialists: Contract specialists negotiate, administer, extend, terminate, and renegotiate contracts with suppliers. They may approve or reject requests for deviations from contract specifications and delivery schedules, and may arbitrate claims or complaints occurring in completion of contracts.

Communications personnel: Communications personnel are workers concerned with the development and distribution of favorable material in order to promote goodwill, develop credibility, or create favorable public image for a wholesaler. This includes workers involved in advertising, marketing, and public relations.

Nonperishable goods can be stored for indefinite periods of time. This allows the wholesaler to keep an adequate supply of goods to satisfy any order.

Distribution workers: Distribution workers handle, store, and transport merchandise between producers and consumers. Distribution workers mainly work in warehouses or drive delivery trucks.

Administrative workers: Administrative workers provide administrative support, such as keeping records of sales transactions and supplying credit information. Increasingly, administrative workers use computer systems to provide support services.

Education

The educational requirements for people involved in wholesaling are varied. There are some people in wholesaling who did not receive formal training in wholesaling, but the majority of wholesalers today have at least an undergraduate college degree in business administration, marketing, or a related field. Most wholesalers also have experience in their particular line of work. Most entry-level positions

Retailers always check the goods that they have ordered before officially accepting them from wholesalers.

also includes extensive on-the-job training, because each company runs its operations somewhat differently.

There is no established route for being a success in the wholesaling industry. There are plenty of people who have worked their way up from clerical positions to become merchant wholesalers. Wholesalers need to be good at planning, astute business people, and have a good deal of experience in buying or selling the product or products that they represent. On-the-job training is often the best method of gaining experience.

While it is not necessary for wholesale sales workers to have a college degree, an increasingly large percentage of salespeople do graduate from college. While large wholesalers tend to prefer those with degrees in business administration or marketing, firms are usually ready to consider graduates from a wide spectrum of majors. Sales workers can come from a variety of disciplines, but those selling products (electronic equipment, for example), should probably have training in that particular field.

For some of the highly technical and advanced scientific equipment, master's and doctoral degrees are required. It is important that the wholesaler have a clear understanding of what each product is used for.

In general, those involved in wholesaling need to be good decision makers and be able to handle the stress of conducting price negotiations. Those involved with ordering and processing merchandise should have a strong mathematical background and also understand business statistics.

Industry outlook

Approximately 60 percent of all product distribution in the United States is through wholesalers, and this share is expected to grow to 63 percent by 1995. Opportunities in wholesaling are, to a large extent, tied to the economy. If the economy is growing at a healthy rate, there figures to be more buying and selling and therefore more opportunities for wholesalers. However, even in slow periods of growth, there will always be an opportunity for someone with skill, experience, and a little bit of creativity. All wholesaling companies, whether large or small, need organized, thoughtful people who can find appropriate markets for their products or purchase quality products for their customers.

While successful wholesalers can expect to earn very good wages, the nature of the business may mean a fluctuation in earnings from year to year and even month to month. For a better understanding of individual industries, see the other articles on this volume.

Because wholesaling offers the possibility of good earnings, and an exciting lifestyle, positions in this field are likely to remain competitive through the 1990s.

◇ SOURCES OF ADDITIONAL INFORMATION

National Association of Wholesaler-Distributors
1725 K Street, NW
Washington, DC 20006

National Association of Service Merchandising
118 South Clinton Street
Suite 300
Chicago, IL 60606

General Merchandise Distributors Council
1275 Lake Plaza Drive
Colorado Springs, CO 80906

Manufacturer's Agents National Association
23016 Mill Creek Road
PO Box 3467
Laguna Hills, CA 92653

Many companies have specific organizations servicing their own area of wholesaling. Look up local wholesaling companies in your community and contact them for information.

◇ **RELATED ARTICLES**

Volume 1: Accounting; Advertising; Business Administration; Foreign Trade; Franchising; Human Resources; Marketing; Packaging; Personal and Consulting Services; Retailing; Transportation

Volume 2: Accountants and auditors; Buyers, wholesale and retail; Cost estimators; Economists; Export-import specialists; General managers and top executives; Management analysts and consultants; Management trainees; Marketing, advertising, and public relations managers; Purchasing agents; Retail business owners; Retail managers

Volume 3: Billing clerks; Bookkeeping and accounting clerks; Clerical supervisors and managers; Door-to-door sales workers; Industrial-truck operators; Retail sales workers; Route drivers; Shipping and receiving clerks; Stock clerks; Traffic agents and clerks; Wholesale trade sales workers

Wood

General information

Wood is the primary product of the forest. It is used to build houses, furniture, flooring, shipping containers, tools, and many other products. When wood is used to produce commercial products it is referred to as lumber. Lumbering processes include the harvesting and removal of trees, the conversion of the raw material into finished products, and the marketing and distribution of these products. Wood is also used to produce the pulp used in making paper. This article will primarily focus on the lumbering industry. Please refer to the Pulp and Paper article in this volume for a discussion of pulpwood.

Throughout history, wood has been used as a source of heat and as material for shelter and other types of construction. The Phoenicians and other early civilizations used wood to build boats and rafts and to make the pilings used in docks and piers. The early Romans used thin slices of wood called veneer for ornamental and other purposes. (Today, veneer is still used in this manner.)

As civilizations advanced technologically, the uses of wood changed to meet the needs of the day. With the growth of the railroad, wood was used in the cross ties used to build railroad tracks. With the advances in wood chemistry, wood was used in clothes, plastics, and a host of other products. In many of the world's poorer countries, wood continues to be used as an important fuel source.

Forests covered huge areas in North America when the Pilgrims first arrived. These early settlers first had to clear the forests so they could build shelters and farm the land. As expansion moved westward, large portions of the forested area were cleared, and most of the trees suitable for prime lumber were removed.

As the population grew and land-clearing spread during the nineteenth century, foresighted people began to realize that unless forests were protected, they would disappear. Laws enacted by Congress and state governments slowed down forest destruction. In 1905, the U.S. Forest Service was established in the Department of Agriculture, and in 1907 the Forest Service assumed responsibility for the newly-proclaimed national forests.

Up until recently, trees were cut with axes, saws, and other hand tools. In the United States and other developed countries, motor-powered tools are now used in harvesting operations.

Most of the nation's lumber production comes from commercial forests. There are about half a billion acres of commercial forests in the United States and it produces about nine-tenths of the country's lumber requirements.

In the United States, portions of Europe, and other areas, the last several decades have seen a vast improvement in forest management techniques. In earlier years, loggers would simply cut down all the trees in a particular area, often destroying vast forests. As foresters and others became to realize that the forests had to be managed, trained forest scientists were used to protect the forests from fire, insects, and diseases and manage the forests so that only the proper types and numbers of trees were removed.

Many lumber companies also began to maintain tree nurseries. The young trees from the nurseries were often replanted in forests. In many cases, more trees are replanted than were removed.

Although forests are now better managed, there is still a degree of controversy regarding foresting techniques. Many old-growth forests support wildlife and plant life that can not exist in any other ecosystem. In Oregon and other parts of the country, there is a continuing debate over how much old-growth forest should be cut down for economic purposes and how much old-growth forest should be retained for environmental reasons.

In the United States, the lumber industry is primarily located in the Northwest, Northeast, the South, and around the Great Lakes.

Lumber is divided into two main classes: *hardwood* and *softwood*. These terms do not refer to the hardness or softness of the wood, but rather to the type of tree from which the lumber comes. Hardwoods come from deciduous trees, which have broad leaves that fall off in autumn. Hardwoods used for lumber include oak, birch, maple, and elm. Softwoods come from conifers, which keep their leave throughout the year. Softwoods are also called evergreens. Softwoods used for lumber include pines, Douglas firs, redwood, and spruce.

Lumber is sawed to a variety of widths and thicknesses depending on its final use. *Factory and shop lumber* will be recut in the manufacture of furniture, baseball bats, and other objects. *Yard lumber* is any piece of lumber less than five inches thick. It is used for general building purposes. *Timbers* are large pieces more than five inches wide or thick. Timber is widely used in the construction industry.

The structure of the wood industry

The vast majority of lumber is used by the construction industry to construct houses and other buildings. Lumber is used for flooring, siding, doors, and other parts of houses. The rest of the lumber is used in the manufacturing of toys, shipping containers, boxes, boats, furniture, and many other products.

The harvesting of trees is called logging. Trees are cut in large numbers from designated forests. The timber cutting and logging process begins when foresters, assisted by forestry technicians, decide when and which trees will be harvested. After an appropriate area has been found and the trees suitable for cutting have been marked, the next step in logging is the felling of the trees. The wood harvester (often called a cutter) usually uses a chain saw to cut the trees. The felled trees are usually then moved to a clearing, from where they are loaded onto trucks or train cars for transport to processing mills. Large trees are bucked, or cut into shorter logs, so they can be loaded more easily. With small trees, only the branches and tops of the tree are removed.

In many areas of the United States and Europe, much of the logging is done by mechanical harvesters. Trees are commonly felled and bunched by machines called skidders or shearers. These mechanized operations are decreasing the amount of chain saw work needed to be done.

A faller uses a powerful chain saw to cut a large tree that has been marked for harvesting.

At the sawmill, the logs are turned into lumber. A moving conveyor carries the logs from the truck or train up a chute into the mill. Strong streams of water are used to remove sand or dirt from the wood. A laser scanner is used to provide the exact dimensions of a log. These dimensions are used to determine the best way to cut the wood so that it yields the most planks. As the log proceeds on a conveyor, it is usually debarked by a mechanical debarker. The wood is then run through a series of four saws—a circular saw, a headsaw, a resaw, and a trimmer saw. The circular saw cuts large logs into shorter lengths. The headsaw then slices each log into boards or other types of lumber. The resaw is then used to cut lumber to its proper width and thickness. Side edgers are used to make the sides straight and even. The trimmer saw then makes the ends of the board square and cuts the lumber to standard lengths.

After the lumber is cut by the saws, it moves along a conveyor belt and is manually graded by graders according to its quality, size, and type of wood. Hardwoods are usually graded on a scale from one to eight, with one

A machine debarks a slender log. This mechanism not only removes bark but gives the log a uniform surface for slicing as well.

The finer woods are made into furniture. Furniture making requires wood shaped in various sizes. Often, fine woods such as mahogany and ebony are imported. The use of thin layers of veneer may be utilized to produce beautiful wood at a lower cost.

As with a host of other industries, the lumber industry is making greater use of computers in the production process. For example, computers are being used in the highly complicated task of determining how to best cut a log and in the automation of inventory control.

Careers

There are a variety of career options available for those interested in pursuing a career in the wood industry. Some of the jobs require highly-skilled workers, while other jobs offer the opportunity for on-the-job training. Many of the careers require outside work, and most are physically demanding. A sampling of career opportunities follows below.

Foresters: Foresters manage and develop forest land for timber production and other uses. They map forest areas, estimate the volume of standing timber, and plan cutting programs. Foresters also assist in planning and implementing projects to control flooding, soil erosion, and tree disease.

Cruisers: Cruisers survey forests to help determine the value of the standing timber. They collect data for use in determining the best and safest places to fell the trees. Cruisers also collect information for use in determining where to locate a logging camp and how to best get the timber to the sawmill.

Forest engineers: Forest engineers design and direct operations for felling and removing timber. They help determine how best to reach and leave logging areas and how to store timber.

Fallers: Fallers, or cutters, cut down the trees. Using various techniques, a faller cuts notches in a tree to make it fall in a particular direction.

Buckers: Buckers trim off the branches and tops of trees and may buck (cut) the resulting logs into specified lengths.

Harvester operators: Harvester operators run a machine that mechanically does the same job as cutters and buckers. Harvester machines aid in the felling, limbing, and bucking processes.

Forestry technicians: Forestry technicians help plan the harvesting and replanting of forests and often assist in the marketing of forest products. They also help manage forests and

being the highest grade of wood. Softwoods are generally graded from one to five, again with one being the highest grade.

Rough lumber may be transported from the sawmill to mills that finish and shape the boards and produce other lumber products. Often, wholesalers buy lumber in large quantities and then resell it to retail lumber yards or other large users of the lumber. The retailers and others then sell the lumber to individual customers.

Seasoning is the process by which moisture is removed from the wood. Since wood cut in the forest has a large moisture content, it is often necessary to remove some of the moisture. Lumber can be seasoned by air drying or kiln drying. (A kiln is a large oven used to dry or fire a substance.) With air drying, the lumber is piled outside and left to dry by the sun and wind. Kiln drying is quicker, but can harm the wood if left in too long. Different woods are dried at different temperatures and speeds. Woods are also dried according to where they will be used. For example, wood being used in a dry climate will be seasoned to a lesser moisture than wood being used in a moist climate.

other wildlife areas. Forestry technicians work under the direction of a forester or other professional forest scientist.

Graders: Graders sort lumber according to size, quality, and the kind of wood.

Log scalers: Log scalers determine the amount of timber in logs. They use scale rules, scaling stick, or tape to make these measurements.

Logging tractor operators: Logging tractor operators run a tractor equipped with a grapple for skidding (dragging) trees, logs, or other harvested wood.

Delimber operators: Delimber operators run equipment that mechanically removes the limbs from harvested trees.

Chipper operators: Chipper operators run loading and chipping machines that reduce trees to wood chips.

Wood scientists: Wood scientists discover new ways to dry, preserve, and make things out of wood. For example, they may develop new ways to dry, or cure, wood so that it will last longer.

Wood technologists: Wood technologists test wood-related materials and equipment, such as kilns and sawmill machinery. They often work for lumber companies.

Wood products technicians: Wood products technicians supervise the operation of kilns, saws, and other equipment and make sure it is operating properly. They may run tests on wood to check its quality.

Education

Historically, the lumber industry has been open to those from a wide variety of educational backgrounds, including those who did not finish high school. As the industry has become more automated, however, there is a move to hire those with at least a high-school diploma.

In addition to meeting educational requirements, it is extremely important that those involved in the logging industry are physically fit and able to work for long periods of times in forests or other remote areas. Many companies require a comprehensive physical examination as a part of the hiring process.

Foresters and other forest management scientists normally have a college degree in forestry or a related major. Course work includes classes in silviculture (the art of tending and reproducing forests), forest utilization (the harvesting and marketing of forest crops), forest management, and related subjects. Forest management education includes training in management of forest fires. Usually thought harm-

A wood scientist for the U.S. government tests the strength and flexibility of different types of wood.

ful by the public, controlled fires may be benign or even helpful to the health and growth of forests. Aspiring foresters need a good background in chemistry, botany, zoology, soil science, mathematics, and physics. Most college degrees include an internship, during which foresters receive on-the-job experience. Many foresters have graduate degrees in forestry, botany, or a similar field.

Forestry technicians often attend community colleges and receive an associate's degree in forestry. Technicians study forest surveying, dendrology (tree identification), forest soils, botany of forests, and related subjects.

Logging industry workers often receive on-the-job training in their area of specialization. For example, an aspiring tree harvester would work under the guidance of an experienced harvester for several weeks or months before assuming full cutting responsibilities. Often, supervisors in the logging industry come from experienced workers. A worker might begin felling trees with a chain saw, advance to operating a mechanical harvester, and then be promoted to a supervisory position, such as foreman or camp manager. Supervisors often receive additional training in the areas of personnel management and administrative tasks.

Wood harvesters do not generally need college degrees, but many cutters do complete a twenty-six week training program in wood harvesting. The program includes courses in chain saw operations, wood scaling, woods safety, and other related subjects. Many wood harvesters also gain on-the-job training with small companies and independent operators.

Log scalers must often obtain a state license to keep records of timber volume.

To ensure ample supplies of trees in the future, lumber companies plant millions of seedlings annually.

Industry outlook

The wood industry in the United States produces more lumber than any other country. In the early 1990s, annual lumber production in the United States totaled some forty million board feet. (The Soviet Union produces the next highest lumber total.) The U.S. lumber industry employs thousands of people in all stages of production.

The use of wood as a raw material should continue to play an important role in the world economy through the coming decades. Because wood is a renewable resource, is relatively inexpensive, is fairly abundant, and can be used in the manufacturing of such a wide range of products, many consider the wood industry to hold great potential for growth into the twenty-first century.

Although demand for wood products should rise in the future, employment should remain steady. This is because improved technology will lessen the demand for workers. For example, the increased computerization of the timber industry will lead to a reduction in the number of workers needed in processing logs. Analysts estimate that a fully computerized mill can reduce its work force by about 25 percent. Computers can now be used to do such highly-skilled work as sorting logs on a conveyor belt and determining the most cost-effective method of cutting logs.

There is also an ongoing controversy between loggers and those who want to protect old-growth forests. In Oregon and other locations, loggers and environmentalists are bat-tling over whether these forests should be harvested. Environmentalists maintain that these forests are an important part of the ecosystem and as such provide an important habitat for wildlife and plants. Loggers maintain that local economies would suffer if loggers can not harvest these trees. The ongoing debate on this issue will affect employment in some parts of the wood industry.

The international aspect of the wood industry also will influence the prospects of various parts of the industry. For example, the lumber industry is expected to benefit from the signing of a trade pact with Canada, which purchases about 30 percent of U.S. lumber exports. If efforts to reduce harvesting the rain forest are successful, this will reduce the supply of wood coming out of Central and South America. Experts estimate that the lumber industry should grow by about 10 percent in the early 1990s. Since not all of the lumber is processed in the United States, other parts of the industry (sawmills, for example) may not see as much growth in the 1990s.

◇ **SOURCES OF ADDITIONAL INFORMATION**

U.S. Forest Service
Department of Agriculture
Washington, DC 20250

American Wood Council
1250 Connecticut Avenue, NW, Suite 230
Washington, DC 20036

Society of American Foresters
5400 Grosvenor Lane
Bethesda, MD 20814

Forest Products Research Society
2801 Marshall Court
Madison, WI 53705

Society of Wood Science and Technology
PO Box 5062
Madison, WI 53705

North American Wholesale Lumber Association
2340 South Arlington Heights Road, Suite 680
Arlington Heights, IL 60005

Wood Products Manufacturers Association
52 Racette Avenue
Gardner, MA 01440

◇ **RELATED ARTICLES**

Photographic Credits

Index

527

534

Travel agents, **1:** 496, **3:** 185-89

Travel and tourism, **1:** 493-98

Travel consultants, **1:** 496

Traveler's checks sales representatives, **3:** 178

Treasurers, **1:** 3, 91

Tree-fruit-and-nut crops farmers, **3:** 346

Tree movers, **4:** 308

Tree-nursery management assistants, **4:** 300

Tree pruners, **3:** 370-71

Tree-services proprietors, **4:** 308

Tree-shear operators, **3:** 374

Tree-supply salespeople, **4:** 308

Tree surgeons, **3:** 370, **4:** 308, 310

Tree trimmers, **3:** 370-71

Tree trimming supervisors, **3:** 370

Trees pruners and trimmers, **4:** 308

Trimmers, **3:** 427, 603

Troubleshooters, **3:** 791

   instrumentation technicians, **4:** 205

   metallurgical, **4:** 219

Truant officers, **2:** 288

Truck and bus dispatchers, **1:** 489

Truck body builders, **3:** 476

Truck drivers

   local and over the road, **3:** 793-97

Truck loaders, **3:** 784

Truck washers, **3:** 435

Truckload checkers, **3:** 86

Trust clerks, **3:** 36

Trust-evaluation supervisors, **3:** 36

Trust-mail clerks, **3:** 36

Trust officers, **2:** 232

Trust securities clerks, **3:** 36

Trust-vault clerks, **3:** 36

Tube drawers, **3:** 424

Tuber machine operators, **1:** 437

Tubing machine operators, **3:** 424

Tubular splitting machine tenders, **3:** 531

Tune-up mechanics, **3:** 481

Turbine operators, **3:** 767

Turfgrass consultants, **4:** 307

Turfgrass maintenance supervisors, **4:** 307

Turfgrass research and development technicians, **4:** 307

Turfgrass technicians, **4:** 307

TV. *See* Television

Twisters, **3:** 390

Typesetters, **1:** 79, **3:** 495-99

Typing section chiefs, **3:** 125

Typists and work processors, **3:** 124-29

Umpires, **1:** 457

Undertakers, **2:** 248

Underwriters, **1:** 246, **2:** 687-90

Union business agents, **1:** 482; **2:** 341-44

Union organizers, **1:** 482

Unions

   division directors, **1:** 483

   international representatives, **1:** 482

   trade, **1:** 479-485

University faculty, **2:** 105-10

Unleavened dough mixers, **3:** 390

Upholsterers, **3:** 579

Upholstery and furniture sales representatives, **3:** 179

Upholstery repairers, **3:** 579

Upper-leather sorters, **3:** 599

Upsetters, **1:** 297, **3:** 511

Urban and regional planners, **2:** 690-94

Urban anthropologists, **2:** 33-34

Urban geographers, **2:** 262

Urban planners, **2:** 98, 99

Urban sociologists, **2:** 634

Urologists, **2:** 496

Used car renovators, **3:** 476

Ushers, **3:** 755

Utilities business specialists, **1:** 393

Utility company workers, **3:** 790

Utility technicians, **4:** 126

Utilization engineers, **2:** 208

Vacation tour guides, **1:** 496

Vacuum-kettle cooks, **3:** 394

Vacuum testers, **3:** 394

Valets, **3:** 303

Valuation engineers, **1:** 315

Valuer-generals, **2:** 45

Van drivers, **3:** 740

Varnish inspectors, **3:** 442

Varnish makers, **3:** 441

Vault attendants, **3:** 36

Vault workers, **3:** 86

Vegetable farmers, **3:** 346

Vending machine mechanics, **3:** 565

Vendors, **3:** 140

Ventilation technicians, **4:** 149-50

Ventriloquists, **2:** 7

Verifier operators, **3:** 30

Veterans' coordinators, **2:** 118

Veterinarians, **2:** 694-98

Veterinarians' assistants, **4:** 289

Veterinary anatomists, **2:** 695

Veterinary bacteriologists, **2:** 695

Veterinary epidemiologists, **2:** 695

Veterinary live-stock inspectors, **2:** 287

Veterinary meat-inspectors, **2:** 287, 695

Veterinary medicine, **1:** 20

Veterinary parasitologists, **2:** 695

Veterinary pathologists, **2:** 695

Veterinary pharmacologists, **2:** 695

Veterinary physiologists, **2:** 695

Veterinary science technicians, **4:** 377-81

Veterinary virus-serum inspectors, **2:** 287, 695

Video-control technicians, **4:** 372

Video directors, **1:** 85

Video engineers, **1:** 86

Video-tape recording technicians, **4:** 372

Video technicians, **4:** 372

Violin repairers, **3:** 592

Vocational education teachers, **2:** 16-20

Vocational-rehabilitation counselors, **2:** 186-87

Vocational training instructors, **2:** 17

Volcanologists, **2:** 270

Voucher clerks, **3:** 71

Wafer machine operators, **3:** 390

Wage-hour compliance inspectors, **2:** 288

Waiters and waitresses, **1:** 181, **3:** 251-56

Wall cleaners, **3:** 272

Washing machine operators, **3:** 226

Wastewater-treatment plant chemists, **2:** 91

Wastewater treatment plant operators, **3:** 797

Waste management, **1:** 499-505

Watch and clock repair clerks, **3:** 24

Watch assembly instructors, **2:** 17

Watch repairers, **3:** 614-17

Watchmakers, **3:** 614-17

Water and waste water treatment plant operators, **1:** 503

Water and wastewater treatment technicians, **4:** 267-68

Water-pollution control, **2:** 287

Water-pollution control inspectors, **2:** 287

Water pollution-control technicians, **4:** 91-92

Water-purification plant chemists, **2:** 91

Water resources technicians, **4:** 144

Water treatment plant operators, **3:** 798

Waterworks pump station operators, **3:** 798

Weapons and ammunition technicians, **4:** 268-69

Weaving instructors, **2:** 17

Weed inspectors, **3:** 370

Weight analysts, **2:** 396

Weir fishers, **3:** 359

Welders, **1:** 273, **3:** 718-23

Welding engineers, **2:** 209

Welding machine operators, **3:** 718

Welding technicians, **4:** 269-73

Wharf laborers, **3:** 393

Wholesale buyers. *See* Buyers

Wholesale florist assistants, **4:** 306

Wholesale route drivers, **3:** 172

Wholesale sales workers, **1:** 509

Wholesale trade sales workers, **3:** 189-93

Wholesalers, **2:** 223

Wholesaling, **1:** 506-11

Wideband and protected communications technicians lasers, **4:** 50

Wig dressers, **3:** 214

Wildlife technicians, **4:** 300

Winch operators, **3:** 784

Wind instrument repairers, **3:** 593

Window clerks, 3;63

Window display managers, **1:** 433

Window unit air-conditioning installer services, **3:** 570